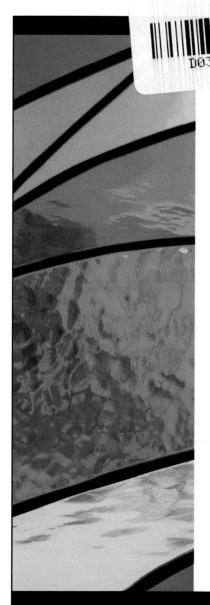

WORKING TOGETHER TO END POVERTY

Christian Aid is all about partnership. Partnership within the communities where we work and with the churches here in Scotland, who enable us to make a difference to the lives of some of the world's poorest, most vulnerable people.

When you fundraise, campaign or pray with Christian Aid, you are helping people living in poverty to achieve:
• the power to change institutions
• the right to essential services
• fair shares in a constrained world
• equality for all
• a means to tackle violence and build peace.

Please join us in striving together to achieve equality, dignity and freedom for all, regardless of faith or nationality.

For the latest news and resources:
• visit **christianaid.org.uk/scotland** where you can sign up for regular emails
• 'like' our Facebook page **(facebook.com/ChristianAidScotland)**
• call **0141 221 7475**, email **glasgow@christian-aid.org** or write to Christian Aid, Sycamore House, 290 Bath Street, Glasgow G2 4JR.

Thank you for your ongoing support.

Photo: Andu Bai distils vinegar made from berries gathered in the forest. Scottish Government funding has enabled Christian Aid to work in partnership with Samarthak Samiti, which helps adivasis forest people to process, package and secure a good price for the produce they collect

UK registered charity no. 1105851 Company no. 5171525 Scot charity no. SC039150 The Christian Aid name and logo are trademarks of Christian Aid; Poverty Over is a trademark of Christian Aid. © Christian Aid July 2012 13-499-J591

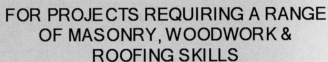

PITCAIRLIE
HOLIDAY
APARTMENTS

Pitcairlie is a 16th century castle set within a 120 acre estate of woods, wildflowers, streams, parklands and two ornamental lakes. There are four luxury self-catering holiday apartments within the Victorian Wing and one cottage in the grounds, all with use of our heated swimming pool.

A venue for groups, weddings or corporate/business events; we're open all year. Heating and linen are inclusive in the price.

PITCAIRLIE HOUSE, By Auchtermuchty, Newburgh,
Fife KY14 6EU. T: 01337 827418. M: 0783164657.
www.pitcairlie-leisure.co.uk   reservations@pitcairlie-leisure.co.uk

We accept most credit/debit cards

© John Young/YoungMedia

The Right Reverend Albert O. Bogle BD MTh

MODERATOR

The Church of Scotland
YEAR BOOK
2012/2013

Editor
Douglas Galbraith

Production Editor
Ivor Normand

Published on behalf of
THE CHURCH OF SCOTLAND
by SAINT ANDREW PRESS
121 George Street, Edinburgh EH2 4YN

THE OFFICES OF THE CHURCH

121 George Street
Edinburgh EH2 4YN

Tel: 0131-225 5722
Fax: 0131-220 3113
Website: www.churchofscotland.org.uk/

Office Hours:
Facilities Manager:

Monday–Friday 9:00am–5:00pm
Carole Tait 0131-240 2214

THE COUNCILS OF THE CHURCH

The following five Councils of the Church operate from the Church Offices, 121 George Street, Edinburgh EH2 4YN (Tel: 0131-225 5722):

- The Council of Assembly
- The Church and Society Council
- The Ministries Council
- The Mission and Discipleship Council
- The World Mission Council

E-mail: churchandsociety@cofscotland.org.uk
E-mail: ministries@cofscotland.org.uk
E-mail: mandd@cofscotland.org.uk
Fax: 0131-226 6121
E-mail: world@cofscotland.org.uk

The Social Care Council (CrossReach) operates from Charis House, 47 Milton Road East, Edinburgh EH15 2SR

Tel: 0131-657 2000
Fax: 0131-657 5000
E-mail: info@crossreach.org.uk
Website: www.crossreach.org.uk

SCOTTISH CHARITY NUMBERS

The Church of Scotland: unincorporated Councils and Committees	SC011353
The Church of Scotland General Trustees	SC014574
The Church of Scotland Investors Trust	SC022884
The Church of Scotland Trust	SC020269

(For the Scottish Charity Numbers of congregations, see Section 7)

First published in 2012 by SAINT ANDREW PRESS, 121 George Street, Edinburgh EH2 4YN on behalf of THE CHURCH of SCOTLAND

Copyright © THE CHURCH of SCOTLAND, 2012

ISBN 978 0 86153 697 9

It is the Publisher's policy only to use papers that are natural and recyclable and that have been manufactured from timber grown in renewable, properly managed forests. All of the manufacturing processes of the papers are expected to conform to the environmental regulations of the country of origin.

Acceptance of advertisements for inclusion in the *Church of Scotland Year Book* does not imply endorsement of the goods or services or of any views expressed within the advertisements.

British Library Cataloguing in Publication Data
A catalogue record for this book is available from the British Library.

Printed and bound by Bell and Bain Ltd, Glasgow

QUICK DIRECTORY

A.C.T.S. 01259 216980
Christian Aid London 020 7620 4444
Christian Aid Scotland 0141-221 7475
Church and Society Council 0131-240 2275
Church of Scotland Insurance Co. Ltd 0131-220 4119
CrossReach 0131-657 2000
Eco-Congregation Scotland 0131-240 2274
Gartmore House 01877 382991
Glasgow Lodging House Mission 0141-552 0285
Media Relations Team (Press Office) 0131-240 2204/2268
Pension Trustees (E-mail: pensions@cofscotland.org.uk) 0131-240 2255
Place for Hope 0131-240 2258
Priority Areas Office 0141-248 2905
Safeguarding Office (item 31 in Assembly Committee list) 0131-240 2256
Scottish Churches Parliamentary Office 0131-220 0246
Scottish Storytelling Centre/John Knox House 0131-556 9579
Trust Housing Association Ltd (formerly Kirk Care) 0131-444 4949
Year Book Editor. 01592 752403

Pulpit Supply: Fee and Expenses
Details of the current fee and related expenses in respect of Pulpit Supply will be found as the last item in
number 3 (the Ministries Council) on page 9.

All correspondence regarding the *Year Book* should be sent to
The Editor, *Church of Scotland Year Book*,
Saint Andrew Press, 121 George Street, Edinburgh EH2 4YN
Fax: 0131-220 3113
[E-mail: yearbookeditor@cofscotland.org.uk]

GENERAL ASSEMBLY OF 2013
The General Assembly of 2013 will convene on
Saturday, 18 May 2013

CONTENTS

FROM THE MODERATOR

We are all familiar with the old adage 'you can't tell a book by its cover'. I think this would be true of the present *Church of Scotland Year Book*. It's too easy to dismiss this book as the same every year – simply a book of statistics and telephone numbers.

The truth is: it's much more. It's a book that contains the names and addresses of ministers and church leaders, congregations and trust funds. They are listed because of the potential we all have to be connected to each other and to work together as a community to serve the cause of Christ in the world.

It's a book that invites us to contextualise the text beyond statistics, to see behind every figure and every name a person or an organisation that is seeking to serve the Kingdom of God.

So, why not use the *Year Book* a little differently this year? Make it a prayer book! Why not pray for two or three ministers and administrators, congregations and trusts from this book on a daily basis?

This year sees the appointment of a new editor, Rev. Dr Douglas Galbraith, with Ivor Normand continuing in a new role as production editor. I'm sure we all wish to extend our gratitude to the new team for the work that has gone into making the *Year Book* such a useful tool for mission and prayer and practical day-to-day ministry.

I am happy to commend this *Year Book* for 2012/13 to you.

Rev. Albert Bogle

ON MHODERATOR

Tha sinn uile eòlach air an t-seann ràdh, 'Chan urrainn dhuinn leabhar a mheas o chòmhdach an leth a-muigh'. Saoilidh mi gum faodadh sin a bhith fìor mun *Leabhar Bliadhnail* seo. Tha e furasta dìmeas a dhèanamh air an leabhar seo le bhith ag ràdh nach eil ann ach an t-aon rud a h-uile bliadhna – dìreach leabhar anns a bheil àireamhan agus fiosan-fòn.

Ma dh'innsear an fhìrinn tha cus a bharrachd air sin ann. 'S e a tha ann leabhar anns a bheil ainmean agus seòlaidhean mhinistearan agus cheannardan-eaglais, choitheanalan agus urrasan. Tha iad air an clàradh mar chomharadh air mar a tha e comasach dhuinn uile a bhith air ar ceangal ri chèile agus a bhith ag obrachadh còmhla mar choimhearsnachd airson seirbheis a dhèanamh do dh'adhbhar Chrìosd anns an t-saoghal.

'S e a tha ann leabhar a tha ag iarraidh oirnn a bhith a' gabhail beachd air dè as ciall do na h-àireamhan, a bhith a' faicinn air cùl gach àireamh agus gach ainm neach no buidheann a tha a' miannachadh a bhith a' dèanamh seirbheis do Rìoghachd Dhè.

Mar sin, carson nach cleachd sibh an *Leabhar* ann an dòigh beagan eadar-dhealaichte am bliadhna? Dèan leabhar-ùrnaigh dheth! Carson nach dèan sibh ùrnaigh gach latha airson a dhà no trì de na ministearan agus na rianadairean, na coitheanalan agus na h-urrasan a gheibhear anns an leabhar seo?

Am bliadhna chaidh fear-deasachaidh ùr a stèidheachadh, an t-Oll. Urr. Dùbhghlas Mac a' Bhreatnaich, agus Iamhair Normand ga chuideachadh mar dheasaiche dealbhachaidh. Tha mi cinnteach gum bi sinn uile airson taing a thoirt don sgiobaidh ùir airson na rinn iad de dh'obair ann a bhith a' dèanamh an leabhair seo 'na ghoireas cho feumail a thaobh misein agus ùrnaigh agus ministrealachd o latha gu latha.

Tha mi toilichte *Leabhar Bliadhnail* 2012/13 a mholadh dhuibh.

An t-Urr. Albert Bogle

FROM THE EDITOR

Prefaces are generally avoided by readers, except perhaps by friends of the author who may wish to see if they are listed among the author's inspirations. Those, however, who have postponed the temptations of congregational statistics and the remits of Assembly committees, and who have turned first to this preface, will realise with dismay that with the departing Editor have departed also the acerbic wit and pointed observations about developments in the Church and in society which have made the *Year Book* prefaces of the last twelve years so entertaining.

Ronald Blakey's knowledge of the Church of Scotland is deep and thorough, arising from his distinguished tenure of key posts in Assembly committees and councils. In his hands, the *Year Book* developed into the useful and comprehensive resource it is today. However, if he has done great service to the Church, he has not so well served Editors who have to succeed him, particularly in the penning of prefaces. I rather fear it is not within the capacity of the new Editor to keep up the chorus of chortles in church vestries, the sniggers in the studies of the nation's manses, the slipped masks quickly regained behind the desks of 121 George Street. I did think, following the example of heroes of the Premier League, of re-employing my predecessor as ghostwriter. Happily, he is far from being a ghost, except that he would rightly deserve a fee that would make a Stewardship Director blush.

Each *Year Book* offers a snapshot of its times, not simply through its lists and figures but also in what is implied by the articles and features included. The earliest *Year Book* on my shelves is dated 1918 – already the thirty-third of the title. Full and detailed explanations of the old-age pension provision and of 'Income-tax – its incidence and abatement' suggest that, where now one might apply to Google, in earlier days it would be to the manse door that one might go for such information and support. An interesting feature is a list of publications of ministers in the previous year, the two who head the list being composers of secular songs, *A Litany of the Sea* (Kirkcaldy: St James's) and *A Mother's Goodbye* (Hamilton: Old). The list also reveals that no fewer than seventeen ministers were editors of religious papers and magazines, reminding us of the important role of printed material in the life of the Church of the time. And then there are the 'Fiars Prices', the average price for grain and meal for each county – a matter of existential interest to ministers.

The present volume similarly acts as a lens for picking out current movements and developments in the Church. At such a time in the Church's history, every year has become a year of change. Perhaps the phrase used in the 2012 Ministries Council report to the General Assembly, echoed by that of the Ecumenical Relations Committee, is right – that we are living through not an age of change but a change of age. There is plenty of evidence in these pages that what was called for particularly in the 1960s and 1970s – more flexible patterns of ministry, church life and witness, with financial and governance structures to enable these – is now beginning to become a reality. New titles for ministerial posts, new groupings of congregations, new ecclesial entities, new kinds of central funds to be channelled into local situations, offer to refresh the Church's engagement with today's society.

Perhaps the most far-reaching of changes, however, one whose implications may not yet be fully appreciated, is that sketched in the short *Joint Report of the Committee on Ecumenical Relations and the Ministries Council on Article III*, given to the same Assembly. Following earlier work, the Assembly had asked that an exploration be made into how the ideal of a territorial ministry, as expressed in that Declaratory Article, might, in these straitened times, be worked out in partnership with other denominations. The instruction that an audit of ecumenical activity in Presbyteries be initiated, and the invitation to other denominations to undertake a similar task, could be the precursor of a new and more effective presence in every parish when other denominations share the role of the 'parish church'.

The volume of the *Year Book* I quoted from earlier was pre-Union. The Union edition of 1930 carried a message from the Moderator, Dr John White, in which he expressed the hope that the volume would 'serve to introduce us to each other'. This continues to be one of the functions of the publication – indeed, the current Moderator has underlined this in his call for it to be a prayer book as well as a book of information. The few changes that have been made in the present edition are intended to facilitate its use and to help people find their way through both book and Church.

The Editor is glad to thank the many who have contributed to the book's compilation. Dr Roddy MacLeod, as always, has provided the important Gaelic component of the book. Roy Pinkerton has made available his wide knowledge of the history of Scotland and its Church. Sandy Gemmill, formerly of the Stewardship and Finance Department, has undertaken the laborious business of bringing congregational statistics up to date. The Rev. Douglas Aitken, formerly of the BBC, has willingly made available the digest of events of the General Assembly that he prepared for the Church's website. Thanks are due also for the ready and willing response of Presbytery Clerks, secretaries and administrators at the Church Offices, and the many others who provided material. Thanks go too to Grant Hutchison, the Church's Head of Communications, whose department is now responsible for the Church's part in the publication – as well as to our publisher, Ann Crawford, for her continuing guidance, and to Lawrie Law for managing the typesetting, print and scheduling of the publication. Finally, particular thanks are due to our meticulous production editor, Ivor Normand, who asks questions, makes connections and gets the detail right.

In these days, the question is inevitably raised as to the balance of print and electronic media. Discussions are taking place about the form in which the information currently stored in this volume may best be circulated – and it is possible that the *Year Book*, first published in 1886, will soon appear in a different format, or in more than one format.

It is unlikely, however, that any new format will have the capability expressed in this anecdote from our Gaelic adviser, who heard about a minister in Argyll many years ago who did not have a degree. The minister above him in the list had a long name, so his MA had to be carried over to the next line. When that minister died, the MA was added to the other minister's name, and he had it for the rest of his life.

Douglas Galbraith
July 2012

SECTION 1

Assembly Councils, Committees, Departments and Agencies

[Note: Years, where given, indicate the year of appointment]

1. THE COUNCIL OF ASSEMBLY

The voting members of the Council of Assembly act as the Charity Trustees for the Unincorporated Councils and Committees of the General Assembly: Scottish Charity No. SC011353.

Remit (as amended May 2011)
The Council of Assembly shall be a standing Committee of the General Assembly, to which it shall be directly accountable and to which it shall report through its Convener. The General Assembly has conferred on the Council the powers as described in the following remit and in particular the powers of supervision of its Agencies (said Agencies being as defined in the Appendix) in the matters as detailed therein.

Membership
The Council shall comprise the following:
1. Convener, Vice-Convener and ten members appointed by the General Assembly on the Report of the Nomination Committee.
2. The Conveners of the Councils, namely Church and Society, Ministries, Mission and Discipleship, Social Care and World Mission together with the Convener of the Panel on Review and Reform.
3. The Secretaries of the following Councils, namely Church and Society, Ministries, Mission and Discipleship, Social Care and World Mission, all with a right to speak on matters affecting the interest of their Council, but not to vote or make a motion.
4. The Principal Clerk, the General Treasurer and the Solicitor of the Church without a right to vote or make a motion.
5. The Secretary to the Council of Assembly without a right to vote or make a motion.
6. The Ecumenical Officer, the Head of Communications and the Head of Human Resources and Information Technology to be in attendance without a right to vote or make a motion.

Remit and Powers
1. To advise the General Assembly on matters of reorganisation and structural change, including adjustments to the membership and remits of relevant Agencies of the General Assembly.
2. To keep under review the central administration of the Church, with particular regard to resolving issues of duplication of resources.
3. To monitor, evaluate and co-ordinate the work of the Agencies of the General Assembly, within the context of policy determined by the Assembly.
4. To advise the General Assembly on the relative importance of work being undertaken by its various Agencies.
5. To receive reports from, offer guidance to and issue instructions to Agencies of the General Assembly as required from time to time on matters of management, organisation and administration.
6. To oversee the implementation and development of the Co-ordinated Communication Strategy across the Church.
7. To determine policy in relation to:
    (a) the teaching and promotion of Christian stewardship throughout the Church;
    (b) Ministries and Mission Contributions from congregations, subject to the approval of Regulations by the General Assembly.

8. To determine annually the stipend rate, having regard to the recommendation thereanent of the Ministries Council, said determination to be made by the voting members of the Council of Assembly with the exception of those members in receipt of either a salary or stipend from the Parish Ministries Fund.

9. To bring recommendations to the General Assembly concerning the total amount of the Church's Co-ordinated Budget for the Parish Ministries Fund and the Mission and Renewal Fund for the following financial year, and to determine the allocation of the budget for the Mission and Renewal Fund among the relevant Agencies of the General Assembly and Ecumenical Bodies.

10. To prepare and present to the General Assembly an indicative Rolling Budget for the following five financial years.

11. To receive and distribute unrestricted legacies and donations among the Agencies of the General Assembly with power to specify the use to which the same are to be applied.

12. To approve and submit annually to the General Assembly the audited Report and Financial Statements of the Unincorporated Councils and Committees of the General Assembly.

13. To determine the types and rates of expenses which may be claimed by members serving on Councils, Committees and Statutory Corporations.

14. Through its oversight of the Stewardship and Finance Department, to be responsible for:
    (a) providing support to Presbyteries and congregations in the teaching and promotion of Christian stewardship;
    (b) determining with Presbyteries the Ministries and Mission Contributions required annually from congregations;
    (c) providing assistance to Presbyteries and congregations in adhering to financial standards required by charity law and by Regulations of the General Assembly;
    (d) setting standards of financial management and providing financial services for the Councils and Committees, Statutory Corporations and other Agencies of the General Assembly.

15. To consider and decide on proposals from Agencies of the General Assembly to purchase heritable property or any other asset (except investments) valued in excess of £50,000 or lease any heritable property where the annual rental exceeds £25,000 per annum, declaring that no Agency save those referred to in section 24 hereof shall proceed to purchase or lease such property without prior approval from the Council.

16. To consider and decide on proposals from Agencies of the General Assembly, save those referred to in section 24 hereof, to sell or lease for a period in excess of five years or otherwise dispose of any heritable property, or sell or otherwise dispose of any asset (except investments) valued in excess of £50,000, held by or on behalf of that Agency, with power to allocate all or part of the sale or lease proceeds to another Agency or Agencies in terms of section 18 hereof.

17. To consider and decide on proposals from Agencies of the General Assembly to enter into an agreement or contract (with the exception of contracts of employment or those relating to property transactions) with a total actual or potential financial commitment in excess of £50,000, declaring that no Agency shall proceed to enter into such an agreement or contract without prior approval from the Council.

18. To reallocate, following upon consultation with the Agency or Agencies affected, unrestricted funds held by or on behalf of any of the Agencies of the General Assembly to another Agency or Agencies with power to specify the use to which the same are to be applied.

19. To determine staffing and resourcing requirements of Agencies of the General Assembly, including inter-Departmental sharing or transfer of staff, in accordance with policies drawn

up by the Council of Assembly in line with priorities approved by the General Assembly, it being declared that the term 'staffing' shall not include those appointed or employed to serve in particular Parishes or overseas or by the Social Care Council in service-provision facilities around the country.

20. To consult with the relative Councils and Agencies in their appointment of Council Secretaries to the Church and Society, Ministries, Mission and Discipleship, Social Care and World Mission Councils, to appoint the Ecumenical Officer, the Head of Stewardship, the Head of Communications and the Head of Human Resources and Information Technology and to nominate individuals to the General Assembly for appointment to the offices of Principal Clerk of the General Assembly, Depute Clerk of the General Assembly, Secretary to the Council of Assembly, General Treasurer of the Church and Solicitor of the Church.

21. To attend to the general interests of the Church in matters which are not covered by the remit of any other Agency.

22. To deal with urgent issues arising between meetings of the General Assembly, provided that (a) these do not fall within the jurisdiction of the Commission of Assembly or of any Presbytery or Kirk Session, (b) they are not of a legislative or judicial nature and (c) any action taken in terms of this clause shall be reported to the next General Assembly.

23. To encourage all Agencies of the General Assembly to work ecumenically wherever possible and to have regard to the international, evangelical and catholic nature of the Church.

24. For the avoidance of doubt, sections 15 and 16 shall not apply to the Church of Scotland General Trustees, the Church of Scotland Housing and Loan Fund for Retired Ministers and Widows and Widowers of Ministers and the Ministries Council Emerging Ministries Task Group, all of which may deal with heritable property and other assets without the approval of the Council.

Appendix to Remit
For the purposes only of this remit, the term 'Agencies' shall mean the following bodies being Standing Committees of the General Assembly, namely:
• The following Councils: Church and Society, Ministries, Mission and Discipleship, Social Care, World Mission.
• The following Committees: Assembly Arrangements, Central Services, Chaplains to Her Majesty's Forces, Ecumenical Relations, Legal Questions, Panel on Review and Reform, Parish Development Fund, Safeguarding.

Convener: Rev. S. Grant Barclay LLB DipLP BD MSc PhD (2012)
Vice-Convener: Iain Johnston BA (2012)
Secretary: Mrs Pauline Weibye MA DPA Chartered FCIPD

---

2. THE CHURCH AND SOCIETY COUNCIL

Remit
The remit of the Church and Society Council is to facilitate the Church of Scotland's engagement with, and comment upon, national, political and social issues through:
• the development of theological, ethical and spiritual perspectives in the formulation of policy on such issues;

- the effective representation of the Church of Scotland in offering on its behalf appropriate and informed comment on political and social issues;
- the building, establishing and maintaining of a series of networks and relationships with leaders and influence-shapers in civic society, and engaging long-term in dialogue and the exchange of ideas with them;
- the support of the local church in its mission and engagement by offering professional and accessible resources on contemporary issues;
- the conducting of an annual review of progress made in discharging the remit and the provision of a written report to the Council of Assembly.

Membership
Convener, Vice-Convener, 28 members appointed by the General Assembly, one of whom will also be appointed to the Ecumenical Relations Committee, and one member appointed from and by the Social Care Council and the Guild. The Nomination Committee will ensure that the Council membership contains at least five individuals with specific expertise in each of the areas of Education, Societal/Political, Science and Technology and Social/Ethical. This number may include the Convener and Vice-Convener of the Council.

Convener: Rev. Sally Foster-Fulton BA BD (2012)
Vice-Convener: Rev. J. Christopher Wigglesworth MBE BSc PhD BD (2012)
Secretary: Rev. Ewan R. Aitken BA BD

3. THE MINISTRIES COUNCIL
Tel: 0131-225 5722; Fax: 0131-240 2201
E-mail: ministries@cofscotland.org.uk

Ministries Council Remit
The remit of the Ministries Council is the enabling of ministries in every part of Scotland, giving special priority to the poorest and most marginalised, through the recruitment, training and support of recognised ministries of the Church and the assessment and monitoring of patterns of deployment of those ministries.

In the fulfilment of this remit, the Council offers strategic leadership in the development of patterns of collaborative ministry which enable the Church of Scotland to be effective in its missionary calling and faithful in its participation in the one ministry of Jesus Christ, and operates within the following spheres of work:

Priority Areas – following the Gospel imperative of priority to the poor
- Working directly in support of the poorest parishes in Scotland to enable and resource ministries and to build communities of hope;
- Assisting the whole Church in fulfilling its responsibility to the Gospel imperative of giving priority to the poorest and most marginalised in society;
- Enabling and supporting work in partnership with ecumenical, inter-faith and statutory agencies to achieve the goal of alleviating poverty in Scotland.

Education and Support – recruitment, training and support of ministries personnel
- Developing and implementing patterns of enquiry and assessment and vocational guidance which enable the identification of appropriately called and gifted people to train for recognised ministries;

- Developing and implementing training patterns for those accepted into training for the recognised ministries of the Church;
- Enabling the transfer of people from other denominations into the ministries of the Church;
- Delivering pastoral support to those involved in the recognised ministries of the Church through the development and resourcing of local pastoral networks, direct one-to-one engagement and the provision of occupational health support, counselling, mediation and conflict-resolution services;
- Promoting and providing vocational guidance and lifelong learning opportunities for ministries personnel through in-service events, self-appraisal processes and a study-leave programme.

Partnership Development – working with Presbyteries and other partners in planning and resourcing ministries
- Working with Presbyteries for effective deployment of ministries to meet the needs of the parishes of Scotland and charges in the Presbytery of England, including consulting with congregations and other denominations where appropriate;
- Working in partnership with other agencies of the Church and ecumenical partners, to enable the emergence of ministries to meet the needs of the people of Scotland in every part;
- Supporting those engaged in chaplaincy services both directly employed by the Council and employed by other agencies;
- Ensuring best practice in the employment, care and support of staff, including setting appropriate terms and conditions, offering developmental training to staff and those responsible for their management.

Finance – ensuring good management of funds and monitoring budgets
- Planning strategically for the future funding of the recognised ministries of the Church;
- Managing the funds and overseeing the budgeting processes of the Council to ensure that maximum benefit is derived for the Church's ministries through the use of income and capital;
- Preparing recommendations on the level of stipends and salaries and liaising with Pension Trustees on matters relating to the setting of the Standard Annuity and discretionary increases in pension, and negotiating and reaching agreement with Pension Trustees on funding rates.

Membership
Convener, four Vice-Conveners, 38 members appointed by the General Assembly, one of whom will also be appointed to the Ecumenical Relations Committee, and one member appointed from and by the General Trustees, the Housing and Loan Fund, the Committee on Chaplains to Her Majesty's Forces and the Diaconate Council. For the avoidance of doubt, where a representative of these other bodies is a member of staff, he or she will have no right to vote.

Convener:	Rev. Neil J. Dougall BD
Vice-Conveners:	Rev. Neil Glover
	Rev. Anne S. Paton BA BD
	Mr David A. Stewart MA DipEd
	Rev. Derek H.N. Pope BD

Staff

Council Secretary:	Rev. Martin Scott DipMusEd RSAM BD PhD
	(Tel: ext. 2389; E-mail: mscott@cofscotland.org.uk)
Education and Support Secretary:	Rev. Marjory Macaskill LLB BD
	(Tel: ext. 2315; E-mail: mmacaskill@cofscotland.org.uk)

Partnership Development Secretary:	Rev. Angus R. Mathieson MA BD (Tel: ext. 2312; E-mail: amathieson@cofscotland.org.uk)
Priority Areas Secretary:	Rev. H. Martin J. Johnstone MA BD MTh PhD (Tel: 0141-248 2905; E-mail: mjohnstone@cofscotland.org.uk)
Strategic Projects Manager:	Ms Catherine Skinner BA MA (Tel: ext. 2274; cskinner@cofscotland.org.uk)
Ministries Support Officers:	Mr Ronald Clarke BEng MSc PGCE (Tel: ext. 2242; E-mail: rclarke@cofscotland.org.uk) Rev. Jane Denniston MA BD (Tel: ext. 2204; E-mail: jdenniston@cofscotland.org.uk) Rev. Gavin J. Elliott MA BD (Tel: ext. 2255; E-mail: gelliott@cofscotland.org.uk) Miss Carol-Anne Frame BA (Tel: ext. 2348; E-mail: caframe@cofscotland.org.uk) Mrs Anne Law MA (Tel: ext. 2379; E-mail: alaw@cofscotland.org.uk) Mr Noel Mathias BA BTh MA (Tel: 0141-248 2905; E-mail: nmathias@cofscotland.org.uk) Mr John Thomson (Tel: ext. 2248; E-mail: jthomson@cofscotland.org.uk) Mrs Joyce Watkinson CQSW COSCA, Accredited Counsellor (Tel: ext. 2225; E-mail: jwatkinson@cofscotland.org.uk) Mrs Moira Whyte MA (Tel: ext. 2266; E-mail: mwhyte@cofscotland.org.uk)
Go For It Fund Co-ordinator:	Ms Shirley Grieve (Tel: ext. 2357; E-mail: sgrieve@cofscotland.org.uk)
Training and Development Worker:	Miss Catherine McIntosh (Tel: ext. 2319; E-mail: cmcintosh@cofscotland.org.uk)
A Chance to Thrive Project Co-ordinator:	Rev. Russell McLarty MA BD (Tel: 01875 614496)

Ministries Council
Further information about the Council's work and services is obtainable through the Ministries Council at the Church Offices. Information is available on a wide range of matters including the Consolidated Stipend Fund, National Stipend Fund, endowment grants, travelling and other expenses, pulpit supply, study leave, ministries development conferences, pastoral care services (including occupational health), Enquiry and Assessment, Education and Training, Presbytery Planning, Priority Areas, New Charge Development, Area Team Ministry, Interim Ministry, Readership, Chaplaincies, the Diaconate, Presbytery and Parish Workers (PPWs), the *Go For It* Fund, Emerging Church, and all aspects of work connected with ministers and the ministry of word and sacrament.

Committees
The policy development and implementation of the work of the Ministries Council is managed under the following committees:

1. Strategic Planning Group

Convener: Rev. Neil J. Dougall BD

The Strategic Planning Group comprises the Convener, Vice-Conveners and senior staff of all four areas (including Finance) of the Council and is empowered by the Council to engage in broad-ranging thinking regarding the future outlook and plans of the Council. It reports directly to Council and brings forward to it ideas and consultation papers offering options as to the future strategic direction of the Council's work. Though a key part of the Council's work, it is a consultative and advisory group rather than a decision-making one.

2. Priority Areas Committee

Convener: Rev. Derek H.N. Pope BD

The Priority Areas Committee implements the policy of the Council in developing, encouraging and overseeing strategy within Priority Area parishes. It is empowered to develop resources to enable congregations to make appropriate responses to the needs of people living in poverty in their parishes, and to raise awareness of the effects of poverty on people's lives in Scotland. It also co-ordinates the strategy of the wider Church in its priority to Scotland's poorest parishes.

3. Education and Support Committee

Convener: Rev. Anne S. Paton BA BD

The Education and Support Committee is responsible for the development and oversight of policy in relation to the enquiry and assessment process for ministers of Word and Sacrament (full-time and ordained local ministry), Deacons and Readers, together with the admission and readmission of ministers. It is further responsible for the supervision of those in training for those recognised ministries of the Church and operates with powers in relation to both of these areas of work to make recommendations on suitability for training and readiness to engage in ministries at the end of a training period. It also implements Council policies on pastoral care for all recognised ministries, the integration of Occupational Health with ministries support services, and the oversight of the working of those Acts relating to long-term illness of ministers in charges. It promotes development opportunities for those engaged in recognised ministries, including study leave and accompanied reviews.

4. Partnership Development Committee

Convener: Mr David A. Stewart MA DipEd

The Partnership Development Committee is responsible for maintaining and developing relationships with Presbyteries and other agencies and partners in the planning and resourcing of ministries. This includes the overall planning of the deployment of the Church's ministries, primarily through the ongoing monitoring of the development of Presbytery Plans. The Committee also oversees work on emerging ministries (including New Charge Development work). It deals further with the work of Interim Ministry and Area Team Ministry, and with all aspects of chaplaincy work. The Committee also oversees the Church of Scotland *Go For It* Fund; see page 32.

5. Finance Committee

Convener: Rev. Neil Glover

The Finance Committee operates with powers to deal with the Parish Ministries Fund, the National Stipend Scheme, Vacancy Schedules, Maintenance Allowances, Hardship Grants and Bursaries, Stipend Advances, management of investments, writing-off shortfalls and the granting of further endowments. It also maintains an oversight of the budgets for all recognised ministries.

The Council also has several *ad hoc* Groups, which report to the Committees and implement specific policies of the Council, as follows:

Recruitment Task Group
Leader: Rev. Andrea E. Price

Training Task Group
Leader: Rev. Donald G.B. McCorkindale BD DipMin

***Go For It* Fund Committee**
Convener: Rev. Rolf H. Billes BD

Joint Emerging Church Group (with Mission and Discipleship Council)
Leader: Rev. David C. Cameron BD CertMin

Interim Ministries Task Group
Leader: Rev. James Reid BD

Chaplaincies Forum
Leader: Rev. C. Graham Taylor BSc BD FIAB

Pastoral and Vocational Care Task Group
Leader: Mrs Sandra Holt

Presbytery Planning Task Group
Leader: Rev. Alison A. Meikle BD

Other Related Bodies:
Chaplains to HM Forces
See separate entry at number 10.

The Church of Scotland Housing and Loan Fund
See separate entry at number 12.

Pulpit Supply: Fee and Expenses
The General Assembly of 2011 approved new regulations governing the amount of Supply Fee and Expenses. These were effective from 1 April 2012 and are as follows:
1. In Charges where there is only one diet of worship, the Pulpit Supply Fee shall be a Standard Fee of £55 (or as from time to time agreed by the Ministries Council).
2. In Charges where there are additional diets of worship on a Sunday, the person fulfilling the Supply shall be paid £15 for each additional Service (or as from time to time agreed by the Ministries Council).
3. Where the person is unwilling to conduct more than one diet of worship on a given Sunday, he or she shall receive a pro-rata payment based on the total available Fee shared on the basis of the number of Services conducted.
4. The Fee thus calculated shall be payable in the case of all persons permitted to conduct Services under Act II 1986.
5. In all cases, Travelling Expenses shall be paid. Where there is no convenient public conveyance, the use of a private car shall be paid for at the Committee rate of Travelling Expenses. In exceptional circumstances, to be approved in advance, the cost of hiring a car may be met.
6. Where weekend board and lodging are agreed as necessary, these may be claimed for the weekend at a maximum rate of that allowed when attending the General Assembly. The Fee and Expenses should be paid to the person providing the Supply before he or she leaves on the Sunday.

4.   THE MISSION AND DISCIPLESHIP COUNCIL

Remit
The remit of the Mission and Discipleship Council is:
* to take a lead role in developing and maintaining an overall focus for mission in Scotland, and to highlight its fundamental relationships with worship, service, doctrine, education and nurture;
* to take a lead role in developing strategies, resources and services in Christian education and nurture, recognising these as central to both mission and discipleship;
* to offer appropriate servicing and support nationally, regionally and locally in the promotion of nurturing, worshipping and witnessing communities of faith;
* to introduce policy on behalf of the Church in the following areas: adult education and elder training, church art and architecture, congregational mission and development, doctrine, resourcing youth and children's work, worship;
* to establish and support the Mission Forum with representatives of relevant Councils;
* to encourage appropriate awareness of, and response to, the requirements of people with particular needs including physical, sensory and/or learning disabilities;
* to conduct an annual review of progress made in discharging the remit and provide a written report to the Council of Assembly.

Statement of Purpose
Resourcing Christ's Mission: to enable and empower people to engage in Christ's mission through resourcing worship, witness and discipleship in the context of the changing contemporary culture of Scotland and beyond.
Specifically, we will:
* stimulate critical reflection and development of places and practice of worship = WORSHIP
* communicate Christ's message lovingly, effectively and relevantly = WITNESS
* nurture and develop learning and growth within congregations and communities = DISCIPLESHIP.

Membership
Convener, three Vice-Conveners and 24 members appointed by the General Assembly, one of whom will also be appointed to the Ecumenical Relations Committee, the Director of Stewardship, one member appointed from and by the General Trustees, the Guild and the Scottish Community Trust, and the Convener or Vice-Convener of the Committee on Church Art and Architecture as that Committee shall determine. The Nomination Committee will ensure that the Council membership contains individuals with specific expertise in the areas of Mission, Education, Worship, Doctrine and Publishing.

Convener:	Rev. Colin A.M. Sinclair BA BD
Vice-Conveners:	Rev. Roderick G. Hamilton MA BD
	Rev. David C. Cameron BD CertMin
	Mr John Hawthorn BSc

Staff

Council Secretary:	Appointment awaited
Faith Expressions Team Leader:	Rev. Nigel Robb FCP MA BD ThM MTh
	(E-mail: nrobb@cofscotland.org.uk)
Church Without Walls Team Leader:	Mrs Lesley Hamilton-Messer MA
	(E-mail: lhamilton-messer@cofscotland.org.uk)
Congregational Learning Team Leader:	Appointment awaited

Mission Development Workers
Mission Development Workers are tasked with supporting local congregations to help them become more resourceful so that they can engage effectively with their communities. They are:

Mr Steve Aisthorpe BA   (E-mail: saisthorpe@cofscotland.org.uk)
Mr Robert Rawson BA   (E-mail: rrawson@cofscotland.org.uk)
Mr Iain Campbell BA PGDE   (E-mail: icampbell@cofscotland.org.uk)

Specialist Development Workers
The following staff members provide specialist advice and support to congregations on key areas of work:

Mr Graham Fender-Allison BA   Worship Development Worker
                                      (E-mail: gfender-allison@cofscotland.org.uk)
Ms Suzi Farrant BSc BA   Children and Young People Development Worker
                                      (E-mail: sfarrant@cofscotland.org.uk)

The Netherbow: Scottish Storytelling Centre: The integrated facilities of the **Netherbow Theatre** and the **John Knox House Museum**, together with the outstanding new conference and reception areas, are an important cultural and visitor centre on the Royal Mile in Edinburgh and provide advice and assistance nationally in the use of the arts in mission, education and worship. 'Story Source', 'Scriptaid' and other resources are available. Contact the Director, The Netherbow: Scottish Storytelling Centre, 43–45 High Street, Edinburgh EH1 1SR (Tel: 0131-556 9579; E-mail; donald@scottishstorytellingcentre.com; Website: www.scottishstorytellingcentre.co.uk).

Life and Work
(Tel: 0131-225 5722; Fax: 0131-240 2207; E-mail: magazine@lifeandwork.org)
Life and Work is the Church of Scotland's monthly magazine. Its purpose is to keep the Church informed about events in church life at home and abroad and to provide a forum for Christian opinion and debate on a variety of topics. It has an independent editorial policy. Contributions which are relevant to any aspect of the Christian faith are welcome.
    The price of *Life and Work* this year is £1.80. With a circulation of around 25,000, it also offers advertisers a first-class opportunity to reach a discerning readership in all parts of Scotland.

Saint Andrew Press
Saint Andrew Press is now managed on behalf of the Church of Scotland by Hymns Ancient and Modern.
    The Saint Andrew Press catalogue includes the updated and freshly redesigned series of New Testament commentaries, *The New Daily Study Bible*, by the late Professor William Barclay, which has been read by many millions of people around the world. Bestsellers include the widely acclaimed *George Mackay Brown: The Wound and the Gift* by Ron Ferguson, William Barclay's inspiring *Insights* series, *A Glasgow Bible* by Jamie Stuart, *Outside Verdict* by Harry Reid, *Iona* by Kenneth Steven, *My Father: Reith of the BBC* by Marista Leishman and *Silent Heroes* by John Miller. Other popular titles include the practical *Who Needs Words?: A Christian Communications Handbook* by Richard Littledale, *Will You Follow Me?* by Leith Fisher, Beginners' Guides to the Old and New Testaments, a series of *Sacred Places* guides to all of Scotland's churches, and the Church of Scotland's *Pray Now*.

Saint Andrew Press invites readers to join its website mailing list in order to receive regular information on its publications, news of authors and special events and offers. Up-to-date information on all Saint Andrew Press titles can be found at www.standrewpress.com

All new proposals for publication should be sent to the Senior Commissioning Editor in the form of a two-page description of the book and its readership, together with one sample chapter. The Senior Commissioning Editor (ann@hymnsam.co.uk) is always happy to offer help and advice. For further information, please refer to www.standrewpress.com and go to 'Submission Guidelines' on the 'Contact Us' tab.

Committee on Church Art and Architecture
Convener: Dr J.G. Roberts MA
Membership
The Committee shall comprise a Convener, Vice-Convener and 15 members appointed by the General Assembly.

Remit
This Committee replaced the Committee on Artistic Matters and will take forward that Committee's remit, which is in the following terms:

The Committee advises congregations and Presbyteries regarding the most appropriate way of carrying out renovations, alterations and reordering of interiors, having regard to the architectural quality of Church buildings. It also advises on the installation of stained glass, tapestries, memorials, furniture and furnishings, and keeps a list of accredited artists and craftsworkers.

Any alteration to the exterior or interior of a Church building which affects its appearance must be referred to the Committee for approval, which is given through the General Trustees. Congregations contemplating alterations are urged to consult the Committee at an early stage.

Members of the Committee are prepared, when necessary, to visit churches and meet office-bearers. The Committee's services are given free.

The Committee seeks the conservation of the nation's heritage as expressed in its Church buildings, while at the same time helping to ensure that these buildings continue to serve the worship and witness of the Church in the present day.

In recent years, the General Assembly has conferred these additional duties on the Committee:
1. preparation of reports on the architectural, historical and aesthetic merit of the buildings of congregations involved in questions of readjustment
2. verification of the propriety of repair and renovation work forming the basis of grant applications to public bodies
3. the offering of advice on the maintenance and installation of organs
4. facilitating the transfer of unwanted furnishings from one church to another through *Exchange and Transfer*
5. the processing of applications from congregations for permission to dispose of surplus communion plate, and the carrying out of an inventory of sacramental vessels held by congregations.

Work with Rural Churches
The Council aims to affirm, support and resource rural churches and is responsible for planning for a Church presence at the Royal Highland Show. It seeks to reflect the full extent of rural experience, encompassing farming, fishing, tourism, forestry and other professions/industries

that have a bearing on rural life. This will involve collaboration with ecumenical partners and responding periodically to requests for submissions to government consultations.

5. THE SOCIAL CARE COUNCIL
SOCIAL CARE (CrossReach)
Charis House, 47 Milton Road East, Edinburgh EH15 2SR
Tel: 0131-657 2000; Fax: 0131-657 5000
E-mail: info@crossreach.org.uk; Website: www.crossreach.org.uk

The Social Care Council, known as CrossReach, provides social-care services as part of the Christian witness of the Church to the people of Scotland.

Remit
The remit of the Social Care Council is:
* as part of the Church's mission, to offer services in Christ's name to people in need;
* to provide specialist resources to further the caring work of the Church;
* to identify existing and emerging areas of need, to guide the Church in pioneering new approaches to relevant problems and to make responses on issues arising within the area of the Council's concern through appropriate channels such as the Church's Church and Society Council, the Scottish Government and the like;
* to conduct an annual review of progress made in discharging the remit and provide an annual written report to the General Assembly;
* to oversee an appropriate corporate management and support service to deliver the above and be responsible for funding all salaries and related costs;
* to set and review terms and conditions of staff and establish appropriate internal governance systems.

Membership
Convener, two Vice-Conveners and 28 members appointed by the General Assembly, one of whom will also be appointed to the Ecumenical Relations Committee. The Council shall have power to appoint such Committees and Groups as it may from time to time determine to be appropriate to ensure that the Council's Remit is fulfilled.

Convener:	Rev. Sydney S. Graham (2009)
Vice-Conveners:	Ian Huggan (2011)
	Rev. Ramsay Shields (2009)

Staff
Chief Executive Officer: Peter Bailey (peter.bailey@crossreach.org.uk)

Management Structure
The management structure is service-based. There are three Operational Directors, each with a specialist area of responsibility. They are supported by Heads of Service, who have lead roles for particular types of service and client groups.

Director of Services to Older People: Marlene Smith (marlene.smith@crossreach.org.uk)

Heads of Service:	Brenda Fraser (East) Allan Logan (West) Annie McDonald (North)
Director of Adult Care Services: Heads of Service:	Calum Murray (calum.murray@crossreach.org.uk) George McNeilly, Dave Clark, Viv Dickenson
Director of Children and Families: Head of Service Residential Schools:	Chris McNaught (chris.mcnaught@crossreach.org.uk) Paul Gilroy
Director of Finance and Resources: Business Partners:	Ian Wauchope (ian.wauchope@crossreach.org.uk) Arthur Akugbo, Eoin McDunphy, Robert Murray
Director of Human Resources and Organisational Development: Business Partners:	 Mari Rennie (mari.rennie@crossreach.org.uk) Jane Allan, Ronnie Black
Head of Estates and Health and Safety:	David Reid (david.reid@crossreach.org.uk)
Health and Safety Manager:	Richard Park
Business, Compliance and Improvement Head of Service:	 Claire Hay (claire.hay@crossreach.org.uk)
Business Development Head of Service:	Elizabeth Hay (elizabeth.hay@crossreach.org.uk)

List of Services
CrossReach operates 75 services across Scotland, and a list of these can be obtained from Charis House on 0131-657 2000, or from the CrossReach website: www.crossreach.org.uk

---

6.   THE WORLD MISSION COUNCIL
Tel: 0131-225 5722; Fax: 0131-226 6121
E-mail: world@cofscotland.org.uk

Remit
The remit of the World Mission Council is:
*   to give life to the Church of Scotland's understanding that it is part of Jesus Christ's Universal Church committed to the advance of the Kingdom of God throughout the world;
*   to discern priorities and form policies to guide the Church of Scotland's ongoing worldwide participation in God's transforming mission, through the Gospel of Jesus Christ;
*   to develop and maintain mutually enriching relationships with the Church of Scotland's partner churches overseas through consultation in the two-way sharing of human and material resources;
*   to equip and encourage Church of Scotland members at local, Presbytery and national levels to become engaged in the life of the world Church;
*   to help the people of Scotland to appreciate the worldwide nature of the Christian faith;

- to keep informed about the cultural, political, social, economic, religious and ecclesiastical issues of relevance to worldwide mission;
- to recruit, train and support paid staff and volunteers to work overseas;
- to direct the work of the Council's centres in Israel;
- to foster and facilitate local partnerships between congregations and Presbyteries and the partner churches;
- to undertake the responsibilities of the former Board of World Mission in regard to the Presbytery of Europe and its congregations as set out in the relevant Assembly legislation;
- to conduct an annual review of progress made in discharging the remit and provide a written report to the Council of Assembly.

Membership
Convener, two Vice-Conveners, 24 members appointed by the General Assembly, one of whom will also be appointed from the Committee on Ecumenical Relations, and one member appointed by the Presbytery of Europe.

Convener:	Very Rev. Andrew R.C. McLellan CBE MA BD STM DD (2010)
Vice-Conveners:	Rev. Iain D. Cunningham MA BD (2011)
	Rev. Christine Sime BSc BD (2012)

Departmental Staff
Council Secretary:	Rev. Ian Alexander
Secretaries:	Jennie Chinembiri (Africa and Caribbean)
	Carol Finlay (Twinning and Local Development)
	Sandy Sneddon (Asia)
Administration:	Donna Maclean
Finance:	Catriona Scrimgeour (Assistant Treasurer)
Human Resources:	Kelly Smith
	Angela Ocak

Strategic Commitments:
Mission in a New Mode – Local to Local
- **Evangelism** – working with partner churches on new initiatives in evangelism
- **Reconciliation** – working for justice, peace and reconciliation in situations of conflict or threat
- **The Scandal of Poverty** – resourcing the Church to set people free from the oppression of poverty.

World Mission and World Resources
Sharing in the mission of God worldwide requires a continuing commitment to sharing the Church of Scotland's resources of people and money for mission in six continents as contemporary evidence that it is 'labouring for the advancement of the Kingdom of God throughout the world' (First Article Declaratory). Such resource-sharing remains an urgent matter because most of our overseas work is in the developing world, or 'South', in nations where the effects of the widening gap between rich and poor is *the* major issue for the Church. Our partner churches in Africa, the Middle East, most of Asia and the Caribbean are desperately short of financial and technical resources, which we can to some extent meet with personnel and grants. However, they are more than willing to share the resources of their Christian faith with us, including things

which the Church in the West often lacks: enthusiasm in worship, hospitality and evangelism, and a readiness to suffer and struggle for righteousness, and in many areas a readiness to sink denominational differences. Mutual sharing in the world Church witnesses to its international nature and has much to offer a divided world, not least in Scotland. Much fruit has been borne since the beginning of the twinning programme, and many congregations are experiencing and sharing the challenges and opportunities of their connection with the World Church. Information and support are available from Carol Finlay (Twinning and Local Development Secretary: E-mail: cfinlay@cofscotland.org.uk).

Vacancies Overseas
The Council welcomes enquiries from men and women interested in serving in the Church overseas. Vacancies for mission partner appointments in the Church's centrally supported partnerships, volunteer programme and opportunities with other organisations can all be considered. Those interested in more information are invited to contact the Human Resources Department at the Church Offices (E-mail: hr@cofscotland.org.uk).

HIV Programme
The Programme aims to raise awareness in congregations about the impact of HIV and AIDS and seeks to channel urgently needed support to partner churches. For further information, contact Marjorie Clark, Co-ordinator, HIV Programme (E-mail: mclark@cofscotland.org.uk).

Christian Aid Scotland
Christian Aid is the official relief and development agency of 41 Churches in Britain and Ireland. Christian Aid's mandate is to challenge and enable us to fulfil our responsibilities to the poor of the world. Half a million volunteers and collectors make this possible, with money given by millions of supporters. The Church of Scotland marks its commitment as a Church to this part of its mission through an annual grant from the Mission and Renewal Fund, transmitted through the World Mission Council, which keeps in close touch with Christian Aid and its work. Up-to-date information about projects and current emergency relief work can be obtained from:
*   The Head of Christian Aid Scotland, Rev. Dr Kathy Galloway: Christian Aid Scotland, Sycamore House, 290 Bath Street, Glasgow G2 4JR (Tel: 0141-221 7475)
*   The Director: Loretta Minghella, Christian Aid Office, PO Box 100, London SE1 7RT (Tel: 020 7620 4444)

Pilgrimage
The Church of Scotland encourages visitors and pilgrims to visit the Christian Community of Israel and Palestine, to walk with them in fellowship and build relationships to help understand their life, witness and situation.

There are two Church of Scotland Residential Centres in Israel which provide comfortable accommodation for pilgrims and visitors to the Holy Land. Further information on planning a pilgrimage experience which includes meetings with the local Christian community and others is available from the ministers: George Shand (E-mail: stachjer@netvision.net.il) and Colin Johnston (E-mail: revcdj60@gmail.com).
(a)   St Andrew's Guest House, 1 David Remez Street, PO Box 8619, Jerusalem 91086, Israel (Tel: 00 972 2 6732401; Fax: 00 972 2 6731711; E-mail: standjer@netvision.net.il)
(b)   The Scots Hotel, St Andrew's, Galilee: 1 Gdud Barak Street, PO Box 104, Tiberias 14100, Israel (Tel: 00 972 4 671 0759; Fax: 00 972 4 672 5282; E-mail: scottie@ netvision.net.il)

A list of Overseas Appointments will be found in List K in Section 6.

A *World Mission Year Book* is available with more details of our partner churches and of people currently serving abroad, including those with ecumenical bodies and para-church bodies.

A list of Retired Missionaries will be found in List L in Section 6.

7. Assembly Arrangements Committee

Membership

Convener, Vice-Convener and ten members appointed by the General Assembly on the Report of the Nomination Committee; the Convener and Vice-Convener also to serve as Convener and Vice-Convener of the General Assembly's Business Committee.

The Clerks are non-voting members of the Assembly Arrangements Committee, and the Moderator and Moderator Designate are members of the Committee.

Convener:	Rev. Janet S. Mathieson MA BD
Vice-Convener:	Rev. E. Lorna Hood MA BD
Secretary:	The Principal Clerk

Remit

The Committee's remit is:

- to make all necessary arrangements for the General Assembly;
- to advise the Moderator on his or her official duties if so required;
- to be responsible to the General Assembly for the care and maintenance of the Assembly Hall and the Moderator's flat;
- to be responsible to the General Assembly for all arrangements in connection with the letting of the General Assembly Hall;
- to conduct an annual review of progress made in discharging the remit and provide a written report to the Council of Assembly.

8. Central Properties Department

Staff

Property, Health and Safety Manager:	Colin Wallace
Property Health and Safety Officer:	Jacqueline Collins
Property Officer:	Eunice Hessell
Support Assistant:	Joyce McMurdo

Remit

The Central Properties Department has the remit to provide Property, Facilities and Health and Safety services to the Councils and Departments of the central administration of the Church. This includes:

- management of properties owned by the Councils and Departments
- procurement of land for new-build projects
- delivery of new-build projects including new church buildings
- delivery of major refurbishment programmes

- management of the furlough housing estate for World Mission
- management of facilities and procurement of work equipment
- development and ongoing review of the Health and Safety policy
- provision of Health and Safety management for employing agencies of the Church
- provision of Health and Safety training
- administration of the Health and Safety Committee
- support for arbitrations in the case of parish readjustment.

Contact: Central Properties Department, 121 George Street, Edinburgh EH2 4YN (Tel: 0131-240 2254; E-mail: cpd@cofscotland.org.uk).

---

9. Central Services Committee

Membership
(13 members: nine appointed by the General Assembly, and four *ex officiis* and non-voting, namely the Secretary to the Council of Assembly, the Solicitor of the Church, the General Treasurer and the Head of Human Resources and Information Technology)

Convener:	Mr Angus Macpherson MA BSc DPSA (2010)
Vice-Conveners:	Mr Bill Steele (2010)
	Mr Philip Craig MA MEd MSc DipRE (2010)

Staff

Administrative Secretary:	Mrs Pauline Wilson
	(E-mail: pwilson@cofscotland.org.uk)

Remit
- To be responsible for the proper maintenance and insurance of the Church Offices at 117–123 George Street and 21 Young Street, Edinburgh ('the Church Offices');
- To be responsible for matters relating to Health and Safety within the Church Offices;
- To be responsible for matters relating to Data Protection within the Church Offices and with respect to the General Assembly Councils based elsewhere;
- To be responsible for the allocation of accommodation within the Church Offices and the annual determination of rental charges to the Councils and other parties accommodated therein;
- To oversee the delivery of central services to departments within the Church Offices, to Councils of the General Assembly and, where appropriate, to the Statutory Corporations, Presbyteries and Congregations, namely:
  1. Those facilities directly managed by the Facilities Manager;
  2. Information Technology (including the provision of support services to Presbytery Clerks);
  3. Human Resources;
  4. Legal Services (as delivered by the Law Department and subject to such oversight not infringing principles of 'client/solicitor' confidentiality);
  5. Property Services (as delivered by the Central Properties Department).
- The Committee shall act as one of the employing agencies of the Church and shall, except in so far as specifically herein provided, assume and exercise the whole rights, functions and responsibilities of the former Personnel Committee;

- While the Committee shall *inter alia* have responsibility for determining the terms and conditions of the staff for whom it is the employing agency, any staff who are members of the Committee or who are appointed directly by the General Assembly shall not be present when matters solely relating to their own personal terms and conditions of employment/office are under consideration;
- To conduct an annual review of progress made in discharging this remit and provide a written report to the Council of Assembly.

10. Chaplains to HM Forces

Convener: Rev. Neil N. Gardner MA BD
Vice-Convener: Rev. Jackie G. Petrie
Secretary: Mr John K. Thomson, Ministries Council, 121 George Street, Edinburgh EH2 4YN

Recruitment
The Chaplains' Committee is entrusted with the task of recruitment of Chaplains for the Regular, Reserve and Auxiliary Forces. Vacancies occur periodically, and the Committee is happy to receive enquiries from all interested ministers.

Forces Registers
The Committee maintains a Register of all those who have been baptised and/or admitted to Communicant Membership by Service Chaplains.

Parish Ministers are asked to take advantage of the facilities by applying for Certificates, where appropriate, from the Secretary of the Committee.

Full information may be obtained from the Secretary, Mr John K. Thomson (Tel: 0131-225 5722; E-mail: jthomson@cofscotland.org.uk).

A list of Chaplains will be found in List B in Section 6.

11. The Church of Scotland Guild

National Office-bearers and Executive Staff
Convener: Mrs Mary Ford
Vice-Convener: Marjorie Paton
General Secretary: Iain W. Whyte BA DCE DMS
Information Officer: Mrs Fiona J. Punton MCIPR
                       (E-mail: fpunton@cofscotland.org.uk)
                       (Tel: 0131-225 5722 ext. 2317 or 0131-240 2217)

The Church of Scotland Guild is a movement within the Church of Scotland whose aim is '**to invite and encourage both women and men to commit their lives to Jesus Christ and to enable them to express their faith in worship, prayer and action**'. Membership of the Guild is open to all who subscribe to that aim.

Groups at congregational level are free to organise themselves under the authority of the Kirk Session, as best suits their own local needs and circumstances. Large groups with frequent meetings and activities continue to operate with a committee or leadership team, while other, smaller groups simply share whatever tasks need to be done among the membership as a whole. Similarly, at Presbyterial Council level, frequency and style of meetings vary according to local needs, as do leadership patterns. Each Council may nominate one person to serve at national level, where five committees take forward the work of the Guild in accordance with the stated Aim.

These committees are:

- National Executive
- Finance and General Purposes
- Projects and Topics
- Programmes and Resources
- Marketing and Publicity.

There has always been a close relationship between the Guild and other Departments of the Church, and members welcome the opportunity to contribute to the Church's wider mission through the Project Partnership Scheme and other joint ventures. The Guild is represented on both the Church and Society Council and the Mission and Discipleship Council.

The project scheme affords groups at congregational level the opportunity to select a project, or projects, from a range of up to six, selected from proposals submitted by a wide range of Church Departments and other Church-related bodies. A project partner in each group seeks ways of promoting the project locally, increasing awareness of the issues raised by it, and encouraging support of a financial and practical nature. Support is available from the Project Co-ordinator at Council level and the Information Officer based at the Guild Office.

The Guild is very aware of the importance of good communication in any large organisation, and regularly sends mailings to its groups to pass on information and resources to the members. In addition, the Newsletter, sent to members three times per session, is a useful communication tool, as is the website (www.cos-guild.org.uk). These are a means of sharing experiences and of communicating something of the wider interest and influence of the Guild, which participates in other national bodies such as the Network of Ecumenical Women in Scotland and the Scottish Women's Convention.

Each year, the Guild follows a Theme and produces a resources pack covering worship and study material. There is also a related Discussion Topic with supporting material and background information. The theme, topic and projects all relate to a common three-year strategy which, for 2012–15, is **'Whose we are and Whom we Serve'**, the Guild's motto being chosen in recognition of the fact that 2012 sees the celebration of 125 years of the Guild. The first theme within the strategy will be **'A Faith to Proclaim'**, to be followed by **'A Fellowship to Build'** and **'A World to Serve'** in the next two years. At the same time, the Guild will embark on six new Partnership Projects, each chosen to reflect something of the strategy and the themes for the triennium. The related discussion topic for 2012–13 will be **'Being Christian in Today's World'**, allowing members to consider and reflect upon what it means to be a Christian in our time and how that might be demonstrated through worship, prayer and action.

Further information is available from the Guild Office (Tel: 0131-225 5722 ext. 2317, or 0131-240 2217) or from the website (www.cos-guild.org.uk).

12. The Church of Scotland Housing and Loan Fund for Retired Ministers and Widows and Widowers of Ministers

Membership
The Trustees shall be a maximum of 11 in number, being:
1. four appointed by the General Assembly on the nomination of the Trustees, who, having served a term of four years, shall be eligible for reappointment;
2. three ministers and one member appointed by the Ministries Council;
3. three appointed by the Baird Trust.

Chairman: Mr J.G. Grahame Lees MA LLB NP
Deputy Chairman: Rev. Ian Taylor BD ThM
Secretary: Miss Lin J. Macmillan MA

Staff
Property Manager: Miss Hilary J. Hardy
Property Assistant: Mr John Lunn

Remit
The Fund, as established by the General Assembly, facilitates the provision of housing accommodation for retired ministers and widows, widowers and separated or divorced spouses of Church of Scotland ministers. When provided, help may take the form of either a house to rent or a house-purchase loan.

The Trustees may grant tenancy of one of their existing houses or they may agree to purchase for rental occupation an appropriate house of an applicant's choosing. Leases are normally on very advantageous terms as regards rental levels. Alternatively, the Trustees may grant a housing loan of up to 70 per cent of a house-purchase price but with an upper limit. Favourable rates of interest are charged.

The Trustees are also prepared to consider assisting those who have managed to house themselves but are seeking to move to more suitable accommodation. Those with a mortgaged home on retirement may be granted a loan to enable them to repay such a mortgage and thereafter to enjoy the favourable rates of interest charged by the Fund.

Ministers making application within five years of retirement, upon their application being approved, will be given a fairly firm commitment that, in due course, either a house will be made available for renting or a house-purchase loan will be offered. Only within nine months of a minister's intended retiral date will the Trustees initiate steps to find a suitable house; only within one year of that date will a loan be advanced. Applications submitted about ten years prior to retirement have the benefit of initial review and, if approved, a place on the preliminary applications list for appropriate decision in due time.

Donations and legacies over the years have been significant in building up this Fund. Congregational contributions have been, and will continue to be, an essential backbone.

The Board of Trustees is a completely independent body answerable to the General Assembly, and enquiries and applications are dealt with in the strictest confidence.

Further information can be obtained from the Secretary, Miss Lin J. Macmillan MA, at the Church of Scotland Offices, 121 George Street, Edinburgh EH2 4YN (Tel: 0131-225 5722 ext. 2310; E-mail: lmacmillan@cofscotland.org.uk; Website: www.churchofscotland.org.uk).

13. Church of Scotland Investors Trust

Membership
(Trustees are appointed by the General Assembly, on the nomination of the Investors Trust)
Chairman: Mr A.W.T. Gibb BA
Vice-Chairman: Mrs I.J. Hunter MA
Treasurer: Mr I.W. Grimmond BAcc CA
Deputy Treasurer: Mrs A.F. Macintosh BA CA
Secretary: Miss N. Laing

Remit
The Church of Scotland Investors Trust was established by the Church of Scotland (Properties and Investments) Order Confirmation Act 1994 – Scottish Charity Number SC022884 – and offers investment services to the Church of Scotland and to bodies and trusts within or connected with the Church. It offers simple and economical facilities for investment in its three Funds, and investors receive the benefits of professional management, continuous portfolio supervision, spread of investment risk and economies of scale.
    The three Funds are:

1. Deposit Fund
The Deposit Fund is intended for short-term investment and seeks to provide a competitive rate of interest while preserving nominal capital value. It is invested mainly in short-term loans to banks and building societies. Interest is calculated quarterly in arrears and paid gross on 15 May and 15 November. Withdrawals are on demand. The Fund is managed by Thomas Miller Investments Limited, Edinburgh and London.

2. Growth Fund
The Growth Fund is a unitised fund, largely equity-based, intended to provide a growing annual income sufficient to meet the Trustees' target distributions and to provide an increase in the value of capital long term. Units can only be purchased or sold on a monthly dealing date, and income is distributed gross on 15 May and 15 November. The Fund is managed by Newton Investment Management Limited, London.

3. Income Fund
The Income Fund is a unitised fund, invested predominantly in fixed-interest securities, intended to provide a high and sustainable income at a level as agreed between the Trustees and the manager from time to time and to protect the long-term nominal value of capital. Units can only be purchased or sold on a monthly dealing date, and income is distributed gross on 15 March and 15 September. The Fund is managed by Royal London Asset Management, London.

    Further information and application forms for investment are available on the Church of Scotland website or by writing to the Secretary, The Church of Scotland Investors Trust, 121 George Street, Edinburgh EH2 4YN (E-mail: nlaing@cofscotland.org.uk).

14.   The Church of Scotland Pension Trustees

Chairman: Mr W.J. McCafferty ACII APFS TEP
Vice-Chairman: Mr A.J. Priestly FCII
Secretary: Mr S.D. Kaney BSc MPMI

Staff
Pensions Manager: Mr Steve D. Kaney BSc MPMI
Pensions Administrators: Mrs Louise Donn
                                        Miss Fiona McCulloch
                                        Mr Andrew McKenna
                                        Miss Marshall Paterson
Team Secretary: Mrs Nancy Harper

Remit
The body acts as Trustees for the Church of Scotland's three Pension Schemes:
1.   The Church of Scotland Pension Scheme for Ministers and Overseas Missionaries
2.   The Church of Scotland Pension Scheme for Staff
3.   The Church of Scotland Pension Scheme for Presbytery and Parish Workers.
The Trustees have wide-ranging duties and powers detailed in the Trust Law, Pension Acts and other regulations, but in short the Trustees are responsible for the administration of the Pension Schemes and for the investment of the Scheme Funds. Six Trustees are appointed by the General Assembly, and members nominate up to three Trustees for each Scheme.
    The investment of the Funds is delegated to external Investment Managers under the guidelines and investment principles set by the Trustees: Baillie Gifford & Co., Newton Investment Management Ltd, Aviva, Black Rock, Aegon, Rogge and Legal & General.
    The benefits provided by the three Pension Schemes differ in detail, but all provide a pension to the Scheme member and dependants on death of the member, and a lump-sum death benefit on death in service. Scheme members also have the option to improve their benefits by paying additional voluntary contributions (AVCs) to arrangements set up by the Trustees with leading Insurance Companies.
    Further information on any of the Church of Scotland Pension Schemes or on individual benefits can be obtained from the Pensions Manager, Church of Scotland Offices, 121 George Street, Edinburgh EH2 4YN (Tel: 0131-240 2255; Fax: 0131-240 2220; E-mail: pensions@ cofscotland.org.uk).

---

15.   The Church of Scotland Trust

Membership
(Members are appointed by the General Assembly, on the nomination of the Trust)
Chairman: Mr Robert Brodie CB WS
Vice-Chairman: Mr Christopher N. Mackay WS
Treasurer: Mr Iain W. Grimmond BAcc CA
Secretary and Clerk: Mrs Jennifer M. Hamilton BA

Remit

The Church of Scotland Trust was established by Act of Parliament in 1932 and has Scottish Charity Number SC020269. The Trust's function since 1 January 1995 has been to hold properties outwith Scotland and to act as Trustee in a number of third-party trusts.

Further information can be obtained from the Secretary and Clerk of The Church of Scotland Trust, 121 George Street, Edinburgh   EH2 4YN (Tel: 0131-240 2222; E-mail: jhamilton@cofscotland.org.uk).

---

16. Committee on Church Art and Architecture

See entry in full under **The Mission and Discipleship Council** (number 4).

---

17. Communications Unit

Communications Department
Head of Communications: Grant Hutchison

Communications and Media Relations Team
Senior Media Relations Officer: Nick Jury
Communications Officer: Fiona Lang

Programmes Co-ordinator: Virginia Cano

Web Team
Web Editor: Narelle McGowan
Web Developer: Alan Murray

Design Services
Senior Graphic Designer: Claire Bewsey
Senior Graphic Designer: Chris Flexen

The Communications Department has responsibility for providing and promoting effective internal and external communications across the Church of Scotland.

The Media Relations Team services local, regional, national, UK and international media. News releases are issued on a regular basis to a large network of media contacts, and staff provide advice and information on media matters within the Church. Media Relations staff can be contacted on 0131-240 2204/2268 during office hours, or on 07854 783539 after hours, at weekends and on public holidays.

The Web Team is responsible for developing and updating the Church's website (www.churchofscotland.org.uk) and managing the Church's social-media channels. The Design Team creates printed and online material for the Church.

18.   The Department of the General Assembly

The Department of the General Assembly supports the General Assembly and the Moderator, the Council of Assembly and the Ecumenical Relations Committee. In addition, Departmental staff service the following Committees: Assembly Arrangements, Legal Questions, the Committee to Nominate the Moderator, the Nomination Committee, the Committee on Overtures and Cases, the Committee on Classifying Returns to Overtures and the Central Services Committee. The Clerks of Assembly are available for consultation on matters of Church Law, Practice and Procedure.

Staff

Principal Clerk of the General Assembly:	Rev. John P. Chalmers BD CPS
Depute Clerk of the General Assembly*:	Rev. George J. Whyte BSc BD DMin
Secretary to the Council of Assembly:	Mrs Pauline Weibye MA DPA Chartered FCIPD
Ecumenical Officer:	Very Rev. Sheilagh M. Kesting BA BD DD
Personal Assistant to the Principal Clerk:	Mrs Linda Jamieson
Senior Administration Officer:	Mrs Alison Murray MA
(Assembly Arrangements and Moderatorial Support)	
Senior Administration Officer:	Mrs Pauline Wilson
(Council of Assembly, Central Services Committee and Nomination Committee)	
Senior Administrator:	Miss Rosalind Milne
(Ecumenical Relations)	

Contact Details:

Principal Clerk:	0131-240 2240
Secretary to the Council of Assembly:	0131-240 2229
Ecumenical Officer:	0131-240 2208
Linda Jamieson:	0131-240 2240
Rosalind Milne:	0131-225 5722 ext. 2370
Alison Murray:	0131-225 5722 ext. 2250
Pauline Wilson:	0131-240 2229
Office Fax number:	0131-240 2239
Office E-mail address:	pcoffice@cofscotland.org.uk

Note: the office of Depute Clerk is part-time, and the office-holder is not based in the Church Offices. Contact should be made through the Principal Clerk.

19.   Design Services

For further details, see Communications Unit at number 17.

20. Ecumenical Relations Committee

Remit
- to advise the General Assembly on matters of policy affecting ecumenical relations;
- to ensure that the members on the Committee serving on the other Councils are appropriately informed and resourced so as to be able to represent the ecumenical viewpoint on the Council on which they serve;
- to ensure appropriate support for the Ecumenical Officer's representative function in the event of his or her absence, whether through illness, holidays or other commitments;
- to nominate people from across the work of the Church of Scotland to represent the Church in Assemblies and Synods of other churches, ecumenical consultations and delegations to ecumenical assemblies and so on;
- to call for and receive reports from representatives of the Church of Scotland attending Assemblies and Synods of other churches and those ecumenical conferences and gatherings which are held from time to time;
- to ensure that appropriate parts of such reports are made available to relevant Councils;
- to ensure that information is channelled from and to ecumenical bodies of which the Church of Scotland is a member;
- to ensure that information is channelled from and to other churches in Scotland and beyond;
- to ensure the continued development of ecumenical relations by means of the Web and other publications;
- to ensure personal support for the Ecumenical Officer;
- to approve guidelines for the setting up and oversight of Local Ecumenical Partnerships.

Membership
a) Five members appointed by the General Assembly, each to serve as a member of one of the five Councils of the Church.
b) A Convener who is not a member of any of the other Councils and who will act as a personal support for the Ecumenical Officer, and a Vice-Convener, appointed by the General Assembly.
c) A representative of the United Free Church of Scotland appointed by that Church.
d) A representative of the Roman Catholic Church in Scotland appointed by the Bishops' Conference and one representative from each of three churches drawn from among the member churches of ACTS and the Baptist Union of Scotland, each to serve for a period of four years.
e) The Committee shall co-opt Church of Scotland members elected to the central bodies of Churches Together in Britain and Ireland (CTBI), the Conference of European Churches (CEC), the World Council of Churches (WCC), the World Communion of Reformed Churches (WCRC) and the Community of Protestant Churches in Europe (CPCE, formerly the Leuenberg Fellowship of Churches).
f) The General Secretary of ACTS shall be invited to attend as a corresponding member.
g) For the avoidance of doubt, while, for reasons of corporate governance, only Church of Scotland members of the Committee shall be entitled to vote, before any vote is taken the views of members representing other churches shall be ascertained.

Convener:	Rev. Alan D. Falconer MA BD DLitt (2009)
Vice-Convener:	Rev. Alison P. McDonald MA BD (2011)
Secretary and Ecumenical Officer:	Very Rev. Sheilagh M. Kesting BA BD DD
Senior Administrator:	Miss Rosalind Milne

INTER-CHURCH ORGANISATIONS

World Council of Churches

The Church of Scotland is a founder member of the World Council of Churches, formed in 1948. As its basis declares, it is 'a fellowship of Churches which confess the Lord Jesus Christ as God and Saviour according to the Scriptures, and therefore seek to fulfil their common calling to the glory of the one God, Father, Son and Holy Spirit'. Its member Churches, which number over 300, are drawn from all continents and include all the major traditions – Eastern and Oriental Orthodox, Reformed, Lutheran, Anglican, Baptist, Disciples, Methodist, Moravian, Friends, Pentecostalist and others. Although the Roman Catholic Church is not a member, there is very close co-operation with the departments in the Vatican.

The World Council holds its Assemblies every seven years. The last, held in Porto Alegre, Brazil, in February 2006, had the theme 'God, in your grace, transform the world'. At that Assembly, Mr Graham McGeoch was elected to the new Executive and to the Central Committee of the Council.

The WCC is divided into six programme areas:
* WCC and the Ecumenical Movement in the 21st Century
* Unity, Mission, Evangelism and Spirituality
* Public Witness: Addressing Power, Affirming Peace
* Justice, Diakonia and Responsibility for Creation
* Education and Ecumenical Formation
* Inter-Religious Dialogue and Co-operation.

The General Secretary is Rev. Dr Olav Fykse Tveit, PO Box 2100, 150 route de Ferney, CH-1211 Geneva 2, Switzerland (Tel: 00 41 22 791 61 11; Fax: 00 41 22 791 03 61; E-mail: infowcc@wcc-coe.org; Website: www.oikumene.org).

World Communion of Reformed Churches

The Church of Scotland was a founder member of 'The Alliance of the Reformed Churches Throughout the World Holding the Presbyterian System', which began in 1875. As the World Alliance of Reformed Churches, it included also Churches of the Congregational tradition. In June 2010, WARC merged with the Reformed Ecumenical Council and became the World Communion of Reformed Churches.

The World Communion of Reformed Churches (WCRC) brings together 80 million Reformed Christians in 108 countries around the world – united in their commitment to mission, church unity and justice. WCRC links Presbyterian, Reformed, Congregational, Waldensian, United and Uniting Churches.

The WCRC works in four main areas:
* Communication (fostering church unity and interfaith dialogue)
* Justice (helping churches to act for social and economic rights and care of the environment)
* Mission (facilitating mission renewal and empowerment)
* Partnership (providing funds for church unity, mission and justice projects).

The Uniting General Council was held in Grand Rapids, Michigan, USA from 18–28 June 2010. The theme was 'Unity of the Spirit in the Bond of Peace'.

The General Secretary is Rev. Dr Setri Nyomi, PO Box 2100, 150 route de Ferney, CH-1211 Geneva 2, Switzerland (Tel: 00 41 22 791 62 40; Fax: 00 41 22 791 65 05; E-mail: wcrc@wcrc.ch; Website: www.wcrc.ch).

Conference of European Churches

The Church of Scotland is a founder member of the Conference of European Churches, formed in 1959 and until recently the only body which involved in common membership representatives of every European country (except Albania) from the Atlantic to the Urals. More than 100 Churches, Orthodox and Protestant, are members. Although the Roman Catholic Church is not a member, there is very close co-operation with the Council of European Catholic Bishops' Conferences. With the removal of the long-standing political barriers in Europe, the Conference has now opportunities and responsibilities to assist the Church throughout the continent to offer united witness and service.

CEC held its thirteenth Assembly in Lyons, France from 15–21 July 2009. The theme was 'Called to One Hope in Christ'.

The General Secretary is Rev. Dr Guy Liagre, PO Box 2100, 150 route de Ferney, CH-1211 Geneva 2, Switzerland (Tel: 00 41 22 791 61 11; Fax: 00 41 22 791 62 27; E-mail: cec@cec-kek.org; Website: www.ceceurope.org).

CEC: Church and Society Commission
The Church of Scotland was a founder member of the European Ecumenical Commission for Church and Society (EECCS). The Commission owed its origins to the Christian concern and vision of a group of ministers and European civil servants about the future of Europe. It was established in 1973 by Churches recognising the importance of this venture. Membership included Churches and ecumenical bodies from the European Union. The process of integration with CEC was completed in 2000, and the name, Church and Society Commission (CSC), established. In Brussels, CSC monitors Community activity, maintains contact with MEPs and promotes dialogue between the Churches and the institutions. It plays an educational role and encourages the Churches' social and ethical responsibility in European affairs. It has a Director, a study secretary and an executive secretary in Brussels and a small office in Strasbourg.

The Director is Rev. Rüdiger Noll, Ecumenical Centre, 174 rue Joseph II, B-1000 Brussels, Belgium (Tel: 00 32 2 230 17 32; Fax: 00 32 2 231 14 13; E-mail: ved@cec-kek.be).

Community of Protestant Churches in Europe
The Church of Scotland is a founder member of the Community of Protestant Churches in Europe (CPCE), which was formerly known as the Leuenberg Church Fellowship. The Fellowship came into being in 1973 on the basis of the Leuenberg Agreement between the Reformation churches in Europe; the name was changed to the CPCE in 2003. The Leuenberg Agreement stipulates that a common understanding of the Gospel based on the doctrine of Justification by Faith, and interpreted with reference to the proclamation of the Word of God, Baptism and the Lord's Supper, is sufficient to overcome the Lutheran–Reformed church division.

Over 100 Protestant churches in Europe, and a number of South American churches with European origin, have been signatories to the Leuenberg Agreement, including Lutheran, Reformed, United and Methodist Churches, as well as pre-Reformation Waldensian, Hussite and Czech Brethren, and they grant each other pulpit and table fellowship. Most of the CPCE member churches are minority churches, and this imparts a particular character to their life and witness. A General Assembly is held every six years – the sixth General Assembly was held in Budapest in 2006 – and a thirteen-member Council carries on the work of the CPCE in the intervening period.

The General Secretary is Bishop Professor Dr Michael Bunker, Severin-Schreiber-Gasse 3, A-1180 Vienna, Austria (Tel: 00 43 1 4791523 900; Fax: 00 43 1 4791523 110; E-mail: office@leuenberg.eu; Website: www.leuenberg.eu).

Churches Together in Britain and Ireland (CTBI)
In September 1990, Churches throughout Britain and Ireland solemnly committed themselves to one another, promising to one another to do everything possible together. To provide frameworks for this commitment to joint action, the Churches established CTBI for the United Kingdom and Ireland, and, for Scotland, ACTS, with sister organisations for Wales and for England.

Churches Together in Britain and Ireland works with member churches to co-ordinate responses, share resources and learn from each other's experiences.

There are currently eight subject-based work areas:
- Church and Public Issues
- Theology and Unity
- Mission
- China Desk
- Inter-Religious
- International Students
- Racial Justice
- Action on Asylum and Refugees.

There are also three theme-based work areas:
- Environment and Climate Change
- Culture, Identity and the Public Square
- Migration and Movements of People.

The General Secretary is Rev. Bob Fyffe, 39 Eccleston Square, London SW1V IBX (Tel: 0845 680 6851; Fax: 0845 680 6852; E-mail: info@ctbi.org.uk; Website: www.ctbi.org.uk).

Action of Churches Together in Scotland (ACTS)

ACTS is governed by a Board of Trustees which consults with the Members' Meeting. The Members' Meeting is composed of representatives from the nine trustee member Churches. There are four Networks: Church Life, Faith Studies, Mission, and Church and Society. Contributing to the life of the Networks are associated ecumenical groups. Such groups are expressions of the Churches' commitment to work together and to bring together key people in a defined field of interest or expertise. ACTS is an expression of the commitment of the Churches to one another.

ACTS is staffed by a General Secretary, an Assistant General Secretary and two Network Officers. Their offices are based in Alloa.

These structures facilitate regular consultation and intensive co-operation among those who frame the policies and deploy the resources of the Churches in Scotland and throughout Britain and Ireland. At the same time, they afford greater opportunity for a wide range of members of different Churches to meet in common prayer and study.

The General Secretary is Brother Stephen Smyth fms, 7 Forrester Lodge, Inglewood House, Alloa FK10 2HU (Tel: 01259 216980; Fax: 01259 215964; E-mail: ecumenical@acts-scotland. org; Website: www.acts-scotland.org).

21. Facilities Management Department

Staff

Facilities Manager: Carole Tait
                (Tel: 0131-240 2214)

The responsibilities of the Facilities Manager's Department include:
- management of a maintenance budget for the upkeep of the Church Offices at 121 George Street, Edinburgh;
- responsibility for all aspects of health and safety for staff, visitors and contractors working in the building;

- managing a team of staff providing the Offices with security, reception, mail room, print room, switchboard, day-to-day maintenance services and Committee room bookings;
- overseeing all sub-contracted services to include catering, cleaning, boiler-room maintenance, intruder alarm, fire alarms, lifts and water management;
- maintaining building records in accordance with the requirements of statutory legislation;
- overseeing all alterations to the building and ensuring, where applicable, that they meet DDR, Planning and Building Control regulations.

22. General Treasurer's Department

The General Treasurer's Department and the Stewardship Department have merged to form the Stewardship and Finance Department. See number 31.

23. General Trustees

Membership
(New Trustees are appointed, as required, by the General Assembly, on the recommendation of the General Trustees)

Chairman: Rev. James A.P. Jack BSc BArch BD DMin RIBA ARIAS
                                   (2010)
Vice-Chairman: Mr Iain C. Douglas RD BArch FRIAS RIBA (2010)
Secretary and Clerk: Mr David D. Robertson LLB NP
Depute Secretary and Clerk: Mr Keith S. Mason LLB NP

Committees:
Fabric Committee
Convener: Mr Roger G.G. Dodd DipBldgCons(RICS) FRICS (2010)

Chairman's Committee
Convener: Rev. James A.P. Jack BSc BArch BD DMin RIBA ARIAS
                                   (2010)

Glebes Committee
Convener: Mr William M. Lawrie (2012)

Finance Committee
Convener: Mr Peter F. King LLB MCIBS (2010)

Audit Committee
Convener: Dr J. Kenneth Macaldowie LLD CA (2005)

Law Committee
Convener: Rev. Alistair G.C. McGregor BA LLB BD QC WS (2008)

Staff

Secretary and Clerk:	Mr David D. Robertson LLB NP
Depute Secretary and Clerk:	Mr Keith S. Mason LLB NP
Assistant Secretaries:	Mr Keith J. Fairweather LLB (Glebes)
	Mrs Morag J. Menneer BSc MRICS (Glebes)
	Mr Brian D. Waller LLB (Ecclesiastical Buildings)
Treasurer:	Mr Iain W. Grimmond BAcc CA
Deputy Treasurer:	Mrs Anne F. Macintosh BA CA
Assistant Treasurer:	Mr Robert A. Allan ACMA CPFA

Remit

The General Trustees are a Property Corporation created and incorporated under the Church of Scotland (General Trustees) Order Confirmation Act 1921. They have Scottish Charity Number SC014574. Their duties, powers and responsibilities were greatly extended by the Church of Scotland (Property & Endowments) Acts and Orders 1925 to 1995, and they are also charged with the administration of the Central Fabric Fund (see below) and the Consolidated Fabric Fund and the Consolidated Stipend Fund in which monies held centrally for the benefit of individual congregations are lodged.

The scope of the work of the Trustees is broad, covering all facets of property administration, but particular reference is made to the following matters:

1. **ECCLESIASTICAL BUILDINGS.** The Trustees' Fabric Committee considers proposals for work at buildings, regardless of how they are vested, and plans of new buildings. Details of all such projects should be submitted to the Committee before work is commenced. The Committee also deals with applications for the release of fabric monies held by the General Trustees for individual congregations, and considers applications for assistance from the Central Fabric Fund from which grants and/or loans may be given to assist congregations faced with expenditure on fabric. Application forms relating to consents for work and possible financial assistance from the Central Fabric Fund are available from the Secretary of the Trustees and require to be submitted through Presbytery with its approval. The Committee normally meets on the first or second Tuesday of each month, apart from July, when it meets on the second last Tuesday, and August, when there is no meeting.

2. **SALE, PURCHASE AND LETTING OF PROPERTIES.** All sales or lets of properties vested in the General Trustees fall to be carried out by them in consultation with the Financial Board of the congregation concerned, and no steps should be taken towards any sale or let without prior consultation with the Secretary of the Trustees. Where property to be purchased is to be vested in the General Trustees, it is essential that contact be made at the earliest possible stage with the Solicitor to the Trustees, who is responsible for the lodging of offers for such properties and all subsequent legal procedure.

3. **GLEBES.** The Trustees are responsible for the administration of Glebes vested in their ownership. All lets fall to be granted by them in consultation with the minister concerned. It should be noted that neither ministers nor Kirk Sessions may grant lets of Glebe land vested in the General Trustees. As part of their Glebe administration, the Trustees review regularly all Glebe rents.

4. **INSURANCE.** Properties vested in the General Trustees must be insured with the Church of Scotland Insurance Co. Ltd, a company wholly owned by the Church of Scotland whose profits are applied for Church purposes. Insurance enquiries should be sent directly to the Company at 67 George Street, Edinburgh EH2 2JG (Tel: 0131-220 4119; Fax: 0131-220 4120; E-mail: enquiries@cosic.co.uk).

24. *Go For It* Fund

Funding change in church and community
Go For It brings together work of the Parish Development Fund, the Emerging Ministries Fund and the Priority Areas Staffing Fund.

The Committee comprises members appointed by the Nominations Committee to the Ministries Council, as well as a number of co-opted members with appropriate skills and knowledge. The Mission and Discipleship Council and the Church and Society Council are also represented.

Convener: Rev. Rolf H. Billes BD
Co-ordinator: Shirley Grieve
Training and Development: Catherine McIntosh

The purpose of the Church of Scotland's *Go For It* Fund is to encourage and support creative initiatives which address needs in local communities and/or encourage new ways of being the Church in Scotland today.

There will be five criteria for receiving funding. To be able to apply, a proposal needs to meet at least two of these criteria. These are:

• meeting identified needs in a community
• nurturing Christian faith within and beyond the Church
• tackling poverty and/or social injustice
• developing new ecclesial/Christian communities
• creating work which is genuinely innovative, developing good practice that can be shared.

The Fund will give grants totalling in the region of £1 million per annum. Awards of up to £45,000 (over a three-year period) will be available to part-fund locally based work. Additional support will be available for schemes which can clearly demonstrate that they are engaged with the very poorest members of Scottish society. Relevant proposals that are unable to attract funding from other sources will also be considered for additional funding.

Successful applications will be either from Church of Scotland congregations or from organisations very closely associated with them. They will need to show how they are actively working with other partners, including other churches, to bring about change.

We want to encourage local Christians to have creative ideas and then, with the support and help of the Fund, to turn these ideas into practice – to really *Go For It.*

Additional information is available by calling the *Go For It* Team within the Church of Scotland's Ministries Council on 0131-225 5722 or by e-mailing goforit@cofscotland.org.uk

---

25. Human Resources Department

Staff
Head of Human Resources and
    Information Technology: Mike O'Donnell Chartered FCIPD
Human Resources Manager: Karen Tait Chartered CIPD

Remit
The Human Resources Department has responsibility for Recruitment and Selection, Learning and Development, and producing and updating HR Policies and Procedures to ensure that the Central Services Committee, the Ministries Council and the World Mission Council, as employing agencies, are in line with current employment-law legislation. The Department produces contracts

of employment and advises on any changes to an individual employee's terms and conditions of employment. It also provides professional Human Resources advice to the organisation on Employee Relations matters, Performance Management and Diversity and Equality.

Our main aim is to work closely with Councils within the organisation to influence strategy so that each Council is making best use of its people and its people opportunities. We take a consultancy role that facilitates and supports each Council's own initiatives and help each other share and work together in consultation with Unite.

26. Information Technology Department

Staff

Head of Human Resources and Information Technology: Mike O'Donnell
Information Technology Manager: David Malcolm

The Department provides computer facilities to Councils and Departments within 121 George Street and to Presbytery Clerks and other groups within the Councils. It is also responsible for the telephone service within 121 George Street and the provision of assistance and advice on this to other groups.

The facilities provided include:
* the provision and maintenance of data and voice networks
* the purchase and installation of hardware and software
* support for problems and guidance on the use of hardware and software
* development of in-house software
* maintenance of data within some central systems.

27. Law Department

Staff

Solicitor of the Church and of the General Trustees:	Mrs Janette Wilson LLB NP
Depute Solicitor:	Miss Mary Macleod LLB NP
Solicitors:	Mrs Jennifer Hamilton BA NP
	Mrs Elspeth Annan LLB NP
	Miss Susan Killean LLB NP
	Mrs Anne Steele LLB NP
	Miss Lesa Burns LLB NP
	Miss Jennifer Sharp LLB NP
	Mr Gregor Buick LLB WS NP

The Department's team of experienced solicitors is available to provide legal advice and assistance to all congregations, Presbyteries, Councils, Committees and Courts of the Church. It also represents the Church of Scotland General Trustees, the Church of Scotland Trust and the Church of Scotland Investors Trust. The solicitors in the Department act exclusively on behalf of Church of Scotland bodies and therefore have an understanding and experience of the law as it relates to the Church which cannot be equalled elsewhere. They also have an awareness of wider policy and financial issues affecting both congregations and central Church bodies.

The Department is committed to meeting the particular needs of the Church. It provides a large number of free resources for congregations, which are available to download from the Church website (www.churchofscotland.org.uk/resources/subjects/law_circulars). These include style documents and circulars covering matters such as contracts of employment; guidance on the Bribery Act 2010 as it affects congregations; guidance on the Data Protection Act; charity law; licensing matters and the letting of church halls.

The solicitors in the Department can offer tailored advice on most areas of the law, including:
- marketing properties for sale
- commercial and residential conveyancing
- commercial and residential leasing
- employment issues
- trusts and executries
- charity law
- litigation and dispute resolution
- data protection
- contract law
- planning law
- agricultural law
- licensing and regulatory matters
- mobile-phone installations.

Contact details: E-mail: lawdept@cofscotland.org.uk; Tel: 0131-225 5722 ext. 2230; Fax: 0131-240 2246.

---

28.   Legal Questions Committee

Membership
Convener, Vice-Convener and ten members appointed by the General Assembly on the Report of the Nomination Committee.

Convener:	Rev. Alan J. Hamilton LLB BD
Vice-Convener:	Rev. Sheila M. Kirk BA LLB BD
Secretary:	The Principal Clerk

The Assembly Clerks, Procurator and Solicitor of the Church are non-voting members of the Legal Questions Committee.

Remit
- to advise the General Assembly on questions of Church Law and of Constitutional Law affecting the relationship between Church and State;
- to advise and assist Agencies of the General Assembly in the preparation of proposed legislation and on questions of interpretation, including interpretation of and proposed changes to remits;
- to compile the statistics of the Church, except Youth and Finance; and to supervise on behalf of the General Assembly all arrangements for care of Church Records and for Presbytery visits;
- to conduct an annual review of progress made in discharging the remit and provide a written report to the Council of Assembly.

29.   Nomination Committee

Membership
(Convener, Vice-Convener and 24 members)
Convener: Rev. James Dewar MA BD (2011)
Vice-Convener: Iain McLarty BSc MMus AMusTCL (2011)
Secretary: The Secretary to the Council of Assembly

Remit
1.   To bring before the General Assembly names of persons to serve on the Councils and
     Standing Committees of the General Assembly.
2.   To identify and interview suitable candidates for membership of the Council of Assembly,
     bringing before the General Assembly the names of persons to serve as charity trustees of
     the Unincorporated Councils and Committees.
3.   To work with the main Councils of the General Assembly to ensure an open, fair and
     robust process for identifying suitable persons to serve as Conveners of such Councils,
     engaging with those so identified to ensure their suitability to serve as charity trustees of
     the Unincorporated Councils and Committees.

30.   Panel on Review and Reform

Membership
(10 members appointed by the General Assembly)
Convener: Rev. Donald Campbell (2011)
Vice-Convener: Rev. Jack Holt (2011)
(The Ecumenical Officer attends but without the right to vote or make a motion.)

Staff
Senior Administrator: Mrs Valerie A. Cox
                                             (Tel: 0131-225 5722 ext. 2336;
                                             E-mail: vcox@cofscotland.org.uk)

Remit
The remit of the Panel on Review and Reform, as determined by the General Assembly of
2004, is as follows:
*   To listen to the voices of congregations, Presbyteries, Agencies and those beyond the
     Church of Scotland.
*   To present a vision of what a Church in need of continual renewal might become and to
     offer paths by which congregations, Presbyteries and Agencies might travel towards that
     vision.
*   To consider the changing needs, challenges and responsibilities of the Church.
*   To have particular regard to the Gospel imperative of priority for the poor, needy and
     marginalised.

31. Stewardship and Finance Department

The General Treasurer's Department and the Stewardship Department merged to form the Stewardship and Finance Department on 1 June 2009. This Department is accountable to the Council of Assembly through its Finance Group.

The Departmental e-mail address is: sfadmin@cofscotland.org.uk

Staff based at the Church Offices

General Treasurer:	Mr Iain W. Grimmond BAcc CA
Deputy Treasurer:	Mrs Anne F. Macintosh BA CA
Head of Stewardship:	Rev. Alan W. Gibson BA BD
Finance Managers:	
Congregational Finance	Mr Archie McDowall BA CA
General Trustees	Mr Robert A. Allan ACMA CPFA
Ministries	Mr Kenneth C.M. Roger BA CA
World Mission	Mrs Catriona M. Scrimgeour BSc ACA
Management and Pensions Accountant:	Mrs Kay C. Hastie BSc CA

Regional Staff

Stewardship Consultants:

- Mrs Margot R. Robertson BA (Tel: 01620 893459) for the Presbyteries of:
  Edinburgh, West Lothian, Lothian, Melrose and Peebles, Duns, Jedburgh
- Mrs Edith Scott (Tel: 01357 520503) for the Presbyteries of:
  Annandale and Eskdale, Dumfries and Kirkcudbright, Wigtown and Stranraer, Ayr, Irvine and Kilmarnock, Ardrossan, Lanark, Greenock and Paisley, Hamilton
- Mr Stuart G. Sangster (Tel: 01360 622302) for the Presbyteries of:
  Glasgow, Dumbarton, Argyll, Stirling, Lochaber
- Mrs Sandra Holt BSc for the Presbyteries of:
  Falkirk, Dunfermline, Kirkcaldy, St Andrews, Dunkeld and Meigle, Perth, Dundee
- Mrs Fiona Penny (Tel: 01771 653442) for the Presbyteries of:
  Aberdeen, Kincardine and Deeside, Gordon, Buchan, Moray, Abernethy, Inverness

Stewardship requests from congregations in the Presbyteries of Angus, Ross, Sutherland, Caithness, Lochcarron – Skye, Uist, Lewis, Orkney, Shetland, England and Europe should be addressed to the Head of Stewardship at the Church Offices in the first instance.

Main Responsibilities of the Stewardship and Finance Department

- Teaching and promoting Christian stewardship throughout the Church;
- Planning and delivery of stewardship programmes in congregations;
- Calculating the annual Ministries and Mission Contribution for each congregation, and processing payments;
- Providing support, training and advice on financial and accounting matters to Congregational Treasurers;
- Providing management and financial accounting support for the Councils, Committees and Statutory Corporations;
- Providing banking arrangements and operating a central banking system for the Councils, Committees and Statutory Corporations;
- Receiving and discharging legacies and bequests on behalf of the Councils, Committees and Statutory Corporations;

- Making VAT returns and tax recoveries on behalf of the Councils, Committees and Statutory Corporations;
- Payroll processing for the Ministries Council, Central Services Committee and the Pension Schemes.

---

32. The Church of Scotland Safeguarding Office
Tel: 0131-240 2256; Fax: 0131-220 3113
E-mail: www.churchofscotland.org.uk

Convener: Ranald Mair (2010)
Vice-Convener: Rev. Karen Campbell BD MTh (2010)

Staff
Head of Safeguarding: Richard Crosse MA (Cantab) MSW CQSW
Assistant Head of Safeguarding: Jennifer Milligan CQSW DipSW

The Church of Scotland Safeguarding Service:
What we aim to do and how we provide the service

Introduction
Harm or abuse of children **and** 'adults at risk' can happen anywhere – even in church communities. We have a duty 'to ensure a safe church for all'. The Church of Scotland has a zero-tolerance approach to harm or abuse of people: any type or level is unacceptable.

The possibility of harm or abuse cannot be eliminated, but the safeguarding structures in the Church and the work of the Safeguarding Service seek to minimise the risk of harm occurring or not being responded to appropriately. The Safeguarding Committee, with representation from across the Church, ensures accountability back to the General Assembly, and also provides a forum for shaping policy and direction.

Remit
The Church of Scotland Safeguarding Service aims to:
- ensure best practice in preventing harm or abuse, and
- ensure that the Church makes a timely and appropriate response when harm or abuse is witnessed, suspected or reported.

Preventing harm and abuse
The Safeguarding Service aims to prevent harm or abuse through ensuring that there is good recognition and reporting. It does this by providing:
- information, support and advice on everyday safeguarding matters where there is not an incident of suspected or reported harm or abuse
- advice and support for the **safe recruitment and selection** of all paid staff and volunteers
- the process of applying for membership of the Protection of Vulnerable Groups (Scotland) Act 2007 Scheme for those working with children or 'protected adults'.

Safe recruitment
Safe recruitment is about ensuring that only people suitable to work with children and 'adults at risk' are employed. There is a comprehensive range of safeguarding training programmes to meet

the particular learning needs of different groups of people in the Church, including, for example, volunteers, Kirk Sessions, Safeguarding Co-ordinators, Ministries Council, Parish Development Fund and CrossReach services.

Responding to disclosures of harm or abuse or risk of abuse
The Safeguarding Service provides:
*   verbal and written advice in situations where harm or abuse is suspected, witnessed or reported to members of the Church. This service is also provided for CrossReach Social Care Council services
*   support for Safeguarding Panels working with **convicted sex offenders** to ensure their safe inclusion in worship.

In summary, harm or abuse in the Church is rare, and thankfully the vast majority of people will have no knowledge or experience of it, but even one case is one too many. Our key message is: *'if you suspect or witness harm or abuse, or it is reported to you, you must immediately report it to your Safeguarding Co-ordinator or line manager'.*
Contact can be made with the Safeguarding Office at the address, telephone number, e-mail address and website shown at the head of this article.

---

33.   Scottish Churches Parliamentary Office
Tel: 0131-220 0246
E-mail: chloe@actsparl.org

The Scottish Churches Parliamentary Officer is Chloe Clemmons MA MA. The office is at 44 Hanover Street, Edinburgh EH2 2DR.

The Church of Scotland and the Gaelic Language

Duilleagan Gàidhlig
Ro-ràdh
Ann an 2008, airson a' chiad turais riamh, bha duilleagan air leth againn ann an Gàidhlig anns an *Leabhar Bhliadhnail*, agus a rèir iomraidh rinn mòran toileachadh ris a' ghluasad ùr seo. Tha sinn fo fhiachan am bliadhna a-rithist don Fhear-dheasachaidh airson a bhith cho deònach cuibhreann Ghàidhlig a bhith an lùib na Beurla. An deidh a bhith a' crìonadh fad ghrunn ghinealach, tha a' Ghàidhlig a-nis a' dèanamh adhartais. Tha e cudthromach gum bi Eaglais na h-Alba a' toirt cùl-taic don leasachadh seo, agus gu dearbha tha i aig teis-meadhan a' ghluasaid seo. Ma bheir sinn sùil air eachdraidh, chì sinn nuair a bha a' Ghàidhlig a' fulang làmhachais-làidir anns na linntean a dh'fhalbh, gu robh an Eaglais glè shoirbheachail ann a bhith a' gabhail ceum-tòisich airson an cànan a dhìon.

Eachdraidh
Bha na thachair an dèidh Blàr Chùil Lodair 'na bhuille chruaidh don Ghàidhlig. Cha do chuidich Achd an Fhòghlaim ann an 1872 le cùisean, Achd nach tug fiù 's iomradh air a' Ghàidhlig. Mar

thoradh air seo bha a' Ghàidhlig air a fuadach à sgoiltean na h-Alba. Ach bha a' Ghàidhlig air a cleachdadh anns an Eaglais agus bha sin na mheadhan air a cumail o bhith a' dol à sealladh mar chainnt làitheil.

Poileataics
Tha Pàrlamaid na h-Eòrpa a' toirt inbhe don Ghàidhlig mar aon de na mion-chànanan Eòrpach a tha i a' smaoineachadh a bu chòir a cuideachadh agus a h-altram. Beagan bhliadhnachan air ais chuir iad lagh an gnìomh a bha a' cur mar dhleasdanas air Pàrlamaid Bhreatainn àite a thoirt don Ghàidhlig. Ann an 2005, thug Pàrlamaid na h-Alba Achd Gàidhlig na h-Alba air adhart a' cur na Gàidhlig air stèidh mar chainnt nàiseanta, leis an aon spèis ris a' Bheurla.

Cultar
Tha An Comunn Gàidhealach agus buidhnean eile air obair ionmholta a dhèanamh bho chionn fada ann a bhith a' cur na Gàidhlig air adhart mar nì cudthromach nar cultar. Bho chionn ghoirid chuir An Comunn air bhonn co-chruinneachadh de riochdairean o na h-Eaglaisean airson dòighean a lorg air a bhith a' cleachdadh na Gàidhlig ann an adhradh follaiseach. Fad còrr is fichead bliadhna chaidh adhartas mòr a dhèanamh ann am fòghlam tro mheadhan na Gàidhlig, an toiseach tro chròileagain, bun-sgoiltean, agus a-nis ann an àrd-sgoiltean. Thàinig seo gu ìre nuair a stèidhicheadh Sabhal Mòr Ostaig ann am fòghlam àrd-ìre. Bidh an Sabhal Mòr mar phàirt chudthromach de dh'Oilthigh ùr na Gàidhealtachd agus nan Eilean. Tha Comann Albannach a' Bhìobaill glè dhealasach ann a bhith a' sìor thoirt taic don Ghàidhlig le bhith a' foillseachadh nan Sgriobtar anns a' chànan. Rinn Gàidheil toileachadh mòr ris an eadar-theangachadh ùr de Shoigeul Eòin ann an Gàidhlig an latha an-diugh a thàinig a-mach bho chaidh an *Leabhar Bliadhnail* mu dheireadh fhoillseachadh.

Eaglais na h-Alba
1.   Air feadh na dùthcha, tha adhradh air a chumail ann an Gàidhlig, air Ghàidhealtachd agus air Ghalldachd. (Mar eisimpleir, anns na bailtean mòra tha seirbheis Ghàidhlig air a cumail gach Sàbaid ann an Eaglais Ghàidhealach nam Manach Liatha ann an Dùn Eideann, agus ann an Eaglais Chaluim Chille agus Eaglais Sràid a' Ghàradair ann an Glaschu.) Tha còir gum biodh fios aig Clèireach na Clèire air eaglaisean far a bheil seirbheisean Gàidhlig air an cumail. Thug an t-Àrd-sheanadh ann an 2008 misneachadh do Chlèirean coitheanalan freagarrach ainmeachadh far am bu chòir a' Ghàidhlig a bhith air a cleachdadh ann an adhradh nuair a bha iad a' cur phlànaichean-clèire air bhonn. A bharrachd air sin, tha goireasan ann a bheir cuideachadh don fheadhainn a tha airson Gàidhlig a chleachdadh ann an adhradh.
2.   Cha mhòr bho stèidhicheadh *Life and Work* tha *Na Duilleagan Gàidhlig* air a bhith rim faotainn as-asgaidh do neach sam bith a tha gan iarraidh.
3.   Tha Eaglais na h-Alba, mar phàirt de dh'Iomairt Chonaltraidh na h-Eaglais, airson a bhith a' brosnachadh cleachdadh na Gàidhlig. Tha duilleagan Gàidhlig air leth air an làraich-lìn.
4.   Bho chionn beagan bhliadhnachan tha an t-Àrd-sheanadh air na nithean cudthromach seo a mholadh co-cheangailte ris a' Ghàidhlig.
      (i)   Tha an t-Àrd-sheanadh a' cur mealadh-naidheachd air Pàrlamaid na h-Alba airson Achd a' Chànain Ghàidhlig (Alba) a stèidheachadh; tha e a' brosnachadh a' BhBC ach an toir iad cùl-taic do OFCOM a tha ag iarraidh craoladh na Gàidhlig a leudachadh; tha e duilich gu bheil chleachdadh na Gàidhlig a' dol an lughad anns an Eaglais, agus tha e a' toirt cuiridh do Chomhairlean na h-Eaglais, far a bheil sin freagarrach, rannsachadh a dhèanamh air dòighean a lorg a bheir don Ghàidhlig an t-àite sònraichte a chleachd a bhith aice ann am beatha spioradail na h-Alba.
      (ii)   Tha an t-Àrd-sheanadh a' cur ìmpidh air Comhairle a' Mhisein agus na Deisciobalachd, ann an co-bhoinn ri Comhairle na Ministrealachd, rannsachadh a

dhèanamh air inbhe na Gàidhlig ann an Eaglais na h-Alba ann an dùil ri aithisg a thoirt air beulaibh an Àrd-sheanaidh ann an 2008 air mar a ghabhas leasachadh a dhèanamh air cleachdadh na Gàidhlig anns an Eaglais.

(iii) Tha an t-Àrd-sheanadh a' gabhail beachd air àireamh nan sgìrean Gàidhlig, agus tha e a' cur ìmpidh Comhairle na Ministrealachd slatan-tomhais a thoirt chun an Ard-sheanaidh ann an 2008 airson gun tèid na sgìrean seo a chomharrachadh anns na bliadhnachan air thoiseach.

(iv) Tha an t-Àrd-sheanadh a' cur ìmpidh air Comhairle an Àrd-sheanaidh cumail romhpa a bhith a' toirt cùl-taic don Ghàidhlig an taobh a-staigh na h-Eaglais, am measg rudan eile a bhith a' còmhradh ri buidhnean maoineachaidh freagarrach.

(v) Tha an t-Àrd-sheanadh a' dèanamh toileachaidh ris an Aithisg air Leasachadh ann an Cleachdadh na Gàidhlig, agus tha e a' brosnachadh Comhairle a' Mhisein agus na Deisciobalachd na plànaichean a tha aca airson an ama air thoiseach a chur an gnìomh.

(vi) Tha an t-Àrd-sheanadh a' dèanamh toileachaidh ris an naidheachd gu bheil Seanal Digiteach Gàidhlig ga chur air bhog, agus tha e a' cur ìmpidh air Comhaire na h-Eaglais agus na Coimhearsnachd, ann an co-bhoinn ri Comhairle an Àrd-sheanaidh, a bhith a' còmhradh ri Comhairle nam Meadhanan Gàidhlig mun àite shònraichte a bu chòir a bhith aig prògraman spioradail anns na prògraman a bhios iad a' cur a-mach.

'S e àm air leth inntinneach a tha seo don Ghàidhlig, agus tha an Eaglais airson a bhith a' gabhail a h-àite anns an iomairt as leth ar cànain. 'S iad na duilleagan seo aon de na dòighean anns a bheil sinn a' dèanamh sin.

An t-Àrd-sheanadh 2012

Bha an t-Urr. Coinneach Dòmhnallach, ministear-cuideachaidh, air ceann seirbheis Ghàidhlig an Ard-sheanaidh ann an Eaglais nam Manach Liath. Leugh an Siorram Ruairidh Iain MacLeòid na Sgriobtaran. A' togail an fhuinn bha Alasdair MacLeòid. Sheinn Còisir Ghàidhlig Lodainn aig toiseach agus aig deireadh na seirbheis. Rinn am Moderàtor am Beannachadh ann an Gàidhlig.

Tha dìreach dà cheud bliadhna bho chaochail am bàrd ainmeil, Donnchadh Bàn Mac an t-Saoir. Bhiodh Donnchadh a' frithealadh na h-Eaglais Ghàidhlig an dèidh dha a dhachaigh a dhèanamh ann am baile Dhùn Eideann. An dèidh seirbheis an Ard-sheanaidh chumadh seirbheis ghoirid aig uaigh a' bhàird ann an cladh nam Manach Liath a' comharrachadh gu bheil dà cheud bliadhna bho shiubhail e.

Bha cuid mhath an làthair aig Coinneamh Ghàidhealach na bliadhna seo air Diceudaoin an Ard-sheanaidh. Chualas òraid inntinneach, le dealbhannan, on Urr. Dòmhnall MacGuaire air na ceanglaichean spioradail a tha eadar an cuan, bàtaichean agus sluagh taobh siar na Gàidhealtachd.

Anns an dealachadh

Tha *Na Duilleagan Gàidhlig* aig *Life and Work* air an leughadh le Gàidheil agus luchd-ionnsachaidh air feadh an t-saoghail. Gheibhear iad an-asgaidh an lùib na h-iris Beurla ma chuirear sibh fios gu oifis *Life and Work*.

Introduction

The *Year Book 2008/2009*, for the first time ever, featured dedicated pages in Gaelic; and this innovation was very well received. Again, appreciation is expressed to the Editor for his willing co-operation. After many generations of decline, Gaelic is once more moving forward. It is important that the Church of Scotland is seen to be encouraging this progress and indeed is part of it. History teaches that, in the past, when the Gaelic language has been under political oppression, the Church has stood successfully in the vanguard of the defence of the language.

History
The events of Culloden in 1746, as part of the Jacobite rebellion, dealt a cruel blow to the Gaelic language. This was compounded by the Education (Scotland) Act of 1872, which made no mention of the Gaelic language and, indeed, resulted in the outlawing of Gaelic in Scottish schools. The continued use of Gaelic in the Church proved to be the only formal antidote to the disappearance of Gaelic as a viable language.

Politics
The European Parliament recognises Gaelic as one of the minority European languages it sees as important to support and nurture. Some years ago, it passed appropriate legislation laying some responsibility on the United Kingdom Parliament. In 2005, the Scottish Parliament delivered the Gaelic (Scotland) Act, establishing Gaelic as a national language given the same respect as English.

Culture
Traditionally, An Comunn Gaidhealach has done an excellent job in promoting the cultural importance of Gaelic. In recent years, it convened a gathering of representatives from Churches to research how they could help promote the use of Gaelic in public worship. For over twenty years now, there has been substantial growth in Gaelic-medium education, first of all through nurseries, then primary schools and now secondary schools. This has moved on to the establishing of Sabhal Mòr Ostaig in the tertiary sector. The Church of Scotland welcomes the granting of a charter to the University of the Highlands and Islands, and looks forward to the Sabhal Mòr being a vital part of the University. The Scottish Bible Society is also eager to continue its support of Gaelic through the provision of Scriptures. Since the last *Year Book* appeared, Gaelic-speakers and learners have warmly welcomed the publication of John's Gospel in modern Gaelic.

The Church of Scotland and its ongoing support for Gaelic
1. Across the nation, public worship continues to be conducted in Gaelic. The General Assembly of 2008 encouraged Presbyteries, as part of their planning, to identify appropriate congregations in which Gaelic must be used regularly in public worship. Furthermore, resources are available to encourage the use of Gaelic in worship in all congregations.
2. Almost since its inception, *Na Duilleagan Gàidhlig*, as part of *Life and Work*, has been available free of charge to any who request it with their *Life and Work* subscription. This is still very much alive.
3. The Church of Scotland, as part of its Communication Strategy, is concerned to promote the use of Gaelic. There are dedicated Gaelic pages on the website.
4. Recent years have seen the General Assembly approve a number of important Deliverances relating to Gaelic. For example:
    (i)   The General Assembly congratulate the Scottish Parliament on its passing of the Gaelic Language (Scotland) Bill, encourage the BBC to support OFCOM in its desire for the extension of Gaelic broadcasting, express regret at the substantial decrease in the use of Gaelic in the Church and invite Councils of the Church, where appropriate, to explore ways in which Gaelic can resume its distinctive place within the religious life of Scotland.
    (ii) The General Assembly instructed the Mission and Discipleship Council, in collaboration with the Ministries Council, to undertake an investigation into the present status of Gaelic in the Church of Scotland with a view to reporting to

the 2008 General Assembly on the strategic development of the use of the language in the Kirk.

(iii)   The General Assembly note the statistics regarding Gaelic-speaking charges and instructed the Ministries Council to bring to the General Assembly of 2008 an agreed set of criteria for future determination of such designations.

(iv)   The General Assembly instruct the Council of Assembly to continue to support the development of Gaelic within the Church, including discussions with appropriate funding bodies.

(v)   The General Assembly welcome the Report on the Strategic Development of the Use of Gaelic and encourage the Mission and Discipleship Council to develop its future plans.

(vi)   The General Assembly welcome the launch of the Gaelic Digital Broadcasting channel and instruct the Church and Society Council, in co-operation with the Council of Assembly, to discuss with the Gaelic Media Council the significant place of religious programmes in its output.

These are exciting times for the Gaelic language, and the Church is responding to the challenge of our day.

The General Assembly 2012
The preacher at this year's General Assembly Gaelic service in Greyfriars Tolbooth and Highland Kirk (where worship takes place in Gaelic every Sunday) was Rev. Kenneth MacDonald, retired Auxiliary Minister. Scripture lessons were read by Sheriff Roddy John MacLeod. The precentor was Alasdair MacLeod. Lothian Gaelic Choir sang at the beginning and end of the service, and the Moderator pronounced the Benediction in Gaelic.

The great Gaelic poet, Duncan Bàn McIntyre, died 200 years ago – the bicentenary of his funeral was the day before the Gaelic service. The bard attended the Gaelic church during his years in Edinburgh, and he is buried in Greyfriars churchyard. After the General Assembly service, there was a short service at Duncan Bàn's grave to mark the bicentenary of his death.

As usual, there was a good attendance at the annual Highland Meeting on Wednesday of Assembly week. Rev. Donald MacQuarrie gave a fascinating illustrated talk on the spiritual links between sea, boats and the people of the West Highlands.

In conclusion
The Gaelic Supplement of *Life and Work* is read by Gaels and learners of Gaelic all over the world. The monthly Supplement is available on request free of charge along with the main *Life and Work*.

SECTION 2

General Information

(1) OTHER CHURCHES IN THE UNITED KINGDOM

THE UNITED FREE CHURCH OF SCOTLAND
General Secretary: Rev. John Fulton BSc BD, United Free Church Offices, 11 Newton Place, Glasgow G3 7PR (Tel: 0141-332 3435; E-mail: office@ufcos.org.uk).

THE FREE CHURCH OF SCOTLAND
Principal Clerk: Rev. James MacIver, 15 North Bank Street, The Mound, Edinburgh EH1 2LS (Tel: 0131-226 5286; E-mail: principal.clerk@freechurch.org).

FREE CHURCH OF SCOTLAND (CONTINUING)
Clerk of Assembly: Rev. John MacLeod, Free Church Manse, Portmahomack, Tain IV20 1YL (Tel: 01862 891467; E-mail: principalclerk@fccontinuing.org).

THE FREE PRESBYTERIAN CHURCH OF SCOTLAND
Clerk of Synod: Rev. John MacLeod, 6 Church Avenue, Sidcup, Kent DA14 6BU (E-mail: jmacl265@aol.com).

ASSOCIATED PRESBYTERIAN CHURCHES
Clerk of Presbytery: Rev. Archibald N. McPhail, APC Manse, Polvinister Road, Oban PA34 5TN (Tel: 01631 567076; E-mail: archibald.mcphail@virgin.net).

THE REFORMED PRESBYTERIAN CHURCH OF SCOTLAND
Clerk of Presbytery: Rev. Andrew Quigley, Church Offices, 48 North Bridge Street, Airdrie ML6 6NE (Tel: 01236 620107; E-mail: sandrewq@aol.com).

THE PRESBYTERIAN CHURCH IN IRELAND
Clerk of the General Assembly and General Secretary: Rev. Dr Donald J. Watts, Church House, Fisherwick Place, Belfast BT1 6DW (Tel: 02890 322284; E-mail: clerk@presbyterianireland.org).

THE PRESBYTERIAN CHURCH OF WALES
General Secretary: Rev. W. Bryn Williams, Tabernacle Chapel, 81 Merthyr Road, Whitchurch, Cardiff CF14 1DD (Tel: 02920 627465; Fax: 02920 616188; E-mail: swyddfa.office@ebcpcw.org.uk).

THE UNITED REFORMED CHURCH
General Secretary: Rev. Roberta Rominger, 86 Tavistock Place, London WC1H 9RT (Tel: 020 7916 8646; Fax: 020 7916 2021; E-mail: roberta.rominger@urc.org.uk).

UNITED REFORMED CHURCH SYNOD OF SCOTLAND
Synod Clerk: Mr Patrick Smyth, 113 West Regent Street, Glasgow G1 2RU (Tel: 0141-248 5382; E-mail: psmyth@urcscotland.org.uk).

BAPTIST UNION OF SCOTLAND
General Director: Rev. Alan Donaldson, 48 Speirs Wharf, Glasgow G4 9TH (Tel: 0141-423 6169; E-mail: director@scottishbaptist.org.uk).

CONGREGATIONAL FEDERATION IN SCOTLAND
Secretary: Rev. May-Kane Logan, 93 Cartside Road, Busby, Glasgow G76 8QD (Tel: 0141-237 1349; E-mail: maycita@talktalk.net).

RELIGIOUS SOCIETY OF FRIENDS (QUAKERS)
Robin Waterston, Clerk to the General Meeting for Scotland, 128 North Street, St Andrews KY16
9AF (Tel: 01334 474129; E-mail: robin.waterston128@gmail.com).

ROMAN CATHOLIC CHURCH
Rev. Paul Conroy, General Secretary, Bishops' Conference of Scotland, 64 Aitken Street,
Airdrie ML6 6LT (Tel: 01236 764061; Fax: 01236 762489; E-mail: gensec@
bpsconfscot.com).

THE SALVATION ARMY
Lt-Col. Alan Burns, Divisional Commander and Scotland Secretary, Headquarters and
Scotland Secretariat, 12A Dryden Road, Loanhead EH20 9LZ (Tel: 0131-440 9101;
E-mail: alan.burns@salvationarmy.org.uk).

SCOTTISH EPISCOPAL CHURCH
Secretary General: Mr John F. Stuart, 21 Grosvenor Crescent, Edinburgh EH12 5EL (Tel: 0131-
225 6357; E-mail: secgen@scotland.anglican.org).

THE SYNOD OF THE METHODIST CHURCH IN SCOTLAND
District Administrator: Mrs Fiona Inglis, Methodist Church Office, Scottish Churches House,
Kirk Street, Dunblane FK15 0AJ (Tel/Fax: 01786 820295; E-mail: meth@
scottishchurcheshouse.org).

GENERAL SYNOD OF THE CHURCH OF ENGLAND
Secretary General: Mr William Fittall, Church House, Great Smith Street, London SW1P 3NZ
(Tel: 020 7898 1360; E-mail: william.fittall@churchofengland.org).

---

(2) OVERSEAS CHURCHES

PRESBYTERIAN CHURCH IN CANADA
Clerk of Assembly: 50 Wynford Drive, Toronto, Ontario M3C 1J7, Canada (E-mail:
pccadmin@presbycan.ca; Website: www.presbycan.ca).

UNITED CHURCH OF CANADA
General Secretary: Suite 300, 3250 Bloor Street West, Toronto, Ontario M8X 2Y4, Canada
(E-mail: info@united-church.ca; Website: www.united-church.ca).

PRESBYTERIAN CHURCH (USA)
Stated Clerk: 100 Witherspoon Street, Louisville, KY 40202-1396, USA (E-mail:
presbytel@pcusa.org; Website: www.pcusa.org).

UNITING CHURCH IN AUSTRALIA
General Secretary: PO Box A2266, Sydney South, New South Wales 1235, Australia (E-mail:
enquiries@nat.uca.org.au; Website: www.uca.org.au).

PRESBYTERIAN CHURCH OF AUSTRALIA
Clerk of Assembly: PO Box 2196, Strawberry Hills, NSW 2012; 168 Chalmers Street,
Surry Hills, NSW 2010, Australia (E-mail: general@pcnsw.org.au; Website:
www.presbyterian.org.au).

PRESBYTERIAN CHURCH OF AOTEAROA, NEW ZEALAND
Executive Secretary: PO Box 9049, Wellington, New Zealand (E-mail: aes@presbyterian.org.nz; Website: www.presbyterian.org.nz).

EVANGELICAL PRESBYTERIAN CHURCH, GHANA
Synod Clerk: PO Box 18, Ho, Volta Region, Ghana.

PRESBYTERIAN CHURCH OF GHANA
Director of Ecumenical and Social Relations: PO Box 1800, Accra, Ghana.

PRESBYTERIAN CHURCH OF EAST AFRICA
Secretary General: PO Box 27573, 00506 Nairobi, Kenya.

CHURCH OF CENTRAL AFRICA PRESBYTERIAN
Secretary General, General Assembly: PO Box 30398, Lilongwe 3, Malawi.
General Secretary, Blantyre Synod: PO Box 413, Blantyre, Malawi.
General Secretary, Livingstonia Synod: PO Box 112, Mzuzu, Malawi.
General Secretary, Nkhoma Synod: PO Box 45, Nkhoma, Malawi.

IGREJA EVANGELICA DE CRISTO EM MOÇAMBIQUE (EVANGELICAL CHURCH OF CHRIST IN MOZAMBIQUE)
(Nampula) General Secretary: Cx. Postale 284, Nampula 70100, Mozambique.

PRESBYTERIAN CHURCH OF NIGERIA
Principal Clerk: 26–29 Ehere Road, Ogbor Hill, PO Box 2635, Aba, Abia State, Nigeria.

UNITING PRESBYTERIAN CHURCH IN SOUTHERN AFRICA (SOUTH AFRICA)
General Secretary: PO Box 96188, Brixton 2019, Johannesburg, South Africa (postal address); 28 Rhodes Avenue, Parktown 2193, South Africa (street address).

UNITING PRESBYTERIAN CHURCH IN SOUTHERN AFRICA (ZIMBABWE)
Presbytery Clerk: PO Box CY224, Causeway, Harare, Zimbabwe.

PRESBYTERIAN CHURCH OF SOUTH SUDAN
Head Office: PO Box 40, Malakal, Sudan.

UNITED CHURCH OF ZAMBIA
General Secretary: Nationalist Road at Burma Road, PO Box 50122, 15101 Ridgeway, Lusaka, Zambia.

CHURCH OF BANGLADESH
Moderator: Synod Office, Church of Bangladesh, 54/1 Barobag, Mirpur-2, Dhaka 1216, Bangladesh.

BURMA: PRESBYTERIAN CHURCH OF MYANMAR
Tahan, Kalaymyo, Myanmar.

CHINA
- Amity Foundation, 71 Hankou Road, Nanjing, JS 210008, China.
- China Christian Council, 219 Jiujiang Road, Shanghai 200002, China.
- Nanjing Union Theological Seminary, 100 Qiaoge Lu, Jiangning, Nanjing 211112, China.

CHURCH OF NORTH INDIA
General Secretary: Synod Office, PO Box 311, 16 Pandit Pant Marg, New Delhi 110 001, India.

CHURCH OF SOUTH INDIA
General Secretary: Synod Office, 5 White's Road, Royapettah, Chennai 600 114, India.

PRESBYTERIAN CHURCH OF KOREA
General Secretary: 135 Yunji Dong, Chongno-Gu, Seoul 110 470, Korea.

PRESBYTERIAN CHURCH IN THE REPUBLIC OF KOREA
General Secretary: Academy House San 76, Suyu 6-dong, Kangbuk-Ku, Seoul 142070, Korea.

THE UNITED MISSION TO NEPAL
Executive Director: PO Box 126, Kathmandu, Nepal.

CHURCH OF PAKISTAN
Moderator: Bishop Sammy Azariah, Diocese of Raiwind, 17 Warris Road, Lahore 54000, Pakistan.

PRESBYTERY OF LANKA
Moderator: 127/1 D S Senanayake Veedyan, Kandy 2000, Sri Lanka.

PRESBYTERIAN CHURCH IN TAIWAN
General Secretary: 3 Lane 269 Roosevelt Road, Sec. 3, Taipei, Taiwan 10763, ROC.

CHURCH OF CHRIST IN THAILAND
General Secretary: 109 CCT Building, 328 Payathai Road, Ratchatheu, Bangkok 10400, Thailand.

UNITED CHURCH IN JAMAICA AND THE CAYMAN ISLANDS
General Secretary: 12 Carlton Crescent, PO Box 359, Kingston 10, Jamaica (E-mail: generalsecretary@ucjci.com).

PRESBYTERIAN CHURCH IN TRINIDAD AND TOBAGO
General Secretary: Box 187, Paradise Hill, San Fernando, Trinidad (E-mail: pctt@tstt.net.tt).

PRESBYTERIAN REFORMED CHURCH IN CUBA
General Secretary: Evangelical Theological Seminary of Matanzas, Apartada 149, Dos de Mayofinal, Matanzas, Cuba.

EVANGELICAL CHURCH OF THE CZECH BRETHREN
Moderator: Jungmannova 9, PO Box 466, CZ-11121 Praha 1, Czech Republic (E-mail: ekumena@srcce.cz; Website: www.srcce.cz).

HUNGARIAN REFORMED CHURCH
General Secretary: PF Box 5, H-1440 Budapest, Hungary (E-mail: tz@zsinatiiroda.hu; Website: www.reformatus.hu).

WALDENSIAN CHURCH
Moderator: Via Firenze 38, 00184 Rome, Italy (E-mail: moderatore@chiesavaldese.org; Website: www.chiesavaldese.org).

PROTESTANT CHURCH IN THE NETHERLANDS
Joseph Haydnlaan 2A, Postbus 8504, NL-3503 RM Utrecht. Landelijk Dienstcentrum Samen op
Weg-Kerken, Postbus 8504, NL-3503 RM Utrecht (Tel/Fax: +31 30 880 1880; Website:
www.protestantchurch.nl).

SYNOD OF THE NILE OF THE EVANGELICAL CHURCH OF EGYPT
General Secretary: Synod of the Nile of the Evangelical Church, PO Box 1248, Cairo, Egypt
(E-mail: epcegypt@yahoo.com).

DIOCESE OF THE EPISCOPAL CHURCH IN JERUSALEM AND THE MIDDLE EAST
Bishop's Office: PO Box 19122, Jerusalem 91191, via Israel (E-mail: development@j-diocese.org;
Website: www.j.diocese.org).

NATIONAL EVANGELICAL SYNOD OF SYRIA AND LEBANON
General Secretary: PO Box 70890, Antelias, Lebanon (E-mail: nessl@synod-sl.org).

MIDDLE EAST COUNCIL OF CHURCHES
General Secretary: PO Box 5376, Deeb Building, Makhoul Street, Lebanon (E-mail:
mecc@cyberia.net.lb).

[**Full information on Churches overseas may be obtained from the World Mission Council.**]

---

(3) SCOTTISH DIVINITY FACULTIES
[* denotes a Minister of the Church of Scotland]
[(R) Reader   (SL) Senior Lecturer   (L) Lecturer]

ABERDEEN
(School of Divinity, History and Philosophy)
King's College, Old Aberdeen AB24 3UB
(Tel: 01224 272380; Fax: 01224 273750; E-mail: divinity@abdn.ac.uk)

Master of Christ's College:	Rev. John Swinton* BD PhD RNM RNMD
	(E-mail: christs-college@abdn.ac.uk)
Head of School:	Rev. Philip Ziegler BA MA MDiv ThD
Deputy Head of School:	Rev. Christopher Brittain BA MDiv PhD

Professors:

Tom Greggs MA(Oxon) PhD(Cantab) (Historical and Doctrinal
Theology)
Steve Mason BA MA PhD (New Testament Exegesis)
Robert Segal BA MA PhD (Religious Studies)
Rev. Joachim Schaper DipTheol PhD (Old Testament)
Rev. John Swinton* BD PhD RNM RNMD (Practical Theology
and Pastoral Care)
Rev. Bernd Wannenwetsch MA DrTheol DrTheolHabil
(Theological Ethics)
John Webster MA PhD DD (Systematic Theology)

Senior Lecturers:	Andrew Clarke BA MA PhD (New Testament) Martin Mills MA PhD (Religious Studies) Rev. Philip Ziegler BA MA MDiv ThD (Systematic Theology)
Lecturers:	Kenneth Aitken BD PhD (Hebrew Bible) Thomas Bokedal ThD MTh (New Testament) Rev. Christopher Brittain BA MDiv PhD (Practical Theology) Brian Brock BS MA DipTheol DPhil (Moral and Practical Theology) Marie-Luise Ehrenschwendtner DrTheol PhD (Church History) Jane Heath BA PhD (New Testament) Jutta Leonhardt-Balzer DipTheol PhD (New Testament) Lukas Pokorny MA PhD (Religious Studies) Lena-Sofia Tiemeyer BA MA MPhil (Old Testament/Hebrew Bible) Will Tuladhar-Douglas BA MA MPhil DPhil (Religious Studies) Donald Wood BA MA MPhil DPhil (Systematic Theology)

ST ANDREWS
(University College of St Mary)
St Mary's College, St Andrews, Fife KY16 9JU
(Tel: 01334 462850/1; Fax: 01334 462852)

Principal, Dean and Head of School:	I.J. Davidson MA PhD MTh
Chairs:	M.I. Aguilar OSB Cam Obl BA MA STB PhD FRSA FRAS FRAI FIAI (Religion and Politics) D.W. Brown MA PhD DPhil FBA FRSE (Theology, Aesthetics and Culture and Wardlaw Professor) I.J. Davidson MA PhD MTh (Systematic and Historical Theology) J.R. Davila BA MA PhD (Early Jewish Studies) K. De Troyer STB MA STL PhD (Old Testament/Hebrew Bible) T.A. Hart BA PhD (Divinity) R.A. Piper BA BD PhD (Christian Origins) A.J. Torrance* MA BD DrTheol (Systematic Theology) N.T. Wright MA DPhil DD (New Testament and Early Christianity)
Readers:	I.C. Bradley* BA MA BD DPhil (Church History and Practical Theology) S.R. Hafemann BA MA DrTheol (New Testament) N. MacDonald MA MPhil PhD (Old Testament and Hebrew)
Senior Lecturers:	M.W. Elliott BA BD PhD (Church History) S.R. Holmes BA MA MTh PGDip PhD (Theology)

Lecturers: G.R. Hopps BA MPhil PhD (Literature and Theology)
                        K.R. Iverson BS ThM PhD (New Testament)
                        G. Macaskill BSc DipTh PhD (New Testament)
                        E. Stoddart BD PhD (Practical Theology)
                        W.A. Tooman BA MA MA PhD (Old Testament/Hebrew Bible)

EDINBURGH
(School of Divinity and New College)
New College, Mound Place, Edinburgh EH1 2LX
(Tel: 0131-650 8900; Fax: 0131-650 7952; E-mail: divinity.faculty@ed.ac.uk)

Head of School: Professor Stewart J. Brown BA MA PhD FRHistS FRSE
Principal of New College: Rev. Professor David A.S. Fergusson* MA BD DPhil FRSE
Assistant Principal of
New College: Rev. Frances M. Henderson* BA BD PhD
Chairs: Professor Hans Barstad DrTheol (Hebrew and Old Testament)
                              Professor Stewart J. Brown BA MA PhD FRHistS FRSE
                                (Ecclesiastical History)
                              Professor Jane E.A. Dawson BA PhD DipEd
                                (John Laing Professor of Reformation History)
                              Rev. Professor David A.S. Fergusson* MA BD DPhil FRSE
                                (Divinity)
                              Professor Timothy Lim BA MPhil DPhil (Biblical Studies)
                              Professor Jolyon Mitchell BA MA PhD (Communications, Arts
                                and Religion)
                              Professor Michael S. Northcott MA PhD (Ethics)
                              Professor Mona Siddiqui OBE FRSE FRSA DCivil Laws (hon)
                                DLitt (hon) (Islamic and Interreligious Studies)
                              Professor Brian Stanley MA PhD (World Christianity)

Readers, Senior Lecturers and Lecturers:

Biblical Studies: David J. Reimer BTh BA MA DPhil (SL)
                              Graham Paul Foster PhD MSt BD (SL)
                              Helen K. Bond MTheol PhD (SL)
                              Matthew Novenson BA MDiv ThM PhD (L)

Theology and Ethics: Nicholas Adams MA PhD (SL)
                              Cecelia Clegg BD MSc PhD (SL)
                              Rev. Ewan Kelly* MB ChB BD PhD (SL) (part-time)
                              Paul Nimmo MA BD DipIA ThM PhD (L)
                              Michael Purcell MA PhD PhL PhB (SL)
                              Sara Parvis BA PhD (L)
                              Mark Harris MA PhD MA (L)
                              David Grumett BA MPhil PhD (L)

Ecclesiastical History: Susan Hardman Moore MA PhD (SL)

Religious Studies: Elizabeth Koepping MA PhD (SL)
Steven Sutcliffe BA MPhil PhD (SL)
Hannah Holtschneider MPhil PhD (SL)
Afeosemime U. Adogame BA MA PhD (SL)
Naomi Appleton BA MPhil DPhil (L)

Fulton Lecturer in Speech and Communication:
Richard Ellis BSc MEd LGSM

GLASGOW
School of Critical Studies
Theology and Religious Studies Subject Area
4 The Square, University of Glasgow, Glasgow G12 8QQ
(Tel: 0141-330 6526; Fax: 0141-330 4943;
Website: www.gla.ac.uk/departments/theology)

Head of Subject: Dr Lloyd Ridgeon
Head of School: Prof. Nigel Leask

Trinity College
Principal of Trinity College: Rev. Dr Doug Gay*
Clerk to Trinity College: Rev. Dr Akma Adam

Chairs: Rev. Prof. David Jasper (Theology and Literature)
Prof. Richard King (Religious Studies)
Prof. Yvonne Sherwood (Biblical Studies)

Readers, Senior Lecturers, Lecturers and Fellows etc.
Biblical Studies: Rev. Dr Akma Adam (L)
Dr Ward Blanton (SL)
Mrs Linda Knox (Language Tutor)
Dr Sarah Nicholson (L)
Church History: Rev. Canon Dr Charlotte Methuen
Catholic Theology: Ms Julie Clague (L)
Practical Theology: Rev. Dr Doug Gay* (L)
Dr Heather Walton (SL)
Rev. Dr Leah Robinson
Islamic Studies: Dr Lloyd Ridgeon (SL)

Associate Staff (Free Church of Scotland College, Edinburgh)
Rev. Donald M. MacDonald
Rev. Prof. John R. McIntosh
Rev. Prof. John L. Mackay
Rev. Alasdair I. MacLeod
Rev. Prof. Donald Macleod
Rev. John A. MacLeod
Rev. Neil MacMillan
Rev. Duncan Peters

HIGHLAND THEOLOGICAL COLLEGE UHI
High Street, Dingwall IV15 9HA
(Tel: 01349 780000; Fax: 01349 780201;
E-mail: htc@uhi.ac.uk)

Principal of HTC: Rev. Hector Morrison* BSc BD MTh
Vice-Principal of HTC: Jamie Grant PhD MA LLB

Lecturers: Hector Morrison* BSc BD MTh (Old Testament and Hebrew)
Jamie Grant PhD MA LLB (Biblical Studies)
Jason Maston BA MA PhD (New Testament)
Innes Visagie MA BTh BA PhD (Pastoral Theology)
Nick Needham BD PhD (Church History)
Robert Shillaker BSc BA PhD (Systematic Theology)

(4) SOCIETIES AND ASSOCIATIONS

The undernoted list shows the name of the Association, along with the name and address of the Secretary.

1. INTER-CHURCH ASSOCIATIONS

The FELLOWSHIP OF ST ANDREW: The fellowship promotes dialogue between Churches of the east and the west in Scotland. Further information available from the Secretary, Rev. John G. Pickles, 1 Annerley Road, Annan DG12 6HE (Tel: 01461 202626; E-mail: jgpickles@hotmail.com).

The FELLOWSHIP OF ST THOMAS: An ecumenical association formed to promote informed interest in and to learn from the experience of Churches in South Asia (India, Pakistan, Bangladesh, Nepal, Sri Lanka and Burma (Myanmar)). Secretary: Rev. Murdoch MacKenzie, 'Torridon', 4 Ferryfield Road, Connel, Oban PA37 1SR (Tel: 01631 710550; E-mail: mackenziema@ymail.com).

FRONTIER YOUTH TRUST: Encourages, resources and supports churches, organisations and individuals working with young people (in particular, disadvantaged young people). Through the StreetSpace initiative, the Trust is able to help churches to explore new ways of engaging young people in the community around mission and fresh expressions of church. All correspondence to: Frontier Youth Trust, Office S15b, St George's Community Hub, Great Hampton Row, Newtown, Birmingham B19 3JG (Tel: 0121-687 3505; E-mail: frontier@fyt.org.uk; Website: www.fyt.org.uk). For information on StreetSpace, contact Richard Passmore (07830 197160).

INTERSERVE SCOTLAND: We are part of Interserve, an international, evangelical and interdenominational organisation with over 150 years of Christian service. The purpose of Interserve is 'to make Jesus Christ known through *wholistic* ministry in partnership with the global church, among the neediest peoples of Asia and the Arab world', and our vision is 'Lives and communities transformed through encounter with Jesus Christ'. Interserve supports over 800 people in cross-cultural ministry in a wide range of work including children and youth, the environment, evangelism, Bible training, engineering, agriculture, business development and health. We rely on supporters in Scotland and throughout the UK to join us. Director: Grace Penney, 4 Blairtummock Place, Panorama Business Village, Queenslie, Glasgow G33 4EN (Tel: 0141-781 1982; Fax: 0141-781 1572; E-mail: info@ isscot.org; Website: www.interservescotland.org.uk).

IONA COMMUNITY: An ecumenical Christian community of men and women from different walks of life and different traditions in the Church, committed to the gospel of Jesus Christ and to following where that leads, even into the unknown; engaged together, and with people of goodwill across the world, in acting, reflecting and praying for justice, peace and the integrity of creation; convinced that the inclusive community we seek must be embodied in the community we practise. The Iona Community's work with young people, Wild Goose Resource Group and Wild Goose Publications, is based in the Glasgow office. The Community also runs residential centres at the Abbey and MacLeod Centre, Iona and Camas, Mull. Leader: Rev. Peter Macdonald, 4th Floor, Savoy House, 140 Sauchiehall Street, Glasgow G2 3DH (Tel: 0141-332 6343; Fax: 0141-332 1090; E-mail: admin@ iona.org.uk; Website: www.iona.org.uk). Centres Director: Rev. Joanna Anderson, Iona Abbey, Isle of Iona, Argyll PA76 6SN (Tel: 01681 700404).

PLACE FOR HOPE: An initiative with its roots in the Church of Scotland, offering a different way of addressing our differences. It is a network of professionally trained individuals, equipped to facilitate some of our more difficult conversations, offering the means of restoring broken relationships. To Kirk Sessions, Presbyteries and any other groups, we provide training in the skills which can lead to more effective conversations with one another, recognising and valuing our differences. We encourage and enable dialogue – rather than debate – and a means of enabling all voices to be heard. We seek to work across denominations and offer our skills and resources into the community. We operate on a confidential basis, and would be pleased to have a conversation at any time on how we might be of help. Visit www. placeforhope.org.uk or contact Dorothy Davidson on 0131-240 2258.

The ST COLM'S FELLOWSHIP: An association for all from any denomination who have trained, studied or been resident at St Colm's, either when it was a college or later as International House. There is an annual retreat and annual lecture; and some local groups meet on a regular basis. Hon. Secretary: Margaret Nutter, 'Kilmorich', Balloch Road, Balloch G83 8SR (Tel: 01389 754505; E-mail: mnutter@blueyonder.co.uk).

SCOTTISH CHURCHES HOUSING ACTION: Unites the Scottish Churches in tackling homelessness; supports local volunteering to assist homeless people; advises on using property for affordable housing. Chief Executive: Alastair Cameron, 44 Hanover Street, Edinburgh EH2 2DR (Tel: 0131-477 4500; E-mail: info@churches-housing.org; Website: www.churches-housing.org).

SCOTTISH JOINT COMMITTEE ON RELIGIOUS AND MORAL EDUCATION: This is an interfaith body that began as a joint partnership between the Educational Institute of Scotland and the Church of Scotland to provide resources, training and support for the work of religious and moral education in schools. Rev. Ewan R. Aitken, 121 George Street, Edinburgh EH2 4YN (Tel: 0131-225 5722), and Mr Lachlan Bradley, 6 Clairmont Gardens, Glasgow G3 7LW (Tel: 0141-353 3595).

SCRIPTURE UNION SCOTLAND: 70 Milton Street, Glasgow G4 0HR (Tel: 0141-332 1162; Fax: 0141-352 7600; E-mail: info@suscotland.org.uk; Website: www.suscotland.org.uk). Scripture Union Scotland's vision is to see all the children and young people in Scotland exploring the Bible and responding to the significance of Jesus. SU Scotland works in schools running Christian Focus Weeks, taking part in assemblies and supporting extra-curricular groups. It also offers 'Classroom Outdoors', an outdoor education programme for school groups that is based around Curriculum for Excellence. These events take place at its two activity centres, Lendrick Muir (near Kinross) and Altnacriche (near Aviemore), which also cater for church or school groups throughout the year. During the school holidays and at weekends, it runs an extensive programme of events for school-age children – including residential holidays (some focused on disadvantaged children and young people), missions and church-based holiday clubs. In addition, it runs discipleship and training programmes for young people and is committed to promoting prayer for, and by, the young people of Scotland through a range of national prayer events and the *Pray for Schools Scotland* initiative. *Ignite* is SU Scotland's online discipleship website for young people, providing a safe space for them to delve deeper into the Bible and the Christian faith, ask questions and join online discussions.

STUDENT CHRISTIAN MOVEMENT: National Co-ordinator: Hilary Topp, SCM, 504F The Big Peg, 120 Vyse Street, Hockley, Birmingham B18 6NE (Tel: 0121-200 3355; E-mail: scm@movement.org.uk; Website: www.movement.org.uk). The Student Christian Movement (SCM) is a student-led community passionate about living out our faith in the real world. We have a network of groups around the country and organise national events.

UCCF: THE CHRISTIAN UNIONS: Blue Boar House, 5 Blue Boar Street, Oxford OX1 4EE (Tel: 01865 253678; E-mail: email@uccf.org.uk). UCCF is a family of students, staff and supporters. Christian Unions are mission teams operating in universities and colleges, supported by the local church, and resourced by UCCF staff. This family exists to proclaim the gospel of Jesus Christ in the student world.

WORLD DAY OF PRAYER: SCOTTISH COMMITTEE: Convener: Christian Williams, 61 McCallum Gardens, Strathview Estate, Bellshill ML4 2SR. Secretary: Marjorie Paton, 'Lindisfarne', 19 Links Road, Lundin Links, Leven KY8 6AS (Tel: 01333 329830; E-mail: marjoriepaton.wdp@btinternet.com; Website: www.wdpscotland.org.uk).

YMCA SCOTLAND: Offers support, training and guidance to churches seeking to reach out to love and serve community needs. National General Secretary: Mr Peter Crory, James Love House, 11 Rutland Street, Edinburgh EH1 2DQ (Tel: 0131-228 1464; E-mail: ian@ymcascotland.org; Website: www.ymcascotland.org).

2. CHURCH OF SCOTLAND SOCIETIES

CHURCH OF SCOTLAND ABSTAINER'S ASSOCIATION: Recognising that alcohol is a major – indeed a growing – problem within Scotland, the aim of the Church of Scotland Abstainer's Association, with its motto 'Abstinence makes sense', is to encourage more people to choose a healthy alcohol-free lifestyle. Further details are available from 'Blochairn', 17A Culduthel Road, Inverness IV24 4AG (Website: www.kirkabstainers.org.uk).

The CHURCH OF SCOTLAND CHAPLAINS' ASSOCIATION: The Association consists of serving and retired chaplains to HM Forces. It holds an annual meeting and lunch, and organises the annual Service of Remembrance in St Giles' Cathedral on Chaplains' Day of the General Assembly. Hon. Secretary: Rev. Neil N. Gardner MA BD, The Manse of Canongate, Edinburgh EH8 8BR (Tel: 0131-556 3515).

The CHURCH OF SCOTLAND RETIRED MINISTERS' ASSOCIATION: Hon. Secretary: Rev. Murray Chalmers, 8 Easter Warriston, Edinburgh EH7 4QX (Tel: 0131-552 4211; E-mail: murr46mers@btopenworld.com).

CHURCH OF SCOTLAND WORLD MISSION COUNCIL OVERSEAS ASSOCIATION (previously AROS): Secretary: Mr Walter Dunlop, 50 Oxgangs Road North, Edinburgh EH13 9DR (Tel: 07854 487376).

The CHURCH SERVICE SOCIETY: Secretary: Rev. Dr Douglas Galbraith, 34 Balbirnie Street, Markinch, Glenrothes KY7 6DA (Tel: 01592 752403; E-mail: dgalbraith@hotmail.com; Website: www.churchservicesociety.org).

FORUM OF GENERAL ASSEMBLY AND PRESBYTERY CLERKS: Secretary: Rev. Rosemary Frew, 83 Milton Road, Kirkcaldy KY1 1TP (Tel: 01592 260315; E-mail: kirkcaldy@cofscotland.org.uk).

FORWARD TOGETHER: An organisation for evangelicals within the Church of Scotland. Chairman: Rev. Steven Reid BAcc CA BD, 74 Lanark Road, Crossford, Carluke ML8 5RE (Tel: 01555 860415; Website: www.forwardtogether.org.uk).

The FRIENDS OF TABEETHA SCHOOL, JAFFA: President: Miss Eileen Robertson. Hon. Secretary: Rev. Iain F. Paton, 'Lindisfarne', 19 Links Road, Lundin Links, Leven KY8 6AS (Tel: 01333 320765).

The IRISH GATHERING: Secretary: Rev. Eric G. McKimmon BA BD MTh PhD, 1F1, 279 Easter Road, Edinburgh EH6 8LQ (Tel: 0131-554 9317; E-mail: mckimmonceres@aol.com).

SCOTTISH CHURCH SOCIETY: Secretary: Rev. W. Gerald Jones MA BD MTh, The Manse, Patna Road, Kirkmichael, Maybole KA19 7PJ (Tel: 01655 750286; Website: www.scottishchurchsociety.org.uk).

SCOTTISH CHURCH THEOLOGY SOCIETY: Rev. Mary M. Cranfield MA BD DMin, The Manse, Daviot, Inverurie AB51 0HY (Tel: 01467 671241; E-mail: marymc@ukgateway.net). The Society encourages theological exploration and discussion of the main issues confronting the Church in the twenty-first century.

SOCIETY OF FRIENDS OF ST ANDREW'S JERUSALEM: Hon. Secretary: Major J.M.K. Erskine MBE, World Mission Council, 121 George Street, Edinburgh EH2 4YN. Hon. Treasurer: Mrs Anne Macintosh BA CA, Assistant Treasurer, The Church of Scotland, 121 George Street, Edinburgh EH2 4YN (Tel: 0131-225 5722).

3. BIBLE SOCIETIES

The SCOTTISH BIBLE SOCIETY: Chief Executive: Elaine Duncan, 7 Hampton Terrace, Edinburgh EH12 5XU (Tel: 0131-347 9813; E-mail: info@scottishbiblesociety.org).

WEST OF SCOTLAND BIBLE SOCIETY: Secretary: Rev. Finlay MacKenzie, 51 Rowallan Gardens, Glasgow G11 7LH (Tel: 0141-563 5276; E-mail: f.c.mack51@ntlworld.com).

4. GENERAL

The BOYS' BRIGADE: Scottish Headquarters, Carronvale House, Carronvale Road, Larbert FK5 3LH (Tel: 01324 562008; Fax: 01324 552323; E-mail: scottishhq@ boys-brigade.org.uk).

BROKEN RITES: Support group for divorced and separated clergy spouses (Tel: 01896 759254 or 01257 423893; Website: www.brokenrites.org).

CHRISTIAN AID SCOTLAND: Kathy Galloway, Head of Christian Aid Scotland, Sycamore House, 290 Bath Street, Glasgow G2 4JR (Tel: 0141-221 7475; Fax: 0141-241 6145; E-mail: glasgow@christian-aid.org). Edinburgh Office: Tel: 0131-220 1254. Perth Office: Tel: 01738 643982.

CHRISTIAN ENDEAVOUR IN SCOTLAND: Winning, Teaching and Training Youngsters for Christ and the Church: 16 Queen Street, Alloa FK10 2AR (Tel: 01259 215101; E-mail: admin@cescotland.org; Website: www.cescotland.org).

DAYONE CHRISTIAN MINISTRIES (THE LORD'S DAY OBSERVANCE SOCIETY): Ryelands Road, Leominster, Herefordshire HR6 8NZ. Contact Mark Roberts for further information (Tel: 01568 613740; E-mail: info@dayone.co.uk).

ECO-CONGREGATION SCOTLAND: 121 George Street, Edinburgh EH2 4YN (Tel: 0131-240 2274; E-mail: manager@ecocongregationscotland.org; Website: www.ecocongregationscotland.org). Eco-Congregation Scotland is the largest movement of community-based environment groups in Scotland. We offer a programme to help congregations reduce their impact on climate change and live sustainably in a world of limited resources.

FEED THE MINDS: Park Place, 12 Lawn Lane, London SW8 1UD (Tel: 020 7582 3535; E-mail: asach@feedtheminds.org).

GIRLGUIDING SCOTLAND: 16 Coates Crescent, Edinburgh EH3 7AH (Tel: 0131-226 4511; Fax: 0131-220 4828; E-mail: administrator@girlguiding-scot.org.uk).

The GIRLS' BRIGADE IN SCOTLAND: 11A Woodside Crescent, Glasgow G3 7UL (Tel: 0141-332 1765; E-mail: enquiries@girls-brigade-scotland.org.uk; Website: www.girls-brigade-scotland.org.uk).

The LEPROSY MISSION SCOTLAND: Suite 2, Earlsgate Lodge, Livilands Lane, Stirling FK8 2BG (Tel: 01786 449266; E-mail: contactus@tlmscotland.org.uk; Website: www.tlmscotland.org.uk). National Director: Linda Todd. Communications Manager: Stuart McAra.

RELATIONSHIPS SCOTLAND: Chief Executive: Mr Stuart Valentine, 18 York Place, Edinburgh EH1 3EP (Tel: 0845 119 2020; Fax: 0845 119 6089; E-mail: enquiries@ relationships-scotland.org.uk; Website: www.relationships-scotland.org.uk).

SCOTTISH CHURCH HISTORY SOCIETY: Hon. Secretary: Christine Lumsden BA MA PhD, 80/3 Slateford Road, Edinburgh EH11 1QU (Tel: 0131-337 3644; E-mail: christinaclumsden@gmail.com).

SCOTTISH EVANGELICAL THEOLOGY SOCIETY: Secretary: Rosemary Dowsett, 4 Borden Road, Glasgow G13 1QX (Tel: 0141-959 4976; E-mail: dickandrosedowsett@ googlemail.com; Website: www.s-e-t-s.org.uk).

The SCOTTISH REFORMATION SOCIETY: Chairman: Rev. Dr S. James Millar. Vice-Chairman: Rev. John J. Murray. Secretary: Rev. Dr Douglas Somerset. Treasurer: Rev. Andrew W.F. Coghill, The Magdalen Chapel, 41 Cowgate, Edinburgh EH1 1JR (Tel: 0131-220 1450; E-mail: info@scottishreformationsociety.org.uk; Website: www.scottishreformationsociety.org.uk).

The SCOUT ASSOCIATION: Scottish Headquarters, Fordell Firs, Hillend, Dunfermline KY11 7HQ (Tel: 01383 419073; E-mail: shq@scouts-scotland.org.uk; Website: www.scouts-scotland.org.uk).

The SOCIETY IN SCOTLAND FOR PROPAGATING CHRISTIAN KNOWLEDGE: Chairman: Rev. Andrew Anderson; Honorary Secretary: Philip Halford-MacLeod. Address: SSPCK, c/o Tods Murray LLP, Edinburgh Quay, 133 Fountainbridge, Edinburgh EH3 9AG (Tel: 0131-656 2000; Website: www.sspck.co.uk; E-mail: philip_h@madasafish.com).

TEARFUND: 100 Church Road, Teddington TW11 8QE (Tel: 0845 355 8355). Director: Lynne Paterson, Tearfund Scotland, Challenge House, 29 Canal Street, Glasgow G4 0AD (Tel: 0141-332 3621; E-mail: scotland@tearfund.org; Website: www.tearfund.org).

The WALDENSIAN MISSIONS AID SOCIETY FOR WORK IN ITALY: David A. Lamb SSC, 36 Liberton Drive, Edinburgh EH16 6NN (Tel: 0131-664 3059; E-mail: david@ dlamb.co.uk).

YOUTH SCOTLAND: Balfour House, 19 Bonnington Grove, Edinburgh EH6 4BL (Tel: 0131-554 2561; Fax: 0131-454 3438; E-mail: office@youthscotland.org.uk).

YWCA SCOTLAND: National Co-ordinator: Kim Smith, 4B Gayfield Place, Edinburgh EH7 4AB (Tel: 0131-558 8000; E-mail: reception@ywcascotland.org; Website: www. ywcascotland.org).

---

(5) TRUSTS AND FUNDS

The ABERNETHY TRUST: Offers residential accommodation and outdoor activities for Youth Fellowships, Church family weekends and Bible Classes at four outdoor centres in Scotland. Further details from the Executive Director, Abernethy Trust, Nethy Bridge PH25 3ED (Tel: 01479 821279; Website: www.abernethy.org.uk).

The ARROL TRUST: The Arrol Trust gives small grants to young people between the ages of 16 and 25 for the purposes of travel which will provide education or work experience. Potential recipients would be young people with disabilities or who would for financial reasons be otherwise unable to undertake projects. It is expected that projects would be beneficial not only to applicants but also to the wider community. Application forms are available from Callum S. Kennedy WS, Lindsays WS, Caledonian Exchange, 19A Canning Street, Edinburgh EH3 8HE (Tel: 0131-229 1212).

The BAIRD TRUST: Assists in the building and repair of churches and halls, and generally assists the work of the Church of Scotland. Apply to Iain A.T. Mowat CA, 182 Bath Street, Glasgow G2 4HG (Tel: 0141-332 0476; Fax: 0141-331 0874; E-mail: info@bairdtrust.org.uk; Website: www.bairdtrust.org.uk).

The Rev. Alexander BARCLAY BEQUEST: Assists mother, daughter, sister or niece of deceased minister of the Church of Scotland who at the time of his death was acting as his housekeeper and who is in needy circumstances. Apply to Robert Hugh Allan LLB DipLP NP, Pomphreys, 79 Quarry Street, Hamilton ML3 7AG (Tel: 01698 891616).

BELLAHOUSTON BEQUEST FUND: Gives grants to Protestant evangelical denominations in the City of Glasgow and certain areas within five miles of the city boundary for building and repairing churches and halls and the promotion of religion. Apply to Mr Donald B. Reid, Mitchells Roberton, 36 North Hanover Street, Glasgow G1 2AD.

BEQUEST FUND FOR MINISTERS: Assists ministers in outlying districts with manse furnishings, pastoral efficiency aids, and their own and family medical or educational costs, including university. Apply to A. Linda Parkhill CA, 60 Wellington Street, Glasgow G2 6HJ (Tel: 0141-226 4994; E-mail: mail@parkhillmackie.co.uk).

CARNEGIE TRUST FOR THE UNIVERSITIES OF SCOTLAND: In cases of hardship, the Carnegie Trust is prepared to consider applications by students of Scottish birth or extraction (at least one parent born in Scotland), or who have had at least two years' education at a secondary school in Scotland, for financial assistance with the payment of their fees for a first degree at a Scottish university. For further details, students should apply to the Secretary, Carnegie Trust for the Universities of Scotland, Andrew Carnegie House, Pittencrieff Street, Dunfermline KY12 8AW (Tel: 01383 724990; Fax: 01383 749799; E-mail: jgray@carnegie-trust.org; Website: www.carnegie-trust.org).

CHURCH OF SCOTLAND INSURANCE CO. LTD: Undertakes insurance of Church property and pays all its distributable profits to the Church of Scotland by way of Gift Aid. It is authorised and regulated by the Financial Services Authority. The company is also an intermediary and can arrange other classes of business including household insurance for members and adherents of the Church of Scotland. At 67 George Street, Edinburgh EH2 2JG (Tel: 0131-220 4119; Fax: 0131-220 4120; E-mail: enquiries@cosic.co.uk; Website: www.cosic.co.uk).

CHURCH OF SCOTLAND MINISTRY BENEVOLENT FUND: Makes grants to retired men and women who have been ordained or commissioned for the ministry of the Church of Scotland and to widows, widowers, orphans, spouses or children of such, who are in need. Apply to the Assistant Treasurer (Ministries), 121 George Street, Edinburgh EH2 4YN (Tel: 0131-225 5722).

The CINTRA BEQUEST: The Trust provides financial assistance towards the cost of accommodation in Scotland for missionaries on leave, or for ministers on temporary holiday, or on rest. In addition, due to additional funds generously donated by the Tod Endowment Trust (q.v.), grants can be given to defray the cost of obtaining rest and recuperation in Scotland. In appropriate cases, therefore, the cost of travel within Scotland may also be met. Applications should be made to Mrs J.S. Wilson, Solicitor, 121 George Street, Edinburgh EH2 4YN.

CLARK BURSARY: Awarded to accepted candidate(s) for the ministry of the Church of Scotland whose studies for the ministry are pursued at the University of Aberdeen. Applications or recommendations for the Bursary to the Clerk to the Presbytery of Aberdeen, Mastrick Church, Greenfern Road, Aberdeen AB16 6TR by 16 October annually.

CRAIGCROOK MORTIFICATION: Pensions are paid to poor men and women over 60 years old, born in Scotland or who have resided in Scotland for not less than ten years. At present, pensions amount to £1,000–£1,500 p.a.
  Ministers are invited to notify the Clerk and Factor, Mrs Fiona M.M. Watson CA, Exchange Place 3, Semple Street, Edinburgh EH3 8BL (Tel: 0131-473 3500; E-mail: charity@scott-moncrieff.com) of deserving persons and should be prepared to act as a referee on the application form.

CROMBIE SCHOLARSHIP: Provides grants annually on the nomination of the Deans of Faculty of Divinity of the Universities of St Andrews, Glasgow, Aberdeen and Edinburgh, who each nominate one matriculated student who has taken a University course in Greek (Classical or Hellenistic) and Hebrew. Award by recommendation only.

The DRUMMOND TRUST: Makes grants towards the cost of publication of books of 'sound Christian doctrine and outreach'. The Trustees are also willing to receive grant requests towards the cost of audio-visual programme material, but not equipment. Requests for application forms should be made to the Secretaries, Hill and Robb, 3 Pitt Terrace, Stirling FK8 2EY (Tel: 01786 450985; E-mail: douglaswhyte@hillandrobb.co.uk). Manuscripts should *not* be sent.

The DUNCAN TRUST: Makes grants annually to students for the ministry in the Faculties of Arts and Divinity. Preference is given to those born or educated within the bounds of the former Presbytery of Arbroath. Applications not later than 31 October to Thorntons Law LLP, Brothockbank House, Arbroath DD11 1NE (reference: G.J.M. Dunlop; Tel: 01241 872683; E-mail: gdunlop@thorntons-law.co.uk).

ESDAILE TRUST: Assists the education and advancement of daughters of ministers, missionaries and widowed deaconesses of the Church of Scotland between 12 and 25 years of age. Applications are to be lodged by 31 May in each year with the Clerk and Treasurer, Mrs Fiona M.M. Watson CA, Exchange Place 3, Semple Street, Edinburgh EH3 8BL (Tel: 0131-473 3500; E-mail: charity@scott-moncrieff.com).

FERGUSON BEQUEST FUND: Assists with the building and repair of churches and halls and, more generally, with the work of the Church of Scotland. Priority is given to the Counties of Ayr, Kirkcudbright, Wigtown, Lanark, Dunbarton and Renfrew, and to Greenock, Glasgow, Falkirk and Ardrossan; applications are, however, accepted from across Scotland. Apply to Iain A.T. Mowat CA, 182 Bath Street, Glasgow G2 4HG (Tel: 0141-332 0476; Fax: 0141-331 0874; E-mail: info@fergusonbequestfund.org.uk; Website: www.fergusonbequestfund.org.uk).

GEIKIE BEQUEST: Makes small grants to students for the ministry, including students studying for entry to the University, preference being given to those not eligible for SAAS awards. Apply to the Assistant Treasurer (Ministries), 121 George Street, Edinburgh EH2 4YN by September for distribution in November each year.

James GILLAN'S BURSARY FUND: Bursaries are available for male or female students for the ministry who were born or whose parents or parent have resided and had their home for not less than three years continually in the old counties (not Districts) of Moray or Nairn. Apply to R. and R. Urquhart LLP, 117–121 High Street, Forres IV36 1AB.

The GLASGOW SOCIETY OF THE SONS AND DAUGHTERS OF MINISTERS OF THE CHURCH OF SCOTLAND: The Society's primary purpose is to grant financial assistance to children (no matter what age) of deceased ministers of the Church of Scotland. Applications are to be submitted by 1 February in each year. To the extent that funds are available, grants are also given for the children of ministers or retired ministers, although such grants are normally restricted to university and college students. These latter grants are considered in conjunction with the Edinburgh-based Society. Limited funds are also available for individual application for special needs or projects. Applications are to be submitted by 31 May in each year. Emergency applications can be dealt with at any time when need arises. Application forms may be obtained from the Secretary and Treasurer, Mrs Fiona M.M. Watson CA, Exchange Place 3, Semple Street, Edinburgh EH3 8BL (Tel: 0131-473 3500; E-mail: charity@scott-moncrieff.com).

HAMILTON BURSARY TRUST: Awarded, subject to the intention to serve overseas under the Church of Scotland World Mission Council or to serve with some other Overseas Mission Agency approved by the Council, to a student at the University of Aberdeen. Preference is given to a student born or residing in (1) Parish of Skene, (2) Parish of Echt, (3) the Presbytery of Aberdeen, Kincardine and Deeside, or Gordon; failing which to Accepted Candidate(s) for the Ministry of the Church of Scotland whose studies for the Ministry are pursued at Aberdeen University. Applications or recommendations for the Bursary to the Clerk to the Presbytery of Aberdeen by 16 October annually.

Martin HARCUS BEQUEST: Makes annual grants to candidates for the ministry resident within the City of Edinburgh. Applications to the Clerk to the Presbytery of Edinburgh, 10/1 Palmerston Place, Edinburgh EH12 5AA by 15 October (E-mail: edinburgh@cofscotland.org.uk).

The HOPE TRUST: Gives some support to organisations involved in combating drink and drugs, and has as its main purpose the promotion of the Reformed tradition throughout the world. There is also a Scholarship programme for Postgraduate Theology Study in Scotland. Apply to Robert P. Miller SSC LLB, 31 Moray Place, Edinburgh EH3 6BY (Tel: 0131-226 5151).

KEAY THOM TRUST: The principal purposes of the Keay Thom Trust are:
1.   To benefit the widows, daughters or other dependent female relatives of deceased ministers, or wives of ministers who are now divorced or separated, all of whom have supported the minister in the fulfilment of his duties and who, by reason of death, divorce or separation, have been required to leave the manse. The Trust can assist them in the purchase of a house or by providing financial or material assistance whether it be for the provision of accommodation or not.

2.   To assist in the education or training of the above female relatives or any other children of deceased ministers.
Further information and application forms are available from Miller Hendry, Solicitors, 10 Blackfriars Street, Perth PH1 5NS (Tel: 01738 637311).

LADIES' GAELIC SCHOOLS AND HIGHLAND BURSARY ASSOCIATION: Distributes money to students, preferably with a Highland/Gaelic background, who are training to be ministers in the Church of Scotland. Apply by 15 October in each year to the Secretary, Donald J. Macdonald, 35 Durham Avenue, Edinburgh EH15 1RZ (E-mail: djandanne@btinternet.com).

The LYALL BEQUEST: Scottish Charity Number SC005542. Makes available the following benefits to ministers of the Church of Scotland:
1.   A grant towards the cost of holiday accommodation in or close to the town of St Andrews may be paid to any minister and to his or her spouse at the rate of £150 per week each for a stay of one week or longer. Grants for a stay of less than one week may also be paid, at the rate of £21 per day each. Due to the number of applications which the Trustees now receive, an applicant will not be considered to be eligible if he or she has received a grant from the Bequest during the three years prior to the holiday for which the application is made. Applications prior to the holiday should be made to the Secretaries. Retired ministers are not eligible for grants.
2.   Grants towards costs of sickness and convalescence so far as not covered by the National Health Service or otherwise may be available to applicants, who should apply to the Secretaries giving relevant details.
All communications should be addressed to Pagan Osborne Ltd, Solicitors, Secretaries to the Lyall Bequest, 106 South Street, St Andrews KY16 9QD (Tel: 01334 475001; E-mail: elcalderwood@pagan.co.uk).

Gillian MACLAINE BURSARY FUND: Open to candidates for the ministry of the Church of Scotland of Scottish or Canadian nationality. Preference is given to Gaelic-speakers. Application forms available from Rev. George G. Cringles BD, Depute Clerk of the Presbytery of Argyll, St Oran's Manse, Connel, Oban PA37 1PJ. Closing date for receipt of applications is 31 October.

The E. McLAREN FUND: The persons intended to be benefited are widows and unmarried ladies, preference being given to ladies above 40 years of age in the following order:
(a) Widows and daughters of Officers in the Highland Regiment, and
(b) Widows and daughters of Scotsmen.
Further details from the Secretary, The E. McLaren Fund, Messrs BMK Wilson, Solicitors, 90 St Vincent Street, Glasgow G2 5UB (Tel: 0141-221 8004; Fax: 0141-221 8088; E-mail: rrs@bmkwilson.co.uk).

The Misses Ann and Margaret McMILLAN BEQUEST: Makes grants to ministers of the Free and United Free Churches, and of the Church of Scotland, in charges within the Synod of Argyll, with income not exceeding the minimum stipend of the Church of Scotland. Apply by 30 June in each year to Rev. Samuel McC. Harris, 36 Adam Wood Court, Troon KA10 6BP.

MORGAN BURSARY FUND: Makes grants to candidates for the Church of Scotland ministry studying at the University of Glasgow. Apply to the Clerk to the Presbytery of Glasgow, 260 Bath Street, Glasgow G2 4JP (Tel: 0141-332 6606).

NOVUM TRUST: Provides small short-term grants – typically between £200 and £2,500 – to initiate projects in Christian action and research which cannot readily be financed from other sources. Trustees welcome applications from projects that are essentially Scottish, are distinctively new, and are focused on the welfare of young people, on the training of lay people or on new ways of communicating the Christian faith. The Trust cannot support large building projects, staff salaries or individuals applying for maintenance during courses or training. Application forms and guidance notes from novumt@cofscotland.org.uk or Mrs Susan Masterton, Blair Cadell WS, The Bond House, 5 Breadalbane Street, Edinburgh EH6 5JH (Tel: 0131-555 5800).

PARK MEMORIAL BURSARY FUND: Provides grants for the benefit of candidates for the ministry of the Church of Scotland from the Presbytery of Glasgow under full-time training. Apply to the Clerk to the Presbytery of Glasgow, 260 Bath Street, Glasgow G2 4JP (Tel: 0141-332 6606).

PATON TRUST: Assists ministers in ill health to have a recuperative holiday outwith, and free from the cares of, their parishes. Apply to Alan S. Cunningham CA, Alexander Sloan, Chartered Accountants, 38 Cadogan Street, Glasgow G2 7HF (Tel: 0141-204 8989; Fax: 0141-248 9931; E-mail: alan.cunningham@alexandersloan.co.uk).

PRESBYTERY OF ARGYLL BURSARY FUND: Open to students who have been accepted as candidates for the ministry and the readership of the Church of Scotland. Preference is given to applicants who are natives of the bounds of the Presbytery, or are resident within the bounds of the Presbytery, or who have a strong connection with the bounds of the Presbytery. Application forms available from Rev. George G. Cringles BD, Depute Clerk of the Presbytery of Argyll, St Oran's Manse, Connel, Oban PA37 1PJ. Closing date for receipt of applications is 31 October.

Margaret and John ROSS TRAVELLING FUND: Offers grants to ministers and their spouses for travelling and other expenses for trips to the Holy Land where the purpose is recuperation or relaxation. Applications should be made to the Secretary and Clerk, The Church of Scotland Trust, 121 George Street, Edinburgh EH2 4YN (Tel: 0131-240 2222; E-mail: jhamilton@cofscotland.org.uk).

SCOTLAND'S CHURCHES TRUST (formerly Scottish Churches Architectural Heritage Trust): Assists congregations of any denomination in the preservation of the fabric of buildings in regular use for public worship. Also supports costs for the playing of church organs. Requests for application forms through www.sctrust.org.uk or from Scotland's Churches Trust, 15 North Bank Street, The Mound, Edinburgh EH1 2LP (Tel: 0131-225 8644; E-mail: info@scaht.org.uk).

SMIETON FUND: Makes small holiday grants to ministers. Administered at the discretion of the pastoral staff, who will give priority in cases of need. Applications to the Associate Secretary (Support and Development), Ministries Council, 121 George Street, Edinburgh EH2 4YN.

Mary Davidson SMITH CLERICAL AND EDUCATIONAL FUND FOR ABERDEENSHIRE: Assists ministers who have been ordained for five years or over and are in full charge of a congregation in Aberdeen, Aberdeenshire and the north, to purchase books, or to travel for educational purposes, and assists their children with scholarships for further education or vocational training. Apply to Alan J. Innes MA LLB, 100 Union Street, Aberdeen AB10 1QR.

The SOCIETY FOR THE BENEFIT OF THE SONS AND DAUGHTERS OF THE CLERGY OF THE CHURCH OF SCOTLAND: Annual grants are made to assist in the education of the children (normally between the ages of 12 and 25 years) of ministers of the Church of Scotland. The Society also gives grants to aged and infirm daughters of ministers and ministers' unmarried daughters and sisters who are in need. Applications are to be lodged by 31 May in each year with the Secretary and Treasurer, Mrs Fiona M.M. Watson CA, Exchange Place 3, Semple Street, Edinburgh EH3 8BL (Tel: 0131-473 3500; E-mail: charity@scott-moncrieff. com).

The Nan STEVENSON CHARITABLE TRUST FOR RETIRED MINISTERS: Provides houses, or loans to purchase houses, for retired ministers or missionaries on similar terms to the Housing and Loan Fund, with preference given to those with a North Ayrshire connection. Secretary and Treasurer: Mrs Ann Turner, 62 Caledonia Road, Saltcoats KA21 5AP.

Miss M.E. SWINTON PATERSON'S CHARITABLE TRUST: The Trust can give modest grants to support smaller congregations in urban or rural areas who require to fund essential maintenance or improvement works at their buildings. Apply to Mr Callum S. Kennedy WS, Messrs Lindsays WS, Caledonian Exchange, 19A Canning Street, Edinburgh EH3 8HE (Tel: 0131-229 1212).

SYNOD OF GRAMPIAN CHILDREN OF THE CLERGY FUND: Makes annual grants to children of deceased ministers. Apply to Rev. Iain U. Thomson, Clerk and Treasurer, 4 Keirhill Gardens, Westhill AB32 6AZ.

SYNOD OF GRAMPIAN WIDOWS FUND: Makes annual grants (currently £225 p.a.) to widows or widowers of deceased ministers who have served in a charge in the former Synod. Apply to Rev. Iain U. Thomson, Clerk and Treasurer, 4 Keirhill Gardens, Westhill AB32 6AZ.

TOD ENDOWMENT TRUST: CINTRA BEQUEST: MINISTRY BENEVOLENT FUND: The Trustees of the Cintra Bequest and of the Church of Scotland Ministry Benevolent Fund can consider an application for a grant from the Tod Endowment funds from any ordained or commissioned minister or deacon in Scotland of at least two years' standing before the date of application, to assist with the cost of the beneficiary and his or her spouse or partner and dependants obtaining rest and recuperation in Scotland. The Trustees of the Church of Scotland Ministry Benevolent Fund can also consider an application from an ordained or commissioned minister or deacon who has retired. Application forms are available from Mrs J.S. Wilson, Solicitor (for the Cintra Bequest), and from the Assistant Treasurer (Ministries) (for the Ministry Benevolent Fund). The address in both cases is 121 George Street, Edinburgh EH2 4YN (Tel: 0131-225 5722). (Attention is drawn to separate individual entries for both the Cintra Bequest and the Church of Scotland Ministry Benevolent Fund.)

YOUNG MINISTERS' FURNISHING LOAN FUND: Makes loans (of £1,000) to ministers in their first charge to assist with furnishing the manse. Apply to the Assistant Treasurer (Ministries), 121 George Street, Edinburgh EH2 4YN.

The undernoted hotels provide special terms as described. Fuller information may be obtained from the establishments:

CRIEFF HYDRO Ltd and MURRAYPARK HOTEL: The William Meikle Trust Fund and

Paton Fund make provision whereby active ministers and their spouses and members of the Diaconate may enjoy hotel and self-catering accommodation all year round. BIG Country provides supervised childcare for children aged 2 to 12 years. (Free supervised childcare is not available for guests staying at the Murraypark Hotel.) For all our guests, Crieff Hydro offers a wide range of inclusive leisure facilities such as leisure pool, gym, cinema and entertainment programme. Over-60 on-site activities are also available at great prices. To make a reservation, please contact Accommodation Sales on 01764 651670 between 8am and 9pm daily, quoting your *Church of Scotland Year Book* page number. Alternatively, you can e-mail your enquiry to sales@crieffhydro.com. If you are unable to quote your *Year Book* page number at the time of booking, you must ask the Church of Scotland's Human Resources Department to e-mail Crieff Hydro to verify your eligibility. Only e-mails originated from the Church of Scotland address will be accepted.

(6) RECENT LORD HIGH COMMISSIONERS
TO THE GENERAL ASSEMBLY

1969	Her Majesty the Queen attended in person
1970	The Rt Hon. Margaret Herbison PC
1971/72	The Rt Hon. Lord Clydesmuir of Braidwood CB MBE TD
1973/74	The Rt Hon. Lord Ballantrae of Auchairne and the Bay of Islands GCMG GCVO DSO OBE
1975/76	Sir Hector MacLennan Kt FRCPGLAS FRCOG
1977	Francis David Charteris, Earl of Wemyss and March KT LLD
1978/79	The Rt Hon. William Ross MBE LLD
1980/81	Andrew Douglas Alexander Thomas Bruce, Earl of Elgin and Kincardine KT DL JP
1982/83	Colonel Sir John Edward Gilmour BT DSO TD
1984/85	Charles Hector Fitzroy Maclean, Baron Maclean of Duart and Morvern KT GCVO KBE
1986/87	John Campbell Arbuthnott, Viscount of Arbuthnott KT CBE DSC FRSE FRSA
1988/89	Sir Iain Mark Tennant KT FRSA
1990/91	The Rt Hon. Donald MacArthur Ross FRSE
1992/93	The Rt Hon. Lord Macfarlane of Bearsden KT FRSE
1994/95	Lady Marion Fraser LT
1996	Her Royal Highness the Princess Royal LT LG GCVO
1997	The Rt Hon. Lord Macfarlane of Bearsden KT FRSE
1998/99	The Rt Hon. Lord Hogg of Cumbernauld
2000	His Royal Highness the Prince Charles, Duke of Rothesay KG KT GCB OM
2001/02	The Rt Hon. Viscount Younger of Leckie
	Her Majesty the Queen attended the opening of the General Assembly of 2002
2003/04	The Rt Hon. Lord Steel of Aikwood KT KBE
2005/06	The Rt Hon. Lord Mackay of Clashfern KT
2007	His Royal Highness the Prince Andrew, Duke of York KG KCVO
2008/09	The Rt Hon. George Reid KT MA
2010/11	Lord Wilson of Tillyorn KT GCMG PRSE
2012	The Rt Hon. Lord Selkirk of Douglas QC MA LLB

(7) RECENT MODERATORS
OF THE GENERAL ASSEMBLY

1969	T.M. Murchison MA DD, Glasgow: St Columba Summertown
1970	Hugh O. Douglas CBE LLD DD, Dundee: St Mary's
1971	Andrew Herron MA BD LLB LLD DD, Clerk to the Presbytery of Glasgow
1972	R.W.V. Selby Wright CVO TD DD FRSE JP, Edinburgh: Canongate
1973	George T.H. Reid MC MA BD DD, Aberdeen: Langstane
1974	David Steel MA BD LLD DD, Linlithgow: St Michael's
1975	James G. Matheson MA BD DD, Portree
1976	Thomas F. Torrance MBE DLitt DD FRSE, University of Edinburgh
1977	John R. Gray VRD MA BD ThM DD, Dunblane: Cathedral
1978	Peter P. Brodie MA BD LLB DD, Alloa: St Mungo's
1979	Robert A.S. Barbour KCVO MC MA BD STM DD, University of Aberdeen
1980	William B. Johnston MA BD DLitt DD, Edinburgh: Colinton
1981	Andrew B. Doig BD STM DD, National Bible Society of Scotland
1982	John McIntyre CVO DLitt DD FRSE, University of Edinburgh
1983	J. Fraser McLuskey MC DD, London: St Columba's
1984	John M.K. Paterson MA BD DD ACII, Milngavie: St Paul's
1985	David M.B.A. Smith MA BD DUniv, Logie
1986	Robert Craig CBE DLitt LLD DD, Emeritus of Jerusalem
1987	Duncan Shaw of Chapelverna *Bundesverdienstkreuz* PhD ThDr Drhc, Edinburgh: Craigentinny St Christopher's
1988	James A. Whyte MA LLD DD DUniv, University of St Andrews
1989	William J.G. McDonald MA BD DD, Edinburgh: Mayfield
1990	Robert Davidson MA BD DD FRSE, University of Glasgow
1991	William B.R. Macmillan MA BD LLD DD, Dundee: St Mary's
1992	Hugh R. Wyllie MA DD FCIBS, Hamilton: Old Parish Church
1993	James L. Weatherhead CBE MA LLB DD, Principal Clerk of Assembly
1994	James A. Simpson BSc BD STM DD, Dornoch Cathedral
1995	James Harkness KCVO CB OBE MA DD, Chaplain General (Emeritus)
1996	John H. McIndoe MA BD STM DD, London: St Columba's linked with Newcastle: St Andrew's
1997	Alexander McDonald BA DUniv CMIWSc, General Secretary, Department of Ministry
1998	Alan Main TD MA BD STM PhD DD, Professor of Practical Theology at Christ's College, University of Aberdeen
1999	John B. Cairns LTh LLB LLD DD, Dumbarton: Riverside
2000	Andrew R.C. McLellan CBE MA BD STM DD, Edinburgh: St Andrew's and St George's
2001	John D. Miller BA BD DD, Glasgow: Castlemilk East
2002	Finlay A.J. Macdonald MA BD PhD DD, Principal Clerk of Assembly
2003	Iain R. Torrance TD DPhil DD DTheol LHD CorrFRSE, University of Aberdeen
2004	Alison Elliot OBE MA MSc PhD LLD DD FRSE, Associate Director CTPI
2005	David W. Lacy BA BD DLitt, Kilmarnock: Henderson
2006	Alan D. McDonald LLB BD MTh DLitt DD, Cameron linked with St Andrews: St Leonard's
2007	Sheilagh M. Kesting BA BD DD, Secretary of Ecumenical Relations Committee
2008	David W. Lunan MA BD DUniv DLitt DD, Clerk to the Presbytery of Glasgow

2009	William C. Hewitt BD DipPS, Greenock: Westburn
2010	John C. Christie BSc BD MSB CBiol, Interim Minister
2011	A. David K. Arnott MA BD, St Andrews: Hope Park with Strathkinness
2012	Albert O. Bogle BD MTh, Bo'ness: St Andrew's

MATTER OF PRECEDENCE

The Lord High Commissioner to the General Assembly of the Church of Scotland (while the Assembly is sitting) ranks next to the Sovereign and the Duke of Edinburgh and before the rest of the Royal Family.

The Moderator of the General Assembly of the Church of Scotland ranks next to the Lord Chancellor of Great Britain and before the Keeper of the Great Seal of Scotland (the First Minister) and the Dukes.

(8) HER MAJESTY'S HOUSEHOLD IN SCOTLAND
ECCLESIASTICAL

Dean of the Chapel Royal: Very Rev. John B. Cairns LTh LLB LLD DD

Dean of the Order of the Thistle: Very Rev. Gilleasbuig Macmillan
CVO MA BD Drhc DD

Domestic Chaplains: Rev. Kenneth I. Mackenzie BD CPS
Rev. Neil N. Gardner MA BD

Chaplains in Ordinary: Very Rev. Gilleasbuig Macmillan
CVO MA BD Drhc DD
Rev. Norman W. Drummond MA BD
Rev. Alastair H. Symington MA BD
Very Rev. Prof. Iain R. Torrance
TD DPhil DD DTheol LHD CorrFRSE
Very Rev. Finlay A.J. Macdonald MA BD PhD DD
Rev. James M. Gibson TD LTh LRAM
Rev. Angus Morrison MA BD PhD
Rev. E. Lorna Hood MA BD
Rev. Alistair G. Bennett BSc BD
Rev. Susan M. Brown BD DipMin

Extra Chaplains: Rev. Kenneth MacVicar MBE DFC TD MA
Very Rev. Prof. Robert A.S. Barbour
KCVO MC BD STM DD
Rev. Alwyn Macfarlane MA
Very Rev. William J. Morris KCVO PhD LLD DD JP
Rev. John MacLeod MA
Very Rev. James L. Weatherhead CBE MA LLB DD
Very Rev. James A. Simpson BSc BD STM DD

Very Rev. James Harkness KCVO CB OBE MA DD
Rev. John L. Paterson MA BD STM
Rev. Charles Robertson LVO MA JP

(9) LONG SERVICE CERTIFICATES

Long Service Certificates, signed by the Moderator, are available for presentation to elders and others in respect of not less than thirty years of service. It should be noted that the period is years of *service*, not (for example) years of ordination in the case of an elder.

In the case of Sunday School teachers and Bible Class leaders, the qualifying period is twenty-one years of service.

Certificates are not issued posthumously, nor is it possible to make exceptions to the rules, for example by recognising quality of service in order to reduce the qualifying period, or by reducing the qualifying period on compassionate grounds, such as serious illness.

A Certificate will be issued only once to any particular individual.

Applications for Long Service Certificates should be made in writing to the Principal Clerk at 121 George Street, Edinburgh EH2 4YN by the parish minister, or by the session clerk on behalf of the Kirk Session. Certificates are not issued from this office to the individual recipients, nor should individuals make application themselves.

(10) LIBRARIES OF THE CHURCH

GENERAL ASSEMBLY LIBRARY AND RECORD ROOM
Most of the books contained in the General Assembly Library have been transferred to the New College Library. Records of the General Assembly, Synods, Presbyteries and Kirk Sessions are now in HM Register House, Edinburgh.

CHURCH MUSIC
The Library of New College contains a selection of works on Church music.

(11) RECORDS OF THE CHURCH OF SCOTLAND

Church records more than fifty years old, unless still in use, should be sent or delivered to the Principal Clerk for onward transmission to the National Records of Scotland. Where ministers or session clerks are approached by a local repository seeking a transfer of their records, they should inform the Principal Clerk, who will take the matter up with the National Records of Scotland.

Where a temporary retransmission of records is sought, it is extremely helpful if notice can be given three months in advance so that appropriate procedures can be carried out satisfactorily.

SECTION 3

Church Procedure

(1) THE MINISTER AND BAPTISM

The administration of Baptism to infants is governed by Act V 2000 as amended by Act IX 2003. A Statement and Exposition of the Doctrine of Baptism may be found at page 13/8 in the published volume of Reports to the General Assembly of 2003.

The Act itself is as follows:

3.   Baptism signifies the action and love of God in Christ, through the Holy Spirit, and is a seal upon the gift of grace and the response of faith.
   (a)   Baptism shall be administered in the name of the Father and of the Son and of the Holy Spirit, with water, by sprinkling, pouring, or immersion.
   (b)   Baptism shall be administered to a person only once.
4.   Baptism may be administered to a person upon profession of faith.
   (a)   The minister and Kirk Session shall judge whether the person is of sufficient maturity to make personal profession of faith, where necessary in consultation with the parent(s) or legal guardian(s).
   (b)   Baptism may be administered only after the person has received such instruction in its meaning as the minister and Kirk Session consider necessary, according to such basis of instruction as may be authorised by the General Assembly.
   (c)   In cases of uncertainty as to whether a person has been baptised or validly baptised, baptism shall be administered conditionally.
5.   Baptism may be administered to a person with learning difficulties who makes an appropriate profession of faith, where the minister and Kirk Session are satisfied that the person shall be nurtured within the life and worship of the Church.
6.   Baptism may be administered to a child:
   (a)   where at least one parent, or other family member (with parental consent), having been baptised and being on the communion roll of the congregation, will undertake the Christian upbringing of the child;
   (b)   where at least one parent, or other family member (with parental consent), having been baptised but not on the communion roll of the congregation, satisfies the minister and Kirk Session that he or she is an adherent of the congregation and will undertake the Christian upbringing of the child;
   (c)   where at least one parent, or other family member (with parental consent), having been baptised, professes the Christian faith, undertakes to ensure that the child grows up in the life and worship of the Church and expresses the desire to seek admission to the communion roll of the congregation;
   (d)   where the child is under legal guardianship, and the minister and Kirk Session are satisfied that the child shall be nurtured within the life and worship of the congregation;
   and, in each of the above cases, only after the parent(s), or other family member, has received such instruction in its meaning as the minister and Kirk Session consider necessary, according to such basis of instruction as may be authorised by the General Assembly.
7.   Baptism shall normally be administered during the public worship of the congregation in which the person makes profession of faith, or of which the parent or other family member is on the communion roll, or is an adherent. In exceptional circumstances, baptism may be administered elsewhere (e.g. at home or in hospital). Further, a minister may administer baptism to a person resident outwith the minister's parish, and who is not otherwise

connected with the congregation, only with the consent of the minister of the parish in which the person would normally reside, or of the Presbytery.

8. In all cases, an entry shall be made in the Kirk Session's Baptismal Register and a Certificate of Baptism given by the minister. Where baptism is administered in a chaplaincy context, it shall be recorded in the Baptismal Register there, and, where possible, reported to the minister of the parish in which the person resides.

9. Baptism shall normally be administered by an ordained minister. In situations of emergency,
    (a) a minister may, exceptionally, notwithstanding the preceding provisions of the Act, respond to a request for baptism in accordance with his or her pastoral judgement, and
    (b) baptism may be validly administered by a person who is not ordained, always providing that it is administered in the name of the Father and of the Son and of the Holy Spirit, with water.
    In every occurrence of the latter case, of which a minister or chaplain becomes aware, an entry shall be made in the appropriate Baptismal Register and where possible reported to the Clerk of the Presbytery within which the baptism was administered.

10. Each Presbytery shall form, or designate, a committee to which reference may be made in cases where there is a dispute as to the interpretation of this Act. Without the consent of the Presbytery, no minister may administer baptism in a case where to his or her knowledge another minister has declined to do so.

11. The Church of Scotland, as part of the Universal Church, affirms the validity of the sacrament of baptism administered in the name of the Father and of the Son and of the Holy Spirit, with water, in accordance with the discipline of other members of the Universal Church.

---

(2) THE MINISTER AND MARRIAGE

1. BACKGROUND
Prior to 1939, every marriage in Scotland fell into one or other of two classes: regular or irregular. The former was marriage by a minister of religion after due notice of intention had been given; the latter could be effected in one of three ways: (1) declaration *de presenti*, (2) by promise *subsequente copula*, or (3) by co-habitation with habit and repute.

The Marriage (Scotland) Act of 1939 put an end to (1) and (2) and provided for a new classification of marriage as either religious or civil. Marriage by co-habitation with habit and repute was abolished by the Family Law (Scotland) Act 2006.

The law of marriage as it was thus established in 1939 had two important limitations to the celebration of marriage: (1) certain preliminaries had to be observed; and (2) in respect of religious marriage, the service had to be conducted according to the forms of either the Christian or the Jewish faith.

2. THE MARRIAGE (SCOTLAND) ACT 1977
These two conditions were radically altered by the Marriage (Scotland) Act 1977.

Since 1 January 1978, in conformity with the demands of a multi-racial society, the benefits of religious marriage have been extended to adherents of other faiths, the only requirements being the observance of monogamy and the satisfaction of the authorities with the forms of the vows imposed.

Since 1978, the calling of banns has also been discontinued. The couple themselves must each complete a Marriage Notice form and return this to the District Registrar for the area in which they are to be married, irrespective of where they live, at least fifteen days before the ceremony is due to take place. The form details the documents which require to be produced with it.

If everything is in order, the District Registrar will issue, not more than seven days before the date of the ceremony, a Marriage Schedule. This must be in the hands of the minister officiating at the marriage ceremony before the service begins. Under no circumstances must the minister deviate from this rule. To do so is an offence under the Act.

Ministers should note the advice given by the Procurator of the Church in 1962, that they should not officiate at any marriage until at least one day after the 16th birthday of the younger party.

Furthermore, a marriage involving someone who is not an EU citizen involves extra registration requirements, and initial contact should be made with the local Registrar several months before the intended date of marriage.

3. THE MARRIAGE (SCOTLAND) ACT 2002

Although there have never been any limitations as to the place where a religious marriage can be celebrated, civil marriage originally could take place only in the Office of a Registrar. The Marriage (Scotland) Act 2002 permits the solemnisation of civil marriages at places approved by Local Authorities. Regulations have been made to specify the kinds of place which may be 'approved' with a view to ensuring that the places approved will not compromise the solemnity and dignity of civil marriage and will have no recent or continuing connection with any religion so as to undermine the distinction between religious and civil ceremonies.

4. PROCLAMATION OF BANNS

Proclamation of banns is no longer required in Scotland; but, in the Church of England, marriage is governed by the provisions of the Marriage Act 1949, which requires that the parties' intention to marry has to have been proclaimed and which provides that in the case of a party residing in Scotland a Certificate of Proclamation given according to the law or custom prevailing in Scotland shall be sufficient for the purpose. In the event that a minister is asked to call banns for a person resident within the registration district where his or her church is situated, the proclamation needs only to be made on one Sunday if the parties are known to the minister. If they are not, it should be made on two Sundays. In all cases, the Minister should, of course, have no reason to believe that there is any impediment to the marriage.

Proclamation should be made at the principal service of worship in this form:

There is a purpose of marriage between AB (Bachelor/Widower/Divorced), residing at .... in this Registration District, and CD (Spinster/Widow/Divorced), residing at .... in the Registration District of ...., of which proclamation is hereby made for the first and only (second and last) time.

Immediately after the second reading, or not less than forty-eight hours after the first and only reading, a Certificate of Proclamation signed by either the minister or the Session Clerk should be issued in the following terms:

At .... the ...... day of ...... 20 ....

It is hereby certified that AB, residing at ...., and CD, residing at ...., have been duly proclaimed in order to marriage in the Church of .... according to the custom of the Church of Scotland, and that no objections have been offered.

Signed .... minister or

Signed .... Session Clerk

5. MARRIAGE OF FOREIGNERS

Marriages in Scotland of foreigners, or of foreigners with British subjects, are, if they satisfy the requirements of Scots Law, valid within the United Kingdom and the various British overseas territories; but they will not necessarily be valid in the country to which the foreigner belongs. This will be so only if the requirements of the law of his or her country have also been complied with. It is therefore most important that, before the marriage, steps should be taken to obtain from the Consul, or other diplomatic representative of the country concerned, a satisfactory assurance that the marriage will be accepted as valid in the country concerned.

6. REMARRIAGE OF DIVORCED PERSONS

By virtue of Act XXVI 1959, a minister of the Church of Scotland may lawfully solemnise the marriage of a person whose former marriage has been dissolved by divorce and whose former spouse is still alive. The minister, however, must carefully adhere to the requirements of the Act which, as slightly altered in 1985, are briefly as follows:

1. The minister should not accede as a matter of routine to a request to solemnise such a marriage. To enable a decision to be made, he or she should take all reasonable steps to obtain relevant information, which should normally include the following:
    (a) Adequate information concerning the life and character of the parties. The Act enjoins the greatest caution in cases where no pastoral relationship exists between the minister and either or both of the parties concerned.
    (b) The grounds and circumstances of the divorce case.
    (c) Facts bearing upon the future well-being of any children concerned.
    (d) Whether any other minister has declined to solemnise the proposed marriage.
    (e) The denomination to which the parties belong. The Act enjoins that special care should be taken where one or more parties belong to a denomination whose discipline in this matter may differ from that of the Church of Scotland.
2. The minister should consider whether there is danger of scandal arising if he or she should solemnise the remarriage, at the same time taking into careful consideration before refusing to do so the moral and spiritual effect of a refusal on the parties concerned.
3. As a determinative factor, the minister should do all he or she can to be assured that there has been sincere repentance where guilt has existed on the part of any divorced person seeking remarriage. He or she should also give instruction, where needed, in the nature and requirements of a Christian marriage.
4. A minister is not required to solemnise a remarriage against his or her conscience. Every Presbytery is required to appoint certain individuals with one of whom ministers in doubt as to the correct course of action may consult if they so desire. The final decision, however, rests with the minister who has been asked to officiate.

---

(3) CONDUCT OF MARRIAGE SERVICES
(CODE OF GOOD PRACTICE)

The code which follows was submitted to the General Assembly in 1997. It appears, on page 1/10, in the Volume of Assembly Reports for that year within the Report of the Board of Practice and Procedure.

1. *Marriage in the Church of Scotland is solemnised by an ordained minister in a religious ceremony wherein, before God, and in the presence of the minister and at least two competent witnesses, the parties covenant together to take each other as husband and wife as long as they both shall live, and the minister declares the parties to be husband and wife. Before solemnising a marriage, a minister must be assured that the necessary legal requirements are being complied with and that the parties know of no legal impediment to their marriage, and he or she must afterwards ensure that the Marriage Schedule is duly completed.* (Act I 1977)

2. Any ordained minister of the Church of Scotland who is a member of Presbytery or who holds a current Ministerial Certificate may officiate at a marriage service (see Act II 1987).

3. While the marriage service should normally take place in church, a minister may, at his or her discretion, officiate at a marriage service outwith church premises. Wherever conducted, the ceremony will be such as to reflect appropriately both the joy and the solemnity of the occasion. In particular, a minister shall ensure that nothing is done which would bring the Church and its teaching into disrepute.

4. A minister agreeing to conduct a wedding should endeavour to establish a pastoral relationship with the couple within which adequate pre-marriage preparation and subsequent pastoral care may be given.

5. 'A minister should not refuse to perform ministerial functions for a person who is resident in his or her parish without sufficient reason' (Cox, *Practice and Procedure in the Church of Scotland*, sixth edition, page 55). Where either party to the proposed marriage has been divorced and the former spouse is still alive, the minister invited to officiate may solemnise such a marriage, having regard to the guidelines in the Act anent the Remarriage of Divorced Persons (Act XXVI 1959 as amended by Act II 1985).

6. A minister is acting as an agent of the National Church which is committed to bringing the ordinances of religion to the people of Scotland through a territorial ministry. As such, he or she shall not be entitled to charge a fee or allow a fee to be charged for conducting a marriage service. When a gift is spontaneously offered to a minister as a token of appreciation, the above consideration should not be taken to mean that he or she should not accept such an unsolicited gift. The Financial Board of a congregation is at liberty to set fees to cover such costs as heat and light, and in addition Organists and Church Officers are entitled to a fee in respect of their services at weddings.

7. A minister should not allow his or her name to be associated with any commercial enterprise that provides facilities for weddings.

8. A minister is not at liberty to enter the bounds of another minister's parish to perform ministerial functions without the previous consent of the minister of that parish. In terms of Act VIII 1933, a minister may 'officiate at a marriage or funeral by private invitation', but, for the avoidance of doubt, an invitation conveyed through a commercial enterprise shall not be regarded as a 'private invitation' within the meaning of that Act.

9. A minister invited to officiate at a Marriage Service where neither party is a member of his or her congregation or is resident within his or her own parish or has any connection with the parish within which the service is to take place should observe the following courtesies:
    (a) he or she should ascertain from the parties whether either of them has a Church of Scotland connection or has approached the appropriate parish minister(s);
    (b) if it transpires that a ministerial colleague has declined to officiate, then he or she (the invited minister) should ascertain the reasons therefor and shall take these and all other relevant factors into account in deciding whether or not to officiate.

(4) CONDUCT OF FUNERAL SERVICES: FEES

The General Assembly of 2007 received the Report of the Legal Questions Committee which included a statement regarding fees for funerals. That statement had been prepared in the light of approaches from two Presbyteries seeking guidance on the question of the charging of fees (on behalf of ministers) for the conduct of funerals. It had seemed to the Presbyteries that expectations and practice were unacceptably varied across the country, and that the question was complicated by the fact that, quite naturally and legitimately, ministers other than parish ministers occasionally conduct funeral services.

The full text of that statement was engrossed in the Minutes of the General Assembly, and it was felt that it would be helpful to include it also in the *Year Book*.

The statement
The (Legal Questions) Committee believes that the question is two-fold, relating firstly to parish ministers (including associate and assistant ministers, deacons and the like) within their regular ministry, and secondly to ministers and others taking an occasional funeral, for instance by private invitation or in the course of pastoral cover of another parish.

Ministers in receipt of a living
The Committee believes that the position of the minister of a parish, and of other paid staff on the ministry team of a parish, is clear. The Third Declaratory Article affirms the responsibility of the Church of Scotland to provide the ordinances of religion through its territorial ministry, while the stipend system (and, for other staff members, the salary) provides a living that enables that ministry to be exercised without charging fees for services conducted. The implication of this principle is that no family in Scotland should ever be charged for the services of a Church of Scotland minister at the time of bereavement. Clearly, therefore, no minister in receipt of a living should be charging separately (effectively being paid doubly) for any such service. The Committee is conscious that the position of congregations outside Scotland may be different, and is aware that the relevant Presbyteries will offer appropriate superintendence of these matters.

A related question is raised about the highly varied culture of gift-giving in different parts of the country. The Committee believes it would be unwise to seek to regulate this. In some places, an attempt to quash a universal and long-established practice would seem ungracious, while in other places there is no such practice, and encouragement in that direction would seem indelicate.

A second related question was raised about Funeral Directors charging for the services of the minister. The Committee believes that Presbyteries should make it clear to Funeral Directors that, in the case of Church of Scotland funerals, such a charge should not be made.

Ministers conducting occasional services
Turning to the position of ministers who do not receive a living that enables them to conduct funerals without charge, the Committee's starting point is the principle articulated above that no bereaved person should have to pay for the services of a minister. The territorial ministry and the parish system of this Church mean that a bereaved family should not find itself being contingently charged because the parish minister happens to be unavailable, or because the parish is vacant.

Where a funeral is being conducted as part of the ministry of the local parish, but where for any reason another minister is taking it and not otherwise being paid, it is the responsibility of the congregation (through its financial body) to ensure that appropriate fees and expenses are met.

Where that imposes a financial burden upon a congregation because of the weight of pastoral need, the need should be taken into account in calculating the resource-needs of that parish in the course of updating the Presbytery Plan.

It is beyond the remit of the Legal Questions Committee to make judgements about the appropriate level of payment. The Committee suggests that the Ministries Council should give the relevant advice on this aspect of the issue.

The Committee believes that these principles could be applied to the conduct of weddings and are perfectly compatible with the Guidelines on that subject which are reproduced in the *Year Book* at item 3 of section 3 dealing with Church Procedure.

(5) THE MINISTER AND WILLS

The Requirements of Writing (Scotland) Act 1995, which came into force on 1 August 1995, has removed the power of a minister to execute wills notarially. Further clarification, if required, may be obtained from the Solicitor of the Church.

(6) PROCEDURE IN A VACANCY

Procedure in a vacancy is regulated by Act VIII 2003 as amended by Acts IX and X 2004, II 2005, V 2006, I, IV and VI 2008 and II and V 2009. The text of the most immediately relevant sections is given here for general information. Schedules of Intimation referred to are also included. The full text of the Act and subsequent amendments can be obtained from the Principal Clerk.

1. Vacancy Procedure Committee

(1) Each Presbytery shall appoint a number of its members to be available to serve on Vacancy Procedure Committees and shall provide information and training as required for those so appointed.

(2) As soon as the Presbytery Clerk is aware that a vacancy has arisen or is anticipated, he or she shall consult the Moderator of the Presbytery and they shall appoint a Vacancy Procedure Committee of five persons from among those appointed in terms of subsection (1), which Committee shall (a) include at least one minister and at least one elder and (b) exclude any communicant member or former minister of the vacant charge or of any constituent congregation thereof. The Vacancy Procedure Committee shall include a Convener and Clerk, the latter of whom need not be a member of the Committee but may be the Presbytery Clerk. The same Vacancy Procedure Committee may serve for more than one vacancy at a time.

(3) The Vacancy Procedure Committee shall have a quorum of three for its meetings.

(4) The Convener of the Vacancy Procedure Committee may, where he or she reasonably believes a matter to be non-contentious, consult members individually, provided that reasonable efforts are made to consult all members of the Committee. A meeting shall be held at the request of any member of the Committee.

(5)   Every decision made by the Vacancy Procedure Committee shall be reported to the next meeting of Presbytery, but may not be recalled by Presbytery where the decision was subject to the provisions of section 2 below.

2. Request for Consideration by Presbytery

Where in this Act any decision by the Vacancy Procedure Committee is subject to the provisions of this section, the following rules shall apply:

(1)   The Presbytery Clerk shall intimate to all members of the Presbytery by mailing or at a Presbytery meeting the course of action or permission proposed, and shall arrange for one Sunday's pulpit intimation of the same to be made to the congregation or congregations concerned, in terms of Schedule A. The intimation having been made, it shall be displayed as prominently as possible at the church building for seven days.

(2)   Any four individuals, being communicant members of the congregation or full members of the Presbytery, may give written notice requesting that action be taken in terms of subsection (3) below, giving reasons for the request, within seven days after the pulpit intimation.

(3)   Upon receiving notice in terms of subsection (2), the Presbytery Clerk shall sist the process or permission referred to in subsection (1), which shall then require the approval of the Presbytery.

(4)   The Moderator of the Presbytery shall in such circumstances consider whether a meeting *pro re nata* of the Presbytery should be called in order to avoid prejudicial delay in the vacancy process.

(5)   The Presbytery Clerk shall cause to have served upon the congregation or congregations an edict in terms of Schedule B citing them to attend the meeting of Presbytery for their interest.

(6)   The consideration by Presbytery of any matter under this section shall not constitute an appeal or a Petition, and the decision of Presbytery shall be deemed to be a decision at first instance subject to the normal rights of appeal or dissent-and-complaint.

3. Causes of Vacancy

The causes of vacancy shall normally include:

(a)   the death of the minister of the charge;

(b)   the removal of status of the minister of the charge or the suspension of the minister in terms of section 20(2) of Act III 2001;

(c)   the dissolution of the pastoral tie in terms of Act I 1988 or Act XV 2002;

(d)   the demission of the charge and/or status of the minister of the charge;

(e)   the translation of the minister of the charge to another charge;

(f)   the termination of the tenure of the minister of the charge in terms of Act VI 1984.

4. Release of Departing Minister

The Presbytery Clerk shall be informed as soon as circumstances have occurred that cause a vacancy to arise or make it likely that a vacancy shall arise. Where the circumstances pertain to section 3(d) or (e) above, the Vacancy Procedure Committee shall

(1)   except in cases governed by subsection (2) below, decide whether to release the minister from his or her charge and, in any case involving translation to another charge or introduction to an appointment, instruct him or her to await the instructions of the Presbytery or another Presbytery;

(2)   in the case of a minister in the first five years of his or her first charge, decide whether there are exceptional circumstances to justify releasing him or her from his or her charge and proceeding in terms of subsection (1) above;

(3)   determine whether a vacancy has arisen or is anticipated and, as soon as possible, determine the date upon which the charge becomes actually vacant, and

(4)   inform the congregation or congregations by one Sunday's pulpit intimation as soon as convenient.

(5)   The provisions of section 2 above shall apply to the decisions of the Vacancy Procedure Committee in terms of subsections (1) and (2) above.

5. Demission of Charge

(1)   Subject to the provisions of subsection (2) below, when a vacancy has occurred in terms of section 3(c), (d) or (f) above, the Presbytery shall determine whether the minister is, in the circumstances, entitled to a seat in the Presbytery in terms of section 16 of Act III 2000 (as amended).

(2)   In the case where it is a condition of any basis of adjustment that a minister shall demit his or her charge to facilitate union or linking, and the minister has agreed in writing in terms of the appropriate regulations governing adjustments, formal application shall not be made to the Presbytery for permission to demit. The minister concerned shall be regarded as retiring in the interest of adjustment, and he or she shall retain a seat in Presbytery unless in terms of Act III 2000 (as amended) he or she elects to resign it.

(3)   A minister who demits his or her charge without retaining a seat in the Presbytery shall, if he or she retains status as a minister, be subject to the provisions of sections 5 to 15 of Act II 2000 (as amended).

6. Appointment of Interim Moderator

(1)   At the same time as the Vacancy Procedure Committee makes a decision in terms of section 4 above, or where circumstances pertain to section 3(a), (b), (c) or (f) above, the Vacancy Procedure Committee shall appoint an Interim Moderator for the charge and make intimation thereof to the congregation subject to the provisions of section 2 above. The Interim Moderator shall be either a ministerial member of the Presbytery in terms of Act III 2000 or Act V 2001 or a member of the Presbytery selected from a list of those who have received such preparation for the task as the Ministries Council shall from time to time recommend or provide, and he or she shall not be a member in the vacant charge nor a member of the Vacancy Procedure Committee. The name of the Interim Moderator shall be forwarded to the Ministries Council.

(2)   If the Interim Moderator appointed is a ministerial member of Presbytery, it is understood that, in accepting the appointment, he or she is thereby disqualified from becoming an applicant or accepting an invitation to be considered in the current vacancy.

7. Duties of Interim Moderator

(1)   It shall be the duty of the Interim Moderator to preside at all meetings of the Kirk Session (or of the Kirk Sessions in the case of a linked charge) and to preside at all congregational meetings in connection with the vacancy, or at which the minister would have presided had the charge been full. In the case of a congregational meeting called by the Presbytery in connection with adjustment, the Interim Moderator, having constituted the meeting, shall relinquish the chair in favour of the representative of the Presbytery, but he or she shall be at liberty to speak at such a meeting. In consultation with the Kirk Session and the Financial Court, he or she shall make arrangements for the supply of the vacant pulpit.

(2)   The Interim Moderator appointed in a prospective vacancy may call and preside at meetings of the Kirk Session and of the congregation for the transaction of business relating to the

said prospective vacancy. He or she shall be associated with the minister until the date of the actual vacancy; after that date, he or she shall take full charge.

(3) The Interim Moderator shall act as an assessor to the Nominating Committee, being available to offer guidance and advice. If the Committee so desire, he or she may act as their Convener, but in no case shall he or she have a vote.

(4) In the event of the absence of the Interim Moderator, the Vacancy Procedure Committee shall appoint a member of the Presbytery who is not a member of the vacant congregation to fulfil any of the rights and duties of the Interim Moderator.

(5) The Interim Moderator shall have the same duties and responsibilities towards all members of ministry teams referred to in section 16 of Act VII 2003 as if he or she were the parish minister, both in terms of this Act and in respect of the terms and conditions of such individuals.

8. Permission to Call

When the decision to release the minister from the charge has been made and the Interim Moderator appointed, the Vacancy Procedure Committee shall consider whether it may give permission to call a minister in terms of Act VII 2003, and may proceed subject to the provisions of section 2 above. The Vacancy Procedure Committee must refer the question of permission to call to the Presbytery if:

(a) shortfalls exist which in the opinion of the Committee require consideration in terms of section 9 hereunder;

(b) the Committee has reason to believe that the vacancy schedule referred to in section 10 below will not be approved;

(c) the Committee has reason to believe that the Presbytery will, in terms of section 11 below, instruct work to be carried out on the manse before a call can be sustained, and judges that the likely extent of such work warrants a delay in the granting of permission to call, or

(d) the Committee has reason to believe that the Presbytery may wish to delay or refuse the granting of permission for any reason.

Any decision by Presbytery to refuse permission to call shall be subject to appeal or dissent-and-complaint.

9. Shortfalls

(1) As soon as possible after intimation of a vacancy or anticipated vacancy reaches the Presbytery Clerk, the Presbytery shall ascertain whether the charge has current or accumulated shortfalls in contributions to central funds, and shall determine whether and to what extent any shortfalls that exist are justified.

(2) If the vacancy is in a charge in which the Presbytery has determined that shortfalls are to any extent unjustified, it shall not resolve to allow a call of any kind until:

(a) the shortfalls have been met to the extent to which the Presbytery determined that they were unjustified, or

(b) a scheme for the payment of the unjustified shortfall has been agreed between the congregation and the Presbytery and receives the concurrence of the Ministries Council and/or the Stewardship and Finance Committee for their respective interests, or

(c) a fresh appraisal of the charge in terms of Act VII 2003 has been carried out, regardless of the status of the charge in the current Presbytery plan:

(i) During such appraisal, no further steps may be taken in respect of filling the vacancy, and the Presbytery shall make final determination of what constitutes such steps.

(ii) Following such appraisal and any consequent adjustment or deferred adjustment, the shortfalls shall be met or declared justifiable or a scheme shall be agreed in terms of subsection (b) above; the Presbytery shall inform the Ministries Council and the Stewardship and Finance Committee of its decisions in terms of this section; and the Presbytery shall remove the suspension-of-vacancy process referred to in sub-paragraph (i).

10. Vacancy Schedule

(1) When in terms of sections 4 and 6 above the decision to release the minister from the charge has been made and the Interim Moderator appointed, there shall be issued by the Ministries Council a Schedule or Schedules for completion by the responsible Financial Board(s) of the vacant congregation(s) in consultation with representatives of the Presbytery, setting forth the proposed arrangements for payment of ministerial expenses and for provision of a manse, showing the ministry requirements and details of any endowment income. The Schedule, along with an Extract Minute from each relevant Kirk Session containing a commitment fully and adequately to support the ministry, shall be forwarded to the Presbytery Clerk.

(2) The Schedule shall be considered by the Vacancy Procedure Committee and, if approved, transmitted to the Ministries Council by the Presbytery Clerk. The Vacancy Procedure Committee or Presbytery must not sustain an appointment and call until the Schedule has been approved by them and by the Ministries Council, which shall intimate its decision within six weeks of receiving the schedule from the Presbytery.

(3) The accuracy of the Vacancy Schedule shall be kept under review by the Vacancy Procedure Committee.

(4) The provisions of section 2 above shall apply to the decisions of the Vacancy Procedure Committee.

11. Manse

As soon as possible after the manse becomes vacant, the Presbytery Property Committee shall inspect the manse and come to a view on what work, if any, must be carried out to render it suitable for a new incumbent. The views of the Property Committee should then be communicated to the Presbytery, which should, subject to any modifications which might be agreed by that Court, instruct the Financial Board of the congregation to have the work carried out. No induction date shall be fixed until the Presbytery Property Committee has again inspected the manse and confirmed that the work has been undertaken satisfactorily.

12. Advisory Committee

(1) As soon as possible after intimation of a vacancy or anticipated vacancy reaches the Presbytery Clerk, the Vacancy Procedure Committee shall appoint an Advisory Committee of three, subject to the following conditions:

(a) at least one member shall be an elder and at least one shall be a minister;

(b) the Advisory Committee may comprise members of the Vacancy Procedure Committee and act as a support committee to congregations in a vacancy;

(c) the Advisory Committee may contain individuals who are not members of the Presbytery;

(d) the appointment shall be subject to section 2 above.

(2) The Advisory Committee shall meet:

(a) before the election of the Nominating Committee, with the Kirk Session (or Kirk Sessions both separately and together) of the vacant charge, to consider together in the light of the whole circumstances of the parish or parishes (i) what kind of ministry would be best suited to their needs and (ii) which system of election of the Nominating Committee described in paragraph 14(2)(d) hereunder shall be used;

(b)   with the Nominating Committee before it has taken any steps to fill the vacancy, to consider how it should proceed;

(c)   with the Nominating Committee before it reports to the Kirk Session and Presbytery the identity of the nominee, to review the process followed and give any further advice it deems necessary;

(d)   with the Kirk Session(s) as soon as an application is made for permission to proceed in terms of section 25A of this Act, to ensure that the requirements of that section are fulfilled;

(e)   with the Nominating Committee at any other time by request of either the Nominating Committee or the Advisory Committee.

In the case of charges which are in the opinion of the Presbytery remote, it will be adequate if the Interim Moderator (accompanied if possible by a member of the Nominating Committee) meets with the Advisory Committee for the purposes listed in paragraphs (a) to (c) above.

13. Electoral Register

(1)   It shall be the duty of the Kirk Session of a vacant congregation to proceed to make up the Electoral Register of the congregation. This shall contain (1) as communicants the names of those persons (a) whose names are on the communion roll of the congregation as at the date on which it is made up and who are not under Church discipline, (b) whose names have been added or restored to the communion roll on revision by the Kirk Session subsequently to the occurrence of the vacancy, and (c) who have given in valid Certificates of Transference by the date specified in terms of Schedule C hereto; and (2) as adherents the names of those persons who, being parishioners or regular worshippers in the congregation at the date when the vacancy occurred, and not being members of any other congregation, have claimed (in writing in the form prescribed in Schedule D and within the time specified in Schedule C) to be placed on the Electoral Register, the Kirk Session being satisfied that they desire to be permanently connected with the congregation and knowing of no adequate reasons why they should not be admitted as communicants should they so apply.

(2)   At a meeting to be held not later than fourteen days after intimation has been made in terms of Schedule C hereto, the Kirk Session shall decide on the claims of persons to be placed on the Electoral Register, such claims to be sent to the Session Clerk before the meeting. At this meeting, the Kirk Session may hear parties claiming to have an interest. The Kirk Session shall thereupon prepare the lists of names and addresses of communicants and of adherents which it is proposed shall be the Electoral Register of the congregation, the names being arranged in alphabetical order and numbered consecutively throughout. The decision of the Kirk Session in respect of any matter affecting the preparation of the Electoral Register shall be final.

(3)   The proposed Electoral Register having been prepared, the Interim Moderator shall cause intimation to be made on the first convenient Sunday in terms of Schedule E hereto that on that day an opportunity will be given for inspecting the Register after service, and that it will lie for inspection at such times and such places as the Kirk Session shall have determined; and further shall specify a day when the Kirk Session will meet to hear parties claiming an interest and will finally revise and adjust the Register. At this meeting, the list, having been revised, numbered and adjusted, shall on the authority of the court be attested by the Interim Moderator and the Clerk as the Electoral Register of the congregation.

(4) This Register, along with a duplicate copy, shall without delay be transmitted to the Presbytery Clerk, who, in name of the Presbytery, shall attest and return the principal copy, retaining the duplicate copy in his or her own possession. For all purposes connected with this Act, the congregation shall be deemed to be those persons whose names are on the Electoral Register, and no other.

(5) If after the attestation of the Register any communicant is given a Certificate of Transference, the Session Clerk shall delete that person's name from the Register and initial the deletion. Such a Certificate shall be granted only when application for it has been made in writing, and the said written application shall be retained until the vacancy is ended.

(6) When a period of more than six months has elapsed between the Electoral Register being attested and the congregation being given permission to call, the Kirk Session shall have power, if it so desires, to revise and update the Electoral Register. Intimation of this intention shall be given in terms of Schedule F hereto. Additional names shall be added to the Register in the form of an Addendum which shall also contain authority for the deletions which have been made; two copies of this Addendum, duly attested, shall be lodged with the Presbytery Clerk, who, in name of the Presbytery, shall attest and return the principal copy, retaining the duplicate copy in his or her own possession.

14. Appointment of Nominating Committee

(1) When permission to call has been given and the Electoral Register has been attested, intimation in terms of Schedule G shall be made that a meeting of the congregation is to be held to appoint a Committee of its own number for the purpose of nominating one person to the congregation with a view to the appointment of a minister.

(2) (a) The Interim Moderator shall preside at this meeting, and the Session Clerk, or in his or her absence a person appointed by the meeting, shall act as Clerk.

(b) The Interim Moderator shall remind the congregation of the number of members it is required to appoint in terms of this section and shall call for Nominations. To constitute a valid Nomination, the name of a person on the Electoral Register has to be proposed and seconded, and assurance given by the proposer that the person is prepared to act on the Committee. The Clerk shall take a note of all Nominations in the order in which they are made.

(c) When it appears to the Interim Moderator that the Nominations are complete, they shall be read to the congregation and an opportunity given for any withdrawals. If the number of persons nominated does not exceed the maximum fixed in terms of subsection (4) below, there is no need for a vote, and the Interim Moderator shall declare that these persons constitute a Nominating Committee.

(d) If the number exceeds the maximum, the election shall proceed by one of the following means, chosen in advance by the Kirk Session, and being either (i) the submission of the names by the Interim Moderator, one by one as they appear on the list, to the vote of the congregation, each member having the right to vote for up to the maximum number fixed for the Committee, and voting being by standing up, or (ii) a system of written ballot devised by the Kirk Session to suit the size of the congregation and approved by the Vacancy Procedure Committee or the Presbytery. In either case, in the event of a tie for the last place, a further vote shall be taken between or among those tying.

(e) The Interim Moderator shall, at the same meeting or as soon thereafter as the result of any ballot has been determined, announce the names of those thus elected to serve on the Nominating Committee, and intimate to them the time and place of their first meeting, which may be immediately after the congregational meeting provided that has been intimated along with the intimation of the congregational meeting.

(3)   Where there is an agreement between the Presbytery and the congregation or congregations that the minister to be inducted shall serve either in a team ministry involving another congregation or congregations, or in a designated post such as a chaplaincy, it shall be competent for the agreement to specify that the Presbytery shall appoint up to two representatives to serve on the Nominating Committee.

(4)   The Vacancy Procedure Committee shall, subject to the provisions of section 2 above, determine the number who will act on the Nominating Committee, being an odd number up to a maximum of thirteen.

(5)   When the vacancy is in a linked charge, or when a union or linking of congregations has been agreed but not yet effected, or when there is agreement to a deferred union or a deferred linking, or where the appointment is to more than one post, the Vacancy Procedure Committee shall, subject to the provisions of section 2 above, determine how the number who will act on the Nominating Committee will be allocated among the congregations involved, unless provision for this has already been made in the Basis of Union or Basis of Linking as the case may be.

(6)   The Nominating Committee shall not have power to co-opt additional members, but the relevant Kirk Session shall have power when necessary to appoint a replacement for any of its appointees who ceases, by death or resignation, to be a member of the Nominating Committee, or who, by falling ill or by moving away from the area, is unable to serve as a member of it.

15. Constitution of the Nominating Committee

It shall be the duty of the Interim Moderator to summon and preside at the first meeting of the Nominating Committee, which may be held at the close of the congregational meeting at which it is appointed and at which the Committee shall appoint a Convener and a Clerk. The Clerk, who need not be a member of the Committee, shall keep regular minutes of all proceedings. The Convener shall have a deliberative vote (if he or she is not the Interim Moderator) but shall in no case have a casting vote. If the Clerk is not a member of the Committee, he or she shall have no vote. At all meetings of the Committee, only those present shall be entitled to vote.

16. Task of the Nominating Committee

(1)   The Nominating Committee shall have the duty of nominating one person to the congregation with a view to the election and appointment of a minister. It shall proceed by a process of announcement in a monthly vacancy list, application and interview, and may also advertise, receive recommendations and pursue enquiries in other ways.

(2)   The Committee shall give due weight to any guidelines which may from time to time be issued by the Ministries Council or the General Assembly.

(3)   The Committee shall make themselves aware of the roles of the other members of any ministry team as described in section 16 of Act VII 2003 and may meet with them for this purpose, but shall not acquire responsibility or authority for the negotiation or alteration of their terms and conditions.

17. Eligibility for Election

The following categories of persons, and no others, are eligible to be nominated, elected and called as ministers of parishes in the Church of Scotland, but always subject, where appropriate, to the provisions of Act IX 2002:

(1)   A minister of a parish of the Church, a minister holding some other appointment that entitles him or her to a seat in Presbytery or a minister holding a current Practising Certificate in terms of Section 5 of Act II 2000 (as amended).

(2)   A minister of the Church of Scotland who has retired from a parish or appointment as above, provided he or she has not reached his or her 65th birthday (or, subject to the provisions of Regulations II 2004, his or her 70th birthday).

(3)   (a)   A licentiate of the Church of Scotland who has satisfactorily completed, or has been granted exemption from, his or her period of probationary service.

       (b)   A graduate candidate in terms of section 22 of Act X 2004.

(4)   A minister, licentiate or graduate candidate of the Church of Scotland who, with the approval of the World Mission Council, has entered the courts of an overseas Church as a full member, provided he or she has ceased to be such a member.

(5)   A minister, licentiate or graduate candidate of the Church of Scotland who has neither relinquished nor been judicially deprived of the status he or she possessed and who has served, or is serving, furth of Scotland in any Church which is a member of the World Alliance of Reformed Churches.

(6)   The holder of a Certificate of Eligibility in terms of Act IX 2002. The holder of a Certificate of Eligibility who is a national outside the European Economic Area and Switzerland shall be eligible to apply for charges only in terms of section 25A of this Act.

(7)   For the avoidance of doubt, anyone who has served as an Interim Moderator in the current vacancy shall not be eligible to apply or to be considered as an applicant.

18. Ministers of a Team

Ministers occupying positions within a team ministry in the charge, or larger area including the charge, and former holders of such positions, shall be eligible to apply and shall not by virtue of office be deemed to have exercised undue influence in securing the call. A *locum tenens* in the vacant charge shall not by virtue of office be deemed to have exercised undue influence in securing the call. Any Interim Moderator in the current vacancy shall not be eligible to apply.

19. Ministers of Other Churches

(1)   Where a minister of a church furth of Scotland, who holds a certificate of eligibility in terms of Act IX 2002, is nominated, the nominee, Kirk Session and Presbytery may agree that he or she shall be inducted for a period of three years only and shall retain status as a minister of his or her denomination of origin.

(2)   Upon induction, such a minister shall be accountable to the Presbytery for the exercise of his or her ministry and to his or her own church for matters of life and doctrine. He or she shall be awarded corresponding membership of the Presbytery.

(3)   With the concurrence of the Presbytery and the Ministries Council, and at the request of the congregation, the period may be extended for one further period of not more than three years.

(4)   The provisions of this section shall apply in the case of an appointment as a member of a ministry team as defined in section 16(2)(a) of Act VII 2003 (as amended), provided that the appointment is one which the Presbytery deems must be held by a Ministry of Word and Sacrament.

20. Nomination

(1)   Before the candidate is asked to accept Nomination, the Interim Moderator shall ensure that the candidate is given an adequate opportunity to see the whole ecclesiastical buildings (including the manse) pertaining to the congregation, and to meet privately with all members of staff of the charge or of any wider ministry team, and shall be provided with a copy of the constitution of the congregation, a copy of the current Presbytery Plan and

of any current Basis of Adjustment or Basis of Reviewable Tenure, and the most recent audited accounts and statement of funds, and the candidate shall acknowledge receipt in writing to the Interim Moderator.

(2)   Before any Nomination is intimated to the Kirk Session and Presbytery Clerk, the Clerk to the Nominating Committee shall secure the written consent thereto of the nominee.

(3)   Before reporting the Nomination to the Vacancy Procedure Committee, the Presbytery Clerk shall obtain from the nominee or Interim Moderator evidence of the eligibility of the nominee to be appointed to the charge.

(a)   In the case of a minister not being a member of any Presbytery of the Church of Scotland, this shall normally constitute an Exit Certificate in terms of Act X 2004, or evidence of status from the Ministries Council, or a current practising certificate, or certification from the Ministries Council of eligibility in terms of Act IX 2002.

(b)   In the case of a minister in the first five years of his or her first charge, this shall consist of an extract minute either from the Vacancy Procedure Committee of his or her current Presbytery, or from that Presbytery, exceptionally releasing the minister.

21. Preaching by Nominee

(1)   The Interim Moderator, on receiving notice of the Committee's Nomination, shall arrange that the nominee conduct public worship in the vacant church or churches, normally within four Sundays, and that the ballot take place immediately after each such service.

(2)   The Interim Moderator shall thereupon cause intimation to be made on two Sundays regarding the arrangements made in connection with the preaching by the nominee and the ballot thereafter, all in terms of Schedule H hereto.

22. Election of Minister

(1)   The Interim Moderator shall normally preside at all congregational meetings connected with the election which shall be in all cases by ballot and shall normally be in charge of the ballot.

(2)   The Interim Moderator may invite one or more persons (not being persons whose names are on the Electoral Register of the vacant congregation) to assist him or her in the conduct of a ballot vote when he or she judges this desirable.

(3)   When a linking or a deferred union or deferred linking is involved, the Interim Moderator shall consult and reach agreement with the minister or Interim Moderator of the other congregation regarding the arrangements for the conduct of public worship in these congregations by the nominee as in section 21(1) above. The Interim Moderator shall in writing appoint a member of Presbytery to take full charge of the ballot vote for the other congregation. In the case of a deferred union or deferred linking, the minister already inducted shall not be so appointed, nor shall he or she be in any way involved in the conduct of the election.

23. Ballot Procedure

(1)   The Kirk Session shall arrange to have available at the time of election a sufficient supply of voting-papers printed in the form of Schedule I hereto, and these shall be put into the custody of the Interim Moderator who shall preside at the election, assisted as in section 22 above. He or she shall issue on request to any person whose name is on the Electoral Register a voting-paper, noting on the Register that this has been done. Facilities shall be provided whereby the voter may mark the paper in secrecy, and a ballot-box shall be available wherein the paper is to be deposited when marked. The Interim Moderator may assist any person who asks for help in respect of completing the voting-paper, but no other person whatever shall communicate with the voter at this stage. The Interim Moderator, or

the deputy appointed by him or her, shall be responsible for the safe custody of ballot-box, papers and Electoral Register.

(2)   As soon as practicable, and at latest within twenty-four hours after the close of the voting, the Interim Moderator shall constitute the Kirk Session, or the joint Kirk Sessions when more than one congregation is involved, and in presence of the Kirk Session shall proceed with the counting of the votes, in which he or she may be assisted as provided in section 22 above. When more than one ballot-box has been used and when the votes of more than one congregation are involved, all ballot-boxes shall be emptied and the voting-papers shall be mixed together before counting begins so that the preponderance of votes in one area or in one congregation shall not be disclosed.

(3)   A voting-paper shall only be considered as spoilt and the vote not counted where the intention of the voter is unclear, and in no other circumstances. It shall be for the Kirk Session, on the recommendation of the Interim Moderator, to determine whether the intention of the voter is clear.

(4)   If the number voting For exceeds the number voting Against, the nominee shall be declared elected and the Nominating Committee shall be deemed to be discharged.

(5)   If the number voting For is equal to or less than the number voting Against, the Interim Moderator shall declare that there has been failure to elect and that the Nominating Committee is deemed to have been discharged. He or she shall proceed in terms of section 26(b) without further reference to the Presbytery.

(6)   After the counting has been completed, the Interim Moderator shall sign a declaration in one of the forms of Schedule J hereto, and this shall be recorded in the minute of the Kirk Session or of the Kirk Sessions. An extract shall be affixed to the notice-board of the church, or of each of the churches, concerned. In presence of the Kirk Session, the Interim Moderator shall then seal up the voting-papers along with the marked copy of the Electoral Register, and these shall be transmitted to the Presbytery Clerk in due course along with the other documents specified in section 27 below.

24. Withdrawal of Nominee

(1)   Should a nominee intimate withdrawal before he or she has preached as nominee, the Nominating Committee shall continue its task and seek to nominate another nominee.

(2)   Should a nominee intimate withdrawal after he or she has been elected, the Interim Moderator shall proceed in terms of sections 23(4) above and 26(b) below without further reference to the Presbytery.

25. The Call

(1)   The Interim Moderator shall, along with the intimation regarding the result of the voting, intimate the arrangements made for members of the congregation over a period of not less than eight days to subscribe the Call (Schedule K). Intimation shall be in the form of Schedule L hereto.

(2)   The Call may be subscribed on behalf of a member not present to sign in person, provided a mandate authorising such subscription is produced as in Schedule M. All such entries shall be initialled by the Interim Moderator or by the member of the Kirk Session appending them.

(3)   Those eligible to sign the call shall be all those whose names appear on the Electoral Register. A paper of concurrence in the Call may be signed by regular worshippers in the congregation and by adherents whose names have not been entered on the Electoral Register.

25A. Ministers from Non-EEA Countries excluding Switzerland

(1)   Six months after the vacancy has first appeared in a monthly vacancy list, and provided

there are no applications currently under the consideration of the Nominating Committee, the Kirk Session (or in the case of a linkage the Kirk Sessions in agreement) may apply to the Presbytery to have the charge listed for the purposes of this section.

(2)   Such applications shall be considered by the whole Presbytery, and shall not form part of the remit of the Vacancy Procedure Committee.

(3)   The Presbytery must be satisfied that there are no outstanding issues of superintendence, or other factors that would make such listing inappropriate, and must consult with the Ministries Council before deciding whether to permit the listing. The Presbytery Clerk shall within seven days send an extract minute of the decision to the Ministries Council.

(4)   Upon receiving notification of the listing from the Presbytery, the Nominating Committee shall proceed again from section 16 of this Act, and holders of Certificates of Eligibility who are nationals of countries outwith the EEA and Switzerland shall now be eligible to apply.

(5)   For the avoidance of doubt, the Nominating Committee (a) must always dispose of any competent applications received in terms of section 17 of this Act before considering those made in terms of this section, but (b) shall not be obliged to make a nomination from any particular group of applicants.

(6)   When a Presbytery withdraws permission to call, or the permission lapses in terms of section 26 of this Act, the Presbytery shall decide whether permission to proceed in terms of this section remains in force during the ensuing process to make a nomination.

26. Failure to Nominate
The exercise by a congregation of its right to call a minister shall be subject to a time-limit of one year; this period shall be calculated from the date when intimation is given of the agreement to grant leave to call. If it appears that an appointment is not to be made within the allotted time (allowing one further calendar month for intimation to the Presbytery), the congregation may make application to the Presbytery for an extension, which will normally be for a further six months. For clear cause shown, a further extension of six months may be granted. If no election has been made and intimated to the Presbytery by the expiry of that time, the permission to call shall be regarded as having lapsed. The Presbytery may thereupon look afresh at the question of adjustment. If the Presbytery is still satisfied that a minister should be appointed, it shall itself take steps to make such an appointment, proceeding in one of the following ways:

(a)   (i)   The Presbytery may discharge the Nominating Committee, strengthen the Advisory Committee which had been involved in the case by the appointment of an additional minister and elder, instruct that Committee to bring forward to a subsequent meeting the name of an eligible individual for appointment to the charge and intimate this instruction to the congregation. If satisfied with the recommendation brought by the Advisory Committee, the Presbytery shall thereupon make the appointment.

(ii)   The Presbytery Clerk shall thereupon intimate to the person concerned the fact of his or her appointment, shall request him or her to forward a letter of acceptance along with appropriate Certificates if these are required in terms of section 27 below, and shall arrange with him or her to conduct public worship in the vacant church or churches on an early Sunday.

(iii)   The Presbytery Clerk shall cause intimation to be made in the form of Schedule N that the person appointed will conduct public worship on the day specified and that a Call in the usual form will lie with the Session Clerk or other suitable person for not less than eight free days to receive the signatures of the congregation. The conditions governing the signing of the Call shall be as in section 25 above.

(iv) At the expiry of the time allowed, the Call shall be transmitted by the Session Clerk to the Presbytery Clerk who shall lay it, along with the documents referred to in sub-paragraph (ii) above, before the Presbytery at its first ordinary meeting or at a meeting *in hunc effectum*.

(b) Otherwise, the Presbytery shall instruct that a fresh Nominating Committee be elected in terms of section 14 above. The process shall then be followed in terms of this Act from the point of the election of the Nominating Committee.

27. Transmission of Documents

(1) After an election has been made, the Interim Moderator shall secure from the person appointed a letter of acceptance of the appointment.

(2) The Interim Moderator shall then without delay transmit the relevant documents to the Presbytery Clerk. These are: the minute of Nomination by the Nominating Committee, all intimations made to the congregation thereafter, the declaration of the election and appointment, the voting-papers, the marked copy of the Register and the letter of acceptance. He or she shall also inform the Clerk of the steps taken in connection with the signing of the Call, and shall arrange that, at the expiry of the period allowed for subscription, the Call shall be transmitted by the Session Clerk to the Presbytery Clerk.

(3) After the person elected has been inducted to the charge, the Presbytery Clerk shall:

(a) deliver to him or her the approved copy of the Vacancy Schedule referred to in section 10(2) above, and

(b) destroy the intimations and voting-papers lodged with him or her in terms of subsection (2) above and ensure that confidential documents and correspondence held locally are destroyed.

28. Sustaining the Call

(1) All of the documents listed in section 27 above shall be laid before the Vacancy Procedure Committee, which may resolve to sustain the call and determine arrangements for the induction of the new minister, subject to (a) a request for the release, if appropriate, of the minister from his or her current charge in terms of this Act and (b) the provisions of section 2 above. The Moderator of the Presbytery shall, if no ordinary meeting of the Presbytery falls before the proposed induction date, call a meeting *pro re nata* for the induction.

(2) In the event that the matter comes before the Presbytery in terms of section 2 above, the procedure shall be as follows:

(a) The Call and other relevant documents having been laid on the table, the Presbytery shall hear any person whom it considers to have an interest. In particular, the Advisory Committee shall be entitled to be heard if it so desires, or the Presbytery may ask for a report from it. The Presbytery shall then decide whether to sustain the appointment in terms of subsection (1) above, and in doing so shall give consideration to the number of signatures on the Call. It may delay reaching a decision and return the Call to the Kirk Session to give further opportunity for it to be subscribed.

(b) If the Presbytery sustain an appointment and Call to a Graduate Candidate, and there be no appeal tendered in due form against its judgement, it shall appoint the day and hour and place at which the ordination and induction will take place.

(c) If the Presbytery sustain an appointment and Call to a minister of the Church of Scotland not being a minister of a parish, or to a minister of another denomination, and there be no ecclesiastical impediment, the Presbytery shall appoint the day and hour and place at which the induction will take place.

(3) In the event that the Call is not sustained, the Presbytery shall determine either (a) to give

more time for it to be signed in terms of section 25 above or (b) to proceed in terms of subsection (a) or (b) of section 26 above.

29. Admission to a Charge

(1) When the Presbytery has appointed a day for the ordination and induction of a Graduate Candidate, or for the induction of a minister already ordained, the Clerk shall arrange for an edict in the form of Schedule O to be read to the congregation on the two Sundays preceding the day appointed.

(2) At the time and place named in the edict, the Presbytery having been constituted, the Moderator shall call for the return of the edict attested as having been duly served. If the minister is being translated from another Presbytery, the relevant minute of that Presbytery or of its Vacancy Procedure Committee agreeing to translation shall also be laid on the table. Any objection, to be valid at this stage, must have been intimated to the Presbytery Clerk at the objector's earliest opportunity, must be strictly directed to life or doctrine and must be substantiated immediately to the satisfaction of the Presbytery, in which case procedure shall be sisted and the Presbytery shall take appropriate steps to deal with the situation that has arisen. Otherwise, the Presbytery shall proceed with the ordination and induction, or with the induction, as hereunder.

(3) The Presbytery shall proceed to the church where public worship shall be conducted by those appointed for the purpose. The Clerk shall read a brief narrative of the cause of the vacancy and of the steps taken for the settlement. The Moderator, having read the Preamble, shall, addressing him or her by name, put to the person to be inducted the questions prescribed (*see the Ordinal of the Church as authorised from time to time by the General Assembly*). Satisfactory answers having been given, the person to be inducted shall sign the Formula. If he or she has not already been ordained, the person to be inducted shall then kneel, and the Moderator by prayer and the imposition of hands, in which members of the Presbytery, appointed by the Presbytery for the purpose, and other ordained persons associated with it, if invited to share in such imposition of hands, shall join, shall ordain him or her to the office of the Holy Ministry. Prayer being ended, the Moderator shall say: 'I now declare you to have been ordained to the office of the Holy Ministry, and in name of the Lord Jesus Christ, the King and Head of the Church, and by authority of this Presbytery, I induct you to this charge, and in token thereof we give you the right hand of fellowship'. The Moderator with all other members of Presbytery present and those associated with it shall then give the right hand of fellowship. The Moderator shall then put the prescribed question to the members of the congregation. Suitable charges to the new minister and to the congregation shall then be given by the Moderator or by a minister appointed for the purpose.

(4) *[This subsection is to be construed in conformity with Act III 2004.]* When an ordained minister is being inducted to a charge, the act of ordination shall not be repeated, and the relevant words shall be omitted from the declaration. In other respects, the procedure shall be as in subsection (3) above.

(5) When the appointment is for a limited or potentially limited period (including Reviewable Tenure, or an appointment in terms of section 19 above), the service shall proceed as in subsections (3) or (4) above, except that in the declaration the Moderator shall say: 'I induct you to this charge on the Basis of [specific Act and Section] and in terms of Minute of Presbytery of date . . .'.

(6) After the service, the Presbytery shall resume its session, when the name of the new minister shall be added to the Roll of Presbytery, and the Clerk shall be instructed to send certified intimation of the induction to the Session Clerk to be engrossed in the minutes of

the first meeting of Kirk Session thereafter, and, in the case of a translation from another Presbytery or where the minister was prior to the induction subject to the supervision of another Presbytery, to the Clerk of that Presbytery.

30. Service of Introduction

(1)   When a minister has been appointed to a linked charge, the Presbytery shall determine in which of the churches of the linking the induction is to take place. This shall be a service of induction to the charge, in consequence of which the person inducted shall become minister of each of the congregations embraced in the linking. The edict regarding the induction, which shall be in terms of Schedule O, shall be read in all of the churches concerned. There shall be no other service of induction; but, if the churches are far distant from one another, or for other good reason, the Presbytery may appoint a service of introduction to be held in the other church or churches. Intimation shall be given of such service, but not in edictal form.

(2)   In any case of deferred union or deferred linking, the minister elected and appointed shall be inducted 'to the vacant congregation of A in deferred union (or linking) with the congregation of B' and there shall be no need for any further act to establish his or her position as minister of the united congregation or of the linked congregation as the case may be. The Presbytery, however, shall in such a case arrange a service of introduction to the newly united congregation of AB or the newly linked congregation of B. Intimation shall be given of such service, but not in edictal form.

(3)   When an appointment has been made to an extra-parochial office wholly or mainly under control of the Church (community ministry, full-time chaplaincy in hospital, industry, prison or university, full-time clerkship and so on), the Presbytery may deem it appropriate to arrange a service of introduction to take place in a church or chapel suitable to the occasion.

(4)   When an appointment has been made to a parochial appointment other than that of an inducted minister, the Presbytery may arrange a service of introduction to take place within the parish. If ordination is involved, suitable arrangements shall be made and edictal intimation shall be given in terms of Schedule P.

(5)   A service of introduction not involving ordination shall follow the lines of an induction except that, instead of putting the normal questions to the minister, the Moderator shall ask him or her to affirm the vows taken at his or her ordination. Where the service, in terms of subsection (3) or (4) above, includes the ordination of the minister, the vows shall be put in full. In either case, in the declaration, the Moderator in place of 'I induct you to . . .' shall say: 'I welcome you as . . .'.

31. Demission of Status

If a minister seeks to demit his or her status as a minister of the Church of Scotland, any accompanying demission of a charge will be dealt with by the Vacancy Procedure Committee in terms of section 4 of this Act without further delay, but the question of demission of status shall be considered by the Presbytery itself. The Moderator of Presbytery, or a deputy appointed by him or her, shall first confer with the minister regarding his or her reasons and shall report to the Presbytery if there appears to be any reason not to grant permission to demit status. Any decision to grant permission to demit status shall be immediately reported to the Ministries Council.

32. Miscellaneous

For the purposes of this Act, intimations to congregations may be made (a) verbally during every act of worship or (b) in written intimations distributed to the whole congregation provided that the congregation's attention is specifically drawn to the presence of an intimation there in terms of this Act.

For the purposes of this Act, attestation of all intimations to congregations shall consist of certification thereof by the Session Clerk as follows:

(a)   Certification that all intimations received have been duly made on the correct number of Sundays shall be sent to the Presbytery Clerk before the service of induction or introduction.

(b)   Certification that any particular intimation received has been duly made on the correct number of Sundays shall be furnished on demand to the Vacancy Procedure Committee or the Presbytery Clerk.

(c)   Intimation shall be made immediately to the Presbytery Clerk in the event that intimation has not been duly made on the appropriate Sunday.

33. Repeals and Amendments

(1)   Act V 1984 (as amended) is hereby repealed; it is hereby provided that all other legislation prior to this Act shall be construed in conformity with this Act.

(2)   Earlier Acts and Regulations are amended as follows:

(a)   In sections 2 and 7 of Act XVIII 1932, delete the latter sentence of section 2 and all of subsection 7(b).

(b)   In Act IV 1999, delete 'Act V 1984 section 25(3)' and substitute 'section 29(3) of Act VIII 2003'.

(c)   In section 19(2) of Act II 2000, delete 'section 2(3) of Act V 1984' and substitute 'section 7 of Act VIII 2003'.

(d)   In section 9 of Act XV 2002, delete 'in terms of section 27 of Act V 1984'.

(e)   In section 12(i) of Act XIII 2000 and in section 2(i) of Regulations V 2000, delete 'sections 6-8 of Act V 1984' and substitute section 13 of Act VIII 2003'.

(f)   In section 2(2) of Act IV 2001, delete 'in terms of Act V 1984 section 27' and 'in terms of the said Act V 1984'.

(g)   In paragraph 1 of Schedule 3 to Act V 2002, delete 'section 13 of Act V 1984' and substitute 'section 17 of Act VIII 2003'.

(h)   In paragraph 2(ii) of Schedule 3 to Act V 2002, delete 'Sections 6 to 8 of Act V 1984' and substitute 'section 13 of Act VIII 2003'.

(i)   In section 2 of Act VII 2002, delete 'Act V 1984 section 25' and substitute 'section 29 of Act VIII 2003'.

(j)   In section 9 of Act XV 2002, delete 'in terms of section 27 of Act V 1984'.

(k)   In Regulations II 1996, delete reference to Act V 1984 (as amended) and substitute Act VIII 2003.

(3)   Notwithstanding subsection (1) above, the repeal of Act V 1984 as amended shall not affect the operation of the said Act (or Deliverances of the General Assembly in pursuance thereof) prior to the repeal of the said Act, or anything done or suffered under the said Act or Deliverances; and any rights or obligations acquired or incurred thereunder shall have effect as if the said Act had not been repealed.

34. Interpretation

For the purposes of this Act, the Interpretation section (section 1) of Act VII 2003 will apply.

SCHEDULES

A INTIMATION OF ACTION OR DECISION OF VACANCY PROCEDURE COMMITTEE – Section 2(1)

To be read on one Sunday

The Vacancy Procedure Committee of the Presbytery of .... proposes [here insert action or permission proposed]....... Any communicant member of the congregation(s) of A [and B] may submit to the Presbytery Clerk a request for this proposal to be considered at the next meeting of the Presbytery: where such requests are received from four individuals, being communicant members of the congregation(s) or full members of the Presbytery, the request shall be met. Such request should be submitted in writing to [name and postal address of Presbytery Clerk] by [date seven days after intimation].

A .... B ....   Presbytery Clerk

B EDICT CITING A CONGREGATION TO ATTEND – Section 2(5)

To be read on one Sunday

Intimation is hereby given that, in connection with the [anticipated] vacancy in this congregation, a valid request has been made for the matter of [here insert action or permission which had been proposed] to be considered by the Presbytery. [The proposed course of action] is in the meantime sisted.

Intimation is hereby further given that the Presbytery will meet to consider this matter at .... on .... the .... day of .... at .... o'clock and that the congregation are hereby cited to attend for their interests.

A .... B ....   Presbytery Clerk

C PREPARATION OF ELECTORAL REGISTER – Section 13(1) and (2)

To be read on two Sundays

Intimation is hereby given that in view of the [1]anticipated vacancy, the Kirk Session is about to make up an Electoral Register of this congregation. Any communicant whose name is not already on the Communion Roll as a member should hand in to the Session Clerk a Certificate of Transference, and anyone wishing his or her name added to the Register as an adherent should obtain from the Session Clerk, and complete and return to him or her, a Form of Adherent's Claim. All such papers should be in the hands of the Session Clerk not later than .... The Kirk Session will meet in .... on .... at .... to make up the Electoral Register, when anyone wishing to support his or her claim in person should attend.

C .... D ....   Interim Moderator

[1] This word to be included where appropriate – otherwise to be deleted

D FORM OF ADHERENT'S CLAIM – Section 13(1)

I, [1] .... of [2] ...., being a parishioner or regular worshipper in the Church of ....
and not being a member of any other congregation in Scotland, claim to have my name put on
the Electoral Register of the parish of .... as an adherent.

Date ....   (Signed).......................

[1] Here enter full name in block capitals
[2] Here enter address in full

E INSPECTION OF ELECTORAL REGISTER – Section 13(3)

To be read on one Sunday

Intimation is hereby given that the proposed Electoral Register of this congregation has now been
prepared and that an opportunity of inspecting it will be given today in .... at the close of
this service, and that it will be open for inspection at .... on .... between the hours of
.... and .... each day. Any questions regarding entries in the Register should be brought
to the notice of the Kirk Session which is to meet in .... on .... at .... o'clock,
when it will finally make up the Electoral Register.

C .... D ....   Interim Moderator

F REVISION OF ELECTORAL REGISTER – Section 13(6)

To be read on two Sundays

Intimation is hereby given that, more than six months having elapsed since the Electoral Register
of this congregation was finally made up, it is now proposed that it should be revised. An
opportunity of inspecting the Register will be given in .... at the close of this service, and
also at .... on .... between the hours of .... and .... each day. Anyone wishing
his or her name added to the Electoral Register as a member should give in a Transference
Certificate, or as an adherent should give in a Form of Adherent's Claim (copies of which may
be had from the Session Clerk) not later than .... The Kirk Session will meet in .... on
.... at .... o'clock, when it will finally make up the Revised Register.

C .... D ....   Interim Moderator

G INTIMATION OF ELECTION OF NOMINATING COMMITTEE – Section 14(1)

To be read on two Sundays

Intimation is hereby given that a meeting of this congregation will be held in the Church [or other
arrangement may be given here] on Sunday .... at the close of morning worship for the purpose
of appointing a Nominating Committee which will nominate one person to the congregation with
a view to the appointment of a minister.

C .... D ....   Interim Moderator

H MINUTE OF NOMINATION BY NOMINATING COMMITTEE – Section 21

To be read on two Sundays

(1)   The Committee chosen by this congregation to nominate a person with a view to the election and appointment of a minister, at a meeting held at .... on ...., resolved to name and propose [1] ...., and they accordingly do name and propose the said ....

Date ....

E .... F ....   Convener of Committee

[1] The name and designation of the person should at this point be entered in full

(2)   Intimation is therefore hereby given that the Nominating Committee having, as by minute now read, named and proposed [Name], arrangements have been made whereby public worship will be conducted in this Church by him or her on Sunday the .... day of .... at .... o'clock; and that a vote will be taken by voting-papers immediately thereafter; and that electors may vote For or Against electing and appointing the said [Name] as minister of this vacant charge.

C .... D ....   Interim Moderator

I VOTING-PAPER – Section 23

FOR Electing [Name]	
AGAINST Electing [Name]	

Directions to Voters: If you are in favour of electing [Name], put a cross (x) on the upper right-hand space. If you are not in favour of electing [Name], put a cross (x) in the lower right-hand space. Mark your voting-paper in this way with a cross and put no other mark on your voting-paper, or your vote may not be counted.

Note: The Directions to Voters must be printed prominently on the face of the voting-paper.

J DECLARATION OF ELECTION RESULT – Section 23(5)

First Form (Successful Election)

I hereby declare that the following are the results of the voting for the election and appointment of a minister to the vacant charge of [1] .... and that the said [Name] has accordingly been elected and appointed subject to the judgement of the courts of the Church.

Date ....   C .... D ....   Interim Moderator

[1] Here enter details

FOR Electing [Name]
AGAINST Electing [Name]

Second Form (Failure to Elect)

I hereby declare that the following are the results of the voting for the election and appointment of a minister to the vacant charge of [1] .... and that in consequence of this vote there has been a failure to elect, and the Nominating Committee is deemed to have been discharged. [Continue in terms of Schedule G if appropriate.]

Date ....   C .... D ....   Interim Moderator

[1] Here enter details

FOR Electing [*Name*]
AGAINST Electing [*Name*]

K THE CALL – Section 25(1)

Form of Call

We, members of the Church of Scotland and of the congregation known as ...., being without a minister, address this Call to be our minister to you, ..., of whose gifts and qualities we have been assured, and we warmly invite you to accept this Call, promising that we shall devote ourselves with you to worship, witness, mission and service in this parish, and also to the furtherance of these in the world, to the glory of God and for the advancement of His Kingdom.

Paper of Concurrence

We, regular worshippers in the congregation of the Church of Scotland known as ...., concur in the Call addressed by that congregation to .... to be their minister.

Note: The Call and Paper of Concurrence should be dated and attested by the Interim Moderator before they are transmitted to the Clerk of the Presbytery.

L SUBSCRIBING THE CALL – Section 25(1)

To be read on at least one Sunday

Intimation is hereby given that this congregation having elected [*Name*] to be their minister, a Call to the said [*Name*] has been prepared and will lie in .... on .... the .... day of .... between the hours of .... and ...., when those whose names are on the Electoral Register of the congregation may sign in person or by means of mandates. Forms of mandate may be obtained from the Session Clerk.

A Paper of Concurrence will also be available for signature by persons who are connected with the congregation but whose names are not on the Electoral Register of the congregation.

C .... D ....   Interim Moderator

M MANDATE TO SIGN CALL – Section 25(2)

I, ... of ...., being a person whose name is on the Electoral Register of the congregation, hereby authorise the Session Clerk, or other member of Session, to add my name to the Call addressed to [Name] to be our minister.

(Signed) ....

N CITATION IN CASE OF NOMINATION BY PRESBYTERY – Section 26(a)(iii)

To be read on one Sunday

Intimation is hereby given that [Name], whom the Presbytery has appointed to be minister of this congregation, will conduct public worship in the Church on Sunday the .... day of .... at .... o'clock.

Intimation is hereby further given that a Call addressed to the said [Name] will lie in .... on .... the .... day of .... between the hours of .... and .... during the day and between the hours of .... and .... in the evening, when members may sign in person or by means of mandates, forms of which may be had from the Session Clerk.

Intimation is hereby further given that the Presbytery will meet to deal with the appointment and Call at .... on .... the .... day of .... at .... o'clock and that the congregation are hereby cited to attend for their interests.

A .... B ....   Presbytery Clerk

O EDICTAL INTIMATION OF ADMISSION – Section 29

To be read on two Sundays

- The Presbytery of .... has received a Call from this congregation addressed to [Name] to be their minister, and the Call has been sustained as a regular Call, and has been accepted by him/her[1];
- The Presbytery, having judged the said [Name] qualified[2] for the ministry of the Gospel and for this charge, has resolved to proceed to his or her[3] ordination and induction on .... the .... day of .... at .... o'clock unless something occur which may reasonably impede it:

Notice is hereby given to all concerned that if they, or any of them, have anything to object to in the life or doctrine of the said [Name], they should intimate their objection at their earliest opportunity to the Presbytery Clerk, with evidence of substantiation of the objection.

The Presbytery is to meet at [time] on [date as above]. In accordance with section 29 of Act VIII 2003, an objection first brought at that time must be immediately substantiated, and the objector must satisfy the Presbytery that there was no earlier opportunity to bring the objection to the attention of the Presbytery Clerk. Otherwise the Presbytery shall proceed without further delay.

By order of the Presbytery

A .... B .... Presbytery Clerk

[1] add, where appropriate, 'and his or her translation has been agreed to by the Presbytery of ....'
[2] omit 'for the ministry of the Gospel and' if the minister to be inducted has been ordained previously
[3] omit, where appropriate, 'ordination and'

P EDICTAL INTIMATION OF ORDINATION IN CASE OF INTRODUCTION – Section 30(1)

To be read on two Sundays

* Whereas [narrate circumstances requiring service of introduction]
* And whereas the Presbytery, having found the said [Name] to have been regularly appointed and to be qualified for the ministry of the Gospel and for the said appointment, has resolved to proceed to his or her ordination to the Holy Ministry and to his or her introduction as [specify appointment] on .... the .... day of .... at .... o'clock unless something occur which may reasonably impede it:

Notice is hereby given to all concerned that if they, or any of them, have anything to object to in the life or doctrine of the said [Name], they may appear at the Presbytery which is to meet at .... on .... the .... day of .... at .... o'clock; with certification that if no relevant objection be then made and immediately substantiated, the Presbytery will proceed without further delay.

By order of the Presbytery

A .... B ....   Presbytery Clerk

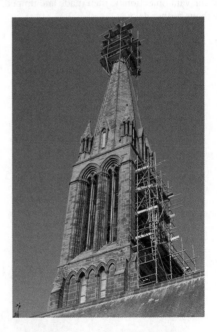

SECTION 4

The
General Assembly
of 2012

(1) THE GENERAL ASSEMBLY

The Lord High Commissioner:	The Rt Hon. Lord Selkirk of Douglas QC MA LLB
Moderator:	Right Rev. Albert O. Bogle BD MTh
Chaplains to the Moderator:	Rev. Iain D. Cunningham MA BD Rev. William McPherson BD DipEd
Principal Clerk:	Rev. John P. Chalmers BD
Depute Clerk:	Rev. George J. Whyte BSc BD DMin
Procurator:	Ms Laura Dunlop QC
Law Agent:	Mrs Janette S. Wilson LLB NP
Convener of the Business Committee:	Rev. Janet S. Mathieson MA BD
Vice-Convener of the Business Committee:	Rev. E. Lorna Hood MA BD
Precentor:	Rev. Douglas Galbraith MA BD BMus MPhil ARSCM PhD
Assembly Officer:	Mr David McColl
Assistant Assembly Officer:	Mr Craig Marshall

(2) THE MODERATOR

The Right Reverend Albert O. Bogle BD MTh

In the year 2000, in the Assembly Hall, the writer and speaker, Adrian Plass, famously said of Albert Bogle: 'Not every church has an Albert!'

But we are glad that the Church of Scotland has, and that he has been chosen to be the Moderator of the General Assembly of 2012.

Albert Bogle has been the parish minister at Bo'ness St Andrew's since 1981 – a long time in his only charge. However, Albert is quick to point out that during that time he has exercised at least five different ministries, developing new skills in response to changing circumstances. He is both an innovator and an imaginative adapter of ideas, and has created a highly skilled team of professionals and volunteers who continue to make an impact on the local Bo'ness community and all around the world by enabling the local and global to influence each other.

Albert was born in the St George's Cross area of Glasgow and attended Grove Street Primary School and Woodside Senior Secondary School. He then worked for seven years at Bank of Scotland, taking his banking exams and building up an expertise in finance that he has used to great effect for the Church's mission at home and abroad.

He began his journey of Christian discipleship as a child in St Silas' Episcopal Church, and his spiritual upbringing in both church and family laid a solid foundation for what has to date been a remarkably innovative, faithful and effective ministry in Bo'ness.

In answering the call to ministry, he entered the Divinity Faculty at Glasgow University in 1975 and gained an honours degree in Ecclesiastical History, which, combined with Systematic Theology taught by Dr John Zizioulas (and a later MTh from Edinburgh University in the theology of media and ethics), has continued to inform his thoughtful engagement with the postmodern world.

One of the earliest projects that Albert set up in Bo'ness (as a community response to the famine in Ethiopia and Sudan) was a not-for-profit gift shop called Branches. A charitable trust, called the Vine Trust, was set up at the same time to provide grants to various local and international projects using the money raised by the shop.

Rev. Willie McPherson became a member of the board of the Vine Trust – and, in the late 1990s through their joint leadership, it began to expand its vision and scope. Rather than simply being a grant-giving organisation, the Vine Trust began to attract funding and sponsorship from outside bodies and to form partnerships with various businesses and public-sector bodies, and soon became a venture that initiates its own innovative and transformative projects around the world. It is now a multi-million-pound international, interdenominational volunteering charity that enables volunteers to make a real and significant difference to some of the poorest children and communities in the world.

Its motto of 'connecting people to change lives' has been the recurrent theme that runs through all the aspects of Albert's own ministry, including several major social-outreach programmes engaged in by the local congregation. These include work with vulnerable families, programmes for children and teenagers, a project for dementia sufferers and their families, a storehouse food initiative in partnership with local supermarkets helping those in poverty, and counselling services based in the local health centre.

Work with film and multimedia, which began in Bo'ness St Andrew's as a way of connecting with young people and bringing them back into the life of the Church, has developed into the media company Sanctus Media.

Albert has also served the wider work of the Church, in Falkirk Presbytery as Education Convener and as its Moderator, and in the General Assembly as a member of the Panel on Worship and the Board of National Mission. He was also a member of the Special Commission on Review and Reform that produced the *Church Without Walls Report*; and he became convener of the Church Without Walls Planning Group, which organised two National Gatherings and a number of Re-Energise Conferences for church leaders.

He was also very much involved in the Carberry Festival for many years, helping to pioneer new forms of worship and expressions of Christian community that engage with the creative arts.

Albert has always had a profound passion for sharing his faith, and in 1998 was officially recognised as an evangelist in the Church of Scotland.

As a songwriter and musician who is also deeply interested in visual media (especially film) and who is sensitive to contemporary culture, he is always searching out new ways to communicate faith effectively in a changing world, but always through making connections with people where they are and using language they can understand. Most of all, Albert is greatly skilled at making and keeping friends. Albert has been married to Martha since 1977, and they have a daughter, Sarah Jane, and a son, Stephen.

It is a great honour for us to have been asked to act as Albert's chaplains during his term of office as Moderator. We look forward to his Moderatorial year, in which we are confident he will bring to the whole Church and to wider society his gifts of insight, energy, enthusiasm, inspiration and encouragement.

Iain Cunningham and Willie McPherson
Chaplains

(3) DIGEST OF ASSEMBLY DECISIONS

Continuing the practice of recent years, this section of the *Year Book* contains the Editor's personal selection of the decisions of the most recent General Assembly which, in his view at the time of writing, seemed likely to be of most immediate or practical interest to those who will read it.

With the brief headline approach that the constraints of space dictate, full justice cannot be done to every important topic that was raised – and so, as before, there may be some surprise that this or that decision has been included or omitted. By the same token, important Deliverances of the Assembly are on occasion framed with reference to some particular Act of Assembly to the extent that the Act in question would require to be quoted at some length to enable the full significance of one year's changes to be appreciated. It has never been and surely should never be the practice in this section to venture either comment or commentary, to express either approval or apprehension in regard to what the Assembly decided.

Those who wish to explore more fully the Assembly's Reports and Deliverances can obtain from the office of the Principal Clerk the relevant volumes and papers. In addition, individual Departments and those who were Commissioners to the Assembly are often happy to make this material available on loan.

The General Assembly of 2012 continued the innovative pattern of its predecessor by spilling over into Princes Street Gardens on the Sunday afternoon, when it was joined by congregations from all parts of Scotland and by members of the public, rather more than 5,000 in all, celebrating the faith with 'Heart and Soul'. They did so through story, through rhythm and song, in the sharing of local initiatives in mission and service, in hearing at first hand of the experience of Christians from overseas, and learning more of the work of the Church's councils and committees. It ended with a service of worship at the bandstand, with a choir of over 250 from churches up and down the country, and a rousing address from the Moderator.

The Assembly itself was notable for the visit of the Archbishop of Canterbury, whose address was received with acclamation. (The Archbishop's address is published in the July 2012 issue of *Life and Work*.) Worship this year was enriched by an Assembly Choir (based on a core group of singers from '121'), by the Saturday-night visit of singer/songwriter Ian White, and indeed by the singing of the Moderator himself! Its debates were, as always, enhanced by the presence of some fifty delegates from other Churches in the United Kingdom and across the world, who were received by the Moderator on the Saturday evening, and whose contributions to debates were welcomed.

What follows is a digest of some of the events and decisions of the Assembly. We are grateful to the Rev. Douglas Aitken for permission to adapt this from the podcast he prepared each day as part of the streaming of the Assembly on the Church of Scotland's website. The complete podcasts may still be accessed there.

Saturday, 19 May
After the election of the Moderator and the reading of the Commission to His Grace and of Her Majesty's Letter, the **Lord High Commissioner**, Lord Selkirk, addressed the Assembly, including reminiscence of his being a pageboy at the Queen's Coronation, and of the Cameronians' custom of posting sentries before worship. He recalled, as an officer, marching into worship, sword in hand, and saying: 'Reverend Sir, no enemy is in sight, worship may proceed', citing this as an example of how free worship was to be treasured.

A new system of electronic voting was inaugurated, which would allow instantaneous results when votes were taken, and which also recorded Commissioners' attendance. The

Legal Questions Committee had been considering the office of Moderator in terms both of the Moderator's duties and of the length of time a Moderator should serve. No change in the duration of the office was proposed, but it was recommended that Conveners of Councils use the Moderator as spokesperson wherever possible and that the immediate past Moderator attend the Council of Assembly for the year following and be available to Councils, Departments and Presbyteries. During the report, a request that an Act be prepared which, in what was now an inter-faith society, required that all worship within Church property be limited to the worship of the one God, Father, Son and Holy Spirit, was defeated by 289 votes to 253.

The **Council of Assembly** noted that givings had risen, with congregations providing 98.1 per cent of what they were required to give. Councils were congratulated on absorbing the required cuts in their budgets over the past year, with special mention made of the Social Care Council, which has to work daily with local authorities, whose own budgets are under pressure. The importance of engaging with the new communications channels like Facebook, Twitter and YouTube was being addressed. The review of the place and priority of theological reflection and doctrine in the Church of Scotland was continuing. The **World Mission Council** report focused on Asia, and China in particular. The Assembly celebrated the renewal of the church in China and resolved to build links with that church, not least through the Amity Foundation, represented at the Assembly by Mrs Helen Zhao. There were resolutions also about minorities, violence against women, and Pakistan's blasphemy laws. During the report, as previously, the Assembly was invited to sing a new hymn by one of the Council's Vice Conveners, Iain Cunningham, which was based on the motto of the Amity Foundation, 'love never ends'. In the evening, before the reception of the overseas and ecumenical delegates, the Retiring Moderator, the Very Rev. David Arnott, reviewed his year in office, speaking movingly of his visits to Gaza, Afghanistan, Assisi and China, as well as those made within Scotland.

Monday, 21 May
The previous day had seen the Assembly service in St Giles' Cathedral and the 'Heart and Soul' event in Princes Street Gardens. Following the Sacrament of Holy Communion, and the report of the **Housing and Loan Fund**, the Assembly heard from the **Iona Community Board** of the plans for the 1,450th anniversary of the landing of St Columba on Iona, which was also the 75th anniversary of the founding of the Community. The **Church and Society Council**, as always, occupied the larger part of the day with reports on a wide range of issues which included climate change, neuroethics, sustainable agriculture, action on poverty, Sunday sporting activities, congregational carbon footprints, domestic abuse, human trafficking, sectarianism, homelessness, literacy, nuclear disarmament, and Gaza. On the matter of the campaign for a living wage for all, the Church was asked to ensure that its suppliers were companies paying the living wage and to raise the wages of all its own employees to at least that level (£7.20 per hour) by 2015 or to have a plan in place by then to do so (to give leeway to the Social Care Council, who might otherwise have to close some services and make staff redundant). The retiring Convener, the Rev. Ian Galloway, was warmly thanked for his work over that previous four years. The **Special Commission on the Purposes of Economic Activity**, whose report was given by the Convener, Professor Charles Munn, urged four priorities on the Church, society and government: *reducing inequality*, *ending poverty*, *ensuring sustainability* and *promoting mutuality*. The Assembly discussed and made resolutions in relation to the establishment of credit unions, the tax system (including tax avoidance), the effect of the economy on health (particularly that of the poor), preaching and teaching about money, international aid, the bonus culture, the social impact of business models, and local work with families of young children.

Tuesday, 22 May
The **Church of Scotland Guild** had, over the last three years, given more than £700,000 to its projects. Over the next three years, the projects were to be:
- **Heart for Art**, with CrossReach, looking at the use of art therapy in the care of those with dementia;
- **A Passage from India**, dealing with micro financing for enterprises in Urban Priority Areas;
- **Mary's Meals**, working in Liberia, one of the world's poorest countries, to provide food and resources for schoolchildren;
- **Out of Africa into Malta**, addressing the problem of refugees from several serious situations who are moving to Malta for security;
- **Comfort Rwanda**, helping a project in which people responsible for the genocide are building new homes for their victims;
- **The Julius Project,** a project of the Scottish Churches Housing Action dealing with the support needed for people moving into social housing after a period of homelessness.

The Convener then referred to an additional project to celebrate their 125th year: the **Golden Age Project**, which looks at how we regard older people and make use of their skills for the mission of the Church. The **Panel on Review and Reform** had been looking at the implications of the digital revolution, the possibilities inherent in the consensus system in the Church's decision-making, and the nurturing of new growth in the Church. The **National Youth Assembly** this year had explored *Sexualisation and Commercialisation of Children*, *Mission and Discipleship's working group on Marriage*, and *Priority Areas*. Out of each of these debates came numerous sections of a deliverance. A major internal review had led to the **Mission and Discipleship Council** ending 2011 with a surplus rather than 2010's substantial deficit. The Assembly heard about the expansion of resources over a wide range of work: the 'Church without Walls' project, 'Pray it Forward' and the events organised by the 'Why Believe?' group; the training of elders and other congregational leaders; rural deprivation; new developments in children's work and youth work; resources for worship and prayer, and the continuing work of the Scottish Storytelling Centre; and printed and electronic resources, including *Life and Work* and Saint Andrew Press. The Council also offered a substantial report on marriage, now available on the Church of Scotland's website. During the course of the report, Ronald Blakey was thanked for his distinguished service as Editor of the *Church of Scotland Year Book*.

Wednesday, 23 May
The morning began with the visit of the **Archbishop of Canterbury**, who was a Guest of the Lord High Commissioner. Dr Williams gave an address, which was warmly received (see the introduction to this section). As well as the report of the **Committee on Ecumenical Relations** itself, in which it was acknowledged that existing patterns of ecumenical co-operation were being tested and new possibilities were being explored, the Joint Report of the Committee on Ecumenical Relations and the Ministries Council on **Declaratory Article III** called for an audit of ecumenical work in the Presbyteries and invited other denominations to do the same. The report was the result of the Assembly's request to explore the idea of territorial ministry as one that could be shared with other denominations, and such audits would be the first step in testing the feasibility of the idea. The **Ministries Council** announced a new 'Go For It' fund, which amalgamated the former Parish Development, Emerging Ministries and Priority Areas Staffing funds. The new fund would be able to give grants totalling close to £1 million in the next year. The Council were seeking new perspectives on the Diaconate, reviewing the Enquiry and Assessment scheme for potential ministers, continuing with strategies for the affirmation of the parish ministry, re-examining the provision of manses, and continuing

to work on the development of the Ordained Local Ministry. The Assembly agreed, while retaining a compulsory **retirement age for ministers**, to raise this to 75 years, although it was expected that the majority of ministers would choose to retire at the state pension age (and the Council would offer its full support to them in doing so). Any eligible minister under the age of 75, whether currently in post or already retired, would be able to apply for induction to a charge. Permission would no longer need to be sought to remain in post beyond 65. However, Presbyteries would retain the right to effect adjustments already agreed to take place at a time when the minister(s) concerned would previously have been expected to retire.

Thursday, 24 May
During the **Committee on Chaplains to HM Forces**, the Assembly reaffirmed the support of the Church for the Chaplains to the forces and their families. Many more chaplains were needed, particularly in the Navy and the Air Force. The desire of the forces to have chaplains is as strong now as it ever was. The Assembly was addressed by Lieutenant General Andrew Graham, who is Colonel of the Royal Regiment of Scotland. The **Pension Trustees** reported that they were still in the position in which ministers whose service was pre-1997 were unlikely to receive any increase in their pensions in the near future. Pension increases for service between 1997 and 2005 and post-2005, however, are set by law. The **Social Care Council** reported that it had over the past year moved close to a break-even budget. Despite budgetary pressures, most of the Council's units had improved their gradings. In partnership with other bodies, new provision had been made in the fields of addiction and the care of the elderly, and for those in early years. A major priority is to provide opportunities for local members and congregations to partner the Council in initiatives; an example was a new parenting scheme based in a district of Glasgow, which aims to improve the health, early literacy and language skills of vulnerable children, particularly in families affected by poverty or drug abuse. The Council was to convene a working group to develop a 'tool kit' for churches who wish to develop local social-care initiatives. Volunteer involvement was encouraged.

Friday, 25 May
The **General Trustees** reported that, while the zero-rated VAT repairs provision for listed buildings had been withdrawn, a listed places-of-worship VAT grant scheme would be expanded from 2012 to enable congregations to recover the whole amount of VAT incurred on both repairs and alterations. The Trustees again emphasised that all manses should be maintained to an appropriate standard. An Overture from the Presbytery of Dumfries and Kirkcudbright asked the General Trustees to have the insurance of church buildings spread over the whole Church, each congregation paying according to its ability. In response, it was pointed out that there is no reason why a Presbytery should not have a fund to assist congregations. However, this would be treated by the Trustees as an ongoing issue. The main issue explored in the report of the **Safeguarding Committee** was the government's new Protection of Vulnerable Groups scheme, which meant an increase in the number of volunteers. Presbyteries and Kirk Sessions were instructed to ensure that all formally recruited Congregational Pastoral Care Visiting Group members who support 'protected adults' had the opportunity to attend safeguarding training. During this report, the Assembly heard from Mr Iain Livingstone, Assistant Chief Constable of the Lothian and Borders Police Force. Matters aired during the report of the **Central Services Committee** included a pay award for the staff at 121 George Street and the closure of the canteen. The Convener regretted that, in the case of the latter, staff had not been properly consulted but that the Committee were responding to this situation.

After addresses from the Moderator and Lord Selkirk, the Assembly took its leave of the Lord High Commissioner and resolved to meet again on Saturday, 18 May 2013.

Roland Mitton Stained Glass

Tel: 01738 812810 • Email: rm.stainglass@virgin.net
The Garden House • Old Main Street
Forgandenny PH2 9EL

www.rolandmitton.co.uk

SECTION 5

Presbytery Lists

See overleaf for an explanation of the two parts of each list; a Key to Abbreviations; and a list of the Presbyteries in their numerical order.

SECTION 5 – PRESBYTERY LISTS

In each Presbytery list, the congregations are listed in alphabetical order. In a linked charge, the names appear under the first named congregation. Under the name of the congregation will be found the name of the minister and, where applicable, that of an associate minister, auxiliary minister and member of the Diaconate. The years indicated after a minister's name in the congregational section of each Presbytery list are the year of ordination (column 1) and the year of current appointment (column 2). Where only one date is given, it is both the year of ordination and the year of appointment.

In the second part of each Presbytery list, those named are listed alphabetically. The first date is the year of ordination, and the following date is the year of appointment or retirement. If the person concerned is retired, then the appointment last held will be shown in brackets.

KEY TO ABBREVIATIONS

(E)   Indicates a Church Extension charge. New Charge Developments are separately indicated.
(GD)   Indicates a charge where it is desirable that the minister should have a knowledge of Gaelic.
(GE)   Indicates a charge where public worship must be regularly conducted in Gaelic.
(H)   Indicates that a Hearing Aid Loop system has been installed. In Linked charges, the (H) is placed beside the appropriate building as far as possible.
(L)   Indicates that a Chair Lift has been installed.
(T)   Indicates that the minister has been appointed on the basis of Terminable Tenure.

PRESBYTERY NUMBERS

1	Edinburgh	18	Dumbarton
2	West Lothian	19	Argyll
3	Lothian	20	
4	Melrose and Peebles	21	
5	Duns	22	Falkirk
6	Jedburgh	23	Stirling
7	Annandale and Eskdale	24	Dunfermline
8	Dumfries and Kirkcudbright	25	Kirkcaldy
9	Wigtown and Stranraer	26	St Andrews
10	Ayr	27	Dunkeld and Meigle
11	Irvine and Kilmarnock	28	Perth
12	Ardrossan	29	Dundee
13	Lanark	30	Angus
14	Greenock and Paisley	31	Aberdeen
15	Glasgow	32	Kincardine and Deeside
16		33	Gordon
17	Hamilton	34	Buchan
35	Moray		
36	Abernethy		
37	Inverness		
38	Lochaber		
39	Ross		
40	Sutherland		
41	Caithness		
42	Lochcarron – Skye		
43	Uist		
44	Lewis		
45	Orkney		
46	Shetland		
47	England		
48	Europe		
49	Jerusalem		

(1) EDINBURGH

The Presbytery meets:
- at Palmerston Place Church, Edinburgh, on 6 November and 11 December 2012, and on 5 February, 12 March, 30 April and 18 June 2013;
- in the church of the Moderator on 11 September 2012.

	Clerk:	REV. GEORGE J. WHYTE BSc BD DMin		10/1 Palmerston Place, Edinburgh EH12 5AA [E-mail: edinburgh@cofscotland.org.uk]	0131-225 9137
1	**Edinburgh: Albany Deaf Church of Edinburgh (H) (0131-444 2054)**				
	Alistair F. Kelly BL (Locum)	1961		19 Avon Place, Edinburgh EH4 6RE [E-mail: alistair_kelly@hotmail.co.uk]	0131-317 9877
2	**Edinburgh: Balerno (H)**				
	Louise J. Duncan (Mrs) BD	2005	2010	3 Johnsburn Road, Balerno EH14 7DN [E-mail: bpc-minister@btconnect.com]	0131-449 3830
3	**Edinburgh: Barclay Viewforth (0131-229 6810) (E-mail: admin@barclaychurch.org.uk)**				
	Samuel A.R. Torrens BD	1995	2005	113 Meadowspot, Edinburgh EH10 5UY [E-mail: minister@barclayviewforth.org.uk]	0131-478 2376
	Howard Espie (Mission Facilitator and Enabler)	2011		Barclay Viewforth Parish Church, 1 Barclay Place, Edinburgh EH10 4HW	0131-229 6810
4	**Edinburgh: Blackhall St Columba's (0131-332 4431) (E-mail: secretary@blackhallstcolumba.org.uk)**				
	Alexander B. Douglas BD	1979	1991	5 Blinkbonny Crescent, Edinburgh EH4 3NB [E-mail: alexandjill@douglas.net]	0131-343 3708
5	**Edinburgh: Bristo Memorial Craigmillar**				
	James Patterson BSc BD	2003	2006	72 Blackchapel Close, Edinburgh EH15 3SL [E-mail: patterson@jimandmegan.force9.co.uk]	0131-657 3266
6	**Edinburgh: Broughton St Mary's (H) (0131-556 4786)**				
	Vacant			103 East Claremont Street, Edinburgh EH7 4JA	0131-556 7313
7	**Edinburgh: Canongate (H)**				
	Neil N. Gardner MA BD	1991	2006	The Manse of Canongate, Edinburgh EH8 8BR [E-mail: nng22@btinternet.com]	0131-556 3515

8   **Edinburgh: Carrick Knowe (H) (0131-334 1505) (E-mail: ckchurch@talktalk.net)**
Fiona M. Mathieson (Mrs)   1988   2001   21 Traquair Park West, Edinburgh EH12 7AN   0131-334 9774
BEd BD PGCommEd MTh   [E-mail: fiona.mathieson@ukgateway.net]

9   **Edinburgh: Colinton (H) (0131-441 2232) (E-mail: church.office@colinton-parish.com)**
Rolf H. Billes BD   1996   2009   The Manse, Colinton, Edinburgh EH13 0JR   0131-466 8384
                                                            [E-mail: rolf.billes@colinton-parish.com]
Gayle J.A. Taylor (Mrs) MA BD (Assoc)   1999   2009   Colinton Parish Church, Dell Road, Edinburgh EH13 0JR   0131-441 2232
                                                            [E-mail: gayle.taylor@colinton-parish.com]

10 **Edinburgh: Colinton Mains (H)**
Vacant   17 Swanston Green, Edinburgh EH10 7EW   0131-445 3451

11 **Edinburgh: Corstorphine Craigsbank (H) (0131-334 6365)**
Stewart M. McPherson BD CertMin   1991   2003   17 Craigs Bank, Edinburgh EH12 8HD   0131-467 6826
                                                            [E-mail: smcpherson@blueyonder.co.uk]   07814 901429 (Mbl)
Stephen Manners MA BD (Assoc)   1989   2009   124 Fernieside Crescent, Edinburgh EH17 7DH   0131-620 0589
                                                            [E-mail: sk.manners@blueyonder.co.uk]   07747 821458 (Mbl)

12 **Edinburgh: Corstorphine Old (H) (0131-334 7864) (E-mail: corold@aol.com)**
Moira McDonald MA BD   1997   2005   23 Manse Road, Edinburgh EH12 7SW   0131-476 5893
                                                            [E-mail: moira-mc@live.co.uk]

13 **Edinburgh: Corstorphine St Anne's (0131-316 4740) (E-mail: office@stannes.corstorphine.org.uk)**
MaryAnn R. Rennie (Mrs) BD MTh   1998   2002   23 Belgrave Road, Edinburgh EH12 6NG   0131-334 3188
                                                            [E-mail: maryann.r.rennie@gmail.com]

14 **Edinburgh: Corstorphine St Ninian's (H) (0131-539 6204) (E-mail: office@st-ninians.co.uk)**
Alexander T. Stewart MA BD FSAScot   1975   1995   17 Templeland Road, Edinburgh EH12 8RZ   0131-334 2978
                                                            [E-mail: alextstewart@blueyonder.co.uk]

15 **Edinburgh: Craigentinny St Christopher's (0131-258 2759)**
Caroline R. Lockerbie BA MDiv DMin   2007   61 Milton Crescent, Edinburgh EH15 3PQ   0131-258 2759
                                                            [E-mail: carolinelockerbie@blueyonder.co.uk]

16 **Edinburgh: Craiglockhart (H) (E-mail: office@craiglockhartchurch.org.uk)**
Gordon Kennedy BSc BD MTh   1993   2012   75A Woodfield Avenue, Edinburgh EH13 0QP
                                                            [E-mail: gordonkennedy15@gmail.com]

17	**Edinburgh: Craigmillar Park (H) (0131-667 5862) (E-mail: cpkirk@btinternet.com)**			
	John C.C. Urquhart MA MA BD	2010	14 Hallhead Road, Edinburgh EH16 5QJ	0131-667 1623
			[E-mail: jccurquhart@gmail.com]	
18	**Edinburgh: Cramond (H) (E-mail: cramond.kirk@blueyonder.co.uk)**			
	G. Russell Barr BA BD MTh DMin	1979 1993	Manse of Cramond, Edinburgh EH4 6NS	0131-336 2036
			[E-mail: rev.r.barr@blueyonder.co.uk]	
19	**Edinburgh: Currie (H) (0131-451 5141) (E-mail: currie_kirk@btconnect.com)**			
	Lezley J. Stewart BD ThM MTh	2000 2008	43 Lanark Road West, Currie EH14 5JX	0131-449 4719
			[E-mail: lezleystewart@btinternet.com]	
	Margaret Gordon (Mrs) DCS		92 Lanark Road West, Currie EH14 5LA	0131-449 2554
20	**Edinburgh: Dalmeny linked with Edinburgh: Queensferry**			
	David C. Cameron BD CertMin	1993 2009	1 Station Road, South Queensferry EH30 9HY	0131-331 1100
			[E-mail: minister@qpcweb.org]	
21	**Edinburgh: Davidson's Mains (H) (0131-312 6282) (E-mail: life@dmainschurch.plus.com)**			
	Jeremy R.H. Middleton LLB BD	1981 1988	1 Hillpark Terrace, Edinburgh EH4 7SX	0131-336 3078
			[E-mail: life@dmainschurch.plus.com]	
22	**Edinburgh: Dean (H)**			
	Mark M. Foster BSc BD	1998	1 Ravelston Terrace, Edinburgh EH4 3EF	0131-332 5736
			[E-mail: markmfoster@mac.com]	
23	**Edinburgh: Drylaw (0131-343 6643)**			
	Patricia Watson (Mrs) BD	2005	15 House o' Hill Gardens, Edinburgh EH4 2AR	0131-343 1441
			[E-mail: p.g.watson@blueyonder.co.uk]	07969 942627 (Mbl)
24	**Edinburgh: Duddingston (H) (E-mail: dodinskirk@aol.com)**			
	James A.P. Jack BSc BArch BD DMin RIBA ARIAS	1989 2001	Manse of Duddingston, Old Church Lane, Edinburgh EH15 3PX	0131-661 4240
			[E-mail: jamesjack2829@aol.com]	
25	**Edinburgh: Fairmilehead (H) (0131-445 2374) (E-mail: fairmilehead.p.c@btconnect.com)**			
	John R. Munro BD	1976 1992	6 Braid Crescent, Edinburgh EH10 6AU	0131-446 9363
			[E-mail: revjohnmunro@hotmail.com]	
	Hayley O'Connor BS MDiv (Assist)	2009	19 Caiystane Terrace, Edinburgh EH10 6SR	0131-629 1610
			[E-mail: oconnorhe@gmail.com]	

26 Edinburgh: Gorgie Dalry (H) (0131-337 7936)
Peter I. Barber MA BD 1984 90 Myreside Road, Edinburgh EH10 5BZ
[E-mail: pjbarber@toucansurf.com] 0131-337 2284

27 Edinburgh: Granton (H) (0131-552 3033)
Norman A. Smith MA BD 1997 2005 8 Wardie Crescent, Edinburgh EH5 1AG
[E-mail: norm@familysmith.biz] 0131-551 2159

28 Edinburgh: Greenbank (H) (0131-447 9669) (E-mail: greenbankchurch@btconnect.com; Website: www.greenbankchurch.org)
Alison I. Swindells (Mrs) LLB BD 1998 2007 112 Greenbank Crescent, Edinburgh EH10 5SZ
[E-mail: alisonswindells@blueyonder.co.uk] 0131-447 4032
William H. Stone BA MDiv ThM 2012 19 Caivstane Terrace, Edinburgh EH10 6SR
(Youth Minister) [E-mail: billstoneiii@gmail.com] 0131-629 1610
  07883 815598 (Mbl)

29 Edinburgh: Greenside (H) (0131-556 5588)
Vacant 80 Pilrig Street, Edinburgh EH6 5AS 0131-554 3277 (Tel/Fax)

30 Edinburgh: Greyfriars Tolbooth and Highland Kirk (GE) (H) (0131-225 1900) (E-mail: enquiries@greyfriarskirk.com)
Richard E. Frazer BA BD DMin 1986 2003 12 Tantallon Place, Edinburgh EH9 1NZ
[E-mail: minister@greyfriarskirk.com] 0131-667 6610

31 Edinburgh: High (St Giles') (0131-225 4363) (E-mail: info@stgilescathedral.org.uk)
Gilleasbuig Macmillan 1969 1973 St Giles' Cathedral, Edinburgh EH1 1RE
CVO MA BD Drhc DD [E-mail: minister@stgilescathedral.org.uk] 0131-225 4363
Helen J.R. Alexander BD DipSW (Assist) 1981 2012 7 Polwarth Place, Edinburgh EH11 1LG
[E-mail: st_giles_cathedral@btconnect.com] 0131-346 0685

32 Edinburgh: Holyrood Abbey (H) (0131-661 6002)
Philip R. Hair BD 1980 1998 100 Willowbrae Avenue, Edinburgh EH8 7HU
[E-mail: phil@holyroodabbey.f2s.com] 0131-652 0640

33 Edinburgh: Holy Trinity (H) (0131-442 3304)
Kenneth S. Borthwick MA BD 1983 2005 16 Thorburn Road, Edinburgh EH13 0BQ
[E-mail: kennysamuel@aol.com] 0131-441 1403
Ian MacDonald (Assoc) 2005 12 Sighthill Crescent, Edinburgh EH11 4QE
[E-mail: ianafrica@hotmail.com] 0131-453 6279
Oliver M.H. Clegg BD (Youth Minister) 2003 256/5 Lanark Road, Edinburgh EH14 2LR
[E-mail: ollieclegg@btinternet.com] 0131-443 0825

34 Edinburgh: Inverleith St Serf's (H)
Joanne G. Finlay (Mrs)
DipTMus BD AdvDipCouns   1996   2012   24 East Lillypot, Edinburgh EH5 3BH   0131-552 3874
[E-mail: joanne.finlay196@btinternet.com]
(New charge formed by the union of Edinburgh: Inverleith and Edinburgh: Leith St Serf's)

35 Edinburgh: Juniper Green (H)
James S. Dewar MA BD   1983   2000   476 Lanark Road, Juniper Green, Edinburgh EH14 5BQ   0131-453 3494
[E-mail: jim.dewar@blueyonder.co.uk]

36 Edinburgh: Kaimes Lockhart Memorial linked with Edinburgh: Liberton
John N. Young MA BD PhD   1996   7 Kirk Park, Edinburgh EH16 6HZ   0131-664 3067
[E-mail: LLLjyoung@btinternet.com]
David Rankin (Assoc)   2009   Office: 76 Lasswade Road, Edinburgh EH16 6SF   07827 815599 (Mbl)
[E-mail: davebobrankin@gmail.com]

37 Edinburgh: Kirkliston
Margaret R. Lane (Mrs) BA BD MTh   2009   43 Main Street, Kirkliston EH29 9AF   0131-333 3298
[E-mail: margaretlane@btinternet.com]   07795 481441 (Mbl)

38 Edinburgh: Kirk o' Field (T) (H)
Ian D. Maxwell MA BD PhD   1977   1996   31 Hatton Place, Edinburgh EH9 1UA   0131-667 7954
[E-mail: i.d.maxwell@quista.net]

39 Edinburgh: Leith North (H) (0131-553 7378) (E-mail: nlpc-office@btinternet.com)
Alexander T. McAspurren BD MTh   2002   2011   6 Craighall Gardens, Edinburgh EH6 4RJ   0131-551 5252
[E-mail: alexander.mcaspurren@btinternet.com]

40 Edinburgh: Leith St Andrew's (H)
Vacant   30 Lochend Road, Edinburgh EH6 8BS   0131-554 7695

41 Edinburgh: Leith South (H) (0131-554 2578) (E-mail: slpc@dial.pipex.com)
John S. (Iain) May   2012   37 Claremont Road, Edinburgh EH6 7NN   0131-554 3062
[E-mail: johnsmay@blueyonder.co.uk]

42 Edinburgh: Leith Wardie (H) (0131-551 3847) (E-mail: churchoffice@wardie.org.uk)
Brian C. Hilsley LLB BD   1990   35 Lomond Road, Edinburgh EH5 3JN   0131-552 3328
[E-mail: minister@wardie.org.uk]

43 Edinburgh: Liberton (H) See Edinburgh: Kaimes Lockhart Memorial

44 Edinburgh: Liberton Northfield (H) (0131-551 3847)
John M. McPake LTh 2000
9 Claverhouse Drive, Edinburgh EH16 6BR 0131-658 1754
[E-mail: john_mcpake9@yahoo.co.uk]

45 Edinburgh: London Road (H) (0131-661 1149)
Sigrid Marten 1997 2006
26 Inchview Terrace, Edinburgh EH7 6TQ 0131-669 5311
[E-mail: minister@londonroadchurch.com]

46 Edinburgh: Marchmont St Giles' (H) (0131-447 4359)
Karen K. Campbell BD MTh 1997 2002
2 Trotter Haugh, Edinburgh EH9 2GZ 0131-447 2834
[E-mail: karen@marchmontstgiles.org.uk]

47 Edinburgh: Mayfield Salisbury (0131-667 1522)
Scott S. McKenna BA BD MTh 1994 2000
26 Seton Place, Edinburgh EH9 2JT 0131-667 1286
[E-mail: ScottSMcKenna@aol.com]

48 Edinburgh: Morningside (H) (0131-447 6745) (E-mail: office@morningsideparishchurch.org.uk)
Derek Browning MA BD DMin 1987 2001
20 Braidburn Crescent, Edinburgh EH10 6EN 0131-447 1617
[E-mail: minister@morningsideparishchurch.org.uk]

49 Edinburgh: Morningside United (H) (0131-447 3152)
John R. Smith MA BD 1973 1998
1 Midmar Avenue, Edinburgh EH10 6BS 0131-447 8724
[E-mail: office@jrsmith.eu]

50 Edinburgh: Muirhouse St Andrew's (E) (Website: www.stampc.co.uk)
Linda J. Dunbar BSc BA BD PhD FRHS 2000 2011
(Full-time Locum)
35 Silverknowes Road, Edinburgh EH4 5LL 0131-312 7773
[E-mail: lindatheleither@googlemail.com] 07801 969995 (Mbl)

51 Edinburgh: Murrayfield (H) (0131-337 1091) (E-mail: mpchurch@btconnect.com)
William D. Brown BD CQSW 1987 2001
45 Murrayfield Gardens, Edinburgh EH12 6DH 0131-337 5431
[E-mail: wdb@talktalk.net]

52 Edinburgh: Newhaven (H)
Peter Bluett 2007
158 Granton Road, Edinburgh EH5 3RF 0131-476 5212
[E-mail: peterbluett@sky.com]

53   Edinburgh: New Restalrig (H) (0131-661 5676)
David L. Court BSc BD   1989   19 Abercorn Road, Edinburgh EH8 7DP   0131-661 4045
[E-mail: david@dlc.org.uk]

54   Edinburgh: Old Kirk (H) (0131-332 4354) (E-mail: minister.oldkirk@btinternet.com)
Tony McLean-Foreman   1987   24 Pennywell Road, Edinburgh EH4 4HD   0131-332 4354
[E-mail: tony@foreman.org.uk]

55   Edinburgh: Palmerston Place (H) (0131-220 1690) (E-mail: admin@palmerstonplacechurch.com)
Colin A.M. Sinclair BA BD   1981   30B Cluny Gardens, Edinburgh EH10 6BJ   0131-447 9598
[E-mail: colins.ppc@virgin.net]   0131-225 3312 (Fax)

56   Edinburgh: Pilrig St Paul's (0131-553 1876)
John M. Tait BSc BD   1985   78 Pilrig Street, Edinburgh EH6 5AS   0131-554 1842
[E-mail: j.m.tait@blueyonder.co.uk]

57   Edinburgh: Polwarth (H) (0131-346 2711) (E-mail: polwarthchurch@tiscali.co.uk)
Jack Holt BSc BD MTh   1985   88 Craiglockhart Road, Edinburgh EH14 1EP   0131-441 6105
[E-mail: jack9holt@gmail.com]

58   Edinburgh: Portobello Old (H)
Andrew R.M. Patterson MA BD   1985   6 Hamilton Terrace, Edinburgh EH15 1NB   0131-657 5545
[E-mail: apatt@tiscali.co.uk]

59   Edinburgh: Portobello St James' (H)
Peter Webster BD   1977   34 Brighton Place, Edinburgh EH15 1LT   0131-669 1767
[E-mail: peterwebster101@hotmail.com]

60   Edinburgh: Portobello St Philip's Joppa (H) (0131-669 3641)
Stewart G. Weaver BA BD PhD   2003   6 St Mary's Place, Edinburgh EH15 2QF   0131-669 2410
[E-mail: stewartweaver@btinternet.com]

61   Edinburgh: Priestfield (H) (0131-667 5644)
Jared W. Hay BA MTh DipMin DMin   1987   13 Lady Road, Edinburgh EH16 5PA   0131-468 1254
[E-mail: jared.hay@blueyonder.co.uk]

62   Edinburgh: Queensferry (H) See Edinburgh: Dalmeny

63 Edinburgh: Ratho
Ian J. Wells BD — 1999 — 2 Freelands Road, Ratho, Newbridge EH28 8NP [E-mail: ianjwells@btinternet.com] — 0131-333 1346

64 Edinburgh: Reid Memorial (H) (0131-662 1203) (E-mail: reid.memorial@btinternet.com)
Brian M. Embleton BD — 1976 — 1985 — 20 Wilton Road, Edinburgh EH16 5NX [E-mail: brianembleton@btinternet.com] — 0131-667 3981

65 Edinburgh: Richmond Craigmillar (H) (0131-661 6561)
Elizabeth M. Henderson (Mrs) MA BD MTh — 1985 — 1997 — Manse of Duddingston, Old Church Lane, Edinburgh EH15 3PX [E-mail: lizhende@tiscali.co.uk] — 0131-661 4240

66 Edinburgh: St Andrew's and St George's West (H) (0131-225 3847) (E-mail: info@standrewsandstgeorges.org.uk)
Ian Y. Gilmour BD — 1985 — 2011 — 25 Comely Bank, Edinburgh EH4 1AJ [E-mail: ianyg2@gmail.com] — 0131-332 5848

67 Edinburgh: St Andrew's Clermiston
Alistair H. Keil BD DipMin — 1989 — 87 Drum Brae South, Edinburgh EH12 8TD [E-mail: ahkeil@blueyonder.co.uk] — 0131-339 4149

68 Edinburgh: St Catherine's Argyle (H) (0131-667 7220)
Robin S. Sydserff PhD — 5 Palmerston Road, Edinburgh EH9 1TL [E-mail: robin@stcaths.org] — 0131-667 9344

69 Edinburgh: St Cuthbert's (H) (0131-229 1142) (E-mail: office@stcuthberts.net)
David W. Denniston BD DipMin — 1981 — 2008 — 34A Murrayfield Road, Edinburgh EH12 6ER [E-mail: denniston.david@googlemail.com] — 0131-337 6637 / 07903 926727 (Mbl)

70 Edinburgh: St David's Broomhouse (H) (0131-443 9851)
Robert A. Mackenzie LLB BD — 1993 — 2005 — 33 Traquair Park West, Edinburgh EH12 7AN [E-mail: rob.anne@blueyonder.co.uk] — 0131-334 1730
Liz Crocker (Mrs) DipComEd DCS — 77C Craigcrook Road, Edinburgh EH4 3PH — 0131-332 0227

71 Edinburgh: St John's Oxgangs
Vacant — 2 Caiystane Terrace, Edinburgh EH10 6SR — 0131-445 1688

72 Edinburgh: St Margaret's (H) (0131-554 7400) (E-mail: stm.parish@virgin.net)
Carol H.M. Ford DSD RSAMD BD   2003   43 Moira Terrace, Edinburgh EH7 6TD
                                                        [E-mail: revcford@btinternet.com]   0131-669 7329
Pauline Rycroft-Sadi (Mrs) DCS   6 Ashville Terrace, Edinburgh EH6 8DD
                                                        [E-mail: prycroft-sadi@blueyonder.co.uk]   0131-554 6564

73 Edinburgh: St Martin's
Russel Moffat BD MTh PhD   1986 2008   5 Duddingston Crescent, Edinburgh EH15 3AS
                                                        [E-mail: rbmoffat@tiscali.co.uk]   0131-657 9894

74 Edinburgh: St Michael's (H) (E-mail: office@stmichaels-kirk.co.uk)
James D. Aitken BD   2002 2005   9 Merchiston Gardens, Edinburgh EH10 5DD
                                                        [E-mail: james.aitken2@btinternet.com]   0131-346 1970

75 Edinburgh: St Nicholas' Sighthill
Alan R. Cobain BD   2000 2008   122 Sighthill Loan, Edinburgh EH11 4NT
                                                        [E-mail: erinbro@hotmail.co.uk]   0131-442 2510

76 Edinburgh: St Stephen's Comely Bank (0131-315 4616)
Jonathan de Groot BD MTh CPS   2007   8 Blinkbonny Crescent, Edinburgh EH4 3NB
                                                        [E-mail: jonathan@comelybankchurch.com]   0131-332 3364

77 Edinburgh: Slateford Longstone
Michael W. Frew BSc BD   1978 2005   50 Kingsknowe Road South, Edinburgh EH14 2JW
                                                        [E-mail: minister@slatefordlongstone.org.uk] 0131-466 5308

78 Edinburgh: Stenhouse St Aidan's
Keith Edwin Graham MA PGDip BD   2008   65 Balgreen Road, Edinburgh EH12 5UA
                                                        [E-mail: minister@ssapc.org.uk]   0131-337 7711

79 Edinburgh: Stockbridge (H) (0131-552 8738) (E-mail: stockbridgechurch@btconnect.com)
Anne T. Logan (Mrs) MA BD MTh DMin   1981 1993   19 Eildon Street, Edinburgh EH3 5JU
                                                        [E-mail: annetlogan@blueyonder.co.uk]   0131-557 6052

80 Edinburgh: The Tron Kirk (Gilmerton and Moredun)
Cameron Mackenzie BD   1997 2010   467 Gilmerton Road, Edinburgh EH17 7JG
                                                        [E-mail: mackenz550@aol.com]   0131-664 7538

Abernethy, William LTh   1979 1993   (Glenrothes: St Margaret's)   120/1 Willowbrae Road, Edinburgh EH8 7HW   0131-661 0390
Aitken, Alexander R. MA   1965 1997   (Newhaven)   36 King's Meadow, Edinburgh EH16 5JW   0131-667 1404

Name			Position	Address	Tel
Aitken, Ewan R. BA BD	1992	2002	Church and Society Council	159 Restalrig Avenue, Edinburgh EH7 6PJ	0131-467 1660
Alexander, Ian W. BA BD STM	1990	2010	General Secretary: World Mission Council	World Mission Council, 121 George Street, Edinburgh EH2 4YN [E-mail: iwalexander@gmail.com]	0131-225 5722
Anderson, Andrew F. MA BD	1981	2011	(Edinburgh: Greenside)	58 Reliance Way, Oxford OX4 2FG [E-mail: andrew@pilrig.fsnet.co.uk]	01865 778397
Anderson, Robert S. BD	1988	1997	(Scottish Churches World Exchange)		
Armitage, William L. BSc BD	1976	2006	(Edinburgh: London Road)	Flat 7, 4 Papermill Wynd, Edinburgh EH7 4GJ [E-mail: bill@billarm.plus.com]	0131-558 8534
Baird, Kenneth S. MSc PhD BD MIMarEST				3 Maule Terrace, Gullane EH31 2DB	01620 843347
Barrington, Charles W.H. MA BD	1998	2009	(Edinburgh: Leith North)	502 Lanark Road, Edinburgh EH14 5DH	0131-453 4826
Beckett, David M. BA BD	1997	2007	(Associate: Edinburgh: Balerno)	1F1, 31 Sciennes Road, Edinburgh EH9 1NT [E-mail: davidbeckett3@aol.com]	0131-667 2672
Blakey, Ronald S. MA BD MTh	1964	2002	(Edinburgh: Greyfriars, Tolbooth and Highland Kirk)	5 Moss Side Road, Biggar ML12 6GF	01899 229226
Booth, Jennifer (Mrs) BD	1962	2000	(The Council of Assembly)	39 Lilyhill Terrace, Edinburgh EH8 7DR	0131-661 3813
Boyd, Kenneth M. MA BD PhD FRCPE	1996	2004	(Associate: Leith South)	1 Doune Terrace, Edinburgh EH3 6DY	0131-225 6485
Brady, Ian D. BSc ARCST BD	1970	1996	University of Edinburgh: Medical Ethics	28 Frankfield Crescent, Dalgety Bay, Dunfermline KY11 9LW [E-mail: pidb@dbay28.fsnet.co.uk]	01383 825104
Brown, William D. MA	1967	2001	(Edinburgh: Corstorphine Old)	9/3 Craigend Park, Edinburgh EH16 5XY [E-mail: wdbrown@surefish.co.uk]	0131-672 2936
Cameron, G. Gordon MA BD STM	1963	1989	(Wishaw: Thornlie)	4 Ladywell Grove, Clackmannan FK10 4JQ	01259 723769
Cameron, John W.M. MA BD	1957	1997	(Juniper Green)	10 Plewlands Gardens, Edinburgh EH10 5JP	0131-447 1277
Chalmers, Murray MA	1957	1996	(Liberton)	8 Easter Warriston, Edinburgh EH7 4QX	0131-552 4211
Clinkenbeard, William W. BSc BD STM	1965	2006	(Hospital Chaplain)	3/17 Western Harbour Breakwater, Edinburgh EH6 6PA [E-mail: bjclinks@compuserve.com]	
Cook, John MA BD	1966	2000	(Edinburgh: Carrick Knowe)	26 Silverknowes Court, Edinburgh EH4 5NR	0131-312 8447
Cook, John Weir MA BD	1967	2005	(Edinburgh: Leith St Andrew's)	74 Pinkie Road, Musselburgh EH21 7QT [E-mail: johnweircook@gmail.com]	0131-653 0992
Curran, Elizabeth M. (Miss) BD	1962	2002	(Edinburgh: Portobello St Philip's Joppa)	27 Captain's Road, Edinburgh EH17 8HR [E-mail: ecurran8@aol.com]	0131-664 1358
Cuthell, Tom C. MA BD MTh	1995	2008	(Aberlour)	Flat 10, 2 Kingsburgh Crescent, Waterfront, Edinburgh EH5 1JS	0131-476 3864
Davidson, D. Hugh MA	1965	2007	(Edinburgh: St Cuthbert's)	Flat 1/2, 22 Summerside Place, Edinburgh EH6 4NZ [E-mail: dhd39@btinternet.com]	0131-554 8420
Davidson, Ian M.P. MBE MA BD	1965	2009	(Edinburgh: Inverleith)	13/8 Craigend Park, Edinburgh EH16 5XX	0131-664 0074
Dawson, Michael S. BTech BD	1957	1994	(Stirling: Allan Park South with Church of the Holy Rude)	9 The Broich, Alva FK12 5NR [E-mail: mixpen.dawson@btinternet.com]	01259 769309
Denniston, Jane M. MA BD	1979	2005	(Associate: Edinburgh: Holy Trinity)	34A Murrayfield Road, Edinburgh EH12 6ER	0131-337 6637
Dilbey, Mary D. (Miss) BD	2002		Ministries Council	41 Bonaly Rise, Edinburgh EH13 0QU	0131-441 9092
Donald, Alistair P. MA PhD BD	1997	2002	(West Kirk of Calder)		
	1999	2009	Chaplain: Heriot-Watt University	The Chaplaincy, Heriot-Watt University, Edinburgh EH14 4AS [E-mail: a.p.donald@hw.ac.uk]	0131-451 4508

Name	Year	Year	Role / Position	Address	Telephone
Dougall, Elspeth G. (Mrs) MA BD	1989	2001	(Edinburgh: Marchmont St Giles')	60B Craigmillar Park, Edinburgh EH16 5PU	0131-668 1342
Douglas, Colin R. MA BD STM	1969	2007	(Livingston Ecumenical Parish)	34 West Pilton Gardens, Edinburgh EH4 4EQ [E-mail: colinrdouglas@btinternet.com]	0131-551 3808
Doyle, Ian B. MA BD PhD	1946	1991	(Department of National Mission)	21 Lygon Road, Edinburgh EH16 5QD	0131-667 2697
Drummond, Rhoda (Miss) DCS			(Deaconess)	Flat K, 23 Grange Loan, Edinburgh EH9 2ER	0131-668 3631
Dunn, W. Iain C. DA LTh	1983	1998	(Pilrig and Dalmeny Street)	10 Fox Covert Avenue, Edinburgh EH12 6UQ	0131-334 1665
Elliott, Gavin J. MA BD	1976	2004	Ministries Council	c/o 121 George Street, Edinburgh EH2 4YN	0131-225 5722
Embleton, Sara R. (Mrs) BA BD MTh	1987	2010	(Edinburgh: Leith St Serf's)	20 Wilton Road, Edinburgh EH16 5NX [E-mail: sara.embleton@blueyonder.co.uk]	0131-478 1624
Evans, Mark BSc RGN DCS	2006		Chaplain: Queen Margaret Hospital, Dunfermline	13 Easter Drylaw Drive, Edinburgh EH4 2QA [E-mail: MarkEvansDCS@aol.com]	(Home) 0131-343 3089 (Office) 01383 674136
Farquharson, Gordon MA BD DipEd	1998	2007	(Stonehaven: Dunnottar)	26 Learmonth Court, Edinburgh EH4 1PB [E-mail: gfarqu@talktalk.net]	0131-343 1047
Faulds, Norman L. MA BD FSAScot	1968	2000	(Aberlady with Gullane)	10 West Fenton Court, West Fenton, North Berwick EH39 5AE	01620 842331
Fergusson, David A.S. MA BD DPhil FRSE	1984	2000	University of Edinburgh	23 Riselaw Crescent, Edinburgh EH10 6HN	0131-447 4022
Foggitt, Eric W. MA BSc BD	1991	2009	(Dunbar)	49/3 Falcon Avenue, Edinburgh EH10 4AN [E-mail: ericleric3@btinternet.com]	0131-447 7712
Forrester, Duncan B. MA BD DPhil DD FRSE	1962	1978	(University of Edinburgh)	25 Kingsburgh Road, Edinburgh EH12 6DZ [E-mail: dbforrester@rosskeen.org.uk]	0131-337 5646
Forrester, Margaret R. (Mrs) MA BD	1974	2003	(Edinburgh: St Michael's)	25 Kingsburgh Road, Edinburgh EH12 6DZ [E-mail: margaret@rosskeen.org.uk]	0131-337 5646
Fraser, Shirley A. (Miss) MA BD	1992	2008	(Scottish Field Director: Friends International)	6/50 Roseburn Drive, Edinburgh EH12 5NS	0131-347 1400
Gardner, John V.	1997	2003	(Glamis, Inverarity and Kinnettles)	75/1 Lockharton Avenue, Edinburgh EH14 1BD [E-mail: jvg66@hotmail.com]	0131-443 7126
Gordon, Margaret (Mrs) DCS	1974	2009	(Edinburgh: Corstorphine St Ninian's)	92 Lanark Road West, Currie EH14 5LA	0131-449 2554
Gordon, Tom MA BD	1967	2008	(Chaplain: Marie Curie Hospice, Edinburgh)	22 Gosford Road, Port Seton, Prestonpans EH32 0HF	01875 812262
Graham, W. Peter MA BD	1967	2008	(Presbytery Clerk)	23/6 East Coniston, Edinburgh EH10 6RZ	0131-445 5763
Harkness, James CB OBE QHC MA DD	1961	1995	(Chaplain General: Army)	13 Saxe Coburg Place, Edinburgh EH3 5BR	0131-343 1297
Hill, J. William BA BD	1967	2001	(Edinburgh: Corstorphine St Anne's)	33/9 Murrayfield Road, Edinburgh EH12 6EP	0131-441 3384
Irving, William D. LTh	1985	2005	(Golspie)	122 Swanston Muir, Edinburgh EH10 7HY	0131-229 7815
Jeffrey, Eric W.S. JP MA	1954	1994	(Edinburgh: Bristo Memorial)	18 Gillespie Crescent, Edinburgh EH10 4HT	0131-466 2607
Kant, Everard FVCM MTh	1953	1988	(Kinghorn)	10/1 Maxwell Street, Edinburgh EH10 5GZ	0131-551 7706
Kelly, Ewan R. MB ChB BD PhD	1994	2006	NHS Education for Scotland	15 Boswall Road, Edinburgh EH5 3RW [E-mail: ewan.kelly@nes.scot.nhs.uk]	
Lawson, Kenneth C. MA BD	1963	1999	(Adviser in Adult Education)	56 Easter Drylaw View, Edinburgh EH4 2QP	0131-539 3311
McCaskill, George L.L. MA BD	1953	1990	(Religious Education)	19 Tyler's Acre Road, Edinburgh EH12 7HY	0131-334 7451
Macdonald, Finlay A.J. MA BD PhD DD	1971	2010	(Principal Clerk)	8 St Ronan's Way, Innerleithen EH44 6RG	01896 831631
Macdonald, Peter J. BD	1986	2009	Leader of the Iona Community	63 Jim Bush Drive, Prestonpans EH32 9GB [E-mail: petermacdonald@iona.org.uk] [E-mail: petermacdonald16@btinternet.com]	(Office) 0141-332 6343 (Mbl) 07946 715166 01875 819655

Name			Position	Address	Telephone
Macdonald, William J. BD	1976	2002	(Board of National Mission: New Charge Development)	1/13 North Werber Park, Edinburgh EH4 1SY	0131-332 0254
McFadzean, Iain MA BD	1989	2010	National Director: Workplace Chaplaincy	2 Lowfield Crescent, Luncarty, Perth PH1 3FG [E-mail: iain.mcfadzean@wpcscotland.co.uk]	
MacGregor, Margaret S. (Miss) MA BD DipEd	1985	1994	(Calcutta)	16 Learmonth Court, Edinburgh EH4 1PB	0131-332 1089
McGregor, Alistair G.C. QC BD	1987	2002	(Edinburgh: Leith North)	22 Primrose Bank Road, Edinburgh EH5 3JG	0131-551 2802
McGregor, T. Stewart MBE MA BD	1957	1998	(Chaplain: Edinburgh Royal Infirmary)	19 Lonsdale Terrace, Edinburgh EH3 9HL [E-mail: cetsm@uwclub.net]	0131-229 5332
MacKay, Stewart A.	2009		Chaplain: Army	2 Bn The Parachute Regiment, Merville Barracks, Colchester CO2 7UT	
McLarty, R. Russell MA BD	1985	2011	A Chance to Thrive – Project Co-ordinator	9 Sanderson's Wynd, Tranent EH33 1DA	01875 614496
Maclean, Ailsa G. (Mrs) BD DipCE	1979	1988	Chaplain: George Heriot's School	28 Swan Spring Avenue, Edinburgh EH10 6NJ	0131-445 1320
MacMurchie, F. Lynne LLB BD	1998	2003	Healthcare Chaplain	Edinburgh Community Mental Health Chaplaincy, 41 George IV Bridge, Edinburgh EH1 1EL	0131-220 5150
McPheat, Elspeth DCS	1953	1993	Deaconess: CrossReach	11/5 New Orchardfield, Edinburgh EH6 5ET	0131-554 4143
McPhee, Duncan C. MA BD	1958	1996	(Department of National Mission)	8 Belvedere Park, Edinburgh EH6 4LR	0131-552 6784
Macpherson, Colin C.R. MA BD	1993	2012	(Dunfermline St Margaret's)	7 Eva Place, Edinburgh EH9 3ET	0131-667 1456
McQuarrie, Ian A. BD			(Edinburgh: Colinton Mains)	41 Lochnagar Road, Motherwell ML1 2PG [E-mail: ianmcquarrie1@btinternet.com]	01698 262000
Mathieson, Angus R. MA BD	1988	1998	Ministries Council	21 Traquair Park West, Edinburgh EH12 7AN	0131-334 9774
Moir, Ian A. MA BD	1962	2000	(Adviser for Urban Priority Areas)	28/6 Comely Bank Avenue, Edinburgh EH4 1EL	0131-332 2748
Monteith, W. Graham BD PhD	1974	1994	(Flotta and Fara with Hoy and Walls)	20/3 Grandfield, Edinburgh EH6 4TL	0131-552 2564
Morrice, William G. MA BD STM PhD	1957	1991	(St John's College Durham)	Flat 37, The Cedars, 2 Manse Road, Edinburgh EH12 7SN [E-mail: w.g.morrice@btinternet.com]	0131-316 4845
Morrison, Mary B. (Mrs) MA BD DipEd	1978	2000	(Edinburgh: Stenhouse St Aidan's)	14 Eildon Terrace, Edinburgh EH3 5LU	0131-556 1962
Morton, Andrew R. MA BD DD	1956	1994	(Board of World Mission and Unity)	7A Laverockbank Terrace, Edinburgh EH5 3DJ	0131-538 7049
Moyes, Sheila A. (Miss) DCS			(Deaconess)	158 Pilton Avenue, Edinburgh EH5 2JZ	0131-551 1731
Mulligan, Anne MA DCS			Deaconess: Hospital Chaplain	27A Craigour Avenue, Edinburgh EH17 1NH	0131-664 3426
Munro, George A.M.	1968	2000	(Edinburgh: Cluny)	108 Caiyside, Edinburgh EH10 7HR	0131-445 5829
Munro, John P.L. MA BD PhD	1977	2007	(Kinross)	5 Marchmont Crescent, Edinburgh EH9 1HN [E-mail: jplmunro@yahoo.co.uk]	0131-623 0198
Murrie, John BD	1953	1996	(Kirkliston)	31 Nicol Road, The Whins, Broxburn EH52 6JJ	01506 852464
Musgrave, Clarence W. BA BD ThM	1966	2006	(Jerusalem: St Andrew's)	4 Ravelston Heights, Edinburgh EH4 3LX [E-mail: clarencejoan@talktalk.net]	0131-332 6337
Page, Ruth MA BD DPhil	1976	2000	(University of Edinburgh)	22/5 West Mill Bank, West Mill Road, Edinburgh EH13 0QT	0131-441 3740
Paterson, Douglas S. MA BD	1976	2010	(Edinburgh: St Colm's)	4 Ards Place, High Street, Aberlady EH32 0DB	01875 870192
Plate, Maria A.G. (Miss) LTh BA	1983	2000	(South Ronaldsay and Burray)	Flat 29, 77 Barnton Park View, Edinburgh EH4 6EL	0131-339 8539
Rennie, Agnes M. (Miss) DCS			(Deaconess)	3/1 Craigmillar Court, Edinburgh EH16 4AD	0131-661 8475
Ridland, Alistair K. MA BD	1982	2000	Chaplain: Western General Hospital	13 Stewart Place, Kirkliston EH29 0BQ	0131-333 2711
Ritchie, Andrew BD DipMin DMin	1984	2011	(Edinburgh: Craiglockhart)	2A Falcon Terrace Lane, Glasgow G20 0BW [E-mail: andrewritchie@talk21.com]	
Robertson, Charles LVO MA	1965	2005	(Edinburgh: Canongate)	3 Ross Gardens, Edinburgh EH9 3BS	0131-662 9025

Name			Role	Address	Telephone
Robertson, Norma P. (Miss) BD DMin MTh	1993	2002	(Kincardine O'Neil with Lumphanan)	Flat 5, 2 Burnbrae Drive, Grovewood Hill, Edinburgh EH12 8AS	0131-339 6701
Ronald, Norma A. (Miss) MBE DCS	1960	2000	(Deaconess)	2B Saughton Road North, Edinburgh EH12 7HG	0131-334 8736
Schofield, Melville F. MA	1965	2006	(Chaplain: Western General Hospitals)	25 Rowantree Grove, Currie EH14 5AT	0131-449 4745
Scott, Ian G. BSc BD STM			(Edinburgh: Greenbank)	50 Forthview Walk, Tranent EH33 1FE [E-mail: igscott50@btinternet.com]	01875 612907
Scott, Martin DipMusEd RSAM BD PhD	1986	2000	Ministries Council	The Manse, Culross, Dunfermline KY12 8JD	01383 880231
Shewan, Frederick D. MA BD	1970	2005	(Edinburgh: Muirhouse St Andrew's)	38 Tremayne Place, Dunfermline KY12 9YH	01383 734354
Slorach, Alexander CA BD	1970	2002	(Kirk of Lammermuir with Langton and Polwarth)		
Smith, Angus MA LTh	1965	2006	(Chaplain to the Oil Industry)	61 Inverleith Row, Edinburgh EH3 5PX	0131-667 1761
Steele, Marilynn J. (Mrs) BD DCS			(Deaconess)	3/7 West Powburn, West Savile Gait, Edinburgh EH9 3EW 2 Northfield Gardens, Prestonpans EH32 9LQ [E-mail: marilynnsteele@aol.com]	01875 811497
Stephen, Donald M. TD MA BD ThM	1962	2001	(Edinburgh: Marchmont St Giles')	10 Hawkhead Crescent, Edinburgh EH16 6LR	0131-658 1216
Stevenson, John MA BD PhD	1963	2001	(Department of Education)	12 Swanston Gardens, Edinburgh EH10 7DL	0131-445 3960
Stirling, A. Douglas BSc	1956	1994	(Rhu and Shandon)	162 Avontoun Park, Linlithgow EH49 6QH	01506 845021
Taylor, Howard G. BSc BD MTh	1971	1998	(Chaplain: Heriot Watt University)	17 Waid Terrace, Anstruther KY10 3EZ [E-mail: HowardTaylor1944@live.co.uk]	
Taylor, William R. MA BD	1983	2003	Chaplaincy Co-ordinator: Scottish Prison Service	33 Kingsknowe Drive, Edinburgh EH14 2JY	0131-336 3113
Teague, Yvonne (Mrs) DCS			(Board of Ministry)	46 Craigcrook Avenue, Edinburgh EH4 3PX	0131-242 1997
Telfer, Iain J.M. BD DPS	1978	2001	Chaplain: Royal Infirmary	Royal Infirmary of Edinburgh, 51 Little France Crescent, Edinburgh EH16 4SA	0131-556 5687
Thom, Helen (Miss) DCS			(Deaconess)	84 Great King Street, Edinburgh EH3 6QU	0131-225 9137
Tweedie, Fiona PhD		2011	Presbytery Mission Facilitator	10/1 Palmerston Place, Edinburgh EH12 5AA [E-mail: fjtweedie@yahoo.co.uk]	
Watson, Nigel G. MA	1998	2012	(Associate: East Kilbride: Old/Stewartfield/West)	7 St Catherine's Place, Edinburgh EH9 1NU [E-mail: nigel.g.watson@gmail.com]	0131-662 4191
Whyte, George J. BSc BD DMin	1981	2008	Presbytery Clerk	4 Baberton Mains Lea, Edinburgh EH14 3HB [E-mail: edinburgh@cofscotland.org.uk]	0131-466 1674
Whyte, Iain A. BA BD STM PhD	1968	2001	Community Mental Health Chaplain	14 Carlingnose Point, North Queensferry, Inverkeithing KY11 1ER [E-mail: iainisabel@whytes28.fsnet.co.uk]	01383 410732
Wigglesworth, J. Christopher MBE BSc PhD BD	1968	1999	(St Andrew's College, Selly Oak)	12 Leven Terrace, Edinburgh EH3 9LW	0131-228 6335
Wilkie, James L. MA BD	1959	1998	(Board of World Mission)	7 Comely Bank Avenue, Edinburgh EH4 1EW [E-mail: jl.wilkie@btinternet.com]	0131-343 1552
Wilkinson, John BD MD FRCP DTM&H	1946	1975	(Kikuyu)	70 Craigleith Hill Gardens, Edinburgh EH4 2JH	0131-332 2994
Williams, Jenny M. (Miss) BSc CQSW BD	1996	1997	Christian Fellowship of Healing	16 Blantyre Terrace, Edinburgh EH10 5AE	0131-447 0050
Wilson, John M. MA	1964	1995	(Adviser in Religious Education)	27 Bellfield Street, Edinburgh EH15 2BR	0131-669 5257
Wynne, Alistair T.E. BA BD	1982	2009	(Nicosia Community Church, Cyprus)	Flat 6, 14 Burnbrae Drive, Edinburgh EH12 8AS [E-mail: awynne2@googlemail.com]	0131-339 6462
Young, Alexander W. BD DipMin	1988	1999	Lead Chaplain: NHS Lothian	32 Lindsay Circus, The Hawthorns, Rosewell EH24 9EP	(Work) 0131-242 1997

EDINBURGH ADDRESSES

Albany	82 Montrose Terrace
Balerno	Johnsburn Road, Balerno
Barclay Viewforth	Barclay Place
Blackhall St Columba's	Queensferry Road
Bristo Memorial	Peffermill Road, Craigmillar
Broughton St Mary's	Bellevue Crescent
Canongate	Canongate
Carrick Knowe	North Saughton Road
Colinton	Dell Road
Colinton Mains	Oxgangs Road North
Corstorphine	
Craigsbank	Craig's Crescent
Old	Kirk Loan
St Anne's	Kaimes Road
St Ninian's	St John's Road
Craigentinny St Christopher's	Craigentinny Road
Craiglockhart	Craiglockhart Avenue
Craigmillar Park	Craigmillar Park
Cramond	Cramond Glebe Road
Currie	Kirkgate, Currie
Davidson's Mains	Quality Street
Dean	Dean Path
Drylaw	Groathill Road North
Duddingston	Old Church Lane, Duddingston
Fairmilehead	Frogston Road West, Fairmilehead
Gorgie Dalry	Gorgie Road
Granton	Boswall Parkway
Greenbank	Braidburn Terrace
Greenside	Royal Terrace
Greyfriars Tolbooth and Highland Kirk	Greyfriars Place
High (St Giles')	High Street
Holyrood Abbey	Dalziel Place x London Road
Holy Trinity	Hailesland Place, Wester Hailes
Inverleith St Serf's	Ferry Road
Juniper Green	Lanark Road, Juniper Green
Kaimes Lockhart Memorial	Gracemount Drive
Kirkliston	The Square, Kirkliston
Kirk o' Field	Pleasance
Leith	
North	Madeira Street off Ferry Road
St Andrew's	Easter Road
South	Kirkgate, Leith
Wardie	Primrosebank Road
Liberton	Kirkgate, Liberton
Northfield	Gilmerton Road, Liberton
London Road	London Road
Marchmont St Giles'	Kilgraston Road
Mayfield Salisbury	Mayfield Road x West Mayfield
Morningside	Cluny Gardens
Morningside United	Bruntsfield Place x Chamberlain Road
Muirhouse St Andrew's	Pennywell Gardens
Murrayfield	Abinger Gardens
Newhaven	Craighall Road
New Restalrig	Willowbrae Road
Old Kirk	Pennywell Road
Palmerston Place	Palmerston Place
Pilrig St Paul's	Pilrig Street
Polwarth	Polwarth Terrace x Harrison Road
Portobello	
Old	Bellfield Street
St James'	Rosefield Place
St Philip's Joppa	Abercorn Terrace
Priestfield	Dalkeith Road x Marchhall Place
Queensferry	The Loan, South Queensferry
Ratho	Baird Road, Ratho
Reid Memorial	West Savile Terrace
Richmond Craigmillar	Niddrie Mains Road
St Andrew's and St George's West	George Street and Shandwick Place
St Andrew's Clermiston	Clermiston View
St Catherine's Argyle	Grange Road x Chalmers Crescent
St Cuthbert's	Lothian Road
St David's Broomhouse	Broomhouse Crescent
St John's Oxgangs	Oxgangs Road
St Margaret's	Restalrig Road South
St Martin's	Magdalene Drive
St Michael's	Slateford Road
St Nicholas' Sighthill	Calder Road
St Stephen's Comely Bank	Comely Bank
Slateford Longstone	Kingsknowe Road North
Stenhouse St Aidan's	Chesser Avenue
Stockbridge	Saxe Coburg Street
The Tron Kirk (Gilmerton and Moredun)	Craigour Gardens and Ravenscroft Street

(2) WEST LOTHIAN

Meets in the church of the incoming Moderator on the first Tuesday of September and in St John's Church Hall, Bathgate, on the first Tuesday of every other month, except December, when the meeting is on the second Tuesday, and January, July and August, when there is no meeting.

Clerk: REV. DUNCAN SHAW BD MTh   St John's Manse, Mid Street, Bathgate EH48 1QD   01506 653146
[E-mail: westlothian@cofscotland.org.uk]

Abercorn (H) linked with Pardovan, Kingscavil (H) and Winchburgh (H)
A. Scott Marshall DipComm BD   1984   1998   The Manse, Winchburgh, Broxburn EH52 6TT   01506 890919
[E-mail: pkwla@aol.com]

Armadale (H)

Julia C. Wiley (Ms) MA(CE) MDiv	1998	2010	70 Mount Pleasant, Armadale, Bathgate EH48 3HB [E-mail: preachergrace@gmail.com]	01501 730358
Brenda Robson PhD (Aux)	2005	2012	2 Baird Road, Ratho, Newbridge EH28 8RA [E-mail: brendarobson@hotmail.co.uk]	0131-333 2746

Avonbridge (H) linked with Torphichen (H)

Sandi McGill (Ms) BD	2002	2012	Manse Road, Torphichen, Bathgate EH48 4LT [E-mail: smcgillbox-mail@yahoo.co.uk]	01506 676803

Bathgate: Boghall (H)

Vacant			1 Manse Place, Ash Grove, Bathgate EH48 1NJ	01506 652940

Bathgate: High (H)

Murdo C. Macdonald MA BD	2002	2011	19 Hunter Grove, Bathgate EH48 1NN [E-mail: murdocmacdonald@gmail.com]	01506 652654

Bathgate: St John's (H)

Duncan Shaw BD MTh	1975	1978	St John's Manse, Mid Street, Bathgate EH48 1QD [E-mail: westlothian@cofscotland.org.uk]	01506 653146

Blackburn and Seafield (H)

Robert A. Anderson MA BD DPhil	1980	1998	The Manse, 5 MacDonald Gardens, Blackburn, Bathgate EH47 7RE [E-mail: robertanderson307@btinternet.com]	01506 652825

Blackridge (H) linked with Harthill: St Andrew's (H)

Robert B. Gehrke BSc BD CEng MIEE	1994	2006	East Main Street, Harthill, Shotts ML7 5QW [E-mail: bob.gehrke@gmail.com]	01501 751239

Breich Valley (H)

Vacant			Stoneyburn, Bathgate EH47 8AU	01501 762018

Broxburn (H)

Terry Taylor BA MTh	2005		2 Church Street, Broxburn EH52 5EL [E-mail: terryanntaylor@btinternet.com]	01506 852825

Fauldhouse: St Andrew's (H)

Robert Sloan BD	1997	2011	7 Glebe Court, Fauldhouse, Bathgate EH47 9DX [E-mail: robertsloan@scotnet.co.uk]	01501 771190

Harthill: St Andrew's See Blackridge

Kirknewton (H) and East Calder (H)
Andre Groenewald BA BD MDiv DD — 1995 2009 — 8 Manse Court, East Calder, Livingston EH53 0HF [E-mail: groenstes@yahoo.com] — 01506 884585 / 07588 845814 (Mbl)

Kirk of Calder (H)
John M. Povey MA BD — 1981 — 19 Maryfield Park, Mid Calder, Livingston EH53 0SB [E-mail: revjpovey@aol.com] — 01506 882495

Linlithgow: St Michael's (H) (E-mail: info@stmichaels-parish.org.uk)
D. Stewart Gillan BSc MDiv PhD — 1985 2004 — St Michael's Manse, Kirkgate, Linlithgow EH49 7AL [E-mail: stewart@stmichaels-parish.org.uk] — 01506 842195
John H. Paton BSc BD (Assoc) — 1983 2008 — Cross House, The Cross, Linlithgow EH49 7AL [E-mail: jonymar@globalnet.co.uk] [E-mail: johnny@stmichaels-parish.org.uk] — 01506 842665
Thomas S. Riddell BSc CEng FIChemE (Aux) — 1993 1994 — 4 The Maltings, Linlithgow EH49 6DS [E-mail: tsriddell@blueyonder.co.uk] — 01506 843251

Linlithgow: St Ninian's Craigmailen (H)
W. Richard Houston BSc BD — 1998 2004 — 29 Philip Avenue, Linlithgow EH49 7BH [E-mail: wrichardhouston@blueyonder.co.uk] — 01506 202246

Livingston Ecumenical Parish
Incorporating the Worship Centres at:
Carmondean (H) and Knightsridge
Ronald G. Greig MA BD — 1987 2008 — 2 Eastcroft Court, Livingston EH54 7ET [E-mail: rgglep@gmail.com] — 01506 467426

Craigshill (St Columba's) and Ladywell (St Paul's)
Eileen Thompson BD MTh — 53 Garry Walk, Craigshill, Livingston EH54 5AS [E-mail: ectlepc@gmail.com] — 01506 433451
(Scottish Episcopal Church)
Dedridge (Lanthorn) and Murieston
Helen Jenkins BSc MRES PhD BA MA — 13 Eastcroft Court, Livingston EH54 7ET [E-mail: revhelen@chjenkins.plus.com] — 01506 464567
(The Methodist Church)
Team Leader:
Robin R. Hine MA — 21 Bankton Gardens, Livingston EH54 9DZ [E-mail: robin@hiner.com] — 01506 207360
(The United Reformed Church)

Livingston: Old (H)
Graham W. Smith BA BD FSAScot — 1995 — Manse of Livingston, Charlesfield Lane, Livingston EH54 7AJ [E-mail: gwsmith2011@hotmail.co.uk] — 01506 420227

Pardovan, Kingscavil and Winchburgh See Abercorn

Polbeth Harwood linked with West Kirk of Calder (H)
Vacant
27 Learmonth Crescent, West Calder EH55 8AF
01506 870460

Strathbrock (H)
Marc B. Kenton BTh MTh   1997 2009
1 Manse Park, Uphall, Broxburn EH52 6NX
01506 852550

Torphichen See Avonbridge

Uphall: South (H)
Vacant
8 Fernlea, Uphall, Broxburn EH52 6DF
01506 852788

West Kirk of Calder (H) See Polbeth Harwood

Whitburn: Brucefield (H)
John K. Collard MA BD (Interim)   1986 2012
1 Nelson Terrace, East Kilbride, Glasgow G74 2EY
[E-mail: brucefield.church@unicombox.com]
01355 520093
01501 748666

Whitburn: South (H)
Vacant
5 Mansewood Crescent, Whitburn, Bathgate EH47 8HA
01501 740333

Black, David W. BSc BD   1968 2008 (Strathbrock)
66 Bridge Street, Newbridge EH28 8SH
[E-mail: dw.black666@yahoo.co.uk]
0131-333 2609

Cameron, Richard MA BD   1953 1981 (Kilbrandon and Kilchattan)
Craigellen, West George Street, Blairgowrie PH10 6DZ
01250 872087

Darroch, Richard J.G.
BD MTh MA(CMS)   1993 2010 (Whitburn: Brucefield)
23 Barnes Green, Livingston EH54 8PP
[E-mail: richdarr@aol.com]
01506 436648

Dundas, Thomas B.S. LTh   1969 1996 (West Kirk of Calder)
35 Coolkill, Sandyford, Dublin 18, Republic of Ireland
00353 12953061

Grainger, Alison J. BD   1995 2010 (Acharacle with Ardnamurchan)
2 Harebum Avenue, Avonbridge, Falkirk FK1 2NR
[E-mail: revajgrainger@btinternet.com]
01324 861632

Jamieson, Gordon D. MA BD   1974 2012 (Head of Stewardship)
41 Goldpark Place, Livingston EH54 6LW
[E-mail: gdj1949@talktalk.net]
01506 412020

Kelly, Isobel J.M. (Miss)
MA BD DipEd   1974 2010 (Greenock: St Margaret's)
76 Bankton Park East, Livingston EH54 9BN
01506 438511

Mackay, Kenneth J. MA BD   1971 2007 (Edinburgh: St Nicholas' Sighthill)
46 Chuckethall Road, Livingston EH54 8FB
[E-mail: kmth_mackay@yahoo.com]
01506 410884

MacRae, Norman I. LTh   1966 2003 (Inverness: Trinity)
144 Hope Park Gardens, Bathgate EH48 2QX
[E-mail: normanmacrae@talktalk.com]
01506 635254

Merrilees, Ann (Miss) DCS   (Deaconess)
23 Cuthill Brae, West Calder EH55 8QE
[E-mail: ann@merrilees.freeserve.co.uk]
01501 762909

Morrison, Iain C. BA BD   1990 2003 (Linlithgow: St Ninian's Craigmailen)
Whaligoe, 53 Eastcroft Drive, Polmont, Falkirk FK2 0SU
[E-mail: iain@kirkweb.org]
01324 713249

Nelson, Georgina (Mrs) MA BD PhD DipEd	1990	1995	Hospital Chaplain	63 Hawthorn Bank, Seafield, Bathgate EH47 7EB
Nicol, Robert M.	1984	1996	(Jersey: St Columba's)	59 Kinloch View, Blackness Road, Linlithgow EH49 7HT 01506 670391

[E-mail: revrob.nicol@tiscali.co.uk]

Thomson, Phyllis (Miss) DCS	2003	2010	(Deaconess)	63 Caroline Park, Mid Calder, Livingston EH53 0SJ 01506 883207
Trimble, Robert DCS			(Deacon)	5 Templar Rise, Dedridge, Livingston EH54 6PJ 01506 412504
Walker, Ian BD MEd DipMS	1973	2007	(Rutherglen: Wardlawhill)	92 Carseknowe, Linlithgow EH49 7LG 01506 844412

[E-mail: walk102822@aol.com]

Whitson, William S. MA	1959	1999	(Cumbernauld: St Mungo's)	2 Chapman's Brae, Bathgate EH48 4LH 01506 650027

[E-mail: william_whitson@tiscali.co.uk]

(3) LOTHIAN

Meets at Musselburgh: St Andrew's High Parish Church at 7pm on the last Thursday in February, April, June and November, and in a different church on the last Thursday in September.

Clerk:	MR JOHN D. McCULLOCH DL			20 Tipperwell Way, Howgate, Penicuik EH26 8QP 01968 676300

[E-mail: lothian@cofscotland.org.uk]

Aberlady (H) linked with Gullane (H)
Christine M. Clark (Mrs) BA BD MTh	2006	2009	The Manse, Hummel Road, Gullane EH31 2BG 01620 843192

[E-mail: gcclark20@aol.com]

Athelstaneford linked with Whitekirk and Tyninghame
Joanne H.G. Evans-Boiten BD	2004	2009	The Manse, Athelstaneford, North Berwick EH39 5BE 01620 880378

[E-mail: joanne.evansboiten@gmail.com]

Belhaven (H) linked with Spott
Laurence H. Twaddle MA BD MTh	1977	1978	The Manse, Belhaven Road, Dunbar EH42 1NH 01368 863098

[E-mail: revtwaddle@aol.com]

Bilston linked with Glencorse (H) linked with Roslin (H)
John R. Wells BD DipMin	1991	2005	31A Manse Road, Roslin EH25 9LG 0131-440 2012

[E-mail: wellsjr3@aol.com]

Bolton and Saltoun linked with Humbie linked with Yester (H)
Malcolm Lyon BD		2007	The Manse, Tweeddale Avenue, Gifford, Haddington EH41 4QN 01620 810515

[E-mail: malcolmlyon2@hotmail.com]

Bonnyrigg (H)
John Mitchell LTh CMin   1991   9 Viewbank View, Bonnyrigg EH19 2HU
[E-mail: jmitchell241@tiscali.co.uk]   0131-663 8287 (Tel/Fax)

Cockenzie and Port Seton: Chalmers Memorial (H)
Kristina M. Herbold Ross (Mrs)   2008   2 Links Road, Port Seton, Prestonpans EH32 0HA
[E-mail: khross@btinternet.com]   01875 819254

Cockenzie and Port Seton: Old (H)
Guardianship of the Presbytery   1 Links Road, Port Seton, Prestonpans EH32 0HA   01875 812310

Cockpen and Carrington (H) linked with Lasswade (H) and Rosewell (H)
Matthew Z. Ross LLB BD MTh FSAScot   1998   2009   Braemar Villa, 2 Links Road, Port Seton, Prestonpans EH32 0HA
[E-mail: mzross@btinternet.com]   01875 819544
07711 706950 (Mbl)

Dalkeith: St John's and King's Park (H)
Keith L. Mack BD MTh DPS   2002   13 Weir Crescent, Dalkeith EH22 3JN
[E-mail: kthmacker@aol.com]   0131-454 0206

Dalkeith: St Nicholas' Buccleuch (H)
Alexander G. Horsburgh MA BD   1995   2004   116 Bonnyrigg Road, Dalkeith EH22 3HZ
[E-mail: alexanderhorsburgh@googlemail.com]   0131-663 3036

Dirleton (H) linked with North Berwick: Abbey (H) (Office: 01620 892800) (E-mail: abbeychurch@hotmail.com)
David J. Graham BSc BD PhD   1982   1998   Sydserff, Old Abbey Road, North Berwick EH39 4BP
[E-mail: dirletonkirk@btconnect.com]   01620 840878

Dunbar (H)
Gordon Stevenson BSc BD   2010   The Manse, 10 Bayswell Road, Dunbar EH42 1AB
[E-mail: gstev@btconnect.com]   01368 865482

Dunglass
Suzanne G. Fletcher (Mrs) BA MDiv MA   2001   2011   The Manse, Cockburnspath TD13 5XZ
[E-mail: revfletcher@btinternet.com]   01368 830713

Garvald and Morham linked with Haddington: West (H)
John Vischer   1993   2011   15 West Road, Haddington EH41 3RD
[E-mail: j_vischer@yahoo.co.uk]   01620 822213

Gladsmuir linked with Longniddry (H)
Robin E. Hill LLB BD PhD　2004　The Manse, Elcho Road, Longniddry EH32 0LB　01875 853195
[E-mail: robinailsa@btinternet.com]

Glencorse (H) See Bilston

Gorebridge (H)
Mark S. Nicholas MA BD　1999　100 Hunterfield Road, Gorebridge EH23 4TT　01875 820387
[E-mail: mark@gorepc.com]

Gullane See Aberlady

Haddington: St Mary's (H)
Jennifer Macrae (Mrs) MA BD　1998　2007　1 Nungate Gardens, Haddington EH41 4EE　01620 823109
[E-mail: minister@stmaryskirk.co.uk]

Haddington: West See Garvald and Morham

Howgate (H) linked with Penicuik: South (H)
Ian A. Cathcart BSc BD　1994　2007　15 Stevenson Road, Penicuik EH26 0LU　01968 674692
[E-mail: reviac@yahoo.co.uk]

Humbie See Bolton and Saltoun
Lasswade and Rosewell See Cockpen and Carrington

Loanhead
Graham L. Duffin BSc BD DipEd　1989　2001　120 The Loan, Loanhead EH20 9AJ　0131-448 2459
[E-mail: gduffin@loanheadparishchurch.co.uk]

Longniddry See Gladsmuir

Musselburgh: Northesk (H)
Alison P. McDonald MA BD　1991　1998　16 New Street, Musselburgh EH21 6JP　0131-665 2128
[E-mail: alisonpmcdonald@btinternet.com]

Musselburgh: St Andrew's High (H) (0131-665 7239)
Yvonne E.S. Atkins (Mrs) BD   1997   8 Ferguson Drive, Musselburgh EH21 6XA   0131-665 1124
[E-mail: yesatkins@hotmail.co.uk]

Musselburgh: St Clement's and St Ninian's
Vacant   The Manse, Wallyford Loan Road, Wallyford, Musselburgh EH21 8BU   0131-653 6588

Musselburgh: St Michael's Inveresk
Andrew B. Dick BD DipMin   1986 1999   8 Hope Place, Musselburgh EH21 7QE   0131-665 0545
[E-mail: dixbit@aol.com]

Newbattle (H) (Website: http://freespace.virgin.net/newbattle.focus)
Sean Swindells BD DipMin MTh   1996 2011   112 Greenbank Crescent, Edinburgh EH10 5SZ   0131-447 4032
[E-mail: sswindells@blueyonder.co.uk]   07791 755976 (Mbl)
Gordon R. Steven BD DCS   2004   51 Nantwich Drive, Edinburgh EH7 6RB   0131-669 2054
[E-mail: grsteven@btinternet.com]   07904 385256 (Mbl)

Newton
Vacant   The Manse, Newton, Dalkeith EH22 1SR   0131-663 3845

North Berwick: Abbey See Dirleton

North Berwick: St Andrew Blackadder (H) (E-mail: admin@standrewblackadder.org.uk) (Website: www.standrewblackadder.org.uk)
Neil J. Dougall BD   1991 2003   7 Marine Parade, North Berwick EH39 4LD   01620 892132
[E-mail: neil@standrewblackadder.org.uk]

Ormiston linked with Pencaitland
David J. Torrance BD DipMin   1993 2009   The Manse, Pencaitland, Tranent EH34 5DL   01875 340963
[E-mail: torrance@talktalk.net]

Pencaitland See Ormiston

Penicuik: North (H)
Ruth D. Halley BA BEd   2012   93 John Street, Penicuik EH26 8AG   01968 672213
[E-mail: ruth.halley@googlemail.com]

Penicuik: St Mungo's (H)
Vacant   31A Kirkhill Road, Penicuik EH26 8JB   01968 677040

Penicuik: South See Howgate

Prestonpans: Prestongrange

Charles M. Cameron BA BD PhD	1980	2012	The Manse, East Loan, Prestonpans EH32 9ED [E-mail: minister@prestongrange-church.org.uk]	01875 571579

Roslin See Bilston
Spott See Belhaven

Tranent

Jan Gillies BD	1998	2008	1 Toll House Gardens, Tranent EH33 2QQ [E-mail: jan@tranentparishchurch.co.uk]	01875 824604

Traprain

David D. Scott BSc BD	1981	2010	The Manse, Preston Road, East Linton EH40 3DS [E-mail: revdd.scott@gmail.com]	01620 860227 (Tel/Fax)

Tyne Valley Parish (H)

Vacant			Cranstoun Cottage, Ford, Pathhead EH37 5RE	01875 320314
Andrew Don MBA (Aux)	2006		5 Eskvale Court, Penicuik EH26 8HT [E-mail: a.a.don@btinternet.com]	01968 675766

Whitekirk and Tyninghame See Athelstaneford
Yester See Bolton and Saltoun

Andrews, J. Edward MA BD DipCG	1985	2005	(Armadale)	Dunnichen, 1B Cameron Road, Nairn IV12 5NS [E-mail: edward.andrews@btinternet.com]
Bayne, Angus L. LTh BEd MTh	1969	2005	(Edinburgh: Bristo Memorial Craigmillar)	14 Myredale, Bonnyrig EH19 3NW [E-mail: angus@mccookies.com] (Mbl) 07808 720708 / 0131-663 6871
Berry, Geoff T. BD BSc	2009	2011	Chaplain: Army	38 Muirfield Drive, Gullane EH31 2HJ [E-mail: geofftalk@yahoo.co.uk]
Black, A. Graham MA	1964	2003	(Gladsmuir with Longniddry)	26 Hamilton Crescent, Gullane EH31 2HR [E-mail: grablack@aol.com] 01620 843899
Brown, Ronald H.	1974	1998	(Musselburgh: Northesk)	6 Monktonhall Farm Cottages, Musselburgh EH21 6RZ 0131-653 2531
Brown, William BD	1972	1997	(Edinburgh: Polwarth)	13 Thornyhall, Dalkeith EH22 2ND 0131-654 0929
Buchanan, John DCS			(Deacon)	19 Gillespie Crescent, Edinburgh EH10 4HZ 0131-229 0794
Cairns, John B. LTh LLB LLD DD	1974	2009	(Aberlady with Gullane)	Bell House, Roxburghe Park, Dunbar EH42 1LR [E-mail: johncairns@mail.com] 01368 862501

Name	Ordained/Inducted	Charge	Address	Telephone
Coltart, Ian O. CA BD	1988 2010	(Arbirlot with Carmyllie)	25 Bothwell Gardens, Dunbar EH42 1PZ	01368 860064
Dutton, David W. BA	1973 2008	(Stranraer: High Kirk)	13 Acredales, Haddington EH41 4NT [E-mail: dutton_sr@yahoo.co.uk]	
Forbes, Iain M. BSc BD	1964 2005	(Aberdeen: Beechgrove)	69 Dobbie's Road, Bonnyrig EH19 2AY [E-mail: panama.forbes@tiscali.co.uk]	0131-454 0717
Fraser, John W. MA BD	1974 2011	(Penicuik: North)	66 Camus Avenue, Edinburgh EH10 6QX [E-mail: jjiji2005@hotmail.co.uk]	0131-623 0647
Gilfillan, James LTh	1968 1997	(East Kilbride: Old)	15 Long Cram, Haddington EH41 4NS	01620 824843
Glover, Robert L. BMus BD MTh ARCO	1971 2010	(Cockenzie and Port Seton: Chalmers Memorial)	27 Winton Park, Cockenzie, Prestonpans EH32 0JN [E-mail: rlglover@btinternet.com]	01875 818759
Haslett, Howard J. BA BD	1972 2010	(Traprain)	48 The Mallings, Haddington EH41 4EF [E-mail: howard.haslett@btinternet.com]	01620 820292
Hutchison, Alan E.W.	1998 2002	(Deacon)	132 Lochbridge Road, North Berwick EH39 4DR [E-mail: revamjones@aol.com]	01620 894077
Jones, Anne M. (Mrs) BD		(Hospital Chaplain)	7 North Elphinstone Farm, Tranent EH33 2ND	01875 61442
Lithgow, Anne R. (Mrs) MA BD	1992 2009	(Dunglass)	14 Thorntonloch Holdings, Dunbar EH42 1QT [E-mail: anne.lithgow@btinternet.com]	01620 810341
Macdonell, Alasdair W. MA BD	1955 1992	(Haddington: St Mary's)	St Andrews Cottage, Duns Road, Gifford, Haddington EH41 4QW [E-mail: alasdair.macdonell@btinternet.com]	
Manson, James A. LTh	1981 2004	(Glencorse with Roslin)	31 Nursery Gardens, Kilmarnock KA1 3JA [E-mail: james.manson@virgin.net]	01563 535430
Pirie, Donald LTh	1975 2006	(Bolton and Saltoun with Humbie with Yester)	46 Caiystane Avenue, Edinburgh EH10 6SH [E-mail: jasritch_77@msn.com]	0131-445 2654
Ritchie, James McL. MA BD MPhil	1950 1985	(Coalsnaughton)	Flat 2/25, Croft-an-Righ, Edinburgh EH8 8EG [E-mail: jstein@handselpress.org.uk]	0131-557 1084
Stein, Jock MA BD	1973 2008	(Tulliallan and Kincardine)	35 Dunbar Road, Haddington EH41 3PJ [E-mail: margaretestein@hotmail.com]	01620 824896
Stein, Margaret E. (Mrs) DA BD DipRE	1984 2008	(Tulliallan and Kincardine)	35 Dunbar Road, Haddington EH41 3PJ	01620 824896
Swan, Andrew F. BD	1983 2000	(Loanhead)	3 Mackenzie Gardens, Dolphinton, West Linton EH46 7HS	01968 682247
Torrance, David W. MA BD	1955 1991	(Earlston)	38 Forth Street, North Berwick EH39 4JQ [E-mail: torrance103@btinternet.com]	(Tel/Fax) 01620 895109
Underwood, Florence A. (Mrs) BD	1992 2006	(Assistant: Gladsmuir with Longniddry)	18 Covenanters Rise, Pitreavie Castle, Dunfermline KY11 8SQ [E-mail: geoffrey.underwood@homecall.co.uk]	01383 740745
Underwood, Geoffrey H. BD DipTh FPhS	1964 1992	(Cockenzie and Port Seton: Chalmers Memorial)	18 Covenanters Rise, Pitreavie Castle, Dunfermline KY11 8SQ [E-mail: geoffrey.underwood@homecall.co.uk]	01383 740745

(4) MELROSE AND PEEBLES

Meets at Innerleithen on the first Tuesday of February, March, May, October, November and December, and on the fourth Tuesday of June, and in places to be appointed on the first Tuesday of September.

Clerk: REV. VICTORIA LINFORD LLB BD   The Manse, 209 Galashiels Road, Stow, Galashiels TD1 2RE   01578 730237
[E-mail: melrosepeebles@cofscotland.org.uk]

Ashkirk linked with Selkirk (H)

Margaret D.J. Steele (Miss) BSc BD	2000	2011	1 Loanside, Selkirk TD7 4DJ [E-mail: mdjsteele@gmail.com]	01750 23308

Bowden (H) and Melrose (H)

Alistair G. Bennett BSc BD | 1978 1984 | Tweedmount Road, Melrose TD6 9ST [E-mail: agbennettmelrose@aol.com] | 01896 822217

Broughton, Glenholm and Kilbucho (H) linked with Skirling linked with Stobo and Drumelzier linked with Tweedsmuir (H)

Robert B. Milne BTh | 1999 2009 | The Manse, Broughton, Biggar ML12 6HQ [E-mail: rbmilne@aol.com] | 01899 830331

Caddonfoot (H) linked with Galashiels: Trinity (H)

Vacant | | 8 Mossilee Road, Galashiels TD1 1NF | 01896 752420

Carlops linked with Kirkurd and Newlands (H) linked with West Linton: St Andrew's (H)

Thomas W. Burt BD | 1982 1985 | The Manse, West Linton EH46 7EN [E-mail: tomburt@westlinton.com] | 01968 660221

Channelkirk and Lauder

James J. Griggs BD MTh | 2011 | The Manse, Brownsmuir Park, Lauder TD2 6QD [E-mail: clcminister@gmail.com] | 01578 722616

Earlston

Julie M. Woods (Ms) BTh | 2005 2011 | The Manse, High Street, Earlston TD4 6DE [E-mail: missjulie@btinternet.com] | 01896 849236

Eddleston (H) linked with Peebles: Old (H)

Malcolm M. Macdougall BD MTh DipCE | 1981 2001 | The Old Manse, Innerleithen Road, Peebles EH45 8BD [E-mail: calum.macdougall@btopenworld.com] | 01721 720568

Ettrick and Yarrow

Samuel Siroky BA MTh | 2003 | Yarrow Manse, Yarrow, Selkirk TD7 5LA [E-mail: sesiroky@tiscali.co.uk] | 01750 82336

Galashiels: Old and St Paul's (H) (Website: www.oldparishandstpauls.org.uk)

Leslie M. Steele MA BD | 1973 1988 | Woodlea, Abbotsview Drive, Galashiels TD1 3SL [E-mail: leslie@oldparishandstpauls.org.uk] | 01896 752320

Galashiels: St John's (H)
Jane M. Howitt (Miss) MA BD   1996   2006   St John's Manse, Hawthorn Road, Galashiels TD1 2JZ   01896 752573
[E-mail: jane@stjohnsgalashiels.co.uk]

Galashiels: Trinity (H) See Caddonfoot

Innerleithen (H), Traquair and Walkerburn
Janice M. Faris (Mrs) BSc BD   1991   2001   The Manse, 1 Millwell Park, Innerleithen, Peebles   EH44 6JF   01896 830309
[E-mail: revjfaris@hotmail.com]

Kirkurd and Newlands See Carlops

Lyne and Manor linked with Peebles: St Andrew's Leckie (H) (01721 723121)
Malcolm S. Jefferson   2012   Mansefield, Innerleithen Road, Peebles   EH45 8BE   01721 721148
[E-mail: jeffersons02@btinternet.com]

Maxton and Mertoun linked with Newtown linked with St Boswells
Sheila W. Moir (Ms) MTheol   2008   7 Strae Brigs, St Boswells, Melrose   TD6 0DH   01835 822255
[E-mail: sheila377@btinternet.com]

Newtown See Maxton and Mertoun
Peebles: Old See Eddleston
Peebles: St Andrew's Leckie See Lyne and Manor
St Boswells See Maxton and Mertoun
Selkirk See Ashkirk
Skirling See Broughton, Glenholm and Kilbucho
Stobo and Drumelzier See Broughton, Glenholm and Kilbucho

Stow: St Mary of Wedale and Heriot
Victoria J. Linford (Mrs) LLB BD   2010   The Manse, 209 Galashiels Road, Stow, Galashiels   TD1 2RE   01578 730237
[E-mail: victorialinford@yahoo.co.uk]

Tweedsmuir See Broughton, Glenholm and Kilbucho
West Linton: St Andrew's See Carlops

Name	(Charge / Position)	Years	Address / E-mail	Telephone
Arnott, A. David K. MA BD	(St Andrews: Hope Park with Strathkinness)	1971 2010	53 Whitehaugh Park, Peebles EH45 9DB [E-mail: adka53@btinternet.com]	01721 725979 (Mbl) 07759 709205
Bowie, Adam McC.	(Cavers and Kirkton with Hobkirk and Southdean)	1976 1996		
Brown, Robert BSc	(Kilbrandon and Kilchattan)	1962 1997	Glenbield, Redpath, Earlston TD4 6AD; 11 Thornfield Terrace, Selkirk TD7 4DU [E-mail: ruwcb@tiscali.co.uk]	01896 848173 01750 20311
Cashman, P. Hamilton BSc	(Dirleton with North Berwick: Abbey)	1985 1998	38 Abbotsford Road, Galashiels TD1 3HR [E-mail: mcashman@tiscali.co.uk]	01896 752711
Cutler, James S.H. BD CEng MIStructE	(Black Mount with Culter with Libberton and Quothquan)	1986 2011	12 Kittlegairy Place, Peebles EH45 9LW [E-mail: revjc@btinternet.com]	01721 723950
Devenny, Robert P.	Hospital Chaplain	2002	Blakeburn Cottage, Wester Housebyres, Melrose TD6 9BW	01896 822350
Dick, J. Ronald BD	Hospital Chaplain	1973 1996	5 Georgefield Farm Cottages, Earlston TD4 6BH	01896 848956
Dobie, Rachel J.W. (Mrs) LTh	(Broughton, Glenholm and Kilbucho with Skirling with Stobo and Drumelzier with Tweedsmuir)	1991 2008	20 Moss Side Crescent, Biggar ML12 6GE [E-mail: revracheldobie@talktalk.net]	01899 229244
Dodd, Marion E. (Miss) MA BD LRAM	(Kelso: Old and Sprouston)	1988 2010	Esdaile, Tweedmount Road, Melrose TD6 9ST [E-mail: mariondodd@btinternet.com]	01896 822446
Duncan, Charles A. MA	(Heriot with Stow: St Mary of Wedale)	1956 1992	10 Elm Grove, Galashiels TD1 3JA	01896 753261
Hardie, H. Warner BD	(Blackridge with Harthill: St Andrew's)	1979 2005	Keswick Cottage, Kingsmuir Drive, Peebles EH45 9AA [E-mail: hardies@bigfoot.com]	01721 724003
Hogg, Thomas M. BD	(Tranent)	1986 2007	22 Douglas Place, Galashiels TD1 3BT	01896 759381
Hughes, Barry MA	Ordained Local Minister	2011	Dunslair, Cardrona Way, Cardrona, Peebles EH45 9LD [E-mail: gill_baz@hotmail.com]	01896 831197
Kellet, John M. MA	(Leith: South)	1962 1995	4 High Cottages, Walkerburn EH43 6AZ	01896 870351
Kennon, Stanley BA BD RN	Chaplain: Royal Navy	1992 2000	Britannia Royal Naval College, Dartmouth, Devon TQ6 0HJ [E-mail: brnc-csf@fleetfost.mod.uk]	01750 21210
Laing, William F. DSC VRD MA	(Selkirk: St Mary's West)	1952 1986	10 The Glebe, Selkirk TD7 5AB	
MacFarlane, David C. MA	(Eddleston with Peebles: Old)	1957 1997	Lorimer House Nursing Home, 491 Lanark Road, Edinburgh EH14 5DQ	
Milloy, A. Miller DPE LTh DipTrMan	(General Secretary: United Bible Societies)	1979 2012	18 Kittlegairy Crescent, Peebles EH45 9NJ [E-mail: ammilloy@aol.com]	01721 723380
Moore, W. Haisley MA	(Secretary: The Boys' Brigade)	1966 1996	26 Tweedbank Avenue, Tweedbank, Galashiels TD1 3SP	01896 668577
Munson, Winnie (Ms) BD	(Delting with Northmavine)	1996 2006	6 St Cuthbert's Drive, St Boswells, Melrose TD6 0DF	01835 823375
Norman, Nancy M. (Miss) BA MDiv MTh	(Lyne and Manor)	1988 2012	Roseneuk, Tweedside Road, Newtown St Boswells TD6 0PQ [E-mail: nancy.norman1@googlemail.com]	01721 721699
Rae, Andrew W.	(Annan: St Andrew's Greenknowe Erskine)	1951 1987	25 March Street, Peebles EH45 8EP	01835 823783
Rennie, John D. MA	(Broughton, Glenholm and Kilbucho with Skirling with Stobo and Drumelzier with Tweedsmuir)	1962 1996	29/1 Rosetta Road, Peebles EH45 8HJ [E-mail: tworennies@talktalk.net]	01721 720963
Riddell, John A. MA BD	(Jedburgh: Trinity)	1967 2006	Orchid Cottage, Gingham Row, Earlston TD4 6ET	01896 848784
Taverner, Glyn R. MA BD	(Maxton and Mertoun with St Boswells)	1957 1995	Woodcot Cottage, Waverley Road, Innerleithen EH44 6QW	01896 830156
Wallace, James H. MA BD	(Peebles: St Andrew's Leckie)	1973 2011	52 Waverley Mills, Innerleithen EH44 6RH [E-mail: jimwallace121@btinternet.com]	01896 831637

(5) DUNS

Meets at Duns, in the Parish Church hall, normally on the first Tuesday of February, March, April, May, October, November and December, on the last Tuesday in June, and in places to be appointed on the first Tuesday of September.

Clerk: MRS HELEN LONGMUIR — Viewfield, South Street, Gavinton, Duns TD11 3QT — 01361 882728
[E-mail: duns@cofscotland.org.uk]

Ayton (H) and Burnmouth linked with Foulden and Mordington linked with Grantshouse and Houndwood and Reston
Norman R. Whyte BD MTh DipMin — 1982 — 2006 — The Manse, Beanburn, Ayton, Eyemouth TD14 5QY — 01890 781333
[E-mail: burraman@msn.com]

Berwick-upon-Tweed: St Andrew's Wallace Green (H) and Lowick
Adam J.J. Hood MA BD DPhil — 1989 — 2012 — 3 Meadow Grange, Berwick-upon-Tweed TD15 1NW — 01289 332787
[E-mail: minister@sawg.org.uk]

Bonkyl and Preston linked with Chirnside (H) linked with Edrom: Allanton (H)
Duncan E. Murray BA BD — 1970 — 2005 — Parish Church Manse, The Glebe, Chirnside, Duns TD11 3XL — 01890 819109
[E-mail: duncanemurray@tiscali.co.uk]

(From 1 January 2013, Bonkyl and Preston will be linked with Duns and with Edrom: Allanton)

Chirnside See Bonkyl and Preston

Coldingham and St Abb's linked with Eyemouth
Vacant — Victoria Road, Eyemouth TD14 5JD — 01890 750327

Coldstream (H) linked with Eccles
David J. Taverner MCIBS ACIS BD — 1996 — 2011 — 36 Bennecourt Drive, Coldstream TD12 4BY — 01890 883887
[E-mail: rahereuk@hotmail.com]

Duns (H)
Stephen A. Blakey BSc BD — 1977 — 2012 — The Manse, Duns TD11 3DG — 01361 883755
[E-mail: stephenablakey@aol.com]

Eccles See Coldstream
Edrom: Allanton See Bonkyl and Preston
Eyemouth See Coldingham and St Abb's

Fogo and Swinton linked with **Ladykirk** linked with **Leitholm** linked with **Whitsome (H)**

Alan C.D. Cartwright BSc BD	1976		Swinton, Duns TD11 3JJ [E-mail: alan@cartwright-family.co.uk]	01890 860228

Foulden and Mordington See Ayton and Burnmouth

Gordon: St Michael's linked with **Greenlaw (H)** linked with **Legerwood** linked with **Westruther**

Thomas S. Nicholson BD DPS	1982	1995	The Manse, Todholes, Greenlaw, Duns TD10 6XD [E-mail: nst54@hotmail.com]	01361 810316

Grantshouse and Houndwood and Reston See Ayton and Burnmouth

Greenlaw See Gordon: St Michael's

Hutton and Fishwick and Paxton
Guardianship of the Presbytery

Ladykirk See Fogo and Swinton

Langton and Lammermuir Kirk

Ann Inglis (Mrs) LLB BD	1986	2003	The Manse, Cranshaws, Duns TD11 3SJ [E-mail: revainglis@btinternet.com]	01361 890289

Legerwood See Gordon: St Michael's
Leitholm See Fogo and Swinton
Westruther See Gordon: St Michael's
Whitsome See Fogo and Swinton

Gaddes, Donald R.	1961	1994	(Kelso: North and Ednam)	2 Teindhill Green, Duns TD11 3DX [E-mail: drgaddes@btinternet.com]	01361 883172
Gale, Ronald A.A. LTh	1982	1995	(Dunoon: Old and St Cuthbert's)	55 Lennel Mount, Coldstream TD12 4NS [E-mail: rgale89@aol.com]	01890 883699
Graham, Jennifer D. (Mrs) BA MDiv PhD	2000	2011	(Eday with Stronsay: Moncur Memorial)	18 Wheatriggs Avenue, Milfield, Wooler NE71 6HU [E-mail: jdgraham67@gmail.com]	01668 216744
Hay, Bruce J.L.	1957	1997	(Makerstoun and Smailholm with Stichill, Hume and Nenthorn)	Assynt, 1 East Ord Gardens, Berwick-upon-Tweed TD15 2LS	01289 303171
Higham, Robert D. BD	1985	2002	(Tiree)	36 Low Greens, Berwick-upon-Tweed TD15 1LZ	01289 302392
Hope, Geraldine H. (Mrs) MA BD	1986	2007	(Foulden and Mordington with Hutton and Fishwick and Paxton)	4 Well Court, Chirnside, Duns TD11 3UD [E-mail: geraldine.hope@virgin.net]	01890 818134

Name	Dates	(Charge)	Address	Telephone
Kerr, Andrew MA BLitt	1948 1991	(Kilbarchan: West)	4 Lairds Gate, Port Glasgow Road, Kilmacolm PA13 4EX	01507 874852
Landale, William S.	2005	Auxiliary Minister	Green Hope Guest House, Green Hope, Duns TD11 3SG [E-mail: bill@greenhope.co.uk]	01361 890242
Ledgard, J. Christopher BA	1969 2004	(Ayton and Burnmouth with Grantshouse and Houndwood and Reston)	Streonshalh, 8 David Hume View, Chirnside, Duns TD11 3SX	ex-directory
Lindsay, Daniel G. BD	1978 2011	(Coldingham and St Abb's with Eyemouth)	18 Hallidown Crescent, Eyemouth TD14 5TB	
Neill, Bruce F. MA BD	1966 2007	(Maxton and Mertoun with St Boswells)	18 Brierydean, St Abbs, Eyemouth TD14 5PQ [E-mail: bneill@phonecoop.coop]	01890 771569
Paterson, William BD	1977 2001	(Bonkyl and Preston with Chirnside with Edrom: Allanton)	Benachie, Gavinton, Duns TD11 3QT	01361 882727
Walker, Kenneth D.F. MA BD PhD	1976 2008	(Athelstaneford with Whitekirk and Tyninghame)	Allanbank Kothi, Allanton, Duns TD11 3PY [E-mail: kenver.walker@btinternet.com]	01890 817102
Watson, James B. BSc	1968 2009	(Coldstream with Eccles)	49 Lennel Mount, Coldstream TD12 4NS [E-mail: revjamesbwatson@f2s.com]	01890 883149

(6) JEDBURGH

Meets at various venues on the first Wednesday of February, March, May, September, October, November and December and on the last Wednesday of June.

Clerk REV. FRANK CAMPBELL			22 The Glebe, Ancrum, Jedburgh TD8 6UX [E-mail: jedburgh@cofscotland.org.uk]	01835 830318 (Tel) 01835 830262 (Fax)

Ale and Teviot United (H) (Website: www.aleandteviot.org.uk)

Frank Campbell	1989 1991		22 The Glebe, Ancrum, Jedburgh TD8 6UX [E-mail: jedburgh@cofscotland.org.uk]	01835 830318 (Tel) 01835 830262 (Fax)

Cavers and Kirkton linked with Hawick: Trinity

Michael D. Scouler MBE BSc BD	1988 2009		Kerrscroft, Howdenburn, Hawick TD9 8PH [E-mail: michaelscouler@hotmail.co.uk]	01450 378248

Hawick: Burnfoot (Website: www.burnfootparishchurch.org.uk)

Charles J. Finnie LTh DPS	1991 1997		29 Wilton Hill, Hawick TD9 8BA [E-mail: charles.finnie@gmail.com]	01450 373181

Hawick: St Mary's and Old (H)

Vacant			The Manse of St Mary's and Old, Braid Road, Hawick TD9 9LZ	01450 378163

Hawick: Teviot (H) and Roberton
Neil R. Combe BSc MSc BD — 1984 — Teviot Manse, Buccleuch Road, Hawick TD9 0EL [E-mail: neil.combe@btinternet.com] — 01450 372150

Hawick: Trinity (H) See Cavers and Kirkton

Hawick: Wilton linked with Teviothead
Lisa-Jane Rankin (Miss) BD CPS — 2003 — 4 Wilton Hill Terrace, Hawick TD9 8BE [E-mail: revlj@talktalk.net] — 01450 370744 (Tel/Fax)

Hobkirk and Southdean (Website: www.hobkirkruberslaw.org) linked with Ruberslaw (Website: www.hobkirkruberslaw.org)
Douglas A.O. Nicol MA BD — 1974 2009 — The Manse, Denholm, Hawick TD9 8NB [E-mail: daon@lineone.net] — 01450 870268

Jedburgh: Old and Trinity (Website: www.jedburgh-parish.org.uk)
Graham D. Astles BD MSc — 2007 — The Manse, Honeyfield Drive, Jedburgh TD8 6LQ [E-mail: minister@jedburgh-parish.org.uk] — 01835 863417 / 07906 290568 (Mbl)

Kelso Country Churches (Website: www.kelsolinkedchurchescofs.org) linked with Kelso: Old and Sprouston (Website: www.kelsolinkedchurchescofs.org)
Jenny Earl MA BD — 2007 — The Manse, 1 The Meadow, Stichill, Kelso TD5 7TG [E-mail: jennyearl@btinternet.com] — 01573 470607

Kelso: North (H) and Ednam (H) (01573 224154) (E-mail: office@kelsonorthandednam.org.uk) (Website: www.kelsonorthandednam.org.uk)
Tom McDonald BD — 1994 — 20 Forestfield, Kelso TD5 7BX [E-mail: revtom@20thepearlygates.co.uk] — 01573 224677

Kelso: Old (H) and Sprouston See Kelso Country Churches

Linton, Morebattle, Hownam and Yetholm (H) (Website: www.cheviotchurches.org)
Robin D. McHaffie BD — 1979 1991 — The Manse, Main Street, Kirk Yetholm, Kelso TD5 8PF [E-mail: robinmchaffie@btinternet.com] — 01573 420308

Oxnam (Website: www.oxnamkirk.co.uk)
Guardianship of the Presbytery

Ruberslaw See Hobkirk and Southdean
Teviothead See Hawick: Wilton

Auld, A. Graeme MA BD PhD DLitt FSAScot FRSE	1973	(University of Edinburgh)	Nether Swanshiel, Hobkirk, Bonchester Bridge, Hawick TD9 8JU [E-mail: a.g.auld@ed.ac.uk]	01450 860636
McNicol, Bruce	1967 2006	(Jedburgh: Old and Edgerston)	42 Dounehill, Jedburgh TD8 6LJ [E-mail: mcnicol195@btinternet.com]	01835 862991
Rodwell, Anna S. (Mrs) BD DipMin	1998 2003	(Langbank)	The Old Mill House, Hownam Howgate, Kelso TD5 8AJ [E-mail: anna.rodwell@gmail.com]	01573 440761
Shields, John M. MBE LTh	1972 2007	(Channelkirk and Lauder)	12 Eden Park, Ednam, Kelso TD5 7RG	01573 229015
Thomson, E.P. Lindsay MA	1964 2008	(Cavers and Kirkton with Hawick: Trinity)	4 Bourtree Bank, Hawick TD9 9HP [E-mail: eplindsay@btinternet.com]	01450 374318

HAWICK ADDRESSES

Burnfoot	Fraser Avenue
St Mary's and Old	Kirk Wynd
Teviot	off Buccleuch Road
Trinity	Central Square
Wilton	Princes Street

(7) ANNANDALE AND ESKDALE

Meets on the first Tuesday of February, May, September and December, and the third Tuesday of March, June and October. The September meeting is held in the Moderator's charge. The other meetings are held in St Andrew's Parish Church, Gretna.

Clerk:	**REV. C. BRYAN HASTON LTh**		The Manse, Gretna Green, Gretna DG16 5DU [E-mail: annandaleeskdale@cofscotland.org.uk] [E-mail: cbhaston@cofs.demon.co.uk]	01461 338313

Annan: Old (H) linked with Dornock

Hugh D. Steele LTh DipMin	1994	2004	12 Plumdon Park Avenue, Annan DG12 6EY [E-mail: hugdebra@aol.com]	01461 201405

Annan: St Andrew's (H) linked with Brydekirk

John G. Pickles BD MTh MSc	2011	1 Amerley Road, Annan DG12 6HE [E-mail: jgpickles@hotmail.com]	01461 202626

Applegarth, Sibbaldbie (H) and Johnstone linked with Lochmaben (H)
Vacant
The Manse, Barrashead, Lochmaben, Lockerbie DG11 1QF
01387 810066

Brydekirk See Annan: St Andrew's

Canonbie United (H) linked with Liddesdale (H)
Stephen Fulcher BA MA   1993   2009
23 Langholm Street, Newcastleton TD9 0QX
[E-mail: steve@pcmanse.plus.com]
01387 375242

Dalton linked with Hightae linked with St Mungo
Morag A. Dawson BD MTh   1999   2011
The Manse, Hightae, Lockerbie DG11 1JL
[E-mail: moragdawson@yahoo.co.uk]
01387 811499

Dornock See Annan: Old

Gretna: Old (H), Gretna: St Andrew's (H) Half Morton and Kirkpatrick Fleming
C. Bryan Haston LTh   1975
The Manse, Gretna Green, Gretna DG16 5DU
[E-mail: cbhaston@cofs.demon.co.uk]
[E-mail: cbhaston@gretnagreen.eu]
01461 338313

Hightae See Dalton

Hoddom, Kirtle-Eaglesfield and Middlebie
Vacant

Kirkpatrick Juxta linked with Moffat: St Andrew's (H) linked with Wamphray
Adam J. Dillon BD ThM   2003   2008
The Manse, 1 Meadowbank, Moffat DG10 9LR
[E-mail: adamdillon@btinternet.com]
01683 220128

Kirtle-Eaglesfield See Hoddom

Langholm Eskdalemuir Ewes and Westerkirk
I. Scott McCarthy BD   2010
The Manse, Langholm DG13 0BL
[E-mail: iscottmccarthy@gmail.com]
01387 380252

Liddesdale (H) See Canonbie United
Lochmaben See Applegarth, Sibbaldbie and Johnstone

Lockerbie: Dryfesdale, Hutton and Corrie

Alexander C. Stoddart BD	2001	2008	The Manse, 5 Carlisle Road, Lockerbie DG11 2DW [E-mail: sandystoddart@supanet.com]	01576 202361

Middlebie See Hoddom
Moffat: St Andrew's (H) See Kirkpatrick Juxta
St Mungo See Dalton

The Border Kirk (Church office: Chapel Street, Carlisle CA1 1JA; Tel: 01228 591757)

David G. Pitkeathly LLB BD	1996	2007	95 Pinecroft, Carlisle CA3 0DB [E-mail: david.pitkeathly@btinternet.com]	01228 593243

Tundergarth
Guardianship of the Presbytery

Wamphray See Kirkpatrick Juxta

Name			Role/Charge	Address	Telephone
Annand, James M. MA BD	1955	1995	(Lockerbie: Dryfesdale)	Dere Cottage, 48 Main Street, Newstead, Melrose TD6 9DX	
Beveridge, S. Edwin P. BA	1959	2004	(Brydekirk with Hoddom)	19 Rothesay Terrace, Edinburgh EH3 7RY	0131-225 3393
Brown, Jack M. BSc BD	1977	2012	(Applegarth, Sibbaldbie and Johnstone with Lochmaben)	69 Berelands Road, Prestwick KA9 1ER [E-mail: jackm.brown@tiscali.co.uk]	01292 477151
Byers, Alan J.	1959	1992	(Gamrie with King Edward)	Meadowbank, Plumdon Road, Annan DG12 6SJ	01461 206512
Byers, Mairi C. (Mrs) BTh CPS	1992	1998	(Jura)	Meadowbank, Plumdon Road, Annan DG12 6SJ [E-mail: aljbyers@hotmail.com]	01461 206512
Gibb, J. Daniel M. BA LTh	1994	2006	(Aberfoyle with Port of Menteith)	21 Victoria Gardens, Eastriggs, Annan DG12 6TW [E-mail: dannygibb@hotmail.co.uk]	01461 40560
Harvey, P. Ruth (Ms) MA BD	2009	2007	Congregational Facilitator	Croslands, Beacon Street, Penrith CA11 7TZ [E-mail: ruth.harvey@furtherministriesteam.com]	(Mbl) 01768 840749
MacMillan, William M. LTh	1980	1998	(Kilmory with Lamlash)	Balskia, 61 Queen Street, Lochmaben, Lockerbie DG11 1PP	07882 259631
Macpherson, Duncan J. BSc BD	1993	2002	Chaplain: Army	HQ Hereford Garrison, Hereford HR4 7DD	01387 811528
Ross, Alan C. CA BD	1988	2007	(Eskdalemuir with Hutton and Corrie with Tundergarth)	Yarra, Ettrickbridge, Selkirk TD7 5JN [E-mail: alkaross@aol.com]	01750 52324
Seaman, Ronald S. MA	1967	2007	(Dornock)	1 Springfield Farm Court, Springfield, Gretna DG16 5EH	01461 337228
Steenbergen, Pauline (Ms) MA BD	1996	2007	Mission and Discipleship Council	95 Pinecroft, Carlisle CA3 0DB [E-mail: psteenbergen@cofscotland.org.uk]	01228 593243
Swinburne, Norman BA	1960	1993	(Sauchie)	Dameroschay, Birch Hill Lane, Kirkbride, Wigton CA7 5HZ	(Mbl) 07854 711988
Vivers, Katherine A.	2004		Auxiliary Minister	Blacket House, Eaglesfield, Lockerbie DG11 3AA [E-mail: katevivers@yahoo.co.uk]	01697 351497 01461 500412
Williams, Trevor C. LTh	1990	2007	(Hoddom with Kirtle-Eaglesfield with Middlebie with Waterbeck)	c/o Presbytery Clerk [E-mail: revtrev@btinternet.com]	(Mbl) 07748 233011

(8) DUMFRIES AND KIRKCUDBRIGHT

Meets at Dumfries on the last Wednesday of February, June, September and November.

Clerk: REV. WILLIAM T. HOGG MA BD	**St Bride's Manse, Glasgow Road, Sanquhar DG4 6BZ** **[E-mail: dumfrieskirkcudbright@cofscotland.org.uk]**	**01659 50247**
Depute Clerk:		

Auchencairn (H) and Rerrick linked with Buittle (H) and Kelton (H)
Vacant   Auchencairn, Castle Douglas DG7 1QS   01556 640041

Balmaclellan and Kells (H) linked with Carsphairn (H) linked with Dalry (H)
David S. Bartholomew BSc MSc PhD BD   1994   The Manse, Dalry, Castle Douglas DG7 3PJ   01644 430380
[E-mail: dhbart@care4free.net]

Balmaghie linked with Tarff and Twynholm (H)
Christopher Wallace BD DipMin   1988   The Manse, Manse Road, Twynholm, Kirkcudbright DG6 4NY   01557 860381
[E-mail: minister@twynholm.org.uk]

Borgue linked with Gatehouse of Fleet
Valerie J. Ott (Mrs) BA BD   2002   The Manse, Planetree Park, Gatehouse of Fleet,   01557 814233
Castle Douglas DG7 2EQ
[E-mail: dandvott@aol.com]

Buittle and Kelton See Auchencairn and Rerrick

Caerlaverock linked with Dumfries: St Mary's-Greyfriars
Vacant   4 Georgetown Crescent, Dumfries DG1 4EQ   01387 253877

Carsphairn See Balmaclellan and Kells

Castle Douglas (H)
Robert J. Malloch BD   1987 2001   1 Castle View, Castle Douglas DG7 1BG   01556 502171
[E-mail: rojama@live.com]

Closeburn
Guardianship of the Presbytery

Colvend, Southwick and Kirkbean   1984   2003   The Manse, Colvend, Dalbeattie DG5 4QN   01556 630255
James F. Gatherer BD   [E-mail: james@gatherer.net]

Corsock and Kirkpatrick Durham linked with Crossmichael and Parton
Sally Russell BTh MTh   2006   Knockdrocket, Clarebrand, Castle Douglas DG7 3AH   01556 503645
[E-mail: rev.sal@btinternet.com]

Crossmichael and Parton See Corsock and Kirkpatrick Durham

Cummertrees, Mouswald and Ruthwell (H)
Vacant   The Manse, Ruthwell, Dumfries DG1 4NP   01387 870217

Dalbeattie (H) linked with Urr (H)
Vacant   36 Mill Street, Dalbeattie DG5 4HE   01556 610029

Dalry See Balmaclellan and Kells

Dumfries: Maxwelltown West (H)
Vacant   Maxwelltown West Manse, 11 Laurieknowe, Dumfries DG2 7AH   01387 252929

Dumfries: Northwest
Neil G. Campbell BA BD   1988   2006   27 St Anne's Road, Dumfries DG2 9HZ   01387 249964
[E-mail: mail@neilgcampbell.co.uk]

Dumfries: St George's (H)
Donald Campbell BD   1997   9 Nunholm Park, Dumfries DG1 1JP   01387 252965
[E-mail: saint-georges@ukonline.co.uk]

Dumfries: St Mary's-Greyfriars (H) See Caerlaverock

Dumfries: St Michael's and South
Maurice S. Bond MTh BA DipEd PhD   1981   1999   39 Cardoness Street, Dumfries DG1 3AL   01387 253849
[E-mail: mauricebond399@btinternet.com]

Dumfries: Troqueer (H)
William W. Kelly BSc BD   1994   Troqueer Manse, Troqueer Road, Dumfries   DG2 7DF
[E-mail: wwkelly@yahoo.com]   01387 253043

Dunscore linked with Glencairn and Moniaive
Vacant   Wallaceton, Auldgirth, Dumfries   DG2 0TJ   01387 820245

Durisdeer linked with Penpont, Keir and Tynron linked with Thornhill (H)
Vacant   The Manse, Manse Park, Thornhill   DG3 5ER   01848 331191

Gatehouse of Fleet See Borgue
Glencairn and Moniaive See Dunscore

Irongray, Lochrutton and Terregles
Vacant   Shawhead Road, Dumfries   DG2 9SJ   01387 730287

Kirkconnel (H)
Alistair J. MacKichan MA BD   1984   2009   The Manse, 31 Kingsway, Kirkconnel, Sanquhar   DG4 6PN   01659 67241

Kirkcudbright (H)
Douglas R. Irving LLB BD WS   1984   1998   6 Bourtree Avenue, Kirkcudbright DG6 4AU
[E-mail: douglasirving05@tiscali.co.uk]   01557 330489

Kirkgunzeon linked with Lochend and New Abbey
Vacant   The Manse, 28 Main Street, New Abbey, Dumfries   DG2 8BY   01387 850232

Kirkmahoe
David M. Almond BD   1996   2008   The Manse, Kirkmahoe, Dumfries DG1 1ST
[E-mail: almond.david138@googlemail.com]   01387 710572

Kirkmichael, Tinwald and Torthorwald
Willem J. Bezuidenhout BA BD MHEd MEd   1977   2010   Manse of Tinwald, Tinwald, Dumfries DG1 3PL
[E-mail: willembezuidenhout@btinternet.com]   01387 710246

Lochend and New Abbey See Kirkgunzeon
Penpont, Keir and Tynron See Durisdeer

Sanquhar: St Bride's (H)
William T. Hogg MA BD   1979   2000   St Bride's Manse, Glasgow Road, Sanquhar DG6 6BZ   01659 50247
[E-mail: wthogg@yahoo.com]

Tarff and Twynholm See Balmaghie
Thornhill (H) See Durisdeer
Urr See Dalbeattie

Name			Charge	Address	Phone
Bennett, David K.P. BA	1974	2000	(Kirkpatrick Irongray with Lochrutton with Terregles)	53 Anne Arundel Court, Heathhall, Dumfries DG1 3SL	01387 257755
Duncan, Maureen M. (Mrs) BD	1996	2008	(Dunlop)	Dunedin, Whitepark, Castle Douglas DG7 1QA [E-mail: revmo@talktalk.net]	01556 502867
Greer, A. David C. LLB DMin DipAdultEd	1956	1996	(Barra)	17 Duthac Wynd, Tain IV19 1LP [E-mail: kandadc@greer10.fsnet.co.uk]	01862 892065
Hamill, Robert BA	1956	1989	(Castle Douglas: St Ringan's)	11 St Andrew Drive, Castle Douglas DG7 1EW	01556 502962
Hammond, Richard J. BA BD	1993	2007	(Kirkmahoe)	3 Marchfield Mount, Marchfield, Dumfries DG1 1SE [E-mail: libby.hammond@virgin.net]	(Mbl) 07764 465783
Henig, Gordon BSc BD	1997	2003	(Bellie with Speymouth)	4 Galla Crescent, Dalbeattie DG5 4JY	01556 611183
Holland, William MA	1967	2009	(Lochend and New Abbey)	Ardshean, 55 Georgetown Road, Dumfries DG1 4DD [E-mail: billholland55@btinternet.com]	01387 256131 (Mbl) 07766 531732
Kirk, W. Logan MA BD MTh	1988	2000	(Dalton with Hightae with St Mungo)	2 Raecroft Avenue, Collin, Dumfries DG1 4LP	01387 750489
Leishman, James S. LTh BD MA(Div)	1969	1999	(Kirkmichael with Tinwald with Torthorwald)	11 Hunter Avenue, Heathhall, Dumfries DG1 3UX	01387 249241
Mack, Elizabeth A. (Miss) DipEd	1994	2011	(Auxiliary Minister)	24 Roberts Crescent, Dumfries DG2 7RS [E-mail: mackliz@btinternet.com]	01387 264847
McKay, David M. MA BD	1979	2007	(Kirkpatrick Juxta with Moffat: St Andrew's with Wamphray)	20 Auld Brig View, Auldgirth, Dumfries DG2 0XE [E-mail: davidmckay20@tiscali.co.uk]	01387 740013
McKenzie, William M. DA	1958	1993	(Dumfries: Troqueer)	41 Kingholm Road, Dumfries DG1 4SR [E-mail: mckenzie.dumfries@btinternet.com]	01387 253688
Miller, John R. MA BD	1958	1992	(Carsphairn with Dalry)	4 Fairgreen Court, Rhonehouse, Castle Douglas DG7 1SA	01556 680428
Owen, John J.C. LTh	1967	2001	(Applegarth and Sibbaldbie with Lochmaben)	5 Galla Avenue, Dalbeattie DG5 4JZ [E-mail: jj.owen@onetel.net]	01556 612125
Robertson, Ian W. MA BD	1956	1995	(Colvend, Southwick and Kirkbean)	10 Marjoriebanks, Lochmaben, Lockerbie DG11 1QH	01387 810541
Smith, Richmond OBE MA BD	1952	1983	(World Alliance of Reformed Churches)	Aignish, Merse Way, Kippford, Dalbeattie DG5 4LH	01556 620624
Strachan, Alexander E. MA BD	1974	1999	Healthcare Chaplain	2 Leafield Road, Dumfries DG1 2DS [E-mail: aestrachan@aol.com]	01387 279460
Sutherland, Colin A. LTh	1995	2007	(Blantyre: Livingstone Memorial)	71 Caulstran Road, Dumfries DG2 9FJ [E-mail: colin.csutherland@btinternet.com]	01387 279954
Vincent, C. Raymond MA FSAScot	1952	1992	(Stonehouse)	Rosebank, Newton Stewart Road, New Galloway, Castle Douglas DG7 3RT	01644 420451
Wilkie, James R. MA MTh	1957	1993	(Penpont, Keir and Tynron)	31 West Morton Street, Thornhill DG3 5NF	01848 331028

Williamson, James BA BD	1986 2009	(Cummertrees with Mouswald with Ruthwell)	12 Mulberry Drive, Dunfermline KY11 8BZ [E-mail: jimwill@rcmkirk.fsnet.co.uk]	01383 734872
Wotherspoon, Robert C. LTh	1976 1998	(Corsock and Kirkpatrick Durham with Crossmichael and Parton)	7 Hillowton Drive, Castle Douglas DG7 1LL [E-mail: robert.wotherspoon@tiscali.co.uk]	01556 502267
Young, John MTh DipMin	1963 1999	(Airdrie: Broomknoll)	Craigview, North Street, Moniaive, Thornhill DG3 4HR	01848 200318

DUMFRIES ADDRESSES

Maxwelltown West	Laurieknowe	Northwest	Lochside Road	St Michael's and South	St Michael's Street
		St George's	George Street	Troqueer	Troqueer Road
		St Mary's-Greyfriars	St Mary's Street		

(9) WIGTOWN AND STRANRAER

Meets at Glenluce, in the church hall, on the first Tuesday of March, October and December for ordinary business; on the first Tuesday of September for formal business followed by meetings of committees; on the first Tuesday of November, February and May for worship followed by meetings of committees; and at a church designated by the Moderator on the first Tuesday of June for Holy Communion followed by ordinary business.

Clerk:	MRS NICOLA STEEL	Auchengallie Farm, Port William, Newton Stewart DG8 9RQ [E-mail: wigtownstranraer@cofscotland.org.uk]	01988 700534

Ervie Kirkcolm linked with Leswalt

Michael J. Sheppard BD	1997	Ervie Manse, Stranraer DG9 0QZ [E-mail: mjs@uwclub.net]	01776 854225

Glasserton and Isle of Whithorn linked with Whithorn: St Ninian's Priory

Alexander I. Currie BD CPS	1990	The Manse, Whithorn, Newton Stewart DG8 8PT	01988 500267

Inch linked with Stranraer: Town Kirk (H)

John H. Burns BSc BD	1985 1988	Bayview Road, Stranraer DG9 8BE	01776 702383

Kirkcowan (H) linked with Wigtown (H)

Eric Boyle BA MTh	2006	Seaview Manse, Church Lane, Wigtown, Newton Stewart DG8 9HT [E-mail: ecthered@aol.com]	01988 402314

Kirkinner linked with Sorbie (H) Jeffrey M. Mead BD	1978	1986	The Manse, Kirkinner, Newton Stewart DG8 9AL	01988 840643
Kirkmabreck linked with Monigaff (H) Peter W.I. Aiken	1996	2005	Creebridge, Newton Stewart DG8 6NR [E-mail: aikenp@btinternet.com]	01671 403361
Kirkmaiden (H) linked with Stoneykirk Melvyn J. Griffiths BTh DipTheol DMin	1978	2011	Church Road, Sandhead, Stranraer DG9 9JJ [E-mail: mel@thehavyn.wanadoo.co.uk]	01776 830548
Leswalt See Ervie Kirkcolm				
Mochrum (H) Mary C. McLauchlan (Mrs) LTh	1997	2010	Manse of Mochrum, Port William, Newton Stewart DG8 9QP [E-mail: mary@revmother.co.uk]	01988 700871
Monigaff (H) See Kirkmabreck				
New Luce (H) linked with Old Luce (H) Thomas M. McWhirter MA MSc BD	1992	1997	Glenluce, Newton Stewart DG8 0PU	01581 300319
Old Luce See New Luce				
Penninghame (H) Edward D. Lyons BD MTh	2007		The Manse, 1A Corvisel Road, Newton Stewart DG8 6LW [E-mail: edwardlyons@hotmail.com]	01671 404425
Portpatrick linked with Stranraer: St Ninian's (H) Vacant			2 Albert Terrace, London Road, Stranraer DG9 8AB	01776 702443
Sorbie See Kirkinner **Stoneykirk** See Kirkmaiden				
Stranraer: High Kirk (H) Ian McIlroy BSS BD	1996	2009	Stoneleigh, Whitehouse Road, Stranraer DG9 0JB	01776 700616

Stranraer: St Ninian's See Portpatrick
Stranraer: Town Kirk See Inch
Whithorn: St Ninian's Priory See Glasserton and Isle of Whithorn
Wigtown See Kirkcowan

Binks, Mike	2007 2009	Auxiliary Minister	5 Maxwell Drive, Newton Stewart DG8 6EL [E-mail: mike@hollybank.net]	01671 402201 (Mbl) 07590 507917
Crawford, Joseph F. BA	1970 2006	(Bowden with Newtown)	21 South Street, Port William, Newton Stewart DG8 9SH	01988 700761
McGill, Thomas W.	1972 1990	(Portpatrick with Stranraer: St Ninian's)	Westfell, Monreith, Newton Stewart DG8 9LT	01988 700449
Munro, Mary (Mrs) BA	1993 2004	(Auxiliary Minister)	14 Auchneel Crescent, Stranraer DG9 0JH	01776 702305

(10) AYR

Meets on the first Tuesday of every month from September to May, excluding January, and on the fourth Tuesday of June. The June meeting will be held in the Moderator's church. One meeting will be held in a venue to be determined by the Business Committee. Other meetings will be held in Alloway Church Hall.

Clerk:	**REV. KENNETH C. ELLIOTT** **BD BA CertMin**		68 St Quivox Road, Prestwick KA9 1JF [E-mail: ayr@cofscotland.org.uk]	01292 478788
Presbytery Office:			Prestwick South Parish Church, 50 Main Street, Prestwick KA9 1NX [E-mail: ayroffice@cofscotland.org.uk]	01292 678556

Alloway (H)
Neil A. McNaught BD MA	1987	1999	1A Parkview, Alloway, Ayr KA7 4QG [E-mail: nandjmcnaught@btinternet.com]	01292 441252

Annbank (H) linked with Tarbolton
Alexander Shuttleworth MA BD	2004		1 Kirkport, Tarbolton, Mauchline KA5 5QJ [E-mail: revshuttleworth@aol.com]	01292 541236

Auchinleck (H) linked with Catrine
Stephen F. Clipston MA BD	1982	2006	28 Mauchline Road, Auchinleck KA18 2BN [E-mail: steveclipston@btinternet.com]	01290 424776

Ayr: Auld Kirk of Ayr (St John the Baptist) (H)

Name			Address	Telephone
David R. Gemmell MA BD	1991	1999	58 Monument Road, Ayr KA7 2UB [E-mail: drgemmell@hotmail.com]	01292 262580 (Tel/Fax)

Ayr: Castlehill (H)

Name			Address	Telephone
Elizabeth A. Crumlish (Mrs) BD	1995	2008	3 Old Hillfoot Road, Ayr KA7 3LW [E-mail: lizcrumlish@aol.com]	01292 263001
Douglas T. Moore	2003	2009	9 Midton Avenue, Prestwick KA9 1PU [E-mail: douglastmoore@hotmail.com]	01292 671352

Ayr: Newton Wallacetown (H)

Name			Address	Telephone
G. Stewart Birse CA BD BSc	1980	1989	9 Nursery Grove, Ayr KA7 3PH [E-mail: axhp44@dsl.pipex.com]	01292 264251

Ayr: St Andrew's (H)

Name			Address	Telephone
Vacant			31 Bellevue Crescent, Ayr KA7 2DP	01292 261126

Ayr: St Columba (H)

Name			Address	Telephone
Fraser R. Aitken MA BD	1978	1991	3 Upper Crofts, Alloway, Ayr KA7 4QX [E-mail: frasercolumba@msn.com]	01292 443747

Ayr: St James' (H)

Name			Address	Telephone
Robert McCrum BSc BD	1982	2005	1 Prestwick Road, Ayr KA8 8LD [E-mail: robert@stjamesayr.org.uk]	01292 262420

Ayr: St Leonard's (H) linked with Dalrymple

Name			Address	Telephone
Linda Godfrey BSc BD	2012		35 Roman Road, Ayr KA7 3SZ [E-mail: godfreykayak@aol.com]	01292 283825

Ayr: St Quivox (H)

Name			Address	Telephone
Rona M. Young (Mrs) BD DipEd	1991	2009	11 Springfield Avenue, Prestwick KA9 2HA [E-mail: revronyoung@hotmail.com]	01292 478306

Ballantrae (H) linked with St Colmon (Arnsheen Barrhill and Colmonell)

Name			Address	Telephone
Stephen Ogston MPhys MSc BD	2009		The Manse, 1 The Vennel, Ballantrae, Girvan KA26 0NH [E-mail: ogston@macfish.com]	01465 831252

Barr linked with Dailly linked with Girvan: South   1999
Ian K. McLachlan MA BD
30 Henrietta Street, Girvan KA26 9AL
[E-mail: iankmclachlan@yetiville.freeserve.co.uk]
01465 713370

Catrine See Auchinleck

Coylton linked with Drongan: The Schaw Kirk   1998
David Whiteman BD   2008
4 Hamilton Place, Coylton, Ayr KA6 6JQ
[E-mail: davesoo@sky.com]
01292 571442

Craigie linked with Symington   1996
Glenda J. Keating (Mrs) MTh   2008
16 Kerrix Road, Symington, Kilmarnock KA1 5QD
[E-mail: kirkglen@btinternet.com]
01563 830205

Crosshill (H) linked with Maybole   1992
Brian Hendrie BD   2010
The Manse, 16 McAdam Way, Maybole KA19 8FD
[E-mail: hendrie962@btinternet.com]
01655 883710

Dailly See Barr

Dalmellington linked with Patna: Waterside   2008
Fiona A. Wilson (Mrs) BD   2012
4 Carsphairn Road, Dalmellington, Ayr KA6 7RE
[E-mail: weefi12b@hotmail.co.uk]
01292 551503

Dalrymple See Ayr: St Leonard's
Drongan: The Schaw Kirk See Coylton

Dundonald (H)   1982
Robert Mayes BD   1988
64 Main Street, Dundonald, Kilmarnock KA2 9HG
[E-mail: bobmayes@fsmail.net]
01563 850243

Fisherton (H) linked with Kirkoswald   2000
Arrick D. Wilkinson BSc BD   2003
The Manse, Kirkoswald, Maybole KA19 8HZ
[E-mail: arrick@clergy.net]
01655 760210

Girvan: North (Old and St Andrew's) (H)
Vacant — 38 The Avenue, Girvan KA26 9DS — 01465 713203

Girvan: South See Barr

Kirkmichael linked with Straiton: St Cuthbert's
W. Gerald Jones MA BD MTh 1984 1985 — Patna Road, Kirkmichael, Maybole KA19 7PJ
[E-mail: revgerald@jonesg99.freeserve.co.uk] — 01655 750286

Kirkoswald (H) See Fisherton

Lugar linked with Old Cumnock: Old (H)
John W. Paterson BSc BD DipEd 1994 — 33 Barrhill Road, Cumnock KA18 1PJ
[E-mail: ocochurchwow@hotmail.com] — 01290 420769
Nancy Jackson (Aux) 2009 — Cygnet House, Holmfarm Road, Catrine, Mauchline KA5 6TA — 01290 550511

Mauchline (H) linked with Sorn
David A. Albon BA MCS 1991 2011 — 4 Westside Gardens, Mauchline KA5 5DJ
[E-mail: albon@onetel.com] — 01290 518528

Maybole See Crosshill

Monkton and Prestwick: North (H)
David Clarkson BSc BA MTh 2010 — 40 Monkton Road, Prestwick KA9 1AR
[E-mail: revdavidclarkson@gmail.com] — 01292 471379

Muirkirk (H) linked with Old Cumnock: Trinity
Scott M. Rae MBE BD CPS 1976 2008 — 46 Ayr Road, Cumnock KA18 1DW
[E-mail: scottrae1@btopenworld.com] — 01290 422145

New Cumnock (H)
Helen E. Cuthbert MA MSc BD 2009 — 37 Castle, New Cumnock, Cumnock KA18 4AG
[E-mail: helencuthbert@mypostoffice.co.uk] — 01290 338296

Ochiltree linked with Stair
William R. Johnston BD 1998 2009 — 10 Mauchline Road, Ochiltree, Cumnock KA18 2PZ — 01290 700365

Old Cumnock: Old See Lugar
Old Cumnock: Trinity See Muirkirk
Patna: Waterside See Dalmellington

Prestwick: Kingcase (H) (E-mail: office@kingcase.freeserve.co.uk)
T. David Watson BSc BD   1988   1997   15 Bellrock Avenue, Prestwick KA9 1SQ   01292 479571
[E-mail: tdavidwatson@btinternet.com]

Prestwick: St Nicholas' (H)
George R. Fiddes BD   1979   1985   3 Bellevue Road, Prestwick KA9 1NW   01292 477613
[E-mail: gfiddes@stnicholasprestwick.org.uk]

Prestwick: South (H)
Kenneth C. Elliott BD BA CertMin   1989   68 St Quivox Road, Prestwick KA9 1JF   01292 478788
[E-mail: kcelliott@tiscali.co.uk]

St Colmon (Arnsheen Barrhill and Colmonell) See Ballantrae
Sorn See Mauchline
Stair See Ochiltree
Straiton: St Cuthbert's See Kirkmichael
Symington See Craigie
Tarbolton See Annbank

Troon: Old (H)
Vacant   85 Bentinck Drive, Troon KA10 6HZ   01292 313644

Troon: Portland (H)
Jamie Milliken BD   2005   2011   89 South Beach, Troon KA10 6EQ   01292 318929
                                                                       07929 349045 (Mbl)
[E-mail: minister@troonportlandchurch.org.uk]

Troon: St Meddan's (H) (E-mail: st.meddan@virgin.net)
Vacant   27 Bentinck Drive, Troon KA10 6HX   01292 311784

Baker, Carolyn M. (Mrs) BD   1997 2008   (Ochiltree with Stair)   Clanary, 1 Maxwell Drive, Newton Stewart DG8 6EL   01292 261276
[E-mail: cncbaker@btinternet.com]
Blyth, James G.S. BSc BD   1963 1986   (Glenmuick)   40 Robsland Avenue, Ayr KA7 2RW
Bogle, Thomas C. BD   1983 2003   (Fisherton with Maybole: West)   38 McEwan Crescent, Mossblown, Ayr KA6 5DR   01292 521215

Name			Position	Address	Tel
Boyd, Ronald M.H. BD DipTh	1995	2010	Chaplain and Teacher of RMPS: Queen Victoria School, Dunblane	6 Victoria Green, Queen Victoria School, Dunblane FK15 0JY	01786 822288
Cranston, George BD	1976	2001	(Rutherglen: Wardlawhill)	20 Capperview, Prestwick KA9 1BH	01292 476627
Crichton, James MA BD MTh	1969	2010	(Crosshill with Dalrymple)	4B Garden Court, Ayr KA8 0AT [E-mail: crichton.james@btinternet.com]	01292 288978
Dickie, Michael M. BSc	1955	1994	(Ayr: Castlehill)	8 Noltmire Road, Ayr KA8 9ES	01292 618512
Geddes, Alexander J. MA BD	1960	1998	(Stewarton: St Columba's)	2 Gregory Street, Mauchline KA5 6BY [E-mail: sandy.elizabeth@tiscali.co.uk]	01290 518597
Glencross, William M. LTh	1968	1999	(Bellshill: Macdonald Memorial)	1 Lochay Place, Troon KA10 7HH	01292 317097
Grant, J. Gordon MA BD PhD	1957	1997	(Edinburgh: Dean)	33 Fullarton Drive, Troon KA10 6LE	01292 311852
Guthrie, James A.	1969	2005	(Corsock and Kirkpatrick Durham with Crossmichael and Parton)	2 Barrhill Road, Pinwherry, Girvan KA26 0QE [E-mail: p.h.m.guthrie@btinternet.com]	01465 841236
Hannah, William BD MCAM MIPR	1987	2001	(Muirkirk)	8 Dovecote View, Kirkintilloch, Glasgow G66 3HY [E-mail: revbillnews@btinternet.com]	0141-776 1337
Harper, David L. BSc BD	1972	2012	(Troon: St Meddan's)	19 Calder Avenue, Troon KA10 7JT [E-mail: d.l.harper@btinternet.com]	01292 312626
Harris, Samuel McC. OStJ BA BD	1974	2010	(Rothesay: Trinity)	36 Adam Wood Court, Troon KA10 6BP	01292 319603
Helon, George G. BA BD	1984	2000	(Barr linked with Dailly)	9 Park Road, Maxwelltown, Dumfries DG2 7PW	01387 259255
Kent, Arthur F.S.	1966	1999	(Monkton and Prestwick: North)	17 St David's Drive, Evesham, Worcs WR11 6AS [E-mail: afsken@onetel.com]	01386 421562
King, Chris (Mrs) MA BD DCS	1971	2009	Deaconess (Bishopbriggs: Kenmuir)	28 Kilnford Drive, Dundonald, Kilmarnock KA2 9ET	01563 851197
Laing, Iain A. MA BD			(Bishopbriggs: Kenmuir)	9 Annfield Road, Prestwick KA9 1PP [E-mail: iandrlaing@yahoo.co.uk]	01292 471732
Lennox, Lawrie I. MA BD DipEd	1991	2006	(Cromar)	7 Carwinshoch View, Ayr KA7 4AY [E-mail: lawrie@lennox.myzen.co.uk]	
Lochrie, John S. BSc BD MTh PhD	1967	2008	(St Colmon)	Cosyglen, Kilkerran, Maybole KA19 8LS	01465 811262
Lynn, Robert MA BD	1984	2011	(Ayr: St Leonard's with Dalrymple)	8 Kirkbrae, Maybole KA19 7ER	(Mbl) 07771 481698
McCrorie, William	1965	1999	(Free Church Chaplain: Royal Brompton Hospital)	12 Shieling Park, Ayr KA7 2UR [E-mail: billevemccrorie@btinternet.com]	01292 288854
Macdonald, Ian U.	1960	1997	(Tarbolton)	18 Belmont Road, Ayr KA7 2PF	01292 283085
McGurk, Andrew F. BD	1983	2011	(Largs: St John's)	15 Fraser Avenue, Troon KA10 6XF [E-mail: afmcg.largs@talk21.com]	01292 676008
McNidder, Roderick H. BD	1987	1997	Chaplain: NHS Ayrshire and Arran Trust	6 Hollow Park, Alloway, Ayr KA7 4SR	01292 442554
McPhail, Andrew M. BA	1968	2002	(Ayr: Wallacetown)	25 Maybole Road, Ayr KA7 2QA	01292 282108
Matthews, John C. MA BD OBE	1992	2010	(Glasgow: Ruchill Kelvinside)	12 Arrol Drive, Ayr KA7 4AF [E-mail: mejohnmatthews@gmail.com]	01292 264382
Mealyea, Harry B. BArch BD	1984	2011	(Ayr: St Andrew's)	c/o Louise Mealyea, 46 Rosehill Drive, Aberdeen AB24 4JQ [E-mail: mealyea@tiscali.co.uk]	
Mitchell, Sheila M. (Miss) BD MTh	1995	2002	Chaplain: NHS Ayrshire and Arran Trust	Ailsa Hospital, Ayr KA6 6BQ	01292 513197
Morrison, Alistair H. BTh DipYCS	1985	2004	(Paisley: St Mark's Oldhall)	92 St Leonard's Road, Ayr KA7 2PU [E-mail: alistairmorrison@supanet.com]	01292 266021
Ness, David T. LTh	1972	2008	(Ayr: St Quivox)	17 Winston Avenue, Prestwick KA9 2EZ [E-mail: dtness@tiscali.co.uk]	

Russell, Paul R. MA BD	1984 2006	Chaplain: NHS Ayrshire and Arran Trust	23 Nursery Wynd, Ayr KA7 3NZ	01292 618020
Sanderson, Alastair M. BA LTh	1971 2007	(Craigie with Symington)	26 Main Street, Monkton, Prestwick KA9 2QL	01292 475819
			[E-mail: alel@sanderson29.fsnet.co.uk]	
Saunders, Campbell M. MA BD	1952 1989	(Ayr: St Leonard's)	27 St Vincent Crescent, Alloway, Ayr KA7 4QW	01292 441673
Simpson, Edward V. BSc BD	1972 2009	(Glasgow: Giffnock South)	8 Paddock View, Thorntoun, Crosshouse, Kilmarnock KA2 0BH	01563 522841
			[E-mail: eddie.simpson3@talktalk.net]	
Smith, Elizabeth (Mrs) BD	1996 2009	(Fauldhouse: St Andrew's)	16 McIntyre Road, Prestwick KA9 1BE	01292 471588
			[E-mail: smithrevb@btinternet.com]	
Stirling, Ian R. BSc BD	1990 2002	Chaplain: The Ayrshire Hospice	Ayrshire Hospice, 35–37 Racecourse Road, Ayr KA7 2TG	01292 269200
Symington, Alastair H. MA BD	1972 2012	(Troon: Old)	1 Cavendish Place, Troon KA10 6JG	01292 312556
			[E-mail: revdahs@btinternet.com]	
Yorke, Kenneth B.	1982 2009	(Dalmellington with Patna: Waterside)	13 Annfield Terrace, Prestwick KA9 1PS	(Mbl) 07766 320525
			[E-mail: kenneth.yorke@googlemail.com]	

AYR ADDRESSES

Ayr

Auld Kirk	Kirkport (116 High Street)
Castlehill	Castlehill Road x Hillfoot Road
Newton Wallacetown	Main Street
St Andrew's	Park Circus
St Columba	Midton Road x Carrick Park
St James'	Prestwick Road x Falkland Park Road
St Leonard's	St Leonard's Road x Monument Road

Girvan

North	Montgomerie Street
South	Stair Park

Prestwick

Kingcase	Waterloo Road
Monkton and Prestwick North	Monkton Road
St Nicholas	Main Street
South	Main Street

Troon

Old	Ayr Street
Portland	St Meddan's Street
St Meddan's	St Meddan's Street

(11) IRVINE AND KILMARNOCK

The Presbytery meets ordinarily at 6.30pm in the Hall of Howard St Andrew's Church, Kilmarnock, on the first Tuesday of each month from September to May (except January and April), and on the fourth Tuesday in June. The September meeting begins with the celebration of Holy Communion.

Clerk:	MR I. STEUART DEY LLB	72 Dundonald Road, Kilmarnock KA1 1RZ	01563 521686
		[E-mail: irvinekilmarnock@cofscotland.org.uk]	
		[E-mail: steuart.dey@btinternet.com]	
Depute Clerk:	REV. S. GRANT BARCLAY LLB DipLP BD MSc PhD	1 Thirdpart Place, Kilmarnock KA1 1UL	01563 571280
		[E-mail: minister@stkentigern.org.uk]	
Treasurer:	JAMES McINTOSH BA CA	15 Dundonald Road, Kilmarnock KA1 1RU	01563 523552

The Presbytery office is staffed each Tuesday, Wednesday and Thursday from 9am until 12:45pm. The office telephone number is 01563 526295.

Charge / Minister			Address	Telephone
Caldwell linked with Dunlop David Donaldson MA BD DMin	1969	2010	4 Dampark, Dunlop, Kilmarnock KA3 4BZ [E-mail: jd.donaldson@talktalk.net]	01560 483268
Crosshouse T. Edward Marshall BD	1987	2007	27 Kilmarnock Road, Crosshouse, Kilmarnock KA2 0EZ [E-mail: marshall862@btinternet.com]	01563 524089
Darvel (01560 322924) Charles Lines BA	2010		46 West Main Street, Darvel KA17 0AQ [E-mail: cmdlines@tiscali.co.uk]	01560 322924
Dreghorn and Springside Gary E. Horsburgh BA	1976	1983	96A Townfoot, Dreghorn, Irvine KA11 4EZ [E-mail: garyhorsburgh@hotmail.co.uk]	01294 217770
Dunlop See Caldwell				
Fenwick (H) Geoffrey Redmayne BSc BD MPhil	2000		2 Kirkton Place, Fenwick, Kilmarnock KA3 6DW [E-mail: gnredmayne@googlemail.com]	01560 600217
Galston (H) (01563 820136) Graeme R. Wilson MCIBS BD ThM	2006		60 Brewland Street, Galston KA4 8DX [E-mail: graeme.wilson@gmail.com]	01563 820246
Hurlford (H) James D. McCulloch BD MIOP MIP3	1996		12 Main Road, Crookedholm, Kilmarnock KA3 6JT [E-mail: mccullochmanse1@btinternet.com]	01563 535673
Irvine: Fullarton (H) (Website: www.fullartonchurch.co.uk) Neil Urquhart BD DipMin	1989		48 Waterside, Irvine KA12 8QJ [E-mail: neilurquhart@f2s.com]	01294 279909
Irvine: Girdle Toll (H) (Website: www.girdletoll.fsbusiness.co.uk) Vacant			2 Littlestane Rise, Irvine KA11 2BJ	01294 213565

Irvine: Mure (H)
Hugh M. Adamson BD
1976
West Road, Irvine KA12 8RE
[E-mail: hmadamson768@btinternet.com]
01294 279916

Irvine: Old (H) (01294 273503)
Robert Travers BA BD
1993   1999
22 Kirk Vennel, Irvine KA12 0DQ
[E-mail: robert.travers@tesco.net]
01294 279265

Irvine: Relief Bourtreehill (H)
Andrew R. Black BD
1987   2003
4 Kames Court, Irvine KA11 1RT
[E-mail: andrewblack@tiscali.co.uk]
01294 216939

Irvine: St Andrew's (H) (01294 276051)
Ian W. Benzie BD
1999   2008
St Andrew's Manse, 206 Bank Street, Irvine KA12 0YD
[E-mail: revianb@gmail.com]
01294 216139

Fiona Blair (Miss) DCS (Pastoral Assistant)
5 Gilbertfield Place, Irvine KA12 0EY
07977 235168 (Mbl)

Kilmarnock: Henderson (H) (01563 541302) (Website: www.hendersonchurch.org.uk)
David W. Lacy BA BD DLitt
1976   1989
52 London Road, Kilmarnock KA3 7AJ
[E-mail: thelacys@tinyworld.co.uk]
01563 523113 (Tel/Fax)

Kilmarnock: New Laigh Kirk (H)
David S. Cameron BD
2001
1 Holmes Farm Road, Kilmarnock KA1 1TP
[E-mail: dvdcam5@msn.com]
01563 525416

Barbara Urquhart (Mrs) DCS
9 Standalane, Kilmaurs, Kilmarnock KA3 2NB
[E-mail: barbararurquhart@uko2.co.uk]
01563 538289

Kilmarnock: Old High Kirk (H)
Vacant
107 Dundonald Road, Kilmarnock KA1 1UP
01563 525608

Kilmarnock: Riccarton (H)
Colin A. Strong BSc BD
1989   2007
2 Jasmine Road, Kilmarnock KA1 2HD
[E-mail: colinastrong@aol.com]
01563 549490

Kilmarnock: St Andrew's and St Marnock's
James McNaughtan BD DipMin
1983   1989
35 South Gargieston Drive, Kilmarnock KA1 1TB
[E-mail: jmcnaughtan@gmail.com]
01563 521665

Kilmarnock: St John's Onthank (H)
Susan M. Anderson (Mrs)   1997   84 Wardneuk Drive, Kilmarnock KA3 2EX   01563 521815
[E-mail: stjohnthank@talktalk.net]

Kilmarnock: St Kentigern's (Website: www.stkentigern.org.uk)
S. Grant Barclay LLB DipLP BD MSc PhD   1995   1 Thirdpart Place, Kilmarnock KA1 1UL   01563 571280
[E-mail: minister@stkentigern.org.uk]

Kilmarnock: South (01563 524705)
H. Taylor Brown BD CertMin   1997 2002   14 McLelland Drive, Kilmarnock KA1 1SF   01563 529920
[E-mail: htaylorbrown@hotmail.com]
(New charge formed by the union of **Kilmarnock: St Ninian's Bellfield and Kilmarnock: Shortlees**)

Kilmaurs: St Maur's Glencairn (H) (Website: www.jimcorbett.freeserve.co.uk/page2.html)
John A. Urquhart BD   1993   9 Standalane, Kilmaurs, Kilmarnock KA3 2NB   01563 538289
[E-mail: john.urquhart@talktalk.net]

Newmilns: Loudoun (H)
David S. Randall BA BD   2003 2009   Loudoun Manse, 116A Loudoun Road, Newmilns KA16 9HH   01560 320174
[E-mail: dsrandall@sky.com]

Stewarton: John Knox
Gavin A. Niven BSc MSc BD   2010   27 Avenue Street, Stewarton, Kilmarnock KA3 5AP   01560 482418
[E-mail: minister@johnknox.org.uk]

Stewarton: St Columba's (H)
George K. Lind BD MCIBS   1998 2010   1 Kirk Glebe, Stewarton, Kilmarnock KA3 5BJ   01560 482453
[E-mail: gklind@talktalk.net]

Ayrshire Mission to the Deaf
Graeme R. Wilson BD ThM MCIBS   2006   60 Brewland Street, Galston KA4 8DX   01563 820246
 (Chaplain)   [E-mail: graeme.wilson@gmail.com]

Brockie, Colin G.F. BSc(Eng) BD SOSc	1967	2007	(Presbytery Clerk)	36 Braehead Court, Kilmarnock KA3 7AB [E-mail: revcol@revcol.demon.co.uk]	01563 526295
Campbell, George H.	1957	1992	(Stewarton: John Knox)	20 Woodlands Grove, Kilmarnock KA3 1TZ [E-mail: george.campbell13@hotmail.co.uk]	01563 536365
Campbell, John A. JP FIEM	1984	1998	(Irvine: St Andrew's)	Flowerdale, Balmoral Lane, Blairgowrie PH10 7AF [E-mail: exrevjack@aol.com]	01250 872795

Cant, Thomas M. MA BD	1964 2004	(Paisley: Laigh Kirk)	3 Meikle Custraw Farm, Stewarton, Kilmarnock KA3 5HU [E-mail: revtmcant@aol.com]	01560 480566
Christie, Robert S. MA BD ThM	1964 2001	(Kilmarnock: West High)	24 Homeroyal House, 2 Chalmers Crescent, Edinburgh EH9 1TP	01294 312515
Davidson, James BD DipAFH	1989 2002	(Wishaw: Old)	13 Redburn Place, Irvine KA12 9BQ	01563 573994
Davidson Kelly, Thomas A. MA BD FSAScot	1975 2002	(Glasgow: Govan Old)	2 Springhill Stables, Portland Road, Kilmarnock KA1 2EJ [E-mail: dks33@btinternet.com]	
Gillon, C. Blair BD	1980 2007	(Glasgow: Ibrox)	East Muirshield Farmhouse, by Dunlop, Kilmarnock KA3 4EJ [E-mail: blair.gillon2@btinternet.com]	01560 483778
Hall, William M. BD	1972 2010	(Kilmarnock: Old High Kirk)	33 Cairns Terrace, Kilmarnock KA1 1JG [E-mail: revwillie@talktalk.net]	
Hare, Malcolm M.W. BA BD	1956 1994	(Kilmarnock: St Kentigern's)	21 Raith Road, Fenwick, Kilmarnock KA3 6DB	01560 600388
Hay, W.J.R. MA BD	1959 1995	(Buchanan with Drymen)	18 Jamieson Place, Stewarton, Kilmarnock KA3 3AY	01560 482799
Huggett, Judith A. (Miss) BA BD	1990 1998	Hospital Chaplain	4 Westmoor Crescent, Kilmarnock KA1 1TX [E-mail: judith.huggett@aaaht.scotnhs.uk]	
Lamarti, Samuel H. BD MTh PhD	1979 2006	(Stewarton: John Knox)	7 Dalwhinnie Crescent, Kilmarnock KA3 1QS [E-mail: samuel.h2@ukonline.co.uk]	01563 529632
McAlpine, Richard H.M. BA FSAScot	1968 2000	(Lochgoilhead and Kilmorich)	7 Kingsford Place, Kilmarnock KA3 6FG	01563 572075
MacDonald, James M.	1964 1987	(Kilmarnock: St John's Onthank)	29 Carmel Place, Kilmaurs, Kilmarnock KA3 2QU	01563 525254
Scott, Thomas T.	1968 1989	(Kilmarnock: St Marnock's)	6 North Hamilton Place, Kilmarnock KA1 2QN [E-mail: tomtscott@btinternet.com]	01563 531415
Shaw, Catherine A.M. MA	1998 2006	(Auxiliary Minister)	40 Merrygreen Place, Stewarton, Kilmarnock KA3 5EP [E-mail: catherine.shaw@tesco.net]	01560 483352
Sutcliffe, Clare B. BSc BD	2000 2009	(Irvine: Girdle Toll)	4 Dalmailing Avenue, Dreghorn, Irvine KA11 4HX [E-mail: revclare@tesco.net]	
Welsh, Alex M. MA BD	1979 2007	Hospital Chaplain	8 Greenside Avenue, Prestwick KA9 2HB [E-mail: alexanderevelyn@hotmail.com]	01292 475341

IRVINE and KILMARNOCK ADDRESSES

Irvine

Dreghorn and Springside	Townfoot x Station Brae
Fullarton	Marress Road x Church Street
Girdle Toll	Bryce Knox Court
Mure	West Road
Old	Kirkgate
Relief Bourtreehill	Crofthead, Bourtreehill
St Andrew's	Caldon Road x Oaklands Ave

Kilmarnock

Ayrshire Mission to the Deaf	10 Clark Street
Henderson	London Road
New Laigh Kirk	John Dickie Street
Old High Kirk	Church Street x Soulis Street
Riccarton	Old Street
St Andrew's and St Marnock's	St Marnock Street
St John's Onthank	84 Wardneuk Street
St Ninian's Bellfield	Whatriggs Road
Shortlees	Central Avenue

(12) ARDROSSAN

Meets at Saltcoats, New Trinity, on the first Tuesday of February, March, April, May, September, October, November and December, and on the second Tuesday of June.

Clerk:	MR ALAN K. SAUNDERSON		17 Union Street, Largs KA30 8DG [E-mail: ak.dj.saunderson@hotmail.co.uk]	01475 687217 07866 034355 (Mbl)

Ardrossan: Barony St John's (H) (01294 465009) (E-mail: www.baronystjohns.co.uk)

Dorothy A. Granger BA BD	2009		10 Seafield Drive, Ardrossan KA22 8NU [E-mail: dorothygranger61@gmail.com]	01294 463571 07918 077877 (Mbl)

Ardrossan: Park (01294 463711)

Tanya Webster BCom DipAcc BD	2011		35 Ardneil Court, Ardrossan KA22 7NQ [E-mail: tanya.webster@talktalk.net]	01294 538903

Beith (H) (01505 502686)

Roderick I.T. MacDonald BD CertMin	1992	2005	2 Glebe Court, Beith KA15 1ET [E-mail: rodannmac@btinternet.com]	01505 503858

Brodick linked with Corrie linked with Lochranza and Pirnmill linked with Shiskine (H)

Angus Adamson BD	2006		4 Manse Crescent, Brodick, Isle of Arran KA27 8AS [E-mail: s-adamson@corriecraviehome.fsnet.co.uk]	01770 302334

Corrie See Brodick

Cumbrae

Vacant			Marine Parade, Millport, Isle of Cumbrae KA28 0ED	01475 530416

Dalry: St Margaret's

James R. Teasdale BA BD	2009		33 Templand Crescent, Dalry KA24 5EZ [E-mail: jamesrteasdale@hotmail.com]	01294 832747

Dalry: Trinity (H)

Martin Thomson BSc DipEd BD	1988	2004	Trinity Manse, West Kilbride Road, Dalry KA24 5DX [E-mail: martin.thomson40@btinternet.com]	01294 832363

Charge / Minister		Address	Tel
Fairlie (H) Vacant		14 Fairlieburne Gardens, Fairlie, Largs KA29 0ER	01475 568342
Kilbirnie: Auld Kirk (H) Vacant		49 Holmhead, Kilbirnie KA25 6BS	01505 682348
Kilbirnie: St Columba's (H) (01505 685239) Fiona C. Ross (Miss) BD DipMin	1996 2004	Manse of St Columba's, Dipple Road, Kilbirnie KA25 7JU [E-mail: fionaross@calvin78.freeserve.co.uk]	01505 683342
Kilmory linked with Lamlash Gillean P. Maclean (Mrs) BD	1994 2008	Lamlash, Isle of Arran KA27 8LE [E-mail: gillean.maclean@hotmail.co.uk]	01770 600318
Kilwinning: Mansefield Trinity (E) (01294 550746) Morag Garrett (Mrs) BD	2011	21 Foundry Wynd, Kilwinning KA13 6UG	01294 539297
Kilwinning: Old Jeanette Whitecross BD	2002 2011	54 Dalry Road, Kilwinning KA13 7HE [E-mail: jwx@hotmail.co.uk]	01294 552606
Lamlash See Kilmory			
Largs: Clark Memorial (H) (01475 675186) Stephen J. Smith BSc BD	1993 1998	31 Douglas Street, Largs KA30 8PT [E-mail: stephenrevsteve@aol.com]	01475 672370
Largs: St Columba's (01475 686212) Vacant		17 Beachway, Largs KA30 8QH	
Largs: St John's (H) (01475 674468) Vacant			
Lochranza and Pirnmill See Brodick			
Saltcoats: New Trinity (H) (01294 472001) Vacant		1 Montgomerie Crescent, Saltcoats KA21 5BX	01294 461143

Saltcoats: North (01294 464679)
Alexander B. Noble MA BD ThM   1982 2003   25 Longfield Avenue, Saltcoats KA21 6DR   01294 604923

Saltcoats: St Cuthbert's (H)
Vacant   10 Kennedy Road, Saltcoats KA21 5SF

Shiskine (H) See Brodick

Stevenston: Ardeer linked with Stevenston: Livingstone (H)
Vacant   32 High Road, Stevenston KA20 3DR   01294 464180

Stevenston: High (H) (Website: www.highkirk.com)
M. Scott Cameron MA BD   2002   Glencairn Street, Stevenston KA20 3DL   01294 463356
[E-mail: revhighkirk@btinternet.com]

Stevenston: Livingstone (H) See Stevenston: Ardeer

West Kilbride (H)
James J. McNay MA BD   2008   The Manse, Goldenberry Avenue, West Kilbride KA23 9LJ   01294 823186
[E-mail: j.mcnay@lycos.com]

Whiting Bay and Kildonan
Elizabeth R.L. Watson (Miss) BA BD   1981 1982   The Manse, Whiting Bay, Brodick, Isle of Arran KA27 8RE   01770 700289
[E-mail: revewatson@btinternet.com]

Cruickshank, Norman BA BD	1983	2006	(West Kilbride: Overton)	24D Faulds Wynd, Seamill, West Kilbride KA23 9FA — 01294 822239
Currie, Ian S. MBE BD	1975	2010	(The United Church of Bute)	15 Northfield Park, Largs KA30 8NZ — (Mbl) 07764 254300
				[E-mail: ianscurrie@tiscali.co.uk]
Dailly, J.R. BD DipPS	1979	1979	(DACG)	2 Curtis Close, Pound Street, Warminster, Wiltshire BA12 9NN
Downie, Alexander S.	1975	1997	(Ardrossan: Park)	12 Loanhead Road, Ardrossan KA22 8AW — 01294 464097
Drysdale, James H. LTh	1987	2006	(Blackbraes and Shieldhill)	10 John Clark Street, Largs KA30 9AH — 01475 674870
Falconer, Alan D. MA BD DLitt	1972	2011	(Aberdeen: St Machar's Cathedral)	18 North Crescent Road, Ardrossan KA22 8NA — 01294 472991
				[E-mail: alanfalconer@gmx.com]
Forsyth, D. Stuart MA	1948	1992	(Belhelvie)	39 Homemount House, Gogoside Road, Largs KA30 9LS — 01475 673379
Gordon, David C.	1953	1988	(Gigha and Cara)	South Beach House, South Crescent Road, Ardrossan KA22 8DU
Harbison, David J.H.	1958	1998	(Beith: High with Beith: Trinity)	42 Mill Park, Dalry KA24 5BB — 01294 834092
				[E-mail: djh@harbi.fsnet.co.uk]
Hebenton, David J. MA BD	1958	2002	(Ayton and Burnmouth with Grantshouse and Houndwood and Reston)	22B Faulds Wynd, Seamill, West Kilbride KA23 9FA — 01294 829228

Name	Year(s)	Charge	Address	Phone
Howie, Marion L.K. (Mrs) MA ACRS	1992	Auxiliary Minister	51 High Road, Stevenston KA20 3DY [E-mail: marion@howiefamily.net]	01294 466571
Leask, Rebecca M. (Mrs)	1977 1985	(Callander: St Bride's)	20 Strathclyde House, 31 Shore Road, Skelmorlie PA17 5AN [E-mail: rmleask@hotmail.com]	01475 520765
McCallum, Alexander D. BD	1987 2005	(Saltcoats: New Trinity)	59 Woodcroft Avenue, Largs KA30 9EW [E-mail: sandyandjose@madasafish.com]	01475 670133
McCance, Andrew M. BSc	1986 1995	(Coatbridge: Middle)	6A Douglas Place, Largs KA30 8PU	01475 673303
Mackay, Marjory H. (Mrs) BD DipEd CCE	1998 2008	(Cumbrae)	4 Golf Road, Millport, Isle of Cumbrae KA28 0HB [E-mail: mhmackay@tiscali.co.uk]	01475 530388
MacLeod, Ian L.Th BA MTh PhD	1969 2006	(Brodick with Corrie)	Cromla Cottage, Corrie, Isle of Arran KA27 8JB [E-mail: i.macleod829@btinternet.com]	01770 810237
Mitchell, D. Ross BA BD	1972 2007	(West Kilbride: St Andrew's)	11 Dunbar Gardens, Saltcoats KA21 6GJ [E-mail: ross.mitchell@virgin.net]	
Paterson, John H. BD	1977 2000	(Kirkintilloch: St David's Memorial Park)	Creag Bhan, Golf Course Road, Whiting Bay, Isle of Arran KA27 8QT	01770 700569
Roy, Iain M. MA BD	1960 1997	(Stevenston: Livingstone)	2 The Fieldings, Dunlop, Kilmarnock KA3 4AU	01560 483072
Taylor, Andrew S. BTh FPhS	1959 1992	(Greenock Union)	9 Raillies Avenue, Largs KA30 8QY [E-mail: andrew.taylor_123@btinternet.com]	01475 674709
Thomson, Margaret (Mrs)	1988 1993	(Saltcoats: Erskine)	7 Glen Farg, St Leonards, East Kilbride, Glasgow G74 2JW	

(13) LANARK

Meets on the first Tuesday of February, March, May, September, October, November and December, and on the third Tuesday of June.

Clerk:	REV. MRS HELEN E. JAMIESON BD DipEd	120 Clyde Street, Carluke ML8 5BG [E-mail: lanark@cofscotland.org.uk]	01555 771218
Depute Clerk:	REV. BRYAN KERR BA BD	Greyfriars Manse, 3 Bellefield Way, Lanark ML11 7NW	01555 663363

Biggar (H) linked with Black Mount linked with Culter (H) linked with Libberton and Quothquan (H)
Vacant

Black Mount See Biggar

Cairngryffe linked with Symington
Vacant

Carluke: Kirkton (H) (01555 750778) (E-mail: iaindc@btconnect.com)
Iain D. Cunningham MA BD   1979 1987   9 Station Road, Carluke ML8 5AA   01555 771262
    [E-mail: iaindc@btconnect.com]

Carluke: St Andrew's (H)
Helen E. Jamieson (Mrs) BD DipEd   1989   120 Clyde Street, Carluke ML8 5BG   01555 771218
[E-mail: helenejamieson@o2.co.uk]

Carluke: St John's (H) (Website: www.carluke-stjohns.org.uk)
Roy J. Cowieson BD   1979   2007   18 Old Bridgend, Carluke ML8 4HN   01555 752519
[E-mail: roy.cowieson@btinternet.com]

Carnwath (H)
Vacant

Carstairs and Carstairs Junction, The United Church of
Vacant   11 Range View, Kames, Carstairs, Lanark ML11 8TF   01555 871123

Coalburn (H) linked with Lesmahagow: Old (H) (Church office: 01555 892425)
Vacant   9 Elm Bank, Lesmahagow, Lanark ML11 0EA

Crossford (H) linked with Kirkfieldbank (E-mail: s.reid@lanarkpresbytery.org)
Steven Reid BAcc CA BD   1989   1997   74 Lanark Road, Crossford, Carluke ML8 5RE   01555 860415
[E-mail: steven.reid@sky.com]

Culter (H) See Biggar

Forth: St Paul's (H) (Website: www.forthstpauls.com)
Sarah L. Ross (Mrs) BD MTh PGDip   2004   22 Lea Rig, Forth, Lanark ML11 8EA   01555 812832
[E-mail: minister@forthstpauls.com]

Glencaple linked with Lowther
Vacant   66 Carlisle Road, Crawford, Biggar ML12 6TW

Kirkfieldbank See Crossford

Kirkmuirhill (H)
Ian M. Watson LLB DipLP BD   1998   2003   The Manse, 2 Lanark Road, Kirkmuirhill, Lanark ML11 9RB   01555 892409
[E-mail: ian.watson21@btopenworld.com]

Lanark: Greyfriars (Church office: 01555 661510) (Website: www.lanarkgreyfriars.com)
Bryan Kerr BA BD   2002 2007   Greyfriars Manse, 3 Bellefield Way, Lanark ML11 7NW   01555 663363
[E-mail: bryan@lanarkgreyfriars.com]

Lanark: St Nicholas' (H)
Alison A. Meikle (Mrs) BD   1999 2002   2 Kaimhill Court, Lanark ML11 9HU   01555 662600
[E-mail: alison-meikle@sky.com]

Law
Una B. Stewart (Ms) BD DipEd   1995 2009   3 Shawgill Court, Law, Carluke ML8 5SJ   01698 373180
[E-mail: rev.ubs@virgin.net]

Lesmahagow: Abbeygreen
David S. Carmichael   1982   Abbeygreen Manse, Lesmahagow, Lanark ML11 0DB   01555 893384
[E-mail: david.carmichael@abbeygreen.org.uk]

Lesmahagow: Old (H) See Coalburn
Libberton and Quothquan (H) See Biggar
Lowther See Glencaple
Symington See Cairngryffe

The Douglas Valley Church (Church office: Tel/Fax: 01555 850000) (Website: www.douglasvalleychurch.org)
Robert Cleland   1997 2009   The Manse, Douglas, Lanark ML11 0RB   01555 851213
[E-mail: cleland810@btinternet.com]

Cowell, Susan G. (Miss) BA BD	1986 1998	(Budapest)	3 Gavel Lane, Regency Gardens, Lanark ML11 9FB	01555 665509
Craig, William BA LTh	1974 1997	(Cambusbarron: The Bruce Memorial)	31 Heathfield Drive, Blackwood, Lanark ML11 9SR	01555 893710
Easton, David J.C. MA BD	1965 2005	(Glasgow: Burnside-Blairbeth)	Rowanbank, Cormiston Road, Quothquan, Biggar ML12 6ND	01899 308459
			[E-mail: deaston@btinternet.com]	
Findlay, Henry J.W. MA BD	1965 2005	(Wishaw: St Mark's)	2 Alba Gardens, Carluke ML8 5US	01555 759995
Fox, George H.	1959 1977	(Coalsnaughton)	Brachead House, Crossford, Carluke ML8 5NQ	01555 860716
Gauld, Beverly G.D.D. MA BD	1972 2009	(Carnwath)	7 Rowan View, Lanark ML11 9FQ	01555 665765
Gibson, Alan W. BA BD	2001 2012	Head of Stewardship	c/o 121 George Street, Edinburgh EH2 4YN	0131-225 5722
			[E-mail: agibson@cofscotland.org.uk]	
Houston, Graham R. BSc BD MTh PhD	1978 2011	(Cairngryffe with Symington)	3 Alder Lane, Beechtrees, Lanark ML11 9FT	01555 678004
			[E-mail: gandih6156@btinternet.com]	
Lyall, Ann (Miss) DCS	1980 2011	The Biggar Area	17 Mercat Loan, Biggar ML12 6DG	01899 229443
			[E-mail: ann.lyall@btinternet.com]	
Pacitti, Stephen A. MA	1963 2003	(Black Mount with Culter with Libberton and Quothquan)	157 Nithsdale Road, Glasgow G41 5RD	0141-423 5972

Seath, Thomas J.G.	1980 1992	(Motherwell: Manse Road)	Flat 11, Wallace Court, South Vennel, Lanark ML11 7LL	01555 665399
Stewart, John M. MA BD	1964 2001	(Johnstone with Kirkpatrick Juxta)	5 Rathmor Road, Biggar ML12 6QG	01899 220398
Turnbull, John LTh	1994 2006	(Balfron with Fintry)	4 Rathmor Road, Biggar ML12 6QG	01899 221502
Young, David A.	1972 2003	(Kirkmuirhill)	15 Mannachie Rise, Forres IV36 2US	01309 672849
			[E-mail: youngdavid@aol.com]	

(14) GREENOCK AND PAISLEY

Meets on the second Tuesday of September, October, November, December, February, March, April and May, and on the third Tuesday of June.

| Clerk: | REV. PETER McENHILL BD PhD | The Presbytery Office as detailed below [E-mail: greenockpaisley@cofscotland.org.uk] | |
| Presbytery Office: | | 'Homelea', Faith Avenue, Quarrier's Village, Bridge of Weir PA11 3SX | 01505 615033 (Tel) 01505 615088 (Fax) |

Barrhead: Arthurlie (H) (0141-881 8442)

| James S.A. Cowan BD DipMin | 1986 | 1998 | 10 Arthurlie Avenue, Barrhead, Glasgow G78 2BU [E-mail: jim_cowan@ntlworld.com] | 0141-881 3457 |

Barrhead: Bourock (H) (0141-881 9813)

| Vacant | | | 14 Maxton Avenue, Barrhead, Glasgow G78 1DY | 0141-881 1462 |

Barrhead: South and Levern (H) (0141-881 7825)

| Vacant | | | 3 Colinbar Circle, Barrhead, Glasgow G78 2BE | 0141-571 4059 |

Bishopton (H) (Office: 01505 862583)

| Daniel Manastireanu BA MTh | 2010 | | The Manse, Newton Road, Bishopton PA7 5JP [E-mail: daniel@bishoptonkirk.org.uk] | 01505 862161 |

Bridge of Weir: Freeland (H) (01505 612610)

| Kenneth N. Gray BA BD | 1988 | | 15 Lawmarnock Crescent, Bridge of Weir PA11 3AS [E-mail: aandkgray@btinternet.com] | 01505 690918 |

Bridge of Weir: St Machar's Ranfurly (01505 614364)

| Suzanne Dunleavy (Miss) BD DipEd | 1990 | 1992 | 9 Glen Brae, Bridge of Weir PA11 3BH [E-mail: suzanne.dunleavy@btinternet.com] | 01505 612975 |

Elderslie Kirk (H) (01505 323348) Robin N. Allison BD DipMin	1994	2005	282 Main Road, Elderslie, Johnstone PA5 9EF [E-mail: revrobin@sky.com]	01505 321767
Erskine (0141-812 4620) Vacant			The Manse, 7 Leven Place, Linburn, Erskine PA8 6AS	0141-581 0955
Gourock: Old Gourock and Ashton (H) David T. Young BA BD	2007		331 Eldon Street, Gourock PA16 7QN [E-mail: minister@ogachurch.org.uk]	01475 635578
Gourock: St John's (H) Glenn A. Chestnutt BA DASE MDiv ThM PhD	2009		6 Barrhill Road, Gourock PA19 1JX [E-mail: glenn.chestnutt@gmail.com]	01475 632143
Greenock: East End (New Charge Development) David J. McCarthy BSc BD	1985	2003	29 Denholm Street, Greenock PA16 8RH [E-mail: greenockeastendparish@googlemail.com]	01475 722111
Greenock: Lyle Kirk C. Ian W. Johnson MA BD	1997		39 Fox Street, Greenock PA16 8PD [E-mail: ian.ciw.johnson@btinternet.com] (New name for the charge formerly known as Greenock: Lyle Community Kirk)	01475 888277
Greenock: Mount Kirk Francis E. Murphy BEng DipDSE BD	2006		76 Finnart Street, Greenock PA16 8HJ [E-mail: francis_e_murphy@hotmail.com]	01475 722338
Greenock: St Margaret's (01475 781953) Vacant Eileen Manson (Mrs) DipCE (Aux: Locum)	1994	2010	105 Finnart Street, Greenock PA16 8HN 1 Cambridge Avenue, Gourock PA19 1XT [E-mail: rev.eileen@ntlworld.com]	01475 786590 01475 632401
Greenock: St Ninian's Allan G. McIntyre BD	1985		5 Auchmead Road, Greenock PA16 0PY [E-mail: agmcintyre@lineone.net]	01475 631878

Congregation / Minister			Address	Telephone
Greenock: Wellpark Mid Kirk Alan K. Sorensen BD MTh DipMin FSAScot	1983	2000	101 Brisbane Street, Greenock PA16 8PA [E-mail: alan.sorensen@ntlworld.com]	01475 721741
Greenock: Westburn Vacant			50 Ardgowan Street, Greenock PA16 8EP	01475 721048
Houston and Killellan (H) Donald Campbell BD	1998	2007	The Manse of Houston, Main Street, Houston, Johnstone PA6 7EL [E-mail: houstonmanse@btinternet.com]	01505 612569
Howwood David Stewart MA DipEd BD MTh	1977	2001	The Manse, Beith Road, Howwood, Johnstone PA9 1AS [E-mail: revdavidst@aol.com]	01505 703678
Inchinnan (H) (0141-812 1263) Alison McBrier MA BD	2011		The Manse, Inchinnan, Renfrew PA4 9PH	0141-812 1688
Inverkip (H) linked with Skelmorlie and Wemyss Bay Vacant			The Manse, Langhouse Road, Inverkip, Greenock PA16 0BJ	01475 521207
Johnstone: High (H) (01505 336303) Ann C. McCool (Mrs) BD DSD IPA ALCM	1989	2001	76 North Road, Johnstone PA5 8NF [E-mail: ann.mccool@ntlworld.com]	01505 320006
Johnstone: St Andrew's Trinity May Bell (Mrs) LTh	1998	2002	1 Swallow Brae, Inverkip, Greenock PA16 0LF [E-mail: may.bell@ntlbusiness.com]	01475 529312
Johnstone: St Paul's (H) (01505 321632) Alistair N. Shaw MA BD MTh	1982	2003	9 Stanley Drive, Brookfield, Johnstone PA5 8UF [E-mail: ans2006@talktalk.net]	01505 320060
Kilbarchan: East Vacant			East Manse, Church Street, Kilbarchan, Johnstone PA10 2JQ	01505 702621

Kilbarchan: West
Arthur Sherratt BD — 1994 — West Manse, Shuttle Street, Kilbarchan, Johnstone PA10 2JR
[E-mail: arthur.sherratt@ntlworld.com] — 01505 342930

Kilmacolm: Old (H) (01505 873911)
Peter McEnhill BD PhD — 1992 2007 — The Old Kirk Manse, Glencairn Road, Kilmacolm PA13 4NJ
[E-mail: petermcenhill@btinternet.com] — 01505 873174

Kilmacolm: St Columba (H)
R. Douglas Cranston MA BD — 1986 1992 — 6 Churchill Road, Kilmacolm PA13 4LH
[E-mail: robert.cranston@sccmanse.plus.com] — 01505 873271

Langbank (T) linked with Port Glasgow: St Andrew's (H)
Andrew T. MacLean BA BD — 1980 1993 — St Andrew's Manse, Barr's Brae, Port Glasgow PA14 5QA
[E-mail: standrews.pg@me.com] — 01475 741486

Linwood (H) (01505 328802)
Eileen M. Ross (Mrs) BD MTh — 2005 2008 — 1 John Neilson Avenue, Paisley PA1 2SX
[E-mail: eileenmross@btinternet.com] — 0141-887 2801

Lochwinnoch (T)
Vacant — 1 Station Rise, Lochwinnoch PA12 4NA — 01505 843484

Neilston (0141-881 9445)
Vacant — The Manse, Neilston Road, Neilston, Glasgow G78 3NP — 0141-881 1958

Paisley: Abbey (H) (Tel: 0141-889 7654; Fax: 0141-887 3929)
Alan D. Birss MA BD — 1979 1988 — 15 Main Road, Castlehead, Paisley PA2 6AJ
[E-mail: alan.birss@paisleyabbey.com] — 0141-889 3587

Paisley: Glenburn (0141-884 2602)
Graham Nash MA BD — 2006 — 10 Hawick Avenue, Paisley PA2 9LD
[E-mail: gpnash@btopenworld.com] — 0141-884 4903

Paisley: Lylesland (H) (0141-561 7139)

Alistair W. Cook BSc CA BD   2008   36 Potterhill Avenue, Paisley PA2 8BA   0141-561 9277
[E-mail: alistaircook@ntlworld.com]

Greta Gray (Miss) DCS   67 Crags Avenue, Paisley PA3 6SG   0141-884 6178
[E-mail: greta.gray@ntlworld.com]

Paisley: Martyrs' Sandyford (0141-889 6603)

Kenneth A.L. Mayne BA MSc CertEd   1976   2007   27 Acer Crescent, Paisley PA2 9LR   0141-884 7400

Paisley: Oakshaw Trinity (H) (Tel: 0141-889 4010; Fax: 0141-848 5139)

John C. Christie BSc BD MSB CBiol   1990   2012   10 Cumberland Avenue, Helensburgh G84 8QG   01436 674078
(Interim Minister)   [E-mail: rev.jcc@btinternet.com]   07711 336392 (Mbl)

Paisley: St Columba Foxbar (H) (01505 812377)

Drausio Goncalves   2008   13 Corsebar Drive, Paisley PA2 9QD   0141-848 5826
[E-mail: drausiopg@gmail.com]

Paisley: St James' (0141-889 2422)

Ivan C. Warwick TD MA BD   1980   2012   38 Woodland Avenue, Paisley PA2 8BH   0141-884 7978
[E-mail: L70rev@btinternet.com]   07787 535083 (Mbl)

Paisley: St Luke's (H)

D. Ritchie M. Gillon BD DipMin   1994   31 Southfield Avenue, Paisley PA2 8BX   0141-884 6215
[E-mail: revgillon@hotmail.com]

Paisley: St Mark's Oldhall (H) (0141-882 2755)

Robert G. McFarlane BD   2001   2005   36 Newtyle Road, Paisley PA1 3JX   0141-889 4279
[E-mail: robertmcf@hotmail.com]

Paisley: St Ninian's Ferguslie (E) (0141-887 9436) (New Charge Development)

William Wishart DCS   10 Stanely Drive, Paisley PA2 6HE   0141-884 4177
[E-mail: bill@saintninians.co.uk]

Paisley: Sherwood Greenlaw (H) (0141-889 7060)

Vacant   5 Greenlaw Drive, Paisley PA1 3RX   0141-889 3057

Paisley: Stow Brae Kirk
Robert Craig BA BD DipRS — 2008 2012 — 25 John Neilson Avenue, Paisley PA1 2SX
[E-mail: rab-craig@tiscali.co.uk] — 07968 283095 (Mbl)

Paisley: Wallneuk North (0141-889 9265)
Peter G. Gill MA BA — 2008 — 5 Glenville Crescent, Paisley PA2 8TW
[E-mail: petergill18@hotmail.com] — 0141-884 4429

Port Glasgow: Hamilton Bardrainney
James A. Munro BA BD DMS — 1979 2002 — 80 Bardrainney Avenue, Port Glasgow PA14 6HD
[E-mail: james@jmunro33.wanadoo.co.uk] — 01475 701213

Port Glasgow: St Andrew's (H) See Langbank

Port Glasgow: St Martin's
Archibald Speirs BD — 1995 2006 — Clunebraehead, Clune Brae, Port Glasgow PA14 5SL
[E-mail: archiespeirs1@aol.com] — 01475 704115

Renfrew: North (0141-885 2154)
E. Lorna Hood (Mrs) MA BD — 1978 1979 — 1 Alexandra Drive, Renfrew PA4 8UB
[E-mail: lorna.hood@ntlworld.com] — 0141-886 2074

Renfrew: Old
Lilly C. Easton (Mrs) — 1999 2009 — 31 Gibson Road, Renfrew PA4 0RH
[E-mail: revlillyeaston@hotmail.co.uk] — 0141-886 2005

Renfrew: Trinity (H) (0141-885 2129)
Stuart C. Steell BD CertMin — 1992 — 25 Paisley Road, Renfrew PA4 8JH
[E-mail: ssren@tiscali.co.uk] — 0141-886 2131

Skelmorlie and Wemyss Bay See Inverkip

Name		Years	Charge	Address	Tel
Alexander, Douglas N.	MA BD	1961 1999	(Bishopton)	West Morningside, Main Road, Langbank, Port Glasgow PA4 6XP	01475 540249
Armstrong, Gordon B.	BD FIAB BRC	2010	Workplace Chaplain: West of Scotland	52 Balgonie Avenue, Paisley PA2 9LP [E-mail: revgordon@ntlworld.com]	0141-587 3124
Armstrong, William R.	BD	1979 2008	(Skelmorlie and Wemyss Bay)	25A The Lane, Skelmorlie PA17 5AR [E-mail: warmstrong17@tiscali.co.uk]	01475 520891

Name	Years	Charge / Designation	Address	Tel.
Bell, Ian W. LTh	1990 2011	(Erskine)	1 Swallow Brae, Inverkip, Greenock PA16 0LF [E-mail: rviwbepc@ntlworld.com]	01475 529312
Black, Janette M.K. (Mrs) BD	1993 2006	(Assistant: Paisley: Oakshaw Trinity)	5 Craigiehall Avenue, Erskine PA8 7DB	0141-812 0794
Breingan, Mhairi	2011	Ordained Local Minister	6 Park Road, Inchinnan, Renfrew PA4 4QJ	
Cameron, Margaret (Miss) DCS	1973 2009	(Deaconess)	2 Rowans Gate, Paisley PA2 6RD	0141-840 2479
Campbell, John MA BA BSc		(Caldwell)	96 Boghead Road, Lenzie, Glasgow G66 4EN [E-mail: johncampbell.lenzie@gmail.com]	0141-776 0874
Cherry, Alastair J. BA BD FPLD	1982 2009	(Glasgow: Penilee St Andrew's)	6 Upper Abbey Road, Belvedere, Kent DA17 5AJ [E-mail: alastair.j.cherry@btinternet.com]	01322 402818
Chestnut, Alexander MBE BA	1948 1987	(Greenock: St Mark's Greenbank)	5 Douglas Street, Largs KA30 8PS	01475 674168
Copland, Agnes M. (Mrs) MBE DCS		(Deacon)	3 Craigmuschat Road, Gourock PA19 1SE	01475 631870
Coull, Morris C. BD	1974 2011	(Skelmorlie and Wemyss Bay)	Flat 0/1 Toward, The Lighthouses, Greenock Road, Wemyss Bay PA18 6DT	01475 522677
Cubie, John P. MA BD	1961 1999	(Caldwell)	36 Winram Place, St Andrews KY16 8XH	01334 474708
Erskine, Morag (Miss) DCS	1979	(Deacon)	111 Mains Drive, Park Mains, Erskine PA8 7JJ [E-mail: morag.erskine@ntlworld.com]	0141-812 6096
Forrest, Kenneth P. CBE BSc PhD	2006	Auxiliary Minister	5 Carruth Road, Bridge of Weir PA11 3HQ [E-mail: kenpforrest@hotmail.com]	01505 612651
Fraser, Ian C. BA BD	1983 2008	(Glasgow: St Luke's and St Andrew's)	62 Kingston Avenue, Neilston, Glasgow G78 3JG [E-mail: ianandlindafraser@gmail.com]	0141-563 6794
Gardner, Frank J. MA	1966 2007	(Gourock: Old Gourock and Ashton)	1 Levanne Place, Gourock PA16 1AX [E-mail: fjg@clyde-mail.co.uk]	(Tel/Fax) 01475 630187
Hamilton, W. Douglas BD	1975 2009	(Greenock: Westburn)	5 Corse Road, Penilee, Glasgow G52 4DG [E-mail: douglas.hamilton44@hotmail.co.uk]	0141-810 1194
Hetherington, Robert M. MA BD	1966 2002	(Barrhead South and Levern)	31 Brodie Park Crescent, Paisley PA2 6EU [E-mail: r-hetherington@sky.com]	0141-848 6560
Irvine, Euphemia H.C. (Mrs) BD	1972 1988	(Milton of Campsie)	32 Baird Drive, Bargarran, Erskine PA8 6BB	0141-812 2777
Johnston, Mary (Miss) DCS	1989 2001	(Deaconess)	19 Lounsdale Drive, Paisley PA2 9ED	0141-849 1615
Kay, David BA BD MTh	1974 2008	(Paisley: Sandyford: Thread Street)	36 Donaldswood Park, Paisley PA2 8RS [E-mail: david.kay500@o2.co.uk]	0141-884 2080
Leitch, Maureen (Mrs) BA BD	1995 2011	(Barrhead: Bourock)	Rockfield, 92 Paisley Road, Barrhead G78 1NW [E-mail: maureen.leitch@ntlworld.com]	0141-580 2927
Lodge, Bernard P. BD	1967 2004	(Glasgow: Govanhill Trinity)	6 Darluith Park, Brookfield, Johnstone PA5 8DD [E-mail: bernardlodge@yahoo.co.uk]	01505 320378
McBain, Margaret (Miss) DCS	1966 2002		33 Quarry Road, Paisley PA2 7RD	0141-884 2920
MacColl, James C. BSc BD	1989 2001	(Johnstone: St Andrew's Trinity)	Greenways, Winton, Kirkby Stephen, Cumbria CA17 4HL	01768 372290
MacColl, John BD DipMin		Teacher: Religious Education	1 Birch Avenue, Johnstone PA5 0DD	01505 326506
McCully, M. Isobel (Miss) DCS		(Deacon)	10 Broadstone Avenue, Port Glasgow PA14 5BB [E-mail: mi.mccully@btinternet.com]	01475 742240
Macdonald, Alexander MA BD	1966 2006	(Neilston)	35 Lochore Avenue, Paisley PA3 4BY [E-mail: alexmacdonald42@aol.com]	0141-889 0066
McDonald, Alexander BA CMIWSC DUniv	1968 2000	(Department of Ministry)	36 Alloway Grove, Paisley PA2 7DQ [E-mail: amcdonald1@ntlworld.com]	0141-560 1937
Macfarlane, Thomas G. BSc PhD BD	1956 1992	(Glasgow: South Shawlands)	12 Elphinstone Court, Lochwinnoch Road, Kilmacolm PA13 4DW	01505 874962

Name	Dates	Role	Address	Tel
McKaig, William G. BD	1979 2011	(Langbank)	54 Brisbane Street, Greenock PA16 8NT [E-mail: bill.mckaig@virgin.net]	01506 400619
MacLaine, Marilyn (Mrs) LTh	1995 2009	(Inchinnan)	37 Bankton Brae, Livingston EH54 9LA	
Murdoch, Christine	1999 2012	(Lochwinnoch)	Flat 2, The Ponderosa, Shore Road, Kilcreggan, Helensburgh G84 0HQ [E-mail: rev.christine@btinternet.com]	01436 842565
Nicol, Joyce M. (Mrs) BA DCS	1988 2003	(Deacon)	93 Brisbane Street, Greenock PA16 8NY [E-mail: joycenicol@hotmail.co.uk]	01475 723235
Page, John R. BD DipMin	1988 2003	(Gibraltar)	1 The Walton Building, North Street, Mere, Warminster, Wiltshire BA12 6HU	
Palmer, S.W. BD	1980 1991	(Kilbarchan: East)	4 Bream Place, Houston PA6 7ZJ	01505 615280
Prentice, George BA BTh	1964 1997	(Paisley: Martyrs')	46 Victoria Gardens, Corsebar Road, Paisley PA2 9AQ [E-mail: g.prentice04@talktalk.net]	0141-842 1585
Simpson, James H. BD LLB	1964 2004	(Greenock: Mount Kirk)	82 Harbourside, Inverkip, Greenock PA16 0BF [E-mail: jameshsimpson@yahoo.co.uk]	01475 520582
Smillie, Andrew M. LTh	1990 2005	(Langbank)	7 Turnbull Avenue, West Freeland, Erskine PA8 7DL [E-mail: andrewsmillie@talktalk.net]	0141-812 7030
Stevenson, Stuart	2011	Ordained Local Minister	143 Springfield Park, Johnstone PA5 8JT	
Stone, W. Vernon MA BD	1949 1985	(Langbank)	36 Woodrow Court, Port Glasgow Road, Kilmacolm KA13 4QA [E-mail: stone@kilmacolm.fsnet.co.uk]	01505 872644
Watson, Valerie G.C. MA BD STM	1987 2012	(Associate: Beith)	38 Brougham Street, Greenock PA16 8AH [E-mail: vgcwatson@btinternet.com]	01475 888636
Whyte, John H. MA	1946 1986	(Gourock: Ashton)	6 Castle Levan Manor, Cloch Road, Gourock PA19 1AY	01475 636788
Whyte, Margaret A. (Mrs) BA BD	1988 2011	(Glasgow: Pollokshaws)	4 Springhill Road, Barrhead G78 2AA [E-mail: dpwhyte@tiscali.co.uk]	0141-881 4942

GREENOCK ADDRESSES

Gourock
Old Gourock and Ashton — 41 Royal Street
St John's — Bath Street x St John's Road

Greenock
Lyle Kirk — 31 Union Street; Newark Street x Bentinck Street; Esplanade x Campbell Street
(Lyle Kirk is continuing meantime to retain all three buildings)

Mount Kirk — Dempster Street at Murdieston Park
St Margaret's — Finch Road x Kestrel Crescent
St Ninian's — Warwick Road, Larkfield
Wellpark Mid Kirk — Cathcart Square
Westburn — 9 Nelson Street

Port Glasgow
Hamilton Bardrainney — Bardrainney Avenue x Auchenbothie Road
St Andrew's — Princes Street
St Martin's — Mansion Avenue

PAISLEY ADDRESSES

Abbey	Town Centre	Oakshaw Trinity	Churchill	Sandyford (Thread St)	Montgomery Road
Glenburn	Nethercraigs Drive off Glenburn Road	St Columba Foxbar	Amochrie Road, Foxbar	Sherwood Greenlaw	Glasgow Road
Lylesland	Rowan Street off Neilston Road	St James'	Underwood Road	Stow Brae Kirk	Causeyside Street
Martyrs'	King Street	St Luke's	Neilston Road	Wallneuk North	off Renfrew Road
		St Mark's Oldhall	Glasgow Road, Ralston		
		St Ninian's Ferguslie	Blackstoun Road		

(16) GLASGOW

Meets at Govan and Linthouse Parish Church, Govan Cross, Glasgow, on the following Tuesdays: 2012: 11 September, 9 October, 13 November, 11 December; 2013: 12 February, 12 March, 23 April, 14 May, 18 June.

Clerk:	REV. ANGUS KERR BD CertMin ThM DMin	260 Bath Street, Glasgow G2 4JP	0141-332 6606

[E-mail: glasgow@cofscotland.org.uk]   0141-352 6646 (Fax)
[Website: www.presbyteryofglasgow.org.uk]
[E-mail: treasurer@presbyteryofglasgow.org.uk]

Treasurer: DOUGLAS BLANEY

1 Banton linked with Twechar
Vacant

Manse of Banton and Twechar, Banton, Glasgow G65 0QL   01236 826129

2 Bishopbriggs: Kenmure
James Gemmell BD MTh   1999 2010

5 Marchfield, Bishopbriggs, Glasgow G64 3PP   0141-772 1468
[E-mail: revgemmell@hotmail.com]

3 Bishopbriggs: Springfield Cambridge (0141-772 1596)
Ian Taylor BD ThM   1995 2006

64 Miller Drive, Bishopbriggs, Glasgow G64 1FB   0141-772 1540
[E-mail: taylorian@btinternet.com]

4 Broom (0141-639 3528)
James A.S. Boag BD CertMin   1992 2007

3 Laigh Road, Newton Mearns, Glasgow G77 5EX   0141-639 2916 (Tel)
[E-mail: office@broomchurch.org.uk]   0141-639 3528 (Fax)

Margaret McLellan (Mrs) DCS

18 Broom Road East, Newton Mearns, Glasgow G77 5SD   0141-639 6853
[E-mail: office@broomchurch.org.uk]

5	**Burnside Blairbeth (0141-634 4130)**				
	William T.S. Wilson BSc BD	1999	2006	59 Blairbeth Road, Burnside, Glasgow G73 4JD [E-mail: william.wilson@burnsideblairbethchurch.org.uk]	0141-583 6470
	Colin Ogilvie DCS			32 Upper Bourtree Court, Glasgow G73 4HT [E-mail: colin.ogilvie@burnsideblairbethchurch.org.uk]	0141-569 2725
6	**Busby (0141-644 2073)**				
	Jeremy C. Eve BSc BD	1998		17A Carmunnock Road, Busby, Glasgow G76 8SZ [E-mail: j-eve@sky.com]	0141-644 3670
7	**Cadder (0141-772 7436)**				
	Graham S. Finch MA BD	1977	1999	231 Kirkintilloch Road, Bishopbriggs, Glasgow G64 2JB [E-mail: gsf1957@ntlworld.com]	0141-772 1363
8	**Cambuslang: Flemington Hallside**				
	Neil Glover	2005		103 Overton Road, Halfway, Cambuslang, Glasgow G72 7XA [E-mail: neilmglover@gmail.com]	0141-641 1049 07779 280074 (Mbl)
9	**Cambuslang Parish Church**				
	A. Leslie Milton MA BD PhD	1996	2008	74 Stewarton Drive, Cambuslang, Glasgow G72 8DG [E-mail: lesliemilton@btconnect.com]	0141-641 2028
	Hilary N. McDougall (Mrs) MA PGCE BD (Assoc)	2002	2009	86 Stewarton Drive, Cambuslang, Glasgow G72 8DJ [E-mail: hilary.mcdougall@ntlworld.com]	0141-586 4301 07940 455473 (Mbl)
10	**Campsie (01360 310939)**				
	Alexandra Farrington LTh	2003	2011	19 Redhills View, Lennoxtown, Glasgow G66 7BL [E-mail: revsfarrington@aol.co.uk]	01360 238126
11	**Chryston (H) (0141-779 4188)**				
	Mark Malcolm MA BD	1999	2008	The Manse, 109 Main Street, Chryston, Glasgow G69 9LA [E-mail: mark.minister@btinternet.com]	0141-779 1436 07731 737377 (Mbl)
	David J. McAdam BSc BD (Assoc)	1990	2000	12 Dunellan Crescent, Moodiesburn, Glasgow G69 0GA [E-mail: dmca29@hotmail.co.uk]	01236 870472
12	**Eaglesham (01355 302047)**				
	Lynn M. McChlery BA BD	2005		The Manse, Cheapside Street, Eaglesham, Glasgow G76 0NS [E-mail: lsmchlery@btinternet.com]	01355 303495

No.	Name	Ord.	App.	Address	Phone
13	**Fernhill and Cathkin** Margaret McArthur BD DipMin	1995	2002	82 Blairbeth Road, Rutherglen, Glasgow G73 4JA [E-mail: revmaggiemac@hotmail.co.uk]	0141-634 1508
14	**Gartcosh (H) (01236 873770) linked with Glenboig** David G. Slater BSc BA DipThRS		2011	26 Inchnock Avenue, Gartcosh, Glasgow G69 8EA [E-mail: minister@gartcoshchurch.co.uk] [E-mail: minister@glenboigchurch.co.uk]	01236 870331 01236 872274 (Office)
15	**Giffnock: Orchardhill (0141-638 3604)** Chris Vermeulen DipLT BTh MA	1986	2005	23 Huntly Avenue, Giffnock, Glasgow G46 6LW [E-mail: chris@orchardhill.org.uk]	0141-620 3734
16	**Giffnock: South (0141-638 2599)** Catherine J. Beattie (Mrs) BD	2008	2011	19 Westerlands Gardens, Glasgow G77 6YJ [E-mail: catherinejbeat@aol.com]	0141-616 3451
17	**Giffnock: The Park (0141-620 2204)** Calum D. Macdonald BD	1993	2001	41 Rouken Glen Road, Thornliebank, Glasgow G46 7JD [E-mail: parkhoose@msn.com]	0141-638 3023
18	**Glenboig** See Gartcosh				
19	**Greenbank (H) (0141-644 1841)** Jeanne Roddick BD	2003		Greenbank Manse, 38 Eaglesham Road, Clarkston, Glasgow G76 7DJ [E-mail: jeanne.roddick@ntlworld.com]	0141-644 1395
20	**Kilsyth: Anderson** Vacant			Anderson Manse, Kingston Road, Kilsyth, Glasgow G65 0HR	01236 822345
21	**Kilsyth: Burns and Old** Vacant			The Grange, 17 Glasgow Road, Kilsyth, Glasgow G65 9AE	01236 823116
22	**Kirkintilloch: Hillhead** Lily F. McKinnon MA BD PGCE	1993	2011	The Manse, 64 Waverley Park, Kensington Gate, Kirkintilloch, Glasgow G66 2BP [E-mail: lily.mckinnon@yahoo.co.uk]	0141-776 4785

23 Kirkintilloch: St Columba's (H) (0141-578 0016)
David M. White BA BD DMin — 1988 — 14 Crossdykes, Kirkintilloch, Glasgow G66 3EU [E-mail: write.to.me@ntlworld.com] — 0141-578 4357

24 Kirkintilloch: St David's Memorial Park (H) (0141-776 4989)
Bryce Calder MA BD — 1995 2001 — 2 Roman Road, Kirkintilloch, Glasgow G66 1EA [E-mail: ministry100@aol.com] — 0141-776 1434 / 07986 144834 (Mbl)
Sandy Forsyth LLB BD DipLP (Assoc) — 2009 — 48 Kerr Street, Kirkintilloch, Glasgow G66 1JZ [E-mail: sandyforsyth67@hotmail.co.uk] — 0141-777 8194 / 07739 639037 (Mbl)

25 Kirkintilloch: St Mary's (0141-775 1166)
Mark E. Johnstone MA BD — 1993 2001 — St Mary's Manse, 60 Union Street, Kirkintilloch, Glasgow G66 1DH [E-mail: markjohnstone@me.com] — 0141-776 1252

26 Lenzie: Old (H)
Douglas W. Clark LTh — 1993 2000 — 41 Kirkintilloch Road, Lenzie, Glasgow G66 4LB [E-mail: douglaswclark@hotmail.com] — 0141-776 2184

27 Lenzie: Union (H) (0141-776 1046)
Daniel J.M. Carmichael MA BD — 1994 2003 — 1 Larch Avenue, Lenzie, Glasgow G66 4HX [E-mail: minister@lupc.org] — 0141-776 3831

28 Maxwell Mearns Castle (Tel/Fax: 0141-639 5169)
Scott R.McL. Kirkland BD MAR — 1996 2011 — 122 Broomfield Avenue, Newton Mearns, Glasgow G77 5JR [E-mail: scottkirkland@maxwellmearns.org.uk] — 0141-616 0642

29 Mearns (H) (0141-639 6555)
Joseph A. Kavanagh BD DipPTh MTh — 1992 1998 — Manse of Mearns, Mearns Road, Newton Mearns, Glasgow G77 5DE [E-mail: revjoe@hotmail.co.uk] — 0141-616 2410 (Tel/Fax)

30 Milton of Campsie (H)
Julie H.C. Moody BA BD PGCE — 2006 — Dunkeld, 33 Birdston Road, Milton of Campsie, Glasgow G66 8BX [E-mail: jhcwilson@msn.com] — 01360 310548 / 07787 184800 (Mbl)

31 Netherlee (H) (0141-637 2503)
Thomas Nelson BSc BD — 1992 2002 — 25 Ormonde Avenue, Netherlee, Glasgow G44 3QY [E-mail: tomnelson@ntlworld.com] — 0141-585 7502 (Tel/Fax)

No.	Charge / Minister			Address	Telephone
32	**Newton Mearns (H) (0141-639 7373)**				
	Esther J. Ninian (Miss) MA BD	1993	2009	28 Waterside Avenue, Newton Mearns, Glasgow G77 6TJ [E-mail: estherninian5194@btinternet.com]	0141-616 2079
33	**Rutherglen: Old (H)**				
	Vacant			31 Highburgh Drive, Rutherglen, Glasgow G73 3RR	0141-647 6178
34	**Rutherglen: Stonelaw (0141-647 5113)**				
	Alistair S. May LLB BD PhD		2002	80 Blairbeth Road, Rutherglen, Glasgow G73 4JA [E-mail: alistair.may@ntlworld.com]	0141-583 0157
35	**Rutherglen: West and Wardlawhill (0844 736 1470)**				
	Vacant			12 Albert Drive, Rutherglen, Glasgow G73 3RT	0141-569 8547
36	**Stamperland (0141-637 4999) (H)**				
	George C. MacKay BD CertMin CertEd DipPc	1994	2004	109 Ormonde Avenue, Netherlee, Glasgow G44 3SN [E-mail: g.mackay3@btinternet.com]	0141-637 4976 (Tel/Fax)
37	**Stepps (H)**				
	Vacant				
	Linda Walker (Aux)		2008	18 Valeview Terrace, Glasgow G42 9LA [E-mail: walkerlinda@hotmail.com]	0141-649 1340
38	**Thornliebank (H)**				
	Vacant			19 Arthurlie Drive, Giffnock, Glasgow G46 6UR	
39	**Torrance (T) (01360 620970)**				
	Nigel L. Barge BSc BD		1991	1 Atholl Avenue, Torrance, Glasgow G64 4JA [E-mail: nigel.barge@sky.com]	01360 622379
40	**Twechar** See Banton				
41	**Williamwood (0141-638 2091)**				
	Iain M.A. Reid MA BD	1990	2007	125 Greenwood Road, Clarkston, Glasgow G76 7LL [E-mail: reviain.reid@ntlworld.com]	0141-571 7949
42	**Glasgow: Anderston Kelvingrove (0141-221 9408)**				
	Vacant			16 Royal Terrace, Glasgow G3 7NY	0141-332 7704

No.			Year	Year	Address	Telephone
43	**Glasgow: Baillieston Mure Memorial (0141-773 1216)**		1984	2010		
	Malcolm Cuthbertson BA BD				28 Beech Avenue, Baillieston, Glasgow G69 6LF [E-mail: malcuth@aol.com]	0141-771 1217
44	**Glasgow: Baillieston St Andrew's (0141-771 6629)**					
	Vacant					
45	**Glasgow: Balshagray Victoria Park**		1982	2001		
	Campbell Mackinnon BSc BD				20 St Kilda Drive, Glasgow G14 9JN [E-mail: campbell54@btinternet.com]	0141-954 9780
46	**Glasgow: Barlanark Greyfriars (0141-771 6477)**					
	Vacant				4 Rhindmuir Grove, Glasgow G69 6NE	0141-771 1240
47	**Glasgow: Blawarthill**		1982	2009		
	G. Melvyn Wood MA BD				46 Earlbank Avenue, Glasgow G14 9HL [E-mail: gmelvynwood@gmail.com]	0141-579 6521
48	**Glasgow: Bridgeton St Francis in the East (H) (L) (0141-556 2830) (Church House: Tel: 0141-554 8045)**		1982	1984		
	Howard R. Hudson MA BD				10 Albany Drive, Rutherglen, Glasgow G73 3QN [E-mail: howard.hudson@ntlworld.com]	0141-587 8667
	Margaret S. Beaton (Miss) DCS (Deacon and Leader of Centre)				64 Gardenside Grove, Carmyle, Glasgow G32 8EZ [E-mail: margaret@churchhouse.plus.com]	0141-646 2297 / 07796 642382 (Mbl)
49	**Glasgow: Broomhill (0141-334 2540)**					
	Vacant				27 St Kilda Drive, Glasgow G14 9LN	0141-959 3204
50	**Glasgow: Calton Parkhead (0141-554 3866)**		1990	2008		
	Alison Davidge MA BD				98 Drumover Drive, Glasgow G31 5RP [E-mail: adavidge@sky.com]	07843 625059 (Mbl)
51	**Glasgow: Cardonald (0141-882 6264)**		1979	2007		
	Calum MacLeod BA BD				133 Newtyle Road, Paisley PA1 3LB [E-mail: pangur@sky.com]	0141-887 2726
52	**Glasgow: Carmunnock (0141-644 0655)**		1989	2001		
	G. Gray Fletcher BSc BD				The Manse, 161 Waterside Road, Carmunnock, Glasgow G76 9AJ [E-mail: gray.fletcher@virgin.net]	0141-644 1578 (Tel/Fax)

53	**Glasgow: Carmyle linked with Kenmuir Mount Vernon**	1997	1999		
	Murdo Maclean BD CertMin			3 Meryon Road, Glasgow G32 9NW	0141-778 2625
				[E-mail: murdo.maclean@ntlworld.com]	
54	**Glasgow: Carnwadric (E)**				
	Graeme K. Bell BA BD	1983		62 Loganswell Road, Thornliebank, Glasgow G46 8AX	0141-638 5884
				[E-mail: graemekbell@googlemail.com]	
	Mary Gargrave (Mrs) DCS	1989		90 Mount Annan Drive, Glasgow G44 4RZ	0141-561 4681
				[E-mail: mary.gargrave@btinternet.com]	
55	**Glasgow: Castlemilk East (H) (0141-634 2444) linked with Castlemilk West**				
	Sarah Brown (Ms)	2012		156 Old Castle Road, Glasgow G44 5TW	0141-637 5451
	MA BD ThM DipYW/Theol PDCCE			[E-mail: ministercastlemilk@gmail.com]	07532 457245 (Mbl)
56	**Glasgow: Castlemilk West (H) (0141-634 1480)** See Castlemilk East				
57	**Glasgow: Cathcart Old (0141-637 4168)**				
	Neil W. Galbraith BD CertMin	1987	1996	21 Courthill Avenue, Cathcart, Glasgow G44 5AA	0141-633 5248 (Tel/Fax)
				[E-mail: revneilgalbraith@hotmail.com]	
58	**Glasgow: Cathcart Trinity (H) (0141-637 6658)**				
	Iain Morrison BD	1991	2003	82 Merrylee Road, Glasgow G43 2QZ	0141-633 3744
				[E-mail: iain77@tiscali.co.uk]	
	Wilma Pearson (Mrs) BD (Assoc)	2004		90 Newlands Road, Glasgow G43 2JR	0141-632 2491
				[E-mail: wilma.pearson@ntlworld.com]	
59	**Glasgow: Cathedral (High or St Mungo's) (0141-552 6891)**				
	Laurence A.B. Whitley MA BD PhD	1975	2007	41 Springfield Road, Bishopbriggs, Glasgow G64 1PL	0141-762 2719
				[E-mail: labwhitley@btinternet.com]	
60	**Glasgow: Clincarthill (H) (0141-632 4206)**				
	Mike R. Gargrave BD	2008	2010	90 Mount Annan Drive, Glasgow G44 4RZ	0141-561 4681
				[E-mail: mike.gargrave@btinternet.com]	
61	**Glasgow: Colston Milton (0141-772 1922)**				
	Christopher J. Rowe BA BD	2008		118 Birsay Road, Milton, Glasgow G22 7QP	0141-564 1138
				[E-mail: ministercolstonmilton@yahoo.co.uk]	

No.	Charge / Minister	Ord.	Ind.	Address	Telephone
62	**Glasgow: Colston Wellpark (H)** Vacant			16 Bishopsgate Gardens, Colston, Glasgow G21 1XS	0141-589 8866
63	**Glasgow: Cranhill (H) (0141-774 3344)** Muriel B. Pearson (Ms) MA BD PGCE	2004		31 Lethamhill Crescent, Glasgow G33 2SH [E-mail: murielpearson@btinternet.com]	0141-770 6873 07951 888860 (Mbl)
64	**Glasgow: Croftfoot (H) (0141-637 3913)** Robert M. Silver BA BD	1995	2011	4 Inchmurrin Gardens, High Burnside, Rutherglen, Glasgow G73 5RU [E-mail: rob.silver@talktalk.net]	
65	**Glasgow: Dennistoun New (H) (0141-550 2825)** Ian M.S. McInnes BD DipMin	1995	2008	31 Pencaitland Drive, Glasgow G32 8RL [E-mail: ian.liz1@ntlworld.com]	0141-564 6498
66	**Glasgow: Drumchapel St Andrew's (0141-944 3758)** John S. Purves LLB BD	1983	1984	6 Firdon Crescent, Old Drumchapel, Glasgow G15 6QQ [E-mail: john.s.purves@talk21.com]	0141-944 4566
67	**Glasgow: Drumchapel St Mark's** Audrey Jamieson BD MTh	2004	2007	146 Garscadden Road, Glasgow G15 6PR [E-mail: audrey.jamieson2@btinternet.com]	0141-944 5440
68	**Glasgow: Easterhouse St George's and St Peter's (E) (0141-771 8810)** Vacant			3 Barony Gardens, Baillieston, Glasgow G69 6TS	0141-573 8200
69	**Glasgow: Eastwood** Graham R.G. Cartlidge MA BD STM	1977	2010	54 Mansewood Road, Eastwood, Glasgow G43 1TL [E-mail: cartlidge262@btinternet.com]	0141-649 0463
70	**Glasgow: Gairbraid (H)** Donald Michael MacInnes BD	2002	2011	8 Fruin Road, Glasgow G15 6SQ [E-mail: revdmmi@googlemail.com]	0141-258 8683
71	**Glasgow: Gallowgate** Peter L.V. Davidge BD MTh	2003	2009	98 Drumover Drive, Glasgow G31 5RP [E-mail: rev_dav46@yahoo.co.uk]	07765 096599 (Mbl)

No.	Charge / Minister	Ord.	Ind.	Address	Telephone
72	**Glasgow: Garthamlock and Craigend East (E)**				
	Valerie J. Duff (Miss) DMin	1993	1996	9 Craigievar Court, Glasgow G33 5DJ [E-mail: valduff@tiscali.co.uk]	0141-774 6364
	Marion Buchanan (Mrs) MA DCS			16 Almond Drive, East Kilbride, Glasgow G74 2HX [E-mail: marion.buchanan@btinternet.com]	01355 228776
73	**Glasgow: Gorbals**				
	Ian F. Galloway BA BD	1976	1996	44 Riverside Road, Glasgow G43 2EF [E-mail: ianfgalloway@msn.com]	0141-649 5250
74	**Glasgow: Govan and Linthouse**				
	Moyna McGlynn (Mrs) BD PhD	1999	2008	19 Dumbreck Road, Glasgow G41 5LJ [E-mail: moyna_mcglynn@hotmail.com]	0141-419 0308
	Judith Breakey (Ms)	2010		Flat 3/2, 8 Mingarry Street, Glasgow G20 8NT [E-mail: judith.breakey@gmail.com]	07858 507282 (Mbl)
	LizTheol MTh DipEd (Assoc)				
	Paul Cathcart DCS			9 Glen More, East Kilbride, Glasgow G74 2AP [E-mail: paulcathcart@msn.com]	01355 243970 07708 396074 (Mbl)
75	**Glasgow: Govanhill Trinity** Vacant			12 Carlton Gate, Giffnock, Glasgow G46 6NU	0141-637 8399
76	**Glasgow: High Carntyne (0141-778 4186)**				
	Joan Ross (Miss) BSc BD PhD	1999	2005	163 Lethamhill Road, Glasgow G33 2SQ [E-mail: joan@highcarntyne.plus.com]	0141-770 9247
77	**Glasgow: Hillington Park (H)**				
	John B. MacGregor BD	1999	2004	61 Ralston Avenue, Glasgow G52 3NB [E-mail: johnmacgregor61@hotmail.co.uk]	0141-882 7000
78	**Glasgow: Househillwood St Christopher's**				
	May M. Allison (Mrs) BD (retiring in October 2012)	1988	2001	12 Leverndale Court, Crookston, Glasgow G53 7SJ [E-mail: revmayallison@hotmail.com]	0141-810 5953
79	**Glasgow: Hyndland (H) (Website: www.hyndlandparishchurch.org)** Vacant			24 Hughenden Gardens, Glasgow G12 9YH	0141-334 1002
80	**Glasgow: Ibrox (H) (0141-427 0896)**				
	Elisabeth G.B. Spence (Miss) BD DipEd	1995	2008	59 Langhaul Road, Glasgow G53 7SE [E-mail: revelisabeth@spenceweb.net]	0141-883 7744

81 Glasgow: John Ross Memorial Church for Deaf People
(Voice Text: 0141-420 1391; Fax: 0141-420 3778)   1989   1998
Richard C. Durno DSW CQSW   1989
31 Springfield Road, Bishopbriggs, Glasgow G64 1PJ
[E-mail: richard.durno@btinternet.com]
(Voice/Text/Fax) 0141-772 1052
(Voice/Text/Voicemail) (Mbl) 07748 607721

82 Glasgow: Jordanhill (Tel: 0141-959 2496)
Colin C. Renwick BMus BD   1989   1996
96 Southbrae Drive, Glasgow G13 1TZ   0141-959 1310
[E-mail: jordchurch@btconnect.com]

83 Glasgow: Kelvin Stevenson Memorial (0141-339 1750)
Gordon Kirkwood BSc BD PGCE MTh   1987   2003
Flat 2/2, 94 Hyndland Road, Glasgow G12 9PZ   0141-334 5352
[E-mail: gordonkirkwood@tiscali.co.uk]

84 Glasgow: Kelvinside Hillhead (0141-334 2788)
Vacant
39 Athole Gardens, Glasgow G12 9BQ   0141-339 2865

85 Glasgow: Kenmuir Mount Vernon See Carmyle

86 Glasgow: King's Park (H) (0141-636 8688)
Sandra Boyd (Mrs) BEd BD   2007
1101 Aikenhead Road, Glasgow G44 5SL   0141-637 2803
[E-mail: sandraboyd.bofa@btopenworld.com]

87 Glasgow: Kinning Park (0141-427 3063)
Margaret H. Johnston BD   1988   2000
168 Arbroath Avenue, Cardonald, Glasgow G52 3HH   0141-810 3782
[E-mail: marniejohnston7@aol.com]

88 Glasgow: Knightswood St Margaret's (H)
Alexander M. Fraser BD DipMin   1985   2009
26 Airthrey Avenue, Glasgow G14 9LJ   0141-959 7075
[E-mail: sandyfraser2@hotmail.com]

89 Glasgow: Langside (0141-632 7520)
David N. McLachlan BD   1985   2004
36 Madison Avenue, Glasgow G44 5AQ   0141-637 0797
[E-mail: dmclachlan77@hotmail.com]

90 Glasgow: Lansdowne
Roy J.M. Henderson MA BD DipMin   1987   1992
18 Woodlands Drive, Glasgow G4 9EH   0141-339 2794
[E-mail: roy.henderson7@ntlworld.com]

91 Glasgow: Lochwood (H) (0141-771 2649)
Stuart M. Duff BA — 1997 — 42 Rhindmuir Road, Swinton, Glasgow G69 6AZ [E-mail: stuart.duff@gmail.com] — 0141-773 2756

92 Glasgow: Maryhill (H) (0141-946 3512)
Stuart C. Matthews BD MA — 2006 — 251 Milngavie Road, Bearsden, Glasgow G61 3DQ [E-mail: stuart.maryhill@gmail.com] — 0141-942 0804

James Hamilton DCS — 6 Beckfield Gate, Glasgow G33 1SW [E-mail: j.hamilton111@btinternet.com] — 0141-558 3195

93 Glasgow: Merrylea (0141-637 2009)
David P. Hood BD CertMin DiplOB(Scot) — 1997 — 2001 — 4 Pilmuir Avenue, Glasgow G44 3HX [E-mail: dphood3@ntlworld.com] — 0141-637 6700

94 Glasgow: Mosspark (H) (0141-882 2240)
Vacant — 396 Kilmarnock Road, Glasgow G43 2DJ — 0141-632 1247

95 Glasgow: Newlands South (H) (0141-632 3055)
John D. Whiteford MA BD — 1989 — 1997 — 24 Monreith Road, Glasgow G43 2NY [E-mail: jwhiteford@hotmail.com] — 0141-632 2588

96 Glasgow: Partick South (H)
James Andrew McIntyre BD — 2010 — 3 Branklyn Crescent, Glasgow G13 1GJ [E-mail: revpartcksouth@hotmail.co.uk] — 0141-959 3732

97 Glasgow: Partick Trinity (H)
Stuart J. Smith BEng BD MTh — 1994 — 99 Balshagray Avenue, Glasgow G11 7EQ [E-mail: ssmith99@ntlworld.com] — 0141-576 7149

98 Glasgow: Penilee St Andrew (H) (0141-882 2691)
Lyn Peden (Mrs) BD — 2010 — 80 Tweedsmuir Road, Glasgow G52 2RX [E-mail: lynpeden@yahoo.com] — 0141-883 9873

99 Glasgow: Pollokshaws (0141-649 1879)
Vacant — 33 Mannering Road, Glasgow G41 3SW — 0141-649 0458

100 Glasgow: Pollokshields (H)
David R. Black MA BD — 1986 — 1997 — 36 Glencairn Drive, Glasgow G41 4PW [E-mail: minister@pollokshieldschurch.org.uk] — 0141-423 4000

101 Glasgow: Possilpark (0141-336 8028)
Vacant
108 Erradale Street, Lambhill, Glasgow G22 6PT
0141-336 6909

102 Glasgow: Priesthill and Nitshill (0141-881 6541)
Douglas M. Nicol BD CA   1987
36 Springkell Drive, Glasgow G41 4EZ
[E-mail: dougiemnicol@aol.com]
0141-427 7877

103 Glasgow: Queen's Park (0141-423 3654)
David S.M. Malcolm BD   2011
17 Linndale Drive, Carmunnock Grange, Glasgow G45 0QE
[E-mail: DavidSMMalcolm@aol.com]
0141-634 1097

104 Glasgow: Renfield St Stephen's (Tel: 0141-332 4293; Fax: 0141-332 8482)
Peter M. Gardner MA BD   1988   2002
101 Hill Street, Glasgow G3 6TY
[E-mail: peter@rsschurch.net]
0141-353 0349

105 Glasgow: Robroyston (New Charge Development) (0141-558 8414)
Jonathan A. Keefe BSc BD   2009
7 Beckfield Drive, Glasgow G33 1SR
[E-mail: jonathanakeefe@aol.com]
0141-558 2952

106 Glasgow: Ruchazie (0141-774 2759)
Vacant
18 Borthwick Street, Glasgow G33 3UU
0141-774 6860

107 Glasgow: Ruchill Kelvinside (0141-946 0466)
Vacant
9 Kirklee Road, Glasgow G12 0RQ
0141-357 3249

108 Glasgow: St Andrew's East (0141-554 1485)
Barbara D. Quigley (Mrs)   1979   2011
MTheol ThM DPS
43 Broompark Drive, Glasgow G31 2JB
[E-mail: bdquigley@aol.com]
0141-237 7982

109 Glasgow: St Columba (GE) (0141-221 3305)
Vacant
1 Reelick Avenue, Peterson Park, Glasgow G13 4NF
0141-952 0948

110 Glasgow: St David's Knightswood (0141-954 1081)
Graham M. Thain LLB BD   1988   1999
60 Southbrae Drive, Glasgow G13 1QD
[E-mail: graham_thain@btopenworld.com]
0141-959 2904

111 Glasgow: St Enoch's Hogganfield (H) (Tel: 0141-770 5694; Fax: 0870 284 0084) (E-mail: church@st-enoch.org.uk)
     (Website: www.stenochshogganfield.org.uk)
     Graham K. Blount LLB BD PhD   1976   2010   43 Smithycroft Road, Glasgow G33 2RH   0141-770 7593
                                                                [E-mail: graham.blount@yahoo.co.uk]

112 Glasgow: St George's Tron (0141-221 2141)
     Vacant

113 Glasgow: St James' (Pollok) (0141-882 4984)
     John W. Mann BSc MDiv DMin   2004   30 Ralston Avenue, Glasgow G52 3NA   0141-883 7405
                                                     [E-mail: drjohnmann@hotmail.com]

114 Glasgow: St John's Renfield (0141-339 7021) (Website: www.stjohns-renfield.org.uk)
     Fiona L. Lillie (Mrs) BA BD MLitt   1995   2009   26 Leicester Avenue, Glasgow G12 0LU   0141-339 4637
                                                                [E-mail: fionalillie@btinternet.com]

115 Glasgow: St Margaret's Tollcross Park
     Vacant   31 Kenmuir Avenue, Sandyhills, Glasgow G32 9LE   0141-778 5060

116 Glasgow: St Nicholas' Cardonald
     Vacant   104 Lamington Road, Glasgow G52 2SE   0141-882 2065

117 Glasgow: St Paul's (0141-770 8559)
     Vacant

118 Glasgow: St Rollox (0141-558 1809)
     Vacant   42 Melville Gardens, Bishopbriggs, Glasgow G64 3DE   0141-562 6296

119 Glasgow: Sandyford Henderson Memorial (H) (L)
     Vacant   66 Woodend Drive, Glasgow G13 1TG   0141-954 9013

120 Glasgow: Sandyhills (0141-778 3415)
     Graham T. Atkinson MA BD MTh   2006   60 Wester Road, Glasgow G32 9JJ   0141-778 2174
                                                     [E-mail: gtatkinson@o2.co.uk]

121 Glasgow: Scotstoun (T)
     Richard Cameron BD DipMin   2000   15 Northland Drive, Glasgow G14 9BE   0141-959 4637
                                                     [E-mail: rev.rickycam@live.co.uk]

122 Glasgow: Shawlands (0141-649 1773)
Vacant
29 St Ronan's Drive, Glasgow G41 3SQ
0141-649 2034

123 Glasgow: Sherbrooke St Gilbert's (H) (0141-427 1968)
Thomas L. Pollock   1982   2003
BA BD MTh FSAScot JP
114 Springkell Avenue, Glasgow G41 4EW
[E-mail: tompollock06@aol.com]
0141-427 2094

124 Glasgow: Shettleston New (0141-778 0857)
Ronald A.S. Craig BAcc BD   1983   2007
211 Sandyhills Road, Glasgow G32 9NB
[E-mail: rascraig@ntlworld.com]
0141-778 1286

Dot Getliffe (Mrs) DCS BA BD DipEd
(Deacon/Development Co-ordinator)
3 Woodview Terrace, Hamilton ML3 9DP
[E-mail: dgetliffe@aol.co.uk]
01698 423504
07766 910171 (Mbl)

125 Glasgow: Shettleston Old (T) (H) (0141-778 2484)
Vacant
57 Mansionhouse Road, Mount Vernon, Glasgow G32 0RP
0141-778 8904

126 Glasgow: South Carntyne (H) (0141-778 1343)
Vacant
47 Broompark Drive, Glasgow G31 2JB
0141-554 3275

127 Glasgow: South Shawlands (T) (0141-649 4656)
Vacant
391 Kilmarnock Road, Glasgow G43 2NU
0141-632 0013

128 Glasgow: Springburn (H) (0141-557 2345)
Alan A. Ford BD   1977   2000
3 Tofthill Avenue, Bishopbriggs, Glasgow G64 3PA
[E-mail: springburnchurch@fordsall.com]
0141-762 1844
07710 455737 (Mbl)

129 Glasgow: Temple Anniesland (0141-959 1814)
Fiona Gardner (Mrs) BD MA MLitt   1997   2011
76 Victoria Park Drive North, Glasgow G14 9PJ
[E-mail: fionandcolin@hotmail.com]
0141-959 5835

130 Glasgow: Toryglen (H)
Sandra Black (Mrs) BSc BD   1988   2003
36 Glencairn Drive, Glasgow G41 4PW
[E-mail: revsblack@btinternet.com]
0141-423 0867

131 Glasgow: Trinity Possil and Henry Drummond
Richard G. Buckley BD MTh   1990   1995
50 Highfield Drive, Glasgow G12 0HL
[E-mail: richardbuckleyis@hotmail.com]
0141-339 2870

132 Glasgow: Tron St Mary's (0141-558 1011)
P. Jill Clancy (Mrs) BD DipMin   2000   2008   Tron St Mary's Church, 128 Red Road, Balornock, Glasgow G21 4PJ   0141-558 1011
[E-mail: jgibson@totalise.co.uk]

Karen Hamilton (Mrs) DCS   1995   2009   6 Beckfield Gate, Glasgow G33 1SW   0141-558 3195
[E-mail: k.hamilton6@btinternet.com]

133 Glasgow: Victoria Tollcross
Monica Michelin Salomon BD   1999   2007   228 Hamilton Road, Glasgow G32 9QU   0141-778 2413
[E-mail: monica@michelin-salomon.freeserve.co.uk]

134 Glasgow: Wallacewell (New Charge Development)
Daniel Frank BA MDiv DMin   1984   2011   8 Streamfield Gate, Glasgow G33 1SJ   0141-585 0283
[E-mail: daniellouis106@gmail.com]

135 Glasgow: Wellington (H) (0141-339 0454)
David I. Sinclair BSc BD PhD DipSW   1990   2008   31 Hughenden Gardens, Glasgow G12 9YH   0141-334 2343
[E-mail: davidsinclair@btinternet.com]

136 Glasgow: Whiteinch (Website: www.whiteinchcofs.co.uk)
Alan McWilliam BD MTh   1993   2000   65 Victoria Park Drive South, Glasgow G14 9NX   0141-576 9020
[E-mail: alan@whiteinchchurch.org]

Alex W. Smeed MA BD (Assoc)   2008   3/1, 24 Thornwood Road, Glasgow G11 7RB   0141-337 3878
[E-mail: alex@whiteinchchurch.org]   07709 756495 (Mbl)

137 Glasgow: Yoker (T)
Karen E. Hendry BSc BD   2005   15 Coldingham Avenue, Glasgow G14 0PX   0141-952 3620
[E-mail: karen@hendry-k.fsnet.co.uk]

Name				Charge / Role	Address	Phone
Alexander, Eric J. MA BD	1958	1997		(Glasgow: St George's Tron)	77 Norwood Park, Bearsden, Glasgow G61 2RZ	0141-942 4404
Allen, Martin A.W. MA BD ThM	1977	2007		(Chryston)	Lealenge, 85 High Barrwood Road, Kilsyth, Glasgow G65 0EE	01236 826616
Alston, William G.	1961	2009		(Glasgow: North Kelvinside)	Flat 0/2, 5 Knightswood Court, Glasgow G13 2XN [E-mail: williamalston@hotmail.com]	0141-959 3113
Barr, Alexander C. MA BD	1950	1992		(Glasgow: St Nicholas' Cardonald)	25 Fisher Drive, Phoenix Park, Paisley PA1 2TP	0141-848 5941
Barr, John BSc PhD BD	1958	1979		(Kilmacolm: Old)	31 Kelvin Court, Glasgow G12 0AD	0141-357 4338
Bayes, Muriel C. DCS	1963			(Deaconess)	Flat 6, Carlton Court, 10 Fenwick Road, Glasgow G46 6AN	0141-633 0865
Bell, John L. MA BD FRSCM DUniv	1978	1988		Iona Community	Flat 2/1, 31 Lansdowne Crescent, Glasgow G20 6NH	0141-334 0688
Bell, Sandra (Mrs) DCS				Hospital Chaplain	62 Loganswell Road, Glasgow G42 8AX	0141-638 5884
Birch, James PgDip FRSA FIOC	2001	2007		(Auxiliary Minister)	1 Kirkhill Grove, Cambuslang, Glasgow G72 8EH	0141-583 1722
Black, William B. MA BD	1972	2011		(Stornoway: High)	33 Tankerland Road, Glasgow G44 4EN [E-mail: revwillieblack@gmail.com]	0141-637 4717

Name				Address	Tel
Blount, A. Sheila (Mrs) BD BA	1978	2010	(Cupar: St John's and Dairsie United)	43 Smithycroft Road, Glasgow G33 2RH [E-mail: asblount@orange.net]	0141-770 7593
Bradley, Andrew W. BD	1975	2007	(Paisley: Lylesland)	Flat 1/1, 38 Cairnhill View, Bearsden, Glasgow G61 1RP	0141-931 5344
Brain, Isobel J. (Mrs) MA	1987	1997	(Ballantrae)	14 Chesterfield Court, 1240 Great Western Road, Glasgow G12 0BJ	0141-357 2249
Brice, Dennis G. BSc BD	1981		(Taiwan)	8 Parkwood Close, Broxbourne, Herts EN10 7PF [E-mail: dbrice1@comcast.net]	
Bryden, William A. BD	1977	1984	(Yoker: Old with St Matthew's)	145 Bearsden Road, Glasgow G13 1BS	0141-959 5213
Bull, Alister W. BD DipMin	1994	2001	Hospital Chaplain	Chaplaincy Centre Office, First Floor, Queen Mother's Hospital, Yorkhill Division, Dalnair Street, Glasgow G3 8SJ [E-mail: alister.bull@yorkhill.scot.nhs.uk]	0141-201 0000
Campbell, A. Iain MA DipEd	1961	1997	(Busby)	430 Clarkston Road, Glasgow G44 3QF [E-mail: bellmac@sagainternet.co.uk]	0141-637 7460
Campbell-Jack, W.C. BD MTh PhD	1979	2011	(Glasgow: Possilpark)	35 Castle Avenue, Airth, Falkirk FK2 8GA [E-mail: c.c-j@homecall.co.uk]	
Cunningham, Alexander MA BD	1961	2002	Presbytery Clerk	The Glen, 103 Glenmavis Road, Airdrie ML6 0PQ	01236 763012
Cunningham, James S.A. MA BD BLitt PhD	1992	2000	(Glasgow: Barlanark Greyfriars)	'Kirkland', 5 Inveresk Place, Coatbridge ML5 2DA	01236 421541
Dean, Roger A.F. LTh	1983	2004	(Mochrum)	0/2, 20 Ballogie Road, Glasgow G44 4TA	0141-571 6002
Drummond, John W. MA BD	1971	2011	(Rutherglen: West and Wardlawhill)	25 Kingsburn Drive, Rutherglen, Glasgow G73 2AN	0141-570 0614 / (Mbl) 07846 926584
Duff, T. Malcolm F. MA BD	1985	2009	(Glasgow: Queen's Park)	54 Hawkhead Road, Paisley PA1 3NB	0141-588 5868
Ferguson, James B. LTh	1972	2002	(Lenzie: Union)	3 Bridgeway Place, Kirkintilloch, Glasgow G66 3HW	
Ferguson, William B. BA BD	1971	2012	(Glasgow: Broomhill)	20 Swift Crescent, Knightswood Gate, Glasgow G13 4QL [E-mail: revferg@btinternet.com]	0141-954 6655
Finlay, William P. MA BD	1969	2000	(Glasgow: Townhead Blochairn)	High Corrie, Brodick, Isle of Arran KA27 8JB	01770 810689
Fleming, Alexander F. MA BD	1966	1995	(Strathblane)	11 Bankwood Drive, Kilsyth, Glasgow G65 0GZ	01236 821461
Forrest, Martin R. BA MA BD	1988	2012	Prison Chaplain	4/1, 7 Blochairn Place, Glasgow G21 2EB [E-mail: roger.dean4@btopenworld.com]	0141-552 1132
Galloway, Kathy (Mrs) BD DD	1977	2002	(Leader: Iona Community)	20 Hamilton Park Avenue, Glasgow G12 8UU [E-mail: martinrforrest@gmail.com]	0141-357 4079
Gay, Douglas C. MA BD PhD	1998	2005	University of Glasgow	23 Clouston Street, Glasgow G20 8QP [E-mail: doug.gay@glasgow.ac.uk]	0141-330 2073 / (Mbl) 07971 321452
Gibson, H. Marshall MA BD	1957	1996	(Glasgow: St Thomas' Gallowgate)	39 Burntbroom Drive, Glasgow G69 7XG	0141-771 0749
Gibson, Michael BD STM	1974	2001	(Giffnock: The Park)	12 Mile End Park, Pocklington, York YO42 2TH	
Grant, David I.M. MA BD	1969	2003	(Dalry: Trinity)	8 Mossbank Drive, Glasgow G33 1LS	0141-770 7186
Gray, Christine M. (Mrs)			(Deaconess)	11 Woodside Avenue, Thornliebank, Glasgow G46 7HR	0141-571 1008
Green, Alex H. MA BD	1986	2010	(Strathblane)	44 Laburnum Drive, Milton of Campsie, Glasgow G66 8HY [E-mail: lesvert@btinternet.com]	01360 313001
Gregson, Elizabeth M. (Mrs) BD	1996	2001	(Glasgow: Drumchapel St Andrew's)	17 Westfields, Bishopbriggs, Glasgow G64 3PL	0141-563 1918
Haley, Derek BD DPS	1960	1999	(Chaplain: Gartnavel Royal)	9 Kinnaird Crescent, Bearsden, Glasgow G61 2BN	0141-942 9281
Harper, Anne J.M. (Miss) BD STM MTh CertSocPsych	1979	1990	(Hospital Chaplain)	122 Greenock Road, Bishopton PA7 5AS	01505 862466
Harvey, W. John BA BD DD	1965	2002	(Edinburgh: Corstorphine Craigsbank)	501 Shields Road, Glasgow G41 2RF	0141-429 3774

Name	Ord	Ind	Role	Address	Telephone
Haughton, Frank MA BD	1942	2000	(Kirkintilloch: St Mary's)	64 Regent Street, Kirkintilloch, Glasgow G66 1JF	0141-777 6802
Hewitt, William C. BD DipPS	1977	2012	Interim Minister	60 Woodlands Grove, Kilmarnock KA3 1TZ [E-mail: billhewitt1@btinternet.com]	01563 533312
Hope, Evelyn P. (Miss) BA BD	1990	1998	(Wishaw: Thornlie)	Flat 0/1, 48 Moss Side Road, Glasgow G41 3UA	0141-649 1522
Houston, Thomas C. BA	1975	2004	(Glasgow: Priesthill and Nitshill)	63 Broomhouse Crescent, Uddingston, Glasgow G71 7RE	0141-771 0577
Hughes, Helen (Miss) DCS			Deacon	2/2, 43 Burnbank Terrace, Glasgow G20 6UQ	0141-333 9459
Hunter, Alastair G. MSc BD	1976	1980	(University of Glasgow)	487 Shields Road, Glasgow G41 2RG	0141-429 1687
Johnston, Robert W.M. MA BD STM	1964	1999	(Glasgow: Temple Anniesland)	13 Kilmardinny Crescent, Bearsden, Glasgow G61 3NP	0141-931 5862
Johnstone, H. Martin J. MA BD MTh PhD	1989	2000	Priority Areas Secretary	3/1, 952 Pollokshaws Road, Glasgow G41 2ET [E-mail: mjohnstone@cofscotland.org.uk]	0141-636 5819
Keddie, David A. MA BD	1966	2005	(Glasgow: Linthouse St Kenneth's)	21 Ilay Road, Bearsden, Glasgow G61 1QG [E-mail: revkd@hotmail.com]	0141-942 5173
Kerr, Angus BD CertMin ThM DMin	1983	2008	Presbytery Clerk	27 Pelham Court, Thornton Grange, Jackton, East Kilbride, Glasgow G74 5PZ	0141-332 6606 (Mbl) 07968 270391
Lancaster, Craig MA BD	2004	2011	Chaplain: RAF	26 Edinburgh Square, Waddington, Lincs LN5 9NQ [E-mail: craiglancaster@yahoo.co.uk]	0141-944 2240
Lang, I. Pat (Miss) BSc	1996	2003	(Dunoon: The High Kirk)	37 Crawford Drive, Glasgow G15 6TW	0141-620 3492
Levison, C.L. MA BD	1972	1998	(Health Care Chaplaincy Training and Development Officer)	5 Deaconsbank Avenue, Stewarton Road, Glasgow G46 7UN	
Lewis, E.M.H. MA	1962	1993	(Glasgow: Drumchapel St Andrew's)	c/o Mr Kelvin McAlister, 30 Ardbeg Road, Carfin, Motherwell ML1 4FE	
Lloyd, John M. BD CertMin	1984	2009	(Glasgow: Croftfoot)	17 Acacia Way, Cambuslang, Glasgow G72 7ZY	(Mbl) 07879 812816
Locke, David I.W. MA MSc BD	2000	2009	(Glasgow: Barlanark Greyfriars)	Flat 15, 65 Partickhill Road, Glasgow G11 5AD [E-mail: davidlockerev@yahoo.co.uk]	(Mbl) 07776 448301
Luman, David W. MA BD DUniv DLitt DD	1970	2002	(Presbytery Clerk)	30 Mill Road, Banton, Glasgow G65 0RD	01236 824110
Macaskill, Marjory (Mrs) LLB BD MTh	1990	1998	Ministries Council	1/3, 2 Wyndham Court, Glasgow G12 0TY [E-mail: mmacaskill@cofscotland.org.uk]	(Home) 0141-337 6196 (Work) 0131-225 5722
MacBain, Ian W. BD	1971	1993	(Coatbridge: Coatdyke)	24 Thornyburn Drive, Baillieston, Glasgow G69 7ER	0141-771 7030
MacDonald, Anne (Miss) BA DCS	2001	2006	Healthcare Chaplain: Levendale Hospital	c/o Leverndale Hospital, Glasgow G53 7TU	0141-211 6695
MacDonald, Kenneth MA BA			(Auxiliary Minister)	5 Henderland Road, Bearsden, Glasgow G61 1AH	0141-943 1103
MacFadyen, Anne M. (Mrs) BSc BD FSAScot	1995		(Auxiliary Minister)	295 Mearns Road, Glasgow G77 5LT	0141-639 3605
MacKay, Alan H. BD	1974	2010	(Glasgow: Mosspark)	Flat 1/1, 18 Newburgh Street, Glasgow G43 2XR [E-mail: alanhmackay@aol.com]	0141-632 0527
McKay, Johnston R. MA BA PhD	1969	1987	(Religious Broadcasting: BBC)	15 Montgomerie Avenue, Fairlie, Largs KA29 0EE [E-mail: johnston.mckay@btopenworld.com]	01475 568802
MacKinnon, Charles M. BD	1989	2009	(Kilsyth: Anderson)	36 Hilton Terrace, Bishopbriggs, Glasgow G64 3HB [E-mail: cm.ccmackinnon@tiscali.co.uk]	0141-772 3811
McLachlan, Eric BD MTh	1978	2005	(Glasgow: Cardonald)	268 Dyke Road, Knightswood, Glasgow G13 4QX [E-mail: eric.mclachlan@ntlworld.com]	0141-954 1574
McLachlan, Fergus C. BD	1982	2009	(Hospital Chaplain)	46 Queen Square, Glasgow G41 2AZ	0141-423 3830
McLachlan, T. Alastair BSc	1972	2009	(Craignish with Kilbrandon and Kilchattan with Kilninver and Kilmelford)	9 Alder Road, Milton of Campsie, Glasgow G66 8HH [E-mail: talastair@btinternet.com]	01360 319861

Name	Years	Charge	Address	Telephone
McLaren, D. Muir MA BD MTh PhD	1971 2001	(Glasgow: Mosspark)	House 44, 145 Shawhill Road, Glasgow G43 1SX [E-mail: muir44@yahoo.co.uk]	(Mbl) 07931 155779
McLay, Alastair D. BSc BD	1989 2004	(Glasgow: Shawlands)	183 King's Park Avenue, Glasgow G44 4HZ	0141-569 5503
Macleod, Donald BD LRAM DRSAM	1987 2008	(Blairgowrie)	9 Millersneuk Avenue, Lenzie G66 5HJ [E-mail: donmac2@sky.com]	0141-776 6235
MacLeod-Mair, Alisdair T. MEd DipTheol	2001 2012	(Glasgow: Baillieston St Andrew's)	2/2, 44 Leven Street, Pollokshields, Glasgow G41 2JE [E-mail: revalisdair@hotmail.com]	0141-423 9600
Macnaughton, J.A. MA BD	1949 1989	(Glasgow: Hyndland)	62 Lauderdale Gardens, Glasgow G12 9QW	0141-339 1294
MacPherson, James B. DCS		(Deacon)	0/1, 104 Cartside Street, Glasgow G42 9TQ	0141-616 6468
MacQuarrie, Stuart JP BD BSc MBA	1984 2001	Chaplain: Glasgow University	The Chaplaincy Centre, University of Glasgow, Glasgow G12 8QQ	0141-330 5419
MacQuien, Duncan DCS	1988	(Deacon)	35 Criffel Road, Mount Vernon, Glasgow G32 9JE	0141-575 1137
Martindale, John P.F. BD	1994 2005	(Glasgow: Sandyhills)	Flat 3/2, 25 Albert Avenue, Glasgow G42 8RB	0141-433 4367
Miller, John D. BA BD DD	1971 2007	(Glasgow: Castlemilk East)	98 Kirkcaldy Road, Glasgow G41 4LD [E-mail: rev.john.miller@zol.co.zw]	0141-423 0221
Moffat, Thomas BSc BD	1976 2008	(Culross and Torryburn)	Flat 8/1, 8 Cranston Street, Glasgow G3 8GG [E-mail: tom@gallus.org.uk]	0141-248 1886
Moore, William B.		(Prison Chaplain: Low Moss)	10 South Dumbreck Road, Kilsyth, Glasgow G65 9LX	01236 821918
Morrice, Alastair M. MA BD	1968 2002	(Rutherglen: Stonelaw)	5 Brechin Road, Kirriemuir DD8 4BX	
Morris, William J. KCVO PhD LLD DD JP	1951 2005	(Glasgow: Cathedral)	1 Whitehill Grove, Newton Mearns, Glasgow G77 5DH	0141-639 6327
Morton, Thomas MA BD LGSM	1945 1986	(Rutherglen: Stonelaw)	54 Greystone Avenue, Burnside, Rutherglen, Glasgow G73 3SW	0141-647 2682
Muir, Fred C. MA BD ThM ARCM	1961 1997	(Stepps)	20 Alexandra Avenue, Stepps, Glasgow G33 6BP	0141-779 2504
Murray, George M. LTh	1995 2011	(Glasgow: St Margaret's Tollcross Park)	6 Mayfield, Lesmahagow ML11 0FH [E-mail: george.murray7@gmail.com]	
Newlands, George M. MA BD PhD DLit FRSA FRSE	1970 1986	(University of Glasgow)	12 Jamaica Street North Lane, Edinburgh EH3 6HQ	
Philip, George M. MA	1953 1996	(Glasgow: Sandyford Henderson Memorial)		
Raeburn, Alan C. MA BD	1971 2010	(Glasgow: Battlefield East)	44 Beech Avenue, Bearsden, Glasgow G61 3EX	(Mbl) 0141-942 1327 07709 552161
			3 Orchard Gardens, Strathaven ML10 6UN [E-mail: acraeburn@hotmail.com]	
Ramsay, W.G.	1967 1999	(Glasgow: Springburn)	53 Kelvinvale, Kirkintilloch, Glasgow G66 1RD [E-mail: billram@btopenworld.com]	0141-776 2915
Robertson, Archibald MA BD	1957 1999	(Glasgow: Eastwood)	19 Canberra Court, Braidpark Drive, Glasgow G46 6NS	0141-637 7572
Robertson, Blair MA BD ThM	1990 1998	Chaplain: Southern General Hospital	c/o Chaplain's Office, Southern General Hospital, 1345 Govan Road, Glasgow G51 4TF	
Ross, Donald M. MA	1953 1994	(Industrial Mission Organiser)	14 Cartsbridge Road, Busby, Glasgow G76 8DH	0141-201 2357
Ross, James MA BD	1968 1998	(Kilsyth: Anderson)	53 Turnberry Gardens, Westerwood, Cumbernauld, Glasgow G68 0AY	0141-644 2220
Saunders, Keith BD	1983 1999	Hospital Chaplain	Western Infirmary, Dumbarton Road, Glasgow G11 6NT	01236 730501
Shackleton, William	1960 1996	(Greenock: Wellpark West)	3 Tynwald Avenue, Burnside, Glasgow G73 4RN	0141-211 2000
Shanks, Norman J. MA BD DD	1983 2007	(Glasgow: Govan Old)	1 Marchmont Terrace, Glasgow G12 9LT [E-mail: rufuski@btinternet.com]	0141-569 9407
Simpson, Neil A. BA BD PhD	1992 2001	(Glasgow: Yoker Old with Yoker St Matthew's)	c/o Glasgow Presbytery Office	0141-339 4421

Name			(Previous Charge)	Address	Tel/Fax
Smith, G. Stewart MA BD STM	1966	2006	(Glasgow: King's Park)	33 Brent Road, Stewartfield, East Kilbride, Glasgow G74 4RA [E-mail: stewartandmary@googlemail.com]	(Tel/Fax) 01355 226718
Smith, James S.A.	1956	1991		146 Aros Drive, Glasgow G52 1TJ	0141-883 9666
Spencer, John MA BD	1962	2001	(Drongan: The Schaw Kirk)	10 Kinkell Gardens, Kirkintilloch, Glasgow G66 2HJ	0141-777 8935
Spiers, John M. LTh MTh	1972	2004	(Dumfries: Lincluden with Holywood)	58 Woodlands Road, Thornliebank, Glasgow G46 7JQ	(Tel/Fax) 0141-638 0632
Stewart, Diane E. BD	1988	2006	(Giffnock: Orchardhill) (Milton of Campsie)	4 Miller Gardens, Bishopbriggs, Glasgow G64 1FG [E-mail: destewart@givemail.co.uk]	0141-762 1358
Stewart, Norma D. (Miss) MA MEd BD MTh	1977	2000	(Glasgow: Strathbungo Queen's Park)	127 Nether Auldhouse Road, Glasgow G43 2YS	0141-637 6956
Sutherland, Denis I.	1963	1995	(Glasgow: Hutchesontown)	56 Lime Crescent, Cumbernauld, Glasgow G67 3PQ	01236 731723
Sutherland, Elizabeth W. (Miss) BD	1972	1996	(Balornock North with Barmulloch)	20 Kirkland Avenue, Blanefield, Glasgow G63 9BZ [E-mail: ewsutherland@aol.com]	01360 770154
Thomson, Alexander BSc BD MPhil PhD	1973	2012	(Rutherglen: Old)	3 Laurel Wynd, Drumfargard Village, Cambuslang, Glasgow G72 7BH [E-mail: alexander.thomson6@btopenworld.com]	0141-641 2936
Thomson, Andrew BA	1976	2007	(Airdrie: Broomknoll)	46 Keir Street, Pollokshields, Glasgow G41 2LA [E-mail: andrewthomson@hotmail.com]	0141-424 0493
Turner, Angus BD	1976	1998	(Industrial Chaplain)	6 Holmwood Gardens, Uddingston, Glasgow G71 7BH	01698 321108
Tuton, Robert M. MA	1957	1995	(Glasgow: Shettleston Old)	11 Dundas Avenue, Torrance, Glasgow G64 4BD	01360 622281
Walker, A.L.	1955	1988	(Glasgow: Trinity Possil and Henry Drummond)		
Walton, Ainslie MA MEd	1954	1995	(University of Aberdeen)	501 Shields Road, Glasgow G41 2RF [E-mail: revainslie@aol.com]	0141-420 3327
White, C. Peter BVMS BD MRCVS	1974	2011	(Glasgow: Sandyford Henderson Memorial)	2 Hawthorn Place, Torrance, Glasgow G64 4EA [E-mail: revpw@gmail.com]	01360 622680
Whyte, James BD	1981	2011	(Fairlie)	32 Torburn Avenue, Giffnock, Glasgow G46 7RB [E-mail: jameswhyte89@btinternet.com]	
Wilson, John BD	1985	2010	(Glasgow: Temple Anniesland)	4 Carron Crescent, Bearsden, Glasgow G61 1HJ [E-mail: revjwilson@btinternet.com]	0141-931 5609
Younger, Adah (Mrs) BD	1978	2004	(Glasgow: Dennistoun Central)	Flat 0/1, 101 Greenhead Street, Glasgow G40 1HR	0141-550 0878

GLASGOW ADDRESSES

Banton	Kelvinhead Road, Banton
Bishopbriggs Kenmure	Viewfield Road, Bishopbriggs
Bishopbriggs Springfield Cambridge	The Leys, off Springfield Road
Broom	Mearns Road, Newton Mearns
Burnside Blairbeth	Church Avenue, Burnside / Kirkriggs Avenue, Blairbeth
Busby	Church Road, Busby
Cadder	Cadder Road, Bishopbriggs
Cambuslang Flemington Hallside	Hutchinson Place
Cambuslang Parish	Arnott Way
Campsie	Main Street, Lennoxtown
Chryston	Main Street, Chryston
Eaglesham	Montgomery Street, Eaglesham
Fernhill and Cathkin	Neilvaig Drive
Gartcosh	113 Lochend Road, Gartcosh
Giffnock Orchardhill	Church Road
Giffnock South	Eastwood Toll
Giffnock The Park	Ravenscliffe Drive
Glenboig	138 Main Street, Glenboig
Greenbank	Eaglesham Road, Clarkston
Kilsyth Anderson	Kingston Road, Kilsyth
Kilsyth Burns and Old	Church Street, Kilsyth
Kirkintilloch Hillhead	Newdyke Road, Kirkintilloch
Kirkintilloch St Columba's	Waterside Road nr Auld Aisle Road
Kirkintilloch St David's Mem Pk	Alexandra Street
Kirkintilloch St Mary's	Cowgate

Lenzie	
Old	Kirkintilloch Road x Garngaber Ave
Union	65 Kirkintilloch Road
Maxwell	
Mearns Castle	Waterfoot Road
Mearns	Mearns Road, Newton Mearns
Milton of Campsie	Antermony Road, Milton of Campsie
Netherlee	Ormonde Drive x Ormonde Avenue
Newton Mearns	Ayr Road, Newton Mearns
Rutherglen	
Old	Main Street at Queen Street
Stonelaw	Stonelaw Road x Dryburgh Avenue
West and Wardlawhill	3 Western Avenue
Stamperland	Stamperland Gardens, Clarkston
Stepps	Whitehill Avenue
Thornliebank	61 Spiersbridge Road
Torrance	School Road, Torrance
Twechar	Main Street, Twechar
Williamwood	4 Vardar Avenue, Clarkston
Glasgow	
Anderston Kelvingrove	759 Argyle St x Elderslie St
Baillieston	
Mure Memorial	Maxwell Drive, Garrowhill
St Andrew's	Bredisholm Road
Balshagray Victoria Pk	218–230 Broomhill Drive
Barlanark Greyfriars	Edinburgh Rd x Hallhill Rd (365)
Blawarthill	Millbrix Avenue
Bridgeton St Francis in the East	26 Queen Mary Street
Broomhill	64–66 Randolph Rd (x Marlborough Ave)
Calton Parkhead	122 Helenvale Street
Cardonald	2155 Paisley Road West
Carmunnock	Kirk Road, Carmunnock
Carmyle	155 Carmyle Avenue
Carnwadric	556 Boydstone Road, Thornliebank
Castlemilk	
East	Barlia Terrace
West	Carmunnock Road
Cathcart	
Old	119 Carmunnock Road
Trinity	90 Clarkston Road
Cathedral	Cathedral Square, 2 Castle Street
Clincarthill	1216 Cathcart Road
Colston Milton	Egilsay Crescent
Colston Wellpark	1378 Springburn Road
Cranhill	109 Bellrock St (at Bellrock Cr)
Croftfoot	Croftpark Ave x Crofthill Road
Dennistoun New	9 Armadale Street
Drumchapel	
St Andrew's	153 Garscadden Road
St Mark's	281 Kinfauns Drive
Easterhouse St George's and St Peter's	Boyndie Street
Eastwood	Mansewood Road
Gairbraid	1517 Maryhill Road
Gallowgate	David Street
Garthamlock and Craigend East	46 Porchester Street
Govan and Linthouse	Govan Cross
Govanhill Trinity	28 Daisy Street nr Allison Street
High Carntyne	358 Carntynehall Road
Hillington Park	24 Berryknowes Road
Househillwood St Christopher's	Meikle Road
Hyndland	79 Hyndland Rd, opp Novar Dr
Ibrox	Carillon Road x Clifford Street
John Ross Memorial	100 Norfolk Street
Jordanhill	28 Woodend Drive (x Munro Road)
Kelvin Stevenson Mem	Belmont Street at Belmont Bridge
Kelvinside Hillhead	Observatory Road
Kenmuir Mount Vernon	2405 London Road, Mount Vernon
King's Park	242 Castlemilk Road
Kinning Park	Eaglesham Place
Knightswood St Margaret's	2000 Great Western Road
Langside	167–169 Ledard Road (x Lochleven Road)
Lansdowne	416 Gt Western Rd at Kelvin Bridge
Lochwood	2A Liff Place, Easterhouse
Maryhill	1990 Maryhill Road
Merrylea	78 Merrylee Road
Mosspark	167 Ashkirk Drive
Newlands South	Riverside Road x Langside Drive
Partick	
South	259 Dumbarton Road
Trinity	20 Lawrence Street
Penilee St Andrew's	Bowfield Cres x Bowfield Avenue
Pollokshaws	223 Shawbridge Street
Pollokshields	Albert Drive x Shields Road
Possilpark	124 Saracen Street
Priesthill and Nitshill	100 Priesthill Rd (x Muirshiel Cr) Dove Street
Queen's Park	170 Queen's Drive
Renfield St Stephen's	260 Bath Street
Robroyston	34 Saughs Road
Ruchazie	4 Elibank Street (x Milncroft Road)
Ruchill Kelvinside	Shakespeare Street nr Maryhill Rd and 10 Kelbourne Street (two buildings)
St Andrew's East	681 Alexandra Parade
St Columba	300 St Vincent Street
St David's Knightswood	66 Boreland Drive (nr Lincoln Avenue)
St Enoch's Hogganfield	860 Cumbernauld Road
St George's Tron	163 Buchanan Street
St James' (Pollok)	Lyoncross Road x Byrebush Road
St John's Renfield	22 Beaconsfield Road
St Margaret's Tollcross Pk	179 Braidfauld Street
St Nicholas' Cardonald	Hartlaw Crescent nr Gladsmuir Road
St Paul's	30 Langdale St (x Greenrig St)
St Rollox	9 Fountainwell Road
Sandyford Henderson Memorial	Kelvinhaugh Street at Argyle Street
Sandyhills	28 Baillieston Rd nr Sandyhills Rd
Scotstoun	Earlbank Avenue x Ormiston Avenue
Shawlands	Shawlands Cross (1114 Pollokshaws Road)
Sherbrooke St Gilbert's	Nithsdale Rd x Sherbrooke Avenue

Shettleston New	679 Old Shettleston Road
Shettleston Old	99–111 Killin Street
South Carntyne	538 Carntyne Road
South Shawlands	Regwood Street x Deanston Drive
Springburn	180 Springburn Way
Temple Anniesland	869 Crow Road

Toryglen	Glenmore Ave nr Prospecthill Road
Trinity Possil and Henry Drummond	2 Crowhill Street (x Broadholm Street)
Tron St Mary's	128 Red Road
Victoria Tollcross	1134 Tollcross Road

Wallacewell New Charge Development	no building yet obtained
Wellington	University Ave x Southpark Avenue
Whiteinch	35 Inchlee Street
Yoker	10 Hawick Street

(17) HAMILTON

Meets at Motherwell: Dalziel St Andrew's Parish Church Halls, on the first Tuesday of February, March, May, September, October, November and December, and on the third Tuesday of June.

Presbytery Office: 353 Orbiston Street, Motherwell ML1 1QW   01698 259135
[E-mail: hamilton@cofscotland.org.uk]
[E-mail: clerk@presbyteryofhamilton.co.uk]

Clerk: REV. SHAW J. PATERSON BSc BD MSc   c/o The Presbytery Office
Depute Clerk: REV. JOHN L. McPAKE BA BD PhD   c/o The Presbytery Office
Presbytery Treasurer: MR ROBERT A. ALLAN   7 Graham Place, Ashgill, Larkhall ML9 3BA   01698 883246
[E-mail: Fallan3246@aol.com]

1 **Airdrie: Broomknoll (H) (01236 762101) (E-mail: airdrie-broomknoll@presbyteryofhamilton.co.uk)**
linked with Calderbank (E-mail: calderbank@presbyteryofhamilton.co.uk)
Vacant   38 Commonhead Street, Airdrie ML6 6NS   01236 609584

2 **Airdrie: Clarkston (E-mail: airdrie-clarkston@presbyteryofhamilton.co.uk)**
F. Derek Gunn BD   1986   2009   Clarkston Manse, Forrest Street, Airdrie ML6 7BE   01236 769676

3 **Airdrie: Flowerhill (H) (E-mail: airdrie-flowerhill@presbyteryofhamilton.co.uk)**
Gary J. Caldwell BSc BD   2007   31 Victoria Place, Airdrie ML6 9BU   01236 754430
[E-mail: garyjcaldwell@btinternet.com]

4 **Airdrie: High (E-mail: airdrie-high@presbyteryofhamilton.co.uk)**
Ian R. W. McDonald BSc BD PhD   2007   17 Etive Drive, Airdrie ML6 9QL   01236 760023
[E-mail: ian@spingetastic.freeserve.co.uk]

5   **Airdrie: Jackson (E-mail: airdrie-jackson@presbyteryofhamilton.co.uk)**
Kay Gilchrist (Miss) BD   1996   2008   48 Dunrobin Road, Airdrie ML6 8LR
    [E-mail: gilky61@yahoo.co.uk]   01236 760154

6   **Airdrie: New Monkland (H) (E-mail: airdrie-newmonkland@presbyteryofhamilton.co.uk)**
linked with Greengairs (E-mail: greengairs@presbyteryofhamilton.co.uk)
William Jackson BD CertMin   1994   2008   3 Dykehead Crescent, Airdrie ML6 6PU
    [E-mail: newmonkgreengair@aol.com]   01236 763554

7   **Airdrie: St Columba's (E-mail: airdrie-stcolumbas@presbyteryofhamilton.co.uk)**
Margaret F. Currie BEd BD   1980   1987   52 Kennedy Drive, Airdrie ML6 9AW
    [E-mail: margaret_currie250@o2.co.uk]   01236 763173

8   **Airdrie: The New Wellwynd (E-mail: airdrie-newwellwynd@presbyteryofhamilton.co.uk)**
Robert A. Hamilton BA BD   1995   2001   20 Arthur Avenue, Airdrie ML6 9EZ
    [E-mail: revrob13@blueyonder.co.uk]   01236 763022

9   **Bargeddie (H) (E-mail: bargeddie@presbyteryofhamilton.co.uk)**
John Fairful BD   1994   2001   The Manse, Manse Road, Bargeddie, Baillieston, Glasgow G69 6UB
    [E-mail: johnfairful@yahoo.co.uk]   0141-771 1322

10   **Bellshill: Macdonald Memorial (E-mail: bellshill-macdonald@presbyteryofhamilton.co.uk) linked with Bellshill: Orbiston**
Alan McKenzie BSc BD   1988   2001   32 Adamson Street, Bellshill ML4 1DT
    [E-mail: rev.a.mckenzie@btopenworld.com]   01698 849114

11   **Bellshill: Orbiston (E-mail: bellshill-orbiston@presbyteryofhamilton.co.uk)** See Bellshill: Macdonald Memorial

12   **Bellshill: West (H) (01698 747581) (E-mail: bellshill-west@presbyteryofhamilton.co.uk)**
Agnes A. Moore (Miss) BD   1987   2001   16 Croftpark Street, Bellshill ML4 1EY
    [E-mail: revamoore2@tiscali.co.uk]   01698 842877

13   **Blantyre: Livingstone Memorial (E-mail: blantyre-livingstone@presbyteryofhamilton.co.uk)**
Vacant   286 Glasgow Road, Blantyre, Glasgow G72 9DB   01698 823794

14   **Blantyre: Old (H) (E-mail: blantyre-old@presbyteryofhamilton.co.uk)**
Vacant   The Manse, Craigmuir Road, High Blantyre, Glasgow G72 9UA   01698 823130

15 **Blantyre: St Andrew's (E-mail: blantyre-standrews@presbyteryofhamilton.co.uk)**
J. Peter N. Johnston BSc BD   2001
  332 Glasgow Road, Blantyre, Glasgow G72 9LQ
  [E-mail: peter.johnston@standrewsblantyre.com]
  01698 828633

16 **Bothwell (H) (E-mail: bothwell@presbyteryofhamilton.co.uk)**
James M. Gibson TD LTh LRAM   1978   1989
  Manse Avenue, Bothwell, Glasgow G71 8PQ
  [E-mail: jamesmgibson@msn.com]
  01698 853189 (Tel)
  01698 854903 (Fax)

17 **Calderbank** See Airdrie: Broomknoll

18 **Caldercruix and Longriggend (H) (E-mail: caldercruix@presbyteryofhamilton.co.uk)**
George M. Donaldson MA BD   1984   2005
  Main Street, Caldercruix, Airdrie ML6 7RF
  [E-mail: g.donaldson505@btinternet.com]
  01236 842279

19 **Chapelhall (H) (E-mail: chapelhall@presbyteryofhamilton.co.uk)**
Gordon R. Mackenzie BScAgr BD   1977   2009
  The Manse, Russell Street, Chapelhall, Airdrie ML6 8SG
  [E-mail: rev-g.mackenzie@btopenworld.com]
  01236 763439

20 **Chapelton (E-mail: chapelton@presbyteryofhamilton.co.uk)**
linked with Strathaven: Rankin (H) (E-mail: strathaven-rankin@presbyteryofhamilton.co.uk)
Shaw J. Paterson BSc BD MSc   1991
  15 Lethame Road, Strathaven ML10 6AD
  [E-mail: s.paterson195@btinternet.com]
  01357 520019 (Tel)
  01357 529316 (Fax)
Maxine Buck (Aux)   2007
  Brownlee House, Mauldslie Road, Carluke ML8 5HW
  [E-mail: maxinebuck01@aol.com]
  01555 759063

21 **Cleland (H) (E-mail: cleland@presbyteryofhamilton.co.uk)**
John A. Jackson BD   1997
  The Manse, Bellside Road, Cleland, Motherwell ML1 5NP
  [E-mail: johnajackson932@btinternet.com]
  01698 860260

22 **Coatbridge: Blairhill Dundyvan (H) (E-mail: coatbridge-blairhill@presbyteryofhamilton.co.uk)**
Vacant
  18 Blairhill Street, Coatbridge ML5 1PG
  01236 432304

23 **Coatbridge: Calder (H) (E-mail: coatbridge-calder@presbyteryofhamilton.co.uk)**
linked with Coatbridge: Old Monkland (E-mail: coatbridge-oldmonkland@presbyteryofhamilton.co.uk)
Vacant
  26 Bute Street, Coatbridge ML5 4HF
  01236 421516

24 **Coatbridge: Middle (E-mail: coatbridge-middle@presbyteryofhamilton.co.uk)**
Alexander M. Roger BD PhD   1982   2009
  47 Blair Road, Coatbridge ML5 1JQ
  [E-mail: s.roger@btinternet.com]
  01236 432427

25 **Coatbridge: New St Andrew's (E-mail: coatbridge-standrews@presbyteryofhamilton.co.uk)**   1996   2005
Fiona Nicolson BA BD   77 Eglinton Street, Coatbridge ML5 3JF   01236 437271

26 **Coatbridge: Old Monkland** See Coatbridge: Calder

27 **Coatbridge: Townhead (H) (E-mail: coatbridge-townhead@presbyteryofhamilton.co.uk)**   1993   2004
Ecilo Selemani LTh MTh   Crinan Crescent, Coatbridge ML5 2LH   01236 702914
[E-mail: eciloselemani@msn.com]

28 **Dalserf (E-mail: dalserf@presbyteryofhamilton.co.uk)**   1982
D. Cameron McPherson BSc BD DMin   Manse Brae, Dalserf, Larkhall ML9 3BN   01698 882195
[E-mail: revcam@talktalk.net]

29 **East Kilbride: Claremont (H) (01355 238088) (E-mail: ek-claremont@presbyteryofhamilton.co.uk)**   1986   2003
Gordon R. Palmer MA BD STM   17 Deveron Road, East Kilbride, Glasgow G74 2HR   01355 248526
[E-mail: gkrspalmer@blueyonder.co.uk]

30 **East Kilbride: Greenhills (E) (01355 221746) (E-mail: ek-greenhills@presbyteryofhamilton.co.uk)**   1988
John Brewster MA BD DipEd   21 Turnberry Place, East Kilbride, Glasgow G75 8TB   01355 242564
[E-mail: johnbrewster@blueyonder.co.uk]

31 **East Kilbride: Moncreiff (H) (01355 223328) (E-mail: ek-moncreiff@presbyteryofhamilton.co.uk)**   1991   2011
Neil Buchanan BD   16 Almond Drive, East Kilbride, Glasgow G74 2HX   01355 238639
[E-mail: neil.buchanan@talk21.com]

32 **East Kilbride: Mossneuk (E) (01355 260954) (E-mail: ek-mossneuk@presbyteryofhamilton.co.uk)**   1987   2000
John L. McPake BA BD PhD   30 Eden Grove, Mossneuk, East Kilbride, Glasgow G75 8XU   01355 234196
[E-mail: jlm1961@hotmail.co.uk]

33 **East Kilbride: Old (H) (01355 279004) (E-mail: ek-old@presbyteryofhamilton.co.uk)**   2001
Anne S. Paton BA BD   40 Maxwell Drive, East Kilbride, Glasgow G74 4HJ   01355 220732
[E-mail: annepaton@fsmail.net]

34 **East Kilbride: South (H) (E-mail: ek-south@presbyteryofhamilton.co.uk)**   2012
Mark Lowey BD DipTh   7 Clamps Wood, East Kilbride, Glasgow G74 2HB   01355 247993

35 **East Kilbride: Stewartfield (New Charge Development)**
Douglas W. Wallace MA BD   1981   2001   8 Thistle Place, Stewartfield, East Kilbride, Glasgow G74 4RH   01355 260879

36 **East Kilbride: West (H) (E-mail: ek-west@presbyteryofhamilton.co.uk)**
Mahboob Masih BA MDiv MTh   1999   2008   4 East Milton Grove, East Kilbride, Glasgow G75 8FN   01355 224469
[E-mail: m_masih@sky.com]

37 **East Kilbride: Westwood (H) (01355 245657) (E-mail: ek-westwood@presbyteryofhamilton.co.uk)**
Kevin Mackenzie BD DPS   1989   1996   16 Inglewood Crescent, East Kilbride, Glasgow G75 8QD   01355 223992
[E-mail: kevin@westwoodmanse.freeserve.co.uk]

38 **Glasford (E-mail: glassford@presbyteryofhamilton.co.uk) linked with Strathaven: East (E-mail: strathaven-east@presbyteryofhamilton.co.uk)**
William T. Stewart BD   1980   68 Townhead Street, Strathaven ML10 6DJ   01357 521138

39 **Greengairs** See Airdrie: New Monkland

40 **Hamilton: Burnbank (E-mail: hamilton-burnbank@presbyteryofhamilton.co.uk)**
linked with **Hamilton: North (H) (E-mail: hamilton-north@presbyteryofhamilton.co.uk)**
Raymond D. McKenzie BD   1978   1987   9 South Park Road, Hamilton ML3 6PJ   01698 424609
[E-mail: rdmackenzie@hotmail.co.uk]

41 **Hamilton: Cadzow (H) (01698 428695) (E-mail: hamilton-cadzow@presbyteryofhamilton.co.uk)**
John Carswell BS MDiv   1996   2009   3 Carlisle Road, Hamilton ML3 7BZ   01698 426682
[E-mail: revcarswell@gmail.com]

42 **Hamilton: Gilmour and Whitehill (H) (E-mail: hamilton-gilmourwhitehill@presbyteryofhamilton.co.uk)**
Vacant   86 Burnbank Centre, Burnbank, Hamilton ML3 0NA   01698 284201

43 **Hamilton: Hillhouse (E-mail: hamilton-hillhouse@presbyteryofhamilton.co.uk)**
David W.G. Burt BD DipMin   1989   1998   66 Wellhall Road, Hamilton ML3 9BY   01698 422300
[E-mail: dwgburt@blueyonder.co.uk]

44 **Hamilton: North** See Hamilton: Burnbank

45 **Hamilton: Old (H) (01698 281905) (E-mail: hamilton-old@presbyteryofhamilton.co.uk)**
John M.A. Thomson TD JP BD ThM   1978   2001   1 Chateau Grove, Hamilton ML3 7DS   01698 422511
[E-mail: jt@john1949.plus.com]

46 **Hamilton: St Andrew's (T) (E-mail: hamilton-standrews@presbyteryofhamilton.co.uk)**
Norman MacLeod BTh   1999   2005   15 Bent Road, Hamilton ML3 6QB   01698 283264
                                            [E-mail: normanmacleod@blueyonder.co.uk]

47 **Hamilton: St John's (H) (01698 283492) (E-mail: hamilton-stjohns@presbyteryofhamilton.co.uk)**
Joanne C. Hood (Miss) MA BD   2003   2012   9 Shearer Avenue, Ferniegair, Hamilton ML3 7FX   01698 425002
                                            [E-mail: hood137@btinternet.com]

48 **Hamilton: South (H) (01698 281014) (E-mail: hamilton-south@presbyteryofhamilton.co.uk)**
linked with Quarter (E-mail: quarter@presbyteryofhamilton.co.uk)
Donald R. Lawrie   2012   The Manse, Limekilnburn Road, Quarter, Hamilton ML3 7XA   01698 424511

49 **Hamilton: Trinity (01698 284254) (E-mail: hamilton-trinity@presbyteryofhamilton.co.uk)**
Karen E. Harbison (Mrs) MA BD   1991   69 Buchan Street, Hamilton ML3 8JY   01698 425326
                                            [E-mail: calumkaren@yahoo.co.uk]

50 **Hamilton: West (H) (01698 284670) (E-mail: hamilton-west@presbyteryofhamilton.co.uk)**
Elizabeth A. Waddell (Mrs) BD   1999   2005   43 Bothwell Road, Hamilton ML3 0BB   01698 458770
                                            [E-mail: elizabethwaddell@tiscali.co.uk]

51 **Holytown (E-mail: holytown@presbyteryofhamilton.co.uk) linked with New Stevenston: Wrangholm Kirk**
Caryl A.E. Kyle (Mrs) BD DipEd   2008   The Manse, 260 Edinburgh Road, Holytown, Motherwell ML1 5RU   01698 832622
                                            [E-mail: caryl_kyle@hotmail.com]

52 **Kirk o' Shotts (H) (E-mail: kirk-o-shotts@presbyteryofhamilton.co.uk)**
Vacant   The Manse, Kirk o' Shotts, Salsburgh, Shotts ML7 4NS   01698 870208

53 **Larkhall: Chalmers (H) (E-mail: larkhall-chalmers@presbyteryofhamilton.co.uk)**
Vacant   Quarry Road, Larkhall ML9 1HH   01698 882238

54 **Larkhall: St Machan's (H) (E-mail: larkhall-stmachans@presbyteryofhamilton.co.uk)**
Alastair McKillop BD DipMin   1995   2004   2 Orchard Gate, Larkhall ML9 1HG   01698 321976
                                            [E-mail: revicar@blueyonder.co.uk]

55 **Larkhall: Trinity (E-mail: larkhall-trinity@presbyteryofhamilton.co.uk)**
Lindsay Schluter (Miss) ThE CertMin   1995   13 Machan Avenue, Larkhall ML9 2HE   01698 881401

56	**Motherwell: Crosshill (H) (E-mail: mwell-crosshill@presbyteryofhamilton.co.uk) linked with Motherwell: St Margaret's (E-mail: mwell-stmargarets@presbyteryofhamilton.co.uk)**		
	Gavin W.G. Black BD	2006	15 Orchard Street, Motherwell ML1 3JE
			[E-mail: gavin.black12@blueyonder.co.uk]
			01698 263410
57	**Motherwell: Dalziel St Andrew's (H) (01698 264097) (E-mail: mwell-dalzielstandrews@presbyteryofhamilton.co.uk)**		
	Derek W. Hughes BSc BD DipEd	1990 1996	4 Pollock Street, Motherwell ML1 1LP
			[E-mail: derekthecleric@btinternet.com]
			01698 263414
58	**Motherwell: North (E-mail: mwell-north@presbyteryofhamilton.co.uk)**		
	Derek H.N. Pope BD	1987 1995	35 Birrens Road, Motherwell ML1 3NS
			[E-mail: derekpopemotherwell@hotmail.com]
			01698 266716
59	**Motherwell: St Margaret's** See Motherwell: Crosshill		
60	**Motherwell: St Mary's (H) (E-mail: mwell-stmarys@presbyteryofhamilton.co.uk)**		
	David W. Doyle MA BD	1977 1987	19 Orchard Street, Motherwell ML1 3JE
			01698 263472
61	**Motherwell: South (H)**		
	Georgina M. Baxendale (Mrs) BD	1981 2009	62 Manse Road, Motherwell ML1 2PT
			[E-mail: georgiebaxendale6@tiscali.co.uk]
			01698 239245
62	**Newarthill and Carfin (E-mail: newarthill@presbyteryofhamilton.co.uk)**		
	Vacant		Church Street, Newarthill, Motherwell ML1 5HS
			01698 860316
63	**Newmains: Bonkle (H) (E-mail: bonkle@presbyteryofhamilton.co.uk) linked with Newmains: Coltness Memorial (H) (E-mail: coltness@presbyteryofhamilton.co.uk)**		
	Graham Raeburn MTh	2004	5 Kirkgate, Newmains, Wishaw ML2 9BT
			[E-mail: grahamraeburn@tiscali.co.uk]
			01698 383858
64	**Newmains: Coltness Memorial** See Newmains: Bonkle		
65	**New Stevenston: Wrangholm Kirk (E-mail: wrangholm@presbyteryofhamilton.co.uk)** See Holytown		
66	**Overtown (E-mail: overtown@presbyteryofhamilton.co.uk)**		
	Bruce H. Sinclair BA BD	2009	The Manse, 146 Main Street, Overtown, Wishaw ML2 0QP
			[E-mail: brucehsinclair@btinternet.com]
			01698 352090
67	**Quarter** See Hamilton: South		

68 **Shotts: Calderhead Erskine (E-mail: calderhead-erskine@presbyteryofhamilton.co.uk)**
    Allan B. Brown BD MTh   1995   2010   The Manse, 9 Kirk Road, Shotts ML7 5ET
                                                                                                                01501 823204
                                                                                                                07578 448655 (Mbl)

69 **Stonehouse: St Ninian's (H) (E-mail: stonehouse@presbyteryofhamilton.co.uk)**
    Paul G.R. Grant BD MTh   2003   4 Hamilton Way, Stonehouse, Larkhall ML9 3PU
                                                                  [E-mail: minister@st-ninians-stonehouse.org.uk]
                                                                                                                01698 792947

70 **Strathaven: Avendale Old and Drumclog (H) (01357 529748) (E-mail: strathaven-avendaleold@presbyteryofhamilton.co.uk and**
    E-mail: drumclog@presbyteryofhamilton.co.uk)
    Alan B. Telfer BA BD   1983   2010   4 Fortrose Gardens, Strathaven ML10 6SH
                                                                  [E-mail: minister@avendale-drumclog.com]
                                                                                                                01357 523031

71 **Strathaven: East See Glasford**
72 **Strathaven: Rankin See Chapelton**

73 **Uddingston: Burnhead (H) (E-mail: uddingston-burnhead@presbyteryofhamilton.co.uk)**
    Les Brunger BD   2010   90 Laburnum Road, Uddingston, Glasgow G71 5DB
                                                                  [E-mail: lesbrunger@hotmail.co.uk]
                                                                                                                01698 813716

74 **Uddingston: Old (H) (01698 814015) (E-mail: uddingston-old@presbyteryofhamilton.co.uk)**
    Fiona L.J. McKibbin (Mrs) MA BD   2011   1 Belmont Avenue, Uddingston, Glasgow G71 7AX
                                                                  [E-mail: fionamckibbin@sky.com]
                                                                                                                01698 814757

75 **Uddingston: Viewpark (H) (E-mail: uddingston-viewpark@presbyteryofhamilton.co.uk)**
    Michael G. Lyall BD   1993   2001   14 Holmbrae Road, Uddingston, Glasgow G71 6AP
                                                                  [E-mail: michaellyall@blueyonder.co.uk]
                                                                                                                01698 813113

76 **Wishaw: Cambusnethan North (H) (E-mail: wishaw-cambusnethannorth@presbyteryofhamilton.co.uk)**
    Mhorag Macdonald (Ms) MA BD   1989   350 Kirk Road, Wishaw ML2 8LH
                                                                  [E-mail: mhoragmacdonald@btinternet.com]
                                                                                                                01698 381305

77 **Wishaw: Cambusnethan Old (E-mail: wishaw-cambusnethanold@presbyteryofhamilton.co.uk)**
    and Morningside (E-mail: wishaw-morningside@presbyteryofhamilton.co.uk)
    Iain C. Murdoch MA LLB DipEd BD   1995   22 Coronation Street, Wishaw ML2 8LF
                                                                  [E-mail: iaincmurdoch@btopenworld.com]
                                                                                                                01698 384235

78 Wishaw: Craigneuk and Belhaven (H) (E-mail: wishaw-craigneukbelhaven@presbyteryofhamilton.co.uk) linked with Wishaw: Old
Vacant
130 Glen Road, Wishaw ML2 7NP   01698 375134

79 Wishaw: Old (H) (01698 376080) (E-mail: wishaw-old@presbyteryofhamilton.co.uk) See Wishaw: Craigneuk and Belhaven

80 Wishaw: St Mark's (E-mail: wishaw-stmarks@presbyteryofhamilton.co.uk)
Graham Austin BD   1997   2008   The Manse, 302 Coltness Road, Wishaw ML2 7EY   01698 384596
[E-mail: graham.austin4@btinternet.com]

81 Wishaw: South Wishaw (H)
Klaus O.F. Buwert LLB BD DMin   1984   1999   3 Walter Street, Wishaw ML2 8LQ   01698 387292
[E-mail: klaus@buwert.co.uk]

Name				Address	Phone
Barrie, Arthur P. LTh	1973	2007	(Hamilton: Cadzow)	30 Airbles Crescent, Motherwell ML1 3AR [E-mail: elizabethbarrie@ymail.com]	01698 261147
Campbell, Andrew M. BD CertMin	1984	2009	(Motherwell: St Margaret's)	17 Clyde View, Ashgill, Larkhall ML9 3DS [E-mail: drewdorca@hotmail.com]	01698 887974
Carruth, Patricia A. (Mrs) BD	1998	2012	(Coatbridge: Blairhill Dundyvan)	38 Springhill Farm Road, Baillieston, Glasgow G69 6GW	0141-771 3758
Colvin, Sharon E.F. (Mrs) BD LRAM LTCL	1985	2007	(Airdrie: Jackson)	25 Balblair Road, Airdrie ML6 6GQ [E-mail: dibleycol@hotmail.com]	01236 590796
Cook, J. Stanley BD Dip PSS	1974	2001	(Hamilton: West)	Mansend, 137A Old Manse Road, Netherton, Wishaw ML2 0EW [E-mail: stancook@blueyonder.co.uk]	01698 299600
Cullen, William T. BA LTh	1984	1996	(Kilmarnock: St John's Onthank)	6 Laurel Wynd, Cambuslang, Glasgow G72 7BA	0141-641 4337
Currie, David E.P. BSc BD	1983	2012	(Congregational Development Consultant)		
Currie, R. David BSc BD	1984	2004	(Cambuslang: Flemington Hallside)	69 Kethers Street, Motherwell ML1 3HN	01698 323424
Davidson, Amelia (Mrs) BD	2004	2011	(Coatbridge: Calder)	11 St Mary's Place, Saltcoats KA21 5NY	01698 383453
Dick, Roddy S.		2010	Auxiliary Minister	27 Easter Crescent, Wishaw ML2 8XB [E-mail: roddy.dick@btopenworld.com]	
Dunn, W. Stuart LTh	1970	2006	(Motherwell: Crosshill)	10 Macrostie Gardens, Crieff PH7 4LP	01764 655178
Fraser, James P.	1951	1988	(Strathaven: Avendale Old and Drumclog)	26 Hamilton Road, Strathaven ML10 6JA	01357 522758
Grier, James BD	1991	2005	(Coatbridge: Middle)	14 Love Drive, Bellshill ML4 1BY	01698 742545
Hastie, James S.G. CA BD	1990	2009	(Larkhall: Chalmers)	29 Mornington Grove, Blackwood, Kirkmuirhill, Lanark ML11 9GQ [E-mail: jim@jimandros.co.uk]	01555 896965
Hunter, James E. LTh	1974	1997	(Blantyre: Livingstone Memorial)	57 Dalwhinnie Avenue, Blantyre, Glasgow G72 9NQ	01698 826177
Kent, Robert M. MA BD	1973	2011	(Hamilton: St John's)	48 Fyne Crescent, Larkhall ML9 2UX [E-mail: robertmkent@talktalk.net]	01698 769244
Lusk, Alastair S. BD	1974	2010	(East Kilbride: Moncreiff)	9 MacFie Place, Stewartfield, East Kilbride, Glasgow G74 4TY	
McAlpine, John BSc	1988	2004	(Auxiliary Minister)	Braeside, 201 Bonkle Road, Newmains, Wishaw ML2 9AA	01698 384610
McCabe, George	1963	1996	(Airdrie: High)	Flat 8, Park Court, 2 Craighouse Park, Edinburgh EH10 5LD	0131-447 9522
McDonald, John A. MA BD	1978	1997	(Cumbernauld: Condorrat)	17 Thomson Drive, Bellshill ML4 3ND	

Name	Years	Role / Parish	Address	Telephone
McKee, Norman B. BD	1987 2010	(Uddingston: Old)	148 Station Road, Blantyre, Glasgow G72 9BW [E-mail: n.mckee1@btinternet.com]	01698 827358
MacKenzie, Ian C. MA BD	1970 2011	(Interim Minister)	21 Wilson Street, Motherwell ML1 1NP [E-mail: iancmac@blueyonder.co.uk]	01698 301230
Mackenzie, James G. BA BD	1980 2005	(Jersey: St Columba's)	26 Drylaw Crescent, Edinburgh EH4 2AU	01698 385825
Martin, James MA BD DD	1946 1987	(Glasgow: High Carntyne)	9 Magnolia Street, Wishaw ML2 7EQ	01698 427958
Melrose, J.H. Loudon MA BD MEd	1955 1996	(Gourock: Old Gourock and Ashton [Assoc])	1 Laverock Avenue, Hamilton ML3 7DD	01236 754848
Munton, James G. BA	1969 2002	(Coatbridge: Old Monkland)	2 Moorcroft Drive, Airdrie ML6 8ES [E-mail: jacjim@supanet.com]	
Price, Peter O. CBE QHC BA FPhS	1960 1996	(Blantyre: Old)	22 Old Bothwell Road, Bothwell, Glasgow G71 8AW [E-mail: peteroprice@aol.com]	01698 854032
Rogerson, Stuart D. BSc BD	1980 2001	(Strathaven: West)	17 Westfield Park, Strathaven ML10 6XH [E-mail: srogerson@cnetwork.co.uk]	01357 523321
Ross, Keith W. MA BD	1984 2007	Congregational Development Officer for the Presbytery of Hamilton	Easter Bavelaw House, Pentland Hills Regional Park, Balerno EH14 7JS [E-mail: keithross.hamiltonpresbytery@googlemail.com]	(Mbl) 07855 163449
Salmond, James S. BA BD MTh ThD	1979 2003	(Holytown)	165 Torbothie Road, Shotts ML7 5NE	01555 892742
Sharp, John C. BSc BD PhD	1980 2011	(East Kilbride: South)	10 Rogerhill Gait, Kirkmuirhill, Lanark ML11 9XR	01698 870598
Spence, Sheila M. (Mrs) MA BD	1979 2010	(Kirk o' Shotts)	6 Drumbowie Crescent, Salsburgh, Shotts ML7 4NP	01698 817582
Stevenson, John LTh	1998 2006	(Cambuslang: St Andrew's)	20 Knowehead Gardens, Uddingston, Glasgow G71 7PY [E-mail therev20@sky.com]	
Stitt, Ronald J. Maxwell LTh BA ThM BREd DMin FSAScot	1977 2012	(Hamilton: Gilmour and Whitehill)	413 Gilmerton Road, Edinburgh EH17 7JJ	01236 432241
Thorne, Leslie W. BA LTh	1987 2001	(Coatbridge: Clifton)	'Hatherleigh', 9 Chatton Walk, Coatbridge ML5 4FH [E-mail: lesthorne@tiscali.co.uk]	(Mbl) 07963 199921
Wilson, James H. LTh	1970 1996	(Cleland)	21 Austine Drive, Hamilton ML3 7YE	01698 457042
Wyllie, Hugh R. MA DD FCIBS	1962 2000	(Hamilton: Old)	18 Chantinghall Road, Hamilton ML3 8NP [E-mail: wilsonjh@blueyonder.co.uk]	01698 420002
Zambonini, James LIADip	1997	Auxiliary Minister	100 Old Manse Road, Wishaw ML2 0EP	01698 350889

HAMILTON ADDRESSES

Airdrie
Broomknoll — Broomknoll Street
Clarkston — Forrest Street
Flowerhill — 89 Graham Street
High — North Bridge Street
Jackson — Glen Road
New Monkland — Glenmavis
St Columba's — Thrashbush Road
The New Wellwynd — Wellwynd

Coatbridge
Blairhill Dundyvan — Blairhill Street
Calder — Calder Street
Middle — Bank Street
New St Andrew's — Church Street
Old Monkland — Woodside Street
Townhead — Crinan Crescent

East Kilbride
Claremont — High Common Road, St Leonard's
Greenhills — Greenhills Centre
Moncreiff — Calderwood Road
Mossneuk — Eden Drive
Old — Montgomery Street
South — Baird Hill, Murray
West — Kittoch Street
Westwood — Belmont Drive, Westwood

Hamilton
Burnbank — High Blantyre Road
Cadzow — Woodside Walk
Gilmour and Whitehill — Glasgow Road, Burnbank
Whitehill — Abbotsford Road, Whitehill
Hillhouse — Clerkwell Road

North — Windmill Road
Old — Leechlee Road
St Andrew's — Avon Street
St John's — Duke Street
South — Strathaven Road
Trinity — Neilsland Square off North Road
West — Burnbank Road

Motherwell
Crosshill — Windmillhill Street x / Airbles Street

Dalziel St Andrew's — Merry Street and Muir Street
North — Chesters Crescent
St Margaret's — Shields Road
St Mary's — Avon Street
South — Gavin Street

Uddingston
Burnhead — Laburnum Road
Old — Old Glasgow Road
Viewpark — Old Edinburgh Road

Wishaw
Cambusnethan — Kirk Road
North — Kirk Road
Old
Craigneuk and — Craigneuk Street
Belhaven — Main Street
Old — Coltness Road
St Mark's — East Academy Street
South Wishaw

(18) DUMBARTON

Meets at Dumbarton, in Riverside Church Halls, on the first Tuesday of February, September and December, on the second Tuesday of June (and April when the first Tuesday falls in Holy Week), and at the incoming Moderator's church on the first Tuesday of June for the installation of the Moderator.

Clerk: REV. DAVID W. CLARK BA BD   37 Campbell Street, Helensburgh G84 9NH   01436 674063
[E-mail: dumbarton@cofscotland.org.uk]

Alexandria
Elizabeth W. Houston MA BD DipEd   1985   1995   32 Ledrish Avenue, Balloch, Alexandria G83 8JB   01389 751933

Arrochar linked with Luss
H. Dane Sherrard BD DMin   1971   1998   The Manse, Luss, Alexandria G83 8NZ   01436 860240 / 07801 939138 (Mbl)
[E-mail: dane@cadder.demon.co.uk]

Baldernock (H)
Andrew P. Lees BD   1984   2002   The Manse, Bardowie, Milngavie, Glasgow G62 6ES   01360 620471
[E-mail: andrew.lees@yahoo.co.uk]

Bearsden: Baljaffray (H)
Ian McEwan BSc PhD BD FRSE   2008   5 Fintry Gardens, Bearsden, Glasgow G61 4RJ   0141-942 0366
[E-mail: mcewan7@btinternet.com]

Bearsden: Cross (H)
Vacant   61 Drymen Road, Bearsden, Glasgow G61 2SU   0141-942 0507

Bearsden: Killermont (H)
Alan J. Hamilton LLB BD   2003
8 Clathic Avenue, Bearsden, Glasgow G61 2HF
[E-mail: ajh63@o2.co.uk]
0141-942 0021

Bearsden: New Kilpatrick (H) (0141-942 8827) (E-mail: mail@nkchurch.org.uk)
Roderick G. Hamilton MA BD   1992   2011
51 Manse Road, Bearsden, Glasgow G61 3PN
[E-mail: rghamilton@ntlworld.com]
0141-942 0035

Bearsden: Westerton Fairlie Memorial (H) (0141-942 6960)
Christine M. Goldie LLB BD MTh DMin   1984   2008
3 Canniesburn Road, Bearsden, Glasgow G61 1PW
[E-mail: christinegoldie@talktalk.net]
0141-942 2672

Bonhill (H) (01389 756516) linked with Renton: Trinity (H)
Vacant
1 Glebe Gardens, Bonhill, Alexandria G83 9NZ

Cardross (H) (01389 841322)
Vacant

Clydebank: Abbotsford (E-mail: abbotsford@lineone.net) (Website: www.abbotsford.org.uk) linked with Dalmuir: Barclay (0141-941 3988)
Fiona E. Maxwell BA BD   2004
16 Parkhall Road, Dalmuir, Clydebank G81 3RJ
[E-mail: fionamaxi@btinternet.com]
0141-941 3317

Clydebank: Faifley
Gregor McIntyre BSc BD   1991
Kirklea, Cochno Road, Hardgate, Clydebank G81 6PT
[E-mail: mail@gregormcintyre.com]
01389 876836

Clydebank: Kilbowie St Andrew's linked with Clydebank: Radnor Park (H)
Margaret J.B. Yule BD   1992
11 Tiree Gardens, Old Kilpatrick, Glasgow G60 5AT
[E-mail: mjbyule@yahoo.co.uk]
01389 875599

Clydebank: Radnor Park See Clydesbank: Kilbowie St Andrew's

Clydebank: St Cuthbert's (T) linked with Duntocher (H)
Vacant
The Manse, Roman Road, Duntocher, Clydebank G81 6BT
01389 873471

Craigrownie linked with Rosneath: St Modan's (H)
Richard B. West   1994   2008   Edenkiln, Argyll Road, Kilcreggan, Helensburgh G84 0JW   01436 842274
[E-mail: rickangelawest@yahoo.co.uk]

Dalmuir: Barclay   See Clydebank: Abbotsford

Dumbarton: Riverside (H) (01389 742551)
Eleanor J. McMahon BEd BD   1994   2010   81 Moorpark Square, Renfrew PA4 8DB   0141-886 1351
[E-mail: e.mcmahon212@btinternet.com]

Dumbarton: St Andrew's (H) linked with Old Kilpatrick Bowling
Vacant   17 Mansewood Drive, Dumbarton G82 3EU   01389 726715

Dumbarton: West Kirk (H)
Elaine W. McKinnon MA BD   1988   2010   3 Havoc Road, Dumbarton G82 4JW   01389 604840

Duntocher (H)   See Clydebank: St Cuthbert's

Garelochhead (01436 810589)
Alastair S. Duncan MA BD   1989   Old School Road, Garelochhead, Helensburgh G84 0AT   01436 810022
[E-mail: gpc@churchuk.fsnet.co.uk]

Helensburgh: Park (H) (01436 674825)
Vacant

Helensburgh: St Andrew's Kirk (H) (01436 676880)
David W. Clark MA BD   1975   1986   37 Campbell Street, Helensburgh G84 9NH   01436 674063
[E-mail: clarkdw@talktalk.net]
George Vidits BD MTh   2000   2006   46 Suffolk Street, Helensburgh G84 9QZ   01436 672054
[E-mail: george.vidits@btinternet.com]
(New charge formed by the union of Helensburgh: St Columba and Helensburgh: The West Kirk)

Jamestown (H)
Norma Moore MA BD   1995   2004   26 Kessog's Gardens, Balloch, Alexandria G83 8QJ   01389 756447
[E-mail: norma.moore5@btinternet.com]

Kilmaronock Gartocharn
Guardianship of the Presbytery

Luss See Arrochar

Milngavie: Cairns (H) (0141-956 4868)
Andrew Frater BA BD MTh   1987   1994   4 Cairns Drive, Milngavie, Glasgow G62 8AJ   0141-956 1717
[E-mail: office@cairnschurch.org.uk]

Milngavie: St Luke's (0141-956 4226)
Ramsay B. Shields BA BD   1990   1997   70 Hunter Road, Milngavie, Glasgow G62 7BY   0141-577 9171 (Tel)
0141-577 9181 (Fax)
[E-mail: rbs@minister.com]

Milngavie: St Paul's (H) (0141-956 4405)
Fergus C. Buchanan MA BD MTh   1982   1988   8 Buchanan Street, Milngavie, Glasgow G62 8DD   0141-956 1043
[E-mail: f.c.buchanan@ntlworld.com]

Old Kilpatrick Bowling See Dumbarton: St Andrew's
Renton: Trinity See Bonhill

Rhu and Shandon (H)
Vacant   11 Ardenconnel Way, Rhu, Helensburgh G84 8LX   01436 820213

Rosneath: St Modan's See Craigrownie

Booth, Frederick M. LTh	1970	2005	(Helensburgh: St Columba)	Achnashie Coach House, Clynder, Helensburgh G84 0QD	01436 831858
Crombie, William D. MA BD	1947	1987	(Glasgow: Calton New with St Andrew's)	9 Fairview Court, 46 Main Street, Milngavie, Glasgow G62 6BU	0141-956 1898
Davidson, Professor Robert MA BD DD FRSE	1956	1991	(University of Glasgow)	30 Dumgoyne Drive, Bearsden, Glasgow G61 3AP	0141-942 1810
Donaghy, Leslie G. BD DipMin PGCE FSAScot	1990	2004	(Dumbarton: St Andrew's)	53 Oak Avenue, East Kilbride, Glasgow G75 9ED [E-mail: leslie@donaghy.org.uk]	(Mbl) 07809 484812
Easton, I.A.G. MA FIPM	1945	1988	(Lecturer)	6 Edgehill Road, Bearsden, Glasgow G61 3AD	0141-942 4214
Ferguson, Archibald M. MSc PhD CEng FRINA	1989	2004	(Auxiliary Minister)	The Whins, 2 Barrowfield, Station Road, Cardross, Dumbarton G82 5NL [E-mail: archieferguson@supanet.com]	01389 841517

Name			Charge	Address	Tel
Hamilton, David G. MA BD	1971	2004	(Braes of Rannoch with Foss and Rannoch)	79 Finlay Rise, Milngavie, Glasgow G62 6QL [E-mail: davidhamilton@onetel.com]	0141-956 4202
Harris, John W.F. MA	1967	2012	(Bearsden: Cross)	68 Mitre Road, Glasgow G14 9LL [E-mail: jwfh@sky.com]	0141-560 0984
Hudson, Eric V. LTh	1971	2007	(Bearsden: Westerton Fairlie Memorial)	2 Murrayfield Drive, Bearsden, Glasgow G61 1JE	0141-942 6110
Inglis, Donald B.C. MA MEd BD	1975	2000	(Turriff: St Andrew's)	39 Thomson Drive, Bearsden, Glasgow G61 3PA	0141-942 1387
Kemp, Tina MA		2005	Auxiliary Minister	12 Oaktree Gardens, Dumbarton G82 1EU	01389 730477
Lawson, Alexander H. ThM ThD FPhS	1950	1988	(Clydebank: Kilbowie)	Erskine Park Nursing Home, Bishopton PA7	
McIntyre, J. Ainslie MA BD	1963	1984	(University of Glasgow)	60 Bonnaughton Road, Bearsden, Glasgow G61 4DB [E-mail: jamcintyre@hotmail.com]	0141-942 5143 (Mbl) 07050 295103
MacMahon, Janet P.H. (Mrs) MSc BD	1992	2010	(Kilmaronock Gartocharn)	14 Hillfoot Drive, Bearsden, Glasgow G61 3QQ [E-mail: janetmacmahon@yahoo.co.uk]	0141-942 8611
Miller, Ian H. BA BD	1975	2012	(Bonhill)	Derand, Queen Street, Alexandria G83 0AS	01389 753039
Munro, David P. MA BD STM	1953	1996	(Bearsden: North)	14 Birch Road, Killearn, Glasgow G63 9SQ	01360 550098
O'Donnell, Barbara		2007	Auxiliary Minister	Ashbank, 258 Main Street, Alexandria G83 0NU	01389 752356
Ramage, Alistair E. MA BA ADB CertEd	1996	2004	Auxiliary Minister	16 Claremont Gardens, Milngavie, Glasgow G62 6PG [E-mail: ara3@waitrose.com]	0141-956 2897
Speed, David K. LTh	1969	2004	(Glasgow: Shettleston Old)	153 West Princes Street, Helensburgh G84 8EZ	01436 674493
Stewart, Charles E. BSc BD MTh PhD	1976	2010	(Chaplain of the Fleet)	105 Sinclair Street, Helensburgh G84 9HY [E-mail: c.e.stewart@btinternet.com]	01436 678113
Steven, Harold A.M. MStJ LTh FSA Scot	1970	2001	(Baldernock)	9 Cairnhill Road, Bearsden, Glasgow G61 1AT	0141-942 1598
Wright, Malcolm LTh	1970	2003	(Craigrownie with Rosneath: St Modan's)	30 Clairinsh, Drumkinnon Gate, Balloch, Alexandria G83 8SE	01389 720338

DUMBARTON ADDRESSES

Clydebank		**Dumbarton**		**Helensburgh**	
Abbotsford	Town Centre	Riverside	High Street	Park	Charlotte Street
Faifley	Faifley Road	St Andrew's	Aitkenbar Circle	St Andrew's Kirk	Colquhoun Square
Kilbowie St Andrew's	Kilbowie Road	West Kirk	West Bridgend		
Radnor Park	Radnor Street				
St Cuthbert's	Linnvale				

(19) ARGYLL

Meets in the Village Hall, Tarbert, Loch Fyne, Argyll on the first Tuesday or Wednesday of March, June, September and December. For details, contact the Presbytery Clerk.

Clerk:	MR IAN MACLAGAN LLB FSAScot	Carmonadh, Eastlands Road, Rothesay, Isle of Bute PA20 9JZ [E-mail: argyll@cofscotland.org.uk]	01700 503015
Depute Clerk:	REV. GEORGE G. CRINGLES BD	St Oran's Manse, Connel, Oban PA37 1PJ [E-mail: george.cringles@btinternet.com]	01631 710242
Treasurer:	MRS PAMELA A. GIBSON	Allt Ban, Portsonachan, Dalmally PA33 1BJ [E-mail: justpam1@tesco.net]	01866 833344

Appin linked with Lismore Roderick D.M. Campbell OStJ TD BD DMin FSAScot	1975	2008	The Manse, Appin PA38 4DD [E-mail: rdmcampbell@aol.com]	01631 730143
Ardchattan (H) Jeffrey A. McCormick BD	1984		Ardchattan Manse, North Connel, Oban PA37 1RG [E-mail: jeff.mcc@virgin.net]	01631 710364
Ardrishaig (H) linked with South Knapdale David Carruthers BD	1998		The Manse, Park Road, Ardrishaig, Lochgilphead PA30 8HE	01546 603269
Campbeltown: Highland (H) Vacant			Highland Church Manse, Kirk Street, Campbeltown PA28 6BN	01586 551146
Campbeltown: Lorne and Lowland (H) Philip D. Burroughs BSc BTh DTS	1998	2004	Lorne and Lowland Manse, Castlehill, Campbeltown PA28 6AN [E-mail: burroughs@btinternet.com]	01586 552468
Kirsty-Ann Burroughs (Mrs) BA BD CertTheol DRM PhD (Aux)	2007		Lorne and Lowland Manse, Castlehill, Campbeltown PA28 6AN [E-mail: burroughs@btinternet.com]	01586 552468
Coll linked with Connel George G. Cringles BD	1981	2002	St Oran's Manse, Connel, Oban PA37 1PJ [E-mail: george.cringles@btinternet.com]	(Connel) 01631 710242 (Coll) 01879 230366

Colonsay and Oronsay (Website: www.islandchurches.org.uk)
Vacant

Connel See Coll

Craignish linked with Kilbrandon and Kilchattan linked with Kilninver and Kilmelford

Kenneth R. Ross BA BD PhD	1982	2010	The Manse, Kilmelford, Oban PA34 4XA [E-mail: kenneth.ross@btinternet.com]	01852 200565

Cumlodden, Lochfyneside and Lochgair linked with Glenaray and Inveraray

Louis C. Bezuidenhout BA MA BD DD	1978	2009	The Manse, Inveraray PA32 8XT [E-mail: macbez@btinternet.com]	01499 302060

Dunoon: St John's linked with Kirn (H) linked with Sandbank (H)

Sarah E.C. Nicol (Mrs) BSc BD	1985	2009	The Manse, 13 Dhailling Park, Hunter Street, Kirn, Dunoon PA23 8FB [E-mail: kimkirk@btinternet.com]	01369 702256
Glenda M. Wilson (Mrs) DCS	1990	2006	Ardlayne, 23 Bullwood Road, Dunoon PA23 7QJ [E-mail: deacglendamwilson@gmail.com]	01369 700848

Dunoon: The High Kirk (H) linked with Innellan linked with Toward

Aileen M. Robson (Miss) BD	2003	2011	7A Mathieson Lane, Innellan, Dunoon PA23 7SH [E-mail: am65robson@ymail.com]	01369 830276
Ruth I. Griffiths (Mrs) (Aux)	2004		Kirkwood, Mathieson Lane, Innellan, Dunoon PA23 7TA [E-mail: ruthigriffiths@googlemail.com]	01369 830145

Gigha and Cara (H) (GD)

Anne McIvor (Miss) SRD BD	1996	2008	The Manse, Isle of Gigha PA41 7AA [E-mail: annemcivor@btinternet.com]	01583 505245

Glassary, Kilmartin and Ford linked with North Knapdale

Clifford R. Acklam BD MTh	1997	2010	The Manse, Kilmichael Glassary, Lochgilphead PA31 8QA [E-mail: clifford.acklam@btinternet.com]	01546 606926

Glenaray and Inveraray See Cumlodden, Lochfyneside and Lochgair

Glenorchy and Innishael linked with Strathfillan

Elizabeth A. Gibson (Mrs) MA MLitt BD	2003	2008	The Manse, Dalmally PA33 1AA [E-mail: lizgibson@phonecoop.coop]	01838 200207

Innellan (H) See Dunoon: The High Kirk

Iona linked with Kilfinichen and Kilvickeon and the Ross of Mull
Linda E. Pollock (Miss) BD ThM ThM   2001   2010
The Manse, Bunessan, Isle of Mull PA67 6DW   01681 700227
[E-mail: fantazomi@yahoo.co.uk]

Jura (GD)
Vacant
Church of Scotland Manse, Craighouse, Isle of Jura PA60 7XG   01496 820384

Kilarrow (H) linked with Kildalton and Oa (GD) (H)
Robert D. Barlow   2010
BA BSc MSc PhD CChem MRSC
The Manse, Bowmore, Isle of Islay PA43 7LH   01496 810271
[E-mail: rob@miragemedia.co.uk]

Kilberry linked with Tarbert (Loch Fyne) (H)
Thomas M. Bryson BD   1997   2011
The Manse, Campbeltown Road, Tarbert, Argyll PA29 6SX   01880 821012
[E-mail: thomas@bryson3.wanadoo.co.uk]

Kilbrandon and Kilchattan See Craignish

Kilcalmonell linked with Killean and Kilchenzie (H)
Vacant
The Manse, Muasdale, Tarbert, Argyll PA29 6XD   01583 421249

Kilchoman (GD) linked with Kilmeny linked with Portnahaven (GD)
Vacant
The Manse, Port Charlotte, Isle of Islay PA48 7TW   01496 850241

Kilchrenan and Dalavich linked with Muckairn
Robert E. Brookes BD   2009
Muckairn Manse, Taynuilt PA35 1HW   01866 822204
[E-mail: eilanview@uwclub.net]

Kildalton and Oa (GD) (H) See Kilarrow

Kilfinan linked with Kilmodan and Colintraive linked with Kyles (H)
David Mitchell BD DipPTheol MSc   1988   2006
West Cowal Manse, Kames, Tighnabruaich PA21 2AD   01700 811045
[E-mail: revdmitchell@yahoo.co.uk]

Kilfinichen and Kilvickeon and the Ross of Mull See Iona
Killean and Kilchenzie (H) See Kilcalmonell
Kilmeny See Kilchoman
Kilmodan and Colintraive See Kilfinan

Kilmore (GD) and Oban (Website: www.obanchurch.com)
Dugald J.R. Cameron BD DipMin MTh   1990   2007
Kilmore and Oban Manse, Ganavan Road, Oban PA34 5TU
[E-mail: obancofs@btinternet.com]
01631 566253

Kilmun (St Munn's) (H) linked with Strone (H) and Ardentinny
David Mill KJSJ MA BD   1978   2010
The Manse, Blairmore, Dunoon PA23 8TE
[E-mail: revandevmill@aol.com]
01369 840313

Kilninver and Kilmelford See Craignish
Kirn (H) See Dunoon: St John's
Kyles See Kilfinan
Lismore See Appin

Lochgilphead
Hilda C. Smith (Miss) MA BD MSc   1992   2005
Parish Church Manse, Manse Brae, Lochgilphead PA31 8QZ
[E-mail: hilda.smith2@btinternet.com]
01546 602238

Lochgoilhead (H) and Kilmorich linked with Strachur and Strathlachlan
Robert K. Mackenzie MA BD PhD   1976   1998
The Manse, Strachur, Cairndow PA27 8DG
[E-mail: rkmackenzie@strachurmanse.fsnet.co.uk]
01369 860246

Muckairn See Kilchrenan

Mull, Isle of, Kilninian and Kilmore linked with Salen (H) and Ulva
linked with Tobermory (GD) (H) linked with Torosay (H) and Kinlochspelvie
Vacant
The Manse, Gruline Road, Salen, Aros, Isle of Mull PA72 6JF
01680 300001

North Knapdale See Glassary, Kilmartin and Ford
Portnahaven See Kilchoman

Rothesay: Trinity (H) (Website: www.rothesaytrinity.org)
Andrew Barrie BSc BD   1984   2010
12 Crichton Road, Rothesay, Isle of Bute PA20 9JR
[E-mail: drew.barrie@btinternet.com]
01700 503010

Saddell and Carradale (H) linked with Southend (H)
Vacant
St Blaan's Manse, Southend, Campbeltown PA28 6RQ
01586 830274

Salen and Ulva See Mull
Sandbank (H) See Dunoon: St John's

Skipness
Vacant

South Knapdale See Ardrishaig
Southend (H) See Saddell and Carradale
Strachur and Strathlachlan See Lochgoilhead and Kilmorich
Strathfillan See Glenorchy
Strone (H) and Ardentinny See Kilmun
Tarbert (Loch Fyne) See Kilberry

The United Church of Bute

John Owain Jones MA BD FSAScot	1981	2011	10 Bishop Terrace, Rothesay, Isle of Bute PA20 9HF [E-mail: johnowainjones@ntlworld.com]	01700 504502
Raymond Deans DCS	1994	2003	60 Ardmory Road, Rothesay, Isle of Bute PA20 0PG [E-mail: deans@fish.co.uk]	01700 504893

Tiree (GD)

Elspeth J. MacLean (Mrs) BVMS BD	2011	The Manse, Scarinish, Isle of Tiree PA77 6TN [E-mail: ejmaclean@yahoo.co.uk]	01879 220377

Tobermory See Mull
Torosay and Kinlochspelvie See Mull
Toward (H) See Dunoon: The High Kirk

Beautyman, Paul H. MA BD	1993	2009	Team Leader: Youth Education Ministries	59 Alexander Street, Dunoon PA23 7BB [E-mail: paul.beautyman@dunoongrammar.argyll-bute.sch.uk]	
Bell, Douglas W. MA LLB BD BEd HDipRE DipSpecEd	1975	1993	(Alexandria: North)	3 Cairnbaan Lea, Cairnbaan, Lochgilphead PA31 8BA	01546 606815
Bristow, W.H.G.	1951	2002	(Chaplain: Army)	Laith Cottage, Southend, Campbeltown PA28 6RU	01586 830667
Dunlop, Alistair J. MA	1965	2004	(Saddell and Carradale)	8 Pipers Road, Cairnbaan, Lochgilphead PA31 8UF [E-mail: dunrevn@btinternet.com]	01546 600316
Forrest, Alan B. MA	1956	1993	(Uphall: South)	126 Shore Road, Innellan, Dunoon PA23 7SX	01369 830424
Gibson, Frank S. BL BD STM DSWA DD	1963	1995	(Kilarrow with Kilmeny)	163 Gilbertstoun, Edinburgh EH15 2RG	0131-657 5208
Goss, Alister J. BD DMin	1975	2009	(Industrial Chaplain)	24 Albert Place, Ardnadam, Sandbank, Dunoon PA23 8QF [E-mail: scimwest@hotmail.com]	01369 704495
Gray, William LTh	1971	2006	(Kilberry with Tarbert)	Lochnagar, Longsdale Road, Oban PA34 5DZ [E-mail: gray98@hotmail.com]	01631 567471
Henderson, Charles M.	1952	1989	(Campbeltown: Highland)	Springbank House, Askomill Walk, Campbeltown PA28 6EP	01586 552759

Name	Ordained/Inducted	Charge	Address	Tel
Henderson, Grahame McL. BD	1974 2008	(Kirn)	6 Gerhallow, Bullwood Road, Dunoon PA23 7QB [E-mail: ghende5884@aol.com]	01369 702433
Hood, Catriona A.	2006	Auxiliary Minister	'Elyside', Dalintober, Campbeltown PA28 6EB	01586 551490
Hood, H. Stanley C. MA BD	1966 2000	(London: Crown Court)	10 Dalriada Place, Kilmichael Glassary, Lochgilphead PA31 8QA	01546 606168
Lamont, Archibald	1952 1994	(Kilcalmonell with Skipness)	8 Achnaird, Taynuilt PA35 1JJ	01866 822385
Lind, Michael J. LLB BD	1984 2012	(Campbeltown: Highland)	Maybank, Station Road, Conon Bridge, Dingwall IV7 8BJ [E-mail: mijylind@btinternet.com]	
Macfarlane, James PhD	1991 2011	(Lochgoilhead and Kilmorich)	'Lindores', 11 Bullwood Road, Dunoon PA23 7QJ [E-mail: mac.farlane@btinternet.com]	01369 710626
MacLeod, Roderick MA BD PhD(Edin) PhD(Open)	1966 2011	(Cumlodden, Lochfyneside and Lochgair)	Creag-nam-Barnach, Furnace, Inveraray PA32 8XU [E-mail: revroddy@btinternet.com]	01499 500629
Marshall, Freda (Mrs) BD FCII	1993 2005	(Colonsay and Oronsay with Kilbrandon and Kilchattan)	Allt Mhaluidh, Glenview, Dalmally PA33 1BE [E-mail: mail@freda.org.uk]	01838 200693
Millar, Margaret R.M. (Miss) BTh	1977 2008	(Kilchrenan and Dalavich with Muckairn)	Fearnoch Cottage, Fearnoch, Taynuilt PA35 1JB [E-mail: macoje@aol.com]	01866 822416
Morrison, Angus W. MA BD	1959 1999	(Kildalton and Oa)	1 Livingstone Way, Port Ellen, Isle of Islay PA42 7EP	01496 300043
Pollock, William MA BD PhD	1987 2002	(Isle of Mull Parishes)	Correay, Salen, Aros, Isle of Mull PA72 6JF	01680 300507
Ritchie, Walter M.	1973 1999	(Uphall: South)	Hazel Cottage, Barr Mor View, Kilmartin, Lochgilphead PA31 8UN	01546 510343
Shedden, John CBE BD DipPSS	1971 2008	(Fuengirola)	Orchy Cottage, Dalmally PA33 1AX [E-mail: shedden7@googlemail.com]	01838 200535
Stewart, Joseph LTh	1979 2011	(Dunoon: St John's with Sandbank)	7 Glenmorag Avenue, Dunoon PA23 7LG	01369 703438
Taylor, Alan T. BD	1980 2005	(Isle of Mull Parishes)	Erray Road, Tobermory, Isle of Mull PA75 6PS	01688 302496
Watson, James LTh	1968 1994	(Bowden with Lilliesleaf)	7 Lochan Avenue, Kirn, Dunoon PA23 8HT	01369 702851
Wilkinson, W. Brian MA BD	1968 2007	(Glenaray and Inveraray)	3 Achlonan, Taynuilt PA35 1JJ [E-mail: brianwilkinson@f2s.com]	01866 822036

ARGYLL Communion Sundays

Parish	Sundays
Ardrishaig	4th Apr, 1st Nov
Campbeltown	
Highland	1st May, Nov
Lorne and Lowland	1st May, Nov
Craignish	1st Jun, Nov
Cumlodden, Lochfyneside and Lochgair	1st May, 3rd Nov
Dunoon	
St John's	1st Mar, Jun, Nov
The High Kirk	1st Feb, Jun, Oct
Gigha and Cara	1st May, Nov
Glassary, Kilmartin and Ford	1st Apr, Sep
Glenaray and Inveraray	1st Apr, Jul, Oct, Dec
Innellan	1st Mar, Jun, Sep, Dec
Inverlussa and Bellanoch	2nd May, Nov
Jura	Passion Sun., 2nd Jul, 3rd Nov

Parish	Sundays
Kilarrow	1st Mar, Jun, Sep, Dec
Kilberry with Tarbert	1st May, Oct
Kilcalmonell	1st Jul, 3rd Nov
Kilchoman	1st Jul, 2nd Dec, Easter
Kildalton	Last Jan, Jun, Oct, Easter
Kilfinan	Last Apr, Oct
Killean and Kilchenzie	2nd May, 3rd Nov
Kilmeny	1st Apr, Sep
Kilmodan and Colintraive	Last Jun, Nov
Kilmun	Last Feb, Jun, Oct
Kilninver and Kilmelford	2nd Jun, Oct
Kirn	1st May, Nov
Kyles	Last Apr, Oct
Lochgair	2nd Oct (Gaelic)
Lochgilphead	1st Apr, Nov

Parish	Sundays
Lochgoilhead and Kilmorich	2nd Mar, Jun, Sep, Nov
North Knapdale	1st Aug, Easter
Portnahaven	3rd Oct, 2nd May
Rothesay Trinity	3rd Jul
Saddell and Carradale	1st Feb, Jun, Nov
Sandbank	2nd May, 1st Nov
Skipness	1st Jan, May, Nov
Southend	2nd May, Nov
South Knapdale	1st Jun, Dec
Strachur and Strathlachlan	4th Apr, 1st Nov
Strone and Ardentinny	1st Mar, Jun, Oct
Tayvallich	Last Feb, Jun, Oct
The United Church of Bute	2nd May, Nov
Toward	1st Feb, Jun, Nov
	Last Feb, May, Aug, Nov

(22) FALKIRK

Meets at Falkirk Old and St Modan's Parish Church on the first Tuesday of September, December, March and May, on the fourth Tuesday of October and January and on the third Tuesday of June.

Clerk:	REV. ROBERT S.T. ALLAN LLB DipLP BD	9 Major's Loan, Falkirk FK1 5QF	01324 625124
		[E-mail: falkirk@cofscotland.org.uk]	
Treasurer:	MR IAN MACDONALD	1 Jones Avenue, Larbert FK5 3ER	01324 553603
		[E-mail: ian_macdonald1938@hotmail.com]	

Airth (H)

James F. Todd BD CPS	1984	2012	The Manse, Airth, Falkirk FK2 8LS	01324 831474

Blackbraes and Shieldhill linked with Muiravonside

Louise J.E. McClements RGN BD	2008	81 Stevenson Avenue, Polmont, Falkirk FK2 0GU	01324 717757
		[E-mail: louise.mcclements@virgin.net]	

Bo'ness: Old (H)

Douglas I. Campbell BD DPS	2004	2009	10 Dundas Street, Bo'ness EH51 0DG	01506 204585
			[E-mail: douglas@bokonline.org.uk]	

Bo'ness: St Andrew's (Website: www.standonline.org.uk) (01506 825803)

Albert O. Bogle BD MTh	1981	St Andrew's Manse, 11 Erngath Road, Bo'ness EH51 9DP	01506 822195
		[E-mail: albertbogle@mac.com]	
Peter Neilson MA BD MTh	1975	2012	Linne Bheag, 2 School Green, Anstruther KY10 3HF	01333 310477
(Interim Moderator and Locum)		[E-mail: neilson.peter@btinternet.com]	07818 418608 (Mbl)

Bonnybridge: St Helen's (H) (Website: www.bbshmc.com)

George MacDonald BTh	2004	2009	The Manse, 32 Reilly Gardens, High Bonnybridge FK4 2BB	01324 874807
			[E-mail: georgemacdonald1@virginmedia.com]	

Bothkennar and Carronshore

Andrew J. Moore BSc BD	2007	11 Hunter Place, Greenmount Park, Carronshore, Falkirk FK2 8QS	01324 570525
		[E-mail: theminister@themoores.me.uk]	

Brightons (H)

Name			Address	Tel
Murdo M. Campbell BD DipMin	1997	2007	The Manse, Maddiston Road, Brightons, Falkirk FK2 0JP [E-mail: murdocampbell@hotmail.com]	01324 712062

Carriden (H)

Name			Address	Tel
Vacant				
David Wandrum (Aux)	1993	2009	The Spires, Foredale Terrace, Carriden, Bo'ness EH51 9LW 5 Cawder View, Carrickstone Meadows, Cumbernauld, Glasgow G68 0BN	01506 822141 01236 723288

Cumbernauld: Abronhill (H)

Name			Address	Tel
Joyce A. Keyes (Mrs) BD	1996	2003	26 Ash Road, Cumbernauld, Glasgow G67 3ED	01236 723833
Linda Black (Miss) BSc DCS			148 Rowan Road, Cumbernauld, Glasgow G67 3DA	01236 786265

Cumbernauld: Condorrat (H)

Name			Address	Tel
Grace Saunders BSc BTh	2007	2011	11 Rosehill Drive, Cumbernauld, Glasgow G67 4EQ [E-mail: rev-grace.saunders@btinternet.com]	01236 452090

Cumbernauld: Kildrum (H)

Name			Address	Tel
Elinor J. Gordon (Miss) BD	1988	2004	64 Southfield Road, Balloch, Cumbernauld, Glasgow G68 9DZ [E-mail: elinorgordon@aol.com]	01236 723204
David Nicholson DCS			2D Doonside, Kildrum, Cumbernauld, Glasgow G67 2HX [E-mail: deacdave@btinternet.com]	01236 732260

Cumbernauld: Old (H) (Website: www.cumbernauldold.org.uk)

Name			Address	Tel
Catriona Ogilvie (Mrs) MA BD	1999		The Manse, 23 Baronhill, Cumbernauld, Glasgow G67 2SD	01236 721912
Valerie Cuthbertson (Miss) DCS			105 Bellshill Road, Motherwell ML1 3SJ	01698 259001

Cumbernauld: St Mungo's

Name			Address	Tel
Vacant			18 Fergusson Road, Cumbernauld, Glasgow G67 1LS	01236 721513

Denny: Old

Name			Address	Tel
John Murning BD	1988	2002	31 Duke Street, Denny FK6 6NR [E-mail: bridgebuilder@supanet.com]	01324 824508

Denny: Westpark (H) (Website: www.westparkchurch.org.uk)

Name			Address	Tel
Vacant			13 Baxter Crescent, Denny FK6 5EZ	01324 876224

Congregation / Minister	Dates	Address	Telephone
Dunipace (H) Jean W. Gallacher (Miss) BD CMin CTheol DMin	1989	The Manse, 239 Stirling Street, Dunipace, Denny FK6 6QJ	01324 824540
Falkirk: Bainsford Michael R. Philip BD	1978 2001	1 Valleyview Place, Newcarron Village, Falkirk FK2 7JB [E-mail: mrphilip@btinternet.com]	01324 621087
Falkirk: Camelon (Church office: 01324 870011) Stuart Sharp MTheol DipPA Margaret Corrie (Miss) DCS	2001	30 Cotland Drive, Falkirk FK2 7GE 44 Sunnyside Street, Falkirk FK1 4BH	01324 623631 01324 670656
Falkirk: Erskine (H) Vacant		Burnbrae Road, Falkirk FK1 5SD	01324 623701
Falkirk: Grahamston United (H) Ian Wilkie BD PGCE	2001 2007	16 Cromwell Road, Falkirk FK1 1SF [E-mail: yanbluejeans@aol.com]	01324 624461 07877 803280 (Mbl)
Falkirk: Laurieston linked with Redding and Westquarter J. Mary Henderson MA BD DipEd PhD	1990 2009	11 Polmont Road, Laurieston, Falkirk FK2 9QQ [E-mail: jmary.henderson@tiscali.co.uk]	01324 621196
Falkirk: Old and St Modan's (H) Robert S.T. Allan LLB DipLP BD	1991 2003	9 Major's Loan, Falkirk FK1 5QF	01324 625124
Falkirk: St Andrew's West (H) Alastair M. Horne BSc BD	1989 1997	1 Maggiewood's Loan, Falkirk FK1 5SJ	01324 623308
Falkirk: St James' Vacant		13 Wallace Place, Falkirk FK2 7EN	01324 632501
Grangemouth: Abbotsgrange Aftab Gohar MA MDiv PgDip	1995 2010	8 Naismith Court, Grangemouth FK3 9BQ [E-mail: abbotsgrange@aol.com]	01324 482109 07528 143784 (Mbl)

Grangemouth: Kirk of the Holy Rood
David J. Smith BD DipMin | 1992 | 2003 | The Manse, Bowhouse Road, Grangemouth FK3 0EX [E-mail: davidkhrood@tiscali.co.uk] | 01324 471595

Grangemouth: Zetland (H)
Ian W. Black MA BD | 1976 | 1991 | Ronaldshay Crescent, Grangemouth FK3 9JH [E-mail: iwblack@hotmail.com] | 01324 472868
Lorna I. MacDougall (Miss) MA DipGC (Aux) | 2003 | | 34 Millar Place, Carron, Falkirk FK2 8QB | 01324 552739

Haggs (H)
Helen F. Christie (Mrs) BD | 1998 | | 5 Watson Place, Dennyloanhead, Bonnybridge FK4 2BG | 01324 813786

Larbert: East
Melville D. Crosthwaite BD DipEd DipMin | 1984 | 1995 | 1 Cortachy Avenue, Carron, Falkirk FK2 8DH | 01324 562402

Larbert: Old (H)
Andrew M. Randall LLB DipLP BD | 2009 | | The Manse, 38 South Broomage Avenue, Larbert FK5 3ED [E-mail: aandk.randall@hotmail.com] | 01324 872760

Larbert: West (H)
Gavin Boswell BTheol | 1993 | 1999 | 11 Carronvale Road, Larbert FK5 3LZ | 01324 562878

Muiravonside See Blackbraes and Shieldhill

Polmont: Old
Jerome O'Brien BA LLB MTh | 2001 | 2005 | 3 Orchard Grove, Polmont, Falkirk FK2 0XE | 01324 718677

Redding and Westquarter See Falkirk: Laurieston

Slamannan
Raymond Thomson BD DipMin | 1992 | | Slamannan, Falkirk FK1 3EN | 01324 851307

Stenhouse and Carron (H)
William Thomson BD | 2001 | 2007 | The Manse, 21 Tipperary Place, Stenhousemuir, Larbert FK5 4SX | 01324 416628

Blair, Douglas B. LTh | 1969 2004 | (Grangemouth: Dundas) | Flat 6, Hanover Grange, Forth Street, Grangemouth FK3 8LF | 01324 484414

Name	Years	Charge	Address	Telephone
Brown, James BA BD DipHSW DipPsychol	1973 2001	(Abercorn with Dalmeny)	6 Salmon Court, Schoolbrae, Bo'ness EH51 9HF	01506 822454
Brown, T. John MA BD	1995 2006	(Tullibody: St Serf's)	1 Callendar Park Walk, Callendar Grange, Falkirk FK1 1TA	01324 617352
			[E-mail: johnbrown1cpw@talktalk.net]	
Chalmers, George A. MA BD MLitt	1962 2002	(Catrine with Sorn)	3 Cricket Place, Brightons, Falkirk FK2 0HZ	01324 712030
Hardie, Robert K. MA BD	1968 2005	(Stenhouse and Carron)	33 Palace Street, Berwick-upon-Tweed TD15 1HN	
Heriot, Charles R. JP BA	1962 1996	(Brightons)	20 Eastcroft Drive, Polmont, Falkirk FK2 0SU	01324 711352
Hill, Stanley LTh	1967 1998	(Muiravonside)	28 Creteil Court, Falkirk FK1 1UL	01324 634483
Holland, John C.	1976 1985	(Strone and Ardentinny)	7 Polmont Park, Polmont, Falkirk FK2 0XT	01324 880109
Job, Anne J. BSc BD	1993 2010	(Kirkcaldy: Viewforth with Thornton)	5 Carse View, Airth, Falkirk FK2 8NY	01324 832094
			[E-mail: aj@ajjob.co.uk]	
Kesting, Sheilagh M. (Miss) BA BD DD	1980 1993	Ecumenical Relations	12 Glenview Drive, Falkirk FK1 5JU	01324 671489
Macaulay, Glendon BD	1999 2012	(Falkirk: Erskine)	43 Gavin's Lee, Tranent EH33 2AP	
			[E-mail: gd.macaulay@blueyonder.co.uk]	
McCallum, John	1962 1998	(Falkirk: Irving Camelon)	11 Burnbrae Gardens, Falkirk FK1 5SB	
McDonald, William G. MA BD	1959 1975	(Falkirk: Grahamston United)	4 Roome Bay Crescent, Crail, Anstruther KY10 3TT	01324 619766
McDowall, Ronald J. BD	1980 2001	(Falkirk: Laurieston with Redding and Westquarter)	'Kailas', Windsor Road, Falkirk FK1 5EJ	01324 871947
MacKinnon, Ronald M. DCS	1982 2001	(Deacon)	12 Mossywood Court, McGregor Avenue, Airdrie ML6 7DY	01236 763389
Mathers, Daniel L. BD	1955 1995	(Grangemouth: Charing Cross and West)	10 Ercall Road, Brightons, Falkirk FK2 0RS	01324 872253
Maxton, Ronald M. MA		(Dollar: Associate)	5 Rulley View, Denny FK6 6QQ	01324 825441
Miller, Elsie M. (Miss) DCS		(Deaconess)	30 Swinton Avenue, Rowansbank, Baillieston, Glasgow G69 6JR	0141-771 0857
Munroe, Henry BA LTh LTI	1971 1988	(Denny: Dunipace North with Old)	Viewforth, High Road, Maddiston, Falkirk FK2 0BL	01324 712446
Paul, Iain BSc PhD BD PhD	1976 1991	(Wishaw: Craigneuk and Belhaven)	11 Hope Park Terrace, Larbert Road, Bonnybridge FK4 1DY	
Ross, Evan J. LTh	1986 1998	(Cowdenbeath: West with Mossgreen and Crossgates)		
Scott, Donald H. BA BD	1983 2002	Chaplain: HMYOI Polmont	5 Arneil Place, Brightons, Falkirk FK2 0NJ	01324 719936
			14 Gibsongray Street, Falkirk FK2 0AB	01324 722241
			[E-mail: donaldhscott@hotmail.com]	
Smith, Richard BD	1976 2002	(Denny: Old)	Easter Wayside, 46 Kennedy Way, Airth, Falkirk FK2 8GB	01324 831386
			[E-mail: richards@uklinux.net]	
Smith, Ronald W. BA BEd BD	1979 2011	(Falkirk: St James')	1F1, 2 Middlefield, Edinburgh EH7 4PF	0131-553 1174
				(Mbl) 07900 896954
Wilson, Phyllis M. (Mrs) DipCom DipRE	1985 2006	(Motherwell: South Dalziel)	'Landemer', 17 Sneddon Place, Airth, Falkirk FK2 8GH	01324 832257
			[E-mail: thomas.wilson38@btinternet.com]	

FALKIRK ADDRESSES

Blackbraes and Shieldhill	Main St x Anderson Cr		
Bo'ness: Old	Panbrae Road		
St Andrew's	Grahamsdyke Avenue		
Carriden	Carriden Brae		
Cumbernauld: Abronhill	Larch Road	Denny: Old	Denny Cross
Condorrat	Main Road	Westpark	Duke Street
Kildrum	Clouden Road	Dunipace	Stirling Street
Old	Baronhill		
St Mungo's	St Mungo's Road		

Falkirk: Bainsford	Hendry Street, Bainsford	St James'	Thornhill Road x Firs Street	West	Main Street
Camelon	Dorrator Road	Grangemouth: Abbotsgrange	Abbot's Road	Muiravonside	off Vellore Road
Erskine	Cockburn St x Hodge St	Kirk of the Holy Rood	Bowhouse Road	Polmont: Old	Kirk Entry/Bo'ness Road
Grahamston	Bute Street	Zetland	Ronaldshay Crescent	Redding and Westquarter	Main Street
Laurieston	Main Falkirk Road	Hags	Glasgow Road	Slamannan	Manse Place
Old and St Modan's	Kirk Wynd	Larbert: East	Kirk Avenue	Stenhouse and Carron	Church Street
St Andrew's West	Newmarket Street	Old	Denny Road x Stirling Road		

(23) STIRLING

Meets at the Moderator's church on the second Thursday of September, and at Stirling: Allan Park South Church on the second Thursday of February, March, April, May, June, October, November and December.

Clerk:	**REV. ALEXANDER M. MILLAR** **MA BD MBA MCMI**	5 Clifford Road, Stirling FK8 2AQ **01786 469979**
		Presbytery Office, Bridge of Allan Parish Church, 12 Keir Street, Bridge of Allan FK9 4NW [E-mail: stirling@cofscotland.org.uk]
Treasurer:	**MR GILMOUR CUTHBERTSON**	'Denovan', 1 Doune Road, Dunblane FK15 9AR **01786 823487**

Aberfoyle (H) linked with Port of Menteith (H)
Linda Stewart (Mrs) BD   1996   2008   The Manse, Loch Ard Road, Aberfoyle, Stirling FK8 3SZ   01877 382391
[E-mail: lindacstewart@tiscali.co.uk]

Alloa: Ludgate
Elizabeth Clelland (Mrs) BD   2002   30 Claremont, Alloa FK10 2DF   01259 210403
[E-mail: liz_clelland@yahoo.co.uk]
Muriel F. Willoughby (Mrs) MA BD (Assoc)   2006   2010   53 Mary Stevenson Drive, Alloa FK10 2BQ   01259 727927
[E-mail: muriel.willoughby@btinternet.com]

Alloa: St Mungo's (H)
Sang Y. Cha BD   2011   37A Claremont, Alloa FK10 2DG   01259 213872
[E-mail: syc@cantab.com]

Alva
James N.R. McNeil BSc BD   1990   1997   The Manse, 34 Ochil Road, Alva FK12 5JT   01259 760262

Balfron linked with Fintry (H)
Iain M. Goring BSc BD (interim Minister) — 1976 — 2011 — 7 Station Road, Balfron, Glasgow G63 0SX [E-mail: imgoring@tiscali.co.uk] — 01360 440285

Karen Hamilton (Mrs) DCS — 1995 — 2009 — 6 Beckfield Gate, Glasgow G33 1SW [E-mail: k.hamilton6@btinternet.com] — 0141-558 3195

Balquhidder linked with Killin and Ardeonaig (H)
John Lincoln MPhil BD — 1986 — 1997 — The Manse, Killin FK21 8TN [E-mail: eoin22@gmail.com] — 01567 820247

Bannockburn: Allan (H) (Website: www.allanchurch.org.uk)
Jim Landels BD CertMin — 1990 — The Manse, Bogend Road, Bannockburn, Stirling FK7 8NP [E-mail: revjimlandels@btinternet.com] — 01786 814692

Bannockburn: Ladywell (H)
Elizabeth M.D. Robertson (Miss) BD CertMin — 1997 — 57 The Firs, Bannockburn FK7 0EG [E-mail: lizrob@talktalk.net] — 01786 812467

Bridge of Allan (H) (01786 834155)
Gillian Weighton (Mrs) BD STM — 1992 — 2004 — 29 Keir Street, Bridge of Allan, Stirling FK9 4QJ [E-mail: gillweighton@aol.com] — 01786 832753

Buchanan linked with Drymen
Alexander J. MacPherson BD — 1986 — 1997 — Buchanan Manse, Drymen, Glasgow G63 0AQ [E-mail: revalex1@gmail.com] — 01360 870212

Buchlyvie (H) linked with Gartmore (H)
Elaine H. MacRae (Mrs) BD — 1985 — 2004 — The Manse, Kippen, Stirling FK8 3DN [E-mail: ge.macrae@btopenworld.com] — 01786 871170

Callander (H) (Tel/Fax: 01877 331409)
Robert R. Simpson BA BD — 1994 — 2010 — 3 Aveland Park Road, Callander FK17 8FD [E-mail: robert@pansmanse.co.uk] — 01877 330097

Cambusbarron: The Bruce Memorial (H)
Vacant — 14 Woodside Court, Cambusbarron, Stirling FK7 9PH — 01786 450579

Clackmannan (H)
Scott Raby LTh — 1991 — 2007 — The Manse, Port Street, Clackmannan FK10 4JH — [E-mail: s.raby@hotmail.co.uk] — 01259 211255

Cowie (H) and Plean linked with Fallin (Website: www.cowiepleanandfallinchurch.com)
Alan L. Dunnett LLB BD — 1994 — 2008 — 5 Fincastle Place, Cowie, Stirling FK7 7DS — [E-mail: alan.dunnett@sky.com] — 01786 818413
Linda Dunnett (Mrs) BA DCS — 5 Fincastle Place, Cowie, Stirling FK7 7DS — [E-mail: lindadunnett@sky.com] — 01786 818413

Dollar (H) linked with Glendevon linked with Muckhart (Website: www.dollarparishchurch.org.uk)
Alan H. Ward MA BD (Interim Minister) — 1978 — 2010 — Glebe House, Muckhart, Dollar FK14 7JN — [E-mail: revalanward@dollarparishchurch.org.uk] — 01259 781638

Drymen See Buchanan

Dunblane: Cathedral (H)
Colin G. McIntosh MA BD — 1976 — 1988 — Cathedral Manse, The Cross, Dunblane FK15 0AQ — [E-mail: revcolcath4@netscape.net] — 01786 822205
Sally Foster-Fulton (Mrs) BA BD (Assoc) — 1999 — 2007 — 21 Craiglea, Causewayhead, Stirling FK9 5EE — [E-mail: sallyfulton01@gmail.com] — 01786 463060

Dunblane: St Blane's (H)
Alexander B. Mitchell BD — 1981 — 2003 — 49 Roman Way, Dunblane FK15 9DJ — [E-mail: alex.mitchell6@btopenworld.com] — 01786 822268

Fallin See Cowie and Plean
Fintry See Balfron

Gargunnock linked with Kilmadock linked with Kincardine-in-Menteith
Andrew B. Campbell BD DPS MTh — 1979 — 2011 — The Manse, Manse Brae, Gargunnock, Stirling FK8 3BQ — [E-mail: andycampbell53@btinternet.com] — 01786 860678

Gartmore See Buchlyvie
Glendevon See Dollar

Killearn (H)
Lee Messeder BD PgDipMin — 2003 — 2010 — 2 The Oaks, Killearn, Glasgow G63 9SF — [E-mail: lee.messeder@gmail.com] — 01360 550045

Killin and Ardeonaig (H) See Balquhidder
Kilmadock See Gargunnock
Kincardine-in-Menteith See Gargunnock

Charge / Minister			Address	Telephone
Kippen (H) linked with Norrieston Gordon MacRae BD MTh	1985	1998	The Manse, Kippen, Stirling FK8 3DN [E-mail: ge.macrae@btopenworld.com]	01786 870229
Lecropt (H) Alison E.P. Britchfield (Mrs) MA BD	1987	2009	Braehead, 5 Henderson Street, Bridge of Allan, Stirling FK9 4NA [E-mail: lecroptminister@btinternet.com]	01786 832382
Logie (H) R. Stuart M. Fulton BA BD	1991	2006	21 Craiglea, Causewayhead, Stirling FK9 5EE [E-mail: stuart.fulton@btinternet.com]	01786 463060
Anne Shearer BA DipEd (Aux)		2010	10 Colsnaur, Menstrie FK11 7HG [E-mail: anne.f.shearer@btinternet.com]	01259 769176
Menstrie (H) Mairi F. Lovett (Miss) BSc BA DipPS MTh		2005	The Manse, 7 Long Row, Menstrie FK11 7BA [E-mail: mairi@kanyo.co.uk]	01259 761461
Muckhart See Dollar **Norrieston** See Kippen **Port of Menteith** See Aberfoyle				
Sauchie and Coalsnaughton Vacant			19 Graygoran, Sauchie, Alloa FK10 3ET	01259 212037
Stirling: Allan Park South (T) (H) Alistair Cowper BD BSc		2011	22 Laurelhill Place, Stirling FK8 2H [E-mail: alistaircowper@talktalk.net]	01786 471998 (Office tel/fax) 07791 524504 (Mbl)
Stirling: Church of the Holy Rude (H) linked with Stirling: Viewfield Erskine Alan Miller BA MA BD	2000	2010	7 Windsor Place, Stirling FK8 2HY [E-mail: revafmiller@gmail.com]	01786 465166

Stirling: North (H) (01786 463376) (Website: www.northparishchurch.com)

Calum Jack BSc BD	2004	18 Shirra's Brae Road, Stirling FK7 0BA [E-mail: info@northparishchurch.com]	01786 475378

Stirling: St Columba's (H) (01786 449516)

Alexander M. Millar MA BD MBA MCMI	1980 2010	5 Clifford Road, Stirling FK8 2AQ [E-mail: alexmillar0406@gmail.com]	01786 469979

Stirling: St Mark's (Website: www.stmarksstirling.org.uk)

Stuart Davidson BD	2008	176 Drip Road, Stirling FK8 1RR [E-mail: info@stmarksstirling.org.uk]	01786 473716
Jean Porter (Mrs) BD DCS	2006 2008	3 Cochrie Road, Tullibody, Alloa FK10 2RR [E-mail: JayteePorter@aol.com]	07729 316321 (Mbl)

Stirling: St Ninians Old (H)

Gary J. McIntyre BD DipMin	1993 1998	7 Randolph Road, Stirling FK8 2AJ [E-mail: gary.mcintyre7@btinternet.com]	01786 474421

Stirling: Viewfield Erskine (H) See Stirling: Church of the Holy Rude

Strathblane (H)

Richard Begg MA BD	2008 2011	The Manse, Strathblane, Glasgow G63 9AB [E-mail: RBEGG711@aol.com]	01360 770226

Tillicoultry (H)

Vacant		The Manse, Dollar Road, Tillicoultry FK13 6PD	01259 750340

Tullibody: St Serf's (H)

Donald M. Thomson BD	1975 2007	16 Menstrie Road, Tullibody, Alloa FK10 2RG [E-mail: donniethomson@tiscali.co.uk]	01259 729804

Aitken, E. Douglas MA	1961 1998	(Clackmannan)	1 Dolan Grove, Saline, Dunfermline KY12 9UP [E-mail: douglasaitken14@btinternet.com]	01383 852730
Blackley, Jean R.M. (Mrs) BD	1989 2001	(Banton with Twechar)	8 Rodders Grove, Alva FK12 5RR	01259 760198
Brown, James H. BD	1977 2005	(Helensburgh: Park)	14 Gullipen View, Callander FK17 8HN [E-mail: revjimhbrown@yahoo.co.uk]	01877 339425

Name	Charge			Address	Tel
Cloggie, June (Mrs)	(Auxiliary Minister)	1997	2006	11A Tulipan Crescent, Callander FK17 8AR	01877 331021
Cochrane, James L.Th	(Tillicoultry)	1994	2012	12 Sandpiper Meadow, Alloa Park, Alloa FK10 1QU [E-mail: jcochrane1@btinternet.com]	01259 218883
Cook, Helen (Mrs) BD	(Kingussie)	1974	2012	60 Pelstream Avenue, Stirling FK7 0BG [E-mail: revhcook@btinternet.com]	01786 464128
Gaston, A. Ray C. MA BD	(Leuchars: St Athernase)	1969	2002	'Hamewith', 13 Manse Road, Dollar FK14 7AL [E-mail: raygaston@onetel.com]	01259 743202
Gillespie, Irene C. (Mrs) BD	(Tiree)	1991	2007	39 King O'Muirs Drive, Tullibody, Alloa FK10 3AY [E-mail: revicg@btinternet.com]	01259 723937
Gilmour, William M. MA BD	(Lecropt)	1969	2008	14 Pine Court, Doune FK16 6JE [E-mail: heleng_fk9@firefly.uk.net]	01786 842928
Izett, William A.F.	(Law)	1968	2000	1 Duke Street, Clackmannan FK10 4EF	01259 724203
Jack, Alison M. MA BD PhD	Assistant: Carse of Gowrie	1998	2001	5 Murdoch Terrace, Dunblane FK15 9JE	01786 825116
MacCormick, Moira G. BA LTh	(Buchlyvie with Gartmore)	1986	2003	12 Rankine Wynd, Tullibody, Alloa FK10 2UW [E-mail: mgmaccormick@o2.co.uk]	01259 724619
McCreadie, David W.	(Kirkmabreck)	1961	1995	23 Willoughby Place, Callander PH17 8DG	01877 330785
McIntosh, Hamish N.M. MA	(Fintry)	1949	1987	1 Forth Crescent, Stirling FK8 1LE	01786 470453
Malloch, Philip R.M. LLB BD	(Killearn)	1970	2009	8 Michael McParland Drive, Torrance, Glasgow G64 4EE	01360 620089
Millar, Jennifer M. (Mrs) BD DipMin	Teacher: Religious and Moral Education	1986	1995	5 Clifford Road, Stirling FK8 2AQ	01786 469979
Murray, Douglas R. MA BD	(Lausanne)	1965	2004	32 Forth Park, Bridge of Allan, Stirling FK9 5NT [E-mail: d-smurray@supanet.com]	01786 831081
Nicol, John C. MA BD	(Bridge of Allan: Holy Trinity)	1965	2002	37 King O'Muirs Drive, Tullibody, Alloa FK10 3AY [E-mail: jchalmersnicol@aol.com]	01259 212305
Ovens, Samuel B. BD	(Slamannan)	1982	1993	21 Bevan Drive, Alva FK12 5PD	01259 222723
Paterson, John L. MA BD STM	(Linlithgow: St Michael's)	1964	2003	'Kirkmichael', 12 Waterfront Way, Stirling FK9 5GH [E-mail: lorrandian.paterson@virgin.net]	01786 447165
Pryce, Stuart F.A.	(Dumfries: St George's)	1963	1997	36 Forth Park, Bridge of Allan, Stirling FK9 5NT	01786 831026
Russell, Kenneth H. BD CCE	NHS Chaplain: Forth Valley	1986	2010	158 Bannockburn Road, Stirling FK7 0EW [E-mail: kenrussell1000@hotmail.com]	01786 475802
Sangster, Ernest G. BD ThM	(Alva)	1958	1997	6 Law Hill Road, Dollar FK14 7BG	01877 330565
Scott, James F.	(Dyce)	1957	1997	5 Gullipen View, Callander FK17 8HN	01786 825976
Scoular, J. Marshall	(Kippen)	1954	1996	6 Buccleuch Court, Dunblane FK15 0AH	
Sewell, Paul M.N. MA BD	(Berwick-upon-Tweed: St Andrew's Wallace Green and Lowick)	1970	2010	7 Bohum Court, Stirling FK7 7UT	01259 220665
Sherry, George T. LTh	(Menstrie)	1977	2004	37 Moubray Gardens, Silver Meadows, Cambus, Alloa FK10 2NQ [E-mail: georgetaylorsherry@tiscali.co.uk]	
Sinclair, James H. MA BD	(Auchencairn and Rerrick with Buittle and Kelton)	1966	2004	16 Delaney Court, Alloa FK10 1RB	01259 729001
Watson, Jean S. (Miss) MA	(Auxiliary Minister)	1993	2004	29 Strachan Crescent, Dollar FK14 7HL	01259 742872
Webster, Brian G. BSc BD	(Cambusbarron: The Bruce Memorial)	1998	2011	3/1, 57 Albert Road, Gourock PA19 1NG [E-mail: Revwebby@aol.com]	
Wright, John P. BD	(Glasgow: New Govan)	1977	2000	Plane Castle, Airth, Falkirk FK2 8SF	01786 480840

STIRLING ADDRESSES

Allan Park South	Dumbarton Road	St Columba's	Park Terrace	Viewfield Erskine	Barnton Street
Holy Rude	St John Street	St Mark's	Drip Road		
North	Springfield Road	St Ninians Old	Kirk Wynd, St Ninians		

(24) DUNFERMLINE

Meets at Dunfermline in St Andrew's Erskine Church, Robertson Road, on the first Thursday of each month, except January, July and August when there is no meeting, and June when it meets on the last Thursday.

| Clerk: | REV. ELIZABETH S.S. KENNY BD RGN SCM | 5 Cobden Court, Crossgates, Cowdenbeath KY4 8AU
[E-mail: dunfermline@cofscotland.org.uk] | **01383 741495 (Office)**
07831 763494 (Mbl) |

Aberdour: St Fillan's (H) (Website: www.stfillans.presbytery.org)

| Peter S. Gerbrandy-Baird
MA BD MSc FRSA FRGS | 2004 | St Fillan's Manse, 36 Bellhouse Road, Aberdour, Fife KY3 0TL | 01383 861522 |

Beath and Cowdenbeath: North (H)

| David W. Redmayne BSc BD | 2001 | 10 Stuart Place, Cowdenbeath KY4 9BN
[E-mail: beathandnorth@dunfermlinepresbytery.org.uk] | 01383 511033 |

Cairneyhill (H) (01383 882352) linked with Limekilns (H) (01383 873337)

| Norman M. Grant BD | 1990 | The Manse, 10 Church Street, Limekilns, Dunfermline KY11 3HT
[E-mail: nmg57@live.com] | 01383 872341 |

Carnock and Oakley (H)

| Maggie R. Roderick BA BD FRSA FTSI | 2010 | The Manse, Main Street, Carnock, Dunfermline KY12 9JG
[E-mail: maggierroderick@yahoo.co.uk] | 01383 850327 |

Cowdenbeath: Trinity (H)

| Vacant | | 66 Barclay Street, Cowdenbeath KY4 9LD | 01383 515089 |
| John Wyllie (Pastoral Assistant) | | 51 Seafar Street, Kelty KY4 0JX | 01383 839200 |

Culross and Torryburn (H)

| Jayne E. Scott (Mrs) BA MEd MBA | 1988 | 2009 | The Manse, Culross, Dunfermline KY12 8JD
[E-mail: jayne.scott5@btinternet.com] | 01383 880231 |

Dalgety (H) (01383 824092) (E-mail: office@dalgety-church.co.uk) (Website: www.dalgety-church.co.uk)
Christine Sime (Miss) BSc BD   1994   2012   9 St Colme Drive, Dalgety Bay, Dunfermline KY11 9LQ   01383 822316
[E-mail: revsime@btinternet.com]

Dunfermline: Abbey (H) (Website: www.dunfabbey.freeserve.co.uk)
Vacant   12 Garvock Hill, Dunfermline KY12 7UU   01383 721022

Dunfermline: East (New Charge Development)
Andrew A. Morrice MA BD   1999   2010   9 Dover Drive, Dunfermline KY11 8HQ   01383 620704
[E-mail: andrew@morrice5.wanadoo.co.uk]
Elizabeth Philip (Mrs) DCS MA BA PGCSE   12 Torvean Place, Dunfermline KY11 4YY   01383 721054
(New name for the charge formerly known as Dunfermline: St Paul's East)

Dunfermline: Gillespie Memorial (H) (01383 621253) (E-mail: gillespie.church@btopenworld.com)
Iain A. Sutherland BSc BD   1996   2009   4 Killin Court, Dunfermline KY12 7XF   01383 723329
[E-mail: RevISutherland@aol.com]

Dunfermline: North
Ian G. Thom BSc PhD BD   1990   2007   13 Barbour Grove, Dunfermline KY12 9YB   01383 733471
[E-mail: ianthom58@btinternet.com]

Dunfermline: St Andrew's Erskine (01383 841660)
Vacant   71A Townhill Road, Dunfermline KY12 0BN   01383 734657

Dunfermline: St Leonard's (01383 620106) (E-mail: office@stleonardsparishchurch.org.uk) (Website: www.stleonardsparishchurch.org.uk)
Andrew J. Philip BSc BD   1996   2004   12 Torvean Place, Dunfermline KY11 4YY   01383 721054
[E-mail: andrewphilip@minister.com]

Dunfermline: St Margaret's
Iain M. Greenshields   1985   2007   38 Garvock Hill, Dunfermline KY12 7UU   01383 723955
BD DipRS ACMA MSc MTh   [E-mail: revimaclg@hotmail.co.uk]

Dunfermline: St Ninian's
Elizabeth A. Fisk (Mrs) BD   1996   51 St John's Drive, Dunfermline KY12 7TL   01383 722256

Dunfermline: Townhill and Kingseat (H)
Rosemary A. Smith BD   1997   2010   7 Lochwood Park, Kingseat, Dunfermline KY12 0UX   01383 626181
[E-mail: revrosieann@gmail.com]

Inverkeithing linked with North Queensferry (T)
Vacant — 1 Dover Way, Dunfermline KY11 8HR — 01383 432158

Kelty (Website: www.keltykirk.org.uk)
Vacant — 15 Arlick Road, Kelty KY4 0BH — 01383 830291

Limekilns See Cairneyhill

Lochgelly and Benarty: St Serf's
Elisabeth M. Stenhouse (Ms) BD — 2006 — 82 Main Street, Lochgelly KY5 9AA [E-mail: lissten@sky.com] — 01592 780435

North Queensferry See Inverkeithing

Rosyth
Violet C.C. McKay (Mrs) BD — 1988 2002 — 42 Woodside Avenue, Rosyth KY11 2LA [E-mail: v.mckay@btinternet.com] — 01383 412776

Morag Crawford (Miss) MSc DCS — 118 Wester Drylaw Place, Edinburgh EH4 2TG [E-mail: morag.crawford.dcs@blueyonder.co.uk] — 0131-332 2253 / 07970 982568 (Mbl)

Saline and Blairingone
Mrs Lesley P. Risby BD — 1994 2012 — 8 The Glebe, Saline, Dunfermline KY12 9UT [E-mail: mrsrisby@hotmail.com] — 01383 853062

Tulliallan and Kincardine
Vacant — 62 Toll Road, Kincardine, Alloa FK10 4QZ — 01259 730538

Name				Address	Tel
Adams, David G. BD	1991	2011	(Cowdenbeath: Trinity)	13 Fernhill Gardens, Windygates, Leven KY8 5DZ [E-mail: adams69@sky.com]	
Boyle, Robert P. LTh	1990	2010	(Saline and Blairingone)	43 Dunipace Crescent, Dunfermline KY12 7JE [E-mail: boab.boyle@btinternet.com]	01383 740980
Brown, Peter MA BD FRAScot	1953	1987	(Holm)	24 Inchmickery Avenue, Dalgety Bay, Dunfermline KY11 5NF	01383 822456
Chalmers, John P. BD	1979	1995	Principal Clerk	10 Liggars Place, Dunfermline KY12 7XZ	01383 739130
Donald, Kenneth W. BA BD	1982	2011	Service of the Church	24 Fieldfare View, Dunfermline KY11 4FY [E-mail: kenneth@kdonald.freeserve.co.uk]	
Farquhar, William E. BA BD	1987	2006	(Dunfermline: Townhill and Kingseat)	29 Queens Drive, Middlewich, Cheshire CW10 0DG	01606 835097
Jenkins, Gordon F.C. MA BD PhD	1968	2006	(Dunfermline: North)	20 Lumsden Park, Cupar KY15 5YL [E-mail: jenkinsgordon1@sky.com]	01334 652548
Jessamine, Alistair L. MA BD	1979	2011	(Dunfermline: Abbey)	11 Gallowhill Farm Cottages, Strathaven ML10 6BZ [E-mail: chatty.1@talktalk.net]	01357 520934

Name			Position	Address / E-mail	Tel
Johnston, Thomas N. LTh	1972	2008	(Edinburgh: Priestfield)	71 Main Street, Newmills, Dunfermline KY12 8ST [E-mail: tonjohnston@blueyonder.co.uk]	01383 889240
Kenny, Elizabeth S.S. BD RGN SCM	1989	2010	(Carnock and Oakley)	5 Cobden Court, Crossgates, Cowdenbeath KY4 8AU [E-mail: esskenny@btinternet.com]	(Mbl) 07831 763494
Laidlaw, Victor W.N. BD	1975	2008	(Edinburgh: St Catherine's Argyle)	9 Tern Road, Dunfermline KY11 8GA	01383 620134
Leitch, D. Graham MA BD	1974	2012	(Tyne Valley Parish)	9 St Margaret Wynd, Dunfermline KY12 0UT [E-mail: dgrahamleitch@gmail.com]	01383 249245
McLellan, Andrew R.C. CBE MA BD STM DD	1970	2002	(HM Inspector of Prisons)	4 Liggars Place, Dunfermline KY12 7XZ	01383 725959
Melville, David D. BD	1989	2008	(Kirkconnel)	28 Porterfield, Comrie, Dunfermline KY12 9HJ	01383 850075
Orr, J. McMichael MA BD PhD	1949	1986	(Aberfoyle with Port of Menteith)	17a St Ninians Way, Linlithgow EH49 7HL	01506 840515
Paterson, Andrew E. JP	1994		Auxiliary Minister	6 The Willows, Kelty KY4 0FQ	01383 830998
Reid, A. Gordon BSc BD	1982	2008	(Dunfermline: Gillespie Memorial)	7 Arkleston Crescent, Paisley PA3 4TG [E-mail: reid501@fsmail.net]	0141-842 1542 / 07773 300989 (Mbl)
Reid, David MSc LTh FSAScot	1961	1992	(St Monans with Largoward)	North Lethans, Saline, Dunfermline KY12 9TE	01383 733144
Shewan, Frederick D.F. MA BD	1970	2005	(Edinburgh: Muirhouse St Andrew's)	38 Tremayne Place, Dunfermline KY12 9YH	01383 734354
Stuart, Anne (Miss) DCS			(Deaconess)	19 St Colme Crescent, Aberdour, Burntisland KY3 0ST	01383 860049
Vint, Allan S. BSc BD MTh	1989	2008	Mission Development Officer	7 Haldon Grove, Glenboig, Coatbridge ML5 2TP [E-mail: allan@vint.co.uk]	01236 872083 / 07795 483070 (Mbl)
Watt, Robert J. BD	1994	2009	(Dumbarton: Riverside)	101 Birrell Drive, Dunfermline KY11 8FA [E-mail: robertjwatt@blueyonder.co.uk]	07753 683717 (Mbl)
Whyte, Isabel H. (Mrs) BD	1993		(Chaplain: Queen Margaret Hospital, Dunfermline)	14 Carlingnose Point, North Queensferry, Inverkeithing KY11 1ER [E-mail: iainisabel@whytes28.fsnet.co.uk]	01383 410732

(25) KIRKCALDY

Meets at Kirkcaldy, in the St Bryce Kirk Centre, on the first Tuesday of February, March, April (when necessary), May, September, October, November and December, and on the fourth Tuesday of June.

Clerk:	REV. ROSEMARY FREW (Mrs) MA BD		83 Milton Road, Kirkcaldy KY1 1TP [E-mail: kirkcaldy@cofscotland.org.uk]	01592 260315
Depute Clerk:	MR DOUGLAS G. HAMILL BEM		41 Abbots Mill, Kirkcaldy KY2 5PE [E-mail: hamilldg@tiscali.co.uk]	01592 267500

Auchterderran: St Fothad's linked with Kinglassie

Ben Pieterse BA BTh LTh	2001	2010	7 Woodend Road, Cardenden, Lochgelly KY5 0NE	01592 720202

Auchtertool linked with Kirkcaldy: Linktown (H) (01592 641080)

Catriona M. Morrison (Mrs) MA BD	1995	2000	16 Raith Crescent, Kirkcaldy KY2 5NN	01592 265536
			[E-mail: catriona@linktown.org.uk]
Marc Prowe			16 Raith Crescent, Kirkcaldy KY2 5NN	01592 265536
			[E-mail: marc@linktown.org.uk]

Buckhaven (01592 715577) and Wemyss

Wilma Cairns (Miss) BD	1999	2004	33 Main Road, East Wemyss, Kirkcaldy KY1 4RE	01592 712870
			[E-mail: wilcairns@blueyonder.co.uk]
Jacqueline Thomson (Mrs) MTh DCS			1 Barron Terrace, Leven KY8 4DL	01333 301115
			[E-mail: churchdeacon@blueyonder.co.uk]	07806 776560 (Mbl)

Burntisland (H)

Alan Sharp BSc BD	1980	2001	21 Ramsay Crescent, Burntisland KY3 9JL	01592 874303
			[E-mail: alansharp03@aol.com]

Dysart: St Clair (H)

Vacant

(New charge formed by the union of Dysart and Kirkcaldy: Viewforth)

Glenrothes: Christ's Kirk (H)

Alexandra M. Rosener (Mrs)	2007	2010	12 The Limekilns, Glenrothes KY6 3QJ	01592 620536
			[E-mail: alexandrarosener@gmx.de]

Glenrothes: St Columba's (01592 752539) (Rothes Trinity Parish Grouping)

Vacant		40 Liberton Drive, Glenrothes KY6 3PB	01592 741215

Glenrothes: St Margaret's (H) (01592 328162) (Rothes Trinity Parish Grouping)

John P. McLean BSc BPhil BD	1994		8 Alburne Park, Glenrothes KY7 5RB	01592 752241
			[E-mail: john@mcleanmail.me.uk]

Glenrothes: St Ninian's (H) (01592 610560) (E-mail: office@stninians.co.uk)

Allistair Roy BD DipSW PGDip	2007		1 Cawdor Drive, Glenrothes KY6 2HN	01592 611963
			[E-mail: alli@stninians.co.uk]

Kennoway, Windygates and Balgonie: St Kenneth's (01333 351372) (E-mail: administration@st-kenneths.freeserve.co.uk)

Richard Baxter MA BD	1997		2 Fernhill Gardens, Windygates, Leven KY8 5DZ	01333 352329
			[E-mail: richard-baxter@msn.com]

Kinghorn
James Reid BD · 1985 1997 · 17 Myre Crescent, Kinghorn, Burntisland KY3 9UB
[E-mail: jim17reid@aol.com] · 01592 890269

Kinglassie See Auchterderran: St Fothad's

Kirkcaldy: Abbotshall (H)
Rosemary Frew (Mrs) MA BD · 1988 2005 · 83 Milton Road, Kirkcaldy KY1 1TP
[E-mail: rosiefrew@blueyonder.co.uk] · 01592 260315

Kirkcaldy: Bennochy
Robin J. McAlpine BDS BD MTh · 1988 2011 · 25 Bennochy Avenue, Kirkcaldy KY2 5QE
[E-mail: robinmcalpine@blueyonder.co.uk] · 01592 643518

Kirkcaldy: Linktown (01592 641080) See Auchtertool

Kirkcaldy: Pathhead (H) (Tel/Fax: 01592 204635) (E-mail: pathhead@btinternet.com) (Website: www.pathheadparishchurch.co.uk)
Andrew C. Donald BD DPS · 1992 2005 · 73 Loughborough Road, Kirkcaldy KY1 3DD
[E-mail: andrewcdonald@blueyonder.co.uk] · 01592 652215

Kirkcaldy: St Bryce Kirk (H) (01592 640016) (E-mail: office@stbrycekirk.org.uk)
Ken Froude MA BD · 1979 · 6 East Fergus Place, Kirkcaldy KY1 1XT
[E-mail: kenfroude@blueyonder.co.uk] · 01592 264480

Kirkcaldy: Templehall (H)
Anthony J.R. Fowler BSc BD · 1982 2004 · 35 Appin Crescent, Kirkcaldy KY2 6EJ
[E-mail: ajrf@btinternet.com] · 01592 260156

Kirkcaldy: Torbain
Ian Elston BD MTh · 1999 · 91 Sauchenbush Road, Kirkcaldy KY2 5RN
[E-mail: elston667@btinternet.com] · 01592 263015

Leslie: Trinity (Rothes Trinity Parish Grouping)
Vacant

Leven
Gilbert C. Nisbet CA BD — 1993 2007 — 5 Forman Road, Leven KY8 4HH
[E-mail: gcn-leven@blueyonder.co.uk] — 01333 303339

Markinch
Alexander R. Forsyth TD BA MTh — 1973 2002 — 7 Guthrie Crescent, Markinch, Glenrothes KY7 6AY
[E-mail: drostan1949@btinternet.com] — 01592 758264

Methil: Wellesley (H)
Gillian Paterson (Mrs) BD — 2010 — 10 Vetriano Vale, Leven KY8 4GD
[E-mail: gillianpatersonpatolq@supanet.com] — 01333 423147
(New charge formed by the union of Methil and Innerleven: East)

Methilhill and Denbeath
Elisabeth F. Cranfield (Miss) MA BD — 1988 — 9 Chemiss Road, Methilhill, Leven KY8 2BS
[E-mail: ecranfield@btinternet.com] — 01592 713142

Thornton
Guardianship of the Presbytery

Collins, Mitchell BD CPS — 1996 2005 — (Creich, Flisk and Kilmany with Monimail) — 6 Netherby Park, Glenrothes KY6 3PL
[E-mail: collinsmit@aol.com]

Connolly, Daniel BD DipTheol DipMin — 1983 — Chaplain: Army — 36 Engr Regt, Invicta Park Barracks, Maidstone, Kent ME14 2NA

Dick, James S. MA BTh — 1988 1997 — (Glasgow: Ruchazie) — 20 Church Street, Kirkcaldy KY1 2AD
[E-mail: jim.s.dick@googlemail.com] — 01592 260289

Elston, Peter K. — 1963 2000 — (Dalgety) — 6 Cairngorm Crescent, Kirkcaldy KY2 5RF
[E-mail: peterkelston@btinternet.com] — 01592 205622

Ferguson, David J. — 1966 2001 — (Bellie with Speymouth) — 4 Russell Gardens, Ladybank, Cupar KY15 7LT — 01337 831406

Forrester, Ian L. MA — 1964 1996 — (Friockheim, Kinnell with Inverkeilor and Lunan)

Galbraith, Douglas MA BD BMus MPhil ARSCM PhD — 1965 2005 — Editor: *The Year Book* — 8 Bennochy Avenue, Kirkcaldy KY2 5QE
[E-mail: dgalbraith@hotmail.com] — 01592 260251
34 Balbirnie Street, Markinch, Glenrothes KY7 6DA — 01592 752403

Gatt, David W. — 1981 1995 — (Thornton) — 15 Beech Avenue, Thornton, Kirkcaldy KY1 4AT — 01592 774328

Gibson, Ivor MA — 1957 1993 — (Abercorn with Dalmeny) — 15 McInnes Road, Glenrothes KY7 6BA — 01592 759982

Gisbey, John E. MA BD MSc DipEd — 1964 2002 — (Thornhill) — Whitenyre House, 28 St Andrews Road, Largoward, Leven KY9 1HZ — 01334 840540

Gordon, Ian D. LTh — 1972 2001 — (Markinch) — 2 Somerville Way, Glenrothes KY7 5GE — 01592 742487

Houghton, Christine (Mrs) BD — 1997 2010 — (Whitburn: South) — 39 Cedar Crescent, Thornton, Kirkcaldy KY1 4BE
[E-mail: c.houghton1@btinternet.com] — 01592 772823

McLeod, Alistair G. — 1988 2005 — (Glenrothes: St Columba's) — 13 Greenmantle Way, Glenrothes KY6 3QG
[E-mail: aagm@btinternet.com] — 01592 744558

McNaught, Samuel M. MA BD MTh	1968 2002	(Kirkcaldy: St John's)	6 Munro Court, Glenrothes KY7 5GD [E-mail: sjmcnaught@btinternet.com]	01592 742352
Munro, Andrew MA BD PhD	1972 2000	(Glencaple with Lowther)	7 Dunvegan Avenue, Kirkcaldy KY2 5SG [E-mail: am.smm@blueyonder.co.uk]	01592 566129
Paterson, Maureen (Mrs) BSc	1992 2010	(Auxiliary Minister)	91 Dalmahoy Crescent, Kirkcaldy KY2 6TA [E-mail: m.e.paterson@blueyonder.co.uk]	01592 262300
Templeton, James L. BSc BD	1975 2012	(Innerleven: East)	29 Coldstream Avenue, Leven KY8 5TN [E-mail: jamietempleton@btinternet.com]	01333 427102
Thomson, John D. BD	1985 2005	(Kirkcaldy: Pathhead)	3 Tottenham Court, Hill Street, Dysart, Kirkcaldy KY1 2XY [E-mail: j.thomson10@sky.com]	01592 655313 (Mbl) 07885 414979
Tomlinson, Bryan L. TD	1969 2003	(Kirkcaldy: Abbotshall)	2 Duddingston Drive, Kirkcaldy KY2 6JP [E-mail: abbkirk@blueyonder.co.uk]	01592 564843
Webster, Elspeth H. (Miss) DCS		(Deaconess)	82 Broomhill Avenue, Burntisland KY3 0BP	01592 873616
Wilson, Tilly (Miss) MTh	1990 2012	(Dysart)	6 Citron Glebe, Kirkcaldy KY1 2NF [E-mail: tillywilson@blueyonder.co.uk]	01592 263141

KIRKCALDY ADDRESSES

Abbotshall	Abbotshall Road
Bennochy	Elgin Street
Linktown	Nicol Street x High Street
Pathhead	Harriet Street x Church Street
St Bryce Kirk	St Brycedale Avenue x Kirk Wynd
Templehall	Beauly Place
Torbain	Lindores Drive
Viewforth	Viewforth Street x Viewforth Terrace

(26) ST ANDREWS

Meets at Cupar, in St John's Church Hall, on the first Wednesday of February, March, May, September, October, November and December, and on the last Wednesday of May and June.

Clerk:	**REV. JAMES G. REDPATH BD DipP'Th**	**The Manse, Kirk Wynd, Strathmiglo, Cupar KY14 7QS** **[E-mail: standrews@cofscotland.org.uk]**	01337 860256
Depute Clerk:	**MR WILLIAM IMLAY DipCE ACE CPSM BA**	**7 Castle Bank, Newport-on-Tay DD6 8JP** **[E-mail: imlay@btinternet.com]** **Presbytery Office**	01382 543446 01337 858442

Abdie and Dunbog (H) linked with Newburgh (H)

Lynn Brady (Miss) BD DipMin	1996	2002	2 Guthrie Court, Cupar Road, Newburgh, Cupar KY14 6HA [E-mail: lynn@revbrady.freeserve.co.uk]	01337 842228

Anstruther linked with Cellardyke linked with Kilrenny   1997 2009
Arthur A. Christie BD   16 Taeping Close, Cellardyke, Anstruther KY10 3YL   01333 313917
[E-mail: revaac@btinternet.com]

Auchtermuchty (H) linked with Edenshead and Strathmiglo   1988 2006
James G. Redpath BD DipPTh   The Manse, Kirk Wynd, Strathmiglo, Cupar KY14 7QS   01337 860256
[E-mail: james.redpath2@btopenworld.com]

Balmerino (H) linked with Wormit (H)   1982 2004
James Connolly DipTh CertMin MA(Theol)   5 Westwater Place, Newport-on-Tay DD6 8NS   01382 542626
[E-mail: revconnolly@btinternet.com]

Boarhills and Dunino
Guardianship of the Presbytery (in deferred linking with St Andrews: Holy Trinity)

Cameron linked with St Andrews: St Leonard's (01334 478702) (E-mail: stlencam@btconnect.com)
Alan D. McDonald LLB BD MTh DLitt DD   1979 1998   1 Cairnhill Gardens, St Andrews KY16 8QY   01334 472793
[E-mail: alan.d.mcdonald@talk21.com]

Carnbee linked with Pittenweem   2007
Margaret E.S. Rose BD   29 Milton Road, Pittenweem, Anstruther KY10 2LN   01333 312838
[E-mail: mgt.r@btopenworld.com]

Cellardyke (H) See Anstruther

Ceres, Kemback and Springfield   1995 2010
James W. Campbell BD   The Manse, St Andrews Road, Ceres, Cupar KY15 5NQ   01334 829350
[E-mail: revjimashkirk@aol.com]

Crail linked with Kingsbarns (H)   2000 2011
Ann Allison BSc PhD BD   The Manse, St Andrews Road, Crail, Anstruther KY10 3UH   01333 451986
[E-mail: revann@sky.com]

Creich, Flisk and Kilmany linked with Monimail   2006
Neil McLay BA BD   Creich Manse, Brunton, Cupar KY15 4PA   01337 870332
[E-mail: neilmclay@gmail.com]

Charge / Minister			Address	Tel
Cupar: Old (H) and St Michael of Tarvit Kenneth S. Jeffrey BA BD PhD	2002		76 Hogarth Drive, Cupar KY15 5YH [E-mail: ksjeffrey@btopenworld.com]	01334 653196
Cupar: St John's and Dairsie United Jan J. Steyn (Mr)	2011		The Manse, 23 Hogarth Drive, Cupar KY15 5YH [E-mail: jansteyn464@btinternet.com]	01334 650751
Edenshead and Strathmiglo See Auchtermuchty				
Elie (H) Kilconquhar and Colinsburgh (H) Vacant			30 Bank Street, Elie, Leven KY9 1BW	01333 330685
Falkland linked with Freuchie (H) George G. Nicol BD DPhil	1982	2006	1 Newton Road, Falkland, Cupar KY15 7AQ [E-mail: ggnicol@totalise.co.uk]	01337 858557
Freuchie (H) See Falkland				
Howe of Fife William F. Hunter MA BD	1986	2011	The Manse, 83 Church Street, Ladybank, Cupar KY15 7ND [E-mail: mail@billhunter.plus.com]	01337 832717
Kilrenny See Anstruther **Kingsbarns** See Crail				
Largo and Newburn (H) linked with Largo: St David's John A.H. Murdoch BA BD DPSS	1979	2006	The Manse, Church Place, Upper Largo, Leven KY8 6EH [E-mail: jm.largo@btinternet.com]	01333 360286
Largo: St David's See Largo and Newburn				
Largoward (H) linked with St Monans (H) Vacant			The Manse, St Monans, Anstruther KY10 2DD	01333 730258

Leuchars: St Athernase
Caroline Taylor (Mrs) MA BD   1995   2003   7 David Wilson Park, Balmullo, St Andrews KY16 0NP   01334 870038
[E-mail: caro234@btinternet.com]

Monimail See Creich, Flisk and Kilmany
Newburgh See Abdie and Dunbog

Newport-on-Tay (H)
Stanley A. Brook BD MTh   1977   2009   8 Gowrie Street, Newport-on-Tay DD6 8ED   01382 540009
[E-mail: stan_brook@hotmail.com]

Pittenweem See Carnbee

St Andrews: Holy Trinity
Rory MacLeod BA MBA BD   1994   2004   5 Cupar Road, Guardbridge, St Andrews KY16 0UA   01334 838038
[E-mail: annicerory@gmail.com]

St Andrews: Hope Park and Martyrs' (H) linked with Strathkinness
Allan McCafferty BSc BD   1993   2011   20 Priory Gardens, St Andrews KY16 8XX   01334 478287 (Tel/Fax)
[E-mail: amcc@grad.com]

St Andrews: St Leonard's (H) See Cameron
St Monans See Largoward
Strathkinness See St Andrews: Hope Park and Martyrs'

Tayport
Brian H. Oxburgh BSc BD   1980   2011   27 Bell Street, Tayport DD6 9AP   01382 553879
[E-mail: b.oxburgh@btinternet.com]

Wormit See Balmerino

Alexander, James S. MA BD BA PhD   1966 1973   (University of St Andrews)   5 Strathkinness High Road, St Andrews KY16 9RP   01334 472680
Bennett, G. Alestair A. TD MA   1938 1976   (Strathkinness)   Rosturk House Care Home, Carslogie Road, Cupar KY15 4HY (text only)   07709 281804
Bews, James MA   1942 1981   (Dundee: Craigiebank)   21 Balrymonth Court, St Andrews KY16 8XT   01334 476087
Bradley, Ian C. MA BD DPhil   1990 1990   University of St Andrews   4 Donaldson Gardens, St Andrews KY16 9DN   01334 475389
Brown, Harry J. LTh   1991 2009   (Dundee: Menzieshill)   6 Hall Street, Kettlebridge, Cupar KY15 7QF   01337 830088
[E-mail: harrybrown@aol.com]
Brown, Lawson R. MA   1960 1997   (Cameron with St Andrew's: St Leonard's) 10 Park Street, St Andrews KY16 8AQ   01334 473413
Cameron, James K.
MA BD PhD FRHistS   1953 1989   (University of St Andrews)   Priorscroft, 71 Hepburn Gardens, St Andrews KY16 9LS   01334 473996

Name	Years	Charge/Role	Address	Telephone
Cameron, John U. BA BSc PhD BD ThD	1974 2008	(Dundee: Broughty Ferry St Stephen's and West)	10 Howard Place, St Andrews KY16 9HL	01334 474474
Casebow, Brian C. MA BD	1959 1993	(Edinburgh: Salisbury)	c/o 6 Lawhead Place, Penicuik EH26 9JU	
Douglas, Peter C. JP	1966 1993	(Boarhills linked with Dunino)	The Old Schoolhouse, Flisk, Newburgh, Cupar KY14 6HN	01337 870218
Earnshaw, Philip MA BSc BD	1986 1996	(Glasgow: Pollokshields)	22 Castle Street, St Monans, Anstruther KY10 2AP	01333 730640
Edington, George L.	1952 1989	(Tayport)	64B Burghmuir Road, Perth PH1 1LH	
Fairlie, George BD BVMS MRCVS	1971 2002	(Crail with Kingsbarns)	41 Warrack Street, St Andrews KY16 8DR	01334 475868
Fraser, Ann G. BD CertMin	1990 2007	(Auchtermuchty)	24 Irvine Crescent, St Andrews KY16 8LG (Tel/Fax) [E-mail: anngifraser@btinternet.com]	01334 461329
Galloway, Robert W.C. LTh	1970 1998	(Cromarty)	22 Haughgate, Leven KY8 4SG	01333 426223
Gibson, Henry M. MA BD PhD	1960 1999	(Dundee: The High Kirk)	4 Comerton Place, Drumoig, Leuchars, St Andrews KY16 0NQ	01382 542199
Gordon, Peter M. MA BD	1958 1995	(Airdrie: West)	3 Cupar Road, Cuparmuir, Cupar KY15 5RH [E-mail: machrie@madasafish.com]	01334 652341
Hamilton, Ian W.F. BD LTh ALCM AVCM	1978 2012	(Nairn: Old)	Mossneuk, 5 Windsor Gardens, St Andrews KY16 8XL [E-mail: reviwfh@btinternet.com]	01334 477745
Harrison, Cameron	2006	(Auxiliary Minister)	Woodfield House, Priormuir, St Andrews KY16 8LP	01334 478067
Hegarty, John D. LTh ABSC	1988 2004	(Buckie: South and West with Enzie)	26 Montgomery Way, Kinross KY13 8FD [E-mail: john.hegarty@tesco.net]	01577 863829
Learmonth, Walter LTh	1968 1997	(Ceres with Springfield)	14 Marionfield Place, Cupar KY15 5JN	01334 656290
McDowell, Brian S. BA BD	1999 2011	(Elie Kilconquhar and Colinsburgh)	85 Croft Manor, Ballygally, Co. Antrim BT40 2RU [E-mail: bmcdowell@btinternet.com]	02828 583005
MacEwan, Donald G. MA BD PhD	2001 2012	Chaplain: University of St Andrews	Chaplaincy Centre, 3A St Mary's Place, St Andrews KY16 9UY [E-mail: dgm21@st-andrews.ac.uk]	01334 462865 (Mbl) 07713 322036
McGregor, Duncan J. MIFM	1982 1996	(Channelkirk with Lauder: Old)	14 Mount Melville, St Andrews KY16 8NG	01334 478314
Mackenzie, A. Cameron MA	1955 1995	(Biggar)	Hedgerow, 5 Shiels Avenue, Freuchie, Cupar KY15 7JD	01337 857763
McKimmon, Eric G. BA BD MTh PhD	1983 2008	(Ceres, Kemback and Springfield)	1F1, 279 Easter Road, Edinburgh EH6 8LQ [E-mail: mckimmonceres@aol.com]	0131-554 9317
Meager, Peter MA BD CertMgmt(Open)	1971 1998	(Elie with Kilconquhar and Colinsburgh)	7 Lorraine Drive, Cupar KY15 5DY	01334 656991
Neilson, Peter MA BD MTh	1975 2006	Mission Consultant	Linne Bheag, 2 School Green, Anstruther KY10 3HF [E-mail: neilson.peter@btinternet.com]	01333 310477 (Mbl) 07818 418608
Paton, Iain F. BD FCIS	1980 2006	(Elie with Kilconquhar and Colinsburgh)	Lindisfarne, 19 Links Road, Lundin Links, Leven KY8 6AS	01333 320765
Petrie, Ian D. MA BD	1970 2008	(Dundee: St Andrew's)	27 High Street East, Anstruther KY10 3DQ [E-mail: idp-77@hotmail.com]	01333 310181
Reid, Alan A.S. MA BD STM	1962 1995	(Bridge of Allan: Chalmers)	Wayside Cottage, Bridgend, Ceres, Cupar KY15 5LS	01334 828509
Robb, Nigel J. FCP MA BD ThM MTh	1981 1998	Associate Secretary: Mission and Discipleship Council	c/o 121 George Street, Edinburgh EH2 4YN [E-mail: nrobb@cofscotland.org.uk]	0131-225 5722
Roy, Alan J. BSc BD	1960 1999	(Aberuthven with Dunning)	14 Comerton Place, Drumoig, Leuchars, St Andrews KY16 0NQ [E-mail: a.roy225@btinternet.com]	01382 542225
Salters, Robert B. MA BD PhD	1966 1971	(University of St Andrews)	Vine Cottage, 119 South Street, St Andrews KY16 9UH	01334 473198
Stevenson, A.L. LLB MLitt DPA FPEA	1984 1993	(Balmerino linked with Wormit)	41 Main Street, Dairsie, Cupar KY15 4SR	01334 870582
Strong, Clifford LTh	1983 1995	(Creich, Flisk and Kilmany with Monimail)	60 Maryknowe, Gauldry, Newport-on-Tay DD6 8SL	01382 330445

Taylor, Ian BSc LTh DipEd	1983 1997	(Abdie and Dunbog with Newburgh)	Lundie Cottage, Arncroach, Anstruther KY10 2RN	01333 720222
Thrower, Charles G. BSc	1965 2002	(Carnbee with Pittenweem)	Grange House, Wester Grangemuir, Pittenweem, Anstruther KY10 2RB [E-mail: charlesandsteph@btinternet.com]	01333 312631
Torrance, Alan J. MA BD DrTheol	1984 1999	University of St Andrews	Kincaple House, Kincaple, St Andrews KY16 9SH	(Home) 01334 850755 (Office) 01334 462843
Tyre, Robert	1960 1998	(Aberdeen: St Ninian's with Stockethill)	44 Doocot Road, St Andrews KY16 8QP [E-mail: robert@roberttyre.wanadoo.co.uk]	01334 473093
Walker, James B. MA BD DPhil	1975 2011	(Chaplain: University of St Andrews)	5 Priestden Park, St Andrews KY16 8DL	01334 472839
Wotherspoon, Ian G. BA LTh	1967 2004	(Coatbridge: St Andrew's)	12 Cherry Lane, Cupar KY15 5DA [E-mail: wotherspoonrig@aol.com]	01334 650710
Wright, Lynda (Miss) BEd DCS		Deacon: Retreat Leader, Key House	6 Key Cottage, High Street, Falkland, Cupar KY15 7BD	01337 857705
Young, Evelyn M. (Mrs) BSc BD	1984 2003	(Kilmun (St Mun's) with Strone and Ardentinny)	2 Priestden Place, St Andrews KY16 8DP	01334 479662

(27) DUNKELD AND MEIGLE

Meets at Pitlochry on the first Tuesday of September and December, on the third Tuesday of February, April and October, and at the Moderator's church on the third Tuesday of June.

Clerk:	**REV. JOHN RUSSELL MA**	**Kilblaan, Gladstone Terrace, Birnam, Dunkeld PH8 0DP** [E-mail: dunkeldmeigle@cofscotland.org.uk]	**01350 728896**

Aberfeldy (H) linked with Amulree (H) and Strathbraan linked with Dull and Weem (H)

Mark Drane BD	2007	The Manse, Taybridge Terrace, Aberfeldy PH15 2BS [E-mail: mark_drane@hotmail.co.uk]	01887 820656

Alyth (H)

Michael J. Erskine MA BD	1985	2012	The Manse, Cambridge Street, Alyth, Blairgowrie PH11 8AW [E-mail: erskinemike@gmail.com]	01828 632238

Amulree and Strathbraan See Aberfeldy

Ardler, Kettins and Meigle

Vacant	The Manse, Dundee Road, Meigle, Blairgowrie PH12 8SB	01828 640074

Bendochy linked with Coupar Angus: Abbey   1997
Bruce Dempsey BD   Caddam Road, Coupar Angus, Blairgowrie PH13 9EF   01828 627331
[E-mail: revbruce.dempsey@btopenworld.com]

Blair Atholl and Struan linked with Tenandry
Vacant   Blair Atholl, Pitlochry PH18 5SX   01796 481213

Blairgowrie
Harry Mowbray BD CA   2003 2008   The Manse, Upper David Street, Blairgowrie PH10 6HB   01250 872146
[E-mail: hmowbray@viewlands.plus.com]

Braes of Rannoch linked with Foss and Rannoch (H)
Vacant   The Manse, Kinloch Rannoch, Pitlochry PH16 5QA   01882 632381

Caputh and Clunie (H) linked with Kinclaven (H)   2003 2011
Peggy Roberts BA BD   Caputh Manse, Caputh, Perth PH1 4JH   01738 710520
[E-mail: revpeggy.r@googlemail.com]

Coupar Angus: Abbey See Bendochy
Dull and Weem See Aberfeldy

Dunkeld (H)
R. Fraser Penny BA BD   1984 2001   Cathedral Manse, Dunkeld PH8 0AW   01350 727249
[E-mail: fraserpenn@aol.com]

Fortingall and Glenlyon linked with Kenmore and Lawers
Anne J. Brennan BSc BD MTh   1999   The Manse, Balnaskeag, Kenmore, Aberfeldy PH15 2HB   01887 830218
[E-mail: annebrennan@yahoo.co.uk]

Foss and Rannoch See Braes of Rannoch

Grantully, Logierait and Strathtay
Vacant   The Manse, Strathtay, Pitlochry PH9 0PG   01887 840251

Kenmore and Lawers (H) See Fortingall and Glenlyon
Kinclaven See Caputh and Clunie

Kirkmichael, Straloch and Glenshee linked with Rattray (H)
Vacant   The Manse, Alyth Road, Rattray, Blairgowrie PH10 7HF   01250 872462

Pitlochry (H) (01796 472160)
Mary M. Haddow (Mrs) BD   2001 2012   Manse Road, Moulin, Pitlochry PH16 5EP   01796 472774
[E-mail: mary_haddow@btconnect.com]

Rattray See Kirkmichael, Straloch and Glenshee
Tenandry See Blair Atholl and Struan

Name			Charge	Address	Phone
Cassells, Alexander K. MA BD	1961	1997	(Leuchars: St Athernase and Guardbridge)	47 Burghmuir Road, Perth PH1 1JG	01738 637995
Creegan, Christine M. (Mrs) MTh	1993	2005	(Grantully, Logierait and Strathtay)	Lonaig, 28 Lettoch Terrace, Pitlochry PH16 5BA	01796 472422
Duncan, James BTh FSAScot	1980	1995	(Blair Atholl and Struan)	25 Knockard Avenue, Pitlochry PH16 5JE	01796 474096
Ewart, William BSc BD	1972	2010	(Caputh and Clunie with Kinclaven)	Cara Beag, Essendy Road, Blairgowrie PH10 6QU [E-mail: ewe1@btinternet.com]	01250 876897
Frail, Nicola BLE MBA MDiv	2000	2012	Chaplain: Army	84 Simpson Square, Perth PH1 5BW [E-mail: nrfscot@hotmail.com]	
Henderson, John D. MA BD	1953	1992	(Cluny with Monymusk)	Aldersyde, George Street, Blairgowrie PH10 6HP	01250 875181
Knox, John W. MTheol	1992	1997	(Lochgelly: Macainsh)	Heatherlea, Main Street, Ardler, Blairgowrie PH12 8SR	01828 640731
McAlister, D.J.B. MA BD PhD	1951	1989	(North Berwick: Blackadder)	2 Duff Avenue, Moulin, Pitlochry PH16 5EN	01796 473591
MacRae, Malcolm H. MA PhD	1971	2010	(Kirkmichael, Straloch and Glenshee with Rattray)	10B Victoria Place, Stirling FK8 2QU [E-mail: malcolm.macrae1@btopenworld.com]	01786 465547
MacVicar, Kenneth MBE DFC TD MA	1950	1990	(Kenmore with Lawers with Fortingall and Glenlyon)	Illeray, Kenmore, Aberfeldy PH15 2HE	01887 830514
Nelson, Robert C. BA BD	1980	2010	(Isle of Mull, Kilninian and Kilmore with Salen and Ulva with Tobermory with Torosay and Kinlochspelvie)	St Colme's, Perth Road, Birnam, Dunkeld PH8 0BH [E-mail: robertnelson@onetel.net]	01350 727455
Ormiston, Hugh C. BSc BD MPhil PhD	1969	2004	(Kirkmichael, Straloch and Glenshee with Rattray)	Cedar Lea, Main Road, Woodside, Blairgowrie PH13 9NP	01828 670539
Oswald, John BSc PhD BD	1997	2011	(Muthill with Trinity Gask and Kinkell)	1 Woodlands Meadow, Rosemount, Blairgowrie PH10 6GZ [E-mail: revdocoz@bigfoot.com]	01250 872598
Ramsay, Malcolm BA LLB DipMin	1986	2011	Overseas service in Nepal	c/o World Mission Council, 121 George Street, Edinburgh EH2 4YN	0131-225 5722
Robertson, Matthew LTh	1968	2002	(Cawdor with Croy and Dalcross)	Inver, Strathtay, Pitlochry PH9 0PG	01887 840780
Russell, John MA	1959	2000	(Tillicoultry)	Kilblaan, Gladstone Terrace, Birnam, Dunkeld PH8 0DP	01350 728896
Shannon, W.G. MA BD	1955	1998	(Pitlochry)	19 Knockard Road, Pitlochry PH16 5HJ	01796 473533
Tait, Thomas W. BD	1972	1997	(Rattray)	3 Rosemount Park, Blairgowrie PH10 6TZ	01250 874833
White, Brock A. LTh	1971	2001	(Kirkcaldy: Templehall)	1 Littlewood Gardens, Blairgowrie PH10 6XZ	01250 870399
Whyte, William B. BD	1973	2003	(Nairn: St Ninian's)	The Old Inn, Park Hill Road, Rattray, Blairgowrie PH10 7DS	01250 874401
Wilson, John M. MA BD	1965	2004	(Altnaharra and Farr)	Berbice, The Terrace, Blair Atholl, Pitlochry PH18 5SZ	01796 481619
Wilson, Mary D. (Mrs) RGN SCM DTM	1990	2004	(Auxiliary Minister)	Berbice, The Terrace, Blair Atholl, Pitlochry PH18 5SZ	01796 481619
Young, G. Stuart	1961	1996	(Blairgowrie: St Andrew's)	7 James Place, Stanley, Perth PH1 4PD	01738 828473

(28) PERTH

Meets at the Elizabeth Ashton Hall, Scone, at 7:00pm on the second Tuesday of February, March, May, June, November and December, and in the Moderator's church on the second Tuesday of September.

Clerk:	**REV. ALAN D. REID MA BD**	
Presbytery Office:	**209 High Street, Perth PH1 5PB**	**01738 451177**
	[E-mail: perth@cofscotland.org.uk]	

Abernethy and Dron and Arngask
Vacant
3 Manse Road, Abernethy, Perth PH2 9JP
01738 850607

Almondbank Tibbermore linked with Methven and Logiealmond
Philip W. Patterson BMus BD   1999   2008
The Manse, Pitcairngreen, Perth PH1 3EA
[E-mail: philip.patterson@btinternet.com]
01738 583217

Ardoch (H) linked with Blackford (H)
Stuart D.B. Picken MA BD PhD   1966   2005
3 Millhill Crescent, Greenloaning, Dunblane FK15 0LH
[E-mail: picken@eikoku.demon.co.uk]
01786 880217

Auchterarder (H)
Vacant
01764 662210

Auchtergaven and Moneydie linked with Redgorton and Stanley
Adrian J. Lough BD   2012
22 King Street, Stanley, Perth PH1 4ND
[E-mail: lough368e@btinternet.com]
01738 621148

Blackford See Ardoch

Cargill Burrelton linked with Collace
Vacant
Manse Road, Woodside, Blairgowrie PH13 9NQ
01828 670352

Cleish (H) linked with Fossoway: St Serf's and Devonside
Vacant
The Manse, Cleish, Kinross KY13 7LR
01577 850231

Collace See Cargill Burrelton

Comrie (H) linked with Dundurn (H)
Graham McWilliams BSc BD   2005   The Manse, Strowan Road, Comrie, Crieff PH6 2ES
[E-mail: Themansefamily@aol.com]   01764 671045

Crieff (H)
Vacant   8 Strathearn Terrace, Crieff PH7 3AQ   01764 653907

Dunbarney (H) and Forgandenny
Allan J. Wilson BSc MEd BD   2007   Dunbarney Manse, Manse Road, Bridge of Earn, Perth PH2 9DY
[E-mail: allanjwilson@dfpchurch.org.uk]   01738 812463

Dundurn See Comrie

Errol (H) linked with Kilspindie and Rait
Douglas M. Main BD   1986 2005   South Bank, Errol, Perth PH2 7PZ
[E-mail: revdmain@btinternet.com]   01821 642279

Fossoway: St Serf's and Devonside See Cleish

Fowlis Wester, Madderty and Monzie linked with Gask
Eleanor D. Muir (Miss) MTheol DipPTheol   1986 2008   Beechview, Abercairney, Crieff PH7 3NF
[E-mail: eleanordmuir@tiscali.co.uk]   01764 652116

Gask (H) See Fowlis Wester, Madderty and Monzie
Kilspindie and Rait See Errol

Kinross (H) (Office: 01577 862570)
Alan D. Reid MA BD   1989 2009   15 Green Wood, Kinross KY13 8FG
[E-mail: kinrossmanse@tiscali.co.uk]   01577 862952

Methven and Logiealmond See Almondbank Tibbermore

Muthill (H) linked with Trinity Gask and Kinkell
Vacant   The Manse, Station Road, Muthill, Crieff PH5 2AR   01764 681205

Orwell (H) and Portmoak (H) (Office: 01577 862100)
Angus Morrison MA BD PhD   1979   2011   41 Auld Mart Road, Milnathort, Kinross KY13 9FR   01577 863461
[E-mail: morrisonangus@btconnect.com]

Perth: Craigie and Moncreiffe
Carolann Erskine BD   2009   The Manse, 46 Abbot Street, Perth PH2 0EE   01738 623748
[E-mail: erskine13@blueyonder.co.uk]
Robert Wilkie (Aux)   2011   24 Huntingtower Road, Perth PH1 2JS   01738 628301
[E-mail: rwew25879@blueyonder.co.uk]

Perth: Kinnoull (H)
David I. Souter BD   1996   2001   The Broch, 34 Monart Road, Perth PH1 5UQ   01738 626046
[E-mail: d.souter@blueyonder.co.uk]

Perth: Letham St Mark's (H) (Office: 01738 446377)
James C. Stewart BD DipMin   1997   35 Rose Crescent, Perth PH1 1NT   01738 624167
[E-mail: diamondboy09@yahoo.com]
Kenneth McKay DCS   11F Balgowan Road, Perth PH1 2JG   01738 621169
[E-mail: deakendan@gmail.com]   07843 883042 (Mbl)

Perth: North (Office: 01738 622298)
Hugh O'Brien CSS MTheol   2001   2009   127 Glasgow Road, Perth PH2 0LU   01738 625728

Perth: Riverside (Office: 01738 622341)
Grant MacLaughlan BA BD   1998   2007   44 Hay Street, Perth PH1 5HS   01738 631148

Perth: St John's Kirk of Perth (H) (01738 626159) linked with Perth: St Leonard's-in-the-Fields
James K. Wallace MA BD STM   1988   2009   5 Strathearn Terrace, Perth PH2 0LS   01738 621709
[E-mail: revjwspc@hotmail.com]

Perth: St Leonard's-in-the-Fields (H) (01738 632238) See Perth: St John's Kirk of Perth

Perth: St Matthew's (Office: 01738 636757; Vestry: 01738 630725)
Scot Burton BD DipMin   1999   2007   23 Kincarrathie Crescent, Perth PH2 7HH   01738 626828
[E-mail: minister@stmatts.org.uk]

Redgorton and Stanley See Auchtergaven and Moneydie

St Madoes and Kinfauns
Marc F. Bircham BD MTh   2000   Glencarse, Perth PH2 7NF   01738 860837
[E-mail: mark.bircham@btinternet.com]

Scone and St Martins
Vacant
(New charge formed by the union of St Martins, Scone: New and Scone: Old)

The Stewartry of Strathearn (H) (Office: 01738 621674)   Aberdalgie, Perth PH2 0QD
Vacant

Trinity Gask and Kinkell See Muthill

Name	Years	Previous charge	Address	Telephone
Ballentine, Ann M. (Miss) MA BD	1981 2007	(Kirknewton and East Calder)	17 Nellfield Road, Crieff PH7 3DU [E-mail: annballentine@hotmail.com]	01764 652567
Barr, George K. ARIBA BD PhD	1967 1993	(Uddingston: Viewpark)	7 Tay Avenue, Comrie, Crieff PH6 2PE [E-mail: gbarr2@compuserve.com]	01764 670454
Barr, T. Leslie LTh	1969 1997	(Kinross)	8 Fairfield Road, Kelty KY4 0BY	01383 839330
Bertram, Thomas A.	1972 1995	(Patna: Waterside)	3 Scrimgeours Corner, 29 West High Street, Crieff PH7 4AP	01764 652066
Birrell, Isobel (Mrs) BD	1994 2012	(Airdrie: Broomknoll)	'Hiddlehame', 5 Hewat Place, Perth PH1 2UD [E-mail: isobel.birrell@peacenik.co.uk]	01738 443335 07540 797945 (Mbl)
Brown, Elizabeth (Mrs) JP RGN	1996 2007	(Auxiliary Minister)	8 Viewlands Place, Perth PH1 1BS [E-mail: liz.brown@blueyonder.co.uk]	01738 552391
Brown, Marina D. (Mrs) MA BD MTh	2000 2012	(Hawick: St Mary's and Old)	Moneydie School Cottage, Luncarty, Perth PH1 3HZ [E-mail: revmdb1711@btinternet.com]	01738 582163
Buchan, William DipTheol BD	1987 2001	(Kilwinning: Abbey)	34 Bridgewater Avenue, Auchterarder PH3 1DQ [E-mail: wbuchan3@aol.com]	01764 660306
Cairns, Evelyn BD	2004 2012	(Chaplain: Rachel House)	15 Talla Park, Kinross KY13 8AB [E-mail: revelyn@btinternet.com]	01577 863990
Caskie, J. Colin BA BD	1977 2012	(Rhu and Shandon)	13 Anderson Drive, Perth PH1 1JZ [E-mail: colin@jcaskie.eclipse.co.uk]	
Coleman, Sidney H. BA BD MTh	1961 2001	(Glasgow: Merrylea)	'Blaven', 11 Clyde Place, Perth PH2 0EZ [E-mail: sidney.coleman@blueyonder.co.uk]	01738 565072
Craig, Joan H. (Miss) MTheol	1986 2005	(Orkney: East Mainland)	7 Jedburgh Place, Perth PH1 1SJ [E-mail: joanhcraig@bigfoot.com]	01738 580180
Donaldson, Robert B. BSocSc	1953 1997	(Kilchoman with Portnahaven)	11 Strathearn Court, Crieff PH7 3DS	01764 654976
Drummond, Alfred G. BD DMin	1991 2006	Scottish General Secretary: Evangelical Alliance	10 Errochty Court, Perth PH1 2SU [E-mail: frdrmmnd@aol.com]	01738 621305

Name			Charge (retired/other)	Address	Tel
Fleming, Hamish K. MA	1966	2001	(Banchory Ternan: East)	36 Earnmuir Road, Comrie, Crieff PH6 2EY	01764 679178
Galbraith, W. James L. BSc BD MICE	1973	1996	(Kilchrenan and Dalavich with Muckairn)	19 Mayfield Gardens, Milnathort, Kinross KY13 9GD	01577 863887
Graham, Sydney S. DipYL MPhil BD	1987	2009	(Iona with Kilfinichen and Kilvickeon and the Ross of Mull)	'Aspen', Milton Road, Luncarty, Perth PH1 3ES [E-mail: sydgraham@btinternet.com]	01738 829350
Gregory, J.C. LTh	1968	1992	(Blantyre: St Andrew's)	2 Southlands Road, Auchterarder PH3 1BA	01764 664594
Gunn, Alexander M. MA BD	1967	2006	(Aberfeldy with Amulree and Strathbraan with Dull and Weem)	'Navarone', 12 Cornhill Road, Perth PH1 1LR [E-mail: sandygunn@btinternet.com]	01738 443216
Halliday, Archibald R. BD MTh	1964	1999	(Duffus, Spynie and Hopeman)	8 Turretbank Drive, Crieff PH7 4LW [E-mail halliday@pittenzie.wanadoo.co.uk]	01764 656464
Henry, Malcolm N. MA BD	1951	1987	(Perth: Craigie)	Kelton, Castle Douglas DG7 1RU	01556 504144
Hughes, Clifford E. MA BD	1993	2001	(Haddington: St Mary's)	Pavilion Cottage, Briglands, Rumbling Bridge, Kinross KY13 0PS	01577 840506
Kelly, T. Clifford	1973	1995	(Ferintosh)	20 Whinfield Drive, Kinross KY13 8UB	01577 864946
Lawson, James B. MA BD	1961	2002	(South Uist)	4 Cowden Way, Comrie, Crieff PH6 2NW [E-mail: james.lawson7@btopenworld.com]	01764 679180
Lawson, Ronald G. MA BD	1964	1999	(Greenock: Wellpark Mid Kirk)	6 East Brougham Street, Stanley, Perth PH1 4NJ	01738 828871
Low, J.E. Stewart MA	1957	1997	(Tarbat)	15 Stormont Place, Scone, Perth PH2 6SR	01738 552023
McCormick, Alastair F.	1962	1998	(Creich with Rosehall)	14 Balmanno Park, Bridge of Earn, Perth PH2 9RJ	01738 813588
MacDonald, James W. BD	1976	2012	(Crieff)	'Mingulay', 29 Hebridean Gardens, Crieff PH7 3BP [E-mail: rev_up@btinternet.com]	
McGregor, William LTh	1987	2003	(Auchtergaven and Moneydie)	'Ard Choille', 7 Taypark Road, Luncarty, Perth PH1 3FE [E-mail: bill.mcgregor7@btinternet.com]	01738 827866
MacKenzie, Donald W. MA	1941	1983	(Auchterarder: The Barony)	81 Kingswell Terrace, Perth PH1 2DA	01738 633716
MacMillan, Riada M. (Mrs) BD	1991	1998	(Perth: Craigend Moncreiffe with Rhynd)	73 Muirend Gardens, Perth PH1 1JR	01738 628867
McNaughton, David J.H. BA CA	1976	1995	(Killin and Ardeonaig)	30 Hollybush Road, Crieff PH7 3HB	01764 653028
Millar, Archibald E. DipTh	1965	1991	(Perth: St Stephen's)	7 Maple Place, Perth PH1 1RT	01738 621813
Munro, Gillian (Miss) BSc BD	1989	2003	Head of Spiritual Care, NHS Tayside	Royal Victoria Hospital, Liff, Dundee DD2 5NF	01382 423116
Munro, Patricia (Ms) BSc DCS			Perth: St John's Kirk of Perth with Perth: St Leonard's-in-the-Fields	4 Hewat Place, Perth PH1 2UD [E-mail: pat.munrodcs@gmail.com]	01738 443088
Pattison, Kenneth J. MA BD STM	1967	2004	(Kilmuir and Logie Easter)	2 Castle Way, St Madoes, Glencarse, Perth PH2 7NY [E-mail: k_pattison@btinternet.com]	(Mbl) 07814 836314 01738 860340
Reid, David T. BA BD	1954	1993	(Cleish with Fossoway: St Serf's and Devonside)	Benarty, Wester Balgedie, Kinross KY13 9HE	01592 840214
Robertson, Thomas G.M. LTh	1971	2004	(Edenshead and Strathmiglo)	23 Muirend Avenue, Perth PH1 1JL	01738 624432
Ross, William B. LTh CPS	1988	2011	(Muthill with Trinity Gask and Kinkell)	The Manse, Station Road, Muthill, Crieff PH5 2AR [E-mail: williamross278@btinternet.com]	01764 681205
Shirra, James MA	1945	1987	(St Martin's with Scone: New)	17 Dunbarney Avenue, Bridge of Earn, Perth PH2 9BP	01738 812610
Simpson, James A. BSc BD STM DD	1960	2000	(Dornoch Cathedral)	'Dornoch', Perth Road, Bankfoot, Perth PH1 4ED [E-mail: ja@simpsondornoch.co.uk]	01738 787710
Sloan, Robert P. MA BD	1968	2007	(Braemar and Crathie)	1 Broomhill Avenue, Perth PH1 1EN [E-mail: sloans1@btinternet.com]	01738 443904
Stenhouse, W. Duncan MA BD	1989	2006	(Dunbarney and Forgandenny)	32 Sandport Gait, Kinross KY13 8FB [E-mail: duncan.stenhouse@btinternet.com]	01577 866992

Stewart, Anne E. (Mrs) BD CertMin	1998	Prison Chaplain	35 Rose Crescent, Perth PH1 1NT [E-mail: revanne@hotmail.co.uk]	01738 624167
Stewart, Gordon G. MA	1961 2000	(Perth: St Leonard's-in-the-Fields and Trinity)		
Stewart, Robin J. MA BD STM	1959 1995	(Orwell with Portmoak)	'Balnoe', South Street, Rattray, Blairgowrie PH10 7BZ	01250 870626
Tait, Henry A.G. MA BD	1966 1997	(Crieff: South and Monzievaird)	'Oakbrae', Perth Road, Murthly, Perth PH1 4HF	01738 710220
Thomson, J. Bruce MA BD	1972 2009	(Scone: Old)	14 Shieling Hill Place, Crieff PH7 4ER	01764 652325
			47 Elm Street, Errol, Perth PH2 7SQ	01821 641039
			[E-mail: RevBruceThomson@aol.com]	(Mbl) 07850 846404
Thomson, Peter D. MA BD	1968 2004	(Comrie with Dundurn)	34 Queen Street, Perth PH2 0EJ [E-mail: rev.pdt@blueyonder.co.uk]	01738 622418

PERTH ADDRESSES

Craigie	Abbot Street		
Kinnoull	Dundee Rd near Queen's Bridge		
Letham St Mark's	Rannoch Road	St John's	St John's Street
Moncreiffe	Glenbruar Crescent	St Leonard's-in-the-Fields	Marshall Place
North	Mill Street near Kinnoull Street	St Matthew's	Tay Street
Riverside	Bute Drive		

(29) DUNDEE

Meets at Dundee, Meadowside St Paul's Church Halls, Nethergate, on the second Wednesday of February, March, May, September, November and December, and on the fourth Wednesday of June.

Clerk:	**REV. JAMES L. WILSON BD CPS**	**[E-mail: dundee@cofscotland.org.uk]**	**01382 459249 (Home)** **07885 618659 (Mobile)**
Depute Clerk:	**REV. JANET P. FOGGIE MA BD PhD**	**[E-mail: r3vjw@aol.com]** **[E-mail: rev.foggie@btinternet.com]**	**01382 660152**
Presbytery Office:		**Whitfield Parish Church, Haddington Crescent, Dundee DD4 0NA**	**01382 503012**

Abernyte linked with Inchture and Kinnaird linked with Longforgan (H)

Marjory A. MacLean (Miss) LLB BD PhD RNR 1991	2011	The Manse, Longforgan, Dundee DD2 5HB [E-mail: mrjrymcln@aol.com]	01382 360238

Auchterhouse (H) linked with Monikie and Newbigging and Murroes and Tealing (H)

David A. Collins BSc BD	1993 2006	New Kirk Manse, 25 Ballinard Gardens, Broughty Ferry, Dundee DD5 1BZ [E-mail: revdcollins@dsl.pipex.com]	01382 778874

Dundee: Balgay (H)

Vacant	150 City Road, Dundee DD2 2PW	01382 668806

Dundee: Barnhill St Margaret's (H) (01382 737294) (E-mail: church.office@btconnect.com)
Susan Sutherland (Mrs) BD
2009
2 St Margaret's Lane, Barnhill, Dundee DD5 2PQ
[E-mail: susan.sutherland@sky.com]
01382 779278

Dundee: Broughty Ferry New Kirk (H)
Catherine E.E. Collins (Mrs) MA BD
1993   2006
New Kirk Manse, 25 Ballinard Gardens, Broughty Ferry, Dundee DD5 1BZ
[E-mail: revccollins@dsl.pipex.com]
01382 778874

Dundee: Broughty Ferry St James' (H)
Alberto A. de Paula BD MTh
1991   2005
2 Ferry Road, Monifieth, Dundee DD5 4NT
[E-mail: albertodepaula@blueyonder.co.uk]
01382 534468

Dundee: Broughty Ferry St Luke's and Queen Street (01382 770329)
C. Graham Taylor BSc BD FIAB
2001
22 Albert Road, Broughty Ferry, Dundee DD5 1AZ
[E-mail: cgdtaylor@tiscali.co.uk]
01382 779212

Dundee: Broughty Ferry St Stephen's and West (H)
Vacant

Dundee: Camperdown (H) (01382 623958)
Vacant
Camperdown Manse, Myrekirk Road, Dundee DD2 4SF
01382 621383

Dundee: Chalmers Ardler (H)
Kenneth D. Stott MA BD
1989   1997
The Manse, Turnberry Avenue, Dundee DD2 3TP
[E-mail: arkstotts@aol.com]
01382 827439

Dundee: Coldside
Anthony P. Thornthwaite MTh
1995   2011
9 Abercorn Street, Dundee DD4 7HY
[E-mail: tony.thornthwaite@sky.com]
01382 458314

Dundee: Craigiebank (H) (01382 731173) linked with Dundee: Douglas and Mid Craigie
Edith F. McMillan (Mrs) MA BD
1981   1999
19 Americanmuir Road, Dundee DD3 9AA
01382 812423

Dundee: Douglas and Mid Craigie See Dundee: Craigiebank

Dundee: Downfield Mains (H) (01382 810624/812166)
Vacant — 9 Elgin Street, Dundee DD3 8NL — 01382 827207
(New charge formed by the union of Dundee: Downfield South and Dundee: Mains)

Dundee: Dundee (St Mary's) (H) (01382 226271)
Keith F. Hall MA BD — 1980 1994 — 33 Strathern Road, West Ferry, Dundee DD5 1PP — 01382 778808

Dundee: Fintry Parish Church (01382 508191)
Colin M. Brough BSc BD — 1998 2002 — 4 Clive Street, Dundee DD4 7AW [E-mail: colin.brough@blueyonder.co.uk] — 01382 458629

Dundee: Lochee (H)
Hazel Wilson (Ms) MA BD DipEd DMS — 1991 2006 — 32 Clayhills Drive, Dundee DD2 1SX [E-mail: hwilson704@btinternet.com] — 01382 561989

Dundee: Logie and St John's Cross (H) (01382 668514)
David S. Scott MA BD — 1987 1999 — 7 Hyndford Street, Dundee DD2 1HQ [E-mail: david@logies.org] — 01382 641572

Dundee: Meadowside St Paul's (H) (01382 202255)
Maudeen I. MacDougall (Miss) BA BD — 1978 1984 — 36 Blackness Avenue, Dundee DD2 1HH — 01382 668828

Dundee: Menzieshill
Robert Mallinson BD — 2010 — The Manse, Charleston Drive, Dundee DD2 4ED [E-mail: bobmalli1975@hotmail.co.uk] — 01382 667446 / 07595 249089 (Mbl)

Dundee: St Andrew's (H) (01382 224860)
Janet P. Foggie MA BD PhD — 2003 2009 — 39 Tullideph Road, Dundee DD2 2JD [E-mail: rev.foggie@btinternet.com] — 01382 660152

Dundee: St David's High Kirk (H)
Marion J. Paton (Miss) MA BMus BD — 1991 2007 — 6 Adelaide Place, Dundee DD3 6LF [E-mail: sdhkrev@googlemail.com] — 01382 322955

Dundee: Steeple (H) (01382 200031)
David M. Clark MA BD — 1989 2000 — 128 Arbroath Road, Dundee DD4 7HR [E-mail: dmclark72@blueyonder.co.uk] — 01382 455411

Dundee: Stobswell (H) (01382 461397)
William McLaren MA BD — 1990 — 2007 — 23 Shamrock Street, Dundee DD4 7AH [E-mail: williammclaren63@googlemail.com] — 01382 459119

Dundee: Strathmartine (H) (01382 825817)
Stewart McMillan BD — 1983 — 1990 — 19 Americanmuir Road, Dundee DD3 9AA — 01382 812423

Dundee: Trinity (H)
David J.H. Laing BD DPS — 1976 — 2008 — 65 Clepington Road, Dundee DD4 7BQ [E-mail: edlaing@tiscali.co.uk] — 01382 458764

Dundee: West
Andrew T. Greaves BD — 1985 — 2000 — Manse of Dundee West Church, Wards of Keithock, by Brechin DD9 7PZ [E-mail: andrewgreaves2@btinternet.com] — 01356 624479

Dundee: Whitfield (H) (01382 503012)
James L. Wilson BD CPS — 1986 — 2001 — 53 Old Craigie Road, Dundee DD4 7JD [E-mail: r3vjw@aol.com] — 01382 459249

Fowlis and Liff linked with Lundie and Muirhead (H)
Donna M. Hays (Mrs) MTheol DipEd DipTMHA — 2004 — 149 Coupar Angus Road, Muirhead of Liff, Dundee DD2 5QN [E-mail: dmhays32@aol.com] — 01382 580210

Inchture and Kinnaird See Abernyte

Invergowrie (H)
Robert J. Ramsay LLB NP BD — 1986 — 1997 — 2 Boniface Place, Invergowrie, Dundee DD2 5DW [E-mail: s3rjr@tiscali.co.uk] — 01382 561118

Longforgan See Abernyte
Lundie and Muirhead See Fowlis and Liff

Monifieth (H)
Dorothy U. Anderson (Mrs) LLB DipLP BD — 2006 — 2009 — 8 Church Street, Monifieth, Dundee DD5 4JP [E-mail: dorothy@kirkyard.plus.com] — 01382 532607

Monikie and Newbigging and Murroes and Tealing See Auchterhouse

Name			Position/Charge	Address	Tel.
Barrett, Leslie M. BD FRICS	1991	2001	Chaplain: University of Abertay, Dundee	Dunelm Cottage, Logie, Cupar KY15 4SJ [E-mail: l.barrett@abertay.ac.uk]	01334 870396
Campbell, Gordon MA BD CDipAF DipHSM MCMI MHM AFRIN ARSGS FRGS FSAScot	2001		Auxiliary Minister: Chaplain: University of Dundee	2 Falkland Place, Kingoodie, Invergowrie, Dundee DD2 5DY [E-mail: gordon.campbell@dundeepresbytery.org.uk]	01382 561383
Clarkson, Robert G.	1950	1989	(Dundee: Strathmartine)	320 Strathmartine Road, Dundee DD3 8QG [E-mail: rob.gov@virgin.net]	01382 825380
Craik, Sheila (Mrs) BD	1989	2001	(Dundee: Camperdown)	35 Haldane Terrace, Dundee DD3 0HT	01382 802078
Cramb, Erik M. LTh	1973	1989	(Industrial Mission Organiser)	Flat 35, Brachead, Methven Walk, Dundee DD2 3FJ [E-mail: erikcramb@aol.com]	01382 526196
Donald, Robert M. LTh BA	1969	2005	(Kilmodan and Colintraive)	2 Blacklaw Drive, Birkhill, Dundee DD2 5RJ [E-mail: robbie.donald@dundeepresbytery.org.uk]	01382 581337
Douglas, Fiona C. (Ms) MBE MA BD PhD	1989	1997	Chaplain: University of Dundee	10 Springfield, Dundee DD1 4JE	01382 384157
Ferguson, John F. MA BD	1987	2001	(Perth: Kinnoull)	10 Glamis Crescent, Inchture, Perth PH14 9QU	01828 687881
Fraser, Donald W. MA	1958	2010	(Monifieth)	1 Blake Avenue, Broughty Ferry, Dundee DD5 3LH [E-mail: fraserdonald37@yahoo.co.uk]	01382 477491 (Mbl) 07531 863316
Gammack, George BD	1985	1999	(Dundee: Whitfield)	13A Hill Street, Broughty Ferry, Dundee DD5 2JP	01382 778636
Hawdon, John E. BA MTh AICS	1961	1995	(Dundee: Clepington)	53 Hillside Road, Dundee DD2 1QT [E-mail: john.hawdon@dundeepresbytery.org.uk]	01382 646212
Hudson, J. Harrison DipTh MA BD	1961	1999	(Dundee: St Peter's McCheyne)	22 Hamilton Avenue, Tayport DD6 9BW	01382 552052
Ingram, J.R.	1954	1978	(Chaplain: RAF)	48 Marlee Road, Broughty Ferry, Dundee DD5 3EX	01382 736400
Jamieson, David B. MA BD STM	1974	2011	(Monifieth)	8A Albert Street, Monifieth, Dundee DD5 4JS	01382 532772
Kay, Elizabeth (Miss) DipYCS	1993	2007	(Auxiliary Minister)	1 Kintail Walk, Inchture, Perth PH14 9RY [E-mail: liz.kay@dundeepresbytery.org.uk]	01828 686029
Laidlaw, John J. MA	1964	1973	(Adviser in Religious Education)	14 Dalhousie Road, Barnhill, Dundee DD5 2SQ	01382 477458
Lynn, Joyce (Mrs) MIPM BD	1995	1999	(Shapinsay)	Flat 8, 131 St Vincent Street, Broughty Ferry, Dundee DD5 2DA	01382 690556
McLeod, David C. BSc MEng BD	1969	2001	(Dundee: Fairmuir)	6 Carseview Gardens, Dundee DD2 1NE	01382 641371
McMillan, Charles D. LTh	1979	2004	(Elgin: High)	11 Troon Terrace, The Orchard, Ardler, Dundee DD2 3FX	01382 831358
Mair, Michael V.A. MA BD	1967	2007	(Craigiebank with Dundee: Douglas and Mid Craigie)	6 Emmockwoods Drive, Dundee DD4 9FD [E-mail: mike.mair@dundeepresbytery.org.uk]	01382 502114
Martin, Janie (Miss) DCS	1960	1992	(Deaconess)	16 Wentworth Road, Ardler, Dundee DD2 8SD	01382 813786
Milroy, Tom	1987	1996	(Monifieth: St Rule's)	9 Long Row, Westhaven, Carnoustie DD7 6BE	01241 856654
Mitchell, Jack MA BD CTh	1948	1986	(Dundee: Menzieshill)	10 Invergowrie Drive, Dundee DD2 1RF	01382 642301
Mowat, Gilbert M. MA	1969	1995	(Dundee: Albany-Butterburn)	Abbeyfield House, 16 Grange Road, Bearsden, Glasgow G61 3PL	
Powrie, James E. LTh	1968	1983	(Dundee: Chalmers Ardler)	3 Kirktonhill Road, Kirriemuir DD8 4HU	01575 572503
Rae, Robert LTh			(Chaplain: Dundee Acute Hospitals)	14 Neddertoun View, Liff, Dundee DD3 5RU	01382 581790
Randall, David J. MA BD ThM	1971	2010	(Macduff)	5 Applehill Gardens, Wellbank, Broughty Ferry, Dundee DD5 3UG [E-mail: djrandall479@btinternet.com]	01382 351812
Reid, R. Gordon BSc BD MIET	1993	2010	(Carriden)	6 Bayview Place, Monifieth, Dundee DD5 4TN [E-mail: GordonReid@aol.com]	01382 520519 (Mbl) 07952 349884
Robson, George K. LTh DPS BA	1983	2011	(Dundee: Balgay)	11 Ceres Crescent, Broughty Ferry, Dundee DD5 3JN [E-mail: gkrobson@tiscali.co.uk]	01382 901212

Rogers, James M. BA DB DCult	1955 1996	(Gibraltar)	
Rose, Lewis (Mr) DCS	1993	Deacon	
		24 Mansion Drive, Dalclaverhouse, Dundee DD4 9DD	01382 506162
		5 Lyndhurst Avenue, Dundee DD2 3HR	01382 622167
		[E-mail: scimnorth@uk.uumail.com]	
Roy, James A. MA BD	1965 2006	(Dundee: Lochee West)	
		'Beechwood', 7 Northview Terrace, Wormit, Newport-on-Tay DD6 8PP	(Mbl) 07899 790466 / 01382 543578
		[E-mail: jim.roy@dundeepresbytery.org.uk]	
Scott, James MA BD	1973 2010	(Drumoak-Durris)	
		3 Blake Place, Broughty Ferry, Dundee DD5 3LQ	01382 739595
		[E-mail: jimscott73@yahoo.co.uk]	
Scoular, Stanley	1963 2000	(Rosyth)	
		31 Duns Crescent, Dundee DD4 0RY	01382 501653
Strickland, Alexander LTh	1971 2005	(Dairsie with Kemback with Strathkinness)	
		12 Ballumbie Braes, Dundee DD5 0UN	01382 685539
Sutherland, David A.	2001	Auxiliary Minister	
		6 Cromarty Drive, Dundee DD2 2UQ	01382 621473
		[E-mail: revdavesutherland@virginmedia.com]	
Webster, Allan F. MA BD	1978 2008	Workplace Chaplain: Dundee and Tayside	
		42 McCulloch Drive, Forfar DD8 2EB	01307 464252
		[E-mail: allanfwebster@aol.com]	

DUNDEE ADDRESSES

Balgay	200 Lochee Road	Coldside	Isla Street
Barnhill St Margaret's	10 Invermark Terrace	Craigiebank	Craigie Avenue at Greendykes Road
Broughty Ferry		Douglas and Mid Craigie	Balbeggie Place/ Longtown Terrace
New Kirk	370 Queen Street	Downfield South	Haldane Street off Strathmartine Road
St James'	5 Fort Street	Dundee (St Mary's)	Nethergate
St Luke's and Queen Street	5 West Queen Street	Fintry	Fintry Road x Fintry Drive
St Stephen's and West	96 Dundee Road	Lochee	191 High Street, Lochee
Camperdown	22 Brownhill Road	Logie and	
Chalmers Ardler	Turnberry Avenue	St John's Cross	Shaftesbury Rd x Blackness Ave

Mains	Foot of Old Glamis Road
Meadowside St Paul's	114 Nethergate
Menzieshill	Charleston Drive, Menzieshill
St Andrew's	2 King Street
St David's High Kirk	119A Kinghorne Road and 273 Strathmore Avenue
Steeple	Nethergate
Stobswell	170 Albert Street
Strathmartine	507 Strathmartine Road
Trinity	73 Crescent Street
West	130 Perth Road
Whitfield	Haddington Crescent

(30) ANGUS

Meets at Forfar in St Margaret's Church Hall on the first Tuesday of February, March, May, September, November and December, and on the last Tuesday of June.

Clerk: REV. MICHAEL S. GOSS BD DPS [E-mail: michaelgoss@blueyonder.co.uk]
Depute Clerk: REV. IAN A. McLEAN BSc BD DMin [E-mail: iamclean@lineone.net]
Presbytery Office: St Margaret's Church, West High Street, Forfar DD8 1BJ   01307 464224
[E-mail: angus@cofscotland.org.uk]

Aberlemno (H) linked with Guthrie and Rescobie

Brian Ramsay BD DPS MLitt	1980 1984	The Manse, Guthrie, Forfar DD8 2TP	01241 828243

Arbirlot linked with Carmyllie
Stewart J. Lamont BSc BD   1972   2011   The Manse, Arbirlot, Arbroath DD11 2NX   01241 434479

Arbroath: Knox's (H) linked with Arbroath: St Vigeans (H)
Nelu I. Balaj BD MA ThD   2010   The Manse, St Vigeans, Arbroath DD11 4RF
[E-mail: nelu@gmx.co.uk]   01241 873206 / 07954 436879 (Mbl)

Arbroath: Old and Abbey (H) (Church office: 01241 877068)
Valerie L. Allen (Ms) BMus MDiv DMin   1990   1996   51 Cliffburn Road, Arbroath DD11 5BA
[E-mail: VL2allen@aol.com]   01241 872196 (Tel/Fax)

Arbroath: St Andrew's (H) (E-mail: office@arbroathstandrews.org.uk)
W. Martin Fair BA BD DMin   1992   92 Grampian Gardens, Arbroath DD11 4AQ
[E-mail: martin.fair@sky.com]   01241 873238 (Tel/Fax)

Arbroath: St Vigeans See Arbroath: Knox's

Arbroath: West Kirk (H)
Alasdair G. Graham BD DipMin   1981   1986   1 Charles Avenue, Arbroath DD11 2EY
[E-mail: alasdair.graham@tiscali.co.uk]   01241 872244

Barry linked with Carnoustie
Michael S. Goss BD DPS   1991   2003   44 Terrace Road, Carnoustie DD7 7AR
[E-mail: michaelgoss@blueyonder.co.uk]   01241 410194 (Tel/Fax) / 07787 141567 (Mbl)

Brechin: Cathedral (H) (Cathedral office: 01356 629360) (Website: www.brechincathedral.org.uk)
Roderick J. Grahame BD CPS   1991   2010   Chanonry Wynd, Brechin DD9 6JS
[E-mail: rjgrahame@talktalk.net]   01356 624980

Brechin: Gardner Memorial (H) linked with Farnell
Jane M. Blackley MA BD   2009   15 Caldhame Gardens, Brechin DD9 7JJ
[E-mail: jmblackley6@aol.com]   01356 622034

Carmyllie See Arbirlot
Carnoustie See Barry

Carnoustie: Panbride (H)
Matthew S. Bicket BD   1989   8 Arbroath Road, Carnoustie DD7 6BL
[E-mail: matthew@bicket.freeserve.co.uk]   01241 854478 (Tel) / 01241 855088 (Fax)

Colliston linked with Friockheim Kinnell linked with Inverkeilor and Lunan (H)
Peter A. Phillips BA   1995   2004   The Manse, Inverkeilor, Arbroath DD11 5SA
[E-mail: rev.p.phillips@gmail.com]   01241 830464

Dun and Hillside
Linda J. Broadley (Mrs) LTh DipEd   1996   2004   4 Manse Road, Hillside, Montrose DD10 9FB
[E-mail: lindabroadley@btinternet.com]   01674 830288

Dunnichen, Letham and Kirkden
Vacant   7 Braehead Road, Letham, Forfar DD8 2PG

Eassie, Nevay and Newtyle
Carleen Robertson (Miss) BD   1992   2 Kirkton Road, Newtyle, Blairgowrie PH12 8TS
[E-mail: carleen.robertson120@btinternet.com]   01828 650461
(New charge formed by the union of Eassie and Nevay and Newtyle)

Edzell Lethnot Glenesk (H) linked with Fern Careston Menmuir
David T. Gray BArch BD   2010   19 Lethnot Road, Edzell, Brechin DD9 7TG
[E-mail: davidgray64@sky.com]   01356 647846
07789 718622 (Mbl)

Farnell See Brechin: Gardner Memorial
Fern Careston Menmuir See Edzell Lethnot Glenesk

Forfar: East and Old (H)
Barbara Ann Sweetin BD   2011   The Manse, Lour Road, Forfar DD8 2BB
[E-mail: barbara.ann17@talktalk.net]   01307 248228

Forfar: Lowson Memorial (H)
Karen Fenwick PhD MPhil BSc BD   2006   1 Jamieson Street, Forfar DD8 2HY
[E-mail: kmfenwick@talktalk.net]   01307 468585

Forfar: St Margaret's (H) (Church office: 01307 464224)
David Logan BD MA FRSA   2009   St Margaret's Manse, 15 Potters Park Crescent, Forfar DD8 1HH
[E-mail: minister@castleroy.org]   01307 462044

Friockheim Kinnell See Colliston

Glamis (H), Inverarity and Kinnettles
Guardianship of the Presbytery   12 Turfbeg Road, Forfar DD8 3LT   01307 466038

Guthrie and Rescobie See Aberlemno

Inchbrayock linked with Montrose: Melville South
David S. Dixon MA BD   1976   The Manse, Ferryden, Montrose DD10 9SD   01674 672108
                                                      [E-mail: david@inchbrayock.wanadoo.co.uk]

Inverkeilor and Lunan See Colliston

Kirriemuir: St Andrew's (H) linked with Oathlaw Tannadice
John K. Orr BD MTh   2012   26 Quarry Park, Kirriemuir DD8 4DR   01575 572610
                                                      [E-mail: minister@standrews-kirriemuir.org.uk]

Montrose: Melville South See Inchbrayock

Montrose: Old and St Andrew's
Ian A. McLean BSc BD DMin   1981 2008   2 Rosehill Road, Montrose DD10 8ST   01674 672447
                                                      [E-mail: iamclean@lineone.net]

Oathlaw Tannadice See Kirriemuir: St Andrew's

The Glens and Kirriemuir: Old (H) (Church office: 01575 572819) (Website: www.gkopc.co.uk)
Malcolm I.G. Rooney DPE BEd BD   1993 1999   20 Strathmore Avenue, Kirriemuir DD8 4DJ   01575 573724
                                                                                                       07909 993233 (Mbl)
                                                      [E-mail: malcolm@gkopc.co.uk]
Linda Stevens (Mrs) BSc BD PgDip   2006   17 North Latch Road, Brechin DD9 6LE   01356 623415
(Team Minister)   07701 052552 (Mbl)
                                                      [E-mail: linda@gkopc.co.uk]

The Isla Parishes
Brian Ian Murray BD   2002 2010   Balduff House, Kilry, Blairgowrie PH11 8HS   01575 560268
                                                      [E-mail: bentleymurray@googlemail.com]

Anderson, John F. MA BD FSAScot	1966	2006	(Aberdeen: Mannofield)	8 Eider Close, Montrose DD10 9NE [E-mail: jfa941@aol.com]	01674 672029
Brodie, James BEM MA BD STM	1955	1974	(Hurlford)	25A Keptie Road, Arbroath DD11 3ED	01241 873298
Butters, David	1964	1998	(Turriff: St Ninian's and Forglen)	68A Millgate, Friockheim, Arbroath DD11 4TN	01241 828030

Name	Dates	Charge	Address	Tel
Douglas, Iain M. MA BD MPhil DipEd	1960 2002	(Farnell with Montrose: St Andrew's)	Old School House, Kinnell, Friockheim, Arbroath DD11 4UL	01241 828717
Drysdale James P.R.	1967 1999	(Brechin: Gardner Memorial)	51 Airlie Street, Brechin DD9 6JX	01356 625201
Duncan, Robert F. MTheol	1986 2001	(Lochgelly: St Andrew's)	25 Rowan Avenue, Kirriemuir DD11 3ED	01575 573973
Gough, Ian G. MA BD MTh DMin	1974 2009	(Arbroath: Knox's with Arbroath: St Vigeans)	23 Keptie Road, Arbroath DD11 3ED [E-mail: ianggough@btinternet.com]	(Mbl) 07891 838379
Hastie, George I. MA BD	1971 2009	(Mearns Coastal)	23 Borrowfield Crescent, Montrose DD10 9BR	01674 672290
Hodge, William N.T.	1966 1995	(Longside)	19 Craigengar Park, Craigshill, Livingston EH54 5NY	01506 435813
London, Dale BTh FSAScot	2011	Chaplain: Army	39 Morrison Street, Kirriemuir DD8 5DB	01575 573518
Milton, Eric G. RD	1963 1994	(Blairdaff)	16 Bruce Court, Links Parade, Carnoustie DD7 7JE	01241 854928
Morrice, Alastair M. MA BD	1968 2002	(Rutherglen: Stonelaw)	5 Brechin Road, Kirriemuir DD8 4BX [E-mail: ambishkek@swissmail.org]	01575 574102
Norrie, Graham MA BD	1967 2007	(Forfar: East and Old)	'Novar', 14A Wyllie Street, Forfar DD8 3DN [E-mail: grahamnorrie@hotmail.com]	01307 468152
Perry, Joseph B.	1955 1989	(Farnell)	19 Guthrie Street, Letham, Forfar DD8 2PS	01307 818741
Reid, Albert B. BD BSc	1996 2001	(Ardler, Kettins and Meigle)	1 Dundee Street, Letham, Forfar DD8 2PQ [E-mail: abreid@btinternet.com]	01307 818416
Robertson, George R. LTh	1985 2004	(Udny and Pitmedden)	3 Slateford Gardens, Edzell, Brechin DD9 7SX [E-mail: geomag.robertson@btinternet.com]	01356 647322
Searle, David C. MA DipTh	1965 2003	(Warden: Rutherford House)	12 Cairnie Road, Arbroath DD11 3DY [E-mail: dcs@davidsearle.plus.com]	01241 872794
Smith, Hamish G.	1965 1993	(Auchterless with Rothienorman)	11A Guthrie Street, Letham, Forfar DD8 2PS	01307 818973
Thomas, Martyn R.H. CEng MIStructE	1987 2002	(Fowlis and Liff with Lundie and Muirhead of Liff)	14 Kirkgait, Letham, Forfar DD8 2XQ [E-mail: martyn.thomas@mypostoffice.co.uk]	01307 818084
Thomas, Shirley A. (Mrs) DipSocSci AMIA (Aux)	2000 2006	(Auxiliary Minister)	14 Kirkgait, Letham, Forfar DD8 2XQ [E-mail: martyn.thomas@mypostoffice.co.uk]	01307 818084
Watt, Alan G.N. MTh CQSW DipCommEd	1996 2009	(Edzell Lethnot Glenesk with Fern Careston Menmuir)	128 Restenneth Drive, Forfar DD8 2DH [E-mail: watt455@btinternet.com]	01307 461686
Youngson, Peter	1961 1996	(Kirriemuir: St Andrew's)	'Coreen', Woodside, Northmuir, Kirriemuir DD8 4PG	01575 572832

ANGUS ADDRESSES

Arbroath: Knox's	Howard Street	Kirriemuir: Old	High Street
Old and Abbey	West Abbey Street	St Andrew's	Glamis Road
St Andrew's	Hamilton Green		
West Kirk	Keptie Street	Montrose: Melville South	Castle Street
		Old and St Andrew's	High Street
Brechin: Cathedral	Bishops Close		
Gardner Memorial	South Esk Street		
Carnoustie:	Dundee Street		
Panbride	Arbroath Road		
Forfar: East and Old	East High Street		
Lowson Memorial	Jamieson Street		
St Margaret's	West High Street		

(31) ABERDEEN

Meets on the first Tuesday of February, March, May, September, October, November and December, and on the fourth Tuesday of June. The venue varies.

Joint Clerks:	REV. GEORGE S. COWIE BSc BD
	REV. JOHN A. FERGUSON
	BD DipMin DMin

Administrator and Depute Clerk:	MRS MOYRA CAMERON		
Presbytery Office:	Mastrick Church, Greenfern Road, Aberdeen AB16 6TR	01224 698119
	[E-mail: aberdeen@cofscotland.org.uk]	

Aberdeen: Bridge of Don Oldmachar (01224 709299) (Website: www.oldmacharchurch.org)
David J. Stewart BD MTh DipMin   2000   2012   60 Newburgh Circle, Aberdeen AB22 8QZ   01224 701365
[E-mail: brigodon@clara.co.uk]

Aberdeen: Cove (E)
David Swan BVMS BD   2005   4 Charleston Way, Cove, Aberdeen AB12 3FA   01224 899933
[E-mail: david@covechurch.org.uk]

Aberdeen: Craigiebuckler (H) (01224 315649)
Kenneth L. Petrie MA BD   1984   1999   185 Springfield Road, Aberdeen AB15 8AA   01224 315125
[E-mail: patandkenneth@aol.com]

Aberdeen: Ferryhill (H) (01224 213093)
Vacant   54 Polmuir Road, Aberdeen AB11 7RT   01224 586933

Aberdeen: Garthdee (H) linked with Aberdeen: Ruthrieston West (H)
Benjamin D.W. Byun BS MDiv MTh PhD   1992   2008   53 Springfield Avenue, Aberdeen AB15 8JJ   01224 312706
[E-mail: benjamin@byun1.fsnet.co.uk]

Aberdeen: Gilcomston South (H) (01224 647144)
D. Dominic Smart BSc BD MTh   1988   1998   37 Richmondhill Road, Aberdeen AB15 5EQ   01224 314326
[E-mail: dominic.smart@gilcomston.org]

Aberdeen: High Hilton (H) (01224 494717)
James M. Davies BSc BD (Interim Minister)   1982   2011   27 Buchan Drive, Newmachar, Aberdeen AB21 0NR
[E-mail: daviesjim@btinternet.com]
01651 862281
07921 023144 (Mbl)

Aberdeen: Holburn West (H) (01224 571120)
Duncan C. Eddie MA BD   1992   1999   31 Cranford Road, Aberdeen AB10 7NJ
[E-mail: dceddies@tiscali.co.uk]
01224 325873

Aberdeen: Mannofield (H) (01224 310087) (E-mail: office@mannofieldchurch.org.uk)
Keith T. Blackwood BD DipMin   1997   2007   21 Forest Avenue, Aberdeen AB15 4TU
[E-mail: minister@mannofieldchurch.org.uk]
01224 315748

Aberdeen: Mastrick (H) (01224 694121)
Elizabeth J.B. Youngson BD   1996   2011   8 Corse Wynd, Kingswells, Aberdeen AB15 8TP
[E-mail: elizabeth.youngson@btinternet.com]
01224 749346

Aberdeen: Middlefield (H)
Anita van der Wal   2008   25 Kirk Place, Cults, Aberdeen AB15 9RD
[E-mail: vanderwal@btinternet.com]
01224 865195

Aberdeen: Midstocket
Vacant

Aberdeen: New Stockethill (New Charge Development)
Ian M. Aitken MA BD   1999   52 Ashgrove Road West, Aberdeen AB16 5EE
[E-mail: ncdstockethill@uk.uumail.com]
01224 686929

Aberdeen: Northfield
Scott C. Guy BD   1989   1999   28 Byron Crescent, Aberdeen AB16 7EX
[E-mail: scott@waitrose.com]
01224 692332

Aberdeen: Queen Street (01224 643567)
Graham D.S. Deans MA BD MTh DMin   1978   2008   51 Osborne Place, Aberdeen AB25 2BX
[E-mail: graham.deans@btopenworld.com]
01224 646429

Aberdeen: Queen's Cross (H) (01224 644742)
Scott Rennie MA BD STM   1999   2009   1 St Swithin Street, Aberdeen AB10 6XH
[E-mail: minister@queenscrosschurch.org.uk]
01224 322549

Aberdeen: Rubislaw (H) (01224 645477)
Vacant
45 Rubislaw Den South, Aberdeen AB15 4BD
01224 314878

Aberdeen: Ruthrieston West (H) See Aberdeen: Garthdee

Aberdeen: St Columba's Bridge of Don (H) (01224 825653)
Louis Kinsey BD DipMin TD   1991
151 Jesmond Avenue, Aberdeen AB22 8UG
[E-mail: louis@stcolumbaschurch.org.uk]
01224 705337

Aberdeen: St George's Tillydrone (H) (01224 482204)
James Weir BD   1991   2003
127 Clifton Road, Aberdeen AB24 4RH
[E-mail: rjimw@sky.com]
01224 483976

Aberdeen: St John's Church for Deaf People (H) (01224 494566)
Vacant

Aberdeen: St Machar's Cathedral (H) (01224 485988)
Jane L. Barron (Mrs) BA DipEd BD   1999   2011
18 The Chanonry, Old Aberdeen AB24 1RQ
[E-mail: janebarron23@hotmail.com]
01224 483688

Aberdeen: St Mark's (H) (01224 640672)
Diane L. Hobson (Mrs) BA BD   2002   2010
65 Mile-end Avenue, Aberdeen AB15 5PU
[E-mail: dianehobson.rev@btinternet.com]
01224 622470

Aberdeen: St Mary's (H) (01224 487227)
Elsie J. Fortune (Mrs) BSc BD   2003
456 King Street, Aberdeen AB24 3DE
[E-mail: eric.fortune@lineone.net]
01224 633778

Aberdeen: St Nicholas Kincorth, South of
Edward C. McKenna BD DPS   1989   2002
The Manse, Kincorth Circle, Aberdeen AB12 5NX
[E-mail: eddiemckenna@uwclub.net]
01224 872820
Daniel Robertson BA BD (Assoc)   2009   2011
5 Bruce Walk, Nigg, Aberdeen AB12 3LX
[E-mail: dan_robertson100@hotmail.com]
01224 878418
07909 840654 (Mbl)

Aberdeen: St Nicholas Uniting, Kirk of (H) (01224 643494)
B. Stephen C. Taylor BA BBS MA MDiv   1984   2005
12 Louisville Avenue, Aberdeen AB15 4TX
[E-mail: minister@kirk-of-st-nicholas.org.uk]
01224 314318
01224 649242 (Fax)

Aberdeen: St Stephen's (H) (01224 624443)
Maggie Whyte BD — 2010 — 6 Belvidere Street, Aberdeen AB25 2QS
[E-mail: maggiewhyte@aol.com] — 01224 635694

Aberdeen: South Holburn (H) (01224 211730)
George S. Cowie BSc BD — 1991 2006 — 54 Woodstock Road, Aberdeen AB15 5JF
[E-mail: gscowie@aol.com] — 01224 315042

Aberdeen: Summerhill (H) (Website: www.summerhillchurch.org.uk)
Michael R.R. Shewan MA BD CPS — 1985 2010 — 36 Stronsay Drive, Aberdeen AB15 6JL
[E-mail: michaelshewan@btinternet.com] — 01224 324669

Aberdeen: Torry St Fittick's (H) (01224 899183)
Vacant — 11 Devanha Gardens East, Aberdeen AB11 7UH — 01224 588245

Aberdeen: Woodside (H) (01224 277249)
Markus Auffermann DipTheol — 1999 2006 — 322 Clifton Road, Aberdeen AB24 4HQ
[E-mail: mauffermann@yahoo.com] — 01224 484562

Bucksburn Stoneywood (H) (01224 712411)
Nigel Parker BD MTh DMin — 1994 — 25 Gilbert Road, Bucksburn, Aberdeen AB21 9AN
[E-mail: revdr.n.parker@btinternet.com] — 01224 712635

Cults (H)
Ewen J. Gilchrist BD DipMin DipComm — 1982 — 1 Cairnlee Terrace, Bieldside, Aberdeen AB15 9AE
[E-mail: ewengilchrist@btconnect.com] — 01224 861692

Dyce (H) (01224 771295)
Manson C. Merchant BD CPS — 1992 2008 — 144 Victoria Street, Dyce, Aberdeen AB21 7BE
[E-mail: mc.merchant@btinternet.com] — 01224 722380

Kingswells
Vacant — Kingswells Manse, Lang Stracht, Aberdeen AB15 8PL — 01224 740229

Newhills (H) (Tel/Fax: 01224 716161)
Hugh M. Wallace MA BD — 1980 2007 — Newhills Manse, Bucksburn, Aberdeen AB21 9SS
[E-mail: revhugh@hotmail.com] — 01224 712655

Peterculter (H) (01224 735845)

Name	Ordained		Position	Address	Phone
John A. Ferguson BD DipMin DMin	1988	1999		7 Howie Lane, Peterculter AB14 0LJ	01224 735041
				[E-mail: john.ferguson525@btinternet.com]	
Aitchison, James W. BD	1993		Chaplain: Army	84 Wakefords Park, Church Crookham, Fleet, Hampshire GU52 8EZ	
Alexander, William M. BD	1971	1998	(Berriedale and Dunbeath with Latheron)	110 Fairview Circle, Danestone, Aberdeen AB22 8YR	01224 703752
Beattie, Walter G. MA BD	1956	1995	(Arbroath: Old and Abbey)	126 Seafield Road, Aberdeen AB15 7YQ	01224 329259
Campbell, W.M.M. BD CPS	1970	2003	(Hospital Chaplain)	43 Murray Terrace, Aberdeen AB11 7SA	07761 235815
Cowie, Marian (Mrs) MA BD MTh	1990	2012	(Aberdeen: Midstocket)	54 Woodstock Road, Aberdeen AB15 5JF	01224 315042
				[E-mail: mcowieou@aol.com]	
Craig, Gordon T. BD DipMin	1998	2012	Chaplain to UK Oil and Gas Industry	c/o Total E and P (UK) plc, Altens Industrial Estate, Crawpeel Road, Aberdeen AB12 3FG	01224 297532
				[E-mail: gordon.craig@ukoilandgaschaplaincy.com]	
Crawford, Michael S.M. LTh	1966	2002	(Aberdeen: St Mary's)	9 Craigton Avenue, Aberdeen AB15 7RP	
Dick, John H.A. MA MSc BD	1982	2012	(Aberdeen: Ferryhill)	18 Fairfield Road, Kelty KY4 0BY	01224 208341
				[E-mail: jhadick01@talktalk.net]	
Dickson, A. Peter BSc BD	1996	2011	(Aberdeen: High Hilton)	24 Rosehill Drive, Aberdeen AB24 4JJ	01224 484155
				[E-mail: peter@highhilton.com]	
Douglas, Andrew M. MA	1957	1995	(Aberdeen: High Hilton)	219 Countesswells Road, Aberdeen AB15 7RD	01224 311932
Falconer, James B. BD	1982	1991	Hospital Chaplain	3 Brimmond Walk, Westhill AB32 6XH	01224 744621
Garden, Margaret J. (Miss) BD	1993	2009	(Cushnie and Tough)	26 Earns Heugh Circle, Cove Bay, Aberdeen AB12 3PY	
				[E-mail: mj.garden@btinternet.com]	
Gardner, Bruce K. MA BD PhD	1988	2011	(Aberdeen: Bridge of Don Oldmachar)	21 Hopetoun Crescent, Bucksburn, Aberdeen AB21 9QY	
				[E-mail: drbrucekgardner@aol.com]	
Goldie, George D. ALCM	1953	1995	(Aberdeen: Greyfriars)	27 Broomhill Avenue, Aberdeen AB10 6JL	01224 322503
Gordon, Laurie Y.	1960	1995	(Aberdeen: John Knox)	1 Alder Drive, Portlethen, Aberdeen AB12 4WA	01224 782703
Graham, A. David M. BA BD	1971	2005	(Aberdeen: Rosemount)	Elmhill House, 27 Shaw Crescent, Aberdeen AB25 3BT	01224 648041
Grainger, Harvey L. LTh	1975	2004	(Kingswells)	13 St Ronan's Crescent, Peterculter, Aberdeen AB14 0RL	01224 739824
				[E-mail: harveygrainger@tiscali.co.uk]	(Mbl) 07768 333216
Haddow, Angus BSc	1963	1999	(Methlick)	25 Lerwick Road, Aberdeen AB16 6RF	01224 696362
Hamilton, Helen (Miss) BD	1991	2003	(Glasgow: St James' Pollok)	The Cottage, West Tilbouries, Maryculter, Aberdeen AB12 5GD	01224 739632
Harley, Elspeth BA MTh	1991	2010	(Aberdeen: Middlefield)	8 Donmouth Road, Aberdeen AB23 8DT	01224 703017
				[E-mail: eharley@hotmail.com]	
Hutchison, Alison M. (Mrs) BD DipMin	1988	1988	Hospital Chaplain	Ashfield, Drumoak, Banchory AB31 5AG	01330 811309
				[E-mail: amhutch62@aol.com]	
Hutchison, David S. BSc BD ThM	1991	1999	(Aberdeen: Torry St Fittick's)	51 Don Street, Aberdeen AB24 1UH	01224 276122
Johnstone, William MA BD	1963	2001	(University of Aberdeen)	9/5 Mount Alvernia, Edinburgh EH16 6AW	0131-664 3140
Kerr, Hugh F. MA BD	1968	2006	(Aberdeen: Ruthrieston South)	134C Great Western Road, Aberdeen AB10 6QE	01224 580091
Lundie, Ann V. DCS			(Deaconess)	20 Langdykes Drive, Cove, Aberdeen AB12 3HW	01224 898416
				[E-mail: ann.lundie@btopenworld.com]	

Name			Address	Telephone
McCallum, Moyra (Miss) MA BD DCS		(Deaconess)	176 Hilton Drive, Aberdeen AB24 4LT [E-mail: moymac@aol.com]	01224 486240
Maciver, Norman MA BD DMin	1976 2006	(Newhills)	4 Mundi Crescent, Newmachar, Aberdeen AB21 0LY [E-mail: norirene@aol.com]	01651 869434
Main, Alan TD MA BD STM PhD DD	1963 2001	(University of Aberdeen)	Kirkfield, Barthol Chapel, Inverurie AB51 8TD [E-mail: amain@talktalk.net]	01651 806773
Montgomerie, Jean B. (Miss) MA BD	1973 2005	(Forfar: St Margaret's)	12 St Ronan's Place, Peterculter, Aberdeen AB14 0QX [E-mail: revjeanb@tiscali.co.uk]	01224 732350
Phillippo, Michael MTh BSc BVetMed MRCVS	2003	(Auxiliary Minister)	25 Deeside Crescent, Aberdeen AB15 7PT [E-mail: phillippo@btinternet.com]	01224 318317
Richardson, Thomas C. LTh ThB	1971 2004	(Cults: West)	19 Kinkell Road, Aberdeen AB15 8HR [E-mail: thomas.richardson7@btinternet.com]	01224 315328
Rodgers, D. Mark BA BD MTh	1987 2003	Hospital Chaplain	152D Gray Street, Aberdeen AB10 6JW	01224 210810
Sefton, Henry R. MA BD STM PhD	1957 1992	(University of Aberdeen)	25 Albury Place, Aberdeen AB11 6TQ	01224 572305
Sheret, Brian S. MA BD DPhil	1982 2009	(Glasgow: Drumchapel Drumry St Mary's)	59 Airyhall Crescent, Aberdeen AB15 7QS	01224 323032
Stewart, James C. MA BD STM	1960 2000	(Aberdeen: Kirk of St Nicholas)	54 Murray Terrace, Aberdeen AB11 7SB	01224 587071
Swinton, John BD PhD	1999	University of Aberdeen	51 Newburgh Circle, Bridge of Don, Aberdeen AB22 8XA [E-mail: j.swinton@abdn.ac.uk]	01224 825637
Torrance, Iain R. TD DPhil DD DTheol LHD CorrFRSE	1982 2004	President: Princeton Theological Seminary	64 Mercer Street, Princeton, NJ 08542-0803, USA [E-mail: irt@ptsem.edu]	001 609 497 7800
Watson, John M. LTh	1989 2009	(Aberdeen: St Mark's)	20 Greystone Place, Newtonhill, Stonehaven AB39 3UL [E-mail: watson-john18@sky.com]	01569 730604
Wilkie, William E. LTh	1978 2001	(Aberdeen: St Nicholas Kincorth, South of)	32 Broomfield Park, Portlethen, Aberdeen AB12 4XT	(Mbl) 07733 334380
Wilson, Andrew G.N. MA BD DMin	1977 2012	(Aberdeen: Rubislaw)	Auchintarph, Coull, Aboyne AB34 4TT [E-mail: agn.wilson@gmail.com]	01224 782052 / 01339 880918
Wilson, Thomas F. BD	1984 1996	Education	55 Allison Close, Cove, Aberdeen AB12 3WG	01224 873501
Wood, James L.K.	1967 1995	(Aberdeen: Ruthrieston West)	1 Glen Drive, Dyce, Aberdeen AB21 7EN	01224 722543

ABERDEEN ADDRESSES

Church	Address
Bridge of Don Oldmachar	Ashwood Park
Cove	Loirston Primary School, Loirston Avenue
Craigiebuckler	Springfield Road
Cults	Quarry Road, Cults
Dyce	Victoria Street, Dyce
Ferryhill	Fonthill Road x Polmuir Road
Garthdee	Ramsay Gardens
Gilcomston South	Union Street x Summer Street
High Hilton	Hilton Drive
Holburn West	Great Western Road
Kingswells	Old Skene Road, Kingswells
Mannofield	Great Western Road x Craigton Road
Mastrick	Greenfern Road
Middlefield	Manor Avenue
Midstocket	Mid Stocket Road
New Stockethill	
Northfield	Byron Crescent
Peterculter	Craigton Crescent
Queen Street	Queen Street
Queen's Cross	Albyn Place
Rubislaw	Queen's Gardens
Ruthrieston West	Broomhill Road
St Columba's	Braehead Way, Bridge of Don
St George's	Hayton Road, Tillydrone
St John's for the Deaf	at St Mark's
St Machar's	The Chanonry
St Mark's	Rosemount Viaduct
St Mary's	King Street
St Nicholas Kincorth, South of	Kincorth Circle
St Nicholas Uniting, Kirk of	Union Street
St Stephen's	Powis Place
South Holburn	Holburn Street
Summerhill	Stronsay Drive
Torry St Fittick's	Walker Road
Woodside	Church Street, Woodside

(32) KINCARDINE AND DEESIDE

Meets in various locations as arranged on the first Tuesday of September, October, November, December, March and May, and on the last Tuesday of June at 7pm.

Clerk: REV. HUGH CONKEY BSc BD — 39 St Ternans Road, Newtonhill, Stonehaven AB39 3PF — 01569 739297
[E-mail: kincardinedeeside@cofscotland.org.uk]

Aberluthnott linked with Laurencekirk (H)
Ronald Gall BSc BD — 1985 — 2001 — Aberdeen Road, Laurencekirk AB30 1AJ — 01561 378838
[E-mail: ronniegall@tiscali.co.uk]

Aboyne and Dinnet (H) (01339 886989) linked with Cromar (E-mail: aboynedinnet.cos@virgin.net)
Frank Ribbons MA BD DipEd — 1985 — 2011 — 49 Charlton Crescent, Aboyne AB34 5GN — 01339 887267
[E-mail: frankribs@gmail.com]

Arbuthnott, Bervie and Kinneff
Dennis S. Rose LTh — 1996 — 2010 — 10 Kirkburn, Inverbervie, Montrose DD10 0RT — 01561 362560
[E-mail: dennis2327@aol.co.uk]

Banchory-Devenick and Maryculter/Cookney (01224 735983) (E-mail: thechurchoffice@tiscali.co.uk)
Heather M. Peacock BSc PhD BD — 2009 — The Manse, Kirkton of Maryculter, Aberdeen AB12 5FS — 01224 730150
[E-mail: hmpeacock@btinternet.com]

Banchory-Ternan: East (H) (01330 820380) (E-mail: banchoryeastchurchoffice@btconnect.com)
Vacant

Banchory-Ternan: West (H)
Antony Stephen MA BD — 2001 — 2011 — The Manse, 2 Wilson Road, Banchory AB31 5UY — 01330 822811
[E-mail: tony@banchorywestchurch.com]

Birse and Feughside
Vacant — The Manse, Finzean, Banchory AB31 6PB

Braemar and Crathie
Kenneth I. Mackenzie BD CPS — 1990 — 2005 — The Manse, Crathie, Ballater AB35 5UL — 01339 742208
[E-mail: crathiemanse@tiscali.co.uk]

Cromar See Aboyne and Dinnet

Drumoak (H)-Durris (H)
Dolly Purnell BD
2003 2012
26 Sunnyside Drive, Drumoak, Banchory AB31 3EW
[E-mail: revdollypurnell@btinternet.com]
01330 811031

Glenmuick (Ballater) (H)
Anthony Watts BD DipTechEd JP
1999
The Manse, Craigendarroch Walk, Ballater AB35 5ZB
[E-mail: tony.watts6@btinternet.com]
01339 754014

Laurencekirk See Aberluthnott

Mearns Coastal
Colin J. Dempster BD CertMin
1990 2010
The Manse, Kirkton, St Cyrus, Montrose DD10 0BW
[E-mail: coldcoast@btinternet.com]
01674 850880

Mid Deeside
Alexander C. Wark MA BD STM
1982 2012
The Manse, Torphins, Banchory AB31 4GQ
[E-mail: alecwark@yahoo.co.uk]
01339 882276

Newtonhill
Hugh Conkey BSc BD
1987 2001
39 St Ternans Road, Newtonhill, Stonehaven AB39 3PF
[E-mail: hugh@conkey.plus.com]
01569 730143

Portlethen (H) (01224 782883)
Flora J. Munro (Mrs) BD DMin
1993 2004
18 Rowanbank Road, Portlethen, Aberdeen AB12 4NX
[E-mail: floramunro@aol.co.uk]
01224 780211

Stonehaven: Dunnottar (H) linked with Stonehaven: South (H)
Rosslyn P. Duncan BD MTh
2007
Dunnottar Manse, Stonehaven AB39 3XL
[E-mail: rpduncan@btinternet.com]
01569 762166

Stonehaven: Fetteresso (H) (01569 767689) (E-mail: fetteresso.office@btinternet.com)
Fyfe Blair BA BD DMin
1989 2009
11 South Lodge Drive, Stonehaven AB39 2PN
[E-mail: fyfeblair@talktalk.net]
01569 762876

Stonehaven: South See Stonehaven: Dunnottar

West Mearns

Catherine A. Hepburn (Miss) BA BD	1982	2000		West Mearns Parish Church Manse, Fettercairn, Laurencekirk AB30 1UE [E-mail: cahepburn@btinternet.com]	01561 340203
Brown, J.W.S. BTh	1960	1995	(Cromar)	10 Forestside Road, Banchory AB31 5ZH [E-mail: iainisobel@aol.com]	01330 824353
Cameron, Ann J. (Mrs) CerCS DCE TEFL		2005	Auxiliary Minister	Currently resident in Qatar [E-mail: anncameron2@googlemail.com]	
Christie, Andrew C. LTh	1975	2000	(Banchory-Devenick and Maryculter/Cookney)	17 Broadstraik Close, Elrick, Aberdeen AB32 6JP	01224 746888
				Little Ennochie Steading, Finzean, Banchory AB31 6LX [E-mail: johnrose.bbbb@talktalk.net]	01330 850785
Forbes, John W.A. BD	1973	1999	(Edzell Lethnot with Fern, Careston and Menmuir with Glenesk)	21 Glen Tanar, Allachburn, Low Road, Aboyne AB34 5GW	01339 886757
Kinninburgh, Elizabeth B.F. (Miss) MA BD	1970	1986	(Birse with Finzean with Strachan)	130 Denstrath Road, Edzell Woods, Brechin DD9 7XF	01356 648139
Lamb, A. Douglas MA	1964	2002	(Dalry: St Margaret's)	[E-mail: lamb.edzell@talk21.com]	
Smith, Albert E. BD	1983	2006	(Methlick)	42 Haulkerton Crescent, Laurencekirk AB30 1FB [E-mail: aesmith42@googlemail.com]	01561 376111
Taylor, Peter R. JP BD	1977	2001	(Torphins)	42 Beltie Road, Torphins, Banchory AB31 4JT [E-mail: playlor850@btinternet.com]	01339 882780
Tierney, John P. MA	1945	1985	(Peterhead West: Associate)	3 Queenshill Drive, Aboyne AB34 5DG	01339 886741
Walker, Donald K. BD	1979	2010	On secondment to Zimbabwe	St Columba's Presbyterian Church, Mutare, Zimbabwe [E-mail: donaldandjudithwalker@googlemail.com]	
Wallace, William F. BDS BD	1968	2008	(Wick: Pulteneytown and Thrumster)	Lachan Cottage, 29 Station Road, Banchory AB31 5XX [E-mail: williamwallace39@talktalk.net]	01330 822259
Watt, William D. LTh	1978	1996	(Aboyne – Dinnet)	2 West Toll Crescent, Aboyne AB34 5GB [E-mail: wdwatt22@tiscali.co.uk]	01339 886943

(33) GORDON

Meets at various locations on the first Tuesday of February, March, April, May, September, October, November and December, and on the last Tuesday of June.

Clerk:	MR GERALD MOORE	7 Allathan Park, Pitmedden, Ellon AB41 7PX [E-mail: gordon@cofscotland.org.uk]	01651 842526

Barthol Chapel linked with Tarves

Isabel C. Buchan (Mrs) BSc BD RE(PgCE)	1975	2006	8 Murray Avenue, Tarves, Ellon AB41 7LZ [E-mail: buchan.123@btinternet.com]	01651 851250

Charge / Minister			Address	Tel
Belhelvie (H) Paul McKeown BSc PhD BD	2000	2005	Belhelvie Manse, Balmedie, Aberdeen AB23 8YR [E-mail: pmckeown1@btconnect.com]	01358 742227
Blairdaff and Chapel of Garioch D. Brian Dobby MA BA	1999	2008	The Manse, Chapel of Garioch, Inverurie AB51 5HE [E-mail: briandobby@googlemail.com]	01467 681619
Cluny (H) linked with Monymusk (H) G. Euan D. Glen BSc BD	1992		The Manse, 26 St Ninian's, Monymusk, Inverurie AB51 7HF [E-mail: euan.glen_1@btinternet.com]	01467 651470
Culsalmond and Rayne linked with Daviot (H) Mary M. Cranfield (Miss) MA BD DMin	1989		The Manse, Daviot, Inverurie AB51 0HY [E-mail: marymc@ukgateway.net]	01467 671241
Cushnie and Tough (T) (H) Rosemary Legge (Mrs) BSc BD MTh	1992	2010	The Manse, Muir of Fowlis, Alford AB33 8JU [E-mail: cushnietough@aol.com]	01975 581239
Daviot See Culsalmond and Rayne				
Echt linked with Midmar (H) Alan Murray BSc BD PhD	2003		The Manse, Echt, Westhill AB32 7AB [E-mail: ladecottage@btinternet.com]	01330 860004
Ellon Stephen Emery BD DPS	2006		The Manse, 12 Union Street, Ellon AB41 9BA [E-mail: stephen.emery2@btinternet.com]	01358 720476
Fintray Kinellar Keithhall Ellen Larson Davidson BA MDiv	2007		20 Kinmohr Rise, Blackburn, Aberdeen AB21 0LJ [E-mail: larsondavidson@gmail.com]	01224 791350
Foveran W. Kenneth Pryde DA BD	1994	2009	The Manse, Foveran, Ellon AB41 6AP [E-mail: wkpryde@hotmail.com]	01358 789288

Howe Trinity
John A. Cook MA BD — 1986 — 2000 — The Manse, 110 Main Street, Alford AB33 8AD [E-mail: john.cook2@homecall.co.uk] — 01975 562282

Huntly Cairnie Glass
Thomas R. Calder LLB BD WS — 1994 — The Manse, Queen Street, Huntly AB54 8EB [E-mail: cairniechurch@aol.com] — 01466 792630

Insch-Leslie-Premnay-Oyne (H)
Jane C. Taylor (Miss) BD DipMin — 1990 — 2001 — 22 Western Road, Insch AB52 6JR [E-mail: jane.c.taylor@btinternet.com] — 01464 820914

Inverurie: St Andrew's (Website: standrewschurchinverurie.org.uk)
T. Graeme Longmuir OSJ MA BEd FASC — 1976 — 2001 — St Andrew's Manse, 1 Ury Dale, Inverurie AB51 3XW [E-mail: standrews@btinternet.com] — 01467 620468

Inverurie: West
Ian B. Groves BD CPS — 1989 — West Manse, 1 Westburn Place, Inverurie AB51 5QS [E-mail: i.groves@inveruriewestchurch.org] — 01467 620285

Kemnay
John P. Renton BA LTh — 1976 — 1990 — Kemnay, Inverurie AB51 9ND [E-mail: johnrenton@btinternet.com] — 01467 642219 (Tel/Fax)

Kintore (H)
Alan Greig BSc BD — 1977 — 1992 — 28 Oakhill Road, Kintore, Inverurie AB51 0FH [E-mail: greig@kincarr.free-online.co.uk] — 01467 632219

Meldrum and Bourtie
Alison Jaffrey (Mrs) MA BD FSAScot — 1990 — 2010 — The Manse, Urquhart Road, Oldmeldrum, Inverurie AB51 0EX [E-mail: alison@revjaffrey.com] — 01651 872250

Methlick
Matthew C. Canlis BA MDiv MLitt — 2007 — The Manse, Manse Road, Methlick, Ellon AB41 7DG [E-mail: mattcanlis@googlemail.com] — 01651 806215

Midmar (H) See Echt
Monymusk See Cluny

New Machar
Douglas G. McNab BA BD   1999 2010   The New Manse, Newmachar, Aberdeen AB21 0RD
[E-mail: dougie.mcnab@btinternet.com]   01651 862278

Noth
Regine U. Cheyne (Mrs) MA BSc BD   1988 2010   Manse of Noth, Kennethmont, Huntly AB54 4NP   01464 831690

Skene (H)
Stella Campbell MA BD   2012   The Manse, Manse Road, Kirkton of Skene, Westhill AB32 6LX
[E-mail: minister.skeneparish@mail.com]   01224 745955
Marion G. Stewart (Miss) DCS   Kirk Cottage, Kirkton of Skene, Westhill AB32 6XE   01224 743407

Strathbogie Drumblade
Neil I.M. MacGregor BD   1995   49 Deveron Park, Huntly AB54 8UZ   01466 792702

Tarves See Barthol Chapel

Udny and Pitmedden
Vacant   Manse Road, Udny Green, Udny, Ellon AB41 7RS   01651 842052

Upper Donside (H)
Brian Dingwall BTh CQSW   1999 2006   The Manse, Lumsden, Huntly AB54 4GQ
[E-mail: upperdonsideparishchurch@btinternet.com]   01464 861757

Name			Role	Address	Phone
Andrew, John MA BD DipRE DipEd	1961	1995	(Teacher: Religious Education)	Cartar's Croft, Midmar, Inverurie AB51 7NJ	01330 833208
Buchan, Alexander MA BD PGCE	1975	1992	(North Ronaldsay with Sanday)	8 Murray Avenue, Tarves, Ellon AB41 7LZ [E-mail: revabuchan@bluebucket.org]	01651 851250
Craggs, Sheila (Mrs)	2001	2008	(Auxiliary Minister)	7 Morar Court, Ellon AB41 9GG	01358 723055
Craig, Anthony J.D. BD	1987	2009	(Glasgow: Maryhill)	4 Hightown, Collieston, Ellon AB41 8RS [E-mail: craig.glasgow@gmx.net]	01358 751247
Dryden, Ian MA DipEd	1988	2001	(New Machar)	16 Glenhome Gardens, Dyce, Aberdeen AB21 7FG [E-mail: ian@idryden.freeserve.co.uk]	01224 722820
Hawthorn, Daniel MA BD DMin	1965	2004	(Belhelvie)	7 Crimond Drive, Ellon AB41 8BT [E-mail: donhawthorn@compuserve.com]	01358 723981
Jones, Robert A. LTh CA	1966	1997	(Marnoch)	13 Gordon Terrace, Inverurie AB51 4GT	01467 622691
Lyon, Andrew LTh	1971	2007	(Fraserburgh West with Rathen West)	Barmekyn, Keig, Alford AB33 8BH [E-mail: andrew@lyon60.orangehome.co.uk]	01975 562768
Macalister, Eleanor	1994	2006	(Ellon)	2 Crimond Drive, Ellon AB41 8BT [E-mail: maca1lster@aol.com]	01358 722711

Macallan, Gerald B.	1954	1992	(Kintore)	38 Thorngrove House, 500 Great Western Road, Aberdeen AB10 6PF	01224 316125
Mack, John C. JP	1985	2008	(Auxiliary Minister)	The Willows, Auchleven, Insch AB52 6QB	01464 820387
McLeish, Robert S.	1970	2000	(Insch-Leslie-Premnay-Oyne)	19 Western Road, Insch AB52 6JR	01464 820749
Rodger, Matthew A. BD	1978	1999	(Ellon)	15 Meadowlands Drive, Westhill AB32 6EJ	01224 743184
Scott, Allan D. BD	1977	1989	(Culsalmond with Daviot with Rayne)	20 Barclay Road, Inverurie AB51 3QP	01467 625161
Stewart, George C. MA	1952	1995	(Drumblade with Huntly Strathbogie)	104 Scott Drive, Huntly AB54 8PF	01466 792503
Stoddart, A. Grainger	1975	2001	(Meldrum and Bourtie)	6 Mayfield Gardens, Insch AB52 6XL	01464 821124
Thomson, Iain U. MA BD	1970	2011	(Skene)	4 Keirhill Gardens, Westhill AB32 6AZ [E-mail: iainuthomson@googlemail.com]	

(34) BUCHAN

Meets at St Kane's Centre, New Deer, Turriff on the first Tuesday of February, March, May, September, October, November and December, and on the third Tuesday of June.

| Clerk: | MR GEORGE W. BERSTAN | Faithlie, Victoria Terrace, Turriff AB53 4EE [E-mail: buchan@cofscotland.org.uk] | 01888 562392 |

Aberdour linked with Pitsligo
Vacant   The Manse, 49 Pitsligo Street, Rosehearty, Fraserburgh AB43 7JL

Auchaber United linked with Auchterless
Stephen J. Potts BA   2012   The Manse, Auchterless, Turriff AB53 8BA   01888 511058
[E-mail: stevejpotts@hotmail.co.uk]

Auchterless See Auchaber United

Banff linked with King Edward (E-mail: banffkirk@btconnect.com)
Vacant   7 Colleonard Road, Banff AB45 1DZ

Crimond linked with Lonmay
Vacant   The Manse, Crimond, Fraserburgh AB43 8QJ   01346 532431

Cruden (H)
Rodger Neilson BSc BD   1972   1974   Hatton, Peterhead AB42 0QQ   01779 841229
[E-mail: minister@crudenchurch.org.uk]

Deer (H)
Sheila M. Kirk BA LLB BD 2007 2010 The Manse, Old Deer, Peterhead AB42 5JB
[E-mail: sheilamkirk@googlemail.com] 01771 623582

Fordyce
Norman Nicoll BD 2003 2010 The Manse, 4 Seafield Terrace, Portsoy, Banff AB45 2QB
[E-mail: fordycechurch@btinternet.com] 01261 842272

Fraserburgh: Old
Peter B. Park BD MCIBS 1997 2007 4 Robbies Road, Fraserburgh AB43 7AF
[E-mail: peterpark9@btinternet.com] 01346 515332

Fraserburgh: South (H) linked with Inverallochy and Rathen: East
Ronald F. Yule 1982 15 Victoria Street, Fraserburgh AB43 9PJ 01346 518244

Fraserburgh: West (H) linked with Rathen: West
Carol Anne Parker (Mrs) BEd BD 2009 4 Kirkton Gardens, Fraserburgh AB43 8TU
[E-mail: ca.parker76@btinternet.com] 01346 513303

Fyvie linked with Rothienorman
Robert J. Thorburn BD 1978 2004 The Manse, Fyvie, Turriff AB53 8RD
[E-mail: rjthorburn@aol.com] 01651 891230

Gardenstown
Donald N. Martin BD 1996 The Manse, Fernie Brae, Gardenstown, Banff AB45 3YL
[E-mail: ferniebrae@gmail.com] 01261 851256

Inverallochy and Rathen: East See Fraserburgh: South
King Edward See Banff

Longside
Robert A. Fowlie BD 2007 9 Anderson Drive, Longside, Peterhead AB42 4XG
[E-mail: bob.fowlie@googlemail.com] 01779 821224

Lonmay See Crimond

Macduff
Calum Stark LLB BD — 2011 — Sol-y-Mar, Bath Street, Macduff AB44 1SA [E-mail: calumstark@yahoo.co.uk] — 01261 832316

Marnoch
Vacant — Marnoch Manse, 53 South Street, Aberchirder, Huntly AB54 7TS

Maud and Savoch linked with New Deer: St Kane's
Paul R. Read BSc MA(Th) — 2000 2010 — The Manse, New Deer, Turriff AB53 6TD [E-mail: prr747@aol.com] — 01771 644216

Monquhitter and New Byth linked with Turriff: St Andrew's
James Cook MA MDiv — 1999 2002 — Balmellie Road, Turriff AB53 4SP [E-mail: jmscook9@aol.com] — 01888 560304

New Deer: St Kane's See Maud and Savoch

New Pitsligo linked with Strichen and Tyrie
Andrew Fothergill BA — 2012 — Kingsville, Strichen, Fraserburgh AB43 6SQ [E-mail: andrewfothergill@btinternet.com] — 01771 637635

Ordiquhill and Cornhill (H) linked with Whitehills
W. Myburgh Verster BA BTh LTh MTh — 1981 — 6 Craigneen Place, Whitehills, Banff AB45 2NE [E-mail: wverster8910@btinternet.com] — 01261 861317

Peterhead: Old
Gordon A. McCracken BD CertMin DMin — 1988 2012 — 1 Hawthorn Road, Peterhead AB42 2DW [E-mail: gordonangus@btopenworld.com] — 01779 472618
(Interim Minister)

Peterhead: St Andrew's (H)
Abi T. Ngunga GTh LTh MDiv MTh PhD — 2001 2011 — 1 Landale Road, Peterhead AB42 1QN [E-mail: abi.t.ngunga@gmail.com] — 01779 238200

Peterhead: Trinity
Vacant — 18 Landale Road, Peterhead AB42 1QP

Pitsligo See Aberdour
Rathen: West See Fraserburgh: West
Rothienorman See Fyvie

St Fergus
Jeffrey Tippner BA MDiv MCS   1991 2012   26 Newton Road, St Fergus, Peterhead AB42 3DD   01779 838287

Sandhaven
Vacant

Strichen and Tyrie See New Pitsligo
Turriff: St Andrew's See Monquhitter and New Byth

Turriff: St Ninian's and Forglen
Kevin R. Gruer BSc BA   2011   4 Deveronside Drive, Turriff AB53 4SP   01888 563850
[E-mail: kevin@gruer.co.uk]

Whitehills See Ordiquhill and Cornhill

Name				Address	Telephone
Blakie, James BD	1972	1997	(Berwick-on-Tweed: St Andrew's Wallace Green and Lowick)	57 Glenugie View, Peterhead AB42 2BW	01779 490625
Coutts, Fred MA BD	1973	1989	(Hospital Chaplain)	Ladebank, 1 Manse Place, Hatton, Peterhead AB42 0UQ	01779 841320
Fawkes, G.M. Allan BA BSc JP	1979	2000	(Lonmay with Rathen: West)	3 Northfield Gardens, Hatton, Peterhead AB42 0SW	01779 841814
McClenaghan, L. Paul BA	1973	2011	(Peterhead: Trinity)	4 Glendale Gardens, Randalstown, Co. Antrim BT41 3EJ [E-mail: paul.mcclenaghan@gmail.com]	02894 478545
McKay, Margaret MA BD MTh	1991	2003	(Auchaber United with Auchterless)	The Smithy, Knowes of Elrick, Aberchirder, Huntly AB54 7PN [E-mail: elricksmithy@yahoo.co.uk]	(Tel) 01466 780208 (Fax) 01466 780015
McMillan, William J. CA LTh BD	1969	2004	(Sandsting and Aithsting with Walls and Sandness)	7 Ardinn Drive, Turriff AB53 4PR [E-mail: revbillymcmillan@aol.com]	01888 560727
Macnee, Iain LTh BD MA PhD	1975	2011	(New Pitsligo with Strichen and Tyrie)	Wardend Cottage, Alvah, Banff AB45 3TR [E-mail: macneeiain4@googlemail.com]	01261 815647
Noble, George S. DipTh	1972	2000	(Carfin with Newarthill)	Craigowan, 3 Main Street, Inverallochy, Fraserburgh AB43 8XX	01346 582749
Ross, David S. MSc PhD BD	1978	2003	Prison Chaplain Service	3–5 Abbey Street, Old Deer, Peterhead AB42 5LN [E-mail: padsross@btinternet.com]	01771 623994
van Sittert, Paul BA BD	1997	2011	Chaplain: Army	1 Bn The Royal Regiment of Scotland, Dreghorn Barracks, Edinburgh EH13 9QW [E-mail: vansittert@btinternet.com]	

(35) MORAY

Meets at St Andrew's-Lhanbryd and Urquhart on the first Tuesday of February, March, May, September, October, November and December, and at the Moderator's church on the fourth Tuesday of June.

Clerk: REV. HUGH M.C. SMITH LTh   Mortlach Manse, Dufftown, Keith AB55 4AR
[E-mail: moray@cofscotland.org.uk]
[E-mail: clerk@moraypresbytery.plus.com]   01340 820538

Aberlour (H)
Shuna M. Dicks BSc BD   2010   The Manse, Mary Avenue, Aberlour AB38 9QU
[E-mail: revshuna@minister.com]   01340 871687

Alves and Burghead linked with Kinloss and Findhorn
Vacant   The Manse, 4 Manse Road, Kinloss, Forres IV36 3GH   01309 690931

Bellie linked with Speymouth
Alison C. Mehigan BD DPS   2003   11 The Square, Fochabers IV32 7DG
[E-mail: alisonc@mehigan-ug.fsnet.co.uk]   01343 820256
Margaret King MA DCS   2007   56 Murrayfield, Fochabers IV32 7EZ   01343 820937

Birnie and Pluscarden linked with Elgin High
Vacant   Daisy Bank, 5 Forteath Avenue, Elgin IV30 1TQ   01343 542449

Buckie: North (H) linked with Rathven
Vacant   14 St Peter's Road, Buckie AB56 1DL   01542 831328

Buckie: South and West (H) linked with Enzie
Alan Macgregor BA BD PhD   1992   2010   Craigendarroch, 14 Cliff Terrace, Buckie AB56 1LX
[E-mail: buckiesouwester@btconnect.com]
[E-mail: enziekirk@btconnect.com]   01542 833775

Cullen and Deskford (Website: www.cullen-deskford-church.org.uk)
Douglas F. Stevenson BD DipMin   1991   2010   3 Seafield Place, Cullen, Buckie AB56 4UU
[E-mail: dstevenson655@btinternet.com]   01542 841963

Dallas linked with Forres: St Leonard's (H) linked with Rafford
Donald K. Prentice BSc BD   1989   2010   St Leonard's Manse, Nelson Road, Forres IV36 1DR   01309 672380

Duffus, Spynie and Hopeman (H)
Vacant — The Manse, Duffus, Elgin IV30 5QP — 01343 830276

Dyke linked with Edinkillie
John Macgregor BD — 2001 2011 — Manse of Dyke, Brodie, Forres IV36 2TD — 01309 641239

Edinkillie See Dyke
Elgin: High See Birnie and Pluscarden

Elgin: St Giles' (H) and St Columba's South (01343 551501) (E-mail: julie@elginstgandcsth.plus.com)
(Office: Williamson Hall, Duff Avenue, Elgin IV30 1QS)
Vacant — 18 Reidhaven Street, Elgin IV30 1QH — 01343 547208
Anne Attenburrow BSc MB ChB (Aux) — 2006 2008 — 4 Jock Inksons Brae, Elgin IV30 1QE — 01343 552330

Enzie See Buckie: South and West

Findochty linked with Portknockie
Vacant — 20 Netherton Terrace, Findochty, Buckie AB56 4QD — 01542 833484

Forres: St Laurence (H)
Barry J. Boyd LTh DPS — 1993 — 12 Mackenzie Drive, Forres IV36 2JP [E-mail: barryj.boydstlaurence@btinternet.com] — 01309 672260 / 07778 731018 (Mbl)

Forres: St Leonard's See Dallas

Keith: North, Newmill, Boharm and Rothiemay (H) (01542 886390)
G. Hutton B. Steel MA BD — 1982 2010 — North Manse, Church Road, Keith AB55 5BR [E-mail: hsteel57@btinternet.com] — 01542 882559

Keith: St Rufus, Botriphnie and Grange (H)
Ranald S.R. Gauld MA LLB BD — 1991 1995 — Church Road, Keith AB55 5BR [E-mail: rev_gauld@btinternet.com] — 01542 882799
Kay Gauld (Mrs) BD STM PhD (Assoc) — 1999 — Church Road, Keith AB55 5BR [E-mail: kay_gauld@btinternet.com] — 01542 882799

Kinloss and Findhorn See Alves and Burghead

Knockando, Elchies and Archiestown (H) linked with Rothes (Website: www.moraykirk.co.uk)
Robert J.M. Anderson BD FInstLM   1993   2000   The Manse, Rothes, Aberlour AB38 7AF   01340 831381
[E-mail: robert@carmanse.freeserve.co.uk]

Lossiemouth: St Gerardine's High (H)
Vacant   The Manse, St Gerardine's Road, Lossiemouth IV31 6RA   01343 813146

Lossiemouth: St James'
Graham W. Crawford BSc BD STM   1991   2003   The Manse, Prospect Terrace, Lossiemouth IV31 6JS   01343 810676
[E-mail: pictishreiver@aol.com]

Mortlach and Cabrach (H)
Hugh M.C. Smith LTh   1973   1982   Mortlach Manse, Dufftown, Keith AB55 4AR   01340 820380
[E-mail: clerk@moraypresbytery.plus.com]

Pluscarden See Birnie
Portknockie See Findochty
Rafford See Dallas
Rathven See Buckie: North
Rothes See Knockando, Elchies and Archiestown

St Andrew's-Lhanbryd (H) and Urquhart
Andrew J. Robertson BD   2008   2010   39 St Andrews Road, Lhanbryde, Elgin IV30 8PU   01343 843995
[E-mail: ajr247@btinternet.com]

Speymouth See Bellie

Bain, Brian LTh   1980 2007   (Gask with Methven and Logiealmond)   Bayview, 13 Stewart Street, Portgordon, Buckie AB56 5QT   01542 831215
Davidson, A.A.B. MA BD   1960 1997   (Grange with Rothiemay)   11 Sutors Rise, Nairn IV12 5BU
Douglas, Christina A. (Mrs)   1987 1993   (Inveraven and Glenlivet)   White Cottage, St Fillans, Crieff PH6 2ND
Evans, John W. MA BD   1945 1984   (Elgin: High)   15 Weaver Place, Elgin IV30 1HB   01343 543607
Lawrie, Bruce B. BD   1974 2012   (Duffus, Spynie and Hopeman)   5 Thorncroft, Scotts Place, Selkirk TD7 4LN
[E-mail: blawrie@zetnet.co.uk]
Mathew, J. Gordon MA BD   1973 2011   (Buckie: North)   2 Mallard Drive, Montrose DD10 9ND   01674 671310
Morton, Alasdair J. MA BD DipEd FEIS   1960 2000   (Bowden with Newtown)   16 St Leonard's Road, Forres IV36 1DW   01309 671719
[E-mail: alasgilmor@hotmail.co.uk]

Morton, Gillian M. (Mrs) MA BD PGCE	1983	1996	(Hospital Chaplain)	16 St Leonard's Road, Forres IV36 1DW [E-mail: alasgilmor@hotmail.co.uk]	01309 671719
Munro, Sheila BD	1995	2003	Chaplain: RAF	RAF Lossiemouth, Elgin IV31 6SD [E-mail: sheila.munro781@halton.raf.mod.uk]	
Poole, Ann McColl (Mrs) DipEd ACE LTh	1983	2003	(Dyke with Edinkillie)	Kirkside Cottage, Dyke, Forres IV36 2TF	01309 641046
Rollo, George B. BD	1974	2010	(Elgin: St Giles' and St Columba's South)	'Struan', 13 Meadow View, Hopeman, Elgin IV30 5PL [E-mail: rollos@gmail.com]	01343 835226
Scotland, Ronald J. BD	1993	2003	(Birnie with Pluscarden)	7A Rose Avenue, Elgin IV30 1NX	01343 543086
Shaw, Duncan LTh CPS	1984	2011	(Alves and Burghead with Kinloss and Findhorn)		
Wright, David L. MA BD	1957	1998	(Stornoway: St Columba)	73 Woodside Drive, Forres IV36 0UF	01667 451613
Thomson, James M. BA	1952	2000	(Elgin: St Giles' and St Columba's South: Associate)	84 Wyvis Drive, Nairn IV12 4TP	01343 547664
Whittaker, Mary	2011		Auxiliary Minister	48 Mayne Road, Elgin IV30 1PD 11 Templand Road, Lhanbryde, Elgin IV30 8BR	
Whyte, David LTh	1993	2011	(Boat of Garten, Duthil and Kincardine)	1 Lemanfield Crescent, Garmouth, Fochabers IV32 7LS [E-mail: whytedj@btinternet.com]	01343 870667

(36) ABERNETHY

Meets at Boat of Garten on the first Tuesday of February, March, April, June, September, October, November and December.

| Clerk: | MRS CATHERINE A. BUCHAN MA MDiv | The Manse, Fort William Road, Newtonmore PH20 1DG [E-mail: abernethy@cofscotland.org.uk] | 01540 673238 |

Abernethy (H) linked with Cromdale (H) and Advie
Vacant
The Manse, Nethy Bridge PH25 3DG — 01479 821280

Alvie and Insh (T) (H) linked with Rothiemurchus and Aviemore (H)
Ron C. Whyte BD CPS   1990   2007   The Manse, 8 Dalfaber Park, Aviemore PH22 1QF [E-mail: ron4xst@aol.com] — 01479 810280

Boat of Garten (H), Duthil (H) and Kincardine
Vacant
Sheila Wallace (Mrs) DCS BA BD (Locum Deacon)   The Manse, Deshar Road, Boat of Garten PH24 3BN [E-mail: sheilad.wallace@virgin.net] — 01479 831252

Cromdale and Advie See Abernethy

Dulnain Bridge (H) linked with Grantown-on-Spey (H)
Morris Smith BD   1988   The Manse, Golf Course Road, Grantown-on-Spey PH26 3HY   01479 872084
[E-mail: mosmith.themanse@btinternet.com]

Grantown-on-Spey See Dulnain Bridge

Kingussie (H)
Vacant   The Manse, 18 Hillside Avenue, Kingussie PH21 1PA   01540 661311

Laggan linked with Newtonmore (H)
Catherine A. Buchan (Mrs) MA MDiv   2002 2009   The Manse, Fort William Road, Newtonmore PH20 1DG   01540 673238
[E-mail: catherinebuchan567@btinternet.com]

Newtonmore See Laggan
Rothiemurchus and Aviemore (H) See Alvie and Insh

Tomintoul (H), Glenlivet and Inveraven
Vacant   The Manse, Tomintoul, Ballindalloch AB37 9HA   01807 580254

Bardgett, Frank D. MA BD PhD   1987 2001   (Board of National Mission)   Tigh an Iasgair, Street of Kincardine, Boat of Garten PH24 3BY   01479 831751
[E-mail: tigh@bardgett.plus.com]

Bjarnason, Sven S. CandTheol   1975 2011   (Tomintoul, Glenlivet and Inveraven)   14 Edward Street, Dunfermline KY12 0JW   01383 724625
[E-mail: sven@bjarnason.org.uk]

MacEwan, James A.I. MA BD   1973 2012   (Abernethy with Cromdale and Advie)   59 Achilles Road, Engadine, NSW 2233, Australia
[E-mail: wurrus@hotmail.co.uk]

Pickering, John M. BSc BD DipEd   1997 2010   (Dundee: Mains)   Oriole House, Ardbroilach Road, Kingussie PH21 1JY

Ritchie, Christine A.Y. (Mrs) BD DipMin   2002 2012   (Braes of Rannoch with Foss and Rannoch)   25 Beachen Court, Grantown-on-Spey PH26 3JD   01479 873419
[E-mail: cayritchie@btinternet.com]

(37) INVERNESS

Meets at Inverness, in Inverness: Trinity, on the first Tuesday of February, March, April, May, September, October, November and December, and at the Moderator's church on the fourth Tuesday of June.

Clerk: REV. REGINALD F. CAMPBELL BD DipChEd The Manse, Daviot, Inverness IV2 5XL 01463 772242
[E-mail: inverness@cofscotland.org.uk]

Ardersier (H) linked with Petty
Alexander Whiteford LTh 1996 Ardersier, Inverness IV2 7SX 01667 462224
[E-mail: a.whiteford@ukonline.co.uk]

Auldearn and Dalmore linked with Nairn: St Ninian's
Richard Reid BSc BD MTh 1991 2005 The Manse, Auldearn, Nairn IV12 5SX 01667 451675

Cawdor (H) linked with Croy and Dalcross (H)
Janet S. Mathieson MA BD 2003 The Manse, Croy, Inverness IV2 5PH 01667 493217
[E-mail: mathieson173@btinternet.com]

Croy and Dalcross See Cawdor

Culloden: The Barn (H)
James H. Robertson BSc BD 1975 1994 45 Oakdene Court, Culloden IV2 7XL 01463 790504
07595 465838 (Mbl)
[E-mail: jim.robertson@barnchurch.org.uk]

Daviot and Dunlichity linked with Moy, Dalarossie and Tomatin
Reginald F. Campbell BD DipChEd 1979 2003 The Manse, Daviot, Inverness IV2 5XL 01463 772242
[E-mail: campbell578@talktalk.net]

Dores and Boleskine
Vacant

Inverness: Crown (H) (01463 238929)
Peter H. Donald MA PhD BD 1991 1998 39 Southside Road, Inverness IV2 4XA 01463 230537
[E-mail: pdonald7@aol.com]

Charge / Minister		Address	Tel
Inverness: Dalneigh and Bona (GD) (H) Andrew A. McMillan BD	2012	9 St Mungo Road, Inverness IV3 5AS	01463 232339
Inverness: East (H) Andrew T.B. McGowan (Prof.) BD STM PhD	1979 2009	2 Victoria Drive, Inverness IV2 3QD [E-mail: atbmcgowan@gmail.com]	01463 238770
Inverness: Hilton Duncan MacPherson LLB BD	1994	66 Culduthel Mains Crescent, Inverness IV2 6RG [E-mail: duncan@hiltonchurch.org.uk]	01463 231417
Inverness: Inshes (H) Vacant		48 Redwood Crescent, Milton of Leys, Inverness IV2 6HB	01463 772402
Inverness: Kinmylies (H) Vacant		2 Balnafettack Place, Inverness IV3 8TQ	01463 709893
Inverness: Ness Bank (T) (H) Fiona E. Smith (Mrs) LLB BD	2010	15 Ballifeary Road, Inverness IV3 5PJ [E-mail: fiona.denhead@btopenworld.com]	01463 234653
Inverness: Old High St Stephen's Peter W. Nimmo BD ThM	1996 2004	24 Damfield Road, Inverness IV2 3HU [E-mail: peternimmo@minister.com]	01463 250802
Inverness: St Columba (New Charge) (H) Vacant		20 Bramble Close, Inverness IV2 6BS	
Inverness: Trinity (H) Alistair Murray BD	1984 2004	60 Kenneth Street, Inverness IV3 5PZ [E-mail: a.murray111@btinternet.com]	01463 234756
Kilmorack and Erchless Edgar J. Ogston BSc BD	1976 2007	'Roselynn', Croyard Road, Beauly IV4 7DJ [E-mail: edgar.ogston@macfish.com]	01463 782260
Kiltarlity linked with Kirkhill Vacant			
Kirkhill See Kiltarlity			

Moy, Dalarossie and Tomatin See Daviot and Dunlichity

Nairn: Old (H)
Vacant

3 Manse Road, Nairn IV12 4RN
01667 452203

Nairn: St Ninian's (H) See Auldearn and Dalmore

Petty See Ardersier

Urquhart and Glenmoriston (H)
Hugh F. Watt BD DPS   1986 1996   Blairbeg, Drummadrochit, Inverness IV3 6UG
[E-mail: hw@tinyworld.co.uk]
01456 450231

Name			Position	Address	Phone
Black, Archibald T. BSc	1964	1997	(Inverness: Ness Bank)	16 Elm Park, Inverness IV2 4WN	01463 230588
Brown, Derek G. BD DipMin DMin	1989	1994	Chaplain: NHS Highland	Cathedral Manse, Cnoc-an-Lobht, Dornoch IV25 3HN [E-mail: revsbrown@aol.com]	01862 810296
Buell, F. Bart BA MDiv	1980	1995	(Urquhart and Glenmoriston)	6 Towerhill Place, Cradlehall, Inverness IV2 5FN	01463 794634
Chisholm, Archibald F. MA	1957	1997	(Braes of Rannoch with Foss and Rannoch)	32 Seabank Road, Nairn IV12 4EU	01667 452001
Christie, James LTh	1993	2003	(Dores and Boleskine)	20 Wester Inshes Crescent, Inverness IV2 5HL	01463 710534
Fraser, Jonathan MA(Div) MTh ThM		2012	Associate: Inverness: Hilton	20 Moy Terrace, Inverness IV2 4EL [E-mail: jonathan@hiltonchurch.org.uk]	01463 711609 (Home) 01463 233310 (Work)
Frizzell, R. Stewart BD	1961	2000	(Wick: Old)	98 Boswell Road, Inverness IV2 3EW	01463 231907
Hunt, Trevor G. BA BD	1986	2011	(Evie with Firth with Rendall)	7 Woodville Court, Culduthel Avenue, Inverness IV2 6BX [E-mail: revorghunt@yahoo.co.uk]	01463 250355 07753 423333 (Mbl)
Jeffrey, Stewart D. BSc BD	1962	1997	(Banff with King Edward)	10 Grigor Drive, Inverness IV2 4LP [E-mail: stewart.jeffrey@talktalk.net]	01463 230085
Lacey, Eric R. BD	1971	1992	(Creich with Rosehall)	78 Laggan Road, Inverness IV2 4EW	01463 235006
Livesley, Anthony LTh	1979	1997	(Kiltearn)	87 Beech Avenue, Nairn IV12 5SX [E-mail: a.livesley@tesco.net]	01667 455126
Logan, Robert J.V. MA BD	1962	2001	(Abdie and Dunbog with Newburgh)	Lindores, 1 Murray Place, Smithton, Inverness IV2 7PX [E-mail: rjvlogan@btinternet.com]	01463 790226
Macdonald, Aonghas I. MA BD	1967	2007	(Inverness: East)	41 Castlehill Park, Inverness IV2 5GJ [E-mail: aonghas@ukonline.co.uk]	01463 792275
Mackenzie, Seoras L. BD	1996	1998	Chaplain: Army	3 Bn The Black Watch, The Royal Regiment of Scotland, Fort George, Ardersier, Inverness IV1 2TD	
Macritchie, Iain A.M. BSc BD STM PhD	1987	1998	Chaplain: Inverness Hospitals	7 Merlin Crescent, Inverness IV2 3TE	01463 235204
Malcolm, Alistair BD DPS	1976	2012	(Inverness: Inshes)	11 Kinclaven Gardens, Murthly, Perth PH1 4EX [E-mail: amalcolm067@btinternet.com]	01738 710979
Mitchell, Joyce (Mrs) DCS		1994	(Deacon)	Sunnybank, Farr, Inverness IV2 6XG [E-mail: joyce@mitchell71.freeserve.co.uk]	01808 521285

Morrison, Hector BSc BD MTh	1981	1994	Principal: Highland Theological College	24 Oak Avenue, Inverness IV2 4NX	01463 238561
Rettie, James A. BTh	1981	1999	(Melness and Eriboll with Tongue)	2 Trantham Drive, Westhill, Inverness IV2 5QT	01463 798896
Robb, Rodney P.T.	1995	2004	(Stirling: St Mark's)	2A Mayfield Road, Inverness IV2 4AE	
Robertson, Fergus A. MA BD	1971	2010	(Inverness: Dalneigh and Bona)	16 Druid Temple Way, Inverness IV2 6UQ	01463 718462
Stirling, G. Alan S. MA	1960	1999	(Leochel Cushnie and Lynturk with Tough)	97 Lochlann Road, Culloden, Inverness IV2 7HJ	01463 798313
Turner, Fraser K. LTh	1994	2007	(Kiltarlity with Kirkhill)	[E-mail: fraseratq@yahoo.co.uk]	
Waugh, John L. LTh	1973	2002	(Ardclach with Auldearn and Dalmore)	58 Wyvis Drive, Nairn IV12 4TP	(Tel/Fax) 01667 456397
				[E-mail: jswaugh@care4free.net]	
Wilson, Ian M.	1988	1993	(Cawdor with Croy and Dalcross)	17 Spires Crescent, Nairn IV12 5PZ	01667 452977
Younger, Alastair S. BScEcon ASCC	1969	2008	(Inverness: St Columba High)	33 Duke's View, Slackbuie, Inverness IV2 6BB	01463 242873
				[E-mail: younger873@btinternet.com]	

INVERNESS ADDRESSES

Inverness

Crown	Kingsmills Road x Midmills Road
Dalneigh and Bona	St Mary's Avenue
East	Academy Street x Margaret Street
Hilton	Druid Road x Tomatin Road
Inshes	Inshes Retail Park
Kinmylies	Kinmylies Way
Ness Bank	Ness Bank x Castle Road
St Stephen's	Old Edinburgh Road x Southside Road
The Old High	Church Street x Church Lane
Trinity	Huntly Place x Upper Kessock Street

Nairn

Old	Academy Street x Seabank Road
St Ninian's	High Street x Queen Street

(38) LOCHABER

Meets at Caol, Fort William, in Kilmallie Church Hall at 6pm, on the first Tuesday of September and December, on the last Tuesday of October and on the fourth Tuesday of March. The June meeting is held at 6pm on the first Tuesday in the church of the incoming Moderator.

Clerk:	MRS ELLA GILL	5 Camus Inas, Acharacle PH36 4JQ	01967 431834
		[E-mail: lochaber@cofscotland.org.uk]	
Treasurer:	MRS PAT WALKER	Tigh a' Chlann, Inverroy, Roy Bridge PH31 4AQ	01397 712028
		[E-mail: pw-15@tiscali.co.uk]	

Acharacle (H) linked with Ardnamurchan

Fiona Ogg (Mrs) BA BD	2012	The Manse, Acharacle PH36 4JU	01967 431638
		[E-mail: fionaogg@gmail.com]	

Ardgour and Kingairloch linked with Morvern linked with Strontian
Donald G.B. McCorkindale BD DipMin   1992   2011   The Manse, 2 The Meadows, Strontian, Acharacle PH36 4HZ   01967 402234
[E-mail: donald.mccorkindale@sky.com]
[E-mail: donald@aksm.org.uk]

Ardnamurchan See Acharacle

Duror (H) linked with Glencoe: St Munda's (H) (T)
Moira Herkes BD (Interim Minister)   1985   2012   The Manse, Ballachulish PH49 4JG   01855 811878
[E-mail: mossherkes@btinternet.com]

Fort Augustus linked with Glengarry
Tabea Baader   2012   The Manse, Fort Augustus PH32 4BH   01320 366210
[E-mail: tabeabaader@gmx.de]

Fort William: Duncansburgh MacIntosh (H) linked with Kilmonivaig
Adrian P.J. Varwell BA BD PhD   1983   2012   19 Enrick Crescent, Kilmore, Drumnadrochit, Inverness IV63 6TP   01456 459352
(Interim Minister)   [E-mail: adrian.varwell@btinternet.com]

Glencoe: St Munda's See Duror
Glengarry See Fort Augustus

Kilmallie
Richard T. Corbett BSc MSc PhD BD   1992   2005   Kilmallie Manse, Corpach, Fort William PH33 7JS   01397 772736
[E-mail: richard.t.corbett@btinternet.com]

Kilmonivaig See Fort William: Duncansburgh MacIntosh

Kinlochleven (H) linked with Nether Lochaber (H)
Malcolm A. Kinnear MA BD PhD   2010   The Manse, Lochaber Road, Kinlochleven PH50 4QW   01855 831227
[E-mail: malcolmkinnear@live.co.uk]

Morvern See Ardgour
Nether Lochaber See Kinlochleven

North West Lochaber
Vacant   Church of Scotland Manse, Mallaig PH41 4RG   01687 462816

Strontian See Ardgour

Anderson, David M. MSc FCOptom	1984	Ordained Local Minister	'Mirlos', 1 Dumfries Place, Fort William PH33 6UQ [E-mail: david@mirlos.co.uk]	01397 702091
Lamb, Alan H.W. BA MTh	1959 2005	(Associate Minister)	Smiddy House, Arisaig PH39 4NH [E-mail: h.a.lamb@handalamb.plus.com]	01687 450227
MacQuarrie, Donald A. BSc BD	1979 2012	(Fort William: Duncansburgh MacIntosh with Kilmonivaig)	Parkfield, 7 Glasdrum Grove, Fort William PH33 6DE [E-mail: pdmacq@ukgateway.net]	01397 698265
Rae, Peter C. BSc BD	1968 2000	(Beath and Cowdenbeath: North)	8 Wether Road, Great Cambourne, Cambridgeshire CB23 5DT [E-mail: rae.fairview@btinternet.com]	01954 710079
Winning, A. Ann MA DipEd BD	1984 2006	(Morvern)	'Westering', 13C Carnoch, Glencoe, Ballachulish PH49 4HQ [E-mail: awinning009@btinternet.com]	01855 811929

LOCHABER Communion Sundays Please consult the Presbytery website: www.cofslochaber.co.uk

(39) ROSS

Meets on the first Tuesday of September in the church of the incoming Moderator, and in Dingwall: Castle Street Church on the first Tuesday of October, November, December, February, March and May, and on the last Tuesday of June.

Clerk:	**MR RONALD W. GUNSTONE BSc**	**20 Bellfield Road, North Kessock, Inverness IV1 3XU** **[E-mail: ross@cofscotland.org.uk]**	**01463 731337**

Alness

Ronald Morrison BD	1996		27 Darroch Brae, Alness IV17 0SD [E-mail: ranald@rmorrison.plus.com]	01349 882238

Avoch linked with Fortrose and Rosemarkie

Alan T. McKean BD CertMin	1982 2010		5 Nessway, Fortrose IV10 8SS [E-mail: a.mckean2345@btinternet.com]	01381 621433

Contin (H) linked with Fodderty and Strathpeffer (H)

Vacant		The Manse, Contin, Strathpeffer IV14 9ES	01997 423296

Cromarty linked with Resolis and Urquhart

Vacant		The Manse, Culbokie, Dingwall IV7 8JN	01349 877452

Dingwall: Castle Street (H) Bruce Ritchie BSc BD PhD	1977	2006	16 Achany Road, Dingwall IV15 9JB [E-mail: brucezomba@hotmail.com]	01349 867315
Dingwall: St Clement's (H) Russel Smith BD	1994		8 Castlehill Road, Dingwall IV15 9PB [E-mail: russel@stclementschurch.fsnet.co.uk]	01349 861011
Fearn Abbey and Nigg linked with Tarbat David V. Scott BTh	1994	2006	Church of Scotland Manse, Fearn, Tain IV20 1TN	01862 832626 (Tel/Fax)
Ferintosh Andrew F. Graham BTh DPS	2001	2006	Ferintosh Manse, Leanaig Road, Conon Bridge, Dingwall IV7 8BE [E-mail: afg1960@tiscali.co.uk]	01349 861275
Fodderty and Strathpeffer (H) See Contin **Fortrose and Rosemarkie** See Avoch				
Invergordon Kenneth Donald Macleod BD CPS	1989	2000	The Manse, Cromlet Drive, Invergordon IV18 0BA [E-mail: kd-macleod@tiscali.co.uk]	01349 852273
Killearnan (H) linked with Knockbain (H) Iain Ramsden BTh	1999		The Church of Scotland Manse, Coldwell Road, Artafallie, North Kessock, Inverness IV1 3ZE [E-mail: s4rev@sky.com]	01463 731333
Kilmuir and Logie Easter Fraser M.C. Stewart BSc BD	1980	2011	Delny, Invergordon IV18 0NW [E-mail: fraserstewart1955@hotmail.com]	01862 842280
Kiltearn (H) Donald A. MacSween BD	1991	1998	The Manse, Swordale Road, Evanton, Dingwall IV16 9UZ [E-mail: donaldmacsween@hotmail.com]	01349 830472
Knockbain See Killearnan				

Lochbroom and Ullapool (GD)
Vacant — The Manse, Garve Road, Ullapool IV26 2SX — 01854 612050

Resolis and Urquhart See Cromarty

Rosskeen
Robert Jones BSc BD — 1990 — Rosskeen Manse, Perrins Road, Alness IV17 0SX [E-mail: rob2jones@btinternet.com] — 01349 882265

Tain
Vacant — 14 Kingsway Avenue, Tain IV19 1NJ — 01862 894140

Tarbat See Fearn Abbey and Nigg

Urray and Kilchrist
Scott Polworth LLB BD — 2009 — The Manse, Corrie Road, Muir of Ord IV6 7TL [E-mail: scottpolworth@btinternet.com] — 01463 870259

Name			Address	Telephone
Buchan, John BD MTh	1968	1993	(Fodderty and Strathpeffer) 'Faithlie', 45 Swanston Avenue, Inverness IV3 6QW	01463 713114
Dupar, Kenneth W. BA BD PhD	1965	1993	(Christ's College, Aberdeen) The Old Manse, The Causeway, Cromarty IV11 8XJ	01381 600428
Forsyth, James LTh	1970	2000	(Fearn Abbey with Nigg Chapelhill) Rhives Lodge, Golspie, Sutherland KW10 6DD	
Glass, Alexander OBE MA	1998	2009	(Auxiliary Minister) Craigton, Tulloch Avenue, Dingwall IV15 9TU	01349 863258
Holroyd, Gordon BTh FPhS FSAScot	1959	1993	(Dingwall: St Clement's) 22 Stuarthill Drive, Maryburgh, Dingwall IV15 9HU	01349 863379
Horne, Douglas A. BD	1977	2009	(Tain) 151 Holm Farm Road, Culduthel, Inverness IV2 6BF [E-mail: douglas.horne@talktalk.net]	01463 712677
Liddell, Margaret (Miss) BD DipTh	1987	1997	(Contin) 20 Wyvis Crescent, Conon Bridge, Dingwall IV7 8BZ [E-mail: margaretliddell@talktalk.net]	01349 865997
Mackinnon, R.M. LTh	1968	1995	(Kilmuir and Logie Easter) 27 Riverford Crescent, Conon Bridge, Dingwall IV7 8HL	01349 866293
McLean, Gordon LTh	1972	2008	(Contin) Beinn Dhorain, Kinnettas Square, Strathpeffer IV14 9BD	01997 421380
MacLennan, Alasdair J. BD DCE	1978	2001	(Resolis and Urquhart) Airdale, Seaforth Road, Muir of Ord IV6 7TA	01463 870704
Macleod, John MA	1959	1993	(Resolis and Urquhart) 'Benview', 19 Balvaird, Muir of Ord IV6 7RG [E-mail: sheilaandjohn@yahoo.co.uk]	01463 871286
McWilliam, Thomas M. MA BD	1964	2003	(Contin) Flat 3, 13 Culduthel Road, Inverness IV2 4AG [E-mail: tommcwilliam@btconnect.com]	01463 718981
Niven, William W. BTh	1982	1995	(Alness) 4 Obsdale Park, Alness IV17 0TP	01349 882427
Rutherford, Ellen B. (Miss) MBE DCS			(Deaconess) 41 Duncanston, Conon Bridge, Dingwall IV7 8JB	01349 877439
Tallach, John MA MLitt	1970	2010	(Cromarty) 29 Firthview Drive, Inverness IV3 8NS [E-mail: j.tallach@tiscali.co.uk]	01463 418721

(40) SUTHERLAND

Meets at Lairg on the first Tuesday of March, May, September, November and December, and on the first Tuesday of June at the Moderator's church.

Clerk: **MRS MARY J. STOBO**   **Druim-an-Sgairnich, Ardgay IV24 3BG**   **01863 766868**
[E-mail: sutherland@cofscotland.org.uk]

Altnaharra and Farr
Vacant   The Manse, Bettyhill, Thurso KW14 7SS   01641 521208

Assynt and Stoer
Guardianship of the Presbytery   Canisp Road, Lochinver, Lairg IV27 4LH   01571 844342

Clyne (H) linked with Kildonan and Loth Helmsdale (H)
Vacant   Golf Road, Brora KW9 6QS   01408 621239
Michael Macdonald (Aux)   2004   2012   73 Firhill, Alness IV17 0RT   01349 884268
[E-mail: mike_mary@hotmail.co.uk]

Creich   See Kincardine Croick and Edderton

Dornoch Cathedral (H)
Susan M. Brown (Mrs) BD DipMin   1985   1998   Cathedral Manse, Cnoc-an-Lobht, Dornoch IV25 3HN   01862 810296
[E-mail: revsbrown@aol.com]

Durness and Kinlochbervie
John T. Mann BSc BD   1990   1998   Manse Road, Kinlochbervie, Lairg IV27 4RG   01971 521287
[E-mail: jimklb@aol.com]

Eddrachillis
John MacPherson BSc BD   1993   Church of Scotland Manse, Scourie, Lairg IV27 4TQ   01971 502431

Golspie
John B. Sterrett BA BD PhD   2007   The Manse, Fountain Road, Golspie KW10 6TH   01408 633295 (Tel/Fax)
[E-mail: johnbsterrett@yahoo.co.uk]

Kildonan and Loth Helmsdale (H)   See Clyne

Kincardine Croick and Edderton linked with Creich linked with Rosehall

Anthony M. Jones	1994	2010	The Manse, Ardgay IV24 3BG	01863 766285
BD DPS DipTheol CertMin FRSA			[E-mail: revanthonymjones@amserve.com]	
Hilary Gardner (Miss) (Aux)	2010	2012	Cayman Lodge, Kincardine Hill, Ardgay IV24 3DJ	01863 766107
			[E-mail: gardnerhilary@hotmail.com]	

Lairg (H) linked with Rogart (H)

| Vacant | The Manse, Lairg IV27 4EH | 01549 402373 |

Melness and Tongue (H)

| Stewart Goudie BSc BD | 2010 | St Andrew's Manse, Tongue, Lairg IV27 4XL | 01847 611230 (Tel/Fax) |
| | | [E-mail: stewart@goudie.me.uk] | 07957 237757 (Mbl) |

Rogart See Lairg
Rosehall See Kincardine Croick and Edderton

Archer, Nicholas D.C. BA BD	1971	1992	(Dores and Boleskine)	Hillview, Edderton, Tain IV19 4AJ	01862 821494
Chambers, John OBE BSc	1972	2009	(Inverness: Ness Bank)	Bannlagan Lodge, 4 Earls Cross Gardens, Dornoch IV25 3NR	01862 811520
				[E-mail: chambersdornoch@btinternet.com]	
Goskirk, J.L. LTh	1968	2010	(Lairg with Rogart)	Rathvilly, Lairgmuir, Lairg IV27 4ED	01549 402569
				[E-mail: leslie_goskirk@sky.com]	
McCree, Ian W. BD	1971	2011	(Clyne with Kildonan and Loth Helmsdale)	Tigh Ardachu, Mosshill, Brora KW9 6NG	01408 621185
				[E-mail: ian@mccree.f9.co.uk]	
Muckart, Graeme W.M. MTh MSc FSAScot	1983	2009	(Kincardine Croick and Edderton)	Kildale, Clashmore, Dornoch IV25 3RG	
				[E-mail: avqt18@dsl.pipex.com]	

(41) CAITHNESS

Meets alternately at Wick and Thurso on the first Tuesday of February, March, May, September, November and December, and the third Tuesday of June.

| Clerk: | REV. RONALD JOHNSTONE BD | 2 Comlifoot Drive, Halkirk KW12 6ZA | 01847 839033 |
| | | [E-mail: caithness@cofscotland.org.uk] | |

Bower linked with Halkirk Westerdale linked with Watten

| Alastair H. Gray MA BD | 1978 | 2005 | The Manse, Station Road, Watten, Wick KW1 5YN | 01955 621220 |
| | | | [E-mail: alastair.h.gray@btinternet.com] | |

Canisbay linked with Dunnet linked with Keiss
Vacant — The Manse, Canisbay, Wick KW1 4YH — 01955 611756

Dunnet See Canisbay
Halkirk Westerdale See Bower
Keiss See Canisbay

Olrig linked with Thurso: St Peter's and St Andrew's (H)
Fanus Erasmus MA LTh MTh ThD   1978   2010 — The Manse, 40 Rose Street, Thurso KW14 8RF [E-mail: spacosminister@btinternet.com] — 01847 895186

The North Coast Parish
Vacant — Church of Scotland Manse, Reay, Thurso KW14 7RE — 01847 811441

The Parish of Latheron
Gordon Oliver BD   1979   2010 — Central Manse, Main Street, Lybster KW3 6BJ [E-mail: parish-of-latheron@btconnect.com] — 01593 721706

Thurso: St Peter's and St Andrew's See Olrig

Thurso: West (H)
Vacant — Thorkel Road, Thurso KW14 7LW — 01847 892663

Watten See Bower

Wick: Pulteneytown (H) and Thrumster
Stuart Farmes   2011 — The Manse, Coronation Street, Wick KW1 5LS [E-mail: thefarmesfamily@tiscali.co.uk] — 01955 603166

Wick: St Fergus
John Nugent   1999   2011 — Mansefield, Miller Avenue, Wick KW1 4DF [E-mail: johnnugentis@mail2web.com] — 01955 602167

Name				Address	Phone
Craw, John DCS	1998	2009	(Deacon)	Liabost, 8 Proudfoot Road, Wick KW1 4PQ [E-mail: johncraw607@btinternet.com]	01955 603805 (Mbl) 07544 761653
Johnstone, Ronald BD	1977	2011	(Thurso: West)	2 Comlifoot Drive, Halkirk KW12 6ZA [E-mail: ronaldjohnstone@btinternet.com]	01847 839033
Warner, Kenneth BD	1981	2008	(Halkirk and Westerdale)	Kilearnan, Clayock, Halkirk KW12 6UZ [E-mail: wrnkenn@btinternet.com]	01847 831825

CAITHNESS   Communion Sundays

Bower	1st Jul, Dec
Canisbay	1st Jun, Nov
Dunnet	last May, Nov
Halkirk Westerdale	Apr, Jul, Oct
Keiss	1st May, 3rd Nov
Latheron	Apr, Jul, Sep, Nov
North Coast	Mar, Easter, Jun, Sep, Dec
Olrig	last May, Nov
Thurso: St Peter's and St Andrew's	Mar, Jun, Sep, Dec
Watten	4th Mar, Jun, Nov
Wick: Pulteneytown and Thrumster	1st Jul, Dec
West St Fergus	1st Mar, Jun, Sep, Dec
	Apr, Oct

(42) LOCHCARRON – SKYE

Meets in Kyle on the first Tuesday of each month, except January, May, July and August.

Clerk:	**REV. ALLAN J. MACARTHUR BD**		**High Barn, Croft Road, Lochcarron, Strathcarron IV54 8YA** **[E-mail: lochcarronskye@cofscotland.org.uk]** **[E-mail: a.macarthur@btinternet.com]**	**01520 722278 (Tel)** **01520 722674 (Fax)**

Applecross, Lochcarron and Torridon (GD)

David Macleod	2008	The Manse, Colonel's Road, Lochcarron, Strathcarron IV54 8YG [E-mail: david.macleod@me.com]	01520 722829

Bracadale and Duirinish (GD)

Geoffrey D. McKee BA	1997	2009	Duirinish Manse, Dunvegan, Isle of Skye IV55 8WQ [E-mail: geoff.mckee@btinternet.com]	01470 521457

Gairloch and Dundonnell

Derek Morrison	1995	2000	Church of Scotland Manse, The Glebe, Gairloch IV21 2BT [E-mail: derekmorrison1@aol.com]	01445 712053 (Tel/Fax)

Glenelg and Kintail

Roderick N. MacRae BTh	2001	2004	Church of Scotland Manse, Inverinate, Kyle IV40 8HE [E-mail: barvalous@msn.com]	01599 511245

Kilmuir and Stenscholl (GD)

Vacant	Staffin, Portree, Isle of Skye IV51 9JX	01470 562759 (Tel/Fax)

Lochalsh

Vacant	The Manse, Main Street, Kyle IV40 8DA	01599 534294

Portree (GD)

Sandor Fazakas BD MTh	1976	2007	Viewfield Road, Portree, Isle of Skye IV51 9ES [E-mail: fazakass52@yahoo.com]	01478 611868

Snizort (H) (GD)

Vacant			The Manse, Kensaleyre, Snizort, Portree, Isle of Skye IV51 9XE	01470 532453

Strath and Sleat (GD)

Ben Johnstone MA BD DMin	1973	2003	The Manse, 6 Upper Breakish, Isle of Skye IV42 8PY [E-mail: benonskye@onetel.com]	01471 820063
John D. Urquhart BA BD (Part-Time: Gaelic Services)	1998	2003	The Manse, The Glebe, Kilmore, Teangue, Isle of Skye IV44 8RG [E-mail: ministear@hotmail.co.uk]	01471 844469

Beaton, Donald MA BD MTh	1961	2002	(Glenelg and Kintail)	Kilmaluag Croft, North Duntulm, Isle of Skye IV51 9UF	01470 552296
Calhoun, Robert L. BBA MDiv DMin	1974	2012	(Snizort)	145 Lamont, San Antonio, TX 78209, USA [E-mail: drref0911@yahoo.com]	
Kellas, David J. MA BD	1966	2004	(Kilfinan with Kyles)	Buarblach, Glenelg, Kyle IV40 8LA [E-mail: davidkellas@btinternet.com]	01599 522257 (Mbl) 07909 577764
Macarthur, Allan J. BD	1973	1998	(Applecross, Lochcarron and Torridon)	High Barn, Croft Road, Lochcarron, Strathcarron IV54 8YA [E-mail: a.macarthur@btinternet.com]	(Tel) 01520 722278 (Fax) 01520 722674
McCulloch, Alen J.R. MA BD	1990	2012	(Chaplain: Royal Navy)	Aros, 6 Gifford Terrace Road, Plymouth PL3 4JE [E-mail: aviljoen90@hotmail.com]	01752 657290
Macdonald, John M.	2002	2011	(Lochalsh)	Manse, Main Street, Kyle IV40 8DA [E-mail: john.macdonald53@btinternet.com]	01599 534294
Mackenzie, Hector M.	2008		Chaplain: Army	3 Bn The Parachute Regiment, Merville Barracks, Colchester CO2 7UT [E-mail: mackenziehector@hotmail.com]	
Macleod, Donald LTh	1988	2000	(Snizort)	Burnside, Upper Galder, Glenelg, Kyle IV40 8JZ [E-mail: donaldpmacleod_7@btinternet.com]	01599 522265
Martin, George M. MA BD	1987	2005	(Applecross, Lochcarron and Torridon)	8(1) Buckingham Terrace, Edinburgh EH4 3AA	0131-343 3937
Murray, John W.	2003		Auxiliary Minister	1 Totescore, Kilmuir, Portree, Isle of Skye IV51 9YN [E-mail: jwm7@hotmail.co.uk]	01470 542297

LOCHCARRON – SKYE Communion Sundays

Parish	Date	Parish	Date	Parish	Date
Applecross	1st Sep	Glenshiel	1st Jul	Plockton and Kyle	2nd May, 1st Oct
Arnisort	3rd Mar, Sep	Kilmuir	1st Mar, Sep	Portree	Easter, Pentecost, Christmas,
Bracadale	Last Feb	Kintail	3rd Apr, Jul		2nd Mar, Aug, 1st Nov
Broadford	3rd Jan, Easter, 3rd Sep	Kyleakin	Last Sep	Sleat	Last May
Duirinish	4th Jun	Lochalsh and	4th Jan, Jun, Sep, Christmas,	Snizort	1st Jan, 4th Mar
Dundonnell	1st Aug	Stromeferry	Easter	Stenscholl	1st Jun, Dec
Elgol		Lochcarron	Easter; communion held on a	Strath	4th Jan
Gairloch	3rd Jun, Nov	and Shieldaig	revolving basis when there is a	Torridon	
Glenelg	2nd Jun, Nov		fifth Sunday in the month	and Kinlochewe	

In the Parish of Strath and Sleat, Easter communion is held on a revolving basis.

(43) UIST

Meets on the first Tuesday of February, March, September and November in Lochmaddy, and on the third Tuesday of June in Leverburgh.

Clerk:	MR WILSON McKINLAY	Heatherburn Cottage, Rhughasnish, Isle of South Uist HS8 5PE	01870 610393
		[E-mail: uist@cofscotland.org.uk]	

Barra (GD)

Vacant		Cuithir, Castlebay, Isle of Barra HS9 5XD	01871 810230

Benbecula (GD) (H)

Andrew A. Downie BD BSc DipEd DipMin ThB	1994	2006	Church of Scotland Manse, Griminish, Isle of Benbecula HS7 5QA	01870 602180
			[E-mail: andownie@yahoo.co.uk]	

Berneray and Lochmaddy (GD) (H)

Donald Campbell MA BD DipTh	1997	2004	Church of Scotland Manse, Lochmaddy, Isle of North Uist HS6 5AA	01876 500414
			[E-mail: dc@hebrides.net]	

Carinish (GD) (H)

Vacant		Church of Scotland Manse, Clachan, Locheport, Lochmaddy, Isle of North Uist HS6 5HD	01876 580219

Kilmuir and Paible (GE)
Vacant   Paible, Isle of North Uist HS6 5ED   01876 510310

Manish-Scarista (GD) (H)
Vacant   Scarista, Isle of Harris HS3 3HX   01859 550200

South Uist (GD)
Vacant   Daliburgh, Lochboisdale, Isle of South Uist HS8 5SS   01878 700265

Tarbert (GD) (H)
Vacant   The Manse, Manse Road, Tarbert, Isle of Harris HS3 3DF   01859 502231

MacDonald, Angus J. BSc BD	1995	2001	(Lochmaddy and Trumisgarry)	7 Memorial Avenue, Stornoway, Isle of Lewis HS1 2QR	01851 706634
MacInnes, David MA BD	1966	1999	(Kilmuir and Paible)	9 Golf View Road, Kinmylies, Inverness IV3 8SZ	01463 717377
MacIver, Norman BD	1976	2011	(Tarbert)	57 Boswell Road, Wester Inshes, Inverness IV2 3EW	
				[E-mail: norman@n-cmaciver.freeserve.co.uk]	
Macpherson, Kenneth J. BD	1988	2002	(Benbecula)	70 Baile na Cille, Balivanich, Isle of Benbecula HS7 5ND	01870 602751
Morrison, Donald John	2001		Auxiliary Minister	22 Kyles, Tarbert, Isle of Harris HS3 3BS	01859 502341
Petrie, Jackie G.	1989	2011	(South Uist)	7B Malacleit, Sollas, Isle of North Uist HS6 5BX	01878 700265
				[E-mail: jackiegpetrie@yahoo.com]	
Smith, John M.	1956	1992	(Lochmaddy)	Hamersay, Clachan, Locheport, Lochmaddy, Isle of North Uist HS6 5HD	
Smith, Murdo MA BD	1988	2011	(Manish-Scarista)	Aisgeir, 15A Upper Shader, Isle of Lewis HS3 3MX	01876 580332

UIST Communion Sundays

Barra	2nd Mar, June, Sep, Easter, Advent
Benbecula	2nd Mar, Sep
Berneray and Lochmaddy	4th Jun, last Oct
Carinish	4th Mar, Aug
Kilmuir and Paible	1st Jun, 3rd Nov
Manish-Scarista	3rd Apr, 1st Oct
South Uist	
Howmore	1st Jun
Daliburgh	1st Sep
Tarbert	2nd Mar, 3rd Sep

(44) LEWIS

Meets at Stornoway, in St Columba's Church Hall, on the first Tuesday of February, March, June, September and November. It also meets if required in April and December on dates to be decided.

Clerk: REV. THOMAS S. SINCLAIR MA LTh BD
An Caladh, East Tarbert,
Tarbert, Isle of Harris HS3 3DB
[E-mail: lewis@cofscotland.org.uk]
[E-mail: presbytery@tsinclair.com]
01859 502849
07816 455820 (Mbl)

Barvas (GD) (H)
Paul Amed LTh DPS   1992   2008
Barvas, Isle of Lewis HS2 0QY
[E-mail: paulamed@hebrides.net]
01851 840218

Carloway (GD) (H) (01851 643211)
Stephen Macdonald BD MTh   2008
Church of Scotland Manse, Knock, Carloway, Isle of Lewis HS2 9AU
[E-mail: smcarloway@live.co.uk]
01851 643255
07964 080494 (Mbl)

Cross Ness (GE) (H)
Ian Murdo M. Macdonald DPA BD   2001
Cross Manse, Swainbost, Ness, Isle of Lewis HS2 0TB
[E-mail: crosschurch@me.com]
01851 810375

Kinloch (GE) (H)
Iain M. Campbell BD   2004   2008
Laxay, Lochs, Isle of Lewis HS2 9LA
[E-mail: i455@btinternet.com]
01851 830218

Knock (GE) (H)
J.R. Ross Macaskill BA MTh   2011
Knock Manse, Garrabost, Point, Isle of Lewis HS2 0PW
[E-mail: afrobear@hotmail.co.uk]
01851 870368

Lochs-Crossbost (GD) (H)
Vacant
Leurbost, Lochs, Isle of Lewis HS2 9NS
01851 860243

Lochs-in-Bernera (GD) (H) linked with Uig (GE) (H)
Hugh Maurice Stewart DPA BD   2008
4 Seaview, Knock, Point, Isle of Lewis HS2 0PD
(Temporary Manse)
[E-mail: berneralwuig@btinternet.com]
01851 870379

Stornoway: High (GD) (H)

Vacant   1 Goathill Road, Stornoway, Isle of Lewis HS1 2NJ   01851 703106

Stornoway: Martin's Memorial (H) (Church office: 01851 700820)

Thomas MacNeil MA BD   2002   2006   Matheson Road, Stornoway, Isle of Lewis HS1 2LR   01851 704238
                                            [E-mail: tommymacneil@hotmail.com]

Stornoway: St Columba (GD) (H) (Church office: 01851 701546)

Vacant   Lewis Street, Stornoway, Isle of Lewis HS1 2JF   01851 703350

Uig (GE) (H) See Lochs-in-Bernera

Name			(Parish)	Address	Phone
Jamieson, Esther M.M. (Mrs) BD	1984	2002	(Glasgow: Penilee St Andrew)	1 Redburn, Bayview, Stornoway, Isle of Lewis HS1 2UU [E-mail: iandejamieson@btinternet.com]	01851 704789 (Mbl) 07867 602963
Macdonald, James LTh CPS	1984	2001	(Knock)	Elim, 8A Lower Bayble, Point, Isle of Lewis HS2 0QA [E-mail: elim8a@hotmail.co.uk]	01851 870173
Maciver, Iain BD	2007	2012	(Carinish)	5 MacLeod Road, Stornoway, Isle of Lewis HS1 2HJ [E-mail: iain.maciver@hebrides.net]	
Maclean, Donald A. DCS	1975	2006	(Deacon)	8 Upper Barvas, Isle of Lewis HS2 0QX	01851 840454
MacLennan, Donald Angus			(Kinloch)	4 Kestrel Place, Inverness IV2 3YH [E-mail: maclennankinloch@btinternet.com]	01463 243750 (Mbl) 07799 668270
Macleod, William	1957	2006	(Uig)	54 Lower Barvas, Isle of Lewis HS2 0QY	01851 840217
Shadakshari, T.K. BTh BD MTh	1998	2006	Healthcare Chaplain	23D Benside, Newmarket, Stornoway, Isle of Lewis HS2 0DZ [E-mail: tk.shadakshari@nhs.net] [E-mail: shadaks2@yahoo.com]	(Home) 01851 701727 (Office) 01851 704704 (Mbl) 07403 697138
Sinclair, Thomas Suter MA LTh BD	1966	2004	(Stornoway: Martin's Memorial)	An Caladh, East Tarbert, Tarbert, Isle of Harris HS3 3DB [E-mail: lewis@cofscotland.org.uk] [E-mail: thomas@tsinclair.com]	01859 502849 (Mbl) 07816 455820

LEWIS Communion Sundays

Barvas	3rd Mar, Sep	Cross Ness	2nd Mar, Oct	Stornoway: High	3rd Feb, last Aug
Carloway	1st Mar, last Sep	Kinloch	3rd Mar, 2nd Jun, 2nd Sep	Martin's Memorial	3rd Feb, last Aug, 1st Dec, Easter
		Knock	3rd Apr, 1st Nov	Stornoway: St Columba	3rd Feb, last Aug
		Lochs-Crossbost	4th Mar, Sep	Uig	3rd Jun, 4th Oct
		Lochs-in-Bernera	1st Apr, 2nd Sep		

(45) ORKNEY

Normally meets at Kirkwall, in the East Church King Street Halls, on the second Tuesday of September and February, and on the last Tuesday of November. The Presbytery meets in conference on the first Tuesday in May. One meeting is usually held outwith the King Street Halls.

Clerk: REV. JAMES WISHART BD

Upper Westshore, Burray, Orkney KW17 2TE
[E-mail: orkney@cofscotland.org.uk]
[E-mail (personal): jwishart06@btinternet.com]

01856 731672

Birsay, Harray and Sandwick   1997   2001
Andrea E. Price (Mrs)

The Manse, North Biggings Road, Dounby, Orkney KW17 2HZ
[E-mail: andrea@andreaneil.plus.com]

01856 771803

East Mainland
Vacant

West Manse, Holm, Orkney KW17 2SB

01856 781422

Eday linked with Stronsay: Moncur Memorial (H)
Vacant

Manse, Stronsay, Orkney KW17 2AF

01857 616311

Evie (H) linked with Firth (H) linked with Rendall linked with Rousay
Vacant

Manse, Finstown, Orkney KW17 2EG

01856 761328

Firth (H) (01856 761117) See Evie

Flotta linked with Hoy and Walls linked with Orphir and Stenness   1991   2011
Alison H. Burnside (Mrs) MA BD

5 Manse Lane, Stromness, Orkney KW16 3AP
[E-mail: alisonskyona@aol.com]

01856 850203

Hoy and Walls See Flotta

Kirkwall: East (H) linked with Shapinsay
Vacant

East Church Manse, Thoms Street, Kirkwall, Orkney KW15 1PF

01856 875469

Kirkwall: St Magnus Cathedral (H)   1982   2002
G. Fraser H. Macnaughton MA BD

Berstane Road, Kirkwall, Orkney KW15 1NA
[E-mail: fmacnaug@gotadsl.co.uk]

01856 873312

North Ronaldsay linked with Sanday (H)
John L. McNab MA BD	1997 2002	The Manse, Sanday, Orkney KW17 2BW	01857 600429

Orphir (H) and Stenness (H) See Flotta

Papa Westray linked with Westray
Iain D. MacDonald BD	1993	The Manse, Hilldavale, Westray, Orkney KW17 2DW [E-mail: idmacdonald@btinternet.com]	01857 677357 (Tel/Fax) 07710 443780 (Mbl)

Rendall See Evie
Rousay (Church centre: 01856 821271) See Evie
Sanday See North Ronaldsay
Shapinsay (50 per cent part-time) See Kirkwall: East

South Ronaldsay and Burray
Vacant	St Margaret's Manse, Church Road, St Margaret's Hope, Orkney KW17 2SR	01856 831288

Stromness (H)
William A.M. Burnside MA BD PGCE	1990 2011	5 Manse Lane, Stromness, Orkney KW16 3AP	01856 850203

Stronsay: Moncur Memorial See Eday
Westray See Papa Westray

Brown, R. Graeme BA BD	1961 1998	(Birsay with Rousay)	Bring Deeps, Orphir, Orkney KW17 2LX [E-mail: graeme_sibyl@btinternet.com]	(Tel/Fax) 01856 811707
Clark, Thomas L. BD	1985 2008	(Orphir with Stenness)	7 Headland Rise, Burghead, Elgin IV30 5HA [E-mail: toml.clark@btinternet.com]	01343 830144
Tait, Alexander	1967 1995	(Glasgow: St Enoch's Hogganfield)	Ingermas, Evie, Orkney KW17 2PH [E-mail: jen1957@hotmail.co.uk]	01856 751477
Wishart, James BD	1986 2009	(Deer)	Upper Westshore, Burray, Orkney KW17 2TE [E-mail: jwishart06@btinternet.com]	01856 731672

(46) SHETLAND

Meets at Lerwick on the first Tuesday of February, April, June, September, November and December.

Clerk: REV. CHARLES H.M. GREIG MA BD   The Manse, Sandwick, Shetland ZE2 9HW   01950 422468
[E-mail: shetland@cofscotland.org.uk]

Burra Isle linked with Tingwall
Wilma A. Johnston MTheol MTh   2006   2008   The Manse, 25 Hogalee, East Voe, Scalloway, Shetland ZE1 0UU   01595 881157
[E-mail: rev.wilmajohnston@btinternet.com]

Delting linked with Northmavine
Vacant   The Manse, Grindwell, Brae, Shetland ZE2 9QJ   01806 522219
Robert M. MacGregor   2004   Olna Cottage, Brae, Shetland ZE2 9QS   01806 522604
  CMIOSH DipOSH RSP (Aux)   [E-mail: revbobdelting@mypostoffice.co.uk]
Grace Russon (Mrs) (Aux)   2011   Marelda, Park Road, Sandwick, Shetland ZE2 9HP   01950 431207
[E-mail: gracerusson@live.co.uk]

Dunrossness and St Ninian's inc. Fair Isle linked with Sandwick, Cunningsburgh and Quarff
Charles H.M. Greig MA BD   1976   1997   The Manse, Sandwick, Shetland ZE2 9HW   01950 422468
[E-mail: chm.greig@btopenworld.com]

Fetlar linked with Unst linked with Yell
David Cooper BA MPhil   1975   2008   The Manse, Gutcher, Yell, Shetland ZE2 9DF   01957 744258 (Tel/Fax)
(David Cooper is a minister of the Methodist Church)   [E-mail: Reverenddavidcooper@googlemail.com]

Lerwick and Bressay
Vacant   The Manse, 82 St Olaf Street, Lerwick, Shetland ZE1 0ES   01595 692125

Nesting and Lunnasting linked with Whalsay and Skerries
Irene A. Charlton (Mrs) BTh   1994   1997   The Manse, Marrister, Symbister, Whalsay, Shetland ZE2 9AE   01806 566767
[E-mail: irene.charlton@btinternet.com]
Richard M. Charlton (Aux)   2001   The Manse, Marrister, Symbister, Whalsay, Shetland ZE2 9AE   01806 566767
[E-mail: revrm.charlton@btinternet.com]

Northmavine See Delting

Sandsting and Aithsting linked with Walls and Sandness
Vacant   The Manse, Happyhansel, Walls, Shetland ZE2 9PB   01595 809709

Sandwick, Cunningsburgh and Quarff See Dunrossness and St Ninian's
Tingwall See Burra Isle
Unst See Fetlar
Walls and Sandness See Sandsting and Aithsting
Whalsay and Skerries See Nesting and Lunnasting
Yell See Fetlar

Kirkpatrick, Alice H. (Miss) MA BD FSAScot	1987	2000	(Northmavine)	1 Daisy Park, Baltasound, Unst, Shetland ZE2 9EA	
Knox, R. Alan MA LTh AInstAM	1965	2005	(Fetlar with Unst with Yell)	27 Killyvalley Road, Garvagh, Co. Londonderry, Northern Ireland BT51 5LX	02829 58925
Macintyre, Thomas MA BD	1972	2011	(Sandsting and Aithsting with Walls and Sandness)	'Lappideks', South Voxter, Cunningsburgh, Shetland ZE2 9HF [E-mail: the2macs.macintyre@btinternet.com]	01950 477549
Smith, Catherine (Mrs) DCS	1964	2003	(Presbytery Assistant)	21 Lingaro, Bixter, Shetland ZE2 9NN	01595 810207
Williamson, Magnus J.C.	1982	1999	(Fetlar with Yell)	Creekhaven, Houll Road, Scalloway, Shetland ZE1 0XA	01595 880023

(47) ENGLAND

Meets at London, in Crown Court Church, on the second Tuesday of March and December, and at St Columba's, Pont Street, on the second Tuesday of June and October.

Clerk: REV. PETER W. MILLS CB BD DD CPS   43 Hempland Close, Corby NN18 8LR   01536 746429
[E-mail: england@cofscotland.org.uk]

Corby: St Andrew's (H)
Peter W. Mills CB BD DD CPS   1984   2009   43 Hempland Close, Corby NN18 8LR   01536 746429
[E-mail: pwmills@live.co.uk]

Corby: St Ninian's (H) (01536 265245)
Vacant   The Manse, 46 Glyndebourne Gardens, Corby, Northants NN18 0PZ 01536 352430

Guernsey: St Andrew's in the Grange (H)
Graeme W. Beebee BD — 1993 — 2003
The Manse, Le Villocq, Castel, Guernsey GY5 7SB
[E-mail: beehive@cwgsy.net]
01481 257345

Jersey: St Columba's (H)
Randolph Scott MA BD — 1991 — 2006
18 Claremont Avenue, St Saviour, Jersey JE2 7SF
[E-mail: rev.rs@hotmail.com]
01534 730659

Liverpool: St Andrew's
Guardianship of the Presbytery
Session Clerk: Mr Robert Cottle
0151-524 1915

London: Crown Court (H) (020 7836 5643)
Philip L. Majcher BD — 1982 — 2007
53 Sidmouth Street, London WC1H 8JX
[E-mail: minister@crowncourtchurch.org.uk]
020 7278 5022

Timothy E.G. Fletcher BA FCMA (Aux) — 1998
37 Harestone Valley Road, Caterham, Surrey CR3 6HN
[E-mail: fletcherts@btinternet.com]
01883 340826

London: St Columba's (H) (020 7584 2321) linked with Newcastle: St Andrew's (H)
C. Angus MacLeod MA BD — 1996 — 2012
29 Hollywood Road, Chelsea, London SW10 9HT
[E-mail: 959macle@armymail.mod.uk]
020 7584 2321

Dorothy Lunn (Aux) — 2002 — 2002
14 Bellerby Drive, Ouston, Co. Durham DH2 1TW
[E-mail: dorothylunn@hotmail.com]
0191-492 0647

Newcastle: St Andrew's See London: St Columba's

Name			Role	Address	Phone
Bowie, A. Glen CBE BA BSc	1954	1984	(Principal Chaplain: RAF)	16 Weir Road, Hemingford Grey, Huntingdon PE18 9EH	01480 381425
Brown, Scott J. QHC BD	1993	1993	Chaplain of the Fleet: Royal Navy	Principal Church of Scotland and Free Churches Chaplain (Naval), and Director Naval Chaplaincy Service (Capability), MP 1.2, Leach Building, Whale Island, Portsmouth PO2 8BY [E-mail: scott.brown943@mod.uk]	02392 625552 (Mbl) 07769 847876
Cairns, W. Alexander BD	1978	2006	(Corby: St Andrew's)	Kirton House, Kirkton of Craig, Montrose DD10 9TB [E-mail: sandy.cairns@btinternet.com]	(Mbl) 07808 588045
Cameron, R. Neil	1975	1981	(Chaplain: Community)	8 Ashdown Terrace, Tidworth, Wilts SP9 7SQ [E-mail: neilandminacameron@yahoo.co.uk]	01980 842175
Coulter, David G. QHC BA BD MDA PhD CF	1989	1994	Chaplain: Army	[E-mail: padredgcoulter@yahoo.co.uk]	
Cross, Brian F. MA	1961	1998	(Coalburn)	1474 High Road, Whetstone, London N20 9QD	020 8492 9313
Cumming, Alistair MSc CCC FInstLM	2010		Auxiliary Minister: London: St Columba's	64 Prince George's Avenue, London SW20 8BH [E-mail: afcumming@hotmail.com]	020 8540 7365 (Mbl) 07534 943986

Name			Position	Address	Contact
Dalton, Mark BD DipMin RN	2002		Chaplain: Royal Navy	COMDEVFLOT, Shackleton Building MO56, Morice Yard, HMNB Devonport, Plymouth PL2 3BG [E-mail: mark.dalton242@mod.uk]	
Dowswell, James A.M.	1991	2001	(Lerwick and Bressay)	Mill House, High Street, Staplehurst, Tonbridge, Kent TN12 0AU [E-mail: jdowswell@btinternet.com]	01580 891271
Duncan, Denis M. BD PhD	1944	1986	(Editor: *The British Weekly*)	24 Caburn Court, Station Street, Lewes BN7 2DA [E-mail: denisduncan@dits.org.uk]	
Duncan, John C. BD MPhil	1987	2001	Chaplain: Army	3 Yorks, CF NES (S), PB 2, Camp 121, Bastion, Op Herrick, BFPO 792 [E-mail: padrerhf@hotmail.com]	(Mbl) 07825 119227
Fields, James MA BD STM	1988	1997	School Chaplain	The Bungalow, The Ridgeway, Mill Hill, London NW7 1QX	020 8201 1397
Francis, James BD PhD	2002	2009	Chaplain: Army	37 Millburn Road, Coleraine BT52 1QT	02870 353869
Kingston, David V.F. BD DipPTh	1993		Chaplain: Army	The Chaplain's Office, HQ Colchester Garrison, Gryphon House, Merville Barracks, Colchester CO2 7UT [E-mail: d.v.f.k@btinternet.com]	01206 563638 (Mbl) 07802 417947
Langlands, Cameron H. BD MTh ThM PhD MInstLM	1995	2009	Pastoral and Spiritual Care Manager: Lancashire Teaching Hospitals NHS Trust	Department of Pastoral and Spiritual Care, Lancashire Teaching Hospitals NHS Foundation Trust, Royal Preston Hospital, Sharoe Green Lane, Fullwood, Preston PR2 9HT [E-mail: cameron.langlands@lthtr.nhs.uk]	01772 522350
Lugton, George L. MA BD	1955	1997	(Guernsey: St Andrew's in the Grange)	6 Clos de Beauvoir, Rue Cohu, Guernsey GY5 7TE	(Tel/Fax) 01481 254285
Macfarlane, Peter T. BA LTh	1970	1994	(Chaplain: Army)	4 rue de Rives, 37160 Abilly, France	
McIndoe, John H. MA BD STM DD	1966	2000	(London: St Columba's with Newcastle: St Andrew's)	5 Dunlin, Westerlands Park, Glasgow G12 0FE [E-mail: johnandeve@mcindoe555.fsnet.co.uk]	0141-579 1366
MacLeod, Rory N. MA BD	1986	1992	Chaplain: Army	39 Regt, Royal Regiment of Artillery, Albemarle Barracks, Harlow Hill, Newcastle-upon-Tyne NE15 0RF	
McMahon, John K.S. MA BD	1998	2012	Spiritual and Pastoral Care Team Leader	Broadmoor Hospital, Crowthorne, Berkshire RG45 7EG [E-mail: john.mcmahonrev@wlmht.nhs.uk]	(Reception) 01344 773111
Mather, James BA DipArch MA MBA	2010		Auxiliary Minister: University Chaplain	24 Ellison Road, Barnes, London SW13 0AD [E-mail: jsm.johnstonmather@btinternet.com]	(Home) 020 8876 6540 (Work) 020 7361 1670 (Mbl) 07836 715655
Middleton, Paul BMus BD ThM PhD	2000		University Lecturer	97B Whipcord Lane, Chester CH1 4DG	
Munro, Alexander W. MA BD	1978		Chaplain and Teacher of Religious Studies	Columba House, 12 Alexandra Road, Southport PR9 0NB [E-mail: awmunro@tiscali.co.uk]	01704 543044
Pickles, Robert G.D.W. BD MPhil ThD	2003	2010	(Orwell and Portmoak)	Chadacres, 49 Rotton Park Road, Birmingham B16 0SG [E-mail: robert.pickles@btopenworld.com]	0121-454 4046
Rennie, Alistair McR. MA BD	1939	1986	(Kincardine Croick and Edderton)	Noble's Yard, St Mary's Gate, Wirksworth, Derbyshire DE4 4DQ [E-mail: alistairrennie@lineone.net]	01629 820289
Shackleton, Scott J.S. QCVS BA BD PhD RN	1993	2010	Chaplain: Royal Navy	HQ 3 Commando Brigade, RMB Stonehouse, Durnford Street, Plymouth PL1 3QS [E-mail: shackletonscott@hotmail.com]	01752 836397
Thomson, Steven BSc BD RN	2001	2004	Chaplain: Royal Navy	21 Kings Terrace, Southsea, Portsmouth PO5 3AR [E-mail: stevie.thomson1@ntlworld.com]	(Mbl) 07841 368797

Trevorrow, James A. LTh	1971 2003	(Glasgow: Cranhill)	12 Test Green, Corby, Northants NN17 2HA [E-mail: jimtrevorrow@compuserve.com]	01536 264018
Walker, R. Forbes BSc BD ThM	1987 2000	School Chaplain	2 Holmleigh, Priory Road, Ascot, Berks SL5 8EA [E-mail: revfw@gmail.com]	01344 883272
Wallace, Donald S.	1950 1980	(Chaplain: RAF)	7 Dellfield Close, Watford, Herts WD1 3BL	01923 223289
Ward, Michael J. BSc BD PhD MA PGCE	1983 2009	Training and Development Officer: Presbyterian Church of Wales	Apt 6, Bryn Hedd, Conwy Road, Penmaen-mawr, Gwynedd LL34 6BS [E-mail: revmw@btopenworld.com]	(Mbl) 07765 598816
Wood, Peter J. MA BD	1993	(College Lecturer)	97 Broad Street, Cambourne, Cambridgeshire CB23 6DH [E-mail: pejowood@tiscali.co.uk]	01954 715558

ENGLAND – Church Addresses

Corby: St Andrew's Occupation Road
St Ninian's Beanfield Avenue

Liverpool: The Western Rooms,
Anglican Cathedral

London: Crown Court Crown Court WC2
St Columba's Pont Street SW1

Newcastle: Sandyford Road

(48) EUROPE

Clerk: REV. JOHN A. COWIE BSc BD Jan Willem Brouwersstraat 9, NL-1071 LH Amsterdam (Tel) **0031 20 672 2288**
[E-mail: europe@cofscotland.org.uk] (Fax) **0031 842 221513**
[E-mail: j.cowie@chello.nl]

Amsterdam

John A. Cowie BSc BD	1983 1989	Jan Willem Brouwersstraat 9, NL-1071 LH Amsterdam, The Netherlands [E-mail: minister@ercadam.nl]	(Tel) 0031 20 672 2288 (Fax) 0031 842 221513

Brussels (E-mail: secretary@churchofscotland.be)

Andrew Gardner BSc BD PhD	1997 2004	23 Square des Nations, B-1000 Brussels, Belgium [E-mail: minister@churchofscotland.be]	0032 2 672 40 56

Budapest (Church telephone: 0036 1 373 0725)

Aaron Stevens	2010	H-1143, Stefánia út 32, Budapest, Hungary [E-mail: revastevens@yahoo.co.uk]	(Mbl) 0036 70 615 5394

Colombo, Sri Lanka: St Andrew's Scots Kirk
John P.S. Purves MBE BSc BD 1978 73 Galle Road, Colpetty, Colombo 3, Sri Lanka
[E-mail: reverend@sltnet.lk] 0094 (11) 2386774

Costa del Sol
Morris M. Dutch BD BA DipBTI 1998 2011 The Manse, Avenida Jesus Santos Rein, 24 Edf. Lindamar 4 – 3Q,
Fuengirola, 29640 Malaga, Spain
[E-mail: mmdutch@yahoo.co.uk] 0034 951 260 982

Geneva
Ian A. Manson BA BD 1989 2001 20 Ancienne Route, 1218 Grand Saconnex, Geneva, Switzerland
(Office)
[E-mail: cofsg@pingnet.ch] 0041 22 798 29 09
0041 22 788 08 31

Gibraltar
Ewen MacLean BA BD 1995 2009 St Andrew's Manse, 29 Scud Hill, Gibraltar
[E-mail: scotskirk@gibraltar.gi] 00350 200 77040

Lausanne
Ian J.M. McDonald MA BD 1984 2010 26 Avenue de Rumine, CH-1005 Lausanne, Switzerland
[E-mail: minister@scotskirklausanne.ch] 0041 21 323 98 28

Lisbon
Graham G. McGeoch MA BTh MTh 2009 Rua da Arriaga 13, 1200-625 Lisbon, Portugal
[E-mail: cofslx@netcabo.pt] 00351 218 043 410

Malta
T. Douglas McRoberts BD CPS FRSA 1975 2009 La Romagnola, 15 Triq is-Seiqia, Misrah Kola, Attard
ATD 1713, Malta
[E-mail: doug.mcroberts@btinternet.com]
Church address: 210 Old Bakery Street, Valletta, Malta
[E-mail: minister@saintandrewsmalta.com] (Tel/Fax) 00356 214 15465

Paris
James M. Cowie BD 1977 2011 10 Rue Thimmonier, F-75009 Paris, France
[E-mail: jimcowie@europe.com] 0033 1 48 78 47 94

Regensburg (University)

Rhona Dunphy (Mrs) BD DPTheol	2005		Liskircherstrasse 9, D-93049 Regensburg, Germany [E-mail: rhona@dunphy.de]	(Mbl) 0049 (0) 176 83 10 69 67

Rome: St Andrew's

William B. McCulloch BD	1997	2002	Via XX Settembre 7, 00187 Rome, Italy [E-mail: revwbmcculloch@hotmail.com]	(Tel) 0039 06 482 7627 (Fax) 0039 06 487 4370

Rotterdam (Church telephone: 0031 10 412 4779)

Robert A. Calvert BSc BD DMin	1983		Church address: Schiedamse Vest 119–121, NL-2012 BH Rotterdam, The Netherlands / Meeuwenstraat 4A, NL-3071 PE Rotterdam, The Netherlands [E-mail: scotsintchurch@cs.com]	0031 10 220 4199

Turin

Azam John Masih (Locum)			Via S. Pio V 17, 10125 Torino, Italy [E-mail: esc.torino@alice.it]	0039 011 650 5770
			Church address: Via Sant Anselmo 6, 10125 Turin, Italy	0039 011 650 9467

Warwick, Bermuda: Christ Church

Barry W. Dunsmore MA BD	1982	2009	Mailing address: PO Box PG88, Paget PG BX, Bermuda / Church address: Christ Church, Middle Road, Warwick, Bermuda [E-mail: christchurch@logic.bm; Website: www.christchurch.bm] / Manse address: The Manse, 6 Manse Road, Paget PG 01, Bermuda	(Office) 001 441 236 1882

Name	Year 1	Year 2	Address	Phone
Irene Bom (Ordained Local Minister: pastoral training and support)	2008		Bergpolderstraat 53A, NL-3038 KB Rotterdam, The Netherlands [E-mail: ibsalem@xs4all.nl]	0031 10 265 1703
James M. Brown MA BD	1982		Neustrasse 15, D-44787 Bochum, Germany [E-mail: j.brown56@gmx.de]	0049 234 133 65
Professor A.I.C. Heron MA BD DTheol	1975	1987	Priessnitzstrasse 10, D-91056 Erlangen, Germany [E-mail: arheron@gmx.de]	0049 9131 52443
Derek G. Lawson LLB BD	1998	2011	2 Rue Joseph Guillemot, F-87210 Oradour St Genest, France [E-mail: derek.lawson@sfr.fr]	00 33 5 55 68 53 03
Paraic Reamonn BA BD	1982		359B Route de Mandement, CH-1281 Russin, Switzerland [E-mail: paraic.reamonn@gmail.com]	0041 22 776 4834
James Sharp (Ordained Local Minister: training and education)	2005		102 Rue des Eaux-Vives, CH-1207 Geneva, Switzerland [E-mail: jimsharp@bluewin.ch]	0041 22 786 4847
(Turin) Alexander B. Cairns MA	1957	2009	Beechwood, Main Street, Sandhead, Stranraer DG9 9JG	
(Bermuda) T. Alan W. Garrity BSc BD MTh	1969	2008	17 Solomon's View, Dunlop, Kilmarnock KA3 4ES	01560 486879

(Rome)	David F. Huie MA BD	1962	2001	15 Rosebank Gardens, Largs KA30 8TD [E-mail: dfh@davidhuie35.plus.com]	01475 670733
(Brussels)	Charles C. McNeill OBE BD	1962	1991	17 All Saints Way, Beachamwell, Swaffham, Norfolk PE37 8BU	01620 843373
(Brussels)	Thomas C. Pitkeathly MA CA BD	1984	2004	1 Lammermuir Court, Gullane EH31 2HU [E-mail: joostpot@gmail.com]	
(Rotterdam)	Joost Pot BSc (Auxiliary Minister)	1992	2004		
(Budapest)	Bertalan Tamas			Pozsonyi ut 34, Budapest H-1137, Hungary [E-mail: bertalantamas@hotmail.com]	0036 1 239 6315 (Mbl) 0036 30 638 6647

(49) JERUSALEM

Clerk:	MR J.G. MAXWELL			Tabeetha School, PO Box 8170, Jaffa 61081, Israel [E-mail: jmaxwell@churchofscotland.org.il] [E-mail: jimmymaxwell27@yahoo.com]	(Home) 00972 3 657 2003 (Mbl) 00972 52 374 0235

Jerusalem: St Andrew's

George C. Shand MA BD	1981	2009	St Andrew's Scots Memorial Church, 1 David Remez Street, PO Box 8619, Jerusalem 91086, Israel [E-mail: stachjer@netvision.net.il]	(Tel) 00972 2 673 2401

Tiberias: St Andrew's

Colin D. Johnston MA BD	1986	2009	St Andrew's, Galilee, 1 Gdud Barak Street, PO Box 104, Tiberias 14100, Israel [E-mail: revcdj60@gmail.com]	(Tel) 00972 4 671 0759

SECTION 6

Additional Lists of Personnel

LIST A – AUXILIARY MINISTERS

NAME	ORD	ADDRESS	TEL	PR
Attenburrow, Anne BSc MB ChB	2006	4 Jock Inksons Brae, Elgin IV30 1QE	01343 552330	35
Binks, Mike	2007	5 Maxwell Drive, Newton Stewart DG8 6EL	01671 402201	9
Buck, Maxine	2007	Brownlee House, Mauldslie Road, Carluke ML8 5HW	01555 759063	17
Burroughs, Kirsty-Ann (Mrs) BA BD CertTheol DRM PhD	2007	Lorne and Lowland Manse, Castlehill, Campbeltown PA28 6AN	01586 552468	19
Cameron, Ann J. (Mrs) CertCS DCE TEFL	2005	Currently resident in Qatar		32
Campbell, Gordon MA BD CDipAF DipHSM MCMI MHM AFRIN ARSGS FRGS FSAScot	2001	2 Falkland Place, Kingoodie, Invergowrie, Dundee DD2 5DY	01382 561383	29
Charlton, Richard M.	2001	The Manse, Marrister, Symbister, Whalsay, Shetland ZE2 9AE	01806 566767	46
Cumming, Alistair	2010	64 Prince George's Avenue, London SW20 8BH	020 8540 7365 (Mbl) 07534 943986	47
Dick, Roddy S.	2010	27 Easter Crescent, Wishaw ML2 8XB	01698 383453	17
Don, Andrew MBA	2006	5 Eskdale Court, Penicuik EH26 8HT	01968 675766	3
Fletcher, Timothy E.G. BA FCMA	1998	37 Hareston Valley Road, Caterham, Surrey CR3 6HN	01883 340826	47
Forrest, Kenneth P. CBE BSc PhD	2006	5 Carruth Road, Bridge of Weir PA11 3HQ	01505 612651	14
Gardner, Hilary (Miss)	2010	Cayman Lodge, Kincardine Hill, Ardgay IV24 3DJ	01863 766107	40
Griffiths, Ruth I. (Mrs)	2004	Kirkwood, Mathieson Lane, Innellan, Dunoon PA23 7TA	01369 830145	19
Hood, Catriona A.	2006	'Elyside', Dalintober, Campbeltown PA28 6EB	01586 551490	19
Howie, Marion L.K. (Mrs) MA ARCS	1992	51 High Road, Stevenston KA20 3DY	01294 466571	12
Jackson, Nancy	2009	Cygnet House, Holmfarm Road, Catrine, Mauchline KA5 6TA	01290 550511	10
Kemp, Tina MA	2005	12 Oaktree Gardens, Dumbarton G82 1EU	01389 730477	18
Landale, William S.	2005	Green Hope Guest House, Green Hope, Duns TD11 3SG	01361 890242	5
Lunn, Dorothy	2002	14 Bellerby Drive, Ouston, Co. Durham DH2 1TW	0191-492 0647	47
Macdonald, Michael	2004	73 Firhill, Alness IV17 0RT	01349 884268	40
MacDougall, Lorna I. (Miss) MA DipGC	2003	34 Millar Place, Carron, Falkirk FK2 8QB	01324 552739	22
MacGregor, Robert M. CMIOSH DipOSH RSP	2004	Olna Cottage, Brae, Shetland ZE2 9QS	01806 522604	46
Manson, Eileen (Mrs) DipCE	1994	1 Cambridge Avenue, Gourock PA19 1XT	01475 632401	14
Mather, James	2010	24 Ellison Road, Barnes, London SW13 0AD	(Home) 020 8876 6540 (Work) 020 7361 1670 (Mbl) 07836 715655	47
Morrison, Donald John	2001	22 Kyles, Tarbert, Isle of Harris HS3 3BS	01859 502341	43
Murray, John W.	2003	1 Totescore, Kilmuir, Portree, Isle of Skye IV51 9YN	01470 542297	42
O'Donnell, Barbara	2007	Ashbank, 258 Main Street, Alexandria G83 0NU	01389 752356	18
Paterson, Andrew E. JP	1994	6 The Willows, Kelty KY4 0FQ	01383 830998	24
Perry, Marion (Mrs)	2009	0/2, 75 Earl Street, Glasgow G14 0DG	07563 180662	16
Ramage, Alistair E. MA BA ADB CertEd	1996	16 Claremont Gardens, Milngavie, Glasgow G62 6PG	0141-956 2897	18
Riddell, Thomas S. BSc CEng FIChemE	1993	4 The Maltings, Linlithgow EH49 6DS	01506 843251	2
Robson, Brenda (Dr)	2005	2 Baird Road, Ratho, Newbridge EH28 8RA	0131-333 2746	2

NAME	ORD	ADDRESS	TEL	PR
Russon, Grace (Mrs)	2011	Marelda, Park Road, Sandwick, Shetland ZE2 9HP	01950 431207	46
Shearer, Anne BA DipEd	2010	10 Colsnaur, Menstrie FK11 7HG	01259 769176	23
Sutherland, David A.	2001	6 Cromarty Drive, Dundee DD2 2UQ	01382 621473	29
Vivers, Katherine A.	2004	Blacket House, Eaglesfield, Lockerbie DG11 3AA	01461 500412	7
Walker, Linda	2008	18 Valeview Terrace, Glasgow G42 9LA	0141-649 1340	16
Wandrum, David	1993	5 Cawder View, Carrickstone Meadows, Cumbernauld, Glasgow G68 0BN	01236 723288	22
Whittaker, Mary	2011	11 Templand Road, Lhanbryde, Elgin IV30 8BR		35
Wilkie, Robert	2011	24 Huntingtower Road, Perth PH1 2JS	01738 628301	28
Zambonini, James LIADip	1997	100 Old Manse Road, Netherton, Wishaw ML2 0EP	01698 350889	17

AUXILIARY MINISTERS: RETIRED

NAME	ORD	ADDRESS	TEL	PR
Birch, James PgDip FRSA FIOC	2001	1 Kirkhill Grove, Cambuslang, Glasgow G72 8EH	0141-583 1722	16
Brown, Elizabeth (Mrs) JP RGN	1996	8 Viewlands Place, Perth PH1 1BS	01738 552391	28
Cloggie, June (Mrs)	1997	11A Tulipan Crescent, Callander FK17 8AR	01877 331021	23
Craggs, Sheila (Mrs)	2001	7 Morar Court, Ellon AB41 9GG	01358 723055	33
Ferguson, Archibald M. MSc PhD CEng FRINA	1989	The Whins, 2 Barrowfield, Station Road, Cardross, Dumbarton G82 5NL	01389 841517	18
Glass, Alexander OBE MA	1998	Craigton, Tulloch Avenue, Dingwall IV15 9TU	01349 863258	39
Harrison, Cameron	2006	Woodfield House, Priormuir, St Andrews KY16 8LP	01334 478067	26
Jenkinson, John J. JP LTCL ALCM DipEd DipSen	1991	8 Rosehall Terrace, Falkirk FK1 1PY	01324 625498	22
Kay, Elizabeth (Miss) DipYCS	1993	1 Kintail Walk, Inchture, Perth PH14 9RY	01828 686029	29
McAlpine, John BSc	1988	Braeside, 201 Bonkle Road, Newmains, Wishaw ML2 9AA	01698 384610	17
MacDonald, Kenneth MA BA	2001	5 Henderland Road, Bearsden, Glasgow G61 1AH	0141-943 1103	16
MacFadyen, Anne M. (Mrs) BSc BD FSAScot	1995	295 Mearns Road, Glasgow G77 5LT	0141-639 3605	16
Mack, Elizabeth A. (Miss) DipPEd	1994	24 Roberts Crescent, Dumfries DG2 7RS	01387 264847	8
Mack, John C. JP	1985	The Willows, Auchleven, Insch AB52 6QB	01464 820387	33
Mailer, Colin	1996	Innis Chonain, Back Row, Polmont, Falkirk FK2 0RD	01324 712401	22
Munro, Mary (Mrs) BA	1993	14 Auchneel Crescent, Stranraer DG9 0JH	01776 702305	9
Paterson, Maureen (Mrs) BSc	1992	91 Dalmahoy Crescent, Kirkcaldy KY2 6TA	01592 262300	25
Phillippo, Michael MTh BSc BVetMed MRCVS	2003	25 Deeside Crescent, Aberdeen AB15 7PT	01224 318317	31
Pot, Joost BSc	1992	[E-mail: joostpot@gmail.com]		48
Shaw, Catherine A.M. MA	1998	40 Merrygreen Place, Stewarton, Kilmarnock KA3 5EP	01560 483352	11
Thomas, Shirley A. (Mrs) DipSocSci AMIA	2000	14 Kirkgait, Letham, Forfar DD8 2XQ	01307 818084	30
Watson, Jean S. (Miss) MA	1993	29 Strachan Crescent, Dollar FK14 7HL	01259 742872	23
Wilson, Mary D. (Mrs) RGN SCM DTM	1990	Berbice, The Terrace, Bridge of Tilt, Blair Atholl, Pitlochry PH18 5SZ	01796 481619	27

ORDAINED LOCAL MINISTERS

NAME	ORD	ADDRESS	TEL	PR
Anderson, David M. MSc FCOptom	1984	'Mirlos', 1 Dumfries Place, Fort William PH33 6UQ	01397 702091	38
Bom, Irene	2008	Bergpolderstraat 53A, NL-3038 KB Rotterdam, The Netherlands	0031 10 265 1703	48
Breingan, Mhairi	2011	6 Park Road, Inchinnan, Renfrew PA4 4QJ		14
Hughes, Barry MA	2011	Dunslair, Cardrona Way, Cardrona, Peebles EH45 9LD	01896 831197	4
Macdonald, Ishabel	2011	18 Carinish, Isle of North Uist HS6 5HN		43
Sharp, James	2005	102 Rue des Eaux-Vives, CH-1207 Geneva, Switzerland	0041 22 786 4847	48
Stevenson, Stuart	2011	143 Springfield Park, Johnstone PA5 8JT		14
Tweedie, Fiona PhD	2011	44 Campbell Park Crescent, Edinburgh EH13 0HT		1

LIST B – CHAPLAINS TO HM FORCES

NAME	ORD	COM	BCH	ADDRESS
Abeledo, Benjamin J.A. BTh DipTh PTh	1991	1999	A	Army Foundation College, Uniacke Barracks, Penny Pot Lane, Harrogate HG3 2SE
Aitchison, James W. BD	1993		A	HQ101 Log Bde, Buller Barracks, Aldershot, Hants GU11 2BY
Almond, David M. BD	1996		ACF	West Lowland Bn, ACF, Royal Regiment of Scotland, Fusilier House, Seaforth Road, Ayr KA8 9HX
Anderson, David P. BSc BD	2002	2007	A	1 UK ADSR, Hammersmith Barracks, BFPO 15
Andrews, J. Edward MA BD DipCG FSAScot	1985		ACF	Glasgow and Lanark Bn, ACF, Royal Regiment of Scotland, Gilberfield Road, Cambuslang, Glasgow G72 8YP
Berry, Geoff T. BD BSc	2009		OC	4 Scots (The Highlanders)
Blackwood, Keith T. BD DipMin	1997		ACF	Shetland Independent Battery, ACF, TA Centre, Fort Charlotte, Lerwick, Shetland ZE1 0JN
Blakey, Stephen A. BSc BD	1977		TA	6 Bn The Royal Regiment of Scotland (V), Walcheran Barracks, 122 Hotspur Street, Glasgow G20 8LQ
Blakey, Stephen A. BSc BD	1977		OC	Glasgow Universities Officers' Training Corps
Brown, Scott J. QHC BD	1993		RN	The Chaplain of the Fleet, MP 1.2, Navy Command HQ, Whale Island, Portsmouth, Hants PO2 8BY
Bryson, Thomas M. BD	1997		ACF	2 Bn The Highlanders, ACF, Royal Regiment of Scotland, Cadet Training Centre, Rocksley Drive, Boddam, Peterhead AB42 3BA
Campbell, Karen K. BD MTh	1997		OC	Personnel Recovery Unit, Edinburgh
Campbell, Roderick D.M. OStJ TD BD DMin FSAScot	1975		ACF	Argyll and Sutherland Highlanders Bn, ACF, Royal Regiment of Scotland, Harfield House, Bonhill Road, Dumbarton G82 2DG
Connolly, Daniel BD DipTheol DipMin	1983		A	36 Engr Regt, Invicta Park Barracks, Maidstone, Kent ME14 2NA

Name	Ord.	Comm.	Service	Appointment
Coulter, David G. QHC BA BD MDA PhD CF	1989	1994	A	Deputy Chaplain General, MoD Chaplains (Army), HQ Land Forces, 2nd Floor Zone 6, Ramillies Building, Marlborough Lines, Andover, Hants SP11 8HJ
Dalton, Mark BD DipMin RN	2002		RN	Chaplain to the Hydrographic Squadron, COMDEVFLOT, Shackleton Building MO56, Morice Yard, HMNB Devonport, Plymouth PL2 3BG
Davidson, Mark R. MA BD STM RN	2005		RN	The Chaplaincy, HMS *Neptune*, HMNB Clyde, Faslane, Helensburgh G84 8HL
Davidson Kelly, Thomas A. MA BD FSAScot	1975		OC	Army Personnel Centre, Glasgow
Duncan, John C. BD MPhil	1987	2001	A	3 Yorks, CF NES (S), PB 2, Camp 121, Bastion, Op Herrick, BFPO 792
Frail, Nicola BLE MBA MDiv	2000		A	225 General Support Medical Regiment (V), Oliver Barracks, Dalkeith Road, Dundee DD4 7DL
Francis, James BD PhD	2002	2009	A	2 Bn The Royal Anglian Regiment, BFPO 58
Gardner, Neil N. MA BD	1991		OC	Edinburgh Universities Officers' Training Corps
Kellock, Chris N. MA BD	1998		A	7 Para RHA, Merville Barracks, Colchester CO2 7UT
Kennon, Stanley BA BD RN	1992	2000	RN	Church of Scotland and Free Churches Chaplain, Britannia Royal Naval College, Dartmouth, Devon TQ6 0HJ
Kingston, David V.F. BD DipPTh	1993		A	HQ Colchester Garrison, Gryphon House, Merville Barracks, Colchester CO2 7UT
Kinsey, Louis BD DipMin TD	1991		TA	205 (Scottish) Field Hospital (V), Graham House, Whitefield Road, Glasgow G51 6JU
Lancaster, Craig MA BD	2004	2011	RAF	26 Edinburgh Square, Waddington, Lincs LN5 9NQ
MacDonald, Roderick I.T. BD CertMin	1992	2011	ACF	West Lowland Bn, ACF, Royal Regiment of Scotland, Fusilier House, Seaforth Road, Ayr KA8 9HX
McDonald, Ross J. BA BD ThM RNR	1998		RNR	HMS *Dalriada*, Eldon Street, Greenock PA16 7SL
MacKay, Stewart A.	2009		A	2 Bn The Parachute Regiment, Merville Barracks, Colchester CO2 7UT
Mackenzie, Cameron BD	1997		ACF	Lothian and Borders Bn, ACF, Royal Regiment of Scotland, Drumshoreland House, Broxburn EH52 5PF
Mackenzie, Hector M.	2008		A	3 Bn The Parachute Regiment, Merville Barracks, Colchester CO2 7UT
Mackenzie, Seoras L. BD	1996	1998	A	3 Bn The Black Watch, The Royal Regiment of Scotland, Fort George, Ardersier, Inverness IV1 2TD
MacLean, Marjory A. LLB BD PhD RNR	1991	1992	RNR	HMS *Scotia*, MoD Caledonia, Hilton Road, Rosyth, Dunfermline KY11 2XH
MacLeod, Rory N. MA BD	1986		A	39 Regt, Royal Regiment of Artillery, Albemarle Barracks, Harlow Hill, Newcastle-upon-Tyne NE15 0RF
MacPherson, Duncan J. BSc BD	1993	2002	A	HQ Hereford Garrison, Hereford HR4 7DD
Mathieson, Angus R. MA BD	1988	2003	OC	Edinburgh Garrison
Munro, Sheila BD	1995		RAF	RAF Lossiemouth, Elgin IV31 6SD
Rowe, Christopher J. BA BD	2008		TA	32 (Scottish) Signal Regiment (V), 21 Jardine Street, Glasgow G20 6JU
Selemani, Ecilo LTh MTh	1993		ACF	Glasgow and Lanark Bn, ACF, Royal Regiment of Scotland, Gilbertfield Road, Cambuslang, Glasgow G72 8YP
Shackleton, Scott J.S. QCVS BA BD PhD RN	1993	2011	RN	HQ 3 Commando Brigade, RMB Stonehouse, Durnford Street, Plymouth PL1 3QS
Stewart, Fraser M.C. BSc BD	1980	2010	ACF	1 Bn The Highlanders, ACF, Royal Regiment of Scotland, Gordonville Road, Inverness IV2 4SU
Thomson, Steven BSc BD RN	2001		RN	Waterfront Chaplains' Office, Lancelot Building (PP 87), HMNB, Portsmouth PO1 3NT
van Sittert, Paul BA BD	1997		A	1 Bn The Royal Regiment of Scotland, Dreghorn Barracks, Edinburgh EH13 9QW
Warwick, Ivan C. MA BD TD	1980		ACF	1 Bn The Highlanders, ACF, Royal Regiment of Scotland, Gordonville Road, Inverness IV2 4SU
Warwick, Ivan C. MA BD TD	1980		ACF	Orkney Independent Battery, ACF, TA Centre, Weyland Park, Kirkwall KW1 5LP

Whiteford, Alexander LTh	1996	OC	Fort George and Cameron Barracks, Inverness
Wylie, Jonathan		RAF	RAF Leuchars, St Andrews KY16 0JX

LIST C – HOSPITAL CHAPLAINS

NHS LOTHIAN

Lead Chaplain (Community, Mental Health and Primary Care)
  Alexander W. Young   0131-242 1990/1
Spiritual Care Offices: 0131-242 1990; 0131-537 6516

The Royal Infirmary of Edinburgh
51 Little France Crescent, Edinburgh EH16 4SA (0131-536 1000)
Liberton Hospital
113 Lasswade Road, Edinburgh EH16 6UB (0131-536 7800)
  Alexander W. Young   0131-242 1990/1
  Anne Mulligan   0131-242 1996
  Iain Telfer   0131-242 1997
The Western General Hospital
Crewe Road South, Edinburgh EH4 2XU (0131-537 1000)
  Alistair Ridland   0131-537 1400
  Liz Markey   0131-537 1401
The Royal Hospital for Sick Children
9 Sciennes Road, Edinburgh EH9 1LF (0131-536 0000)
  Caroline Applegath   0131-536 0144
St John's Hospital
Howden Road West, Livingston EH54 6PP (01506 523000)
  Georgina Nelson   01506 522188
  Joe Gierasik   01506 522187
The Royal Edinburgh Hospital
Morningside Place, Edinburgh EH10 5HF (0131-537 6000)
  Lynne MacMurchie   0131-537 6368
  Maxwell Reay   0131-537 6366
Edinburgh Community Mental Health (Community Office 0131-220 5159)
  Lynne MacMurchie   0131-537 6368
  Maxwell Reay   0131-537 6366

Corstorphine
136 Corstorphine Road, Edinburgh EH12 6TT (0131-459 7200)
Rosemary Bayne   0131-537 6516
Findlay House
Seafield Street, Edinburgh EH6 7LN (0131-454 2200)
Trisha Murphy-Black   0131-537 6516
Linlithgow St Michael's
Edinburgh Road, Linlithgow EH49 6QS (01506 842053)
Dr Georgina Nelson   01506 522188
Herdmanflat
Aberlady Road, Haddington EH41 3BU (0131-536 8300)
Rosemary Bayne   0131-537 6516
Roodlands
Hospital Road, Haddington EH41 3PF (0131-536 8300)
Rosemary Bayne   0131-537 6516
Bonnyrigg Community Hospital
70 Eskbank Road, Bonnyrigg EH22 3ND (0131-454 1001)
Trisha Murphy-Black   0131-537 6516
Belhaven
Beveridge Row, Dunbar EH42 1TR (01368 862246)
Laurence H. Twaddle   01368 863098
St Columba's Hospice
Kirklands House, Gogarmuir Road, Gogarbank, Edinburgh EH12 9BZ
Michael Paterson   0131-551 1381
Marie Curie Hospice, Edinburgh
Wards 12 and 15, Western General Hospital, Crewe Road South, Edinburgh EH4 2XU
Patrick Ryan   0131-470 2201
(Both hospices are currently in temporary accommodation)

For further information and full details of all e-mail/telephone contacts, see www.nhslothian.scot.nhs.uk

BORDERS

MELROSE –			
BORDERS GENERAL HOSPITAL	Rev. J. Ronald Dick	Chaplaincy Centre, Borders General Hospital, Melrose TD6 9BS	01896 826564
HUNTLYBURN	Post vacant		
HAY LODGE, PEEBLES	Rev. J. Ronald Dick	Chaplaincy Centre, Borders General Hospital, Melrose TD6 9BS	01896 826564
KNOLL	Post vacant		
KELSO	Rev. Robin D. McHaffie	Kirk Yetholm, Kelso TD5 8RD	01573 420308

DUMFRIES AND GALLOWAY

Institution	Chaplain	Address	Telephone
DUMFRIES AND GALLOWAY ROYAL INFIRMARY [01387 241625]			
THOMAS HOPE, LANGHOLM			
LOCHMABEN	Rev. Alexander E. Strachan	The Manse, Barrashead, Lochmaben, Lockerbie DG11 1QF	01387 810066
MOFFAT			
NEW ANNAN	Rev. Jack Brown		
CASTLE DOUGLAS	Rev. Mairi C. Byers	Meadowbank, Plumdon Road, Annan DG12 6SJ	01461 206512
DUMFRIES AND GALLOWAY ROYAL INFIRMARY	Rev. Robert J. Malloch	1 Castle View, Castle Douglas DG7 1BG	01556 502171
KIRKCUDBRIGHT	Rev. Douglas R. Irving	6 Bourtree Avenue, Kirkcudbright DG6 4AU	01557 330489
THORNHILL			
NEWTON STEWART			
STRANRAER: GALLOWAY COMMUNITY			

AYRSHIRE AND ARRAN

Institution	Chaplain	Address	Telephone
AILSA HOSPITAL, AYR	Rev. Sheila M. Mitchell	Ailsa Hospital, Ayr KA6 6BQ	01292 513197
AYR HOSPITAL/BIGGART HOSPITAL	Rev. Paul R. Russell	23 Nursery Wynd, Ayr KA7 3NZ	01292 614587 (Work)
AYRSHIRE CENTRAL	Rev. Alex M. Welsh	8 Greenside Avenue, Prestwick KA9 2HB	01292 826128 (Work)
CROSSHOUSE HOSPITAL, KILMARNOCK	Rev. Alex M. Welsh	8 Greenside Avenue, Prestwick KA9 2HB	01292 826128 (Work)
	Rev. Judith A. Huggett	4 Westmoor Crescent, Kilmarnock KA1 1TX	01563 827301 (Work)
STATE CARE AND OCCUPATIONAL HEALTH	Rev. Roderick H. McNidder	6 Hollow Park, Alloway, Ayr KA7 4SR	01292 442554
EAST AYRSHIRE	Rev. Judith A. Huggett	4 Westmoor Crescent, Kilmarnock KA1 1TX	01563 827301 (Work)
WAR MEMORIAL, ARRAN			
LADY MARGARET, MILLPORT	Rev. Elizabeth R.L. Watson	The Manse, Whiting Bay, Brodick, Isle of Arran KA27 8RE	01770 700289

LANARKSHIRE

Institution	Chaplain	Address	Telephone
Head of Spiritual Care, NHS Lanarkshire	Rev. Robert P. Devenny	Law House, Airdrie Road, Carluke ML8 5ER	01698 377637
LADY HOME	Rev. Susan G. Cowell	3 Gavel Lane, Regency Gardens, Lanark ML11 9FB	01555 665509
LOCKHART	Rev. Alison A. Meikle	2 Kaimhill Court, Lanark ML11 9HU	01555 662600
CLELAND	Rev. John A. Jackson	The Manse, Bellside Road, Cleland, Motherwell ML1 5NP	01698 860260
KELLO	Rev. Susan G. Cowell	3 Gavel Lane, Regency Gardens, Lanark ML11 9FB	01555 665509
WISHAW GENERAL	Rev. Sharon E.F. Colvin	25 Balblair Road, Airdrie ML6 6GQ	01236 590796
	Rev. Mhorag MacDonald	350 Kirk Road, Wishaw ML2 8LH	01698 381305
	Rev. Kathryn Smith-Anderson		01698 366779

STRATHCLYDE

Institution	Chaplain	Address	Telephone
STRATHCLYDE	Rev. David W. Doyle	19 Orchard Street, Motherwell ML1 3JE	01698 263472

HAIRMYRES	Rev. James S.G. Hastie	Chalmers Manse, Quarry Road, Larkhall ML9 1HH	01698 882238
	Rev. Derek Peat		01355 584301
	Rev. Patricia Johnston		01355 584301
	Marian McElhinney		01355 584669
STONEHOUSE	Rev. Marjorie Taylor		01698 794000
UDSTON	Rev. James S.G. Hastie		01698 723200
	Rev. James Bryden		01698 723200
COATHILL	Rev. James Grier		01698 742545
MONKLANDS GENERAL	Rev. James Munton	14 Love Drive, Bellshill ML4 1BY	01236 754848
	Rev. Kay Gilchrist	2 Moorcroft Drive, Airdrie ML6 8ES	01236 760154
	Rev. Helen Mee	48 Dunrobin Road, Airdrie ML6 8LR	01236 712607
WESTER MOFFAT	Rev. Helen Mee		01236 712607
CRAIGHOUSE	Rev. Derek Pope	35 Birrens Road, Motherwell ML1 3NS	01698 266716

GREATER GLASGOW AND CLYDE

Head of Chaplaincy and Spiritual Care	Rev. Blair Robertson	[E-mail: blair.robertson@ggc.scot.nhs.uk]	0141-201 2156
GLASGOW ROYAL INFIRMARY (GRI)	Helen Bunce		0141-211 4661
and THE PRINCESS ROYAL MATERNITY	Rev. Adam Plenderleith		
HOSPITAL	Sandra Bell DCS (p/t)		
BEATSON WEST OF SCOTLAND CANCER	Rev. Keith Saunders and	Glasgow Western Infirmary Chaplains' Office:	0141-211 2812
CENTRE; GARTNAVEL GENERAL	Rev. Anne Dougall	Gartnavel General Hospital Chaplains' Office:	0141-211 3026
HOSPITAL (GGH) and GLASGOW WESTERN			
INFIRMARY; BLAWARTHILL HOSPITAL;			
DRUMCHAPEL HOSPITAL; GLASGOW			
HOMEOPATHIC HOSPITAL			
YORKHILL CHILDREN'S HOSPITAL	Rev. Alister Bull		0141-201 0595
SOUTHERN GENERAL HOSPITAL (SGH)	Rev. Blair Robertson		0141-201 2156
	Rev. Ann Purdie		0141-201 2357
	Mayra Gomez-Sorto		
VICTORIA INFIRMARY (VI);	Rev. Ishaku Bitrus		0141-201 5164
MANSIONHOUSE UNIT; MEARNSKIRK	Imam Mohammed Ishaq (p/t)		
HOSPITAL			
GARTNAVEL ROYAL HOSPITAL (GRH)	Rev. Dr Kevin Franz		0141-211 3686
and Mental Health units in western Glasgow			
STOBHILL HOSPITAL SITE; THE ORCHARDS;	Rev. Jim Meighan		0141-531 5908
BIRDSTON HOSPITAL; PARKHEAD			
HOSPITAL; FOURHILLS NURSING HOME;			
GREENFIELD PARK NURSING HOME			
LEVERNDALE HOSPITAL and Mental Health	Anne MacDonald DCS		0141-211 6695
units in southern Glasgow			

RUTHERGLEN ROWANTREE/RODGER PARK	Anne MacDonald DCS	(Leverndale Hospital Chaplaincy)	0141-211 6695
NURSING HOME NHS Partnership Beds			
DARNLEY COURT NURSING HOME		Carmichael and Fleming Wards: contact Leverndale	
		Hospital Chaplaincy	
		Beaton Ward: contact SGH Chaplaincy	
ROYAL ALEXANDRA HOSPITAL, PAISLEY	Rev. Carol Campbell		0141-314 9561
INVERCLYDE ROYAL HOSPITAL (IRH) and	Paul Graham		01475 504759
RAVENSCRAIG HOSPITAL, GREENOCK			
VALE OF LEVEN HOSPITAL	Rev. Carol Campbell		0141-314 9561
DYKEBAR HOSPITAL and	Rev. Andrew Davis		0141-314 4211
DUMBARTON JOINT HOSPITAL			

FORTH VALLEY

Head of Spiritual Care	Rev. Margery Collin	Forth Valley Royal Hospital, Larbert FK5 4WR	01324 566071
FORTH VALLEY ROYAL	Rev. Robert MacLeod		01324 566073
	Rev. Kenneth G. Russell		01324 566072
	Rev. Helen Christie		01324 813786
MENTAL HEALTH UNITS	Rev. Timothy Njuguna		07824 460903
BO'NESS	Mr Frank Hartley	49 Argyll Place, Kilsyth, Glasgow G65 0PY	01236 824135
FALKIRK COMMUNITY	Rev. Helen Christie	Forth Valley Royal Hospital, Larbert FK5 4WR	01324 813786
BANNOCKBURN	Rev. James Landels	Allan Manse, Bogend Road, Bannockburn, Stirling FK7 8NP	01786 814692
CLACKMANNAN COUNTY	Rev. Kenneth G. Russell	Forth Valley Royal Hospital, Larbert FK5 4WR	01324 566072
STIRLING COMMUNITY	Rev. Robert MacLeod	Forth Valley Royal Hospital, Larbert FK5 4WR	01324 566073

FIFE

QUEEN MARGARET HOSPITAL,	Mr Mark Evans DCS	Queen Margaret Hospital, Whitefield Road, Dunfermline	01383 674136
DUNFERMLINE [01383 674136]		KY12 0SU	
		[E-mail: MarkEvansDCS@aol.com]	
VICTORIA HOSPITAL, KIRKCALDY	Mr Damian Murray	Victoria Hospital, Hayfield Road, Kirkcaldy KY2 5AH	01592 648158
[01592 643355]			
LYNEBANK	Mr Allan Grant	6 Normandy Place, Rosyth, Dunfermline KY11 2HJ	01383 428760
CAMERON; GLENROTHES; RANDOLPH	Miss Lynda Wright	Key Cottage, High Street, Falkland, Cupar KY15 7BU	01337 857705
WEMYSS			
ADAMSON, CUPAR	Rev. Lynn Brady	2 Guthrie Court, Cupar Road, Newburgh, Cupar KY14 6HA	01337 842228
STRATHEDEN, CUPAR	Mr Allan Grant	6 Normandy Place, Rosyth, Dunfermline KY11 2HJ	01383 428760
ST ANDREWS COMMUNITY	Rev. James Connolly	5 Westwater Place, Newport-on-Tay DD6 8NS	01382 542626

TAYSIDE

Head of Spiritual Care
DUNDEE NINEWELLS HOSPITAL

Rev. Gillian Munro	Wellbeing Cottage, Royal Victoria Hospital, Dundee DD2 5NF	01382 423116
Mr David Gordon	Chaplain's Office, Ninewells Hospital, Dundee DD1 9SY	01382 632755
Mr Andrew Bennett	Chaplain's Office, Ninewells Hospital, Dundee DD1 9SY	01382 632755

ROXBURGHE HOUSE — Mr Andrew Bennett — Chaplain's Office, Roxburghe House — 01382 740804

PERTH ROYAL INFIRMARY — Rev. Anne Findlay — Chaplain's Office, Perth Royal Infirmary — 01738 473896

ABERFELDY COMMUNITY — Rev. Anne Brennan — 01382 423110

BLAIRGOWRIE COMMUNITY — Rev. Geoff Williams — Community Chaplain — 01382 423110

PITLOCHRY COMMUNITY — Rev. Geoff Williams — Community Chaplain — 01382 423110

CRIEFF COMMUNITY — 01382 423110

MACMILLAN HOSPICE — Rev. Anne Findlay — Chaplain's Office, Perth Royal Infirmary — 01738 473896

ST MARGARET'S COMMUNITY — Rev. Geoff Williams — 01382 423110

ARBROATH INFIRMARY — 01382 423110

ANGUS CHAPLAIN — Rev. Rona Phillips — Susan Carnegie Centre, Stracathro Hospital — 01382 423110
(Little Cairnie Hospital, Montrose Infirmary, Brechin Infirmary, Stracathro Hospital)

GRAMPIAN

Co-ordinating Chaplain:
Rev. Mark Rodgers, Chaplains' Office, Aberdeen Royal Infirmary, Foresterhill, Aberdeen AB25 2ZN — 01224 553166

1. ACUTE SECTOR
ABERDEEN ROYAL INFIRMARY, ABERDEEN MATERNITY HOSPITAL Aberdeen AB25 2ZN
Chaplains' Office, Aberdeen Royal Infirmary, Foresterhill, Aberdeen AB25 2ZN

Rev. Mark Rodgers	01224 553316
Rev. James Falconer	01224 554905
Rev. Sylvia Spencer	01224 559214
Rev. Elizabeth Campbell	01224 554907
Mrs Trudy Noble (Assistant Chaplain)	01224 554298

ROYAL ABERDEEN CHILDREN'S HOSPITAL
Chaplain's Office, Royal Aberdeen Children's Hospital, Westburn Drive, Aberdeen AB25 2ZG
Rev. James Falconer — 01224 554905

ROXBURGHE HOUSE
Chaplain's Office, Roxburghe House, Ashgrove Road, Aberdeen AB25 2ZH
Rev. Sylvia Spencer — 01224 557077

WOODEND HOSPITAL
Chaplain's Office, Woodend Hospital, Eday Road, Aberdeen AB15 6XS
Rev. Alison M. Hutchison — 01224 556788
Rev. John Duthie (Assistant Chaplain) — 01224 556006 / 01224 556007

DR GRAY'S HOSPITAL, ELGIN — 01343 567262
Rev. Andrew Willis, Deanshaugh Croft, Mulben, Keith AB55 6YJ — 01542 860240
Rev. Norma Milne, 26 Green Road, Huntly AB54 8BE — 01466 793841
Rev. David Young, 15 Mannachie Rise, Forres IV36 2US — 01309 672849

THE OAKS, ELGIN
Post vacant

2. MENTAL HEALTH
ROYAL CORNHILL HOSPITAL, WOODLANDS
Chaplain's Office, Royal Cornhill Hospital, Cornhill Road, Aberdeen AB25 2ZH
Rev. Jim Simpson — 01224 557293
Miss Pamela Adam (Assistant Chaplain) — 01224 557484
Mr Donald Meston (Assistant Chaplain) — 01224 557231

3. COMMUNITY HOSPITALS

Hospital	Chaplain	Address	Telephone
ABOYNE	Rev. John Duthie	Moraine, Inchmarlo, Banchory AB31 4BR	01330 824108
GLEN O' DEE, BANCHORY	Rev. John Duthie	Moraine, Inchmarlo, Banchory AB31 4BR	01330 824108
CHALMERS, BANFF	Mrs Margaret Robb	Chrislouan, Keithhall, Inverurie AB51 0LN	01651 882310
FLEMING, ABERLOUR	Rev. Andrew Willis	Deanshaugh Croft, Mulben, Keith AB55 6YJ	01542 860240
FRASERBURGH	Rev. James Newell	39 Grattan Place, Fraserburgh AB43 9SD	01346 514905
INVERURIE	Rev. Ian B. Groves	1 Westburn Place, Inverurie AB51 5QS	01467 620285
INSCH	Rev. Jane C. Taylor	22 Western Road, Insch AB52 6JR	01464 820914
JUBILEE, HUNTLY	Rev. Norma Milne	26 Green Road, Huntly AB54 8BE	01466 793841
KINCARDINE COMMUNITY, STONEHAVEN	Post vacant		
LEANCHOIL, FORRES	Rev. David Young	15 Mannachie Rise, Forres IV36 2US	01309 672284
MUIRTON	Rev. Andrew Willis	Deanshaugh Croft, Mulben, Keith AB55 6YJ	01542 860240
PETERHEAD COMMUNITY	Rev. David S. Ross	3–5 Abbey Street, Deer, Peterhead AB42 5LN	01771 623994
SEAFIELD, BUCKIE	Rev. Andrew Willis	Deanshaugh Croft, Mulben, Keith AB55 6YJ	01542 860240
STEPHEN, DUFFTOWN	Rev. Hugh M.C. Smith	The Manse, Church Street, Dufftown, Keith AB55 4AR	01340 820380
TURNER, KEITH	Rev. Kay Gauld	The Manse, Church Road, Keith AB55 5BR	01542 882799
TURRIFF	Mrs Margaret Robb	Chrislouan, Keithhall, Inverurie AB51 0LN	01651 882310
UGIE, PETERHEAD	Rev. David S. Ross	3–5 Abbey Street, Deer, Peterhead AB42 5LN	01771 623994

HIGHLAND

Lead Chaplain
THE RAIGMORE HOSPITAL [01463 704000]

Hospital	Name	Address	Tel
THE RAIGMORE HOSPITAL	Rev. Dr Derek Brown	Raigmore Hospital	01463 704463
	Rev. Dr Derek Brown	Cathedral Manse, Cnoc-an-Lobht, Dornoch IV25 3HN	01463 704463
	Mrs Lindsay Rodgers	Raigmore Hospital	01463 704463
	Rev. Maureen Wilson	Raigmore Hospital	01463 704463
	Rev. Canon Michael Hickford	Raigmore Hospital	01479 872084
IAN CHARLES	Rev. Morris Smith	Golf Course Road, Grantown-on-Spey PH26 3HY	01540 661219
ST VINCENT			01463 704000
NEW CRAIGS	Rev. Dr Iain Macritchie		01667 452101
NAIRN TOWN AND COUNTY			01397 702481
BELFORD AND BELHAVEN			
GLENCOE			
ROSS MEMORIAL, DINGWALL	Rev. Russel Smith	8 Castlehill Road, Dingwall IV15 9PB	01349 861011
INVERGORDON COUNTY	Rev. Kenneth D. Macleod	The Manse, Cromlet Drive, Invergordon IV18 0BA	01349 852273
LAWSON MEMORIAL	Mr Karl Weidner		01408 664029
MIGDALE	Mr Karl Weidner		01863 766211
CAITHNESS GENERAL	Mr John Craw DCS	Liabost, 8 Proudfoot Road, Wick KW1 4PQ	01955 603805
			(Mbl) 07544 761653
DUNBAR	Rev. Alastair H. Gray	The Manse, Station Road, Watten, Wick KW1 5YN	01955 621220
	Rev. Alastair H. Gray	The Manse, Station Road, Watten, Wick KW1 5YN	01955 621220
BROADFORD MACKINNON MEMORIAL	Rev. Dr Ben Johnstone	The Manse, 6 Upper Breakish, Isle of Skye IV42 8PY	01471 820063
PORTREE	Rev. Donald G. MacDonald	Free Church Manse, 3 Sluggans, Portree, Isle of Skye IV51 9LY	01478 613256
CAMPBELTOWN	Mrs Andrea Holden		01586 552224
LOCHGILPHEAD	Mrs Margaret Sinclair	2 Quarry Park, Furnace, Inveraray PA32 8XW	01499 500633
ISLAY			01496 301000
DUNOON			01369 704341
ROTHESAY	Mr Raymond Deans	60 Ardmory Road, Rothesay, Isle of Bute PA20 0PG	01700 504893
LORN AND THE ISLANDS DISTRICT GENERAL	Rev. William Gray	Liogh, Glengallan Road, Oban PA34	01631 567500

WESTERN ISLES HEALTH BOARD

Hospital	Name	Address	Tel
UIST AND BARRA HOSPITAL WESTERN ISLES, STORNOWAY	Rev. T.K. Shadakshari	23D Benside, Newmarket, Stornoway, Isle of Lewis HS2 0DZ [E-mail: tk.shadakshari@nhs.net] [E-mail: shadaks2@yahoo.com]	(Home) 01851 701727 (Office) 01851 704704 (Mbl) 07403 697138

ORKNEY HEALTH BOARD

BALFOUR AND EASTBANK   Mrs Marion Dicken   6 Claymore Brae, Kirkwall KW15 1UQ   01856 879509

LIST D – FULL-TIME WORKPLACE CHAPLAINS

NATIONAL DIRECTOR	Rev. Iain McFadzean	iain.mcfadzean@wpcscotland.co.uk	(Mbl) 07969 227696
EDINBURGH AND CENTRAL			
Regional Organiser	Mr Paul Wilson	paul.wilson@wpcscotland.co.uk	(Mbl) 07703 585987
Edinburgh City Centre	Rev. Tony Bryer	tbryer@wpcscotland.co.uk	(Mbl) 07834 748129
Edinburgh West	Rev. James Stewart	james.stewart@wpcscotland.co.uk	(Mbl) 07980 162788
WEST OF SCOTLAND			
Regional Organiser	Rev. Gordon Armstrong	gordon.armstrong@wpcscotland.co.uk	(Mbl) 07999 485109
DUNDEE AND TAYSIDE			
Regional Organiser	Rev. Allan Webster	allan.webster@wpcscotland.co.uk	(Mbl) 07546 276725
ABERDEEN – City Centre	Mrs Cate Adams	cateadams@wpcscotland.co.uk	(Mbl) 07890 954027
	Rev. Alison Harvey	aharvey@wpcscotland.co.uk	(Mbl) 07508 654423
UK OIL AND GAS INDUSTRY	Rev. Gordon Craig	gordon.craig@ukoilandgaschaplaincy.com	01224 297532

LIST E – PRISON CHAPLAINS

ADVISER TO SCOTTISH PRISON SERVICE (NATIONAL)   Rev. William R. Taylor   SPS HQ, Calton House, Edinburgh EH12 9DQ   0131-244 8640

Location	Chaplains	Address	Telephone
ABERDEEN	Rev. Louis Kinsey Rev. Dr David Ross	HM Prison, Aberdeen AB11 8FN	01224 238300
ADDIEWELL	Rev. Bob Paterson Rev. Peter Hall	HM Prison, Addiewell, West Calder EH55 8QA	01506 874500 ext. 3606
CORNTON VALE	Rev. William R. Taylor Ms Deirdre Yellowlees	HM Prison and YOI Cornton Vale, Stirling FK9 5NU	01786 835365
DUMFRIES	Rev. Neil Campbell Rev. Calum Smith	HM Prison, Dumfries DG2 9AX	01387 274214
EDINBURGH: SAUGHTON	Rev. Colin Reid Rev. Dr Bob Akroyd Rev. Chris Currie Rev. Keith Graham	HM Prison, Edinburgh EH11 3LN	0131-444 3115
GLASGOW: BARLINNIE	Rev. Douglas Clark Rev. Alex Wilson Rev. Jonathan Keefe Rev. Ian McInnes	HM Prison, Barlinnie, Glasgow G33 2QX	0141-770 2059
GLENOCHIL	Rev. Graham Bell Rev. Elizabeth Kenny	HM Prison, Glenochil FK10 3AD	01259 760471 ext. 7211 or 7431
GREENOCK	Rev. James Munro	HM Prison, Gateside, Greenock PA16 9AH	01475 787801 ext. 287
INVERNESS	Rev. Peter Donald Rev. Alexander Shaw Rev. Christopher Smart	HM Prison, Inverness IV2 3HN	01463 229020 ext. 244
KILMARNOCK	Rev. Andrew Black Mr Nigel Johns	HMP Kilmarnock, Bowhouse, Mauchline Road, Kilmarnock KA1 5AA	01563 548928
LOW MOSS	Rev. Martin Forrest Mr Craig Bryan Rev. John Craib	HMP Low Moss, Crosshill Road, Bishopbriggs, Glasgow G64 2PZ	0141-762 9727

OPEN ESTATE: CASTLE HUNTLY	Rev. Anne E. Stewart	HMP Open Estate, Castle Huntly, Longforgan, Dundee DD2 5HL	01382 319388
PERTH	Rev. Graham Matthews Ms Deirdre Yellowlees	Chaplaincy Centre, HM Prison, Perth PH2 7JH	01738 458216
PETERHEAD	Rev. Dr David Ross	HM Prison, Peterhead AB42 6YY	01779 485040
POLMONT	Rev. Donald H. Scott Mr Craig Bryan	Chaplaincy Centre, HMYOI Polmont, Falkirk FK2 0AB	01324 722241
SHOTTS	Ms Dorothy Russell Rev. Murdo Maclean	Chaplaincy Centre, HM Prison, Shotts ML7 4LE	01501 824071

LIST F – UNIVERSITY CHAPLAINS

ABERDEEN	Easter Smart MDiv DMin	01224 488396
ABERTAY, DUNDEE	Leslie M. Barrett BD FRICS	01382 308447
CALEDONIAN		0141-558 7451
CAMBRIDGE	Nigel Uden (U.R.C. and C. of S.)	01223 314586
DUNDEE	Fiona C. Douglas MBE MA BD PhD	01382 384157
EDINBURGH	Richard E. Frazer BA BD DMin (Honorary)	0131-650 2595
GLASGOW	Stuart D. MacQuarrie JP BD BSc	0141-330 5419
HERIOT-WATT	Alistair P. Donald MA PhD BD	0131-451 4508
NAPIER	John R. Smith MA BD (Honorary)	0131-447 8724
OXFORD	Carla Grosch-Miller (U.R.C. and C. of S.)	01865 554358
PAISLEY		0141-571 4059
ROBERT GORDON	Daniel French	01224 262000 (ext. 3506)
ST ANDREWS	Donald G. MacEwan MA BD PhD	01334 462866
STIRLING	Gillian Weighton BD STM (Honorary)	01786 832753
STRATHCLYDE		0141-553 4144

LIST G – THE DIACONATE

NAME	COM	APP	ADDRESS	TEL	PRES
Anderson, Janet (Miss) DCS	1979	2006	Creagard, 31 Lower Breakish, Isle of Skye IV42 8QA [E-mail: jaskye31@tiscali.co.uk]	01471 822403	38
Beaton, Margaret (Miss) DCS	1989	1988	64 Gardenside Grove, Carmyle, Glasgow G32 8EZ [E-mail: margaret@churchhouse.plus.com]	0141-646 2297 (Mbl) 07796 642382	16
Bell, Sandra (Mrs) DCS	2001	2004	62 Loganswell Road, Thornliebank, Glasgow G46 8AX	0141-638 5884	16
Black, Linda (Miss) BSc DCS	1993	2004	148 Rowan Road, Abronhill, Cumbernauld, Glasgow G67 3DA [E-mail: lnan@blueyonder.co.uk]	01236 786265	22
Blair, Fiona (Miss) DCS		2010	[E-mail: fiobla12@aol.com]	(Mbl) 07977 235168	11
Buchanan, Marion (Mrs) MA DCS	1983	2006	16 Almond Drive, East Kilbride, Glasgow G74 2HX	01698 292685	16
Burns, Marjory (Mrs) DCS	1997	1998	22 Kirklee Road, Mossend, Bellshill ML4 2QN [E-mail: mburns8070@aol.co.uk]	07792 843922	17
Carson, Christine (Miss) MA DCS	2006		36 Upper Wellhead, Limekilns, Dunfermline KY11 3JQ	(Mbl) 01383 873131 07919 137294	24
Cathcart, John Paul (Mr) DCS	2000		9 Glen More, East Kilbride, Glasgow G74 2AP [E-mail: paulcathcart@msn.com]	01355 243970 (Mbl) 07708 396074	16
Corrie, Margaret (Miss) DCS	1989	1998	44 Sunnyside Street, Camelon, Falkirk FK1 4BH	01324 670656	22
Crawford, Morag (Miss) MSc DCS	1977	1998	118 Wester Drylaw Place, Edinburgh EH4 2TG [E-mail: morag.crawford.dcs@blueyonder.co.uk]	(Tel/Fax) 0131-332 2253 (Mbl) 07970 982563	24
Crocker, Elizabeth (Mrs) DipComEd	1985	2003	77C Craigcrook Road, Edinburgh EH4 3PH	0131-332 0227	1
Cunningham, Ian (Mr) DCS	1994	2002	110 Nelson Terrace, Keith AB55 5FD [E-mail: icunninghamdcs@btinternet.com]		35
Cuthbertson, Valerie (Miss) DipTMus DCS	2003		105 Bellshill Road, Motherwell ML1 3SJ [E-mail: v.cuthbertson333@btinternet.com]	01698 259001	22
Deans, Raymond (Mr) DCS	1994	2003	60 Ardmory Road, Rothesay, Isle of Bute PA20 0PG [E-mail: r.deans93@btinternet.com]	01700 504893	19
Dunnett, Linda (Mrs)	1976	2000	5 Fincastle Place, Cowie, Stirling FK7 7DS [E-mail: lindadunnett@sky.com]	01786 818413	23
Evans, Mark (Mr) BSc RGN DCS	1988	2006	13 Easter Drylaw Drive, Edinburgh EH4 2QA [E-mail: MarkEvansDCS@aol.com]	0131-343 3089 (Office) 01383 674136	1
Gargrave, Mary (Mrs) DCS	1989	2002	The Manse, 90 Mount Annan Drive, Glasgow G44 4RZ [E-mail: mary_gargrave@btinternet.com]	0141-561 4681	16
Getliffe, Dorothy (Mrs) DCS BA BD DipEd	2006		3 Woodview Terrace, Hamilton ML3 9DP [E-mail: dgetliffe@aol.co.uk]	01698 423504 (Mbl) 07766 910171	16
Gordon, Margaret (Mrs) DCS	1998	2001	92 Lanark Road West, Currie EH14 5LA	0131-449 2554	1
Gray, Greta (Miss) DCS	1992	1998	67 Crags Avenue, Paisley PA2 6SG [E-mail: greta.gray@ntlworld.com]	0141-884 6178	14

Name			Address / E-mail	Telephone	No.
Hamilton, James (Mr) DCS	1997	2000	6 Beckfield Gate, Glasgow G33 1SW [E-mail: j.hamilton111@btinternet.com]	0141-558 3195	16
Hamilton, Karen (Mrs) DCS	1995	2009	6 Beckfield Gate, Glasgow G33 1SW [E-mail: k.hamilton6@btinternet.com]	0141-558 3195 (Mbl) 07970 872859	17
King, Margaret (Miss) DCS	2002		56 Murrayfield, Fochabers IV32 7EZ	01343 820937	35
Love, Joanna (Ms) BSc DCS	2006		92 Everard Drive, Glasgow G21 1XQ	0141-563 5859	16
Lyall, Ann (Miss) DCS	1980	2011	17 Mercat Loan, Biggar ML12 6DG [E-mail: ann.lyall@btinternet.com]	01899 229443	13
MacDonald, Anne (Miss) BA DCS	1980	2002	502 Castle Gait, Paisley PA1 2PA	0141-840 1875	16
McKay, Kenneth (Mr) DCS	1996	1998	11F Balgowan Road, Letham, Perth PH1 2JG [E-mail: deakendan@gmail.com]	01738 621169 (Mbl) 07843 883042	28
McLellan, Margaret (Mrs)	1986	2000	18 Broom Road East, Newton Mearns, Glasgow G77 5SD	0141-639 6853	16
McPheat, Elspeth (Miss)	1985	2001	11/5 New Orchardfield, Edinburgh EH6 5ET	0131-554 4143	1
Mulligan, Anne MA DCS	1974	1986	27A Craigour Avenue, Edinburgh EH17 7NH [E-mail: mulliganne@aol.com]	0131-664 3426 (Office) 0131-242 1996	1
Munro, Patricia (Ms) BSc DCS	1986	2002	4 Hewat Place, Perth PH1 2UD [E-mail: pat.munrodcs@gmail.com]	01738 443088 (Mbl) 07814 836314	24
Nicholson, David (Mr) DCS	1994	1993	2D Doonside, Kildrum, Cumbernauld, Glasgow G67 2HX [E-mail: deacdave@btinternet.com]	01236 732260	22
Nicol, Joyce (Mrs) BA DCS	1974	1998	93 Brisbane Street, Greenock PA16 8NY	01475 723235 (Mbl) 07957 642709	14
Ogilvie, Colin (Mr) DCS	1998	2003	32 Upper Bourtree Court, Glasgow G73 4HT	0141-569 2725	16
Philip, Elizabeth (Mrs) DCS MA BA PGCSE			12 Torvean Place, Dunfermline KY11 4YY	01383 721054	24
Porter, Jean (Mrs) HNC BD DCS	2006		3 Cochrie Place, Tullibody, Alloa FK10 2RR [E-mail: jeanjeanniet@aol.com]	(Mbl) 07729 316321	23
Ross, Duncan (Mr) DCS	1996	2006	1 John Neilson Avenue, Paisley PA1 2SX [E-mail: ssornacnud@hotmail.com]	0141-887 2801	14
Rycroft-Sadi, Pauline (Mrs) DCS	2003	2006	6 Ashville Terrace, Edinburgh EH6 8DD [E-mail: prycroft-sadi@blueyonder.co.uk]	0131-554 6564 (Mbl) 07759 436303	1
Steven, Gordon BD DCS	1997	2004	51 Nantwich Drive, Edinburgh EH7 6RB	0131-669 2054 07904 385256 (Mbl)	3
Stewart, Marion (Miss) DCS	1991	1994	Kirk Cottage, Kirkton of Skene, Westhill, Skene AB32 6XE	01224 743407	33
Thomson, Jacqueline (Mrs) MTh DCS	2004	2004	1 Barron Terrace, Leven KY8 4DL [E-mail: churchdeacon@blueyonder.co.uk]	01333 301115 (Mbl) 07806 776560	25
Urquhart, Barbara (Mrs) DCS	1986	2006	9 Standalane, Kilmaurs, Kilmarnock KA3 2NB [E-mail: barbaraurquhart@uko2.co.uk]	01563 538289	11
Wallace, Sheila (Mrs) DCS BA BD	2011	2006		(Mbl) 07733 243046	36
Wilson, Glenda (Mrs) DCS	1990		Ardlayne, 23 Bullwood Road, Dunoon PA23 7QJ [E-mail: deacglendamwilson@gmail.com]	01369 700848	19
Wishart, William (Mr) DCS	1994	2004	10 Stanely Drive, Paisley PA2 6HE [E-mail: bill@saintninians.co.uk]	0141-884 4177 (Mbl) 07846 555654	14

| Wright, Lynda (Miss) BEd DCS | 1979 | 1992 | Key Cottage, High Street, Falkland, Cupar KY15 7BU [E-mail: lynda@keyhouse.org] | 01337 857705 | 26 |

THE DIACONATE (Retired List)

NAME	COM	ADDRESS	TEL	PRES
Allan, Jean (Mrs) DCS	1989	12C Hindmarsh Avenue, Dundee DD3 7LW	01382 827299	29
Bayes, Muriel C. (Mrs) DCS	1963	Flat 6, Carleton Court, 10 Fenwick Road, Glasgow G46 4AN	0141-633 0865	16
Buchanan, John (Mr) DCS	2010	19 Gillespie Crescent, Edinburgh EH10 4HZ	0131-229 0794	3
Cameron, Margaret (Miss) DCS	1961	2 Rowans Gate, Paisley PA2 6RD	0141-840 2479	14
Copland, Agnes M. (Mrs) MBE DCS	1950	Altnacraig House, Lyle Road, Greenock PA16 7XT	01955 603805	14
Craw, John (Mr) DCS	1998	Liabost, 8 Proudfoot Road, Wick KW1 4PQ	(Mbl) 07544 761653	41
Cunningham, Alison W. (Miss) DCS	1961	23 Strathblane Road, Milngavie, Glasgow G62 8DL	0141-563 9232	18
Drummond, Rhoda (Miss) DCS	1960	Flat K, 23 Grange Loan, Edinburgh EH9 2ER	0131-668 3631	1
Erskine, Morag (Miss) DCS	1979	111 Mains Drive, Park Mains, Erskine PA8 7JJ	0141-812 6096	14
Flockhart, Andrew (Mr) DCS	1988	Flat 0/1, 8 Hardie Avenue, Rutherglen, Glasgow G73 3AS	0141-569 0716	16
Forrest, Janice (Mrs)	1990	38 Lochview Drive, Glasgow G33 1QF	0141-770 9611	16
Gordon, Fiona S. (Mrs) MA DCS	1958	Machrie, 3 Cupar Road, Cuparmuir, Cupar KY15 5RH [E-mail: machrie@madasafish.com]	01334 652341	26
Gray, Catherine (Miss) DCS	1969	10C Eastern View, Gourock PA19 1RJ	01475 637479	14
Gray, Christine M. (Mrs) DCS	1969	11 Woodside Avenue, Thornliebank, Glasgow G46 7HR	0141-571 1008	16
Howden, Margaret (Miss) DCS	1954	38 Munro Street, Kirkcaldy KY1 1PY	01592 205913	25
Hughes, Helen (Miss) DCS	1977	2/2, 43 Burnbank Terrace, Glasgow G20 6UQ	0141-333 9459	16
Hutchison, Alan E.W. (Mr) DCS	1988	132 Lochbridge Road, North Berwick EH39 4DR	01620 894077	3
Johnston, Mary (Miss) DCS	1988	19 Lounsdale Drive, Paisley PA2 9ED	0141-849 1615	14
King, Chris (Mrs) DCS	2002	28 Kilnford, Dundonald, Kilmarnock KA2 9ET [E-mail: chrisking99@tiscali.co.uk]	01563 851197	10
Lundie, Ann V. (Miss) DCS	1972	20 Langdykes Drive, Cove, Aberdeen AB12 3HW	01224 898416	31
McBain, Margaret (Miss) DCS	1974	33 Quarry Road, Paisley PA2 7RD	0141-884 2920	14
McCallum, Moyra (Miss) MA BD DCS	1965	176 Hilton Drive, Aberdeen AB24 4LT [E-mail: moymac@aol.com]	01224 486240	31
McCully, M. Isobel (Miss) DCS	1974	10 Broadstone Avenue, Port Glasgow PA14 5BB	01475 742240	14
MacKinnon, Ronald (Mr) DCS	1996	12 Mossywood Court, McGregor Avenue, Airdrie ML6 7DY	01236 763389	22
MacLean, Donald A. (Mr) DCS	1988	8 Upper Barvas, Isle of Lewis HS2 0QX	01851 840454	44
McNaughton, Janette (Miss) DCS	1982	4 Dunellan Avenue, Moodiesburn, Glasgow G69 0GB	01236 870180	22
MacPherson, James B. (Mr) DCS	1988	104 Cartside Street, Glasgow G42 9TQ	0141-616 6468	16

Name	Year	Address	Telephone	No.
MacQuien, Duncan (Mr) DCS	1988	35 Criffel Road, Mount Vernon, Glasgow G32 9JE	0141-575 1137	14
Martin, Janie (Miss) DCS	1979	16 Wentworth Road, Dundee DD2 3SD [E-mail: janimar@aol.com]	01382 813786	29
Merrilees, Ann (Miss) DCS	1994	23 Cuthill Brae, Willow Wood Residential Park, West Calder EH55 8QE [E-mail: ann@merrilees.freeserve.co.uk]	01501 762909	2
Miller, Elsie M. (Miss) DCS	1974	30 Swinton Avenue, Rowanbank, Baillieston, Glasgow G69 6JR	0141-771 0857	22
Mitchell, Joyce (Mrs) DCS	1994	Sunnybank, Farr, Inverness IV2 6XG [E-mail: joyce@mitchell71.freeserve.co.uk]	01808 521285	37
Morrison, Jean (Dr) DCS	1964	45 Corslet Road, Currie EH14 5LZ [E-mail: jean.morrison@blueyonder.co.uk]	0131-449 6859	1
Moyes, Sheila (Miss) DCS	1957	158 Pilton Avenue, Edinburgh EH5 2JZ	0131-551 1731	1
Palmer, Christine (Ms) DCS	2003	39 Fortingall Place, Perth PH1 2NF	01738 587488	28
Ramsay, Katherine (Miss) MA DCS	1958	25 Homeroyal House, 2 Chalmers Crescent, Edinburgh EH9 1TP	0131-667 4791	1
Rennie, Agnes M. (Miss) DCS	1974	3/1 Craigmillar Court, Edinburgh EH16 4AD	0131-661 8475	1
Ronald, Norma A. (Miss) MBE DCS	1961	2B Saughton Road North, Edinburgh EH12 7HG	0131-334 8736	1
Rose, Lewis (Mr) DCS	1993	5 Lyndhurst Avenue, Dundee DD2 3HR [E-mail: scinmorth@uk.uumail.com]	01382 622167 / 07899 790466 (Mbl)	29
Rutherford, Ellen B. (Miss) MBE DCS	1962	41 Duncanston, Conon Bridge, Dingwall IV7 8JB	01349 877439	39
Smith, Catherine (Mrs) DCS	1964	21 Lingaro, Bixter, Shetland ZE2 9NN	01595 810207	46
Steele, Marilynn J. (Mrs) BD DCS	1999	2 Northfield Gardens, Prestonpans EH32 9LQ	01875 811497	1
Stuart, Anne (Miss) DCS	1966	1 Murrell Terrace, Burntisland KY3 0XH	01383 860049	24
Tait, Agnes (Mrs) DCS	1995	10 Carnoustie Crescent, Greenhills, East Kilbride, Glasgow G75 8TE	01389 873196	17
Teague, Yvonne (Mrs) DCS	1965	46 Craigcrook Avenue, Edinburgh EH4 3PX	0131-336 3113	1
Thom, Helen (Miss) BA DipEd MA DCS	1959	84 Great King Street, Edinburgh EH3 6QU	0131-556 5687	1
Thomson, Phyllis (Miss) DCS	2003	63 Caroline Park, Mid Calder, Livingston EH53 0SJ	01506 883207	2
Trimble, Robert DCS	1988	5 Templar Rise, Livingston EH54 6PJ	01506 412504	2
Webster, Elspeth H. (Miss) DCS	1950	82 Broomhill Avenue, Burntisland KY3 0BP	01592 873616	25
Wilson, Muriel (Miss) MA BD DCS	1997	28 Bellevue Crescent, Ayr KA7 2DR [E-mail: muriel.wilson4@btinternet.com]	01292 264939	10

THE DIACONATE (Supplementary List)

Name	Year	Address	Telephone
Gilroy, Lorraine (Mrs) DCS	1988	5 Bluebell Drive, Cheverel Court, Bedward CO12 0GE	02476 366031
Guthrie, Jennifer M. (Miss) DCS		14 Eskview Terrace, Ferryden, Montrose DD10 9RD	01674 674413

NAME	ADDRESS	ORD	TEL	PRES
Harris, Judith (Mrs) DCS	243 Western Avenue, Sandfields, Port Talbot, West Glamorgan SA12 7NF	1993	01639 884855	30
Hood, Katrina (Mrs) DCS	67C Farquhar Road, Edgbaston, Birmingham B18 2QP	1988		
Hudson, Sandra (Mrs) DCS	10 Albany Drive, Rutherglen, Glasgow G73 3QN	1982		
McIntosh, Kay (Mrs) DCS	4 Jacklin Green, Livingston EH54 8PZ [E-mail: kay@backedge.co.uk]	2008	01506 440543	
Muir, Alison M. (Mrs) DCS	77 Arthur Street, Dunfermline KY12 0JJ	1969		
Ramsden, Christine (Miss) DCS	2 Wykeham Close, Bassett, Southampton SO16 7LZ	1978		
Walker, Wikje (Mrs) DCS	24 Brodie's Yard, Queen Street, Coupar Angus PH13 9RA	1970	01828 628251	
Wallace, Catherine (Mrs) DCS	5 Strathearn Terrace, Perth PH2 0LS		01738 621709	

LIST H – MINISTERS HAVING RESIGNED MEMBERSHIP OF PRESBYTERY
(in Terms of Act III 1992)

(Resignation of Presbytery membership does not imply the lack of a practising certificate. Some of those listed do have practising certificates; others do not.)

NAME	ORD	ADDRESS	TEL	PRES
Anderson, Kenneth G. MA BD	1967	8 School Road, Arbroath DD11 2LT	01241 874825	30
Barbour, Robin A.S. KCVO MC MA BD STM DD	1954	Old Fincastle, Pitlochry PH16 5RJ	01796 473209	27
Bartholomew, Julia (Mrs) BSc BD	2002	Kippenhill, Dunning, Perth PH2 0RA	01764 684929	28
Beck, John C. BD	1975	31 The Woodlands, Stirling FK8 2LB		35
Black, W. Graham MA BD	1983	72 Linksview, Linksfield Road, Aberdeen AB24 5RG [E-mail: graham.black@virgin.net]	01224 492491	31
Blane, Quintin A. BSc BD MSc	1979	18D Kirkhill Road, Penicuik EH26 8HZ [E-mail: quintin@qab.org.uk]	01968 670017	3
Brown, Alastair BD	1986	52 Henderson Drive, Kintore, Inverurie AB51 0FB	01467 632787	32
Brown, Joseph MA	1954	The Orchard, Hermitage Lane, Shedden Park Road, Kelso TD5 7AN	01573 223481	6
Caie, Albert LTh	1983	34 Ringwell Gardens, Stonehouse, Larkhall ML9 3QW	01698 792187	32
Campbell, J. Ewen R. MA BD	1967	20 St Margaret's Road, North Berwick EH39 4PJ	01620 893814	25
Campbell, Richard S. LTh	1993	3 River Wynd, Strathallan Park, Stirling FK9 5GN [E-mail: revrichards@btinternet.com]	01786 469622	23
Cooper, George MA BD	1943	8 Leighton Square, Alyth, Blairgowrie PH11 8AQ	01828 633746	1
Craig, Eric MA BD BA	1959	5 West Relugas Road, Edinburgh EH9 2PW	0131-667 8210	1
Craig, Gordon W. MBE MA BD	1972	1 Beley Bridge, Dunino, St Andrews KY16 8LT	01334 880285	26
Crawford, S.G. Victor	1980	Crofton, 65 Main Road, East Wemyss, Kirkcaldy KY1 4RL	01592 712325	25
Cumming, David P.L. MA	1957	Shillong, Tarbat Ness Road, Portmahomack, Tain IV20 1YA	01862 871794	19
Currie, Gordon C.M. MA BD	1975	43 Deanburn Park, Linlithgow EH49 6HA	01506 842759	2

Name	Year	Address / E-mail	Tel	
Davidson, John F. BSc DipEdTech	1970	49 Craigmill Gardens, Carnoustie DD7 6HX \ E-mail: davidson900@btinternet.com]	01241 854566	30
Davies, Gareth W. BA BD	1979	Pitadro House, Fordell Gardens, Dunfermline KY11 7EY	01383 417634	24
Doherty, Arthur James DipTh	1957	1 Murdiston Avenue, Callander FK17 8AY		23
Donaldson, Colin V.	1982	3A Playfair Terrace, St Andrews KY16 9HX	01334 472889	3
Drake, Wendy F. (Mrs) BD	1978	21 William Black Place, South Queensferry EH30 9QR \ E-mail: revwdrake@hotmail.co.uk]	0131-331 1520	1
Drummond, R. Hugh	1953	19 Winton Park, Edinburgh EH10 7EX \ E-mail: hughdrummond1@activemail.co.uk]	0131-445 3634	1
Ferguson, Ronald \ MA BD ThM DUniv	1972	Vinbreck, Orphir, Orkney KW17 2RE \ E-mail: ronbluebrazil@aol.com]	01856 811353	45
Finlay, Quintin BA BD	1975	Ivy Cottage, Greenlees Farm, Kelso TD5 8BT	(Mbl) 07901 981171	6
Finlayson, Duncan MA	1943	Flat 3, Nicholson Court, Kinnettas Road, Strathpeffer IV14 9BG	01997 420014	39
Flockhart, D. Ross \ OBE BA BD DUniv	1955	Longwood, Humbie EH36 5PN \ E-mail: rossflock@ednet.co.uk]	01875 833208	31
Gordon, Alasdair B. BD LLB EdD	1970	Flat 1, 13 Auchingramont Road, Hamilton ML3 6JP \ E-mail: alasdairbgordon@hotmail.com]	01698 200561	31
Greig, James C.G. MA BD STM	1955	Block 2, Flat 2, Station Lofts, Strathblane, Glasgow G63 9BD \ E-mail: james.greig12@btinternet.com]	(Mbl) 07768 897843 \ 01360 771915	16
Grubb, George D.W. \ BA BD BPhil DMin	1962	10 Wellhead Close, South Queensferry EH30 9WA	0131-331 2072	1
Hamilton, David S.M. MA BD STM	1958	49 Paddocks Lane, Cheltenham GL50 4NU	01242 254917	47
Hosie, James MA BD MTh	1959	Hilbre, Baycrofts, Strachur, Cairndow, Argyll PA27 8BY	01369 860634	19
Howie, William MA BD STM	1964	26 Morgan Road, Aberdeen AB16 5JY	01224 483669	31
Hurst, Frederick R. MA	1965	Flat 6, 21 Bulldale Place, Glasgow G14 0NE	0141-959 2604	40
Lambie, Andrew E. BD	1957	1 Mercat Loan, Biggar ML12 6DG	01899 221352	13
Lindsay, W. Douglas BD CPS	1978	3 Drummond Place, Calderwood, East Kilbride, Glasgow G74 3AD	01355 234169	16
McDonald, William J.G. DD	1953	7 Blacket Place, Edinburgh EH9 1RN	0131-667 2100	1
Macfarlane, Alwyn J.C. MA	1951	Flat 12, Homeburn House, 177 Fenwick Road, Giffnock, Glasgow G46 6JD	0141-620 3235	1
McGillivray, A. Gordon MA BD STM	1951	36 Larchfield Neuk, Balerno EH14 7NL		1
Mackenzie, J.A.R. MA	1947	West Lodge, Inverness Road, Nairn IV12 4SD	01667 452827	26
McKenzie, Mary O. (Miss)	1976	4 Dunellan Avenue, Moodiesburn, Glasgow G69 0GB	01236 870180	16
Mackie, John F. BD	1979	1A Halls Close, Weldon, Corby, Northants NN17 3HH		40
Mackinnon, Thomas J.R. \ LTh DipMin	1996	4 Flashadder, Arnisort, Portree, Isle of Skye IV51 9PT	01470 582377	39
McLean, John MA BD	1967	16 Eastside Drive, Westhill AB32 6QN	01224 747701	33
Mair, John BSc	1965	21 Kenilworth Avenue, Helensburgh G84 7JR	01436 671744	18
Millar, John L. MA BD	1981	Flat 0/1, 12 Chesterfield Gardens, Glasgow G12 0BF	0141-339 4098	38
Miller, Irene B. (Mrs) MA BD	1984	5 Braeside Park, Aberfeldy PH15 2DT	01887 829396	27
Morton, Andrew Q. \ MA BSc BD FRSE	1949	Sunnyside, 4A Manse Street, Aberdour, Burntisland KY3 0TY		18
O'Leary, Thomas BD	1983	1 Carter's Place, Irvine KA12 0BU	01294 313274	11

Name	ORD	Address	TEL	PRES
Osbeck, John R. BD	1979	15 Deeside Crescent, Aberdeen AB15 7PT	01224 315595	31
Park, Christopher BSc BD	1977	65 Moubray Road, Dalgety Bay, Dunfermline KY11 9JP [E-mail: chrispark8649@hotmail.com]	01383 821111	24
Ramsay, Alan MA	1967	12 Riverside Grove, Lochyside, Fort William PH33 7NY		38
Reid, Janette G. (Miss) BD	1991	c/o Glasgow Presbytery Office, 260 Bath Street, Glasgow G2 4JP		16
Reid, William M. MA BD	1966	10 Rue Rossini, F-75009 Paris, France		48
Ritchie, Garden W.M.	1961	23 Croft Road, Kelso TD5 7EP	01573 224419	6
Scott, J.A. Miller MA BD FSAScot DD	1949	St Martins, 6 Trinity Place, St Andrews KY16 8SG	01334 479518	26
Scouller, Hugh BSc BD	1985	11 Kirk View, Haddington EH41 4AN [E-mail: h.scouller@btinternet.com]		3
Duncan Shaw of Chapelverna Bundesverdienstkreuz PhD ThDr Drhc	1951	4 Sydney Terrace, Edinburgh EH7 6SL	0131-337 2130	19
Shaw, D.W.D. BA BD LLB WS DD	1960	4/13 Succoth Court, Edinburgh EH12 6BZ	0131-663 1234	26
Smith, Ralph C.P. MA STM	1960	2A Waverley Road, Eskbank, Dalkeith EH22 3DJ [E-mail: rcpsmith@waitrose.com]		1
Spowart, Mary G. (Mrs) BD	1978	Aldersyde, St Abbs Road, Coldingham, Eyemouth TD14 5NR	01890 771697	26
Strachan, Ian M. MA BD	1959	'Cardenwell', Glen Drive, Dyce, Aberdeen AB21 7EN	01224 772028	31
Taylor, David J. MA BD	1982	32 Croft an Righ, Inverkeithing KY11 1PF	01383 413227	24
Thomson, Gilbert L. BA	1965	3 Forthafield, Freuchie, Cupar KY15 7JJ	01337 857431	25
Weatherhead, James L. CBE MA LLB DD	1960	59 Brechin Road, Kirriemuir DD8 4DE	01575 572237	30
Webster, John G. BSc	1964	Plane Tree, King's Cross, Brodick, Isle of Arran KA27 8RG	01770 700747	16
Westmarland, Colin A.	1971	PO Box 5, Cospicua, CSPO1, Malta	00356 216 923552	48
Wilkie, George D. OBE BL	1948	2/37 Barnton Avenue West, Edinburgh EH4 6EB	0131-339 3973	1

LIST I – MINISTERS HOLDING PRACTISING CERTIFICATES (under Act II, as amended by Act VIII 2000)

Not all Presbyteries have stated whether or not some of those listed have taken a seat in Presbytery. There is still some variation in practice.

NAME	ORD	ADDRESS	TEL	PRES
Abeledo, Benjamin J.A. BTh DipTh PTh	1991	Army Foundation College, Uniacke Barracks, Penny Pot Lane, Harrogate HG3 2SE		23
Anderson, David MA BD	1975	Rowan Cottage, Aberlour Gardens, Aberlour AB38 9LD	01340 871906	35
Anderson, David P. BSc BD	2002	1 UK ADSR, Hammersmith Barracks, BFPO 15		
Anderson, Kenneth G. MA BD	1967	8 School Road, Arbroath DD11 2LT	01241 874825	30

Name	Year	Address / E-mail	Telephone	No.
Arbuthnott, Joan E. (Mrs) MA BD	1993	139/1 New Street, Musselburgh EH21 6DH	0131-665 6736	3
Barbour, Robin A.S. KCVO MC MA BD STM DD				
Barclay, Neil W. BSc BEd BD	1954	Old Fincastle, Pitlochry PH16 5RJ	01796 473209	27
Bartholomew, Julia (Mrs) BSc BD	1986	4 Gibsongray Street, Falkirk FK2 7LN	01324 874681	22
Beattie, Warren R. BSc BD MSc PhD	2002	Kippenhill, Dunning, Perth PH2 0RA	01764 684929	28
	1991	Director for Mission Research, OMF International, 2 Cluny Road, Singapore 259570 [E-mail: beattiewarren@omf.net]	0065 6319 4550	1
Bell, Ruth	2009	Flat 2/2, 22 Caledonia Street, Clydebank G81 4ER		18
Biddle, Lindsay (Ms)	1991	30 Ralston Avenue, Glasgow G52 3NA [E-mail: lindsaybiddle@hotmail.com]	0141-883 7405	
Birrell, John M. MA LLB BD	1974	'Hiddlehame', 5 Hewat Place, Perth PH1 2UD [E-mail: john.birrell@nhs.net]	01738 443335	28
Black, James S. BD DPS	1976	7 Breck Terrace, Penicuik EH26 0RJ [E-mail: jsb.black@btopenworld.com]	01968 677559	3
Bonar, Sandy F. LTh	1988	7 Westbank Court, Westbank Terrace, Macmerry, Tranent EH33 1QS [E-mail: sandy.bonar@btinternet.com]	01875 615165	3
Bowman, Norman McG. MA BD	1940	Abbotsford Nursing Home, 98 Eglinton Road, Ardrossan KA22 8NN		12
Boyd, Ian R. MA BD PhD	1989	33 Castleton Drive, Newton Mearns, Glasgow G77 3LE		
Brown, Robert F. MA BD ThM	1971	55 Hilton Drive, Aberdeen AB24 4NJ [E-mail: Bjacob546@aol.com]	01224 491451	31
Caie, Albert LTh	1983	34 Ringwell Gardens, Stonehouse, Larkhall ML9 3QW	01698 792187	17
Carvalho, Jose R. BD	2002	c/o The Ministries Council, 121 George Street, Edinburgh EH2 4YN (Mr Carvalho is currently living in Brazil)	0131-225 5722	28
Coogan, J. Melvyn LTh	1992	19 Glen Grove, Largs KA30 8QQ	01241 854566	12
Davidson, John F. BSc DipEdTech	1970	49 Craigmill Gardens, Carnoustie DD7 6HX [E-mail: davidson900@btinternet.com]		30
Davidson, Mark R. MA BD STM RN	2005	20 Kinmohr Rise, Blackburn, Aberdeen AB21 0LJ [E-mail: mark.davidson122@mod.uk]	01224 791350	33
Dickson, Graham T. MA BD	1985	19/4 Stead's Place, Edinburgh EH6 5DY [E-mail: gtd22@blueyonder.co.uk]	0131-476 0187	1
Donaldson, Colin V.	1982	3A Playfair Terrace, St Andrews KY16 9HX	01334 472889	3
Drake, Wendy F. (Mrs) BD	1978	21 William Black Place, South Queensferry EH30 9QR [E-mail: revwdrake@hotmail.co.uk]	0131-331 1520	1
Drummond, Professor Norman W. MA BD FRSE	1976	c/o Columba 1400 Ltd, Staffin, Isle of Skye IV51 9JY	01478 611400	42
Ellis, David W. GIMechE GIProdE	1962	4 Wester Tarsappie, Rhynd Road, Perth PH2 8PT	01738 449618	16
Ferguson, Ronald MA BD ThM DUniv	1972	Vinbreck, Orphir, Orkney KW17 2RE [E-mail: ronbluebrazil@aol.com]	01856 811353	45
Fowler, Richard C.A. BSc MSc BD	1978	4 Gardentown, Whalsay, Shetland ZE2 9AB	01806 566538	46
Fraser, Ian M. MA BD PhD	1946	Ferndale, Gargunnock, Stirling FK8 3BW	01786 860612	23
Frew, John M. MA BD	1946	17 The Furrows, Walton-on-Thames KT12 3JQ		16

Name	Year	Address	Phone	No.
Gow, Neil BSc MEd BD	1996	Hillhead Lodge, Portknockie, Buckie AB56 4PB	01542 840625	35
Groenewald, Jonanda BA BD MTh DD	1999	8 Manse Court, East Calder, Livingston EH53 0HF [E-mail: jonandagroenewald@yahoo.com]	01506 884585	2
Grubb, George D.W. BA BD BPhil DMin	1962	10 Wellhead Close, South Queensferry EH30 9WA	0131-331 2072	1
Henderson, Frances M. BA BD PhD	2006	Stoneyburn Farm, Crawford, Biggar ML12 6RH [E-mail: frances.henderson@tiscali.co.uk]	01864 502387	3
Hendrie, Yvonne (Mrs) MA BD	1995	The Manse, 16 McAdam Way, Maybole KA19 8FD	01655 883710	10
Hibbert, Frederick W. BD	1986	4 Cemydd Terrace, Senghemydd, Caerphilly, Mid Glamorgan CF83 4HL	02920 831653	47
Homewood, Ivor Maxwell MSc BD	1997	An der Fließwiese 26, D-14052 Berlin, Germany	0049 30 3048722	48
Hosie, James MA BD MTh	1959	Hilbre, Baycrofts, Strachur, Cairndow PA27 8BY	01369 860634	19
Jenkinson, John J. JP LTCL ALCM DipEd DipSen (Aux)	1991	8 Rosehall Terrace, Falkirk FK1 1PY	01324 625498	22
Johnstone, Donald B.	1969	22 Glenhove Road, Cumbernauld, Glasgow G67 2JZ	01236 612479	22
Johnstone, Robert MTheol	1973	59 Cliffburn Road, Arbroath DD11 5BA	01241 439292	30
Kellock, Chris N. MA BD	1998	7 Para RHA, Merville Barracks, Colchester CO2 7UT		3
Kenny, Celia G. BA MTh	1995	37 Grosvenor Road, Rathgar, Dublin 6, Ireland		5
Lawrie, Robert M. BD MSc DipMin LLCM(TD) MCMI	1994	18/1 John's Place, Edinburgh EH6 7EN [E-mail: robert.lawrie@ed.ac.uk]	0131-554 9765	1
Liddiard, F.G.B. MA	1957	34 Trinity Fields Crescent, Brechin DD9 6YF	01356 622966	30
Lindsay, W. Douglas BD CPS	1978	3 Drummond Place, Calderwood, East Kilbride, Glasgow G74 3AD	01355 234169	16
Logan, Thomas M. LTh	1971	3 Duncan Court, Kilmarnock KA3 7TF	01563 524398	11
Lyall, David BSc BD STM PhD	1965	16 Brian Crescent, Tunbridge Wells, Kent TN4 0AP [E-mail: lyall3@gmail.com]	01892 670323	47
Macaskill, Donald MA BD PhD	1994	HMS *Dalriada*, Navy Buildings, Eldon Street, Greenock PA16 7SL	0141-883 7545	16
McDonald, Ross J. BA BD ThM RNR	1998	[E-mail: rossjmcdonald@tiscali.co.uk]	(Mbl) 07952 558767	
McFadyen, Gavin BEng BD	2006	20 Tennyson Avenue, Bridlington YO15 2EP		18
McGillivray, A. Gordon MA BD STM	1951	36 Larchfield Neuk, Balerno EH14 7NL		1
McKean, Martin J. BD DipMin	1984	56 Kingsknowe Drive, Edinburgh EH14 2JX	0131-466 1157	1
MacPherson, Gordon C.	1963	203 Capelrig Road, Patterton, Newton Mearns, Glasgow G77 6ND	0141-616 2107	16
McPherson, William BD DipEd	1993	83 Laburnum Avenue, Port Seton, Prestonpans EH32 0UD	01875 812252	22
Mailer, Colin (Aux)	1996	Innis Chonain, Back Row, Polmont, Falkirk FK2 0RD	01324 712401	22
Main, Arthur W.A. BD	1954	13/3 Eildon Terrace, Edinburgh EH3 5NL	0131-556 1344	16
Masson, John D. MA BD PhD BSc	1984	2 Beechgrove, Craw Hall, Brampton CA8 1TS [E-mail: jmasson96@btinternet.com]	ex-directory	7
Mill, J. Stuart	1976	9 Chatsfield Close, Park View Road, Ealing, London W5 2JD	020 8810 4877	47
Millar, Peter W. MA BD PhD	1971	6/5 Ettrickdale Place, Edinburgh EH3 5JN [E-mail: ionacottage@hotmail.com]	0131-557 0517	1
Miller, Irene B. (Mrs) MA BD	1984	5 Braeside Park, Aberfeldy PH15 2DT	01887 829396	27
Moodie, Alastair R. MA BD	1978	4 Burnbrae Road, Auchinloch, Glasgow G66 5DQ		16

Name	Year	Address	Telephone	No.
Morton, Andrew Q. MA BSc BD FRSE	1949	Sunnyside, 4A Manse Street, Aberdour, Burntisland KY3 0TY		18
Muir, Margaret A. (Miss) MA LLB BD	1989	59/4 South Beechwood, Edinburgh EH12 5YS	0131-313 3240	13
Newell, Alison M. (Mrs) BD	1986	1A Inverleith Terrace, Edinburgh EH3 5NS [E-mail: alinewell@aol.com]	0131-556 3505	1
Newell, J. Philip MA BD PhD	1982	1A Inverleith Terrace, Edinburgh EH3 5NS	0131-556 3505	1
Notman, John R. BSc BD	1990	5 Dovecote Road, Bromsgrove, Worcs B61 7BN		47
Ostler, John H. MA LTh	1975	5 Osborne Terrace, Port Seton, Prestonpans EH32 0BZ	01875 814358	3
Owen, Catherine W. MTh	1984	10 Waverley Park, Kirkintilloch, Glasgow G66 2BP	0141-776 0407	16
Penman, Iain D. BD	1977	33/5 Carnbee Avenue, Edinburgh EH16 6GA [E-mail: iainpenmanklm@aol.com]	0131-664 0673 (Mbl) 07931 993427	1
Perry, Marion (Mrs) (Aux)	2009	0/2, 75 Earl Street, Glasgow G14 0DG [E-mail: perryask@hotmail.com]	0141-434 1280 (Mbl) 07563 180662	16
Provan, Iain W. MA BA PhD	1991	Regent College, 5800 University Boulevard, Vancouver BC V6T 2E4, Canada	001 604 224 3245	1
Roy, Alistair A. MA BD	1955	1 Broaddykes Close, Kingswells, Aberdeen AB15 8UF	01224 743310	31
Sawers, Hugh BA	1968	2 Rosemount Meadows, Castlepark, Bothwell, Glasgow G71 8EL	01698 853960	17
Scott, J.A. Miller MA BD FSAScot DD	1949	St Martins, 6 Trinity Place, St Andrews KY16 8SG	01334 479518	26
Shaw, D.W.D. BA BD LLB WS DD	1960	4/13 Succoth Court, Edinburgh EH12 6BZ	0131-337 2130	26
Stewart, Margaret L. (Mrs) BSc MB ChB BD	1985	28 Inch Crescent, Bathgate EH48 1EU	01506 653428	2
Storrar, William F. MA BD PhD	1984	Director, Centre of Theological Enquiry, 50 Stockton Street, Princeton, NJ 08540, USA		1
Strachan, David G. BD DPS	1978	1 Deeside Park, Aberdeen AB15 7PQ	01224 324101	31
Strachan, Ian M. MA BD	1959	'Cardenwell', Glen Drive, Dyce, Aberdeen AB21 7EN	01224 772028	31
Thomas, W. Colville ChLJ BTh BPhil DPS DSc	1964	11 Muirfield Crescent, Gullane EH31 2HN	01620 842415	3
Tollick, Frank BSc DipEd	1958	3 Bellhouse Road, Aberdour, Burntisland KY3 0TL	01383 860559	24
Turnbull, Julian S. BSc BD MSc CEng MBCS	1980	25 Hamilton Road, Gullane EH31 2HP [E-mail: jules-turnbull@zetnet.co.uk]	01620 842958	3
Weatherhead, James L. CBE MA LLB DD	1960	59 Brechin Road, Kirriemuir DD8 4DE	01575 572237	30
Weir, Mary K. (Mrs) BD PhD	1968	1249 Millar Road RR1, SITEH-46, BC V0N 1G0, Canada	001 604 947 0636	1
Whitton, John P.	1977	115 Sycamore Road, Farnborough, Hants GU14 6RE	01252 674488	47
Yarwood, Derek				48

LIST J – PRESBYTERY/PARISH WORKERS (PPWs)

Associate Ministers and Deacons employed by the Ministries Council and placed in charges appear under the name of the charge. It has not proved easy to compile a fully comprehensive and accurate list of these valued workers. We offer apologies where there are errors or omissions. Where a year is given, this indicates when the appointment referred to was made.

NAME	APP	ADDRESS	APPOINTMENT	TEL
Adam, Pamela BD	2009	Basement Left Flat, 409 Holburn Street, Aberdeen AB10 7GS [E-mail: thekirk@btinternet.com]	Gordon: Ellon	01358 725690 (Work) 07712 674614 (Mbl)
Anderson, Christopher	2008	14 Edmonstone Drive, Danderhall, Dalkeith EH22 1QQ	Newton and Loanhead	0131-663 0819
Atkin, Clare BEd	2009	38 Alford Drive, Glenrothes KY6 2HH [E-mail: clare@stninians.co.uk]	Glenrothes: St Ninian's	01592 565624 07783 685376 (Mbl)
Baker, Paula (Mrs)	2007	Kernow, 18 Main Street, Buckpool, Buckie AB56 1XQ [E-mail: mikepaulabaker@aol.com]	Moray Presbytery: Children's Ministry Training and Development	01542 832662 (Mbl)
Bauer, Alex (Ms)	2001	759A Argyle Street, Glasgow G3 8DS		0141-248 2905 07903 120226 (Mbl)
Beautyman, Paul H. (Rev.) MA BD	2009	59 Alexander Street, Dunoon PA23 7BB [E-mail: paul.beautyman@ dunoongrammar.argyll-bute.sch.uk]	Argyll Presbytery: Team Leader: Youth Education Ministries	
Beggs, Stuart	2009	4 Trondra Place, Glasgow G34 9AX	Glasgow: Lochwood	07793 039656 (Mbl)
Blackwood, Katrina BD	2009	Torry St Fittick's Church, 39 Walker Road, Torry, Aberdeen AB11 8DL [E-mail: beanie.blackwood@btinternet.com]	Aberdeen: Torry St Fittick's: Ministry Assistant (p/t)	01224 315748 07853 053579 (Mbl)
Bruce, Nicola (Mrs) BD MTh	2009	11 South Chesters Lane, Bonnyrigg EH19 3GL [E-mail: overhills@hotmail.com]	Lothian Presbytery: Tranent Cluster: Family and Youth Development Worker	07711 223100 (Mbl)
Bruce, Stuart	2009		Glasgow: Govanhill Trinity	
Buchan, William BSc BD	2009	36 Westdyke Avenue, Elrick, Westhill AB32 6QX [E-mail: will@covechurch.org.uk]	Aberdeen: Cove: Children's and Families Worker	01224 745410
Campbell, Alasdair BA	2000	3 Gellatly Road, Dunfermline KY11 4BH [E-mail: adcam@talktalk.net]	Dunfermline Presbytery: Dalgety/Forth Churches Group: Parish Assistant	01383 726238
Campbell, Neil MA	2010	36 Clovis Duveau Drive, Dundee DD2 5JB [E-mail: neilcampbell98@btinternet.com]	Dundee: Craigiebank with Douglas and Mid Craigie: Youth and Young Adult Development Worker	01382 561171 (Home) 01382 731173 (Work) 07999 349587 (Mbl)
Chaba, Sumtende MSc PgDipCE	2008	61 Anderson Avenue, Aberdeen AB24 4LR [E-mail: astiras@yahoo.com]	Aberdeen: Middlefield	01224 682310

Name	Commenced	Address/Email	Appointment	Tel.
Close, David BA MLitt	2001	34 Currie Place, Glasgow G20 9EQ [E-mail: close.david@rocketmail.com]	PEEK/Secondment PDF	
Cowie, Marjorie (Miss) MA BA	2002	35 Balbirnie Avenue, Markinch, Glenrothes KY7 6BS [E-mail: marjorieh@mhcowiestm.plus.com]	Glenrothes: St Margaret's: Parish Assistant	01592 758402
Crossan, Morag BA	2010	1A Church Hill, Dalmellington, Ayr KA6 7QP [E-mail: morag.crossan@gmail.com]	Dalmellington with Patna Waterside: Youth and Children's Worker	01292 550984 / 07861 736071 (Mbl)
Crumlin, Melodie (Mrs) BA PGMgt DipBusMgt	2000	c/o Gallowgate Parish Church, St Luke's Building, 17 Bain Street, Glasgow G40 2JZ [E-mail: projectmanager@peekproject.co.uk]	PEEK (Possibilities for East End Kids): Project Development Manager	0141-558 2589 (Home) / 0141-552 5757 (Work) / 07904 672891 (Mbl)
Dale-Pimentil, Sheila (Mrs) MA BD	1999/2007	3 Golf Road, Lundin Links, Leven KY8 6BB [E-mail: sdale.pimentil@btinternet.com]	Kennoway, Windygates and Balgonie: St Kenneth's: Parish Assistant	01333 329618 (Home) / 01333 351372 (Work)
Dyer, Eildon BSc MSc RGN DNCert	2008	Ruchazie Parish Church, 4 Eilbank Street, Glasgow G33 3QN [E-mail: eildon@ruchazie.eclipse.co.uk]	Glasgow: Ruchazie Parish Church: Interim Project Manager	0141-774 2759 / 07776 201270 (Mbl)
Finch, John		71 Maxwell Avenue, Westerton, Bearsden, Glasgow G61 1NZ [E-mail: johnfinch10@ntlworld.com]		0141-587 7390 / 07715 119263 (Mbl)
Finegan, Sarah (Mrs) BA	2007	261 Main Street, East Calder, Livingston EH53 0ED	Kirknewton and East Calder: Youth Worker	01506 882628
Forbes, Farquhar	2006/2008	The Heights, Inverarnie, Inverness IV2 4XA [E-mail: f.forbes@live.com]	Inverness: Inshes: Congregational Development Worker	07749 539981 (Mbl)
Gray, Ian	2011	The Mallards, 15 Rossie Island Road, Montrose DD10 9NH [E-mail: iancelia15@aol.com]	Esk Parish Grouping – Angus Presbytery: Pastoral Assistant	01674 677126 (Home) / 07757 888233 (Mbl)
Groenewald, Johannes (Rev.)	2009		Falkirk: Camelon: Associate Minister	
Guy, Helen (Miss)		24D Cattofield Place, Aberdeen AB25 3QL [E-mail: helenjguy@googlemail.com]	Aberdeen: St Columba's Bridge of Don	01224 488686 / 07923 177392 (Mbl)
Haringman, Paul MSc	2010	11 Tower Gardens, Westhill, Inverness IV2 5DQ [E-mail: paul.haringman@barnchurch.org.uk]	Inverness: Culloden: The Barn: Community Worker	01463 798946 (Home) / 01463 795428 (Work) / 07837 903277 (Mbl)
Harper, Kirsty (Mrs) BA	2009	Richmond Craigmillar Church, 227–229 Niddrie Mains Road, Edinburgh EH16 4AR [E-mail: k-harper@richmondshope.org.uk]		0131-661 6561 (Work) / 0131-258 5162 (Home)
Harvey, P. Ruth (Rev.) MA BD	2007	Croslands, Beacon Street, Penrith, Cumbria CA11 7TZ [E-mail: ruth.harvey@furtherministriesteam.com]	Annandale and Eskdale Presbytery: Congregational Facilitator (p/t)	01768 840749 / 07882 259631 (Mbl)
Harvey, Stuart		[E-mail: stuart.harvey@glasgowcathedral.org.uk]		
Hunter, Jean (Mrs)	2006	Manse, Shiskine, Isle of Arran KA27 8EP [E-mail: j.hunter744@btinternet.com]	Brodick with Corrie with Lochranza: Parish Assistant	01770 860380 (Mbl)

Name	Year	Address	Role	Phone
Hutchison, John BA	2001	30/4 West Pilton Gardens, Edinburgh EH4 4EG	Edinburgh: The Old Kirk: Parish Assistant	0131-538 1622
Johnston, Heather	2009	11 Eden Drive, Mossneuk, East Kilbride, Glasgow G75 8XX	East Kilbride: Mossneuk and East Kilbride: Westwood	07894 538340 (Mbl)
Johnstone, Christine	2009	4 Ramsay Avenue, Johnstone PA5 0EU [E-mail: ceejae51@yahoo.co.uk]	East Kilbride: Claremont and South Parishes: Parish Assistant	07974 632112 (Mbl)
Jones, Helen M. (Miss)	2007	Further Ministries Team, Canonbie Church Centre, Canonbie DG14 0RA [E-mail: helen.jones@furtherministriesteam.com]	Annandale and Eskdale Further Ministries Team: Children and Families Facilitator	01387 371037 (Office) 07789 631822 (Mbl)
Keenan, Deborah	2009	St George's and St Peter's Church, 40 Boyndie Street, Easterhouse, Glasgow G34 9JE [E-mail: debbiedkeenan@gmail.com]	Glasgow: Easterhouse St George's and St Peter's	0141-771 8810 (Work) 07928 116142 (Mbl)
MacChoille, Stiubhart MA	2009	61 Don Street, Aberdeen AB24 2RX [E-mail: smacchoille@fsmail.net]	Aberdeen: Craigiebuckler	01224 481359 (Home) 01224 315649 (Work) 07951 846262 (Mbl)
McEwan, Craig	2010	Tarquah, Glasgow Road, Dumfries DG2 9DE	Dumfries: Northwest: Parish Assistant	01387 249964
McIver, Ian LLB DipLP NP	2009	68 York Street, Peterhead AB42 1SP [E-mail: ianmci@hotmail.co.uk]	Aberdeen City Centre Parish Grouping: Community Outreach Worker	01779 479162 (Home) 01224 566451 (Office) 07890 932677 (Mbl)
Mackenzie, Lynn	2009	1990 Maryhill Road, Glasgow G20 0EF [E-mail: l.mackenzie@gmopbuzz.org]	Greater Maryhill Outreach Project	0141-946 3512
Mackenzie, Norman	2009	41 Kilmailing Road, Glasgow G44 5UH [E-mail: mackenzie799@btinternet.com]	Larkhall: Chalmers	0141-637 5958
MacRae, Christopher LLB	2009	Presbytery of Glasgow, 260 Bath Street, Glasgow G2 4JP [E-mail: strategy@presbyteryofglasgow.org.uk]	Presbytery of Glasgow Strategy Officer	0141-332 6606 (Office) 07786 965030 (Mbl)
Montgomery, Rilza (Ms)	2009	71 Glendinning Crescent, Edinburgh EH16 6DN	Edinburgh: Muirhouse St Andrew's	0131-440 4442
Naismith, Kenneth BD	2010	1/1, 29 Napier Drive, Govan, Glasgow G51 2LP [E-mail: kencaitheast@btinternet.com]	Glasgow: Govan and Linthouse: Parish Assistant	07787 764105 (Mbl)
Orr, Gillian BA	2009	'Zippity Do Da', Loch Alvie, Aviemore PH22 1QB [E-mail: gillianorr.cosyouth@googlemail.com]	Presbytery of Abernethy: Youth Worker	01479 811699 07969 457191 (Mbl)
Philip, Darren BSc	2009	29 Traprain Terrace, Haddington EH41 3QE [E-mail: darren@lepyouth.com]	Livingston Ecumenical Parish: Youth and Children's Worker	
Ramsay, Sheila BA JD	2008	18 Morrison Quadrant, Clydebank G81 2SZ [E-mail: sheila.maryhill@yahoo.co.uk]	Glasgow: Maryhill	07794 508544 (Mbl)
Reford, Susan (Miss)	2001	32 Jedburgh Street, Blantyre, Glasgow G72 0SU [E-mail: susan.reford@btopenworld.com]	Glasgow: Springburn and Tron St Mary's	01698 820122
Ross, Duncan DCS	2009	1 John Neilson Avenue, Paisley PA1 2SX [E-mail: ssornacnud@hotmail.com]	Greenock: Lyle Kirk and Paisley: St Columba Foxbar	0141-887 2801
Ross, Keith W. (Rev.) MA BD	2007	Easter Bavelaw House, Pentland Hills Regional Park, Balerno EH14 7JS [E-mail: keithross.hamiltonpresbytery@googlemail.com]	Hamilton Presbytery: Congregational Development Officer	07855 163449 (Mbl)

Name		Address	Position	Tel.
Sanders, Martyn S.	2010	26 Wood Avenue, Annan DG12 6DA [E-mail: martyn.sanders@furtherministriesteam.com]	Annandale and Eskdale Further Ministries Team: Pastoral Assistant	07830 697976 (Mbl)
Smith, David	2003	66 Hendry Road, Kirkcaldy KY2 5DB [E-mail: dave@tibal.org.uk]	Lochgelly and Benarty: Children's and Young People's Development Worker	01592 641823 / 07553 386137 (Mbl)
Stark, Jennifer MA MATheol	2010	South Leith Parish Halls, 6 Henderson Street, Edinburgh EH6 6BS [E-mail: outreach@leithchurchestogether.org.uk]	Edinburgh: Leith Churches Outreach Project: Leader	0131-554 2578
Stewart, Gregor	2010	30 Cairnhill Road, Newtonhill, Stonehaven AB39 3NF [E-mail: gstewart1977@aol.com]	Montrose: Youth and Children's Worker	01569 731518 / 07813 036289 (Mbl)
Stewart, Peter	2009	5 Craigievar Crescent, Glasgow G33 5DN [E-mail: pete@clanstewart.co.uk]	Glasgow: Barlanark Greyfriars	07855 424633 (Mbl)
Stirling, Diane (Miss) BSc DipCPC	2009	28 Kaims Court, Livingston Village EH54 7DB [E-mail: parish.assistant@yahoo.co.uk]	Polbeth Harwood with West Kirk of Calder: Parish Assistant	01506 426887 / 07855 866396 (Mbl)
Taylor, Valerie AssocCIPD PgDip	2010	372 Victoria Road, Torry, Aberdeen AB11 9PA [E-mail: vtaylor.torrystfitticks@gmail.com]	Aberdeen: Torry St Fittick's: PPW	07723 778788 (Mbl)
Thomas, Jason	2009	4 Dairsie Court, Glasgow G44 3JF	Glasgow: St James' Pollok	
Thomson, Andrew (Rev.)	2010	3 Laurel Wynd, Cambuslang, Glasgow G72 7BH	Glasgow: Govan and Linthouse: Pastoral Assistant	0141-641 2936
Thomson, John D. (Rev.) BD	2007	3 Tottenham Court, Hill Street, Dysart, Kirkcaldy KY1 2XY [E-mail: j.thomson10@sky.com]	Kennoway, Windygates and Balgonie: St Kenneth's: Parish Assistant	01592 655313 (Home) / 01333 351372 (Office) / 07885 414979 (Mbl)
Vint, Allan S. (Rev.) BSc BD MTh	2008	7 Haldon Grove, Glenboig, Coatbridge ML5 2TP [E-mail: allan@vint.co.uk]	Dunfermline Presbytery: Mission Development Officer	01236 872083 / 07795 483070 (Mbl)
Wellstod, Keith PGDip MICG	2009	47 Carrington Terrace, Crieff PH7 4DZ [E-mail: keithw2011@btinternet.com]	Perth: Riverside: Community Worker	01764 655678 (Home) / 01738 622341 (Office) / 07963 766782 (Mbl)
White, Ian	2009	4 Gilchrist Walk, Lesmahagow, Lanark ML11 0FQ	Craigneuk and Belhaven with Wishaw: Old	
Willis, Mags	2008	1 Union Place, Dundee DD2 1AA	Dundee: Chalmers Ardler	07513 415835 (Mbl)
Wyllie, John	2007	51 Seafar Drive, Kelty KY4 0JX	Cowdenbeath: Trinity: Pastoral Assistant	01383 839200
Young, Neil James	2001	31 Craigendmuir Street, Blackhill, Glasgow G33 1LG [E-mail: neil.young@bigfoot.com]	Glasgow: St Paul's: Youth Worker	0141-770 8559 / 07748 808488 (Mbl)

LIST K – OVERSEAS LOCATIONS

PRESBYTERY OF EUROPE

AMSTERDAM	The English Reformed Church, The Begijnhof (off the Spui). Service each Sunday at 10:30am. [Website: www.ercadam.nl]
BERMUDA	Christ Church Warwick, Middle Road, Warwick. Sunday services: 8:00am and 11:00am. [Website: www.christchurch.bm]
BOCHUM	English-speaking Christian congregation – ECC Bochum: Pauluskirche, Grabenstraße 9, D-44787 Bochum. Service each Sunday at 12:30pm. [Website: www.ecc-bochum.de]
BRUSSELS	St Andrew's Church, Chaussée de Vleurgat 181 (off Ave. Louise). Service each Sunday at 11:00am. [Website: www.churchofscotland.be]
BUDAPEST	St Columba's Scottish Mission, Vörösmarty utca 51, H-1064 Budapest. (Church Tel) 0036 1 373 0725 Service in English and Sunday School each Sunday at 11:00am. (Tel/Fax) 0036 1 460 0708 [Website: www.scotskirkhungary.com]
COLOMBO	St Andrew's Scots Kirk, 73 Galle Road, Colombo 3, Sri Lanka. Service each Sunday at 9:30am. (Tel) 0034 952 474840 [Website: www.internationalchurchcolombo.info]
COSTA DEL SOL	Services at Lux Mundi Ecumenical Centre, Calle Nueva 7, Fuengirola, Malaga. Service each Sunday at 10:30am. [Website: www.churchofscotlandcostadelsol.eu]
GENEVA	The Calvin Auditoire, Place de la Taconnerie (beside Cathedral of St Pierre). Service each Sunday at 11:00am. [Website: www.churchofscotlandgeneva.com]
GIBRALTAR	St Andrew's Church, Governor's Parade. Service each Sunday at 10:30am. [Website: www.scotskirkgibraltar.com]
LAUSANNE	26 Avenue de Rumine, CH-1005 Lausanne. Service each Sunday at 10:30am. [Website: www.scotskirklausanne.ch]
LISBON	St Andrew's Church, Rua da Arriaga 13–15, Lisbon. Service each Sunday at 11:00am. [Website: www.standrewslisbon.com]
MALTA	St Andrew's Church, 210 Old Bakery Street, Valletta. Service each Sunday at 10:30am. [Website: www.standrewsmalta.com]
PARIS	The Scots Kirk, 17 Rue Bayard, F-75008 Paris (Metro: Roosevelt). Service each Sunday at 11:00am. [Website: www.scotskirkparis.com]
REGENSBURG	English-language congregation: Alumneum, Am Olberg 2, D-93047 Regensburg. Sunday service: second Sunday 10:30am; fourth Sunday 6:00pm. [Website: www.esg-regensburg.de]

ROME — Via XX Settembre 7, 00187 Rome. Service each Sunday at 11:00am.
[Website: www.presbyterianchurchrome.org]

ROTTERDAM — The Scots Kirk, Schiedamsevest 121, Rotterdam. Service each Sunday at 10:30am. Informal service at 9:15am.
[Website: www.scotsintchurch.com]

TURIN — English-speaking congregation of the Waldensian Church in co-operation with the Church of Scotland. Via Principe Tommaso 1, 10125 Torino. Service each Sunday at 10:30am.
[Website: www.torinovaldese.org]

AFRICA AND THE CARIBBEAN

MALAWI

Church of Central Africa Presbyterian
Synod of Blantyre

Dr Ruth Shakespeare (2011) — Mulanje Mission Hospital, PO Box 45, Mulanje, Malawi [E-mail: shakespeareruth@gmail.com]
(Tel) 00265 9922 61569
(Fax) 00265 1 467 022

Synod of Livingstonia

Miss Helen Scott (2000, held previous appointment) — CCAP Girls' Secondary School, PO Box 2, Ekwendeni, Malawi [E-mail: helenms1960@yahoo.co.uk]
(Tel) 00265 1929 1932

Synod of Nkhoma

Dr David Morton (2009) — Nkhoma Hospital, PO Box 48, Nkhoma, Malawi [E-mail: kuluva2@gmail.com]
(Tel) 00265 9940 74022

Mr Rob Jones (2010) — Nkhoma Hospital, PO Box 48, Nkhoma, Malawi [E-mail: robert@thejonesfamily.org.uk]
(Tel) 00265 9918 65705

ZAMBIA

United Church of Zambia

Mr Keith and Mrs Ida Waddell (Ecum) (2008) — Mwandi UCZ Mission, PO Box 60693, Livingstonia, Zambia [E-mail: keith_ida2002@yahoo.co.uk]
(Tel) 00260 977 328 767

Ms Jenny Featherstone (Ecum) (2007) — Mindolo Ecumenical Foundation, PO Box 21493, Kitwe, Zambia [E-mail: jenny.featherstone@googlemail.com]
(Tel) 00260 979 703 130

Mr Glen Lund (2010) — UCZ Theological College, PO Box 20429, Kitwe, Zambia [E-mail: redhair.community@googlemail.com]
(Tel) 00260 978 363 400

TRINIDAD

Rev. Garwell Bacchas — Church of Scotland Greyfriars St Ann's, 50 Frederick Street, Port of Spain, Trinidad [E-mail: garwellbacchas@yahoo.com]
(Tel) 001 868 627 9312

ASIA

BANGLADESH

Church of Bangladesh

Mr James and Mrs Linda Dipty Pender (Ecum) (2004)
Development Consultant, CBSDP – Rajshani
[E-mail: penderjs@gmail.com]
[E-mail: ohenepender@yahoo.co.uk]

Mr David and Mrs Sarah Hall (Ecum) (2005)
c/o St Thomas' Church, 54 Johnston Road, Dhaka 1100, Bangladesh
[E-mail: dhall.dhaka@gmail.com]

Miss Pat Jamieson (Ecum) (2010)
c/o St Thomas' Church, 54 Johnston Road, Dhaka 1100, Bangladesh

PAKISTAN

Ms Susan Clark   (departure date TBC)
Diocese of Raiwind's Women Development and Service Programme
Contact c/o World Mission, 121 George Street, Edinburgh EH2 4YN

MIDDLE EAST

ISRAEL

[NOTE: Church Services are held in St Andrew's Scots Memorial Church, Jerusalem, each Sunday at 10:00am, and at St Andrew's, Galilee each Sunday at 6:00pm]

Jerusalem

Rev. George and Mrs Margaret Shand (2009)
St Andrew's, Jerusalem, 1 David Remez Street, PO Box 8619, Jerusalem 91086, Israel
(Tel: 00 972 2 673 2401; Fax: 00 972 2 673 1711)
[E-mail: stachjer@netvision.net.il]
[Website: www.scotsguesthouse.com]

Mr James and Mrs Nicola Laing (2009)
St Andrew's, Jerusalem, 1 David Remez Street, PO Box 8619, Jerusalem 91086, Israel
(Tel: 00 972 2 673 2401; Fax: 00 972 2 673 1711; Mobile: 00 972 50 202 3773)
[E-mail: jlaing@churchofscotland.org.il]
[Website: www.scotsguesthouse.com]

Tiberias

Rev. Colin D. Johnston (2009)
St Andrew's, Galilee, 1 Gdud Barak Street, PO Box 104, Tiberias 14100, Israel
(Tel: 00 972 4 671 0759; Fax: 00 972 4 672 5282)
[E-mail: revcdj60@gmail.com]
[Website: www.scotshotels.co.il]

Jaffa

Mr Anthony and Mrs Darya Short (2006)
Tabeetha School, 21 Yefet Street, PO Box 8170, Jaffa 61081, Israel
(Tel: 00 972 3 682 1581; Fax: 00 972 3 681 9357; Mobile: 00 972 54 757 2104)
[E-mail: principal@tabeethaschool.org]
[Website: www.tabeethaschool.org]

Mr James Maxwell (2009)
Tabeetha School, 21 Yefet Street, PO Box 8170, Jaffa 61081, Israel
(Tel: 00 972 3 682 1581; Fax: 00 972 3 681 9357)
[E-mail: jmaxwell@churchofscotland.org.il]
[Website: www.tabeethaschool.org]

LIST L – OVERSEAS RESIGNED AND RETIRED MISSION PARTNERS (ten or more years' service)

NAME	APP	RET	AREA	ADDRESS
Anderson, Karen (Mrs)	1992	2006	Israel	23 Allanpark Street, Largs KA30 9AG
Anderson, Kathleen (Mrs)	1955	1968	Pakistan	1A Elms Avenue, Great Shelford, Cambridge CB2 5LN
Archibald, Mary L. (Miss)	1964	1982	Nigeria/Ghana	490 Low Main Street, Wishaw ML2 7PL
Barbour, Edith R. (Miss)	1952	1983	North India	Sunnybrae, Atholl Road, Pitlochry PH16 5AR
Baxter, Mrs Ray	1954	1969	Malawi	91/17 Morningside Road, Edinburgh EH10 4AY
Berkeley, Dr John	1967	1977	Bhutan	Drumbeg, Coylumbridge, Aviemore PH22 1QU
and Dr Muriel	1995	1998	Yemen	
Bone, Mr David and Mrs Isobel	1977	1988	Malawi	315 Blackness Road, Dundee DD2 1SH
Bone, Elizabeth (Mrs)	1950	1964	Malawi	2A Elm Street, Dundee DD2 2AY
	1980	1984	Malawi	
Boyle, Lexa (Miss)	1959	1992	Aden/Yemen/Sudan	7 Maxwell Grove, Glasgow G41 5JP
Brodie, Rev. Jim	1955	1974	North India	25A Keptie Road, Arbroath DD11 3ED
	1996	1998	Nepal	
Brown, Janet H. (Miss)	1967	1980	Pakistan	6 Baxter Park Terrace, Dundee DD4 6NL
Burnett, Dr Fiona	1988	1998	Zambia	The Glenholm Centre, Broughton, Biggar ML12 6JF
Burnett, Dr Robin	1964	1967	Nigeria	79 Bank Street, Irvine KA12 0LL
and Mrs Storm	1968	1977	South Africa	
Burt, M.R.C. (Miss)	1940	1975	Kenya	22 The Loaning, Chirnside, Duns TD11 3YE
Byers, Rev. Alan and Rev. Mairi	1960	1971	Ghana	Meadowbank, Plumdon Road, Annan DG12 6SJ
Campbell, George H.	1957	1971	Livingstonia	20 Woodlands Grove, Kilmarnock KA3 1TZ
Coltart, Rev. Ian O.	1967	1985	North India	The Manse, Arbirlot, Arbroath DD11 2NX
Conacher, Marion (Miss)	1963	1993	India	41 Magdalene Drive, Edinburgh EH15 3BG
Cooper, Rev. George	1966	1986	Kenya	8 Leighton Square, Alyth, Blairgowrie PH11 8AQ
Crosbie, Ann R. (Miss)	1955	1967	Nigeria	21 Fieldhead Square, Glasgow G43 IHL
Dawson, Miss Anne	1976	2000	Malawi	31 Colville Gardens, Alloa FK10 1DU
Dick, Dr James and Mrs Anne	1954	1957	North India	1 Tummel Place, Comrie, Crieff PH6 2PG
	1957	1968	Nepal	
Dodman, Rev. Roy and Mrs Jane	1983	2006	Jamaica	78 Barbican Road, Kingston 6, Jamaica
Drever, Dr Bryan	1962	1982	Aden/Yemen/Pakistan	188 Addison Road, King's Head, Birmingham
Duncan, Mr David and Mrs Allison	1952	1969	Nigeria	7 Newhailes Avenue, Musselburgh EH21 6DW
	1977	1987		
Duncan, Rev. Graham and Mrs Sandra	1998	2006	South Africa	56 Daphne Road, Maroelana, 0081 Pretoria, South Africa

Name	From	To	Country	Address
Dunlop, Mr Walter T. and Mrs Jennifer	1979	1994	Malawi/Israel	50 Oxgangs Road, Edinburgh EH13 9DR
Fauchelle, Mrs Margaret	1991	1999	Zambia, Malawi, Zimbabwe	Flat 3, 22 North Avenue, Devonport, Auckland 1309, New Zealand
Ferguson, Mr John K.P.	1977	1989	Pakistan	15 Ashgrove, Craigshill, Livingston EH54 5JQ
Finlay, Carol (Ms)	1990	2001	Malawi	96 Broomfield Crescent, Edinburgh EH12 7LX
Fischbacher, Dr Colin M. and Mrs Sally	1986	1998	Malawi	11 Barclay Square, Gosforth, Newcastle-upon-Tyne NE3 2JB
Foster, Joyce (Miss) BSc	1968	1972	Kenya	99 Sixth Street, Newtongrange EH22 4LA
Fowler, Rev. Margaret	1972	1981	Malawi	
Fucella, Rev. Mike and Mrs Jane	1988	2007	Jamaica	PO Box 3097, Negril, Westmorland, Jamaica
Gaston, Dr Andrew and Mrs Felicity	1990	2006	Thailand	25 Kimberley Drive, Crown Hill, Plymouth, Devon PL6 5WA
Irvine, Mr Clive and Mrs Su	1997	2008	Malawi	McGregor Flat, 92 Blackford Avenue, Edinburgh EH9 3ES
Karam, Ishbel (Mrs)	1984	1999	Nepal	Hillsgarth, Baltasound, Unst, Shetland ZE2 9DY
King, Mrs Betty	1968	1985	Pakistan	23 Main Street, Newstead, Melrose TD6 9DX
Knowles, Dr John K. and Mrs Heather	1955	1971	North India	Trollopes Hill, Monton Combe, Bath BA2 7HX
Laidlay, Mrs Una	1976	1992	Malawi	Isles View, 5 Bell's Road, Lerwick, Shetland ZE1 0QB
	1961	1968	Yemen	
	1968	1971	Pakistan	
	1971	1978	Yemen	
Liddell, Margaret (Miss)	1964	1980	Zambia	20 Wyvis Crescent, Conon Bridge, Dingwall IV7 8BZ
Logie, Robina (Mrs)	1950	1960	North India	23 Stonefield Drive, Inverurie AB51 9DZ
McCulloch, Lesley (Mrs)	1982	1992	Malawi/Pakistan	316 North Jones Street, Port Angeles, WA 98362-4218, USA
McCutcheon, Agnes W.F. (Miss)	1957	1989	India	10A Hugh Murray Grove, Cambuslang, Glasgow G72 7NG
MacDonald, Dr Alistair and Mrs Freda	1949	1962	Nigeria	10 Millside, Morpeth, Northumberland NE61 1PN
McDougall, Rev. John N.	1935	1960	West Pakistan	Everill Orr Home, Allendale Road, Mount Albert, Auckland 3, New Zealand
McGoff, A.W. (Miss)	1954	1974	Kolhapur	6 Mossvale Walk, Craigend, Glasgow G33 5PF
MacGregor, Rev. Margaret	1959	1994	India	Gordon Flat, 16 Learmonth Court, Edinburgh EH4 1PB
McKenzie, Rev. W.M.	1958	1974	Zambia	Troqueer Road, Dumfries DG2 7DF
MacKinnon, E.L. (Miss)	1952	1972	Nigeria	3 Havoc Road, Dumbarton G82 4JN
McMahon, Mrs Jessie	1959	1976	North India	7 Ridgepark Drive, Lanark ML11 7PG
Malley, Beryl Stevenson (Miss)	1982	1992	Malawi	272/2 Craigcrook Road, Edinburgh EH4 7TF
Marshall, Rev. Fred J.	1946	1992	Bermuda	Flat 3, 31 Oswald Road, Edinburgh EH9 2HT
Millar, Rev. Margaret R.M.	1967	1996	Malawi/Zambia	Fearnoch Cottage, Taynuilt, Argyll PA35 1JB
Millar, Rev. Peter	1976	1989	South India	6/5 Ettrickdale Place, Edinburgh EH3 5JN
Moir, Rev. Ian and Mrs Elsie	1962	1973	South Africa	28/6 Comely Bank Avenue, Edinburgh EH4 1EL
Moore, Rev. J. Wilfred	1943	1957	Ghana	31 Lennox Gardens, Linlithgow EH49 7PZ
Morrice, Mrs Margaret	1971	1998	Buenos Aires/Kenya	104 Baron's Hill Avenue, Linlithgow EH49 7JG
Morton, Rev. Alasdair J. and Mrs Gillian M.	1960	1973	Zambia	St Leonard's, 16 St Leonard's Road, Forres IV36 1DW

Name	From	To	Country	Address
Munro, Harriet (Miss)	1959	1969	Malawi	26 The Forge, Braidpark Drive, Glasgow G46 6LB
Murray, Rev. Douglas and Mrs Sheila	1994	2004	Switzerland	Flat 9, 4 Bonnington Gait, Edinburgh EH6 5NZ
Murray, Mr Ian and Mrs Isabel	1962	2000	Pakistan	17 Piershill Terrace, Edinburgh EH8 7EY
Musgrave, Rev. Clarence W. and Mrs Joan	1966	1980	Zambia	4 Ravelston Heights, Edinburgh EH4 3LX
Musk, Mrs Lily	2000	2006	Jerusalem	1 Tulloch Place, St Andrews KY16 8XJ
	1959	1959	Malawi	
	1959	1974	Zambia	
Nelson, Rev. John and Mrs Anne	1947	1952	Pakistan	7 Manse Road, Roslin EH25 9LF
	1952	1959	North India	
	1959	1973	North India	
Nicholson, Rev. Thomas S.	1981	1995	Taiwan	Todholes, Greenlaw, Duns TD10 6XD
Nicol, Catherine (Miss)	1960	2000	Pakistan	St Columba Christian Girls' RTC, Barah Patthar, Sialkot 2, Pakistan
Nutter, Margaret (Miss)	1966	1979	Pakistan	Kilmorich, 14 Balloch Road, Balloch, Alexandria G83 8SR
Pacitti, Rev. Stephen A.	1977	1996	Taiwan	157 Nithsdale Road, Pollokshields, Glasgow G41 5RD
Pattison, Rev. Kenneth and Mrs Susan	1966	1977	Malawi	2 Castle Way, St Madoes, Glencarse, Perth PH2 7NY
Philip, Mrs Margaret	1951	1968	Nigeria	Penlan, Holm Farm Road, Catrine, Mauchline KA5 6TA
Philpot, Rev. David	1981	1995	WCC Geneva	2/27 Pentland Drive, Edinburgh EH10 6PX
Reid, Dr Ann	1988	1996	Ghana	36 Kingshill Court, Standish, Wigan WN6 0AR
Reid, Margaret I. (Miss)	1964	1982	Malawi	3/1 Coxfield Lane, Edinburgh EH11 2RF
Rennie, Rev. Alistair M.	1939	1976	Malawi	Noble's Yard, St Mary's Gate, Wirksworth, Derbyshire DE4 4DQ
Ritchie, Ishbel M. (Miss)	1955	1996	Eastern Himalaya	8 Ross Street, Dunfermline KY12 0AN
Ritchie, Rev. J.M.	1974	1977	Yemen	Flat 2/25, Croft-an-Righ, Edinburgh EH8 8EG
Ritchie, Mary Scott (Miss)	1968	1991	Malawi/Zambia/Israel	Afton Villa, 1 Afton Bridgend, New Cumnock KA18 4AX
Ross, Rev. Prof. Kenneth and Mrs Hester	1988	1998	Malawi	The Manse, Kilmelford, Oban PA34 4XA
Rough, Mary E. (Miss)	1966	1987	Blantyre	6 Glebe Street, Dumfries DG1 2LF
Roy, Rev. Alan J.	1960	1972	Zambia	14 Comerton Place, Drumoig, St Andrews KY16 0NQ
Russell, M.M. (Miss)	1946	1969	Nigeria	14 Hozier Street, Carluke ML8 5DW
Samuel, Lynda (Mrs)	1974	1990	Madras	28 Braehead, Methven Walk, Dundee DD2 3FJ [E-mail: rasam42@onetel.com]
Shepherd, Dr Clyne	1956	1968	Nigeria	10 Kingsknowe Road South, Edinburgh EH14 2JE
Smith, Mr Harry and Mrs Margaret	1959	1967	Nigeria	31 Woodville Crescent, Sunderland SR4 8RE
Sneddon, Mr Sandy and Mrs Marie	1968	1970	Malawi	84 Greenend Gardens, Edinburgh EH17 7QH
	1986	2003	Pakistan	
Steedman, Martha (Mrs) (née Hamilton)	1955	1966	North India	Muir of Blebo, Blebo Craigs, Cupar KY15 5TZ
Stewart, Marion G. (Miss)	1976	1989	Malawi/Israel	Kirk Cottage, Kirkton of Skene, Westhill, Skene AB32 6XX
Stone, W. Vernon MA BD	1949	1966	Zambia	36 Woodrow Court, Port Glasgow Road, Kilmacolm PA13 4QA
Taylor, Rev. A.T.H.	1938	1972	Nigeria/Jamaica	4 The Pleasance, Strathkinness, St Andrews KY16 9SD

Tennant, Frances (Miss)	1965	1977	Pakistan	101 St John's Road, Edinburgh EH12 6NN
Wallace, A. Dorothy (Miss)	1953	1991	North India	Amberley, Mill Lane, Nethy Bridge PH25 3DR
Walker, Rev. Donald and Mrs Judith				
Westmarland, Rev. Colin	1981	1994	Zambia	c/o Mrs H.J. Yarr, Flat 1/1, 6 Striven Gardens, Glasgow G20 6DU
Wilkie, Rev. James L.	1975	2001	Malta	PO Box 5, Cospicua, CSPOI, Malta
Wilkinson, Dr Alison	1959	1976	Zambia	7 Comely Bank Avenue, Edinburgh EH4 1EW
Wilkinson, Rev. John	1992	2007	Kenya	5 Birch Avenue, Stirling FK8 2PL
Wilson, Irene (Ms)	1946	1975	Kenya	70 Craigleith Hill Gardens, Edinburgh EH4 2JH
Wilson, Rev. Mark	1993	2004	Israel	
	1953	1978	Nagpur	37 Kings Avenue, Longniddry EH32 0QN

LIST M – PARISH ASSISTANTS AND PROJECT WORKERS

Those who in previous years would have been named here are now included in List J – Presbytery/Parish Workers.

LIST N – READERS

1. EDINBURGH

Brown, Ivan
4 St Cuthberts Court, Edinburgh EH13 0LG — 0131-441 1245
[E-mail: j.ivanb@btinternet.com] — (Mbl) 07730 702860

Christie, Gillian L. (Mrs)
32 Allan Park Road, Edinburgh EH14 1LJ — 0131-443 4472
[E-mail: mrsglchristie@aol.com] — (Mbl) 07914 883354

Davies, Ruth (Ms) (attached to Liberton)
4 Hawkhead Grove, Edinburgh EH16 6LS — 0131-664 3608
[E-mail: ruth@mdavies.me.uk]

Farrant, Yvonne (Ms)
Flat 7, 14 Duddingston Mills, Edinburgh EH8 7NF — 0131-661 0672
[E-mail: yvonne.farrant@crossreach.org.uk] — (Mbl) 07747 766405

Farrell, William J.
50 Ulster Crescent, Edinburgh EH8 7JS — 0131-661 1026
[E-mail: w.farrell154@btinternet.com]

Farrow, Edmund
14 Brunswick Terrace, Edinburgh EH7 5PG — 0131-558 8210
[E-mail: edmundfarrow@blueyonder.co.uk]

Johnston, Alan
8/19 Constitution Street, Edinburgh EH6 7BT — 0131-554 1326
[E-mail: alanacj@cairnassoc.wanadoo.co.uk] — (Mbl) 07901 510819

Kerrigan, Herbert A. (Prof.) MA LLB QC
Airdene, 20 Edinburgh Road, Dalkeith EH22 1JY — 0131-660 3007
[E-mail: kerrigan@kerriganqc.com] — (Mbl) 07725 953772

Kinnear, Malcolm A.
25 Thorburn Road, Edinburgh EH13 0BH — 0131-441 3150
[E-mail: andrew@kinnear25.fsnet.co.uk]

Macfarlane, Helen (Mrs) — 5/5 Moat Drive, Edinburgh EH14 1NU [E-mail: h.macfarlane@butterflytrust.org.uk] — 0131-444 1709 / (Mbl) 07986 170802

McKenzie, Janet (Mrs) — 80C Colinton Road, Edinburgh EH14 1DD — 0131-444 2054

McPherson, Alistair — 77 Bonaly Wester, Edinburgh EH13 0RQ [E-mail: jintymck@talktalk.net] — 0131-478 5384

Pearce, Martin — 4 Corbiehill Avenue, Edinburgh EH4 5DR [E-mail: amjhmcpherson@blueyonder.co.uk]

Sherriffs, Irene (Mrs) — 22/2 West Mill Bank, Edinburgh EH13 0QT [E-mail: martin.j.pearce@blueyonder.co.uk] / [E-mail: reenie.sherriffs@blueyonder.co.uk] — 0131-336 4864 / (Mbl) 07801 717222 / 0131-466 9530

Wyllie, Anne (Miss) — 2F3, 46 Jordan Lane, Edinburgh EH10 4QX [E-mail: anne.wyllie@tiscali.co.uk] — 0131-447 9035

2. WEST LOTHIAN

Beatson, David — 'Schiefer Hof', Kepscaith Farm, Longridge, Bathgate EH47 9AL [E-mail: ireneagape@tiscali.co.uk] — 01501 740494 / (Work) 01506 655305

Coyle, Charlotte (Mrs) — 28 The Avenue, Whitburn EH47 0DA [E-mail: paulcharlotte@talktalk.net] — 01501 740687

Elliott, Sarah (Miss) — 105 Seafield Rows, Seafield, Bathgate EH47 7AW [E-mail: sarah.elliott6@btopenworld.com] — 01506 654950

Galloway, Brenda (Dr) — Lochend, 58 St Ninians Road, Linlithgow EH49 7BN [E-mail: bhgallo@yahoo.co.uk] — 01506 842028

Middleton, Alex — 36 Fivestanks Place, Broxburn EH52 6BJ [E-mail: alex.middleton@btinternet.com] — 01506 852645

Salmon, Jeanie (Mrs) — 81 Croftfoot Drive, Fauldhouse, Bathgate EH47 9EH [E-mail: jeaniesalmon@aol.com] — 01501 772468 / (Work) 01501 828509

Scoular, Iain W. — 15 Bonnyside Road, Bonnybridge FK4 2AD [E-mail: iain@iwsconsultants.com] — 01324 812395 / (Mbl) 07717 131596

Wilkie, David — 53 Goschen Place, Broxburn EH52 5JH [E-mail: david-fmu_09@tiscali.co.uk] — 01506 854777

3. LOTHIAN

Evans, W. John IEng MIIE(Elec) — Waterlily Cottage, 10 Fenton Steading, North Berwick EH39 5AF [E-mail: jevans7is@hotmail.com] — 01620 842990

Hogg, David MA — 82 Eskhill, Penicuik EH26 8DQ [E-mail: hogg-d2@sky.com] — 01968 676350 / (Mbl) 07821 693946

Johnston, June E. (Ms) BSc MEd BD — 49 Braeside Road South, Gorebridge EH23 4DL [E-mail: johnston330@btinternet.com] — 01875 823086 / (Mbl) 07754 448889

Millan, Mary (Mrs) — 33 Polton Vale, Loanhead EH20 9DF [E-mail: marymillan@fsmail.net] — 0131-440 1624 / (Mbl) 07814 466104

Trevor, A. Hugh MA MTh — 29A Fidra Road, North Berwick EH39 4NE [E-mail: htrevor@talktalk.net] — 01620 894924

Yeoman, Edward T.N. FSAScot	75 Newhailes Crescent, Musselburgh EH21 6EF [E-mail: edwardyeoman6@aol.com]	0131-653 2291 (Mbl) 07896 517666

4. MELROSE AND PEEBLES

Cashman, Margaret D. (Mrs)	38 Abbotsford Road, Galashiels TD1 3HR [E-mail: mcashman@tiscali.co.uk]	01896 752711
Henderson-Howatt, David	Stoneyknowe, West Linton EH46 7BY [E-mail: stoneyknowe@aol.com]	01968 660677
Selkirk, Frances (Mrs)	2 The Glebe, Ashkirk, Selkirk TD7 4PJ [E-mail: f.selkirk@btinternet.com]	01750 32204

5. DUNS

Taylor, Christine (Mrs)	Rowardennan, Main Street, Gavinton, Duns TD11 3QT [E-mail: ctaylor174@btinternet.com]	01361 882994

6. JEDBURGH

Findlay, Elizabeth (Mrs)	10 Inch Park, Kelso TD5 7EQ [E-mail: elizabeth@findlay8124.fsworld.co.uk]	01573 226641
Knox, Dagmar (Mrs)	3 Stichill Road, Ednam, Kelso TD5 7QQ [E-mail: dagmar.knox.riding@btinternet.com]	01573 224883

7. ANNANDALE AND ESKDALE

Boncey, David	Redbrae, Beattock, Moffat DG10 9RF [E-mail: david.boncey613@btinternet.com]	01683 300613
Brown, Martin J.	Lochhouse Farm, Beattock, Moffat DG10 9SG [E-mail: martin@lochhousefarm.com]	01683 300451
Brown, S. Jeffrey BA	Skara Brae, 8 Ballplay Road, Moffat DG10 9JU [E-mail: sjbrown@btinternet.com]	01683 220475
Chisholm, Dennis A.G. MA BSc	Moss-side, Hightae, Lockerbie DG11 1JR [E-mail: dchis@talktalk.net]	01387 811803
Dodds, Alan	Trinco, Battlehill, Annan DG12 6SN [E-mail: alanandjen46@talktalk.net]	01461 201235
Jackson, Susan (Mrs)	48 Springbells Road, Annan DG12 6LQ [E-mail: peter-jackson24@sky.com]	01461 204159
Morton, Andrew A. BSc	19 Sherwood Park, Lockerbie DG11 2DX [E-mail: andrew.a.morton@btinternet.com]	01576 203164
Sanders, Martyn S.	26 Wood Avenue, Annan DG12 6DA [E-mail: martyn.sanders@furtherministriesteam.com]	(Mbl) 07830 697976
Saville, Hilda A. (Mrs)	32 Crosslaw Burn, Moffat DG10 9LP [E-mail: saville.c@sky.com]	01683 222854

8. DUMFRIES AND KIRKCUDBRIGHT

Carroll, J. Scott — 17 Downs Place, Heathhall, Dumfries DG1 3RF — 01387 265350
[E-mail: scott.carroll@btinternet.com]

Corson, Gwen (Mrs) — 7 Sunnybrae, Borgue, Kirkcudbright DG6 4SJ — 01557 870328

Harvey, Joyce (Mrs) — 4A Allanfield Place, Newton Stewart DG8 6BS — 01387 264267

Ogilvie, D. Wilson MA FSAScot — Lingerwood, 2 Nelson Street, Dumfries DG2 9AY — 01557 820202

Paterson, Ronald M. (Dr) — Mirkwood, Ringford, Castle Douglas DG7 2AL — 01557 860381
[E-mail: mirkwoodtyke@aol.com]

Wallace, Mhairi (Mrs) — The Manse, Manse Road, Twynholm, Kirkcudbright DG6 4NY — (Mbl) 07880 546743
[E-mail: tobythewestie@msn.com]

9. WIGTOWN AND STRANRAER

Comery, Graham — Skellies Knowe West, Ervie, Leswalt, Stranraer DG9 0RY — 01776 854277

McQuistan, Robert — Old School House, Carsluith, Newton Stewart DG8 7DT — 01671 820327
[E-mail: mcquistan@quistaworld.net]

Williams, Roy — 120 Belmont Road, Stranraer DG9 7BG — 01776 705762
[E-mail: roywilliams84@hotmail.com]

10. AYR

Anderson, James (Dr) BVMS PhD DVM FRCPath FIBiol MRCVS — 67 Henrietta Street, Girvan KA26 9AN — 01465 710059 / (Mbl) 07952 512720
[E-mail: jc.anderson@tesco.net]

Black, Sandra (Mrs) — 5 Doon Place, Troon KA10 7EQ — 01292 220075
[E-mail: blacks_troon@hotmail.com]

Gowans, James — 2 Cochrane Avenue, Dundonald, Kilmarnock KA2 9EJ — 01563 850904 / (Mbl) 07985 916814
[E-mail: jim@luker42.freeserve.co.uk]

Jamieson, Ian A. — 2 Whinfield Avenue, Prestwick KA9 2BH — 01242 476898 / 01292 479313
[E-mail: ian@jamieson4189.freeserve.co.uk]

Morrison, James — 27 Monkton Road, Prestwick KA9 1AP — 07773 287852
[E-mail: jim.morrison@talktalk.net]

Murphy, Ian — 56 Lamont Crescent, Netherthird, Cumnock KA18 3DU — (Mbl) 01290 423675
[E-mail: ianm_cumnock@yahoo.co.uk]

Riome, Elizabeth (Mrs) — Monkwood Mains, Minishant, Maybole KA19 8EY — 01292 443440
[E-mail: aj.riome@btinternet.com]

11. IRVINE AND KILMARNOCK

Bircham, James F. — 8 Holmlea Place, Kilmarnock KA1 1UU — 01563 532287

Cooper, Fraser — 5 Balgray Way, Irvine KA11 1RP — 01294 211235
[E-mail: frasercooper@wightcablenorth.net]

Crosbie, Shona (Mrs) — 4 Campbell Street, Darvel KA17 0DA — 01560 322229
[E-mail: fawltytowersdarvel@yahoo.co.uk]

Dempster, Ann (Mrs) — 20 Graham Place, Kilmarnock KA3 7JN — 01563 529361 / (Work) 01563 534080 / (Mbl) 07729 152945
[E-mail: ademp99320@aol.com]

Gillespie, Janice (Miss) — 12 Jeffrey Avenue, Kilmarnock KA1 4EB [E-mail: janice.gillespie@tiscali.co.uk] — 01563 540009

Hamilton, Margaret A. (Mrs) — 59 South Hamilton Street, Kilmarnock KA1 2DT [E-mail: tomhmltn@sky.com] — 01563 534431

Jamieson, John H. BSc DEP AFBPSS — 22 Moorfield Avenue, Kilmarnock KA1 1TS [E-mail: johnhjamieson@tiscali.co.uk] — 01563 534065

McAllister, Anne C. (Mrs) — 39 Bowes Rigg, Stewarton, Kilmarnock KA3 5EN [E-mail: annecmcallister@btinternet.com] — 01560 483191

McGeever, Gerard — 23 Kinloch Avenue, Stewarton, Kilmarnock KA3 3HQ [E-mail: gerard@gmcgeever.freeserve.co.uk] — 01560 484331, (Work) 0141-847 5717

MacLean, Donald — 1 Four Acres Drive, Kilmaurs, Kilmarnock KA3 2ND [E-mail: donannmac@yahoo.co.uk] — 01563 538475

Mills, Catherine (Mrs) — 59 Crossdene Road, Crosshouse, Kilmarnock KA2 0JU [E-mail: cfmills5lib@hotmail.com] — 01563 535305

Raleigh, Gavin — 21 Landsborough Drive, Kilmarnock KA3 1RY [E-mail: gavin.raleigh@lineone.net] — 01563 520836

Robertson, William — 1 Archers Avenue, Irvine KA11 2GB [E-mail: willie.robert@yahoo.co.uk] — 01294 203577

Scott, William BA DipEd — 6 Elgin Avenue, Stewarton, Kilmarnock KA3 3HJ — 01560 484273
Whitelaw, David — 9 Kirkhill, Kilwinning KA13 6NB [E-mail: whitelawfam@talktalk.net] — 01294 551695

12. ARDROSSAN
Barclay, Elizabeth (Mrs) — 2 Jacks Road, Saltcoats KA21 5NT [E-mail: mfiz98@dsl.pipex.com] — 01294 471855

Currie, Archie BD — 55 Central Avenue, Kilbirnie KA25 6JP [E-mail: archiecurrie@yahoo.co.uk] — 01505 681474, (Mbl) 07881 452115

Hunter, Jean C.Q. (Mrs) BD — Church of Scotland Manse, Shiskine, Isle of Arran KA27 3EP [E-mail: j.hunter744@btinternet.com] — 01770 860380

McCool, Robert — 17 McGregor Avenue, Stevenston KA20 4BA — 01294 466548
Mackay, Brenda H. (Mrs) — 19 Eglinton Square, Ardrossan KA22 8LN [E-mail: bremac82@aol.com] — 01294 464491

Nimmo, Margaret (Mrs) — 12 Muirfield Place, Kilwinning KA13 6NL [E-mail: margtmcmn@aol.com] — 01294 553718, (Work) 01292 220336

Ross, Magnus BA MEd — 39 Beachway, Largs KA30 8QH [E-mail: m.b.ross@btinternet.com] — 01475 689572

Smith, Nicola (Mrs) — 5 Kames Street, Millport, Isle of Cumbrae KA28 0BN [E-mail: nsasmith@fsmail.net] — 01475 530747

13. LANARK
Allan, Angus J. — Blackburn Mill, Chapelton, Strathaven ML10 6RR [E-mail: angus.allan@hotmail.com] — 01357 528548

Grant, Alan — 25 Moss-side Avenue, Carluke ML8 5UG [E-mail: amgrant25@aol.com] — 01555 771419

Love, William — 30 Barmore Avenue, Carluke ML8 4PE [E-mail: janbill30@tiscali.co.uk] — 01555 751243

14. GREENOCK AND PAISLEY

Banks, Russell — 18 Aboyne Drive, Paisley PA2 7SJ [E-mail: margaret.banks2@ntlworld.com] — 0141-884 6925

Boag, Jennifer (Miss) — 11 Madeira Street, Greenock PA16 7UJ [E-mail: jenniferboag@hotmail.com] — 01475 720125

Campbell, Tom BA DipCPC — 3 Grahamston Place, Paisley PA2 7BY [E-mail: tomcam38@googlemail.com] — 0141-840 2273

Davey, Charles L. — 16 Divert Road, Gourock PA19 1DT [E-mail: charles.davey@talktalk.net] — 01475 631544

Geddes, Elizabeth (Mrs) — 40 Hazelwood Road, Bridge of Weir PA11 3DT [E-mail: geddes_liz@hotmail.com] — 01505 612639

Glenny, John C. — 49 Cloch Road, Gourock PA19 1AT [E-mail: jacklizg@aol.com] — 01475 636415

Hood, Eleanor (Mrs) — 12 Clochoderick Avenue, Kilbarchan, Johnstone PA10 2AY [E-mail: eleanor.hood.kilbarchan@ntlworld.com] — 01505 704208

Jackson, Nancy (Mrs) — 100 Old Greenock Road, Bishopton PA7 5BB [E-mail: nancyj@ntlworld.com] — 01505 863506

MacDonald, Christine (Ms) — 33 Collier Street, Johnstone PA5 8AG [E-mail: christine.macdonald10@ntlworld.com] — 01505 355779

McFarlan, Elizabeth (Miss) — 20 Fauldswood Crescent, Paisley PA2 9PA [E-mail: elizabeth.mcfarlan@ntlworld.com] — 01505 358411

McGill, David — 21 Mains Hill, Park Mains, Erskine PA8 7JA [E-mail: david.mcgill@ntlworld.com]

McHugh, Jack — 'Earlshaugh', Earl Place, Bridge of Weir PA11 3HA [E-mail: jackmchugh@tiscali.co.uk] — 01505 612789

Marshall, Leon M. — 'Glenisla', Gryffe Road, Kilmacolm PA13 4BA [E-mail: lm@stevenson-kyles.co.uk] — 01505 872417

Maxwell, Sandra A. (Mrs) BD — 2 Grants Avenue, Paisley PA2 6AZ [E-mail: sandra1.maxwell@virgin.net] — 0141-884 3710

Munro, Irene (Mrs) — 80 Bardrainney Avenue, Port Glasgow PA14 6HA [E-mail: irenemunro906@hotmail.com] — 01475 701213

Noonan, Pam (Mrs) — 18 Woodburn Place, Houston, Johnstone PA6 7NA [E-mail: pam.noonan@btinternet.com] — 01505 326254

Orry, Geoff — 'Rhu Ellan', 4 Seaforth Crescent, Barrhead, Glasgow G78 1PL [E-mail: geoff.orry@googlemail.com] — 0141-881 9748

Shaw, Ian — The Grove, 8 Commercial Road, Barrhead, Glasgow G78 1AJ — 0141-881 2038

16. GLASGOW

Armstrong, John (Reader Emeritus) — 44 Eckford Street, Glasgow G32 7AJ — 0141-778 4745

Bremner, David
Greenhill Lodge, 1 Old Humbie Road, Glasgow G77 5DF
[E-mail: david.bremner@tiscali.co.uk]
0141-639 1742

Campbell, Jack T. BD BEd
40 Kenmure Avenue, Bishopbriggs, Glasgow G64 2DE
[E-mail: jack.campbell@ntlworld.com]
0141-563 5837

Dickson, Hector M.K.
'Gwito', 61 Whitton Drive, Giffnock, Glasgow G46 6EF
[E-mail: hectordickson@hotmail.com]
0141-637 0080

Fullarton, Andrew
225 Aros Drive, Glasgow G52 1TJ
0141-883 9518

Galbraith, Iain B. (Dr)
Beechwood, Overton Road, Alexandria G83 0LJ
01389 753563

Grant, George
44 Brownside Road, Cambuslang, Glasgow G72 8NJ
[E-mail: reader.grant@gmail.com]
0141-560 0059

Grieve, Leslie
23 Hertford Avenue, Glasgow G12 0LG
[E-mail: leslie.grieve@gmail.com]
0141-576 1376

Horner, David J.
20 Ledi Road, Glasgow G43 2AJ
[E-mail: djhorner@btinternet.com]
0141-637 7369

Hunt, Roland BSc PhD CertEd
4 Flora Gardens, Bishopbriggs, Glasgow G64 1DS
[E-mail: roland.hunt@ntlworld.com]
0141-563 3257
0141-563 3257 (Evenings and weekends)
0141-429 6733

Joansson, Tordur
1/2, 18 Eglinton Court, Glasgow G5 9NE
[E-mail: to4ljo@yahoo.co.uk]
0141-621 1809

Kilpatrick, Mrs Joan
39 Brent Road, Regent's Park, Glasgow G46 8JG
[E-mail: je-kilpatrick@sky.com]

McChlery, Stuart
The Manse, Cheapside Street, Eaglesham, Glasgow G76 0NS
[E-mail: s.mcchlery@gcu.ac.uk]
01355 303495

McFarlane, Robert
25 Avenel Road, Glasgow G13 2PB
[E-mail: robertmcfrln@yahoo.co.uk]
0141-954 5540

McInally, Gordon
10 Melville Gardens, Bishopbriggs, Glasgow G64 3DF
[E-mail: gmcinally@sky.com]
0141-563 2685

Mackenzie, Norman
Flat 3/2, 41 Kilmailing Road, Glasgow G44 5UH
[E-mail: mackenzie799@btinternet.com]
(Mbl) 07780 733710

McKenzie-Adams, Mary (Mrs)
44 Springcroft Crescent, Glasgow G69 6SB
[E-mail: ma@hsog.co.uk]
0141-771 1957
(Mbl) 07939 889091

McLaughlin, Cathy (Mrs)
8 Lamlash Place, Glasgow G33 3XH
[E-mail: chmclaughlin@talktalk.net]
0141-774 2483

MacLeod, John
2 Shuna Place, Newton Mearns, Glasgow G77 6TN
[E-mail: jmacleod2@sky.com]
0141-639 6862

Maxwell, David
248 Old Castle Road, Glasgow G44 5EZ
[E-mail: david.maxwell7@ntlworld.com]
0141-569 6379

Millar, Kathleen (Mrs)
9 Glenbank Court, Thornliebank, Glasgow G46 7EJ
[E-mail: kathleen.millar@tesco.net]
0141-638 6250
07793 203045
(Mbl) 0141-429 7716

Phillips, John B.
2/3, 30 Handel Place, Glasgow G5 0TP
[E-mail: johnphillips@fish.co.uk]

Queen, Leslie
60 Loch Assynt, East Kilbride, Glasgow G74 2DW
[E-mail: leslie.queen@btopenworld.com]
01355 233932

Rennie, Katherine (Miss)
12 Westside Gardens, 4 Partickhill Road, Glasgow G11 5BL
[E-mail: katherinemrennie@btinternet.com]
0141-339 0540

Robertson, Adam — 423 Amulree Street, Glasgow G32 7SS — 0141-573 6662
Roy, Mrs Shona — 81 Busby Road, Clarkston, Glasgow G76 8BD [E-mail: theroyfamily@yahoo.co.uk] — 0141-644 3713
Stead, Mrs Mary — 9A Carrick Drive, Mount Vernon, Glasgow G32 0RW [E-mail: maystead@hotmail.co.uk] — 0141-764 1016
Stewart, James — 45 Airthrey Avenue, Glasgow G14 9LY [E-mail: jmstewart325@btinternet.com] — 0141-959 5814
Stuart, Alex — 107 Baldorran Crescent, Cumbernauld, Glasgow G68 9EX [E-mail: alexpstuart@btopenworld.com] — 01236 727710
Sturrock, Roger — 36 Thomson Drive, Glasgow G61 3PA [E-mail: rogersturrock@mac.com] — 0141-942 7412
Tindall, Margaret (Mrs) — 23 Ashcroft Avenue, Lennoxtown, Glasgow G65 7EN [E-mail: margarettindall@aol.com] — 01360 310911
Watson, Alan — 56 Baldorran Crescent, Cumbernauld, Glasgow G68 9BL [E-mail: watsonalan@btinternet.com] — 01236 729095
Webster, James — 65 Fruin Avenue, Newton Mearns, Glasgow G77 6HG [E-mail: j.webster139@btinternet.com] — 0141-639 0035
Wilson, George A. — 46 Maxwell Drive, Garrowhill, Baillieston, Glasgow G69 6LS [E-mail: healthandsafety@talk21.com] — 0141-771 3862

17. HAMILTON

Allan, Robert H. — 59 Jennie Lee Drive, Overtown, Wishaw ML2 0EE
Beattie, Richard — 4 Bent Road, Hamilton ML3 6QB [E-mail: richardbeattie1958@hotmail.com] — 01698 420086
Bell, Sheena — 2 Langdale, East Kilbride, Glasgow G74 4RP [E-mail: belljsheena@hotmail.co.uk] — 01355 248217
Clemenson, Anne — 25 Dempsey Road, Lochview, Bellshill ML4 2UF [E-mail: aclemenson@msn.com] — 01698 291019
Codona, Joy (Mrs) — Dykehead Farm, 300 Dykehead Road, Airdrie ML6 7SR [E-mail: jcodona772@btinternet.com] — 01236 767063 / 07810 770609 (Mbl)
Cruickshanks, William — 63 Progress Drive, Caldercruix, Airdrie ML6 7PU — 01236 843352
Haggarty, Frank — 46 Glen Road, Caldercruix, Airdrie ML6 7PZ — 01236 842182
Hastings, William Paul — 186 Glen More, East Kilbride, Glasgow G74 2AN [E-mail: wphastings@hotmail.co.uk] — 01355 521228
Hawthorne, William G. MBE — 172 Main Street, Plains, Airdrie ML6 7JH [E-mail: william@hawthorne1938.freeserve.co.uk] — 01236 842230
Hewitt, Samuel — 3 Corrie Court, Earnock, Hamilton ML3 9XE [E-mail: sambetty1@hotmail.com] — 01698 457403
Hislop, Eric — 1 Castlegait, Strathaven ML10 6FF [E-mail: eric.hislop@tiscali.co.uk] — 01357 520003
Jardine, Lynette — 32 Powburn Crescent, Uddingston, Glasgow G71 7SS [E-mail: lpjardine@blueyonder.co.uk] — 01698 812404

Keir, Dickson	46 Brackenhill Drive, Hamilton ML3 8AY [E-mail: dickson.keir@btinternet.com]	01698 457351
Leckie, Elizabeth	41 Church Street, Larkhall ML9 1EZ [E-mail: elizleckie@blueyonder.co.uk]	01698 308933
McCart, Frances	19 White Cart Tower, East Kilbride, Glasgow G74 2EE [E-mail: francesmccart@yahoo.co.uk]	01355 246939
McCleary, Isaac	719 Coatbridge Road, Bargeddie, Glasgow G69 7PH	0141-236 0158
McIlroy, Stuart	17 Dendale, Stewartfield, East Kilbride, Glasgow G74 4LP [E-mail: s.mcilroy1@btinternet.com]	01355 247958
MacMillan, Georgina	1 Darngaber Gardens, Quarter, Hamilton ML3 7XX [E-mail: georgiemac@talktalk.net]	01698 424040
Murphy, Jim	10 Hillview Crescent, Bellshill ML4 1NX [E-mail: jim.murphy5@btopenworld.com]	01698 740189
Preston, J. Steven	24 Glen Prosen, East Kilbride, Glasgow G74 3TA [E-mail: steven.preston1@btinternet.com]	01355 237359
Stevenson, Thomas	34 Castle Wynd, Quarter, Hamilton ML3 7XD	01698 282263
White, Ian T.	21 Muirhead, Stonehouse, Larkhall ML9 3HG [E-mail: iantwhite@aol.com]	01698 792772

18. DUMBARTON

Foster, Peter	The Forge, Colgrain Steading, Colgrain, Cardross, Dumbarton G82 5JL [E-mail: peterafoster@btopenworld.com]	01389 849200
Giles, Donald (Dr)	Levern House, Stuckenduff, Shandon, Helensburgh G84 8NW [E-mail: don.giles@btopenworld.com]	01436 820565
Harold, Sandy	The Laurels, Risk Street, Clydebank G81 3LW [E-mail: harold996@btinternet.com]	0141-952 3673
Hart, R.J.M. BSc	7 Kidston Drive, Helensburgh G84 8QA [E-mail: rjm7k@yahoo.com]	01436 672039
McCutcheon, John	Flat 2/6 Parkview, Milton Brae, Milton, Dumbarton G82 2TT [E-mail: JMccutc933@aol.com]	01389 739034
Nutter, Margaret (Miss)	14 Balloch Road, Balloch, Alexandria G83 8SR [E-mail: mnutter@blueyonder.co.uk]	01436 754505
Rettie, Sara (Mrs)	86 Dennistoun Crescent, Helensburgh G84 7JF [E-mail: sarajayne.rettie@btinternet.com]	01436 677984
Robertson, Ishbel (Miss)	81 Bonhill Road, Dumbarton G82 2DU [E-mail: ishbelrobertson@blueyonder.co.uk]	01389 763436

19. ARGYLL

Binner, Aileen (Mrs)	'Ailand', North Connel, Oban PA37 1QX [E-mail: binners@ailand.plus.com]	01631 710264
Challis, John O.	Bay Villa, Strachur, Cairndow PA27 8DE [E-mail: strachur@aol.com]	01369 860436
Goodison, Michael	Dalriada Cottage, Bridge of Awe, Taynuilt PA35 1HT [E-mail: dalriada@btinternet.com]	01866 822479

Holden, Robert	Orsay, West Bank Road, Ardrishaig, Lochgilphead PA30 8HG [E-mail: bobby@robertholden.freeserve.co.uk]	01546 603211
Logue, David	3 Braeface, Tayvallich, Lochgilphead PA31 8PN [E-mail: david@loguenet.co.uk]	01546 870647
McLellan, James A.	West Drimvore, Lochgilphead PA31 8SU [E-mail: james.mclellan8@btinternet.com]	01546 606403
Mitchell, James S.	4 Main Street, Port Charlotte, Isle of Islay PA48 7TX	01496 850650
Morrison, John L.	Tigh na Barnashaig, Tayvallich, Lochgilphead PA31 8PN [E-mail: jolomo@thejolomostudio.com]	01546 870637
Ramsay, Mathew M.	Portnastorm, Carradale, Campbeltown PA28 6SB [E-mail: portnastorm@tiscali.co.uk]	01583 431381
Scouller, Alastair	3 Oxford Terrace, Edinburgh EH4 1PX [E-mail: scouller@globalnet.co.uk]	0131-332 9581
Simpson, John	Ardvullin, Longsdale Road, Oban PA34 5JU	01631 562022
Sinclair, Margaret (Mrs)	2 Quarry Place, Furnace, Inveraray PA32 8XW [E-mail: margaret_sinclair@btinternet.com]	01499 500633
Stather, Angela (Mrs)	9 Gartness Cottages, Ballygrant, Isle of Islay PA45 7QN [E-mail: angel.stather@virgin.net]	01496 840527
Thornhill, Christopher R.	4 Ardfern Cottages, Ardfern, Lochgilphead PA31 9QN [E-mail: c.thornhill@btinternet.com]	01852 500674
Waddell, Martin	2 Kilbrandon Cottages, Balvicar, Isle of Seil, Oban PA34 4RA [E-mail: waddell1715@btinternet.com]	01852 300395
Zielinski, Jennifer C. (Mrs)	26 Cromwell Street, Dunoon PA23 7AX [E-mail: jczyefo@aol.com]	01369 706136

22. FALKIRK

Brown, Kathryn (Mrs)	1 Callendar Park Walk, Callendar Grange, Falkirk FK1 1TA [E-mail: kaybrownlcpw@talktalk.net]	01324 617352
Duncan, Lorna M. (Mrs) BA	Richmond, 28 Solway Drive, Head of Muir, Denny FK6 5NS [E-mail: ell.dee@blueyonder.co.uk]	01324 813020
MacDonald, Monica (Mrs)	32 Reilly Gardens, High Bonnybridge, Bonnybridge FK4 2BB [E-mail: monica.macdonald55@googlemail.com]	01324 874807
Mathers, Sandra (Mrs)	10 Ercall Road, Brightons, Falkirk FK2 0RS [E-mail: alexena@btinternet.com]	01324 872253
O'Rourke, Edith (Ms)	16 Achray Road, Condorrat, Cumbernauld G67 4JH [E-mail: o-rourke45@btinternet.com]	01236 732813
Sarle, Andrew BSc BD	114 High Station Road, Falkirk FK1 5LN [E-mail: andrew@sarle.me.uk]	01324 621648
Stewart, Arthur MA	51 Bonnymuir Crescent, Bonnybridge FK4 1GD [E-mail: arthur.stewart1@btinternet.com]	01324 812667
Struthers, Ivar B.	7 McVean Place, Bonnybridge FK4 1QZ [E-mail: ivar.struthers@btinternet.com]	01324 841145 / 07921 778208 (Mbl)

23. STIRLING

Durie, Alastair (Dr)	25 Forth Place, Stirling FK8 1UD [E-mail: acdurie@btinternet.com]	01786 451029
Grier, Hunter	17 Station Road, Bannockburn, Stirling FK7 8LG [E-mail: hunter@xaltmail.com]	01786 815192
Mack, Lynne (Mrs)	36 Middleton, Menstrie FK11 7HD [E-mail: lynnemack36@sky.com]	01259 761465
Ross, Alastair	7 Elm Court, Doune FK16 6JG [E-mail: ross654@btinternet.com]	01786 841648 (Mbl) 07885 598960
Tilly, Patricia (Mrs)	4 Innerdownie Place, Dollar FK14 7BY [E-mail: Trishatilly@aol.com]	01259 742094
Weir, Andrew (Dr)	16 The Oaks, Killearn, Glasgow G63 9SF [E-mail: andrewweir@btinternet.com]	01360 550779 (Mbl) 07534 506075

24. DUNFERMLINE

Adams, William	24 Foulford Street, Cowdenbeath KY4 0EQ [E-mail: william.adams94@yahoo.co.uk]	01383 510540
Arnott, Robert G.K.	25 Sealstrand, Dalgety Bay, Dunfermline KY11 9NG [E-mail: robin.arnott@nibor.org.uk]	01383 822293
Blane, David	10 Ordnance Road, Crombie, Dunfermline KY12 8JZ [E-mail: davidblane@virgin.net]	01383 873002 (Mbl) 07866 543049
Conway, Bernard	4 Centre Street, Kelty KY4 0EQ	01383 830442
Grant, Allan	6 Normandy Place, Rosyth KY11 2HJ [E-mail: allan75@btinternet.com]	01383 428760
McCafferty, Joyce (Mrs)	53 Foulford Street, Cowdenbeath KY4 9AS	01383 515775
McDonald, Elizabeth (Mrs)	Parleyhill, Culross, Dunfermline KY12 8JD	01383 880231
Meiklejohn, Barry	40 Lilac Grove, Dunfermline KY11 8AP [E-mail: barry.meiklejohn@btinternet.com]	01383 731550
Mitchell, Ian G. QC	17 Carlingnose Point, North Queensferry, Inverkeithing KY11 1ER [E-mail: igmitchell@easynet.co.uk]	01383 416240

25. KIRKCALDY

| Allardice, Michael | 20 Parbroath Road, Glenrothes KY7 4TH [E-mail: m.allardice@dundee.ac.uk] | 01592 772280 (Mbl) 07936 203465 |
| Biernat, Ian | 2 Formonthills Road, Glenrothes KY6 3EF [E-mail: ian.biernat@btinternet.com] | 01592 655565 |

26. ST ANDREWS

| Elder, Morag Anne (Ms) | 5 Provost Road, Tayport DD6 9JE [E-mail: benuardin@tiscali.co.uk] | 01382 552218 |
| King, C.M. (Mrs) | 8 Bankwell Road, Anstruther KY10 3DA | 01333 310017 |

Kinnis, W.K.B. (Dr) (Reader Emeritus)
4 Dempster Court, St Andrews KY16 9EU
[E-mail: mail@bkinnis.fsnet.co.uk]
01334 476959

Smith, Elspeth (Mrs)
Whinstead, Dalgairn, Cupar KY15 4PH
[E-mail: elspeth.smith@btopenworld.com]
01334 653269

27. DUNKELD AND MEIGLE

Howat, David
Lilybank Cottage, Newton Street, Blairgowrie PH10 6HZ
[E-mail: davidphowat@btinternet.com]
01250 874715

Peacock, Graham
7 Glenisla View, Alyth, Blairgowrie PH11 8LW
[E-mail: grahampeacock@tiscali.co.uk]
01828 633341

Steele, Grace (Ms)
12A Farragon Drive, Aberfeldy PH15 2BQ
[E-mail: gmfsteele@tiscali.co.uk]
01887 820025

Templeton, Elizabeth (Mrs)
Milton of Pitgur Farmhouse, Dalcapon, Pitlochry PH9 0ND
[E-mail: templeton.e@btinternet.com]
01796 472360

28. PERTH

Archibald, Michael
Wychwood, Culdeesland Road, Methven, Perth PH1 3QE
[E-mail: michael.archibald@gmail.com]
01738 840995

Begg, James
8 Park Village, Turretbank Road, Crieff PH7 4JN
[E-mail: Bjimmy37@aol.com]
01764 655907

Brown, Gordon
Nowell, Fossoway, Kinross KY13 0UW
[E-mail: brown.nowell@hotmail.co.uk]
01577 840248

Brown, Stanley R.
14 Buchan Drive, Perth PH1 1NQ
[E-mail: broonbuchan@supanet.com]
01738 628818

Chappell, Enid (Mrs)
Flat B, Fiscal House, 1 South Street, Perth PH2 8NJ
[E-mail: echappell308@googlemail.com]
01738 587808

Coulter, Hamish (James)
95 Cedar Drive, Perth PH1 1RW
[E-mail: hamish@hamlynperth.co.uk]
(Home) 01738 636761
(Office) 01738 896231

Davidson, Andrew
95 Needless Road, Perth PH2 0LD
[E-mail: andrew_r_davidson@yahoo.co.uk]
01738 620839

Hardman Moore, Susan (Dr)
Hoolie Hoose, Dunira, Crieff PH6 2IZ
[E-mail: s.hardmanmoore@ed.ac.uk]
(Mbl) 01764 670010
07811 345699

Johnstone, David
92 Duncansby Way, Perth PH1 5XF
[E-mail: dehij@fish.co.uk]
01738 442051

Laing, John
10 Graybank Road, Perth PH2 0GZ
[E-mail: johnandmarylaing@hotmail.co.uk]
01738 623888

Livingstone, Alan
Meadowside, Lawmuir, Methven, Perth PH1 3SZ
[E-mail: livingstone24@btinternet.com]
(Mbl) 01738 638866
07860 930154

Michie, Margaret (Mrs)
3 Loch Leven Court, Wester Balgedie, Kinross KY13 9NE
[E-mail: margaretmichie@btinternet.com]
01592 840602

Ogilvie, Brian
67 Whitecraigs, Kinnesswood, Kinross KY13 9JN
[E-mail: brianj.ogilvie1@btopenworld.com]
(Mbl) 01592 840823
07815 759864

Theaker, Phillip — 5 Altamount Road, Blairgowrie PH10 6QL [E-mail: ptheaker@talktalk.net] — 01250 871162

Thorburn, Susan (Mrs) MTh — 3 Daleally Cottages, St Madoes Road, Errol, Perth PH2 7TJ [E-mail: s.thor@yahoo.com] — 01821 642681

Wilkie, Robert — 24 Huntingtower Road, Letham, Perth PH1 2JS [E-mail: rwew25879@blueyonder.co.uk] — 01738 628301

Yellowlees, Deirdre (Mrs) — Ringmill House, Gannochy Farm, Perth PH2 7JH [E-mail: d.yellowlees@btinternet.com] — 01738 633773 / (Mbl) 07920 805399

29. DUNDEE

Baxter, John MA — 2 Garten Street, Broughty Ferry, Dundee DD5 3HH — 01382 739997

Bell, Stephen (Dr) — 10 Victoria Street, Newport-on-Tay DD6 8DJ — 01382 542315

Brown, Isobel (Mrs) — 10 School Wynd, Muirhead, Dundee DD2 5LW [E-mail: isobel73@btinternet.com] — 01382 580545

Brown, Janet (Miss) — G2, 6 Baxter Park Terrace, Dundee DD4 6NL [E-mail: j.herries.brown@blueyonder.co.uk] — 01382 453066

Doig, Andrew A.A. — 6 Lyndhurst Terrace, Dundee DD2 3HP — 01382 610596

Simpson, Webster — 51 Wemyss Crescent, Monifieth, Dundee DD5 4RA [E-mail: webster@randallsimpson.co.uk] — 01382 535218

Webster, Charles A. — 16C Bath Street, Broughty Ferry, Dundee DD5 2BY [E-mail: charliewebster@talktalk.net] — 01382 739520 / (Mbl) 07905 141269

Woodley, Alan G. (Dr) — 67 Marlee Road, Broughty Ferry, Dundee DD5 3EU [E-mail: awoodley@btinternet.com] — 01382 739820

Xenophontos-Hellen, Tim — Aspro Spiti, 23 Ancrum Drive, Dundee DD2 2JG [E-mail: tim.xsf@btinternet.com] — 01382 630355 / (Work) 01382 567756

30. ANGUS

Anderson, Gordon — 33 Grampian View, Ferryden, Montrose DD10 9SU [E-mail: gordon.anderson46@btinternet.com] — 01674 674915

Davidson, Peter I. — 24 Kinnaird Place, Brechin DD9 7HF [E-mail: mail@idavidson.co.uk]

Edwards, Dougal — 25 Mackenzie Street, Carnoustie DD7 6HD [E-mail: dougal.edwards@blueyonder.co.uk] — 01241 852666

Gray, Ian — 'The Mallards', 15 Rossie Island Road, Montrose DD10 9NH [E-mail: iancelia15@aol.com] — 01674 677126

Gray, Linda (Mrs) — 8 Inchgarth Street, Forfar DD8 3LY [E-mail: lindamgray@sky.com] — 01307 464039

Stevens, Peter J. BSc BA — 7 Union Street, Montrose DD10 8PZ [E-mail: peter280stevens@btinternet.com] — 01674 673710

Thompson, Annie (Miss) — 22 Braehead Drive, Carnoustie DD7 7SX [E-mail: look814@gmail.com] — 01241 852084

Wheat, Michael A. — 16A South Esk Street, Montrose DD10 8BJ — 01674 676083

31. ABERDEEN

Anderson, William
1 Farepark Circle, Westhill, Skene AB32 6WJ
[E-mail: bill.anderson6@btinternet.com]
01224 740017
(Mbl) 07708 343891

Gray, Peter (Prof.)
165 Countesswells Road, Aberdeen AB15 7RA
[E-mail: pmdgray165@btinternet.com]
01224 318172

Morgan, Richard
73A Bon Accord Street, Aberdeen AB11 6ED
[E-mail: themorgans@hotmail.co.uk]
01224 210270

32. KINCARDINE AND DEESIDE

Bell, Robert
27 Mearns Drive, Stonehaven AB39 2DZ
[E-mail: r.bell282@btinternet.com]
01569 767173
(Mbl) 07733 014826

Broere, Teresa (Mrs)
3 Balnastraid Cottages, Dinnet, Aboyne AB34 5NE
[E-mail: dirk.broere@talktalk.net]
01339 880058

Coles, Stephen
43 Mearns Walk, Laurencekirk AB30 1FA
[E-mail: steve@sbcco.com]
01561 378400

McCafferty, W. John
Lynwood, Cammachmore, Stonehaven AB39 3NR
[E-mail: wjmccafferty@yahoo.co.uk]
01569 730281

McLuckie, John
7 Monaltrie Close, Ballater AB35 5PT
[E-mail: johnemcluckie@btinternet.com]
01339 755489

Middleton, Robin B. (Capt.)
7 St Ternan's Road, Newtonhill, Stonehaven AB39 3PF
[E-mail: randjmiddleton@tiscali.co.uk]
01569 730852

Platt, David
2 St Michael's Road, Newtonhill, Stonehaven AB39 3RW
[E-mail: daveplatt01@btinternet.com]
01569 730465

Simpson, Elizabeth (Mrs)
Connemara, 33 Golf Road, Ballater AB35 5RS
[E-mail: connemara33@yahoo.com]
01339 755597

33. GORDON

Beddows, Joanne (Mrs)
28 St Ninians, Monymusk, Inverurie AB51 7HF
[E-mail: jobeddows@btopenworld.com]
01467 651261

Bichard, Susanna (Mrs)
Beechlee, Haddo Lane, Tarves, Ellon AB41 7JZ
[E-mail: smbichard@aol.com]
01651 851343

Doak, Alan B.
17 Chievres Place, Ellon AB41 9WH
[E-mail: alanbdoak@aol.com]
01358 721819

Findlay, Patricia (Mrs)
Douglas View, Tullynessle, Alford AB33 8QR
[E-mail: p.a.findlay@btopenworld.com]
01975 562379

Mitchell, Jean (Mrs)
6 Cowgate, Oldmeldrum, Inverurie AB51 0EN
[E-mail: j.g.mitchell@btinternet.com]
01651 872745

Morrison, Alex
58 East Park Street, Huntly AB54 8JF
(Work) 01542 837242

Robb, Margaret (Mrs)
Chrislouan, Keithhall, Inverurie AB51 0LN
[E-mail: Robbminister1@aol.com]
01651 882310

Robertson, James Y. MA
1 Nicol Road, Kintore, Inverurie AB51 0QA
[E-mail: j.robertson833@btinternet.com]
01467 633001

34. BUCHAN

Armitage, Rosaline (Mrs)
Whitecairn, Blackhills, Peterhead AB42 3LR
[E-mail: r.r.armitage@uwclub.co.uk]
01779 477267

Brown, Lillian (Mrs)
45 Main Street, Aberchirder, Huntly AB54 7ST
01779 470242

Davidson, James C.
19 Great Stuart Street, Peterhead AB42 1JX
[E-mail: jim@jcdavidson.com]

Forsyth, Alicia (Mrs)
Rothie Inn Farm, Forgue Road, Rothienorman, Inverurie AB51 8YH
[E-mail: a.forsyth@btinternet.com]
01651 821359

Givan, James
Zimra, Longmanhill, Banff AB45 3RP
[E-mail: jim.givan@btinternet.com]
01261 833318
(Mbl) 07753 458664

Higgins, Scott
St Ninian's, Manse Terrace, Turriff AB53 4BA
[E-mail: scott.higgins@uk.bp.com]

Lumsden, Vera (Mrs)
8 Queen's Crescent, Portsoy, Banff AB45 2PX
[E-mail: ivsd@lumsden77.freeserve.co.uk]
01261 842712

McColl, John
East Cairnchina, Lonmay, Fraserburgh AB43 8RH
[E-mail: info@solomonsfolly.co.uk]
01346 532558
(Mbl) 07757 303195

MacLeod, Alice (Mrs)
11 Pitfour Crescent, Fetterangus, Peterhead AB42 4EL
[E-mail: aliowl@hotmail.com]
01771 622992
(Mbl) 07821 670705

Macnee, Anthea (Mrs)
Wardend Cottage, Alvah, Banff AB45 3TR
[E-mail: macneeiain4@googlemail.com]
01261 815647

Mair, Dorothy L.T. (Miss)
Flat F, 15 The Quay, Newburgh, Ellon AB41 6DA
[E-mail: dorothymair2@aol.com]
(Mbl) 07505 051305

Michie, William D.
34 Seafield Street, Whitehills, Banff AB45 2NR
[E-mail: b.michie@talktalk.net]
01261 861439

Noble, John M.
44 Henderson Park, Peterhead AB42 2WR
[E-mail: j-m-noble@hotmail.co.uk]
01779 472522

Ogston, Norman
Rowandale, 6 Rectory Road, Turriff AB53 4SU
[E-mail: norman.ogston@gmail.com]
01888 560342

Simpson, Andrew C.
10 Wood Street, Banff AB45 1JX
[E-mail: andy.louise1@btinternet.com]
01261 812538

Smith, Jenny (Mrs)
5 Seatown Place, Cairnbulg, Fraserburgh AB43 8WP
[E-mail: jennyfsmith@hotmail.com]
01346 582980

Sneddon, Richard
8 School Road, Peterhead AB42 2BE
[E-mail: richard.sneddon@btinternet.com]
01779 480803

Stewart, William
Denend, Strichen, Fraserburgh AB43 6RN
[E-mail: billandjunes@live.co.uk]
01771 637256

Williams, Paul
20 Soy Burn Gardens, Portsoy, Banff AB45 2QG
[E-mail: paul.williams447@virgin.net]
01261 842338

Yule, Joseph B.
5 Scaffa Street, Peterhead AB42 1NF

35. MORAY

Benson, F. Stewart
8 Springfield Court, Forres IV36 3WY
[E-mail: janetwbenson@hotmail.com]
01309 671525

Finnie, Leslie   83 Robertson Road, Lhanbryde, Elgin IV30 8JQ [E-mail: lesliefinnie@btopenworld.com]   01343 842789   (Mbl) 07595 326558

Forbes, Jean (Mrs)   Greenmoss, Drybridge, Buckie AB56 2JB [E-mail: dancingfeet@tinyworld.co.uk]   01542 831646   (Mbl) 07974 760337

Middleton, Alexander   Coral Cottage, 1 Pilmuir Road West, Forres IV36 2HL [E-mail: amiddleton@trustcorgi.com]   01309 676912

36. ABERNETHY

Bardgett, Alison (Mrs)   Tigh an Iasgair, Street of Kincardine, Boat of Garten PH24 3BY [E-mail: tigh@bardgett.plus.com]   01479 811055

Berkeley, John (Dr)   Drumbeg, Coylumbridge, Aviemore PH22 1QU [E-mail: john@berkeley.freeserve.co.uk]

Duncanson, Mary (Ms)   Glenelg, 72B High Street, Kingussie PH21 1HZ [E-mail: mary1105@hotmail.co.uk]   01540 662075

Thomson, Mary (Mrs)   Riverside Flat, Gynack Street, Kingussie PH21 1EL [E-mail: marythomson835@btinternet.com]   01540 661772

37. INVERNESS

Archer, Morven (Mrs)   42 Firthview Drive, Inverness IV3 8QE [E-mail: morvarch@btinternet.com]   01463 237840

Cazaly, Leonard   9 Moray Park Gardens, Culloden, Inverness IV2 7FY [E-mail: len_cazaly@lineone.net]   01463 794469

Cook, Arnett D.   66 Millerton Avenue, Inverness IV3 8RY [E-mail: arnett.cook@btinternet.com]   01463 224795

Dennis, Barry   50 Holm Park, Inverness IV2 4XU [E-mail: barry.dennis@tiscali.co.uk]   01463 225883   (Work) 01463 663448

MacInnes, Ailsa (Mrs)   Kilmartin, 17 Southside Road, Inverness IV2 3BG [E-mail: ailsa.macinnes@btopenworld.com]   01463 230321   (Mbl) 07704 485055

Ogston, Jean (Mrs)   Roselynn, Croyard Road, Beauly IV4 7DJ [E-mail: jeanogston@googlemail.com]   01463 782260

Robertson, Hendry   Park House, 51 Glenurquhart Road, Inverness IV3 5PB [E-mail: hendry.robertson@connectfree.co.uk]   01463 231858   (Mbl) 07929 766102

Robertson, Stewart J.H.   21 Towerhill Drive, Cradlehall, Inverness IV2 5FD   01463 793144

Roden, Vivian (Mrs)   15 Old Mill Road, Tomatin, Inverness IV13 7YW [E-mail: vroden@btinternet.com]   01808 511355   (Mbl) 07887 704915

Todd, Iain   9 Leanach Gardens, Inverness IV2 5DD [E-mail: itoddyo@aol.com]   01463 791161

38. LOCHABER

Chalkley, Andrew BSc   2 Telford Place, Claggan, Fort William PH33 6QG [E-mail: andrew.chalkley@btinternet.com]   01397 700271

Muirhead, Morag (Mrs)
6 Dunbarton Road, Fort William PH33 6UU
[E-mail: mowgli49@aol.com]
(Mbl) 01397 703643
07899 764643
(Work) 01631 740313

Perkins, Mairi (Mrs)
Ashlea, Cuil Road, Duror, Appin PA38 3DA
[E-mail: m.perkins533@btinternet.com]

Walker, Eric
Tigh a' Chlann, Inverroy, Roy Bridge PH31 4AQ
[E-mail: line15@btinternet.com]
01397 712028

Walker, Pat (Mrs)
Tigh a' Chlann, Inverroy, Roy Bridge PH31 4AQ
[E-mail: pw-15@tiscali.co.uk]
01397 712028

39. ROSS

Finlayson, Michael R.
Amberlea, Glenskiach, Evanton, Dingwall IV16 9UU
[E-mail: finlayson935@btinternet.com]
01349 830598

Greer, Kathleen (Mrs) MEd
17 Duthac Wynd, Tain IV19 1LP
[E-mail: greer2@talktalk.net]
01862 892065

Gunstone, Ronald W.
20 Bellfield Road, North Kessock, Inverness IV1 3XU
[E-mail: ronald.gunstone@virgin.net]
01463 731337
(Mbl) 07974 443948

Jamieson, Patricia A. (Mrs)
9 Craig Avenue, Tain IV19 1JP
[E-mail: hapijam179@yahoo.co.uk]
01862 893154

McAlpine, James
5 Cromlet Park, Invergordon IV18 0RN
[E-mail: jmca1@tinyworld.co.uk]
01349 852801

McCreadie, Frederick
Inchbroom, Highfield Park, Conon Bridge, Dingwall IV7 8AP
01349 862171

Riddell, Keith
2 Station Cottages, Fearn, Tain IV20 1RR
[E-mail: keithriddell@hotmail.co.uk]
01862 832867
(Mbl) 07719 645995

40. SUTHERLAND

Baxter, A. Rosie (Dr)
Creich Old Manse, Bonar Bridge, Ardgay IV24 3AB
[E-mail: drrosiereid@yahoo.co.uk]
01863 766257
(Mbl) 07748 761694

Bruce, Dorothy (Mrs) (Reader Emeritus)
Eastwood, Altass, Rosehall, by Lairg IV27 4EU
[E-mail: dorothymbruce@aol.com]
01549 441285

Innes, Derek
Hill Cottage, 24 Lairg Muir, Lairg IV27 4ED
[E-mail: dereklinnes@btinternet.com]
01549 402215
(Mbl) 07791 125954

Roberts, Irene (Mrs)
Flat 4, Harbour Buildings, Main Street, Portmahomack, Tain IV20 1YG
[E-mail: ireneroberts43@hotmail.com]
01862 871166
(Mbl) 07854 436854

Stobo, Mary (Mrs)
Druim-an-Sgairnich, Ardgay IV24 3BG
[E-mail: sutherland@cofscotland.org.uk]
01863 766868

Weidner, Karl
6 St Vincent Road, Tain IV19 1JR
[E-mail: kweidner@btinternet.com]
01862 894202

41. CAITHNESS

Duncan, Esme (Miss)
Avalon, Upper Warse, Canisbay, Wick KW1 4YD
[E-mail: esmeduncan@btinternet.com]
01955 611455

Rennie, Lyall — The Manse, Canisbay, Wick KW1 4YH
[E-mail: lyall.rennie@btinternet.com] — 01955 611756

Stewart, Heather (Mrs) — Burnthill, Thrumster, Wick KW1 5AX
[E-mail: heatherburnthill@btopenworld.com] — 01955 651717 / (Work) 01955 603333

42. LOCHCARRON – SKYE
Lamont, John H. BD — 6 Tigh na Fiiine, Aultbea, Achnasheen IV22 2JE
[E-mail: jhlamont@btinternet.com] — (Mbl) 07714 720753

MacRae, Donald E. — Nethania, 52 Strath, Gairloch IV21 2DB
[E-mail: Dmgair@aol.com] — 01445 712235

Murray, John W. — 1 Totescore, Kilmuir, Portree, Isle of Skye IV51 9YW — 01470 542297
Ross, R. Ian — St Conal's, Inverinate, Kyle IV40 8HB — 01599 511371

43. UIST
Browning, Margaret (Miss) — 1 Middlequarter, Sollas, Lochmaddy, Isle of North Uist HS6 5BU
[E-mail: margaretckb@tiscali.co.uk] — 01876 560392

Lines, Charles M.D. — Flat 1/02, 8 Queen Margaret Road, Glasgow G20 6DP
MacAulay, John — Fernhaven, 1 Flodabay, Isle of Harris HS3 3HA — 01859 530340
MacNab, Ann (Mrs) — Druim Skilivat, Scolpaig, Lochmaddy, Isle of North Uist HS6 5DH
[E-mail: annabhan@hotmail.com] — 01876 510701

MacSween, John — 5 Scott Road, Tarbert, Isle of Harris HS3 3DL — 01859 502338
Taylor, Hamish — Tigh na Tobair, Flodabay, Isle of Harris HS3 3HA — 01859 530310

44. LEWIS
McAlpin, Robert J.G. — 42A Upper Coll, Back, Isle of Lewis HS2 0LT — 01851 820288
Macleod, Donald — 14 Balmerino Drive, Stornoway, Isle of Lewis HS1 2TD
[E-mail: donaldmacleod25@btinternet.com] — 01851 704516

Macmillan, Iain — 34 Scotland Street, Stornoway, Isle of Lewis HS1 2JR
[E-mail: macmillan@brocair.fsnet.co.uk] — 01851 871114 / (Mbl) 07775 598679

Murray, Angus — 4 Ceann Chilleagraidh, Stornoway, Isle of Lewis HS1 2UJ — 01851 703550

45. ORKNEY
Fidler, David G. — 34 Guardhouse Park, Stromness, Orkney KW16 3DP
[E-mail: dvdfid@yahoo.co.uk] — 01856 850575 / (Mbl) 07900 386473

Prentice, Martin — Cott of Howe, Cairston, Stromness, Orkney KW16 3JU
[E-mail: mwm.prentice@virgin.net] — 01856 851139 / (Mbl) 07795 817213

Robertson, Johan (Mrs) — Old Manse, Eday, Orkney KW17 2AA — 01857 622251
Steer, John — Beckington, Hillside Road, Stromness, Orkney KW16 3AH
[E-mail: johnsteer@aol.com] — 01856 850815

46. SHETLAND

Christie, William C. (Reader Emeritus) — 11 Fullaburn, Bressay, Shetland ZE2 9ET [E-mail: william.christie2@homecall.co.uk] — 01595 820244

Greig, Diane (Mrs) MA — The Manse, Sandwick, Shetland ZE2 9HW [E-mail: mrschm.greig@binternet.com] — (Work) 01950 431244 / 01950 422468

Harrison, Christine (Mrs) BA — Gerdavatn, Baltasound, Unst, Shetland ZE2 9DY [E-mail: chris4242@binternet.com] — 01957 711578

MacGregor, Robert M. — Vistavird, Brae, Shetland ZE2 9SL — 01806 522773

Smith, M. Beryl (Mrs) DCE MSc — Vakterlee, Cumliewick, Sandwick, Shetland ZE2 9HH [E-mail: beryl@brooniestaing.co.uk] — 01950 431280

47. ENGLAND

Houghton, Mark (Dr) — Kentcliffe, Charney Road, Grange-over-Sands, Cumbria LA11 6BP [E-mail: mark@chaplain.me.uk] — 01539 525048

Mackay, Donald (Reader Emeritus) — 90 Hallgarth Street, Elvet, Durham DH1 3AS — (Work) 01629 813505 / 0191-383 2110

Menzies, Rena (Mrs) — 49 Elizabeth Avenue, St Brelade's, Jersey JE3 8GR [E-mail: menzfamily@jerseymail.co.uk] — 01534 741095

Milligan, Elaine (Mrs) — 16 Surrey Close, Corby, Northants NN17 2TG [E-mail: elainemilligan@ntlworld.com] — 01536 205259

Munro, William — 35 Stour Road, Corby, Northants NN17 2HX — 01536 504864

48. EUROPE

Ross, David — Urb. El Campanario, EDF Granada, Esc. 14, Baja B, Ctra Cadiz N-340, Km 168, 29680 Estepona, Malaga, Spain [E-mail: rosselcampanario@yahoo.co.uk] — (Tel/Fax) 0034 952 88 26 34

ASSOCIATE (Ireland)

Binnie, Jean (Miss) — 2 Ailesbury Lawn, Dundrum, Dublin 16, Ireland [E-mail: jeanbinnie@eircom.net] — 00353 1 298 7229

LIST O – REPRESENTATIVES ON COUNCIL EDUCATION COMMITTEES

COUNCIL	NAME	ADDRESS	TEL
ABERDEEN CITY	Mr Peter Campbell	12 Station Road East, Aberdeen AB14 0PT	01224 734245
ABERDEENSHIRE	Dr Eleanor Anderson	Drumblair Cottage, Forgue, Huntly AB54 6DE	01464 871329

Area	Representative	Address	Telephone
ANGUS	Mr David Adams	Glebe House, Farnell, by Brechin DD9 6UH	01674 820227
ARGYLL and BUTE	Mr William Crossan	Gowanbank, Kilkerran Road, Campbeltown PA26 6JL	
BORDERS	Mr Graeme Donald	1 Upper Loan Park, Lauder TD2 6TR [E-mail: graeme.donald@btopenwoprld.com]	01578 722422
CLACKMANNAN	Rev. Sang Y. Cha	37A Claremont, Alloa FK10 2DG [E-mail: syc@cantab.com]	01259 213872
DUMFRIES and GALLOWAY	Mr Robert McQuistan	Kirkdale Schoolhouse, Carsluith, Newton Stewart DG8 7DT [E-mail: mcquistan@quistaworld.net]	01671 820327
DUNDEE	Miss Kathleen Mands	27 Noran Avenue, Dundee DD4 7LE	01382 451140
EAST AYRSHIRE	Mr Ian Rennie	46 Colonsay Place, Wardneuk, Kilmarnock KA3 2JU	
EAST DUNBARTONSHIRE	Mrs Barbara Jarvie	18 Cannerton Crescent, Milton of Campsie, Glasgow G66 8DR [E-mail: bj@bjarvie.fsnet.co.uk]	01360 319729
EAST LOTHIAN	Mrs Marjorie K. Goldsmith	20 St Lawrence, Haddington EH41 3RL	01620 823249
EAST RENFREWSHIRE	Ms Mary McIntyre	5 Buchanan Drive, Glasgow G77 6HT	
EDINBURGH CITY	Mr A. Craig Duncan	2 East Barnton Gardens, Edinburgh EH4 6AR [E-mail: acraigduncan@btinternet.com]	0131-336 4432
EDINBURGH SCRUTINY PANEL	Dr J. Mitchell Manson	17 Huntingdon Place, Edinburgh EH7 4AX [E-mail: MitchellManson@aol.com]	0131-557 1933
FALKIRK	Mrs Margaret Coutts	34 Pirleyhill Gardens, Falkirk FK1 5NB [E-mail: margaret.coutts1@tiscali.co.uk]	01324 628732
FIFE	Rev. Andrew J. Philip	12 Torvean Place, Dunfermline KY11 4YY [E-mail: andrewphilip@minister.com]	01383 721054
GLASGOW CITY	Rev. Graham R.G. Cartlidge	54 Mansewood Road, Eastwood, Glasgow G43 1TL [E-mail: g.cartlidge@ntlworld.com]	0141-649 0463
GLASGOW CITY SCRUTINY PANEL	Rev. David A. Keddie	21 Ilay Road, Bearsden, Glasgow G61 1QG [E-mail: revked@hotmail.com]	0141-942 5173
HIGHLAND	Mr Gordon Smith		
INVERCLYDE	Rev. Andrew T. MacLean	St Andrew's Manse, Barr's Brae, Port Glasgow PA14 5QA [E-mail: standrews.pg@me.com]	01475 741486
MIDLOTHIAN	Mr Paul Hayes	Kingsway Management Services Ltd, 127 Deanburn, Penicuik EH26 0JA [E-mail: paul.hayes@basilicon.com]	
MORAY	Rev. Shuna M. Dicks	The Manse, Mary Avenue, Aberlour AB38 9QU [E-mail: revshuna@minister.com]	01340 871687
NORTH AYRSHIRE			
NORTH LANARKSHIRE	Mr John William Maddock	137 Manse Road, Motherwell ML1 2PS [E-mail: john@maddockfamily.plus.com]	01698 251137
ORKNEY	Rev. William A.M. Burnside	5 Manse Lane, Stromness, Orkney KW16 3AP	01856 850203
PERTH and KINROSS	Mrs Pat Giles	190 Oakbank Road, Perth PH1 1EG [E-mail: patgiles190@yahoo.co.uk]	01738 625805
RENFREWSHIRE	Mr Ian Keith	5 Langside Drive, Kilbarchan PA10 2EL	01505 702564
SHETLAND	Rev. Tom Macintyre	The Rock, Whiteness, Shetland ZE2 9LJ [E-mail: the2macs.macintyre@btinternet.com]	

SOUTH AYRSHIRE	Rev. David R. Gemmell	58 Monument Road, Ayr KA7 2UB [E-mail: drgemmell@hotmail.com]	01292 262580
SOUTH LANARKSHIRE	Rev. Sarah L. Ross	22 Lea Rig, Forth, Lanark ML11 8EA [E-mail: rev_sross@btinternet.com]	01555 812832
STIRLING	Rev. Stuart Fulton	21 Craiglea, Causewayhead, Stirling FK9 5EE [E-mail: stuart.fulton@btinternet.com]	01786 463060
WEST DUNBARTONSHIRE	Miss Sheila Rennie	128 Dumbuie Avenue, Dumbarton G82 2JW [E-mail: sheila_rennie@tiscali.co.uk]	01389 763246
WEST LOTHIAN	Mrs Lynne McEwen	6 Fernlea, Uphall, Broxburn EH52 6DF [E-mail: lynnemcewen@hotmail.co.uk]	01506 855513
WESTERN ISLES	Dr Neil Galbraith	Four Winds, 1 Churchill Drive, Stornoway, Isle of Lewis HS1 2NP [E-mail: n.galbraith@tiscali.net]	01851 702209

LIST P – RETIRED LAY AGENTS

Falconer, Alexander J.	84 Bridge Street, Dollar FK14 7DQ [E-mail: falconer@falconer59.freeserve.co.uk]
Forrester, Arthur A.	158 Lee Crescent North, Bridge of Don, Aberdeen AB22 8FR
Scott, John W.	15 Manor Court, Forfar DD8 1BR

LIST Q – MINISTERS ORDAINED FOR SIXTY YEARS AND UPWARDS

Until 1992, the *Year Book* contained each year a list of those ministers who had been ordained 'for fifty years and upwards'. Such a list was reinstated in the edition for 2002, including the names of those ordained for sixty years and upwards. With ministers, no less than the rest of society, living longer, it was felt reasonable to proceed on that basis. Correspondence made it clear that this list was welcomed, and it has been included in an appropriately revised form each year since then. Again this year, an updated version is offered following the best enquiries that could be made. The date of ordination is given in full where it is known.

1938	29 June	George Alestair Alison Bennett (Strathkinness)
1939	22 December	Alistair McRae Rennie (Kincardine Croick and Edderton)
1940	29 May	Norman McGathan Bowman (Edinburgh: St Mary's)

1941	3 July	Donald William MacKenzie (Auchterarder: The Barony)
1942	15 April	Frank Haughton (Kirkintilloch: St Mary's)
	24 December	James Bews (Dundee: Craigiebank)
1943	2 June	Duncan Finlayson (Morvern)
	3 September	George Cooper (Delting with Nesting and Lunnasting)
1944	21 June	Denis Macdonald Duncan (Editor: *The British Weekly*)
	10 November	Alexander Spence (Elgin: St Giles': Associate)
1945	24 January	Thomas Morton (Rutherglen: Stonelaw)
	4 February	James Shirra (St Martin's with Scone: New)
	27 June	Ian Arthur Girdwood Easton (University of Strathclyde)
	1 August	John Walter Evans (Elgin: High)
	4 September	John Paul Tierney (Peterhead West: Associate)
1946	11 April	James Martin (Glasgow: High Carntyne)
	19 May	John McClymont Frew (Glasgow: Dennistoun)
	23 June	Ian Masson Fraser (Selly Oak Colleges)
	18 September	John Wilkinson (Kikuyu)
	3 October	John Henry Whyte (Gourock: Ashton)
	13 November	Ian Bruce Doyle (Department of National Mission)
1947	22 June	James Alexander Robertson Mackenzie (Largo: St David's)
	27 November	William Duncan Crombie (Glasgow: Calton New with Glasgow: St Andrew's)
1948	31 March	Gilbert Mollison Mowat (Dundee: Albany-Butterburn)
	20 April	Andrew Kerr (Kilbarchan: West)
	6 July	Alexander Chestnut (Greenock: St Mark's Greenbank)
	8 September	David Stuart Forsyth (Belhelvie)
	6 October	George Davidson Wilkie (Kirkcaldy: Viewforth)
1949	5 January	Andrew Queen Morton (Culross and Torryburn)
	14 February	Hamish Norman Mackenzie McIntosh (Fintry)
	17 July	Walter Vernon Stone (Langbank)
	1 September	John Anderson Macnaughton (Glasgow: Hyndland)

22 November	John Alexander Miller Scott (Jerusalem)
18 December	James McMichael Orr (Aberfoyle with Port of Menteith)

1950	
9 July	Alexander Craib Barr (Glasgow: St Nicholas' Cardonald)
10 July	Kenneth MacVicar (Kenmore with Lawers with Fortingall and Glenlyon)
26 July	Alexander Hamilton Lawson (Clydebank: Kilbowie)
27 August	Robert Govan Clarkson (Dundee: Strathmartine)
5 September	James McLaren Ritchie (Coalsnaughton)
28 December	Donald Stewart Wallace (Chaplain: RAF)

1951	
28 January	William Henry Greenway Bristow (Chaplain: Army)
5 June	Malcolm Nicholson Henry (Perth: Craigie)
12 June	Donald John Barker McAlister (North Berwick: Blackadder)
26 July	Duncan Shaw (Edinburgh: Craigentinny St Christopher's)
9 September	Alwyn James Cecil Macfarlane (Glasgow: Newlands South)
1 October	William James Morris (Glasgow: Cathedral)
6 November	Alexander Gordon McGillivray (Edinburgh: Presbytery Clerk)
15 November	Andrew Whittingham Rae (Annan: St Andrew's Greenknowe Erskine)
20 November	Donald Iain McMillan (Bearsden: South)
28 November	James Pringle Fraser (Strathaven: Avendale Old and Drumclog)

1952	
April	William Frederick Laing (Selkirk: St Mary's West)
18 May	Campbell Milne Saunders (Ayr: St Leonard's)
11 June	Archibald Lamont (Kilcalmonell with Skipness)
2 July	George Compton Stewart (Drumblade with Huntly Strathbogie)
4 July	Charles Malcolm Henderson (Campbeltown: Highland)
16 July	James Mercer Thomson (Elgin: St Giles' and St Columba's South: Associate)
27 August	George Richmond Naismith Rendall Knight Smith (World Alliance of Reformed Churches)
13 September	Charles Raymond Vincent (Stonehouse)
24 September	George Levack Edington (Tayport)

LIST R – DECEASED MINISTERS

The Editor has been made aware of the following ministers who have died since the publication of the previous volume of the *Year Book*.

Bailey, Wellesley Grahame	(Ladykirk with Whitsome)
Bell, Charles James Grant	(Resolis and Urquhart)
Bowie, Alfred	(Alford with Keig with Tullynessle and Forbes)

Brough, Robert — (Whitburn: Brucefield)
Cameron, Alexander (Alasdair) Francis — (Paisley: Sherwood Greenlaw)
Carmichael, James Alexander — (Ardgour with Strontian)
Christman, William James — (Ayr: St Columba)
Crichton, Thomas — (Hospital Chaplain)
Cruickshank, Alistair Booth — (Auxiliary Minister)
Currie, Robert — (Community Minister, Glasgow)
Dick, Thomas — (Dunkeld)
Donn, Thomas Mackenzie — (Duthil)
Dougall, Ian Cunningham — (Kenya)
Duncan, Robert Howat — (Glasgow: Drumchapel St Mark's)
Ferguson, Robert — (Glasgow: North Kelvinside)
Fleming, Thomas Graham — (Slamannan)
Grimstone, Alexander Francis — (Glasgow: Calton Parkhead)
Hill, Robert — (Lisbon)
Houston, Alexander McRae — (Tibbermore)
Hutchison, Alexander Scott — (Hospital Chaplain)
Johnston, Kenneth Lindsay — (Annbank)
Lafferty, John Marshall Morton — (Stevenston: Ardeer with Stevenston: Livingstone)
Levison, Leon David — (Ormiston with Pencaitland)
Levison, Mary Irene — (Edinburgh: St Andrew's and St George's: Associate)
MacFarlane, Donald — (Inverness: East)
Macintyre, William John — (Crail with Kingsbarns)
MacKelvie, John — (Greenock: West)
MacPherson, Allan Stewart — (Chaplain: Merchiston Castle School)
McQuilken, John Ernest — (Glenaray and Inveraray)
Macrae, Norman Christopher — (Loanhead)
Mappin, Michael Graeme — (Bower with Watten)
Massie, Robert William — (Monifieth: St Rule's)
Miller, John Groom — (Port Glasgow: St Martin's)
Miller, Charles Wilmar — (Fowlis and Liff)
Morton, William Scott — (Bearsden: South)
Ogilvy, Oliver Marshall — (Leswalt)
Robertson, James — (Newton)
Robertson, John Archibald — (Strath and Sleat)
Roy, James — (Irvine: Girdle Toll)
Savage, Gordon Matthew Alexander — (Dumfries: Maxwelltown West)
Scott, Ernest Martin — (Port Glasgow: St Andrew's)
Scroggie, John Clark — (Dundee: Mains)
Stewart, Jean Elizabeth — (Kildalton and Oa)
Taylor, John Henry Bindon — (Associate: Galston)
Taylor, William — (Buckie: North)

Thomson, Pauline Mary
Turnbull, James Johnstone
Warnock, Denis
Whiteford, Robert Stockbridge

Peterhead: Old
(Arbirlot with Colliston)
(Kirkcaldy: Torbain)
(Shapinsay)

SECTION 7

Legal Names and Scottish Charity Numbers for Individual Congregations

(All congregations in Scotland, and congregations furth of Scotland which are registered with OSCR, the Office of the Scottish Charity Regulator)

EXPLANATORY NOTE:

All documents, as defined in the Charities References in Documents (Scotland) Regulations 2007, must specify the Charity Number, Legal Name of the congregation, any other name by which the congregation is commonly known and the fact that it is a Charity.

For more information, please refer to the Law Department circular on the Regulations on the Church of Scotland website.

SCOTTISH CHARITY NUMBER	NEW LEGAL NAME
1.	**Presbytery of Edinburgh**
SC018012	Balerno Church of Scotland
SC001554	Edinburgh Currie Kirk (Church of Scotland)
SC010971	Dalmeny Parish Church of Scotland
SC018321	Albany Deaf Church, Edinburgh (Church of Scotland)
SC014757	Edinburgh Barclay Viewforth Church of Scotland
SC008756	Blackhall St Columba's Church of Scotland, Edinburgh
SC011625	Bristo Memorial Church of Scotland, Craigmillar, Edinburgh
SC012642	Edinburgh: Broughton St Mary's Parish Church (Church of Scotland)
SC015251	Canongate Parish Church of Scotland, Edinburgh
SC004783	Carrick Knowe Parish Church of Scotland, Edinburgh
SC010313	Colinton Parish Church of Scotland, Edinburgh
SC015982	Colinton Mains Parish Church of Scotland, Edinburgh
SC014719	Edinburgh: Corstorphine Craigsbank Parish Church (Church of Scotland)
SC016009	Corstorphine Old Parish Church, Church of Scotland, Edinburgh
SC006300	Edinburgh: Corstorphine St Anne's Parish Church (Church of Scotland)
SC016557	Edinburgh: Corstorphine St Ninian's Parish Church (Church of Scotland)
SC003466	Edinburgh: Craigentinny St Christopher's Parish Church of Scotland
SC010545	Craiglockhart Parish Church, Edinburgh (Church of Scotland)
SC017061	Craigmillar Park Church of Scotland, Edinburgh
SC003430	Cramond Kirk, Edinburgh (Church of Scotland)
SC009470	Davidsons Mains Parish Church of Scotland, Edinburgh
SC001692	Dean Parish Church, Edinburgh – The Church of Scotland
SC005744	Drylaw Parish Church of Scotland, Edinburgh
SC016610	Duddingston Kirk (Church of Scotland), Edinburgh
SC015967	Fairmilehead Parish Church of Scotland, Edinburgh
SC009146	Edinburgh: Gorgie Dalry Church of Scotland
SC011985	Granton Parish Church of Scotland, Edinburgh
SC011325	Edinburgh Greenbank Parish Church of Scotland
SC009749	Edinburgh Greenside Church of Scotland
SC003761	Edinburgh: Greyfriars Tolbooth and Highland Kirk (Church of Scotland)
SC003565	St Giles' Cathedral, Edinburgh (Church of Scotland)
SC012562	Holy Trinity Church of Scotland, Edinburgh
SC000052	Holyrood Abbey Parish Church of Scotland, Edinburgh
SC015442	Edinburgh Inverleith St Serf's Church of Scotland
SC005197	Edinburgh Juniper Green Parish Church of Scotland
SC004950	Kaimes: Lockhart Memorial Church of Scotland, Edinburgh
SC014430	Kirk o' Field Parish Church, Edinburgh (Church of Scotland)
SC004932	Edinburgh Leith North Parish Church of Scotland

SC004695	South Leith Parish Church of Scotland, Edinburgh
SC012680	Leith St Andrew's Church of Scotland, Edinburgh
SC008710	Wardie Parish Church of Scotland, Edinburgh
SC011602	Edinburgh: Liberton Kirk (Church of Scotland)
SC008891	Liberton Northfield Parish Church of Scotland, Edinburgh
SC000896	London Road Church of Scotland, Edinburgh
SC009338	Marchmont St Giles Parish Church of Scotland, Edinburgh
SC000785	Mayfield Salisbury Parish (Edinburgh) Church of Scotland
SC034396	Morningside Parish Church of Scotland, Edinburgh
SC015552	Edinburgh: Morningside United Church
SC000871	Muirhouse Parish Church of Scotland, Edinburgh
SC005198	Edinburgh Murrayfield Parish Church of Scotland
SC000963	New Restalrig Church of Scotland, Edinburgh
SC019117	Newhaven Church of Scotland, Edinburgh
SC006457	The Old Kirk of Edinburgh (Church of Scotland)
SC004291	Edinburgh: Palmerston Place Church of Scotland
SC007277	Edinburgh: Pilrig St Paul's Church of Scotland
SC004183	Polwarth Parish Church, Edinburgh (Church of Scotland)
SC002328	Edinburgh: Portobello Old Parish Church of Scotland
SC007372	Edinburgh: Portobello St James' Parish Church of Scotland
SC011728	St Philip's Church of Scotland: Edinburgh
SC014499	Priestfield Parish Church of Scotland, Edinburgh
SC014027	Church of Scotland, Reid Memorial Church, Edinburgh
SC009035	Richmond Craigmillar Parish Church of Scotland, Edinburgh
SC030896	Slateford Longstone Parish Church of Scotland, Edinburgh
SC002748	Edinburgh: St Andrew's Clermiston Church of Scotland
SC009379	St Catherine's Argyle Parish Church of Scotland Edinburgh
SC010592	St Cuthberts Parish Church of Scotland, Edinburgh
SC004746	St Davids Broomhouse Church of Scotland, Edinburgh
SC008990	St Andrew's and St George's West Church of Scotland, Edinburgh
SC030819	St John's Oxgangs Church of Scotland: Edinburgh
SC004779	St Margaret's Church of Scotland: Edinburgh
SC013918	St Martins Church of Scotland, Portobello, Edinburgh
SC009038	St Michaels Parish Church of Scotland, Edinburgh
SC007068	Edinburgh: St Nicholas' Sighthill Parish Church of Scotland
SC004487	St Stephen's Comely Bank Church of Scotland, Edinburgh
SC010004	Stenhouse St Aidan's Parish Church of Scotland: Edinburgh
SC002499	Stockbridge Parish Church of Scotland, Edinburgh
SC009274	Tron Kirk (Gilmerton and Moredun), Edinburgh, Church of Scotland
SC013924	Kirkliston Parish Church of Scotland

SC002329 Queensferry Parish Church of Scotland
SC001169 Ratho Church of Scotland

2.   Presbytery of West Lothian
SC013100 Abercorn Parish Church of Scotland
SC000791 Armadale Parish Church of Scotland
SC007454 Avonbridge Parish Church of Scotland
SC001881 Boghall Parish Church of Scotland, Bathgate
SC007418 Bathgate High Parish Church of Scotland
SC016755 St John's Parish Church of Scotland, Bathgate
SC024154 Blackburn and Seafield Parish Church of
          Scotland
SC006811 Blackridge Parish Church of Scotland
SC000800 Breich Valley Parish Church of Scotland
SC017180 Broxburn Parish Church of Scotland
SC016313 Fauldhouse St Andrews Parish Church of
          Scotland
SC007601 Harthill St Andrew's Parish Church of
          Scotland
SC013461 Kirk of Calder Parish (Church of Scotland)
SC006973 Kirknewton & East Calder Parish Church of
          Scotland
SC016185 St Michaels Parish Church of Scotland:
          Linlithgow
SC011348 St Ninians Craigmailen Parish Church of
          Scotland, Linlithgow
SC011826 Livingston Old Parish Church of Scotland
SC026230 Pardovan, Kingscavil and Winchburgh Parish
          Church of Scotland
SC017373 Polbeth Harwood Parish Church of Scotland
SC006336 Strathbrock Parish Church of Scotland, Uphall
SC021516 Torphichen Parish Church of Scotland
SC024255 Uphall South Parish Church of Scotland
SC004703 West Kirk of Calder (Church of Scotland)
SC003362 Brucefield Parish Church of Scotland,
          Whitburn
SC001053 Whitburn South Parish Church of Scotland

3.   Presbytery of Lothian
SC004580 Aberlady Parish Church (Church of Scotland)
SC009401 Athelstaneford Parish Church (Church of
          Scotland)
SC007231 Belhaven Parish Church (Church of
          Scotland)
SC032180 Bilston Parish Church (Church of Scotland)
SC003230 Bolton and Saltoun Parish Church (Church of
          Scotland)
SC003482 Bonnyrigg Parish Church (Church of Scotland)
SC004630 Cockenzie and Port Seton: Chalmers Memorial
          Parish Church (Church of Scotland)
SC007052 Cockenzie and Port Seton: Old Parish Church
          (Church of Scotland)
SC013139 Cockpen and Carrington Parish Church
          (Church of Scotland)
SC006926 Tyne Valley Parish (Church of Scotland)
SC008958 Dalkeith: St John's and King's Park Parish
          Church (Church of Scotland)
SC014158 Dalkeith: St Nicholas Buccleuch Parish
          Church (Church of Scotland)
SC004533 Dirleton Parish Church (Church of Scotland)
SC000455 Dunbar Parish Church (Church of Scotland)
SC014299 Dunglass Parish Church (Church of Scotland)
SC014972 Garvald and Morham Parish Church (Church
          of Scotland)
SC005996 Gladsmuir Parish Church (Church of Scotland)
SC030433 Glencorse Parish Church (Church of Scotland)
SC004673 Gorebridge Parish Church (Church of
          Scotland)
SC005237 Gullane Parish Church (Church of Scotland)
SC010614 Haddington: St Mary's Parish Church (Church
          of Scotland)

SC022183 Haddington: West Parish Church (Church of
          Scotland)
SC014364 Howgate Parish Church (Church of Scotland)
SC016765 Humbie Parish Church (Church of Scotland)
SC015878 Lasswade and Rosewell Parish Church
          (Church of Scotland)
SC014420 Loanhead Parish Church (Church of Scotland)
SC016556 Longniddry Parish Church (Church of
          Scotland)
SC004722 Musselburgh: Northesk Parish Church (Church
          of Scotland)
SC000129 Musselburgh: St Andrew's High Parish Church
          (Church of Scotland)
SC001726 Musselburgh: St Clement's and St Ninian's
          Parish Church (Church of Scotland)
SC013559 Musselburgh: St Michael's Inveresk Parish
          Church (Church of Scotland)
SC035087 Newbattle Parish Church (Church of Scotland)
SC030879 Newton Parish Church (Church of Scotland)
SC004761 Abbey Church, North Berwick, Church of
          Scotland
SC006421 St Andrew Blackadder, Church of Scotland,
          North Berwick
SC014810 Ormiston Parish Church (Church of
          Scotland)
SC004871 Pencaitland Parish Church (Church of
          Scotland)
SC010902 Penicuik: North Parish Church (Church of
          Scotland)
SC005838 Penicuik: St Mungo's Parish Church (Church
          of Scotland)
SC011871 Penicuik: South Parish Church (Church of
          Scotland)
SC031191 Prestonpans: Prestongrange Parish Church
          (Church of Scotland)
SC005457 Roslin Parish Church (Church of Scotland)
SC008667 Spott Parish Church (Church of Scotland)
SC017423 Tranent Parish Church (Church of Scotland)
SC012277 Traprain Parish Church (Church of Scotland)
SC000494 Whitekirk and Tyninghame Parish Church
          (Church of Scotland)
SC015414 Yester Parish Church (Church of Scotland)

4.   Presbytery of Melrose and Peebles
SC010768 Ashkirk Parish Church of Scotland
SC006480 Bowden and Melrose Church of Scotland
SC030062 Broughton, Glenholm and Kilbucho Church of
          Scotland
SC016990 Caddonfoot Parish Church of Scotland
SC001340 Carlops Parish Church of Scotland
SC009892 Channelkirk and Lauder Church of Scotland
SC003895 Earlston Parish Church of Scotland
SC010081 Eddleston Parish Church of Scotland
SC010389 Old Parish and St Paul's Church of Scotland:
          Galashiels
SC001386 Galashiels Trinity Church of Scotland
SC034662 Ettrick and Yarrow Parish (Church of
          Scotland)
SC000281 St John's Church of Scotland: Galashiels
SC001100 Innerleithen, Traquair and Walkerburn Parish
          Church of Scotland
SC021456 Lyne & Manor Church of Scotland
SC013481 Maxton and Mertoun Parish Church of
          Scotland
SC000575 Newtown Church of Scotland
SC013316 Peebles Old Parish Church of Scotland
SC009159 Church of Scotland St Andrews Leckie Parish:
          Peebles
SC010210 St Boswells Parish Church of Scotland
SC000228 Stow St Mary of Wedale & Heriot Church of
          Scotland

SC004728	Skirling Church of Scotland
SC001866	Stobo and Drumelzier Church of Scotland
SC013564	Tweedsmuir Kirk Church of Scotland
SC003938	St Andrews Parish Church of Scotland: West Linton
SC018087	Kirkurd and Newlands Parish Church of Scotland
SC014883	Selkirk Parish Church of Scotland

5. **Presbytery of Duns**

SC001208	Church of Scotland: Ayton and Burnmouth Parish Church
SC000867	St Andrew's Wallace Green and Lowick Church of Scotland, Berwick-upon-Tweed
SC000246	Bonkyl & Preston Church of Scotland
SC006722	Chirnside Church of Scotland
SC009185	The Church of Scotland, Coldingham Priory
SC001456	Coldstream Parish Church of Scotland
SC005161	Duns Parish Church of Scotland
SC000031	Eccles Parish Church of Scotland
SC007567	Edrom & Allanton Church of Scotland
SC006499	The Church of Scotland, Eyemouth Parish Church
SC002789	Fogo & Swinton Church of Scotland
SC024535	Church of Scotland: Foulden and Mordington Parish Church
SC022349	Gordon St Michael's Church of Scotland
SC016400	Church of Scotland: Grantshouse, Houndwood and Reston Parish Church
SC013136	Greenlaw Parish, Church of Scotland
SC002216	Hutton, Fishwick and Paxton Church of Scotland
SC010680	Langton and Lammermuir Kirk, Church of Scotland
SC009995	Ladykirk Parish Church (Church of Scotland)
SC004582	Legerwood Parish, Church of Scotland
SC005115	Leitholm Parish Church (Church of Scotland)
SC004903	Westruther Parish, Church of Scotland
SC001611	Whitsome Church (Church of Scotland)

6. **Presbytery of Jedburgh**

SC016457	Ale & Teviot United Church of Scotland
SC004550	Cavers and Kirkton Parish Church (Church of Scotland)
SC004517	Hawick Burnfoot Church of Scotland
SC005574	St Mary's & Old Parish Church of Scotland, Hawick
SC005191	Teviot and Roberton Church of Scotland
SC013892	Trinity Parish Church, Hawick (Church of Scotland)
SC017381	Wilton Parish Church of Scotland
SC012830	Hobkirk & Southdean Parish Church of Scotland
SC004530	Jedburgh Old and Trinity Parish Church of Scotland
SC000958	Kelso Country Churches (Church of Scotland)
SC014039	Kelso North and Ednam Parish Church of Scotland
SC010009	Kelso Old & Sprouston Parish Church of Scotland
SC003023	Linton, Morebattle, Hownam and Yetholm Parish Church of Scotland
SC010593	Oxnam Parish Church of Scotland
SC034629	Ruberslaw Parish Church of Scotland
SC006917	Teviothead Parish Church of Scotland

7. **Presbytery of Annandale and Eskdale**

SC010555	Annan Old Parish Church of Scotland
SC010891	St Andrews Parish Church of Scotland, Annan
SC013947	Applegarth, Sibbaldbie & Johnstone Church of Scotland
SC012516	Brydekirk Parish Church of Scotland
SC000717	Canonbie Parish Church of Scotland
SC006344	Dalton Parish Church of Scotland
SC004542	Dornock Parish Church of Scotland
SC016747	Gretna Old, Gretna St Andrew's, Half Morton and Kirkpatrick Fleming Parish Church of Scotland
SC022170	Hightae Parish Church of Scotland
SC005701	Kirkpatrick Juxta Church of Scotland
SC011946	Langholm, Eskdalemuir, Ewes and Westerkirk Church of Scotland
SC006519	Liddesdale Parish Church of Scotland
SC004644	Lochmaben Church of Scotland
SC007116	Lockerbie Dryfesdale, Hutton and Corrie Church of Scotland
SC000722	Hoddom, Kirtle-Eaglesfield and Middlebie Church of Scotland
SC012236	St Andrews Church of Scotland, Moffat
SC001060	St Mungo Parish Church of Scotland, Lockerbie
SC013190	Tundergarth Church of Scotland
SC007536	Wamphray Church of Scotland

8. **Presbytery of Dumfries and Kirkcudbright**

SC016850	Auchencairn & Rerrick Church of Scotland
SC016053	Balmaclellan & Kells Church of Scotland
SC000498	Balmaghie Church of Scotland
SC004450	Borgue Parish Church of Scotland
SC003844	Buittle & Kelton Church of Scotland
SC008648	Caerlaverock Parish Church of Scotland
SC015242	Carsphairn Church of Scotland
SC011037	Castle Douglas Parish Church of Scotland
SC005624	Closeburn Parish Church of Scotland
SC009384	Colvend Southwick & Kirkbean Church of Scotland
SC007152	Corsock & Kirkpatrick Durham Church of Scotland
SC014901	Crossmichael & Parton Church of Scotland
SC002443	Dalbeattie Parish Church of Scotland
SC013121	Dalry Kirkcudbrightshire Church of Scotland
SC010748	Dumfries Northwest Church of Scotland
SC006404	St George's Church of Scotland, Dumfries
SC009432	St Mary's-Greyfriars' Parish Church, Dumfries (Church of Scotland)
SC016201	St Michael's & South Church of Scotland, Dumfries
SC000973	Troqueer Parish Church of Scotland, Dumfries
SC016060	Dunscore Parish Church of Scotland
SC014783	Durisdeer Church of Scotland
SC000961	Gatehouse of Fleet Parish Church of Scotland
SC014663	Glencairn & Moniaive Parish Church of Scotland
SC033058	Irongray Lochrutton & Terregles Parish Church of Scotland
SC014150	Kirkconnel Parish Church of Scotland
SC005883	Kirkcudbright Parish Church of Scotland
SC002286	Kirkgunzeon Church of Scotland
SC010508	Kirkmahoe Parish Church of Scotland
SC030785	Kirkmichael Tinwald & Torthorwald Church of Scotland
SC014590	Lochend and New Abbey Church of Scotland
SC015925	Maxwelltown West Church of Scotland, Dumfries
SC015087	Penpont Keir & Tynron Church of Scotland
SC015399	Cummertrees, Mouswald and Ruthwell Church of Scotland
SC000845	St Bride's Parish Church of Scotland: Sanquhar
SC004475	Tarff & Twynholm Church of Scotland
SC012722	Thornhill Parish Church of Scotland
SC014465	Urr Parish Church of Scotland

9.   **Presbytery of Wigtown and Stranraer**
SC003122   Ervie-Kirkcolm Church of Scotland
SC001705   Glasserton and the Isle of Whithorn Church of
          Scotland
SC007375   Inch Church of Scotland
SC007136   Kirkcowan Parish Church (Church of
          Scotland)
SC001946   Kirkinner Church of Scotland
SC010150   Kirkmabreck Church of Scotland
SC007708   Kirkmaiden Parish Church (Church of
          Scotland)
SC009412   Leswalt Parish Church (Church of Scotland)
SC003300   Mochrum Church of Scotland
SC006014   Monigaff Church of Scotland
SC006316   New Luce Church of Scotland
SC005302   Old Luce Church of Scotland
SC031847   Parish of Penninghame (Church of Scotland)
SC015452   Portpatrick Parish Church (Church of
          Scotland)
SC010621   Sorbie Parish Church of Scotland
SC007346   Stoneykirk Parish Church (Church of
          Scotland)
SC017312   High Kirk of Stranraer (Church of Scotland)
SC002247   Stranraer: St Ninian's Parish Church (Church
          of Scotland)
SC009905   Town Kirk of Stranraer (Church of Scotland)
SC016881   Whithorn: St Ninian's Priory Church of
          Scotland
SC014552   Wigtown Parish Church (Church of Scotland)

10.   **Presbytery of Ayr**
SC012456   Alloway Parish Church of Scotland
SC013225   Annbank Parish Church of Scotland
SC008536   Ballantrae Parish Church of Scotland
SC006707   Auchinleck Parish Church of Scotland
SC001792   Castlehill Parish Church of Scotland: Ayr
SC031474   Dalmellington Parish Church of Scotland
SC001994   Ayr: Newton Wallacetown Church of
          Scotland
SC001757   St Andrew's Parish Church of Scotland: Ayr
SC009336   St James' Parish Church of Scotland: Ayr
SC016860   St Leonard's Parish Church of Scotland: Ayr
SC015366   Barr Parish Church of Scotland
SC013689   Catrine Parish Church of Scotland
SC005283   Coylton Parish Church (Church of Scotland)
SC002633   Craigie Parish Church of Scotland:
          Kilmarnock
SC017520   Crosshill Parish Church (Church of Scotland)
SC012591   Dailly Parish Church of Scotland
SC013503   Dalrymple Parish Church (Church of Scotland)
SC008482   Dundonald Church of Scotland
SC008226   Fisherton Church of Scotland
SC007347   Girvan: North Parish Church of Scotland
SC010381   Girvan South Parish Church of Scotland
SC031952   Kirkmichael Parish Church of Scotland:
          Maybole
SC000213   Kirkoswald Parish Church of Scotland
SC007714   Mauchline Parish Church of Scotland
SC014055   Lugar Parish Church of Scotland
SC004906   St Quivox Parish Church: Ayr (Church of
          Scotland)
SC014794   New Cumnock Parish Church (Church of
          Scotland)
SC010606   Muirkirk Parish Church of Scotland
SC003164   Maybole Parish Church of Scotland
SC034504   Church of Scotland Cumnock Trinity Church
SC000130   Ochiltree Parish Church of Scotland
SC006025   Old Cumnock Old Church of Scotland
SC001940   Kingcase Parish Church of Scotland: Prestwick
SC011750   St Nicholas Parish Church of Scotland:
          Prestwick

SC007403   Prestwick South Church of Scotland
SC004271   Monkton & Prestwick North Parish Church of
          Scotland
SC014381   St Colmon (Arnsheen Barrhill and Colmonell)
          Church of Scotland
SC015899   Sorn Parish Church of Scotland
SC035601   Stair Parish Church (Church of Scotland)
SC013366   Straiton (St Cuthbert's) Parish Church of
          Scotland: Maybole
SC014767   Tarbolton Parish Church of Scotland
SC030714   Drongan: The Schaw Kirk (Church of
          Scotland)
SC007246   Troon Old Parish Church of Scotland
SC003477   Portland Parish Church of Scotland: Troon
SC015019   Troon St Meddan's Parish Church of
          Scotland
SC016648   The Auld Kirk of Ayr Church of Scotland
SC008562   Patna Waterside Parish Church of Scotland
SC002144   Symington Parish Church of Scotland
SC014338   Ayr St Columba Church of Scotland

11.   **Presbytery of Irvine and Kilmarnock**
SC011414   Crosshouse Parish Church (Church of
          Scotland)
SC012014   Darvel Parish Church of Scotland
SC008684   Dreghorn & Springside Parish Church of
          Scotland
SC000447   Dunlop Church of Scotland
SC010062   Fenwick Parish Church (Church of Scotland)
SC010370   Galston Parish Church of Scotland
SC001084   Hurlford Church of Scotland
SC005491   Girdle Toll Church of Scotland, Irvine New
          Town
SC008725   Fullarton Parish Church (Church of Scotland),
          Irvine
SC002299   Mure Parish Church of Scotland, Irvine
SC008345   Irvine Old Parish Church of Scotland
SC002469   Relief Church of Scotland, Irvine
SC010167   St Andrews Church of Scotland: Irvine
SC008154   Kilmarnock: Henderson Parish Church of
          Scotland
SC031334   Kilmarnock: New Laigh Kirk (Church of
          Scotland)
SC008405   Old High Kirk of Kilmarnock (Church of
          Scotland)
SC006040   Kilmarnock Riccarton Church of Scotland
SC029057   Kilmarnock: Shortlees Parish Church of
          Scotland
SC006345   St Andrew's and St Marnock's Parish Church
          of Scotland, Kilmarnock
SC033107   St Johns Parish Church of Scotland – Onthank:
          Kilmarnock
SC001324   St Kentigern's Parish Church of Scotland:
          Kilmarnock
SC012430   Kilmarnock: St Ninian's Bellfield Church of
          Scotland
SC009036   St Maurs Glencairn Church of Scotland,
          Kilmaurs
SC013880   Loudoun Church of Scotland, Newmilns
SC015890   John Knox Parish Church of Scotland,
          Stewarton
SC013595   St Columba's Parish Church of Scotland,
          Stewarton

12.   **Presbytery of Ardrossan**
SC004736   Ardrossan Park Parish Church of Scotland
SC002350   Ardrossan Barony St John's Church of Scotland
SC004660   Beith Parish Church of Scotland
SC012017   Brodick Church of Scotland
SC005030   Corrie Parish Church of Scotland
SC004919   Cumbrae Parish Church of Scotland

SC013170	Dalry St Margaret's Parish Church of Scotland
SC006882	Dalry Trinity Church of Scotland
SC017304	Fairlie Parish Church of Scotland
SC016024	Kilbirnie Auld Kirk (Church of Scotland)
SC013750	St Columbas Parish Church of Scotland: Kilbirnie
SC023602	Kilmory Parish Church of Scotland
SC016499	Kilwinning Mansefield Trinity Church of Scotland
SC001856	Kilwinning Old Parish Church of Scotland
SC015072	Lamlash Church of Scotland
SC002782	Largs Clark Memorial Church of Scotland
SC002294	The Church of Scotland, Largs: St Columba's Parish Church
SC009048	Largs St John's Church of Scotland
SC009377	Lochranza & Pirnmill Church of Scotland
SC023003	Saltcoats New Trinity Parish Church of Scotland
SC003299	Saltcoats North Parish Church of Scotland
SC002905	Saltcoats St Cuthberts Parish Church of Scotland
SC005323	Shiskine Church of Scotland
SC015397	Stevenston Ardeer Parish Church of Scotland
SC009848	Stevenston High Church of Scotland
SC000452	Stevenston Livingstone Parish Church of Scotland
SC013464	West Kilbride Parish Church of Scotland
SC014005	Whiting Bay & Kildonan Church of Scotland

13.   Presbytery of Lanark

SC000333	Biggar Parish Church of Scotland
SC000603	Blackmount Parish Church (Church of Scotland)
SC017001	Cairngryffe Parish Church (Church of Scotland)
SC026539	Kirkton Parish Church, Carluke (Church of Scotland)
SC013968	St Andrews Parish Church of Scotland: Carluke
SC004066	St Johns Church of Scotland: Carluke
SC016360	Carnwath Parish Church of Scotland
SC028124	Carstairs & Carstairs Junction Church of Scotland
SC016493	Coalburn Parish Church (Church of Scotland)
SC014659	Crossford Church of Scotland
SC018252	Culter Parish Church (Church of Scotland)
SC003080	Forth St Paul's Parish Church (Church of Scotland)
SC017506	Glencaple Parish Church (Church of Scotland)
SC011211	Kirkfieldbank Parish Church (Church of Scotland)
SC014451	Kirkmuirhill Parish Church (Church of Scotland)
SC016504	Greyfriars Parish Church, Lanark (Church of Scotland)
SC011368	St Nicholas Parish Church, Lanark (Church of Scotland)
SC013217	Law Parish Church (Church of Scotland)
SC006516	Lesmahagow Abbeygreen (Church of Scotland)
SC017014	Lesmahagow Old Parish Church (Church of Scotland)
SC016304	Libberton & Quothquan Parish Church (Church of Scotland)
SC034654	Lowther Parish Church (Church of Scotland)
SC009095	Symington Parish Church (Church of Scotland)
SC001718	The Douglas Valley Church (Church of Scotland)

14.   Presbytery of Greenock and Paisley

SC015730	Arthurlie Parish Church of Scotland Barrhead
SC016467	Barrhead Bourock Parish Church of Scotland
SC007776	Barrhead South and Levern Church of Scotland
SC006109	Bishopton Parish Church (Church of Scotland)
SC002293	Freeland Church of Scotland, Bridge of Weir
SC003766	Church of Scotland, St Machar's Ranfurly Church, Bridge of Weir
SC008214	Caldwell Parish Church of Scotland
SC015701	Elderslie Kirk (Church of Scotland)
SC017177	Erskine Parish Church of Scotland
SC007324	Old Gourock and Ashton Parish Church of Scotland
SC006412	St Johns Church of Scotland: Gourock
SC010818	Greenock: Lyle Kirk (Church of Scotland)
SC037023	Greenock East End Parish Church of Scotland
SC008357	Greenock The Mount Kirk (Church of Scotland)
SC004855	Old West Kirk, Greenock (Church of Scotland)
SC016711	St Margarets Church of Scotland: Greenock
SC008059	St Ninians Parish Church of Scotland: Greenock
SC001043	Wellpark Mid Kirk of Greenock (Church of Scotland)
SC005106	Greenock Westburn Church of Scotland
SC012822	Houston and Killellan Kirk (Church of Scotland)
SC003487	Howwood Parish Church of Scotland
SC011778	Inchinnan Parish Church (Church of Scotland)
SC001079	Inverkip Church of Scotland
SC009588	Johnstone High Parish Church of Scotland
SC011696	St Andrews Trinity Parish Church of Scotland Johnstone
SC011747	St Pauls Church of Scotland: Johnstone
SC012123	Kilbarchan East Church of Scotland
SC017140	Kilbarchan West Church of Scotland
SC009291	Kilmacolm Old Kirk (Church of Scotland)
SC007992	St Columba Church of Scotland Kilmacolm
SC015085	Langbank Church of Scotland
SC020972	Linwood Parish Church of Scotland
SC014518	Lochwinnoch Parish Church of Scotland
SC035155	Neilston Parish Church of Scotland
SC007633	Paisley Abbey (Church of Scotland)
SC006718	Paisley: Glenburn Parish Church of Scotland
SC006437	Paisley: Stow Brae Kirk (Church of Scotland)
SC012648	Lylesland Parish Church of Scotland, Paisley
SC011798	Paisley: Martyrs Sandyford Church of Scotland
SC005362	Oakshaw Trinity Church, Paisley
SC007484	Sherwood Greenlaw Parish Church of Scotland, Paisley
SC005770	St Columba Foxbar Church of Scotland, Paisley
SC000949	St James's Paisley (Church of Scotland)
SC000558	St Luke's Church of Scotland: Paisley
SC011210	St Marks Church of Scotland (Oldhall): Paisley
SC004753	St Ninians Church of Scotland: Paisley
SC012650	Paisley Wallneuk North Church of Scotland
SC005421	Church of Scotland Port Glasgow: Hamilton Bardrainney Church
SC009018	Port Glasgow: St Andrew's Church of Scotland
SC002410	St Martins Church of Scotland: Port Glasgow
SC006605	Renfrew North Parish Church of Scotland
SC004411	Renfrew Old Parish Church of Scotland
SC003785	Renfrew Trinity (Church of Scotland)
SC003309	Skelmorlie and Wemyss Bay Parish Church of Scotland

16.   Presbytery of Glasgow

SC017638	Banton Parish Church of Scotland
SC012329	Kenmure Parish Church of Scotland
SC005642	Springfield Cambridge Church of Scotland, Bishopbriggs
SC003290	Broom Parish Church of Scotland
SC006633	Burnside Blairbeth Church of Scotland
SC016612	Busby Parish Church of Scotland
SC015193	Cadder Parish Church of Scotland
SC006638	Flemington Hallside Parish Church of Scotland
SC000061	Cambuslang Parish Church of Scotland
SC023596	St Andrews Parish Church of Scotland Cambuslang: Glasgow
SC011456	Trinity St Pauls Church of Scotland, Cambuslang
SC000835	Campsie Parish Church of Scotland
SC006752	Chryston Church of Scotland
SC006377	Eaglesham Parish Church of Scotland
SC001077	Fernhill & Cathkin Church of Scotland
SC007541	Gartcosh Parish Church of Scotland
SC009774	Orchardhill Parish Church of Scotland, Giffnock
SC007807	Giffnock South Parish Church of Scotland
SC002965	Giffnock Park Church of Scotland
SC014631	Anderston Kelvingrove Church of Scotland, Glasgow
SC002220	Glasgow: Mure Memorial Church of Scotland
SC005625	Baillieston St Andrews Church of Scotland, Glasgow
SC000885	Balshagray Victoria Park Parish Church of Scotland, Glasgow
SC025730	Barlanark Greyfriars Parish Church of Scotland, Glasgow
SC006410	Blawarthill Parish Church of Scotland, Glasgow
SC012535	Bridgeton St Francis in the East Church of Scotland, Glasgow
SC007820	Broomhill Church of Scotland, Glasgow
SC006958	Calton Parkhead Parish Church of Scotland, Glasgow
SC010265	Cardonald Parish Church of Scotland, Glasgow
SC011224	Carmunnock Parish Church of Scotland, Glasgow
SC000532	Carmyle Church of Scotland, Glasgow
SC030150	Carnwadric Church of Scotland, Glasgow
SC015309	Castlemilk East Parish Church of Scotland, Glasgow
SC009813	Castlemilk West Church of Scotland, Glasgow
SC002727	Cathcart Old Parish Church of Scotland, Glasgow
SC033802	Cathcart Trinity Church of Scotland, Glasgow
SC013966	Glasgow Cathedral (St Mungo's or High), Church of Scotland
SC012939	Colston Milton Parish Church of Scotland, Glasgow
SC005709	Colston Wellpark Parish Church of Scotland, Glasgow
SC009874	Cranhill Parish Church of Scotland, Glasgow
SC009761	Croftfoot Parish Church of Scotland, Glasgow
SC008824	Glasgow Dennistoun New Parish Church of Scotland
SC022128	Drumchapel St Andrews Parish Church of Scotland, Glasgow
SC008954	St Marks Parish Church of Scotland, Glasgow
SC004642	Glasgow Shettleston New Church of Scotland
SC003021	St Georges & St Peters Parish Church of Scotland: Easterhouse, Glasgow
SC000277	Eastwood Parish Church of Scotland, Glasgow
SC030168	Gairbraid Parish Church of Scotland, Glasgow
SC016862	Garthamlock & Craigend East Parish Church of Scotland, Glasgow

SC002214	Gorbals Parish Church of Scotland, Glasgow
SC004153	Glasgow Govan and Linthouse Parish Church of Scotland
SC012752	Govanhill Trinity Parish Church of Scotland, Glasgow
SC006729	High Carntyne Church of Scotland, Glasgow
SC002614	Hillington Park Church of Scotland, Glasgow
SC007798	St Christophers Church of Scotland: Glasgow
SC002398	Hyndland Parish Church of Scotland, Glasgow
SC009841	Ibrox Parish Church of Scotland, Glasgow
SC027651	John Ross Memorial Church for Deaf People, Glasgow (Church of Scotland)
SC015683	Jordanhill Parish Church of Scotland, Glasgow
SC014414	Kelvin – Stevenson Memorial Parish Church of Scotland, Glasgow
SC006629	Kelvinside Hillhead Parish Church of Scotland, Glasgow
SC008980	Kenmuir Mount Vernon Church of Scotland, Glasgow
SC017040	Kings Park Church of Scotland, Glasgow
SC014895	Kinning Park Parish Church of Scotland, Glasgow
SC007757	Knightswood St Margarets Parish Church of Scotland, Glasgow
SC007055	Langside Parish Church of Scotland, Glasgow
SC015778	Lansdowne Church of Scotland, Glasgow
SC002161	Lochwood Parish Church of Scotland, Glasgow
SC002102	Maryhill Parish Church of Scotland, Glasgow
SC004016	Merrylea Parish Church of Scotland Newlands, Glasgow
SC013281	Mosspark Church of Scotland, Glasgow
SC010138	Glasgow: Clincarthill Church of Scotland
SC000042	Newlands South Church of Scotland, Glasgow
SC008315	Partick South Church of Scotland, Glasgow
SC007632	Partick Trinity Church of Scotland, Glasgow
SC022874	Penilee St Andrew Church of Scotland, Glasgow
SC006683	Pollokshaws Parish Church of Scotland, Glasgow
SC013690	Pollokshields Church of Scotland, Glasgow
SC003241	Possilpark Parish Church of Scotland, Glasgow
SC015858	Priesthill & Nitshill Church of Scotland, Glasgow
SC001575	Queens Park Parish Church of Scotland, Glasgow
SC011423	Renfield St Stephens Parish Church of Scotland, Glasgow
SC032401	Robroyston Church of Scotland, Glasgow
SC003149	Ruchazie Parish Church of Scotland, Glasgow
SC014538	Glasgow: Ruchill Kelvinside Parish Church of Scotland
SC002155	Sandyford Henderson Memorial Church of Scotland, Glasgow
SC009460	Sandyhills Church of Scotland, Glasgow
SC030418	Scotstoun Parish Church of Scotland, Glasgow
SC012969	Shawlands Parish Church of Scotland, Glasgow
SC015155	Sherbrooke St Gilberts Church of Scotland, Glasgow
SC004642	Glasgow Shettleston New Church of Scotland
SC001070	Shettleston Old Parish Church of Scotland, Glasgow
SC010899	South Carntyne Church of Scotland, Glasgow
SC005196	South Shawlands Church of Scotland, Glasgow
SC004397	Springburn Parish Church of Scotland, Glasgow
SC009600	St Andrews East Parish Church, Glasgow (Church of Scotland)

SC006342	St Columbas Gaelic Church of Scotland, Glasgow
SC017297	St Davids Parish Church of Scotland: Glasgow
SC004918	St Enoch's – Hogganfield Parish Church of Scotland, Glasgow
SC004931	St Georges Tron Church of Scotland, Glasgow
SC013313	St James Pollok Parish Church of Scotland: Glasgow
SC012920	St Johns Renfield Church of Scotland, Glasgow
SC032738	Gallowgate Parish Church of Scotland, Glasgow
SC005764	St Margarets Tollcross Church of Scotland: Glasgow
SC011527	St Nicholas Parish Church of Scotland, Cardonald, Glasgow
SC016306	St Pauls Church of Scotland: Provanmill, Glasgow
SC015459	St Rollox Church of Scotland: Glasgow
SC015579	Temple Anniesland Parish Church of Scotland, Glasgow
SC009399	Toryglen Church of Scotland, Glasgow
SC009578	Trinity Possil & Henry Drummond Church of Scotland, Glasgow
SC017015	Tron St Marys Parish Church of Scotland, Glasgow
SC004821	Victoria Tollcross Church of Scotland, Glasgow
SC008840	Glasgow Wallacewell Church of Scotland New Charge
SC000289	Wellington Church of Scotland, Glasgow
SC030362	Whiteinch Church of Scotland, Glasgow
SC017408	Yoker Parish Church of Scotland, Glasgow
SC002834	Glenboig Parish Church of Scotland
SC011453	Greenbank Parish Church of Scotland
SC009866	Kilsyth Anderson Church of Scotland
SC009912	Kilsyth Burns & Old Parish Church of Scotland
SC002424	Kirkintilloch Hillhead Church of Scotland
SC008735	St Columba Parish Church of Scotland, Kirkintilloch
SC007427	St Davids Memorial Park Church of Scotland, Kirkintilloch
SC007260	St Marys Parish Church of Scotland, Kirkintilloch
SC008935	Lenzie Old Parish Church of Scotland
SC015287	Lenzie Union Church of Scotland
SC017317	Maxwell Mearns Church of Scotland
SC007125	Mearns Kirk (Church of Scotland)
SC014735	Milton of Campsie Parish Church of Scotland
SC015303	Netherlee Church of Scotland
SC004219	Newton Mearns Parish Church of Scotland
SC006856	Rutherglen Old Parish Church of Scotland
SC013558	Stonelaw Parish Church of Scotland, Rutherglen
SC007585	Rutherglen West and Wardlawhill Parish Church of Scotland
SC003155	Stamperland Parish Church of Scotland, Clarkston
SC014212	Stepps Parish Church of Scotland, Stepps
SC008426	Thornliebank Parish Church of Scotland
SC016058	Torrance Parish Church of Scotland
SC011672	Twechar Church of Scotland
SC009939	Williamwood Parish Church of Scotland

17.	**Presbytery of Hamilton**
SC016464	Airdrie Broomknoll Parish Church of Scotland
SC011239	Airdrie Clarkston Parish Church of Scotland
SC014555	Airdrie Flowerhill Parish Church of Scotland
SC024357	Airdrie High Parish Church of Scotland
SC004083	Airdrie Jackson Parish Church of Scotland

SC011674	Airdrie New Monkland Parish Church of Scotland
SC002900	Airdrie St Columbas Parish Church of Scotland
SC004209	Bargeddie Parish Church of Scotland
SC012556	Bellshill Macdonald Memorial Parish Church of Scotland
SC006007	Bellshill Orbiston Parish Church of Scotland
SC008340	Bellshill West Parish Church of Scotland
SC005955	Blantyre St Andrew's Parish Church of Scotland
SC004084	Blantyre Livingstone Memorial Parish Church of Scotland
SC018492	Blantyre Old Parish Church of Scotland
SC012944	The New Wellwynd Parish Church of Scotland Airdrie
SC009819	Bothwell Parish Church of Scotland
SC015831	Calderbank Parish Church of Scotland
SC030492	Caldercruix and Longriggend Parish Church of Scotland
SC008486	Chapelhall Parish Church of Scotland
SC011817	Chapelton Parish Church of Scotland
SC017084	Cleland Parish Church of Scotland
SC009704	Coatbridge Blairhill Dundyvan Parish Church of Scotland
SC006854	Coatbridge Calder Parish Church of Scotland
SC016362	Coatbridge Middle Parish Church of Scotland
SC013521	Coatbridge New St Andrew's Parish Church of Scotland
SC010236	Coatbridge Old Monkland Parish Church of Scotland
SC008809	Coatbridge Townhead Parish Church of Scotland
SC016156	Dalserf Parish Church of Scotland
SC007396	East Kilbride Claremont Parish Church of Scotland
SC030300	East Kilbride Greenhills Parish Church of Scotland
SC016751	East Kilbride Moncreiff Parish Church of Scotland
SC000609	East Kilbride Old Parish Church of Scotland
SC008332	East Kilbride South Parish Church of Scotland
SC000250	East Kilbride West Kirk Church of Scotland
SC001857	East Kilbride Westwood Parish Church of Scotland
SC014716	Glassford Parish Church of Scotland
SC012692	East Kilbride Mossneuk Parish Church of Scotland
SC018154	Greengairs Parish Church of Scotland
SC015042	Hamilton Burnbank Parish Church of Scotland
SC006611	Cadzow Parish Church of Scotland, Hamilton
SC011571	Hamilton Gilmour & Whitehill Parish Church of Scotland
SC005376	Hamilton Hillhouse Parish Church of Scotland
SC014508	Hamilton North Parish Church of Scotland
SC010855	Hamilton Old Parish Church of Scotland
SC007145	Hamilton St Andrew's Parish Church of Scotland
SC008779	Hamilton St John's Parish Church of Scotland
SC022166	Hamilton South Parish Church of Scotland
SC007051	Hamilton Trinity Parish Church of Scotland
SC008451	Hamilton West Parish Church of Scotland
SC012888	Holytown Parish Church of Scotland
SC013309	Chalmers Parish Church of Scotland Larkhall
SC002870	St Machan's Parish Church of Scotland Larkhall
SC008611	Trinity Parish Church of Scotland, Larkhall
SC034242	Church of Scotland Stewartfield New Charge Development East Kilbride
SC008810	Motherwell Crosshill Parish Church of Scotland

SC016821	Motherwell North Parish Church of Scotland
SC008601	Motherwell South Parish Church of Scotland
SC010924	Motherwell St Margaret's Parish Church of Scotland
SC012233	Motherwell St Marys Parish Church of Scotland
SC005427	Newarthill and Carfin Parish Church of Scotland
SC006540	Bonkle Parish Church of Scotland
SC001381	Newmains Coltness Memorial Parish Church of Scotland
SC004688	New Stevenston Wrangholm Parish Church of Scotland
SC007360	Overtown Parish Church of Scotland
SC009689	Quarter Parish Church of Scotland
SC015503	Motherwell Dalziel St Andrew's Parish Church of Scotland
SC013269	Kirk o' Shotts Parish Church of Scotland
SC003239	Stonehouse St Ninian's Parish Church of Scotland
SC001956	Strathaven Avendale Old and Drumclog Memorial Parish Church of Scotland
SC015591	Strathaven East Parish Church of Scotland
SC001020	Strathaven Rankin Parish Church of Scotland
SC010039	Uddingston Burnhead Parish Church of Scotland
SC006538	Shotts Calderhead – Erskine Parish Church of Scotland
SC009991	Uddingston Viewpark Parish Church of Scotland
SC013037	Wishaw: Cambusnethan North Parish Church of Scotland
SC011532	Wishaw Cambusnethan Old and Morningside Parish Church of Scotland
SC013841	Wishaw Craigneuk and Belhaven Church of Scotland
SC011253	Wishaw Old Parish Church of Scotland
SC012529	Wishaw St Marks Parish Church of Scotland
SC016893	Uddingston Old Parish Church of Scotland
SC010775	South Wishaw Parish Church of Scotland
18.	**Presbytery of Dumbarton**
SC001268	Alexandria Parish Church of Scotland
SC008929	Arrochar Parish Church of Scotland
SC006355	Baldernock Parish Church of Scotland
SC037739	Bearsden: Baljaffray Parish Church of Scotland
SC009748	Killermont Parish Church (Church of Scotland) Bearsden
SC012997	New Kilpatrick Parish Church of Scotland
SC009082	The Church of Scotland Bearsden Cross Church
SC004489	Westerton Fairlie Memorial Parish Church of Scotland, Bearsden
SC000886	Bonhill Church of Scotland
SC003494	Cardross Parish Church of Scotland
SC004596	Abbotsford, Church of Scotland, Clydebank
SC005108	Faifley Parish Church of Scotland, Clydebank
SC015005	Kilbowie St Andrews Church of Scotland, Clydebank
SC013242	Radnor Park Church of Scotland, Clydebank
SC003077	St Cuthberts Parish Church of Scotland: Clydebank
SC001725	Craigrownie Parish Church of Scotland
SC013599	Dalmuir Barclay Church of Scotland
SC002937	Riverside Parish Church of Scotland, Dumbarton
SC006235	St Andrews Church of Scotland: Dumbarton
SC010474	West Kirk, Dumbarton (Church of Scotland)
SC008854	Duntocher Trinity Parish Church of Scotland
SC016699	Garelochhead Parish Church of Scotland

SC007801	Park Church of Scotland, Helensburgh
SC012053	The Church of Scotland: Helensburgh: St Andrew's Kirk
SC012346	Jamestown Parish Church of Scotland
SC002145	Kilmaronock Gartocharn Church of Scotland
SC017192	Luss Parish Church of Scotland
SC009913	Cairns Church of Scotland, Milngavie
SC003870	St Lukes Church of Scotland: Milngavie
SC002737	St Pauls Parish Church of Scotland: Milngavie
SC011630	Old Kilpatrick Bowling Parish Church of Scotland
SC014833	Renton Trinity Parish Church of Scotland
SC010086	Rhu and Shandon Parish Church of Scotland
SC001510	Rosneath St Modans Church of Scotland
19.	**Presbytery of Argyll**
SC015795	Appin Parish Church (Church of Scotland)
SC000680	Ardchattan (Church of Scotland)
SC010713	Ardrishaig Parish Church (Church of Scotland)
SC002493	Campbeltown: Highland Parish Church of Scotland
SC011686	Campbeltown: Lorne and Lowland Church of Scotland
SC035582	Coll Parish Church (Church of Scotland)
SC031271	Colonsay & Oronsay Church of Scotland
SC006738	Connel Parish Church of Scotland
SC003718	Craignish Parish Church of Scotland
SC016097	Cumlodden, Lochfyneside and Lochgair (Church of Scotland)
SC003216	Dunoon: St John's Church (Church of Scotland)
SC017524	Dunoon: The High Kirk (Church of Scotland)
SC002567	Gigha & Cara Church (Church of Scotland)
SC002121	Glassary, Kilmartin & Ford Parish Church of Scotland
SC016665	Glenaray & Inveraray Parish Church (Church of Scotland)
SC003179	Glenorchy & Innishael Church of Scotland
SC013247	Innellan Church (Church of Scotland)
SC036399	Iona Parish Church (Church of Scotland)
SC002925	Jura Parish Church of Scotland
SC009853	Kilarrow Parish Church of Scotland
SC006941	Kilberry Parish Church (Church of Scotland)
SC017005	Kilbrandon & Kilchattan Parish Church (Church of Scotland)
SC006948	Kilcalmonell Parish Church (Church of Scotland)
SC013203	Kilchoman Parish Church (Church of Scotland)
SC009417	Kilchrenan & Dalavich Parish Church (Church of Scotland)
SC006032	Kildalton & Oa Parish Church (Church of Scotland)
SC003483	Kilfinan Parish Church (Church of Scotland)
SC013473	Kilfinichen & Kilvickeon & the Ross of Mull Church of Scotland
SC016020	Killean & Kilchenzie Parish Church (Church of Scotland)
SC015317	Kilmeny Parish Church of Scotland
SC021449	Kilmodan & Colintraive Parish Church of Scotland
SC011171	Kilmore & Oban Church of Scotland
SC001694	Kilmun: St Munn's Church (Church of Scotland)
SC025506	Kilninian & Kilmore Church of Scotland
SC002458	Kilninver & Kilmelford Parish Church of Scotland
SC001976	Kirn Parish Church (Church of Scotland)
SC014928	Kyles Parish Church (Church of Scotland)
SC030972	Lismore Parish Church (Church of Scotland)

SC016311	Lochgilphead Church of Scotland
SC006458	Lochgoilhead & Kilmorich Church (Church of Scotland)
SC013377	Muckairn Parish Church (Church of Scotland)
SC001002	North Knapdale Parish Church of Scotland
SC004086	Portnahaven Parish Church of Scotland
SC006420	Rothesay: Trinity Church (Church of Scotland)
SC002609	Saddell & Carradale Church (Church of Scotland)
SC026099	Salen and Ulva Church of Scotland
SC006657	Sandbank Church (Church of Scotland)
SC004280	Skipness: St Brendan's Church (Church of Scotland)
SC010782	South Knapdale Parish Church (Church of Scotland)
SC005484	Southend Parish Church (Church of Scotland)
SC001767	Strachur & Strathlachlan Church (Church of Scotland)
SC004088	Strathfillan Parish Church of Scotland
SC003410	Strone & Ardentinny Church (Church of Scotland)
SC002622	Tarbert, Argyll, Church of Scotland
SC030563	The United Church of Bute (Church of Scotland)
SC000878	Tiree Parish Church of Scotland
SC002878	Tobermory Parish Church of Scotland
SC003909	Torosay & Kinlochspelvie Church of Scotland
SC015531	Toward Church (Church of Scotland)

22.	**Presbytery of Falkirk**
SC029326	Cumbernauld Abronhill Church of Scotland
SC011038	Airth Parish Church of Scotland
SC008191	Bo'ness Old Kirk (Church of Scotland)
SC015225	Bonnybridge St Helen's Parish Church of Scotland
SC001385	Brightons Parish Church of Scotland
SC014816	Camelon Parish Church, Church of Scotland
SC011839	Cumbernauld: Condorrat Parish Church of Scotland
SC000877	Cumbernauld Old Parish Church of Scotland
SC016255	Denny Old Parish Church of Scotland
SC007072	Denny Westpark Church of Scotland
SC002943	Dunipace Parish Church of Scotland
SC000652	Falkirk Old & St Modan's Parish Church of Scotland
SC000775	Grangemouth Abbotsgrange Church of Scotland
SC014536	Haggs Parish Church of Scotland
SC004564	Cumbernauld Kildrum Parish Church of Scotland
SC001603	Grangemouth, Kirk of the Holy Rood, Church of Scotland
SC006456	Larbert East Church of Scotland
SC000445	Larbert Old Church of Scotland
SC012251	Larbert West Parish Church of Scotland
SC007383	Laurieston Parish Church of Scotland
SC003421	Polmont Old Parish Church of Scotland
SC008787	Redding & Westquarter Church of Scotland
SC013602	Slamannan Parish Church of Scotland
SC005066	St Andrews West Church of Scotland, Falkirk
SC002263	Stenhouse & Carron Parish Church of Scotland: Stenhousemuir
SC013114	Grangemouth Zetland Parish Church of Scotland
SC036366	St Mungo's Church of Scotland, Cumbernauld
SC007546	The Church of Scotland Falkirk Erskine Parish Church
SC002512	Blackbraes & Shieldhill Parish Church of Scotland

SC007665	St James Church of Scotland, Falkirk
SC016991	Grahamston United Church
SC011448	St Andrew's Church of Scotland, Bo'ness
SC007571	Muiravonside Parish Church of Scotland
SC009754	Bothkennar & Carronshore Parish Church (Church of Scotland)
SC007811	Carriden Parish Church of Scotland
SC004142	Bainsford Parish Church of Scotland, Falkirk

23.	**Presbytery of Stirling**
SC001308	Aberfoyle Parish Church of Scotland
SC007821	St Mungo's Parish Church of Scotland, Alloa
SC007605	Alloa Ludgate Church of Scotland
SC000006	Alva Parish Church of Scotland
SC005335	Balfron Church of Scotland
SC012316	Balquhidder Parish Church of Scotland
SC002953	Allan Church of Scotland, Bannockburn
SC011345	Bannockburn Ladywell Church of Scotland
SC015171	Bridge of Allan Parish Church of Scotland
SC012927	Buchanan Parish Church of Scotland
SC000833	Buchlyvie Church of Scotland
SC000396	Callander Kirk Church of Scotland
SC019113	Cambusbarron Parish Church of Scotland Bruce Memorial
SC002324	Clackmannan Parish Church of Scotland
SC016296	Cowie and Plean Church of Scotland
SC009713	Dollar Parish Church of Scotland
SC004824	Drymen Church of Scotland
SC004454	Dunblane Cathedral Church of Scotland
SC005185	Dunblane: St Blane's Church of Scotland
SC028465	Fallin Parish Church of Scotland
SC012537	Fintry Church of Scotland
SC012154	Gargunnock Parish Church of Scotland
SC009788	Gartmore Parish Church of Scotland
SC003028	Glendevon Parish Church of Scotland
SC012140	Killearn Kirk (Church of Scotland)
SC010198	Killin & Ardeonaig Parish Church of Scotland
SC012031	Kilmadock Parish Church of Scotland, Doune
SC000802	Kincardine in Menteith Church of Scotland, Blair Drummond
SC004286	Kippen Parish Church of Scotland
SC014031	Lecropt Kirk Parish Church of Scotland
SC001298	Logie Kirk Stirling (Church of Scotland)
SC004778	Menstrie Parish Church of Scotland
SC009418	Muckhart Parish Church of Scotland
SC028719	Norrieston Parish Church of Scotland
SC001864	Port of Menteith Church of Scotland
SC018155	Sauchie and Coalsnaughton Parish Church of Scotland
SC001414	Allan Park South Church of Scotland, Stirling
SC011473	Church of the Holy Rude, Stirling (Church of Scotland)
SC011795	Stirling North Parish Church of Scotland
SC013444	St Columba's Church of Scotland Stirling
SC005432	St Marks Parish Church of Scotland: Stirling
SC016320	St Ninians Old Parish Church of Scotland, Stirling
SC007533	Viewfield Erskine Church of Scotland, Stirling
SC007261	Strathblane Parish Church of Scotland
SC016570	Tillicoultry Parish Church of Scotland
SC005918	St Serfs Church of Scotland, Tullibody

24.	**Presbytery of Dunfermline**
SC005851	St Fillans Church of Scotland: Aberdour
SC031695	Beath and Cowdenbeath North Church of Scotland
SC012892	Cairneyhill Parish Church of Scotland
SC010676	Carnock and Oakley Church of Scotland
SC003799	Cowdenbeath Trinity Church of Scotland
SC015149	Culross & Torryburn Church of Scotland

SC020926	Dalgety Parish Church of Scotland
SC016883	The Abbey Church of Dunfermline (Church of Scotland)
SC035690	Dunfermline East Church of Scotland
SC011659	Dunfermline Gillespie Memorial Church of Scotland
SC013226	Dunfermline North Parish Church of Scotland
SC007302	St Andrew's Erskine Church of Scotland, Dunfermline
SC007799	Dunfermline St Leonard's Parish Church of Scotland
SC007080	Dunfermline St Margaret's Parish Church of Scotland
SC007453	St Ninians Church of Scotland: Dunfermline
SC008085	Dunfermline Townhill & Kingseat Parish Church of Scotland
SC000968	Inverkeithing Parish Church of Scotland
SC011004	Kelty Church of Scotland
SC002435	Limekilns Church of Scotland
SC032353	Lochgelly and Benarty St Serf's Parish Church of Scotland
SC007414	North Queensferry Church of Scotland
SC013620	Rosyth Parish Church of Scotland
SC013688	Saline & Blairingone Parish Church of Scotland
SC002951	Tulliallan & Kincardine Parish Church of Scotland
25.	**Presbytery of Kirkcaldy**
SC031143	Auchterderran St Fothads Parish Church of Scotland
SC025310	Auchtertool Kirk (Church of Scotland)
SC009495	Buckhaven and Wemyss Parish Church of Scotland
SC016418	Burntisland Parish Church of Scotland
SC008991	Dysart Kirk (Church of Scotland)
SC007397	Glenrothes Christ's Kirk (Church of Scotland)
SC016386	St Columba's Parish Church of Scotland, Glenrothes
SC009845	St Margaret's Parish Church of Scotland: Glenrothes
SC002472	St Ninian's Parish Church of Scotland: Glenrothes
SC009342	Innerleven East Parish Church of Scotland: Methil
SC016733	Kennoway, Windygates and Balgonie: St Kenneth's Church of Scotland
SC007848	Kinghorn Parish Church of Scotland
SC012030	Kinglassie Parish Church of Scotland
SC002586	Abbotshall Parish Church of Scotland, Kirkcaldy
SC012039	Linktown Church of Scotland, Kirkcaldy
SC002858	Pathhead Parish Church of Scotland, Kirkcaldy
SC031064	St Bryce Kirk, Church of Scotland, Kirkcaldy
SC005628	Bennochy Parish Church of Scotland, Kirkcaldy
SC012756	Templehall Parish Church of Scotland, Kirkcaldy
SC015807	Torbain Parish Church of Scotland, Kirkcaldy
SC004264	Viewforth Parish Church of Scotland, Kirkcaldy
SC014025	Trinity Church of Scotland, Leslie
SC031969	Leven Parish Church of Scotland
SC005820	Markinch Parish Church of Scotland
SC009581	Methil Parish Church of Scotland
SC007949	Methilhill and Denbeath Parish Church of Scotland
SC003417	Thornton Parish Church of Scotland
26.	**Presbytery of St Andrews**
SC004848	Abdie & Dunbog Parish Church of Scotland
SC012986	Anstruther Parish Church of Scotland
SC005402	Auchtermuchty Parish Church of Scotland
SC002542	Balmerino Parish Church of Scotland
SC001108	Boarhills and Dunino Parish Church of Scotland
SC005565	Cameron Parish Church (Church of Scotland)
SC016744	Carnbee Church of Scotland
SC000181	Cellardyke Parish Church of Scotland
SC017442	Ceres, Kemback & Springfield Church of Scotland
SC001601	Crail Parish Church of Scotland
SC001907	Creich, Flisk and Kilmany Church of Scotland
SC013123	Cupar Old & St Michael of Tarvit Parish Church (of Scotland)
SC015721	Cupar St John's and Dairsie United Parish Church of Scotland
SC015226	Edenshead and Strathmiglo Church of Scotland
SC003163	Elie, Kilconquhar and Colinsburgh Church of Scotland
SC012247	Falkland Parish Church of Scotland
SC016622	Freuchie Parish Church of Scotland
SC005381	Howe of Fife Parish Church (Church of Scotland)
SC002653	Kilrenny Parish Church of Scotland
SC012192	Kingsbarns Parish Church of Scotland
SC003465	Largo & Newburn Parish Church of Scotland
SC013075	Largo St David's Church of Scotland
SC009474	Largoward Church of Scotland
SC015677	Leuchars: St Athernase Church of Scotland
SC015182	Monimail Parish (Church of Scotland)
SC004607	Newburgh Parish Church of Scotland
SC006758	Newport-on-Tay Church of Scotland
SC015271	Pittenweem Church of Scotland
SC017173	The Parish Church of the Holy Trinity, St Andrews (Church of Scotland)
SC014934	Hope Park and Martyrs' Parish Church St Andrews (Church of Scotland)
SC013586	St Andrews: St Leonard's Parish Church of Scotland Congregation
SC005556	St Monans Church of Scotland
SC014710	Strathkinness Parish Church of Scotland
SC008659	Tayport Parish Church of Scotland
SC006447	Wormit Parish Church of Scotland
27.	**Presbytery of Dunkeld and Meigle**
SC007899	Aberfeldy Parish Church of Scotland
SC028023	Amulree and Strathbraan Parish Church of Scotland
SC001465	Dull and Weem Parish Church of Scotland
SC000540	Alyth Parish Church of Scotland
SC000098	Ardler Kettins & Meigle Parish Church of Scotland
SC004358	Bendochy Parish Church of Scotland
SC014438	Coupar Angus Abbey Church of Scotland
SC013516	Blair Atholl and Struan Church of Scotland
SC001984	Tenandry Parish Church of Scotland
SC033757	Blairgowrie Parish Church of Scotland
SC011351	Braes of Rannoch Church of Scotland
SC006570	Foss and Rannoch Church of Scotland
SC001957	Caputh and Clunie Church of Scotland
SC009251	Kinclaven Church of Scotland
SC009867	Dunkeld Parish Church of Scotland
SC003310	Fortingall & Glenlyon Church of Scotland
SC006260	Kenmore and Lawers Church of Scotland
SC004275	Grantully Logierait & Strathtay Church of Scotland
SC008021	Kirkmichael Straloch & Glenshee Church of Scotland
SC000323	Rattray Parish Church of Scotland
SC008361	Pitlochry Church of Scotland

28. **Presbytery of Perth**

SC000586	Abernethy and Dron and Arngask Church of Scotland
SC005203	Almondbank Tibbermore Parish Church of Scotland
SC000139	Ardoch Parish Church of Scotland
SC001688	Auchterarder Parish Church of Scotland
SC010247	Auchtergaven and Moneydie Parish Church of Scotland
SC005594	Blackford Parish Church of Scotland
SC007283	Cargill Burrelton Parish Church of Scotland
SC003168	Cleish Parish Church of Scotland
SC009031	Collace Church of Scotland
SC001878	Comrie Parish Church of Scotland
SC004304	Crieff Parish Church of Scotland
SC009638	Dunbarney and Forgandenny Parish Church (Church of Scotland)
SC010311	St Fillans Dundurn Parish Church of Scotland
SC015895	Errol Parish Church of Scotland
SC013157	Fossoway St Serf's & Devonside Parish Church of Scotland
SC002209	Fowlis Wester, Madderty and Monzie Parish Church of Scotland
SC009632	Gask Parish Church of Scotland
SC010838	Kilspindie & Rait Parish Church of Scotland
SC012555	Kinross Parish Church of Scotland
SC010807	Methven and Logiealmond Church of Scotland
SC004984	Muthill Parish Church of Scotland
SC015523	Orwell and Portmoak Parish Church of Scotland
SC001330	Perth: Craigie and Moncreiffe Church of Scotland
SC007509	Kinnoull Parish Church of Scotland, Perth
SC002467	Perth: Letham St Mark's Church of Scotland
SC013014	Perth North, Church of Scotland
SC011113	Perth Riverside Church of Scotland
SC017132	St John's Kirk of Perth (Church of Scotland)
SC002919	Perth St Leonard's-in-the-Fields Church of Scotland
SC016829	Perth: St Matthew's Church of Scotland
SC010629	Redgorton and Stanley Parish Church – Church of Scotland
SC007094	Scone New Church of Scotland
SC014964	St Madoes and Kinfauns Church of Scotland, Glencarse
SC030799	The Church of Scotland: The Stewartry of Strathearn
SC000004	Trinity Gask and Kinkell Church (Church of Scotland)
SC002844	Scone Old Parish Church of Scotland
SC002000	St Martin's Church of Scotland, Perth

29. **Presbytery of Dundee**

SC007847	Abernyte Parish Church of Scotland
SC016717	Auchterhouse Parish Church of Scotland
SC017449	Dundee: Balgay Parish Church of Scotland
SC007031	Broughty Ferry New Kirk (Church of Scotland)
SC003677	Dundee: Camperdown Parish Church of Scotland
SC021763	Chalmers-Ardler Parish Church of Scotland, Dundee
SC012089	Dundee: Coldside Parish Church of Scotland
SC016701	Dundee: Craigiebank Parish Church of Scotland
SC005707	Dundee: Downfield South Church of Scotland
SC010030	Dundee Douglas and Mid Craigie Church of Scotland
SC033313	Dundee Lochee Parish Church of Scotland

SC017136	Dundee: West Church of Scotland
SC002792	Fowlis & Liff Parish Church of Scotland
SC009839	Inchture & Kinnaird Parish Church of Scotland
SC009454	Invergowrie Parish Church of Scotland
SC009115	Dundee: Logie & St John's (Cross) Church of Scotland
SC012230	Longforgan Parish Church of Scotland
SC001085	Lundie and Muirhead Parish Church of Scotland
SC013884	Dundee: Mains Parish Church of Scotland
SC020742	Fintry Parish Church of Scotland, Dundee
SC013162	Dundee: Meadowside St Paul's Church of Scotland
SC004496	Dundee: Menzieshill Parish Church of Scotland
SC012137	Monikie & Newbigging and Murroes & Tealing Church of Scotland
SC011775	Dundee: St Andrew's Parish Church of Scotland
SC000723	St David's High Kirk Dundee (Church of Scotland)
SC005210	St James Church of Scotland: Broughty Ferry
SC000088	St Luke's and Queen Street Church of Scotland: Broughty Ferry
SC011017	Barnhill St Margaret's Parish Church of Scotland
SC002198	Dundee Parish Church (St Mary's) Church of Scotland
SC003714	St Stephen's & West Parish Church of Scotland: Broughty Ferry
SC000384	Stobswell Parish Church of Scotland: Dundee
SC018015	Strathmartine Church of Scotland: Dundee
SC011021	Dundee: Trinity Parish Church of Scotland
SC000316	Dundee: Whitfield Parish Church of Scotland
SC014314	The Steeple Church: Dundee (Church of Scotland)
SC008965	Monifieth Parish Church of Scotland

30. **Presbytery of Angus**

SC018944	Aberlemno Parish Church of Scotland
SC002545	Barry Parish Church of Scotland
SC008630	Brechin Gardner Memorial Church of Scotland
SC015146	Carnoustie Church of Scotland
SC001293	Colliston Church of Scotland
SC007997	Farnell Parish Church of Scotland
SC000572	Dun and Hillside Church of Scotland
SC013105	Edzell Lethnot Glenesk Church of Scotland
SC009017	Inchbrayock Parish Church of Scotland
SC031461	The Isla Parishes Church of Scotland
SC013352	Eassie, Nevay and Newtyle Church of Scotland
SC017413	Arbirlot Parish Church of Scotland
SC006482	Arbroath West Kirk Church of Scotland
SC011361	Arbroath Knox's Parish Church of Scotland
SC005478	Arbroath: St Andrew's Church of Scotland
SC017424	Carmyllie Parish Church of Scotland
SC004594	Carnoustie Panbride Church of Scotland
SC003833	Dunnichen, Letham and Kirkden Church of Scotland
SC004921	Forfar East and Old Parish Church of Scotland
SC002417	Forfar Lowson Memorial Parish Church of Scotland
SC010332	Brechin Cathedral Church of Scotland
SC005085	Friockheim and Kinnell Parish Church of Scotland
SC017785	Inverkeilor and Lunan Church of Scotland
SC004395	Kirriemuir St Andrew's Parish Church of Scotland
SC015123	The Glens and Kirriemuir Old Parish Church of Scotland
SC009016	Montrose Melville South Church of Scotland

SC009934	Montrose: Old and St Andrew's Church of Scotland	SC014112	Aboyne-Dinnet Parish Church of Scotland
SC003049	Arbroath St Vigeans Church of Scotland	SC009239	Arbuthnott, Bervie and Kinneff (Church of Scotland)
SC006317	Oathlaw Tannadice Church of Scotland	SC011251	Banchory-Ternan East Church of Scotland
SC001506	Forfar St Margaret's Church of Scotland	SC003306	Banchory-Ternan West Parish Church of Scotland
SC013052	Arbroath Old and Abbey Church of Scotland		
SC011205	Glamis, Inverarity and Kinnettles Parish Church of Scotland	SC013648	Banchory Devenick & Maryculter-Cookney Parish Church of Scotland
SC017327	Guthrie and Rescobie Church of Scotland	SC018517	Birse & Feughside Church of Scotland
SC003236	Fern, Careston and Menmuir Church of Scotland	SC012075	Braemar and Crathie Parish, The Church of Scotland
		SC015856	Parish of Cromar Church of Scotland
31.	**Presbytery of Aberdeen**	SC033779	Drumoak-Durris Church of Scotland
SC025324	Aberdeen Bridge of Don Oldmachar Church of Scotland	SC005522	Glenmuick (Ballater) Parish Church of Scotland
SC032413	Cove Church of Scotland, Aberdeen	SC007436	Kinneff Church of Scotland
SC017158	Craigiebuckler Church of Scotland, Aberdeen	SC014830	Laurencekirk Church of Scotland
SC010756	Aberdeen Ferryhill Parish Church of Scotland	SC011997	Mearns Coastal Parish Church of Scotland
SC022497	Garthdee Parish Church of Scotland, Aberdeen	SC012967	Mid Deeside Parish, Church of Scotland
SC013916	Gilcomston South Church of Scotland, Aberdeen	SC005679	Newtonhill Parish Church (Church of Scotland)
SC003789	High Hilton Church of Scotland, Aberdeen	SC007420	Portlethen Parish Church of Scotland
SC013318	Holburn West Church of Scotland, Aberdeen	SC013165	Stonehaven Dunnottar Church of Scotland
SC001680	Mannofield Church of Scotland, Aberdeen	SC011191	Stonehaven Fetteresso Church of Scotland
SC013459	Mastrick Parish Church of Scotland, Aberdeen	SC016565	Stonehaven South Church of Scotland
SC010643	Midstocket Parish Church of Scotland, Aberdeen	SC016193	West Mearns Parish Church of Scotland
SC034441	Northfield Parish Church of Scotland, Aberdeen	**33.**	**Presbytery of Gordon**
		SC010960	Barthol Chapel Church of Scotland
SC014117	Queen Street Church of Scotland Aberdeen	SC016387	Belhelvie Church of Scotland
SC002019	Queens Cross Church of Scotland Aberdeen	SC000935	Insch-Leslie-Premnay-Oyne Church of Scotland
SC015841	Rubislaw Parish Church of Scotland, Aberdeen	SC004050	Blairdaff and Chapel of Garioch Church of Scotland
SC013020	Ruthrieston West Church of Scotland, Aberdeen	SC003429	Cluny Church of Scotland
SC017516	Aberdeen South Holburn Church of Scotland	SC010911	Culsalmond and Rayne Church of Scotland
SC027440	Aberdeen Bridge of Don St Columba's Church of Scotland	SC030817	Cushnie and Tough Parish Church of Scotland
		SC003254	Daviot Parish Church of Scotland
SC015451	Aberdeen St Marks Church of Scotland	SC003215	Echt Parish Church of Scotland
SC018173	St Mary's Church of Scotland: Aberdeen	SC008819	Ellon Parish Church of Scotland
SC016043	South St Nicholas & Kincorth Church of Scotland, Aberdeen	SC003115	Fintray Kinellar Keithhall Church of Scotland
		SC011701	Foveran Church of Scotland
SC014120	The Church of Scotland – Aberdeen: St Stephens Church	SC007979	Howe Trinity Parish Church of Scotland
		SC001405	Huntly Cairnie Glass Church of Scotland
SC030587	New Stockethill Church of Scotland, Aberdeen	SC008791	St Andrews Parish Church of Scotland Inverurie
SC007076	Summerhill Parish Church of Scotland, Aberdeen	SC016907	Inverurie West Church of Scotland
		SC014790	Kemnay Parish Church of Scotland
SC001966	Woodside Parish Church of Scotland, Aberdeen	SC001406	Kintore Parish Church of Scotland
		SC015960	Meldrum & Bourtie Parish Church of Scotland
SC017404	Bucksburn Stoneywood Parish Church of Scotland	SC016542	Methlick Parish Church of Scotland
		SC009556	Midmar Parish Church of Scotland
SC017517	Cults Parish Church of Scotland	SC004525	Monymusk Parish Church of Scotland
SC011204	Newhills Parish Church of Scotland	SC024017	Newmachar Parish Church of Scotland
SC001452	Peterculter Parish Church of Scotland	SC007582	Parish of Noth Church of Scotland
SC009020	Torry St Fitticks Parish Church of Scotland, Aberdeen	SC009462	Skene Parish Church of Scotland
		SC017161	Tarves Parish Church of Scotland
SC006865	Kingswells Church of Scotland	SC006056	Udny & Pitmedden Church of Scotland
SC031403	Middlefield Parish Church of Scotland, Aberdeen	SC014679	Upper Donside Parish Church of Scotland
		SC000534	Strathbogie Drumblade Church of Scotland Huntly
SC016950	Dyce Parish Church of Scotland		
SC024795	St Georges Tillydrone Church of Scotland, Aberdeen	**34.**	**Presbytery of Buchan**
		SC007197	Aberdour Church of Scotland
SC008157	St Machar's Cathedral, Aberdeen, Church of Scotland	SC017101	Auchaber United Parish Church of Scotland
		SC009168	Auchterless Parish Church of Scotland
SC021283	St John's Church for Deaf People in the North of Scotland, Church of Scotland	SC015501	Banff Parish Church of Scotland
		SC006889	Crimond Parish Church of Scotland
SC008689	Kirk of St Nicholas Uniting	SC006408	Cruden Parish Church of Scotland
		SC012985	Deer Parish Church of Scotland
32.	**Presbytery of Kincardine and Deeside**	SC000522	Fordyce Parish Church of Scotland
SC016449	Aberluthnott Church of Scotland		

SC013119   Fraserburgh Old Church of Scotland
SC005714   Fraserburgh South Church of Scotland
SC016334   Fraserburgh West Parish Church of Scotland
SC001475   Fyvie Church of Scotland
SC012282   Gardenstown Church of Scotland
SC000375   Inverallochy & Rathen East Parish Church of
           Scotland
SC015077   King Edward Parish Church of Scotland
SC008873   Longside Parish Church of Scotland
SC008813   Lonmay Parish Church of Scotland
SC015786   Macduff Parish Church of Scotland
SC009773   Maud & Savoch Church of Scotland
SC010291   Monquhitter & New Byth Parish Church of
           Scotland
SC007917   New Deer St Kane's Church of Scotland
SC001107   Marnoch Church of Scotland
SC014620   New Pitsligo Parish Church of Scotland
SC001971   Ordiquhill & Cornhill Church of Scotland
SC011147   Peterhead Old Parish Church of Scotland
SC010841   Peterhead St Andrews Church of Scotland
SC009990   Peterhead Trinity Parish Church of Scotland
SC005498   Pitsligo Parish Church of Scotland
SC015604   Rathen West Parish Church of Scotland
SC032016   Rothienorman Parish Church of Scotland
SC000710   St Fergus Parish Church of Scotland
SC024874   Sandhaven Parish Church of Scotland
SC007273   Strichen and Tyrie Parish Church of Scotland
SC015620   St Andrews Parish Church of Scotland,
           Turriff
SC007470   Turriff St Ninians and Forglen Parish Church
           of Scotland
SC002085   Whitehills Parish Church of Scotland

35.   Presbytery of Moray
SC001336   Aberlour Parish Church of Scotland
SC010330   Alves & Burghead Parish Church of Scotland
SC005310   Bellie Parish Church of Scotland
SC016720   Birnie and Pluscarden Church of Scotland
SC001235   Buckie North Church of Scotland
SC005608   Buckie South & West Church of Scotland
SC011231   Cullen & Deskford Church of Scotland
SC015881   St Michael's Parish Church of Scotland, Dallas
SC004853   Duffus Spynie & Hopeman Church of
           Scotland
SC000585   Dyke Parish Church of Scotland
SC009986   Edinkillie Church of Scotland
SC005240   Elgin High Church of Scotland
SC015164   St Giles & St Columbas Church of Scotland,
           Elgin
SC015093   Enzie Parish Church of Scotland
SC010045   Findochty Parish Church of Scotland
SC000711   St Laurence Parish Church of Scotland,
           Forres
SC005094   St Leonard's Church of Scotland, Forres
SC033804   Keith North Newmill Boharm & Rothiemay
           Church of Scotland
SC031791   Kirk of Keith: St Rufus, Botriphnie and
           Grange (Church of Scotland)
SC014557   Kinloss & Findhorn Parish Church of
           Scotland
SC014428   Knockando Elchies & Archiestown Parish
           Church of Scotland
SC009793   St Gerardine's High Church of Scotland,
           Lossiemouth
SC000880   St James Church of Scotland: Lossiemouth
SC010193   Mortlach and Cabrach Church of Scotland
SC014485   Portknockie Parish Church of Scotland
SC022567   Rafford Parish Church of Scotland
SC015906   Rathven Parish Church of Scotland
SC016116   Rothes Parish Church of Scotland
SC007113   Speymouth Parish Church of Scotland

SC008850   St Andrews Lhanbryd & Urquhart Parish
           Church of Scotland, Elgin

36.   Presbytery of Abernethy
SC003652   Abernethy Church of Scotland
SC002884   Cromdale & Advie Church of Scotland
SC010001   Grantown-on-Spey Church of Scotland
SC014015   Dulnain Bridge Church of Scotland
SC021546   Kingussie Church of Scotland
SC003282   Rothiemurchus & Aviemore Church of
           Scotland
SC001802   Tomintoul, Glenlivet and Inveravon Church of
           Scotland
SC000043   Alvie and Insh Church of Scotland
SC008346   Boat of Garten, Duthil and Kincardine Church
           of Scotland
SC008016   Laggan Church of Scotland
SC005490   Newtonmore Church of Scotland

37.   Presbytery of Inverness
SC015446   Ardersier Parish Church of Scotland
SC026653   Auldearn & Dalmore Parish Church of
           Scotland
SC001695   Cawdor Parish Church (Church of Scotland)
SC013601   Croy & Dalcross Parish Church (Church of
           Scotland)
SC000662   The Barn, Church of Scotland, Culloden
SC003301   Daviot & Dunlichity Church of Scotland
SC013579   Dores & Boleskine Church of Scotland
SC018159   Crown Church, Inverness (Church of Scotland)
SC011773   Dalneigh & Bona Parish Church of Scotland,
           Inverness
SC016866   East Church of Scotland Inverness
SC016775   Hilton Parish Church of Scotland, Inverness
SC005553   Inshes Church of Scotland, Inverness
SC010870   Ness Bank Church of Scotland, Inverness
SC035073   Old High St Stephen's Church of Scotland,
           Inverness
SC008109   Inverness: St Columba Church of Scotland
           New Charge
SC015432   Inverness Trinity Church of Scotland
SC008121   Kilmorack & Erchless Church of Scotland
SC014918   Kiltarlity Church of Scotland
SC020888   Kinmylies Church of Scotland, Inverness
SC003866   Kirkhill Church of Scotland
SC015653   Moy Dalarossie & Tomatin Church of
           Scotland
SC000947   Nairn Old Parish Church of Scotland
SC015361   St Ninians Church of Scotland, Nairn
SC004952   Petty Church of Scotland
SC016627   Urquhart & Glenmoriston Church of
           Scotland

38.   Presbytery of Lochaber
SC002916   Acharacle Parish Church of Scotland
SC008222   Ardgour and Kingairloch Parish Church of
           Scotland
SC030394   Ardnamurchan Parish Church of Scotland
SC021584   North West Lochaber Church of Scotland
SC018259   Duror Parish Church of Scotland
SC022635   Fort Augustus Parish Church of Scotland
SC013279   Fort William Duncansburgh MacIntosh Parish
           Church of Scotland
SC005211   Glencoe St Munda's Parish Church of
           Scotland
SC023413   Glengarry Parish Church of Scotland
SC005687   Kilmallie Parish Church of Scotland
SC014745   Kilmonivaig Parish Church of Scotland
SC030288   Kinlochleven Parish Church of Scotland
SC015532   Morvern Parish Church of Scotland
SC006700   Nether Lochaber Parish Church of Scotland

SC008982   Strontian Parish Church of Scotland

39.   Presbytery of Ross
SC015227   Alness Parish Church of Scotland
SC003921   Avoch Parish Church of Scotland
SC011897   Contin Parish Church of Scotland
SC006666   Cromarty Parish Church of Scotland
SC001167   Dingwall Castle Street Church of Scotland
SC001056   Dingwall St Clements Parish Church of
              Scotland
SC009309   Fearn Abbey & Nigg Church of Scotland
SC012675   Ferintosh Parish Church of Scotland
SC003499   Fodderty & Strathpeffer Parish Church of
              Scotland
SC004472   Fortrose & Rosemarkie Parish Church of
              Scotland
SC010964   Invergordon Church of Scotland
SC010319   Killearnan Parish Church of Scotland
SC013375   Kilmuir & Logie Easter Church of Scotland
SC009180   Kiltearn Parish Church of Scotland
SC014467   Knockbain Parish Church of Scotland
SC015631   Lochbroom & Ullapool Church of Scotland
SC013643   Resolis & Urquhart Church of Scotland
SC010093   Rosskeen Parish Church of Scotland
SC012425   Tain Parish Church of Scotland
SC021420   Tarbat Parish Church of Scotland
SC009902   Urray & Kilchrist Church of Scotland

40.   Presbytery of Sutherland
SC016038   Altnaharra & Farr Church of Scotland
SC010171   Assynt & Stoer Parish Church of Scotland
SC004973   Clyne Church of Scotland
SC003840   Creich Parish Church of Scotland
SC000315   Dornoch Cathedral (Church of Scotland)
SC005079   Durness & Kinlochbervie Church of
              Scotland
SC007326   Eddrachillis Parish Church of Scotland
SC004560   Golspie (St Andrews) Church of Scotland
SC004056   Kildonan & Loth Helmsdale Church of
              Scotland
SC016877   Kincardine Croick & Edderton Church of
              Scotland
SC020871   Lairg Church of Scotland
SC014066   Melness & Tongue Church of Scotland
SC010035   Rogart Church of Scotland
SC017558   Rosehall Church of Scotland

41.   Presbytery of Caithness
SC001363   Bower Church of Scotland
SC032164   Canisbay Parish Church of Scotland
SC030261   Dunnet Church of Scotland
SC008544   Halkirk & Westerdale Church of Scotland
SC010874   Keiss Parish Church of Scotland
SC034424   The Parish of Latheron Church of Scotland
SC010296   Olrig Church of Scotland
SC001815   North Coast Parish Church of Scotland
SC016691   Thurso St Peter's & St Andrew's Church of
              Scotland
SC007248   Thurso West Church of Scotland
SC003365   Watten Church of Scotland
SC013840   Wick St Fergus Church of Scotland
SC001291   Pulteneytown & Thrumster Church of Scotland

42.   Presbytery of Lochcarron – Skye
SC032334   Applecross, Lochcarron and Torridon Church
              of Scotland
SC022592   Bracadale and Duirinish Church of Scotland
SC015448   Gairloch and Dundonnell Church of Scotland
SC017510   Glenelg and Kintail Church of Scotland
SC014072   Kilmuir and Stenscholl Church of Scotland
SC016505   Lochalsh Church of Scotland

SC000416   Portree Church of Scotland
SC030117   Snizort Church of Scotland
SC001285   Strath and Sleat Church of Scotland

43.   Presbytery of Uist
SC003980   Barra Church of Scotland
SC002191   Benbecula Church of Scotland
SC016358   Berneray and Lochmaddy Church of
              Scotland
SC016461   Carinish Church of Scotland
SC030955   Kilmuir and Paible Church of Scotland
SC001770   Manish-Scarista Church of Scotland
SC031790   South Uist Church of Scotland
SC004787   Tarbert Church of Scotland

44.   Presbytery of Lewis
SC006563   Barvas Church of Scotland
SC032250   Carloway Church of Scotland
SC000991   Cross Ness Church of Scotland
SC008004   Kinloch Church of Scotland
SC014492   Knock Church of Scotland
SC024236   Lochs Crossbost Parish Church of Scotland
SC008746   Lochs-in-Bernera Church of Scotland
SC010164   Stornoway High Church of Scotland
SC000753   Martins Memorial Church of Scotland,
              Stornoway
SC006777   St Columba Old Parish Church of Scotland,
              Stornoway
SC007879   Uig Parish Church of Scotland

45.   Presbytery of Orkney
SC035048   Birsay Harray & Sandwick Church of Scotland
SC019770   East Mainland Church of Scotland
SC005404   Eday Church of Scotland
SC005062   Evie Church of Scotland
SC013330   Firth Church of Scotland
SC016203   Flotta Parish Church of Scotland
SC023194   Hoy & Walls Parish Church of Scotland
SC018002   Kirkwall East Church, Church of Scotland
SC005322   Kirkwall St Magnus Cathedral (Church of
              Scotland)
SC030098   North Ronaldsay Parish Church of Scotland
SC016221   Orphir and Stenness Church of Scotland
SC013661   Papa Westray Church of Scotland
SC016806   Rendall Church of Scotland
SC001078   Rousay Church of Scotland
SC000271   Sanday Church of Scotland
SC006097   Shapinsay Church of Scotland
SC003298   South Ronaldsay & Burray Church of Scotland
SC003099   Stromness Church of Scotland
SC006572   Moncur Memorial Church of Scotland,
              Stronsay
SC025053   Westray Parish Church of Scotland

46.   Presbytery of Shetland
SC030483   Burra Church of Scotland
SC029873   Delting Parish Church (Church of Scotland)
SC015253   Dunrossness and St Ninian's Parish Church
              (incl. Fair Isle) (Church of Scotland)
SC038365   Fetlar Church of Scotland
SC017535   Lerwick and Bressay Parish Church (Church
              of Scotland)
SC031996   Nesting and Lunnasting Church of Scotland
SC002341   Northmavine Parish Church of Scotland
SC012345   Sandsting and Aithsting Parish Church of
              Scotland
SC014545   Sandwick, Cunningsburgh and Quarff Church
              of Scotland
SC030748   St Paul's Church of Scotland Walls: Shetland
SC032982   Tingwall Parish Church of Scotland
SC007954   Unst Church of Scotland

SC000293 Whalsay and Skerries Parish Church of
Scotland
SC020628 Yell Parish Church of Scotland

47. **Presbytery of England**
SC042648 Crown Court Church of Scotland London
SC042854 Liverpool: St Andrew's Church of Scotland

SECTION 8

Church Buildings: Ordnance Survey National Grid References

NOTE:
The placing of symbols denoting churches may vary according to the edition of published maps. The references which follow should be sufficiently accurate to allow church buildings to be located. The correction of any errors will always be welcomed, and appropriate details should be sent to the Editor of the *Year Book*.

The Churches are listed in the order in which they appear in the Presbytery Lists in the *Year Book*.

1. Presbytery of Edinburgh
Albany Deaf Church of Edinburgh, meets at 82 Montrose Terrace
Balerno, NT163664
Barclay Viewforth, NT249726
Blackhall St Columba's, NT219747
Bristo Memorial Craigmillar, NT287716
Broughton St Mary's, NT256748
Canongate, NT265738
Carrick Knowe, NT203721
Colinton, NT216692
Colinton Mains, NT233692
Corstorphine Craigsbank, NT191730
Corstorphine Old, NT201728
Corstorphine St Anne's, NT204730
Corstorphine St Ninian's, NT198730
Craigentinny St Christopher's, NT292748
Craiglockhart, NT224705
Craigmillar Park, NT269714
Cramond, NT190768
Currie, NT183676
Dalmeny, NT144775
Davidson's Mains, NT207752
Dean, NT238742
Drylaw, NT221754
Duddingston, NT284726
Fairmilehead, NT248683
Gorgie Dalry, NT231724
Granton, NT237766
Greenbank, NT243702
Greenside, NT263745
Greyfriars Tolbooth and Highland, NT256734
High (St Giles'), NT257736
Holyrood Abbey, NT274744
Holy Trinity, NT201700
Inverleith St Serf's, NT248761
Juniper Green, NT199687
Kaimes Lockhart Memorial, NT277684
Kirkliston, NT125744
Kirk o' Field, NT263732
Leith North, NT263765
Leith St Andrew's, NT273757
Leith South, NT271761
Leith Wardie, NT246768
Liberton, NT275695
Liberton Northfield, NT280699
London Road, NT268745
Marchmont St Giles', NT256718
Mayfield Salisbury, NT266717
Morningside, NT246707
Morningside United, NT245719
Muirhouse St Andrew's, NT215763
Murrayfield, NT227733
Newhaven, NT254769
New Restalrig, NT284742
Old Kirk, NT220760
Palmerston Place, NT241734
Pilrig St Paul's, NT266752
Polwarth, NT236719
Portobello Old, NT309738
Portobello St James', NT303738
Portobello St Philip's Joppa, NT313736
Priestfield, NT271721
Queensferry, NT130782
Ratho, NT138710
Reid Memorial, NT261710
Richmond Craigmillar, NT296717
St Andrew's and St George's West, NT255741

St Andrew's Clermiston, NT201746
St Catherine's Argyle, NT257721
St Cuthbert's, NT248736
St David's Broomhouse, NT203714
St John's Oxgangs, NT237687
St Margaret's, NT284745
St Martin's, NT305726
St Michael's, NT234722
St Nicholas' Sighthill, NT194707
St Stephen's Comely Bank, NT241748
Slateford Longstone, NT213707
Stenhouse St Aidan's, NT218716
Stockbridge, NT247748
The Tron Kirk (Gilmerton and Moredun):
    Gilmerton, NT293686
    Moredun, NT294697

2. Presbytery of West Lothian
Abercorn, NT082792
Armadale, NS935684
Avonbridge, NS910730
Bathgate: Boghall, NS996686
Bathgate: High, NS976691
Bathgate: St John's, NS977687
Blackburn and Seafield, NS991655
Blackridge, NS897671
Breich Valley, NS968622
Broxburn, NT085723
Fauldhouse: St Andrew's, NS931607
Harthill: St Andrew's, NS896643
Kirknewton and East Calder:
    Kirknewton, NT106670
    East Calder, NT086678
Kirk of Calder, NT074673
Linlithgow: St Michael's, NT002773
Linlithgow: St Ninian's Craigmailen, NS994771
Livingston Ecumenical Parish:
    Carmondean and Knightsridge, NT048693
    Craigshill (St Columba's) and Ladywell (St Paul's), NT054682
    Dedridge and Murieston: Lanthorn Centre, Dedridge, NT060663
Livingston: Old, NT037669
    Deans, NT021686
Pardovan, Kingscavil and Winchburgh:
    Kingscavil, NT030764
    Winchburgh, NT087750
Polbeth Harwood, NT030641
Strathbrock, NT060722
    Ecclesmachan, NT059737
Torphichen, NS969725
Uphall: South, NT061718
West Kirk of Calder, NT014629
Whitburn: Brucefield, NS948650
Whitburn: South, NS947646

3. Presbytery of Lothian
Aberlady, NT462799
Athelstaneford, NT533774
Belhaven, NT668787
Bilston, NT262647
Bolton and Saltoun:
    Bolton, NT507701
    Saltoun, NT474678
Bonnyrigg, NT307654
Cockenzie and Port Seton: Chalmers Memorial, NT403757
Cockenzie and Port Seton: Old, NT401758
Cockpen and Carrington, NT319642
Dalkeith: St John's and King's Park, NT330670
Dalkeith: St Nicholas' Buccleuch, NT333674

Dirleton, NT513842
Dunbar, NT682786
Dunglass:
  Cockburnspath, NT774711
  Innerwick, NT721739
  Oldhamstocks, NT738707
Garvald and Morham:
  Garvald, NT591709
  Morham, NT557726
Gladsmuir, NT457733
Glencorse, NT247627
Gorebridge, NT343619
Gullane, NT483827
Haddington: St Mary's, NT519736
Haddington: West, NT512739
Howgate, NT248580
Humbie, NT461637
Lasswade and Rosewell:
  Lasswade, NT305661
  Rosewell, NT288624
Loanhead, NT278654
Longniddry, NT442763
Musselburgh: Northesk, NT340727
Musselburgh: St Andrew's High, NT345727
Musselburgh: St Clement's and St Ninian's, NT360727
  Wallyford, NT368722
Musselburgh: St Michael's Inveresk, NT344721
  St John's, Whitecraig, NT351701
Newbattle, NT331661:
  Newtongrange, NT334643
  Easthouses, NT348652
Newton, NT315693
North Berwick: Abbey, NT551853
North Berwick: St Andrew Blackadder, NT553853
Ormiston, NT414693
Pencaitland, NT443690
Penicuik: North, NT234603
Penicuik: St Mungo's, NT237599
Penicuik: South, NT236595
Prestonpans: Prestongrange, NT388746
Roslin, NT270631
Spott, NT673755
Tranent, NT403734
Traprain:
  Prestonkirk, NT592778
  Stenton, NT622743
  Whittingehame, NT603737
Tyne Valley Parish:
  Borthwick, NT369596
  Cranston, Crichton and Ford, NT386656
  Fala and Soutra, NT438609
Whitekirk and Tyninghame, NT596815
Yester, NT535681

4. Presbytery of Melrose and Peebles
Ashkirk, NT466220
Bowden and Melrose:
  Bowden, NT554301
  Melrose, NT544344
Broughton, Glenholm and Kilbucho, NT114357
Caddonfoot, NT451348
Carlops, NT161559
Channelkirk and Lauder:
  Channelkirk, NT482545
  Lauder, NT531475
Earlston, NT581388
Eddleston, NT244472
Ettrick and Yarrow:
  Ettrick, NT259145
  Yarrow, NT356278
  Kirkhope, NT390244

Galashiels: Old and St Paul's, NT492358
Galashiels: St John's, NT509357
Galashiels: Trinity, NT491363
Innerleithen, Traquair and Walkerburn:
  Innerleithen, NT332369
  Traquair, NT320335
Kirkurd and Newlands, NT162467
Lyne and Manor:
  Lyne, NT192405
  Manor, NT220380
Maxton and Mertoun:
  Maxton, NT610303
  Mertoun, NT615318
Newtown, NT581316
Peebles: Old, NT250404
Peebles: St Andrew's Leckie, NT253404
St Boswells, NT594310
Selkirk, NT472287
Skirling, NT075390
Stobo and Drumelzier:
  Stobo, NT183377
  Drumelzier, NT135343
Stow: St Mary of Wedale and Heriot:
  Stow: St Mary of Wedale, NT459444
  Heriot, NT390526
Tweedsmuir, NT101245
West Linton: St Andrew's, NT149516

5. Presbytery of Duns
Ayton and Burnmouth:
  Ayton, NT927609
  Burnmouth, NT956610
Berwick-upon-Tweed: St Andrew's Wallace Green
  and Lowick, NT999532
Bonkyl and Preston, NT808596
Chirnside, NT869561
Coldingham and St Abb's, NT904659
Coldstream, NT843398
Duns, NT786539
Eccles, NT764413
Edrom: Allanton, NT826558
Eyemouth, NT943640
Fogo and Swinton:
  Fogo, NT773492
  Swinton, NT838477
Foulden and Mordington, NT931558
Gordon: St Michael's, NT645432
Grantshouse and Houndwood and Reston:
  Reston, NT878621
  Grantshouse congregation meets in village hall
Greenlaw, NT712462
Hutton and Fishwick and Paxton:
  Hutton and Fishwick, NT907540
  Paxton, NT934532
Ladykirk, NT889477
Langton and Lammermuir:
  Cranshaws, NT692619
  Langton, NT767523
  Longformacus, NT694573
Legerwood, NT594434
Leitholm, NT791441
Westruther, NT633500
Whitsome, NT861504

6. Presbytery of Jedburgh
Ale and Teviot United:
  Ancrum, NT627246
  Crailing, NT682250
  Lilliesleaf, NT539253
Cavers and Kirkton:
  Cavers, NT538159

Kirkton, NT541140
Hawick: Burnfoot, NT510162
Hawick: St Mary's and Old, NT502143
Hawick: Teviot and Roberton:
   Hawick: Teviot, NT501144
   Roberton, NT432142
Hawick: Trinity, NT505147
Hawick: Wilton, NT502153
Hobkirk and Southdean:
   Hobkirk, NT587109
   Southdean, NT624109
Jedburgh: Old and Trinity, NT651203
Kelso Country Churches:
   Makerstoun, NT669331
   Roxburgh, NT700307
   Smailholm, NT649364
   Stichill, NT711383
Kelso: North and Ednam:
   Kelso: North, NT725343
   Ednam, NT737372
Kelso: Old and Sprouston:
   Kelso: Old, NT725343
   Sprouston, NT757353
Linton, Morebattle, Hownam and Yetholm:
   Linton, NT773262
   Hoselaw, NT802318
   Morebattle, NT772250
   Hownam, NT778193
   Yetholm, NT826281
Oxnam, NT701190
Ruberslaw:
   Bedrule, NT599179
   Denholm, NT569186
   Minto, NT567201
Teviothead, NT403052

7. Presbytery of Annandale and Eskdale
Annan: Old, NY197666
Annan: St Andrew's, NY193665
Applegarth, Sibbaldbie and Johnstone, NY104843
Brydekirk, NY183705
Canonbie United, NY395763
Dalton, NY114740
Dornock, NY231660
Gretna: Old, Gretna: St Andrew's, Half Morton and
   Kirkpatrick Fleming:
   Gretna: Old, NY319680
   Gretna: St Andrew's, NY317670
   Kirkpatrick Fleming, NY277701
Hightae, NY090793
Hoddom, Kirtle-Eaglesfield and Middlebie:
   Eaglesfield, NY233743
   Middlebie, NY214762
Kirkpatrick Juxta, NT083009
Langholm Eskdalemuir Ewes and Westerkirk:
   Langholm, NY362844
   Eskdalemuir, NY253979
   Ewes, NY369908
   Westerkirk, NY312903
Liddesdale:
   Castleton, NY482877
   Saughtree, NY562968
Lochmaben, NY084823
Lockerbie: Dryfesdale, Hutton and Corrie
   Hutton and Corrie, NY171908
   Lockerbie: Dryfesdale, NY135818
Moffat: St Andrew's, NT084051
St Mungo, NY143771
The Border Kirk, NY402561
Tundergarth, NY175808
Wamphray, NY131965

8. Presbytery of Dumfries and Kirkcudbright
Auchencairn and Rerrick, NX799512
Balmaclellan and Kells:
   Balmaclellan, NX651791
   Kells, NX632784
Balmaghie, NX722663
Borgue, NX629483
Buittle and Kelton, NX758603
Caerlaverock, NX996688
Carsphairn, NX563932
Castle Douglas, NX765622
Closeburn, NX904923
Colvend, Southwick and Kirkbean:
   Colvend, NX862541
   Southwick, NX927573
Corsock and Kirkpatrick Durham:
   Corsock, NX762760
   Kirkpatrick Durham, NX786699
Crossmichael and Parton:
   Crossmichael, NX729670
   Parton, NX697699
Cummertrees, Mouswald and Ruthwell, NY101683
Dalbeattie, NX831611
Dalry, NX618813
Dumfries: Maxwelltown West, NX967760
Dumfries: North West, NX958774
Dumfries: St George's, NX971764
Dumfries: St Mary's-Greyfriars, NX975763
Dumfries: St Michael's and South, NX975757
Dumfries: Troqueer, NX975751
Dunscore, NX867843
Durisdeer, NS894038
Gatehouse of Fleet, NX602566
Glencairn and Moniaive:
   Glencairn, NX809904
   Moniaive, NX777910
Irongray, Lochrutton and Terregles:
   Irongray, NX915794
   Terregles, NX931771
Kirkconnel, NS728123
Kirkcudbright, NX683509
Kirkgunzeon, NX866667
Kirkmahoe, NX974815:
   Dalswinton, NX942850
Kirkmichael, Tinwald and Torthorwald:
   Kirkmichael, NY005884
   Tinwald, NY003816
   Torthorwald, NY035783
Lochend and New Abbey, NX965660
Penpont, Keir and Tynron, NX849944
Sanquhar: St Bride's, NS779102
Tarff and Twynholm, NX664542
Thornhill, NX883957
Urr, NX817658

9. Presbytery of Wigtown and Stranraer
Ervie Kirkcolm, NX026687
Glasserton and Isle of Whithorn:
   Glasserton, NX421381
   Isle of Whithorn, NX478363
Inch, NX101603
Kirkcowan, NX327610
Kirkinner, NX423514
Kirkmabreck, NX477585
Kirkmaiden, NX125369:
   Drummore, NX135366
Leswalt, NX020638
Mochrum, NX347463
Monigaff, NX410666
New Luce, NX175645
Old Luce, NX197574

Penninghame, NX410654
Portpatrick, NX002544
Sorbie, NX468463
Stoneykirk:
    Sandhead, NX097500
    Ardwell, NX101457
Stranraer: High Kirk, NX057609
Stranraer: St Ninian's, NX060607
Stranraer: Town Kirk, NX064606
Whithorn: St Ninian's Priory, NX444403
Wigtown, NX436555

10. Presbytery of Ayr
Alloway, NS332180
Annbank, NS407243
Auchinleck, NS552216
Ayr: Auld Kirk of Ayr, NS339219
Ayr: Castlehill, NS347203
Ayr: Newton Wallacetown, NS339224
Ayr: St Andrew's, NS338213
Ayr: St Columba, NS337209
Ayr: St James', NS342232
Ayr: St Leonard's, NS338204
Ayr: St Quivox:
    Auchincruive, NS375241
    Dalmilling, NS363229
Ballantrae, NX083825:
    Glenapp, NX075746
Barr, NX275941
Catrine, NS528260
Coylton, NS422198
Craigie, NS427323
Crosshill, NS327068
Dailly, NS271016
Dalmellington, NS481061:
    Bellsbank, NS480046
Dalrymple, NS358144
Drongan: The Schaw Kirk, NS441185
Dundonald, NS366343
Fisherton, NS275175
Girvan: North (Old and St Andrew's), NX187982
Girvan: South, NX183977
Kirkmichael, NS345090
Kirkoswald, NS240073
Lugar, NS591213
Mauchline, NS498272
Maybole, worshipping in Maybole Baptist Church,
    NS299099
Monkton and Prestwick: North, NS353263
Muirkirk, NS701278
New Cumnock, NS617135
Ochiltree, NS504212
Old Cumnock: Old, NS568202
Old Cumnock: Trinity, NS567200:
    Netherthird, NS578187
Patna: Waterside, NS412106
Prestwick: Kingcase, NS348243
Prestwick: St Nicholas', NS351256
Prestwick: South, NS351259
St Colmon (Arnsheen Barrhill and Colmonell):
    Colmonell, NX144857
    Barrhill congregation meets in community
    centre
Sorn, NS550268
Stair, NS439236
Straiton: St Cuthbert's, NS381049
Symington, NS384314
Tarbolton, NS430272
Troon: Old, NS321309
Troon: Portland, NS323308
Troon: St Meddan's, NS323309

11. Presbytery of Irvine and Kilmarnock
Caldwell, NS435552
Crosshouse, NS395384
Darvel, NS563375
Dreghorn and Springside, NS352383
Dunlop, NS405494
Fenwick, NS465435
Galston, NS500367
Hurlford, NS454372
Irvine: Fullarton, NS316389
Irvine: Girdle Toll, NS341409
Irvine: Mure, NS319390
Irvine: Old, NS322387
Irvine: Relief Bourtreehill, NS344392
Irvine: St Andrew's, NS325399
Kilmarnock: Henderson, NS431380
Kilmarnock: New Laigh, NS428379
Kilmarnock: Old High Kirk, NS430382
Kilmarnock: Riccarton, NS428364
Kilmarnock: St Andrew's and St Marnock's, NS427377
Kilmarnock: St John's Onthank, NS433399
Kilmarnock: St Kentigern's, NS442388
Kilmarnock: St Ninian's Bellfield, NS435359
Kilmarnock: Shortlees, NS428353
Kilmaurs: St Maur's Glencairn, NS415408
Newmilns: Loudoun, NS537373
Stewarton: John Knox, NS421460
Stewarton: St Columba's, NS419457
Ayrshire Mission to the Deaf, Kilmarnock, NS430377

12. Presbytery of Ardrossan
Ardrossan: Barony St John's, NS231420
Ardrossan: Park, NS233436
Beith: NS350539
Brodick, NS012359
Corrie, NS024437
Cumbrae, NS160550
Dalry: St Margaret's, NS291496
Dalry: Trinity, NS292494
Fairlie, NS209556
Kilbirnie: Auld Kirk, NS315536
Kilbirnie: St Columba's, NS314546
Kilmory, NR963218
Kilwinning: Mansefield Trinity, NS290432
Kilwinning: Old, NS303433
Lamlash, NS026309
Largs: Clark Memorial, NS202593
Largs: St Columba's, NS203596
Largs: St John's, NS201593
Lochranza and Pirnmill:
    Lochranza, NR937503
    Pirnmill, NR874447
Saltcoats: New Trinity, NS246414
Saltcoats: North, NS252423
Saltcoats: St Cuthbert's, NS244418
Shiskine, NR910295
Stevenston: Ardeer, NS269411
Stevenston: High, NS266422
Stevenston: Livingston, NS268416
West Kilbride, NS207484
Whiting Bay and Kildonan, NS047273

13. Presbytery of Lanark
Biggar, NT040379
Black Mount, NT101464
Cairngryffe, NS923384
Carluke: Kirkton, NS844503
Carluke: St Andrew's, NS844508
Carluke: St John's, NS847503
Carnwath, NS976465:
    Auchengray, NS995540

Tarbrax, NT025549
Carstairs and Carstairs Junction, The United Church of:
  Carstairs, NS938461
  Carstairs Junction, NS954450
Coalburn, NS813345
Crossford, NS827466
Culter, NT027342
Forth: St Paul's, NS942538
Glencaple, NS930234
Kirkfieldbank, NS866438
Kirkmuirhill, NS799429
Lanark: Greyfriars, NS880437
Lanark: St Nicholas', NS881437
Law, NS821527
Lesmahagow: Abbeygreen, NS813402
Lesmahagow: Old, NS814399
Libberton and Quothquan, NS992428
Lowther, NS885148
Symington, NS999352
The Douglas Valley Church:
  Douglas, NS835310
  Douglas Water and Rigside, NS873347

14. Presbytery of Greenock and Paisley
Barrhead: Arthurlie, NS501588
Barrhead: Bourock, NS499589
Barrhead: South and Levern, NS503589
Bishopton, NS445721
Bridge of Weir: Freeland, NS387656
Bridge of Weir: St Machar's Ranfurly, NS392653
Elderslie Kirk, NS441631
Erskine, NS466707
Gourock: Old Gourock and Ashton, NS243775
Gourock: St John's, NS241778
Greenock: East End, meets at Crawfurdsburn Community
  Centre
Greenock: Lyle Kirk:
  Greenock: Ardgowan, NS271768
  Greenock: Finnart St Paul's, NS265774
  Greenock: Old West Kirk, NS273772
Greenock: Mount Kirk, NS271759
Greenock: St Margaret's, NS255764
Greenock: St Ninian's, NS242755
Greenock: Wellpark Mid Kirk, NS279762
Greenock: Westburn, NS273763
Houston and Killellan, NS410671
Howwood, NS396603
Inchinnan, NS479689
Inverkip, NS207720
Johnstone: High, NS426630
Johnstone: St Andrew's Trinity, NS434623
Johnstone: St Paul's, NS424626
Kilbarchan: East, NS403633
Kilbarchan: West, NS401632
Kilmacolm: Old, NS358700
Kilmacolm: St Columba, NS358697
Langbank, NS380734
Linwood, NS432645
Lochwinnoch, NS353587
Neilston, NS480574
Paisley: Abbey, NS486640
Paisley: Glenburn, NS473617
Paisley: Lylesland, NS488626
Paisley: Martyrs' Sandyford:
  Martyrs', NS474639
  Sandyford, NS493657
Paisley: Oakshaw Trinity, NS480641
Paisley: St Columba Foxbar, NS458622
Paisley: St James', NS477644
Paisley: St Luke's, NS482632
Paisley: St Mark's Oldhall, NS511640

Paisley: St Ninian's Ferguslie, NS464644
Paisley: Sherwood Greenlaw, NS492642
Paisley: Stow Brae Kirk, NS483634
Paisley: Wallneuk North, NS486643
Port Glasgow: Hamilton Bardrainney, NS337733
Port Glasgow: St Andrew's, NS319745
Port Glasgow: St Martin's, NS306747
Renfrew: North, NS508678
Renfrew: Old, NS509676
Renfrew: Trinity, NS505674
Skelmorlie and Wemyss Bay, NS192681

16. Presbytery of Glasgow
Banton, NS752788
Bishopbriggs: Kenmure, NS604698
Bishopbriggs: Springfield, NS615702
Broom, NS554563
Burnside Blairbeth:
  Burnside, NS622601
  Blairbeth, NS616603
Busby, NS577563
Cadder, NS616723
Cambuslang: Flemington Hallside, NS663595
Cambuslang Parish Church, NS645605
Campsie, NS629777
Chryston, NS688702:
  Moodiesburn, NS699708
Eaglesham, NS574519
Fernhill and Cathkin, NS624594
Gartcosh, NS698682
Giffnock: Orchardhill, NS563587
Giffnock: South, NS559582
Giffnock: The Park, NS559593
Glenboig, NS723687
Greenbank, NS574568
Kilsyth: Anderson, NS717782
Kilsyth: Burns and Old, NS716778
Kirkintilloch: Hillhead, NS663730
Kirkintilloch: St Columba's, NS664733
Kirkintilloch: St David's Memorial Park, NS653736
Kirkintilloch: St Mary's, NS654739
Lenzie: Old, NS655720
Lenzie: Union, NS654722
Maxwell Mearns Castle, NS553553
Mearns, NS543551
Milton of Campsie, NS652768
Netherlee, NS577590
Newton Mearns, NS537557
Rutherglen: Old, NS613617
Rutherglen: Stonelaw, NS617612
Rutherglen: West and Wardlawhill, NS609618
Stamperland, NS576581
Stepps, NS657686
Thornliebank, NS546588
Torrance, NS620744
Twechar, NS700753
Williamwood, NS566576
Glasgow: Anderston Kelvingrove, NS577655
Glasgow: Baillieston Mure Memorial, NS673643
Glasgow: Baillieston St Andrew's, NS681639
Glasgow: Balshagray Victoria Park, NS549671
Glasgow: Barlanark Greyfriars, NS667649
Glasgow: Blawarthill, NS522683
Glasgow: Bridgeton St Francis in the East, NS611639
Glasgow: Broomhill, NS549674
Glasgow: Calton Parkhead, NS624638
Glasgow: Cardonald, NS526639
Glasgow: Carmunnock, NS599575
Glasgow: Carmyle, NS649618
Glasgow: Carnwadric, NS544599
Glasgow: Castlemilk East, NS607593

Glasgow: Castlemilk West, NS596594
Glasgow: Cathcart Old, NS587606
Glasgow: Cathcart Trinity, NS582604
Glasgow: Cathedral (High or St Mungo's), NS603656
Glasgow: Clincarthill, NS586613
Glasgow: Colston Milton, NS592697
Glasgow: Colston Wellpark, NS606692
Glasgow: Cranhill, NS643658
Glasgow: Croftfoot, NS603602
Glasgow: Dennistoun New, NS613652
Glasgow: Drumchapel St Andrew's, NS523707
Glasgow: Drumchapel St Mark's, NS521719
Glasgow: Easterhouse St George's and St Peter's, NS678657
Glasgow: Eastwood, NS558607
Glasgow: Gairbraid, NS568688
Glasgow: Gallowgate, NS614646
Glasgow: Garthamlock and Craigend East, NS658667
Glasgow: Gorbals, NS593638
Glasgow: Govan and Linthouse, NS555658
Glasgow: Govanhill Trinity, NS587627
Glasgow: High Carntyne, NS636653
Glasgow: Hillington Park, NS534639
Glasgow: Househillwood St Christopher's, NS534616
Glasgow: Hyndland, NS559675
Glasgow: Ibrox, NS560642
Glasgow: John Ross Memorial Church for Deaf People, NS588644
Glasgow: Jordanhill, NS544682
Glasgow: Kelvin Stevenson Memorial, NS576673
Glasgow: Kelvinside Hillhead, NS567673
Glasgow: Kenmuir Mount Vernon, NS655626
Glasgow: King's Park, NS601608
Glasgow: Kinning Park, NS570648
Glasgow: Knightswood St Margaret's, NS536694
Glasgow: Langside, NS582614
Glasgow: Lansdowne, NS576669
Glasgow: Lochwood, NS685663
Glasgow: Maryhill, NS563695
Glasgow: Merrylea, NS575603
Glasgow: Mosspark, NS544633
Glasgow: Newlands South, NS573611
Glasgow: Partick South, NS559665
Glasgow: Partick Trinity, NS563668
Glasgow: Penilee St Andrew, NS518647
Glasgow: Pollokshaws, NS561612
Glasgow: Pollokshields, NS577635
Glasgow: Possilpark, NS592677
Glasgow: Priesthill and Nitshill:
   Priesthill, NS531607
   Nitshill, NS522603
Glasgow: Queen's Park, NS579625
Glasgow: Renfield St Stephen's, NS582659
Glasgow: Robroyston, NS638688
Glasgow: Ruchazie, NS643662
Glasgow: Ruchill Kelvinside, NS573683
Glasgow: St Andrew's East, NS619656
Glasgow: St Columba, NS583657
Glasgow: St David's Knightswood, NS528689
Glasgow: St Enoch's Hogganfield, NS629660
Glasgow: St George's Tron, NS590655
Glasgow: St James' (Pollok), NS530626
Glasgow: St John's Renfield, NS558683
Glasgow: St Margaret's Tollcross Park, NS637631
Glasgow: St Nicholas' Cardonald, NS524646
Glasgow: St Paul's, NS631671
Glasgow: St Rollox, NS603668
Glasgow: Sandyford Henderson Memorial, NS570659
Glasgow: Sandyhills, NS658638
Glasgow: Scotstoun, NS533676
Glasgow: Shawlands, NS572621
Glasgow: Sherbrooke St Gilbert's, NS561636

Glasgow: Shettleston New, NS647642
Glasgow: Shettleston Old, NS649639
Glasgow: South Carntyne, NS630652
Glasgow: South Shawlands, NS569615
Glasgow: Springburn, NS607677
Glasgow: Temple Anniesland, NS547689
Glasgow: Toryglen, NS602615
Glasgow: Trinity Possil and Henry Drummond, NS593687
Glasgow: Tron St Mary's, NS618676
Glasgow: Victoria Tollcross, NS642632
Glasgow: Wallacewell, NS621690
Glasgow: Wellington, NS570667
Glasgow: Whiteinch, NS540668
Glasgow: Yoker, NS511689

17. Presbytery of Hamilton
Airdrie: Broomknoll, NS761653
Airdrie: Clarkston, NS783661
Airdrie: Flowerhill, NS765655
Airdrie: High, NS760658
Airdrie: Jackson, NS782647
Airdrie: New Monkland, NS753678
Airdrie: St Columba's, NS766665
Airdrie: The New Wellwynd, NS759654
Bargeddie, NS692648
Bellshill: Macdonald Memorial, NS738602
Bellshill: Orbiston, NS729593
Bellshill: West, NS727603
Blantyre: Livingstone Memorial, NS687577
Blantyre: Old, NS679565
Blantyre: St Andrew's, NS693573
Bothwell, NS705586
Calderbank, NS770631
Caldercruix and Longriggend, NS819677
Chapelhall, NS783627
Chapelton, NS685485
Cleland, NS797581
Coatbridge: Blairhill Dundyvan, NS726650
Coatbridge: Calder, NS738639
Coatbridge: Middle, NS723646
Coatbridge: Old Monkland, NS718633
Coatbridge: New St Andrew's, NS733653
Coatbridge: Townhead, NS718664
Dalserf, NS800507:
   Ashgill, NS783503
East Kilbride: Claremont, NS653543
East Kilbride: Greenhills, NS616525
East Kilbride: Moncreiff, NS647555
East Kilbride: Mossneuk, NS607532
East Kilbride: Old, NS635545
East Kilbride: South, NS633537
East Kilbride: Stewartfield, meets in a community
   centre at NS643561
East Kilbride: West, NS634547
East Kilbride: Westwood, NS618537
Glasford, NS726470
Greengairs, NS783705
Hamilton: Burnbank, NS699562
Hamilton: Cadzow, NS723550
Hamilton: Gilmour and Whitehill, NS704563
Hamilton: Hillhouse, NS696554
Hamilton: North, NS719558
Hamilton: Old, NS723555
Hamilton: St Andrew's, NS723551
Hamilton: St John's, NS724553
Hamilton: South, NS717538
Hamilton: Trinity, NS711543
Hamilton: West, NS712558
Holytown, NS773608
Kirk o' Shotts, NS843629

Larkhall: Chalmers, NS763499
Larkhall: St Machan's, NS763511
Larkhall: Trinity, NS762513
Motherwell: Crosshill, NS756566
Motherwell: Dalziel St Andrew's, NS752571
Motherwell: North, NS741577
Motherwell: St Margaret's, NS769549
Motherwell: St Mary's, NS750566
Motherwell: South, NS757560
Newarthill and Carfin, NS781597
Newmains: Bonkle, NS837571
Newmains: Coltness Memorial, NS819557
New Stevenston: Wrangholm Kirk, NS760596
Overtown, NS801527
Quarter, NS722512
Shotts: Calderhead Erskine, NS877600:
　Allanton, NS850578
Stonehouse: St Ninian's, NS752467
Strathaven: Avendale Old and Drumclog:
　Avendale Old, NS701443
　Drumclog, NS640389
Strathaven: East, NS702446
Strathaven: Rankin, NS701446
Uddingston: Burnhead, NS717614
Uddingston: Old, NS696603
Uddingston: Viewpark, NS702616
Wishaw: Cambusnethan North, NS808554
Wishaw: Cambusnethan Old, NS806553
Wishaw: Craigneuk and Belhaven, NS773561
Wishaw: Old, NS796552
Wishaw: St Mark's, NS801566
Wishaw: South Wishaw, NS797548

18. Presbytery of Dumbarton
Alexandria, NS387817
Arrochar, NM296037
Baldernock, NS577751
Bearsden: Baljaffray, NS534736
Bearsden: Cross, NS543719
Bearsden: Killermont, NS557713
Bearsden: New Kilpatrick, NS543723
Bearsden: Westerton Fairlie Memorial, NS543706
Bonhill, NS395796
Cardross, NS345775
Clydebank: Abbotsford, NS498703
Clydebank: Faifley, NS502732
Clydebank: Kilbowie St Andrew's, NS499712
Clydebank: Radnor Park, NS495713
Clydebank: St Cuthbert's, NS511704
Craigrownie, NS224811
Dalmuir: Barclay, NS479715
Dumbarton: Riverside, NS398752
Dumbarton: St Andrew's, NS407764
Dumbarton: West Kirk, NS390755
Duntocher, NS494727
Garelochhead, NS239912
Helensburgh: Park, NS300823
Helensburgh: St Andrew's Kirk, NS295825
Jamestown, NS397813
Kilmaronock Gartocharn:
　Kilmaronock, NS452875
　Gartocharn, NS428864
Luss, NS361929
Milngavie: Cairns, NS556748
Milngavie: St Luke's, NS543747
Milngavie: St Paul's, NS557745
Old Kilpatrick Bowling, NS463731
Renton: Trinity, NS390780
Rhu and Shandon, NS267841
Rosneath: St Modan's, NS255832

19. Presbytery of Argyll
Appin, NM938459
Ardchattan, NM944360:
　Benderloch, NM905384
Ardrishaig, NR854852
Campbeltown: Highland, NR720201
Campbeltown: Lorne and Lowland, NR718206
Coll, NM223573
Colonsay and Oronsay, NR390941
Connel, NM914343
Craignish, NM805042
Cumlodden, Lochfyneside and Lochgair:
　Cumlodden, NS015997
　Lochfyneside, NR979962
　Lochgair, NR922905
Dunoon: St John's, NS172769
Dunoon: The High Kirk, NS174765
Gigha and Cara, NR648489
Glassary, Kilmartin and Ford:
　Glassary, NR859935
　Kilmartin, NR834988
　Ford, NM869037
Glenaray and Inveraray, NN095085
Glenorchy and Innishael, NN168275
Innellan, NS151707
Iona, NM285243
Jura, NR527677
Kilarrow, NR312596
Kilberry, NR741620
Kilbrandon and Kilchattan:
　Kilbrandon, NM758155
　Kilchattan, NM743104
Kilcalmonell, NR763561
Kilchoman, NR257596
Kilchrenan and Dalavich:
　Kilchrenan, NN037229
　Dalavich, NM968124
Kildalton and Oa, NR368450
Kilfinan, NR934789
Kilfinichen and Kilvickeon and the Ross of Mull:
　Kilfinichen and Kilvickeon, NM383218
　The Ross of Mull, NM316232
Killean and Kilchenzie, NR681418
Kilmeny, NR390657
Kilmodan and Colintraive:
　Kilmodan, NR995842
　Colintraive, NS045735
Kilmore and Oban:
　Kilmore, NM872258
　Oban: Old, NM861296
　Corran Esplanade, NM856306
Kilmun (St Munn's), NS166821
Kilninian and Kilmore, NM432517
Kilninver and Kilmelford:
　Kilninver, NM825217
　Kilmelford, NM849130
Kirn, NS184783
Kyles, NR973713
Lismore, NM861435
Lochgilphead, NR863882
Lochgoilhead and Kilmorich:
　Lochgoilhead, NN198015
　Kilmorich, NN181108
Muckairn, NN005310
North Knapdale:
　Kilmichael Inverlussa, NR776859
　Bellanoch, NR797923
　Tayvallich, NR742871
Portnahaven, NR168523
Rothesay: Trinity, NS089645
Saddell and Carradale, NR796376

Salen and Ulva, NM573431
Sandbank, NS163803
Skipness, NR902579
South Knapdale, NR781775
Southend, NR698094
Strachur and Strathlachlan:
    Strachur, NN096014
    Strathlachlan, NS022958
Strathfillan:
    Crianlarich, NN387252
    Bridge of Orchy, NN297395
Strone and Ardentinny:
    Strone, NS193806
    Ardentinny, NS188876
Tarbert, NR863686
The United Church of Bute, NS086637
Tiree:
    Heylipol, NL964432
    Kirkapol, NM041468
Tobermory, NM504554
Torosay and Kinlochspelvie, NM721367
Toward, NS135679:
    Inverchaolain, NS091753

22. Presbytery of Falkirk
Airth, NS898878
Blackbraes and Shieldhill, NS899769
Bo'ness: Old, NS994813
Bo'ness: St Andrew's, NT007813
Bonnybridge: St Helen's, NS821804
Bothkennar and Carronshore, NS903834
Brightons, NS928778
Carriden, NT019812:
    Blackness, NT053798
Cumbernauld: Abronhill, NS781758
Cumbernauld: Condorrat, NS732730
Cumbernauld: Kildrum, NS767747
Cumbernauld: Old, NS764760
Cumbernauld: St Mungo's, NS757745
Denny: Old, NS812828
Denny: Westpark, NS809828
Dunipace, NS807833
Falkirk: Bainsford, NS887814
Falkirk: Camelon, NS873804
Falkirk: Erskine, NS884798
Falkirk: Grahamston United, NS889807
Falkirk: Laurieston, NS913794
Falkirk: Old and St Modan's, NS887800
Falkirk: St Andrew's West, NS887801
Falkirk: St James', NS893806
Grangemouth: Abbotsgrange, NS928817
Grangemouth: Kirk of the Holy Rood, NS931805
Grangemouth: Zetland, NS931818
Haggs, NS791793
Larbert: East, NS871829
Larbert: Old, NS856822
Larbert: West, NS863827
Muiravonside, NS956770
Polmont: Old, NS937793
Redding and Westquarter, NS921786
Slamannan, NS856734
Stenhouse and Carron, NS876831

23. Presbytery of Stirling
Aberfoyle, NN514013
Alloa: Ludgate, NS884927
Alloa: St Mungo's, NS883926
Alva, NS882970
Balfron, NS547893
Balquhidder, NN536209
Bannockburn: Allan, NS810903

Bannockburn: Ladywell, NS803907
Bridge of Allan, NS791974
Buchanan, NS443903
Buchlyvie, NS577939
Callander, NN629077:
    Trossachs, NN515066
Cambusbarron: The Bruce Memorial, NS778924
Clackmannan, NS910918
Cowie and Plean:
    Cowie, NS837892
    Plean, NS836867
Dollar, NS964980
Drymen, NS474881
Dunblane: Cathedral, NN782014
Dunblane: St Blane's, NN783014
Fallin, NS844913
Fintry, NS627862
Gargunnock, NS707943
Gartmore, NS521971
Glendevon, NN979051
Killearn, NS523861
Killin and Ardeonaig, NN573332:
    Morenish, NN607356
Kilmadock, NN727016
Kincardine-in-Menteith, NS719988
Kippen, NS650948
Lecropt, NS781979
Logie, NS818968
Menstrie, NS849969
Muckhart, NO001010
Norrieston, NN670001
Port of Menteith, NN583012
Sauchie and Coalsnaughton, NS897945
Stirling: Allan Park South, NS795933
Stirling: Church of the Holy Rude, NS792937
Stirling: North, NS802920
Stirling: St Columba's, NS796930
Stirling: St Mark's, NS791948
Stirling: St Ninian's Old, NS795916
Stirling: Viewfield, NS795938
Strathblane, NS557797
Tillicoultry, NS923968
Tullibody: St Serf's, NS860954

24. Presbytery of Dunfermline
Aberdour: St Fillan's, NT193855
Beath and Cowdenbeath: North, NT166925
Cairneyhill, NT052863
Carnock and Oakley:
    Carnock, NT043890
    Oakley, NT025890
Cowdenbeath: Trinity:
    Cowdenbeath, NT157908
    Crossgates, NT145893
Culross and Torryburn:
    Culross, NS989863
    Torryburn, NT027861
    Valleyfield, NT003866
Dalgety, NT155836
Dunfermline: Abbey, NT090873
Dunfermline: East, NT127864
Dunfermline: Gillespie Memorial, NT090876
Dunfermline: North, NT086879
Dunfermline: St Andrew's Erskine, NT107884
Dunfermline: St Leonard's, NT096869
Dunfermline: St Margaret's, NT114878
Dunfermline: St Ninian's, NT113868
Dunfermline: Townhill and Kingseat:
    Townhill, NT106894
    Kingseat, NT126904
Inverkeithing, NT131830

Kelty, NT144942
Limekilns, NT078833
Lochgelly and Benarty: St Serf's:
  Lochgelly, NT186933
  Ballingry, NT173977
North Queensferry, NT132808
Rosyth, NT114839
Saline and Blairingone, NT023924
Tulliallan and Kincardine, NS933879

25. Presbytery of Kirkcaldy
Auchterderran: St Fothad's, NT214960
Auchtertool, NT207902
Buckhaven and Wemyss:
  Buckhaven, NT358981
  Wemyss, NT336968
  West Wemyss, NT328949
Burntisland, NT234857
Dysart: St Clair:
  Dysart, NT302931
  Kirkcaldy: Viewforth, NT294936
Glenrothes: Christ's Kirk, NO275023
Glenrothes: St Columba's, NO270009
Glenrothes: St Margaret's, NO285002
Glenrothes: St Ninian's, NO257007
Kennoway, Windygates and Balgonie: St Kenneth's:
  Kennoway, NO350027
  Windygates, NO345006
Kinghorn, NT272869
Kinglassie, NT227985
Kirkcaldy: Abbotshall, NT274913
Kirkcaldy: Bennochy, NT275925
Kirkcaldy: Linktown, NT278910
Kirkcaldy: Pathhead, NT291928
Kirkcaldy: St Bryce Kirk, NT279917
Kirkcaldy: Templehall, NT265934
Kirkcaldy: Torbain, NT259939
Leslie: Trinity, NT247015
Leven, NO383009
Markinch, NO297019
Methil: Wellesley, NT370994
Methilhill and Denbeath, NT357999
Thornton, NT289976

26. Presbytery of St Andrews
Abdie and Dunbog, NO257167
Anstruther, NO567037
Auchtermuchty, NO238117
Balmerino, NO368245:
  Gauldry, NO379239
Boarhills and Dunino:
  Boarhills, NO562137
  Dunino, NO541109
Cameron, NO484116
Carnbee, NO532065
Cellardyke, NO574037
Ceres, Kemback and Springfield:
  Ceres, NO399117
  Kemback, NO419151
  Springfield, NO342119
Crail, NO613080
Creich, Flisk and Kilmany:
  Creich, NO328200
  Kilmany, NO388217
Cupar: Old and St Michael of Tarvit,
  NO373143
Cupar: St John's and Dairsie United:
  Cupar: St John's, NO373147
  Dairsie, NO413173
Edenshead and Strathmiglo, NO217103
Elie, Kilconquhar and Colinsburgh:

Elie, NO491001
Kilconquhar, NO485020
Colinsburgh, NO475034
Falkland, NO252074
Freuchie, NO283067
Howe of Fife:
  Collessie, NO287133
  Cults, NO347099
  Kettle, NO310083
  Ladybank, NO302102
Kilrenny, NO575049
Kingsbarns, NO593121
Largo and Newburn, NO423035
Largo: St David's, NO419026
Largoward, NO469077
Leuchars: St Athernase, NO455214
Monimail, NO303142
Newburgh, NO240183
Newport-on-Tay, NO422280
Pittenweem, NO549026
St Andrews: Holy Trinity, NO509167
St Andrews: Hope Park and Martyrs', NO505167
St Andrews: St Leonard's, NO502164
St Monans, NO523014
Strathkinness, NO460163
Tayport, NO458286
Wormit, NO403267

27. Presbytery of Dunkeld and Meigle
Aberfeldy, NN854491
Alyth, NO243488
Amulree and Strathbraan, NN899366
Ardler, Kettins and Meigle:
  Kettins, NO238390
  Meigle, NO287446
Bendochy, NO218415
Blair Atholl, NN874654:
  Struan, NN808654
Blairgowrie, NO177454
Braes of Rannoch, NN507566
Caputh and Clunie:
  Caputh, NO088401
  Clunie, NO109440
Coupar Angus: Abbey, NO223398
Dull and Weem, NN844497
Dunkeld: Cathedral, NO024426:
  Little Dunkeld, NO028423
  Dowally, NO001480
Fortingall and Glenlyon:
  Fortingall, NN742471
  Glenlyon, NN588475
Foss and Rannoch:
  Foss, NN790581
  Rannoch, NN663585
Grantully, Logierait and Strathtay:
  Logierait, NN967520
  Strathtay, NN908532
Kenmore and Lawers, NN772454
Kinclaven, NO151385
Kirkmichael, Straloch and Glenshee:
  Kirkmichael, NO081601
  Glenshee, NO109702
Pitlochry, NO940582
Rattray, NO190457
Tenandry, NN911615

28. Presbytery of Perth
Abernethy and Dron and Arngask:
  Abernethy, NO190164
  Arngask (Glenfarg), NO133104
Almondbank and Tibbermore, NO065264

Ardoch, NO839098
Auchterarder, NN948129
Auchtergaven and Moneydie, NO061347
Blackford, NN899092
Cargill Burrelton, NO202377
Cleish, NT095981
Collace, NO197320
Comrie, NN770221
Crieff, NN867219
Dunbarney and Forgandenny:
    Dunbarney, NO130185
    Forgandenny, NO087183
Dundurn, NN697241
Errol, NO253230
Fossoway: St Serf's and Devonside, NO033001
Fowlis Wester, Madderty and Monzie:
    Fowlis Wester, NN928241
    Madderty, NN947217
    Monzie, NN879250
Gask, NO003203
Kilspindie and Rait, NO220258
Kinross, NO118023
Methven and Logiealmond, NO026260
Muthill, NN868171
Orwell and Portmoak:
    Orwell, NO121051
    Portmoak, NO183019
Perth: Craigie and Moncreiffe:
    Craigie, NO110228
    Moncreiffe, NO113218
Perth: Kinnoull, NO123235
Perth: Letham St Mark's, NO095243
Perth: North, NO116237
Perth: Riverside, NO110256
Perth: St John's Kirk of Perth, NO119235
Perth: St Leonard's-in-the-Fields, NO117232
Perth: St Matthew's, NO121235
Redgorton and Stanley, NO110329
St Madoes and Kinfauns, NO197212
Scone and St Martins:
    Scone, NO136262
    St David's Stormontfield, NO108298
    St Martins, NO154304
The Stewartry of Strathearn:
    Aberdalgie and Dupplin, NO079203
    Aberuthven, NN979155
    Forteviot, NO052175
    Dunning, NO020147
Trinity Gask and Kinkell, NN963183

29. Presbytery of Dundee
Abernyte, NO267311
Auchterhouse, NO342381
Dundee: Balgay, NO385309
Dundee: Barnhill St Margaret's, NO478316
Dundee: Broughty Ferry New Kirk, NO464309
Dundee: Broughty Ferry St James', NO460307
Dundee: Broughty Ferry St Luke's and Queen Street,
    NO457312
Dundee: Broughty Ferry St Stephen's and West,
    NO458309
Dundee: Camperdown, NO363320
Dundee: Chalmers Ardler, NO377333
Dundee: Coldside, NO403316
Dundee: Craigiebank, NO429315
Dundee: Douglas and Mid Craigie, NO444322
Dundee: Downfield South, NO389336
Dundee: Dundee St Mary's, NO401301
Dundee: Fintry, NO423334
Dundee: Lochee, NO377318
Dundee: Logie and St John's Cross, NO386299

Dundee: Mains, NO403337
Dundee: Meadowside St Paul's, NO402300
Dundee: Menzieshill, NO362312
Dundee: St Andrew's, NO404307
Dundee: St David's High Kirk:
    St David's North, NO391318
    High Kirk, NO394313
Dundee: Steeple, NO402301
Dundee: Stobswell, NO411315
Dundee: Strathmartine, NO384343
Dundee: Trinity, NO410310
Dundee: West, NO395297
Dundee: Whitfield, NO435334
Fowlis and Liff:
    Fowlis, NO322334
    Liff, NO333328
Inchture and Kinnaird:
    Inchture, NO281288
    Kinnaird, NO243287
Invergowrie, NO346304
Longforgan, NO309300
Lundie and Muirhead:
    Lundie, NO291366
    Muirhead, NO342345
Monifieth:
    Panmure, NO500327
    St Rule's, NO495323
    South, NO493324
Monikie and Newbigging and Murroes and Tealing:
    Monikie, NO518388
    Murroes, NO461351

30. Presbytery of Angus
Aberlemno, NO523555
Arbirlot, NO602406
Arbroath: Knox's, NO638414
Arbroath: Old and Abbey, NO644413
Arbroath: St Andrew's, NO643414
Arbroath: St Vigean's, NO638429
Arbroath: West Kirk, NO636410
Barry, NO541346
Brechin: Cathedral, NO595601:
    Stracathro, NO617657
Brechin: Gardner Memorial, NO601602
Carmyllie, NO549426
Carnoustie, NO559346
Carnoustie: Panbride, NO570347:
    Panbride, NO572358
Colliston, NO604453
Dun and Hillside:
    Dun, NO664600
    Hillside, NO709609
Dunnichen, Letham and Kirkden, NO528488
Eassie, Nevay and Newtyle:
    Eassie and Nevay, NO333450
    Newtyle, NO296413
Edzell Lethnot Glenesk:
    Edzell Lethnot, NO599693
    Glenesk, NO497795
Farnell, NO627554
Fern Careston Menmuir:
    Fern, NO484616
    Careston, NO528603
Forfar: East and Old, NO457506
Forfar: Lowson Memorial, NO465509
Forfar: St Margaret's, NO454505
Friockheim Kinnell, NO592497
Glamis, Inverarity and Kinnettles:
    Glamis, NO386469
    Inverarity, NO453443
Guthrie and Rescobie:

Guthrie, NO568505
Rescobie, NO509521
Inchbrayock, NO714567
Inverkeilor and Lunan, NO664496
Kirriemuir: St Andrew's, NO386535
Montrose: Melville South, NO713575
Montrose: Old and St Andrew's, NO715578
Oathlaw Tannadice, NO475581
The Glens and Kirriemuir: Old:
    Kirriemuir Old, NO386539
    Cortachy, NO396597
    Glen Prosen, NO328657
    Memus, NO427590
The Isla Parishes:
    Airlie, NO313515
    Glenisla, NO215604
    Kilry, NO246538

31. Presbytery of Aberdeen
Aberdeen: Bridge of Don Oldmachar, NJ928121
Aberdeen: Cove, meets in Loirston Primary School
Aberdeen: Craigiebuckler, NJ907053
Aberdeen: Ferryhill, NJ937051
Aberdeen: Garthdee, NJ918034
Aberdeen: Gilcomston South, NJ935058
Aberdeen: High Hilton, NJ923078
Aberdeen: Holburn West, NJ926052
Aberdeen: Mannofield, NJ917045
Aberdeen: Mastrick, NJ902073
Aberdeen: Middlefield, NJ911088
Aberdeen: Midstocket, NJ919066
Aberdeen: New Stockethill, meets in community
    centre
Aberdeen: Northfield, NJ903085
Aberdeen: Queen Street, NJ943064
Aberdeen: Queen's Cross, NJ925058
Aberdeen: Rubislaw, NJ924058
Aberdeen: Ruthrieston West, NJ924042
Aberdeen: St Columba's Bridge of Don, NJ935104
Aberdeen: St George's Tillydrone, NJ931090
Aberdeen: St John's Church for Deaf People, meets in
    Aberdeen: St Mark's
Aberdeen: St Machar's Cathedral, NJ939088
Aberdeen: St Mark's, NJ937063
Aberdeen: St Mary's, NJ943081
Aberdeen: St Nicholas Kincorth, South of, NJ934033
Aberdeen: St Nicholas Uniting, Kirk of, NJ941063
Aberdeen: St Stephen's, NJ936074
Aberdeen: South Holburn, NJ930042
Aberdeen: Summerhill, NJ904063
Aberdeen: Torry St Fittick's, NJ947050
Aberdeen: Woodside, NJ924088
Bucksburn Stoneywood, NJ897096
Cults, NJ886026
Dyce, NJ887130
Kingswells, NJ869063
Newhills, NJ876095
Peterculter, NJ841007

32. Presbytery of Kincardine and Deeside
Aberluthnott, NO687656:
    Luthermuir, NO655685
Aboyne and Dinnet, NO525983
Arbuthnott, Bervie and Kinneff:
    Arbuthnott, NO801746
    Bervie, NO830727
Banchory-Devenick and
    Maryculter/Cookney:
    Banchory-Devenick, NJ907024
    Maryculter/Cookney, NO857993
Banchory-Ternan: East, NO707958

Banchory-Ternan: West, NO693957
Birse and Feughside, NO605925
Braemar and Crathie:
    Braemar, NO150913
    Crathie, NO265949
Cromar:
    Coull, NJ512024
    Tarland, NJ485047
Drumoak-Durris:
    Drumoak, NO792993
    Durris, NO772965
Glenmuick (Ballater), NO369957
Glengairn, NJ300012
Laurencekirk, NO718717
Mearns Coastal:
    Johnshaven, NO798672
    St Cyrus, NO750648
Mid Deeside:
    Kincardine O'Neil, NO594997
    Torphins, NJ626021
Newtonhill, NO911934
Portlethen, NO924966
Stonehaven: Dunnottar, NO863853
Stonehaven: Fetteresso, NO869864
Stonehaven: South, NO872857
West Mearns:
    Fettercairn, NO651735
    Fordoun, NO726784
    Glenbervie, NO766807

33. Presbytery of Gordon
Barthol Chapel, NJ814339
Belhelvie, NJ957184
Blairdaff and Chapel of Garioch:
    Blairdaff, NJ704173
    Chapel of Garioch, NJ716242
Cluny, NJ685124
Culsalmond and Rayne, NJ698302
Cushnie and Tough:
    Cushnie, NJ530108
    Tough, NJ616129
Daviot, NJ750283
Echt, NJ739057
Ellon, NJ959304:
    Slains, NK042290
Fintray Kinellar Keithhall:
    Fintray, NJ841166
    Keithhall, NJ803210
Foveran, NJ999253
Howe Trinity, NJ582157
Huntly Cairnie Glass, NJ530398
Insch-Leslie-Premnay-Oyne,
    NJ631283
Inverurie: St Andrew's, NJ777211
Inverurie: West, NJ774215
Kemnay, NJ737162
Kintore, NJ793163
Meldrum and Bourtie:
    Meldrum, NJ813273
    Bourtie, NJ804248
Methlick, NJ858372
Midmar, NJ699065
Monymusk, NJ684152
New Machar, NJ887194
Noth, NJ497272
Skene, NJ803077:
    Westhill, NJ833072
Strathbogie Drumblade:
    Strathbogie, NJ531399
    Drumblade, NJ588402
Tarves, NJ868312

Udny and Pitmedden:
  Udny, NJ880264
  Pitmedden, NJ893274
Upper Donside:
  Strathdon, NJ355127
  Towie, NJ440129
  Lumsden, NJ475220

34. Presbytery of Buchan
Aberdour, NJ885634
Auchaber United, NJ632411
Auchterless, NJ713415
Banff, NJ689638
Crimond, NK054568
Cruden, NK071366
Deer, NJ979477:
  Fetterangus, NJ987508
Fordyce, NJ587659
Fraserburgh: Old, NJ998671
Fraserburgh: South, NJ998666
Fraserburgh: West, NJ994667
Fyvie, NJ768377
Gardenstown, NJ801648
Inverallochy and Rathen: East, NK043651
King Edward, NJ716579
Longside, NK037473
Lonmay, NK038602
Macduff, NJ701643
Marnoch, NJ628527
Maud and Savoch, NJ927478
Monquhitter and New Byth, NJ803506
New Deer: St Kane's, NJ886469
New Pitsligo, NJ880562
Ordiquhill and Cornhill, NJ587583
Peterhead: Old, NK131462
Peterhead: St Andrew's, NK131465
Peterhead: Trinity, NK132463:
  Boddam, NK133423
Pitsligo, NJ929673
Rathen: West, NK000609
Rothienorman, NJ723357
St Fergus, NK093519
Sandhaven, NJ963675
Strichen and Tyrie:
  Strichen, NJ945554
  Tyrie, NJ930631
Turriff: St Andrew's, NJ729497
Turriff: St Ninian's and Forglen,
  NJ723500
Whitehills, NJ655653

35. Presbytery of Moray
Aberlour, NJ264428:
  Craigellachie, NJ290451
Alves and Burghead:
  Alves, NJ125616
  Burghead, NJ114688
Bellie, NJ345588
Birnie and Pluscarden:
  Birnie, NJ207587
  Pluscarden, NJ149573
Buckie: North, NJ427657
Buckie: South and West, NJ426654
Cullen and Deskford, NJ507664
Dallas, NJ122518
Duffus, Spynie and Hopeman:
  Duffus, NJ168687
  Spynie, NJ183642
  Hopeman, NJ144693
Dyke, NH990584
Edinkillie, NJ020466

Elgin: High, NJ215627
Elgin: St Giles' and St Columba's South:
  St Giles', NJ217628
  St Columba's South, NJ219623
Enzie, NJ397643
Findochty, NJ464682
Forres: St Laurence, NJ035588
Forres: St Leonard's, NJ038591
Keith: North, Newmill, Boharm and
  Rothiemay:
  Keith: North, NJ433507
  Newmill, NJ439527
  Boharm, NJ355505
  Rothiemay, NJ547483
Keith: St Rufus, Botriphnie and Grange:
  Keith: St Rufus, NJ430508
  Botriphnie, NJ375441
  Grange, NJ481515
Kinloss and Findhorn:
  Kinloss, NJ063617
  Findhorn, NJ042642
Knockando, Elchies and Archiestown, NJ186429
Lossiemouth: St Gerardine's High, NJ233706
Lossiemouth: St James', NJ235707
Mortlach and Cabrach:
  Mortlach, NJ324393
  Lower Cabrach, NJ382313
Portknockie, NJ488684
Rafford, NJ061564
Rathven, NJ444657
Rothes, NJ278492
St Andrew's-Lhanbryd and Urquhart, NJ256622
Speymouth, NJ337607

36. Presbytery of Abernethy
Abernethy, NJ007218:
  Nethy Bridge, NJ003203
Alvie and Insh:
  Alvie, NH864093
  Insh, NH837053
Boat of Garten, Duthil and Kincardine:
  Boat of Garten, NH941190
  Duthil, NH908225
  Kincardine, NH938155
Cromdale and Advie, NJ067289
Dulnain Bridge, NH998249
Grantown-on-Spey, NJ032281
Kingussie, NH761007
Laggan, NN615943
Newtonmore, NN715993
Rothiemurchus and Aviemore:
  Rothiemurchus, NH903108
  Aviemore, NH896130
Tomintoul, Glenlivet and Inveraven:
  Tomintoul, NJ169185
  Inveraven, NJ183376

37. Presbytery of Inverness
Ardersier, NH781553
Auldearn and Dalmore, NH919556
Cawdor, NH844499
Croy and Dalcross, NH797498
Culloden: The Barn, NH719461
Daviot and Dunlichity:
  Daviot, NH722394
  Dunlichity, NH660330
Dores and Boleskine:
  Dores, NH601350
  Boleskine, NH507183
Inverness: Crown, NH671452
Inverness: Dalneigh and Bona:

Dalneigh, NH655450
Bona, NH595377
Inverness: East, NH666455
Inverness: Hilton, NH674436
Inverness: Inshes, NH688441
Inverness: Kinmylies, NH646446
Inverness: Ness Bank, NH665448
Inverness: Old High St Stephen's:
Old High, NH665455
St Stephen's, NH670447
Inverness: St Columba
Inverness: Trinity, NH661458
Kilmorack and Erchless:
Beauly, NH525465
Struy, NH402402
Cannich, NH336318
Kiltarlity, NH513413
Kirkhill, NH553454
Moy, Dalarossie and Tomatin:
Dalarossie, NH767242
Tomatin, NH803290
Nairn: Old, NH879564
Nairn: St Ninian's, NH883563
Petty, NH767502
Urquhart and Glenmoriston,
NH509294

38. Presbytery of Lochaber
Acharacle, NM674683
Ardgour, NN011642:
Kingairloch, NM862526
Ardnamurchan, NM488638
Duror, NM993553
Fort Augustus, NH377090
Fort William: Duncansburgh MacIntosh, NN104741
Glencoe: St Munda's, NN083578
Glengarry, NH304012:
Tomdoun, NH154011
Kilmallie:
Achnacarry, NN181873
Caol, NN106762
Corpach, NN092770
Kilmonivaig, NN212819
Kinlochleven, NN187621
Morvern, NM672452
Nether Lochaber, NN031614
North West Lochaber:
Arisaig, NM661866
Canna, NG277054
Eigg, NM481855
Mallaig: St Columba, NM676967
Strontian, NM817617

39. Presbytery of Ross
Alness, NH647693
Avoch, NH701552
Contin, NH457557:
Kinlochluichart, NH317622
Cromarty, NH786674
Dingwall: Castle Street, NH552588
Dingwall: St Clement's, NH548589
Fearn Abbey and Nigg:
Fearn Abbey, NH837773
Nigg, NH825736
Ferintosh, NH543556
Fodderty and Strathpeffer, NH482580
Fortrose and Rosemarkie:
Fortrose, NH728568
Rosemarkie, NH737576
Invergordon, NH707687
Killearnan, NH577494

Kilmuir and Logie Easter:
Kilmuir, NH758732
Logie Easter, NH779757
Kiltearn, NH607662
Knockbain, NH647530:
Kessock, NH655479
Lochbroom and Ullapool:
Lochbroom, NH177848
Ullapool, NH130942
Resolis and Urquhart, meets in Findon Hall, Culbokie
Rosskeen, NH658697
Tain, NH780820
Tarbat, NH917846
Urray and Kilchrist:
Urray, NH509524
Muir of Ord, NH528507

40. Presbytery of Sutherland
Altnaharra and Farr:
Altnaharra, NC568355
Farr, NC708622
Strathnaver, NC694439
Assynt and Stoer, NC093225
Clyne, NC905044
Creich, NH611917
Dornoch Cathedral, NH797897
Durness and Kinlochbervie:
Durness, NC404669
Kinlochbervie, NC221564
Eddrachillis, NC151443
Golspie, NC837003
Kildonan and Loth Helmsdale, ND025154
Kincardine Croick and Edderton:
Ardgay, NH595910
Croick, NH457915
Edderton, NH710847
Lairg, NC583065
Melness and Tongue:
Melness, NC586634
Tongue, NC591570
Rogart, Pitfure, NC715038:
St Callan's, NC739035
Rosehall, NC484013

41. Presbytery of Caithness
Bower, ND238622
Canisbay, ND343728
Dunnet, ND220712
Halkirk and Westerdale, ND131594
Keiss, ND348611
Olrig, ND191682
The North Coast Parish:
Halladale, NC893558
Reay, NC967648
Strathy, NC843653
The Parish of Latheron:
Lybster, ND248361
Dunbeath, ND157295
Thurso: St Peter's and St Andrew's, ND115683
Thurso: West, ND114681
Watten, ND243547
Wick: Pulteneytown and Thrumster:
Pulteneytown, ND365504
Thrumster, ND333447
Wick: St Fergus, ND362512

42. Presbytery of Lochcarron – Skye
Applecross, Lochcarron and Torridon:
Applecross, NG711417
Lochcarron, NG893391
Shieldaig, NG816542

Torridon, NG864572
Bracadale and Duirinish:
  Bracadale, NG355387
  Duirinish, NG251479
Gairloch and Dundonnell:
  Gairloch, NG807756
  Aultbea, NG875886
  Dundonnell, NH019919
Glenelg and Kintail:
  Glenelg, NG813193
  Kintail, NG930213
Kilmuir and Stenscholl:
  Kilmuir, NG389694
  Stenscholl, NG489673
Lochalsh:
  Kirkton, NG829272
  Kyle of Lochalsh, NG761277
  Plockton, NG801331
  Stromeferry, NG863346
Portree, NG482436
Snizort:
  Arnisort, NG348532
  Kensaleyre, NG420517
  Uig, NG398642
Strath and Sleat:
  Broadford, NG642235
  Elgol, NG523143
  Kilmore, NG657069
  Kyleakin, NG751263

43. Presbytery of Uist
Barra, NF670034
Benbecula, NF800519
Berneray and Lochmaddy:
  Berneray, NF920819
  Lochmaddy, NF918684
Carinish, NF811637
Kilmuir and Paible:
  Kilmuir, NF727703
  Sollas, NF802744
Manish-Scarista:
  Manish, NG102892
  Scaristabeg, NG007927
  Leverburgh, NG020868
South Uist:
  Daliburgh, NF754214
  Howmore, NF758364
Tarbert, NG159998

44. Presbytery of Lewis
Barvas, NB360494
Carloway, NB206424
Cross Ness, NB506619
Kinloch:
  Laxay, NB323220
  Lemreway, NB380118
Knock, NB522336
Lochs-Crossbost, NB382255
Lochs-in-Bernera, NB159366
Stornoway: High, NB427330
Stornoway: Martin's Memorial, NB424327
Stornoway: St Columba, NB426330
Uig, NB087347

45. Presbytery of Orkney
Birsay, Harray and Sandwick, HY314179
East Mainland, HY503019
Eday, HY562328
Evie, HY368255
Firth, HY359138

Flotta, ND366931
Hoy and Walls, ND312908
Kirkwall: East, HY451110
Kirkwall: St Magnus Cathedral, HY449108
North Ronaldsay, congregation meets in community
  school, HY758532
Orphir and Stenness:
  Orphir, HY343059
  Stenness, HY311125
Papa Westray, HY496516
Rendall, HY393206
Rousay, HY442278
Sanday, HY659408
Shapinsay, HY497173
South Ronaldsay and Burray, St Margaret's Hope,
  ND449934:
  St Peter's Eastside, ND472908
Stromness, HY254090
Stronsay: Moncur Memorial, HY654252
Westray, HY457462

46. Presbytery of Shetland
Burra Isle, HU371330
Delting:
  Brae, HU359673
  Togon, HU404637
  Mossbank, HU451753
  Muckle Roe, HU342647
Dunrossness and St Ninian's:
  Bigton, HU384213
  Boddam, HU391151
  Fair Isle, HZ206706
Fetlar, HU607905
Lerwick and Bressay:
  Lerwick, HU478411
  Gulberwick, HU443389
  Bressay, HU493410
Nesting and Lunnasting:
  Nesting, HU487578
  Lunna, HU486690
Northmavine:
  Hillswick, HU282771
  North Roe, HU365895
  Ollaberry, HU366806
Sandsting and Aithsting, HU345556
Sandwick, Cunningsburgh and Quarff:
  Sandwick, HU432237
  Cunningsburgh, HU430293
  Quarff, HU429358
Tingwall:
  Scalloway, HU401395
  Veensgarth, HU419437
  Weisdale, HU394526
Unst:
  Baltasound, HP614088
  Uyeasound, HP601011
Walls and Sandness:
  Walls, HU240493
  Mid Walls, HU220502
  Sandness, HU195571
  Papa Stour, HU177600
  Foula, HT969378
Whalsay and Skerries:
  Whalsay, HU555654
  Skerries, HU680717
Yell:
  Cullivoe, HP544021
  Hamnavoe, HU494804
  Mid Yell, HU515907

SECTION 9

Discontinued Parish
and Congregational Names

The following list updates and corrects the 'Index of Discontinued Parish and Congregational Names' printed in the previous edition of the *Year Book*. As before, it lists the parishes of the Church of Scotland and the congregations of the United Presbyterian Church (and its constituent denominations), the Free Church (1843–1900) and the United Free Church (1900–29) whose names have completely disappeared, largely as a consequence of union.

It should be noted, as has been stressed in previous years, that this list is *not* intended to be 'a comprehensive guide to readjustment in the Church of Scotland'; that would require a considerably larger number of pages. Despite the annual reiteration of this statement, the Editor's attention continues to be drawn to the omission from the list of this or that now-vanished congregation whose name does not in fact fall within the criteria for inclusion given below.

The specific purpose of this list is to assist those who are trying to identify the present-day successor of some former parish or congregation whose name is now wholly out of use and which can therefore no longer be easily traced. Where the former name has not disappeared completely, and the whereabouts of the former parish or congregation may therefore be easily established by reference to the name of some existing parish, the former name has not been included in this list. Present-day names, in the right-hand column of this list, may be found in the 'Index of Parishes and Places' near the end of this book.

The following examples will illustrate some of the criteria used to determine whether a name should be included or not:

*   Where all the former congregations in a town have been united into one, as in the case of Melrose or Selkirk, the names of these former congregations have not been included; but in the case of towns with more than one congregation, such as Galashiels or Hawick, the names of the various constituent congregations are listed.
*   The same principle applies in the case of discrete areas of cities. For example, as Dundee: Lochee and Glasgow: Dennistoun New are now the only congregations in Lochee and Dennistoun respectively, there is no need to list Dundee: Lochee St Ninian's, Glasgow: Dennistoun South or any other congregations which had Lochee or Dennistoun in their names.
*   Where a prefix such as North, Old, Little, Mid or the like has been lost but the substantive part of the name has been retained, the former name has not been included: it is assumed that someone searching for Little Dalton or Mid Yell will have no difficulty in connecting these with Dalton or Yell.
*   Where the present name of a united congregation includes the names of some or all of its constituent parts, these former names do not appear in the list: thus, neither Glasgow: Anderston nor Glasgow: Kelvingrove appears, since both names are easily traceable to Glasgow: Anderston Kelvingrove.

Two other criteria for inclusion or exclusion may also be mentioned:

*   Some parishes and congregations have disappeared, and their names have been lost, as a consequence of suppression, dissolution or secession. The names of rural parishes in this category have been included, together with the names of their Presbyteries to assist with identification, but those in towns and cities have not been included, as there will clearly be no difficulty in establishing the general location of the parish or congregation in question.
*   Since 1929, a small number of rural parishes have adopted a new name (for example, Whitehills, formerly Boyndie). The former names of these parishes have been included, but it would have been too unwieldy to include either the vast numbers of such changes of name in towns and cities, especially those which occurred at the time of the 1900 and 1929 unions, or the very many older names of pre-Reformation parishes which were abandoned in earlier centuries (however fascinating a list of such long-vanished names as Fothmuref, Kinbathock and Toskertoun might have been).

In this list, the following abbreviations have been used:

C of S	Church of Scotland
FC	Free Church
R	Relief Church
RP	Reformed Presbyterian Church
UF	United Free Church
UP	United Presbyterian Church
US	United Secession Church

Name no longer used	Present name of parish
Abbey St Bathan's	Langton and Lammermuir Kirk
Abbotrule	charge suppressed: Presbytery of Jedburgh
Aberargie	charge dissolved: Presbytery of Perth
Aberchirder	Marnoch
Aberdalgie	The Stewartry of Strathearn
Aberdeen: Beechgrove	Aberdeen: Midstocket
Aberdeen: Belmont Street	Aberdeen: St Mark's
Aberdeen: Carden Place	Aberdeen: Queen's Cross
Aberdeen: Causewayend	Aberdeen: St Stephen's
Aberdeen: East	Aberdeen: St Mark's
Aberdeen: Gallowgate	Aberdeen: St Mary's
Aberdeen: Greyfriars	Aberdeen: Queen Street
Aberdeen: Hilton	Aberdeen: Woodside
Aberdeen: Holburn Central	Aberdeen: South Holburn
Aberdeen: John Knox Gerrard Street	Aberdeen: Queen Street
Aberdeen: John Knox's (Mounthooly)	Aberdeen: Queen Street
Aberdeen: King Street	Aberdeen: Queen Street
Aberdeen: Melville	Aberdeen: Queen's Cross
Aberdeen: Nelson Street	Aberdeen: Queen Street
Aberdeen: North	Aberdeen: Queen Street
Aberdeen: North of St Andrew	Aberdeen: Queen Street
Aberdeen: Pittodrie	Aberdeen: St Mary's
Aberdeen: Powis	Aberdeen: St Stephen's
Aberdeen: Ruthrieston (C of S)	Aberdeen: South Holburn
Aberdeen: Ruthrieston (FC)	Aberdeen: Ruthrieston West
Aberdeen: South (C of S)	Aberdeen: South of St Nicholas, Kincorth
Aberdeen: South (FC)	Aberdeen: St Mark's
Aberdeen: St Andrew's	Aberdeen: Queen Street
Aberdeen: St Columba's	Aberdeen: High Hilton
Aberdeen: St Mary's	Aberdeen: St Machar's Cathedral
Aberdeen: St Ninian's	Aberdeen: Midstocket
Aberdeen: Trinity (C of S)	Aberdeen: Kirk of St Nicholas Uniting
Aberdeen: Trinity (FC)	Aberdeen: St Mark's
Aberuthven	The Stewartry of Strathearn
Abington	Glencaple
Addiewell	Breich Valley
Afton	New Cumnock
Airdrie: West	Airdrie: New Wellwynd
Airlie	The Isla Parishes
Aldbar	Aberlemno
Aldcambus	Dunglass
Alford	Howe Trinity
Alloa: Chalmers	Alloa: Ludgate
Alloa: Melville	Alloa: Ludgate
Alloa: North	Alloa: Ludgate
Alloa: St Andrew's	Alloa: Ludgate
Alloa: West	Alloa: Ludgate
Altries	charge dissolved: Presbytery of Kincardine and Deeside
Altyre	Rafford
Alvah	Banff
Ancrum	Ale and Teviot United
Annan: Erskine	Annan: St Andrew's
Annan: Greenknowe	Annan: St Andrew's
Anwoth	Gatehouse of Fleet
Arbroath: East	Arbroath: St Andrew's
Arbroath: Erskine	Arbroath: West Kirk
Arbroath: High Street	Arbroath: St Andrew's
Arbroath: Hopemount	Arbroath: St Andrew's

Name no longer used	Present name of parish
Arbroath: Ladyloan	Arbroath: West Kirk
Arbroath: Princes Street	Arbroath: West Kirk
Arbroath: St Columba's	Arbroath: West Kirk
Arbroath: St Margaret's	Arbroath: West Kirk
Arbroath: St Ninian's	Arbroath: St Andrew's
Arbroath: St Paul's	Arbroath: St Andrew's
Ardallie	Deer
Ardclach	charge dissolved: Presbytery of Inverness
Ardwell	Stoneykirk
Arisaig	North West Lochaber
Ascog	The United Church of Bute
Auchindoir	Upper Donside
Auchmithie	Arbroath: St Vigean's
Auldcathie	Dalmeny
Aultbea	Gairloch and Dundonnell
Ayr: Cathcart	Ayr: St Columba
Ayr: Darlington New	Ayr: Auld Kirk of Ayr
Ayr: Darlington Place	Ayr: Auld Kirk of Ayr
Ayr: Lochside	Ayr: St Quivox
Ayr: Martyrs'	Ayr: Auld Kirk of Ayr
Ayr: Sandgate	Ayr: St Columba
Ayr: St John's	Ayr: Auld Kirk of Ayr
Ayr: Trinity	Ayr: St Columba
Ayr: Wallacetown North	Ayr: Newton Wallacetown
Ayr: Wallacetown South	Ayr: Auld Kirk of Ayr
Back	charge dissolved: Presbytery of Lewis
Badcall	Eddrachillis
Balbeggie	Collace
Balfour	charge dissolved: Presbytery of Dundee
Balgedie	Orwell and Portmoak
Baliasta	Unst
Ballachulish	Nether Lochaber
Ballater	Glenmuick
Ballingry	Lochgelly and Benarty: St Serf's
Balmacolm	Howe of Fife
Balmullo	charge dissolved: Presbytery of St Andrews
Balnacross	Tarff and Twynholm
Baltasound	Unst
Banchory-Ternan: North	Banchory-Ternan: West
Banchory-Ternan: South	Banchory-Ternan: West
Bandry	Luss
Bara	Garvald and Morham
Bargrennan	Penninghame
Barnweil	Tarbolton
Barrhead: Westbourne	Barrhead: Arthurlie
Barrock	Dunnet
Bearsden: North	Bearsden: Cross
Bearsden: South	Bearsden: Cross
Bedrule	Ruberslaw
Belkirk	Liddesdale
Benholm	Mearns Coastal
Benvie	Fowlis and Liff
Berriedale	The Parish of Latheron
Binny	Linlithgow: St Michael's
Blackburn	Fintray Kinellar Keithhall
Blackhill	Longside
Blairlogie	congregation seceded: Presbytery of Stirling
Blanefield	Strathblane

Name no longer used	Present name of parish
Blantyre: Anderson	Blantyre: St Andrew's
Blantyre: Burleigh Memorial	Blantyre: St Andrew's
Blantyre: Stonefield	Blantyre: St Andrew's
Blyth Bridge	Kirkurd and Newlands
Boddam	Peterhead: Trinity
Bonhill: North	Alexandria
Borthwick	Tyne Valley Parish
Bothwell: Park	Uddingston: Viewpark
Bourtreebush	Newtonhill
Bow of Fife	Monimail
Bowmore	Kilarrow
Boyndie	Whitehills
Brachollie	Petty
Braco	Ardoch
Braehead	Forth
Brechin: East	Brechin: Gardner Memorial
Brechin: Maison Dieu	Brechin: Cathedral
Brechin: St Columba's	Brechin: Gardner Memorial
Brechin: West	Brechin: Gardner Memorial
Breich	Breich Valley
Bridge of Teith	Kilmadock
Brora	Clyne
Bruan	The Parish of Latheron
Buccleuch	Ettrick and Yarrow
Burnhead	Penpont, Keir and Tynron
Cairnryan	charge dissolved: Presbytery of Wigtown and Stranraer
Cambuslang: Old	Cambuslang
Cambuslang: Rosebank	Cambuslang
Cambuslang: St Andrew's	Cambuslang
Cambuslang: St Paul's	Cambuslang
Cambuslang: Trinity	Cambuslang
Cambuslang: West	Cambuslang
Cambusmichael	Scone and St Martins
Campbeltown: Longrow	Campbeltown: Lorne and Lowland
Campsail	Rosneath: St Modan's
Canna	North West Lochaber
Carbuddo	Guthrie and Rescobie
Cardenden	Auchterderran: St Fothad's
Carlisle	The Border Kirk
Carmichael	Cairngryffe
Carnoch	Contin
Carnousie	Turriff: St Ninian's and Forglen
Carnoustie: St Stephen's	Carnoustie
Carrbridge	Boat of Garten, Duthil and Kincardine
Carruthers	Hoddom, Kirtle-Eaglesfield and Middlebie
Castle Kennedy	Inch
Castleton	Liddesdale
Caterline	Arbuthnott, Bervie and Kinneff
Chapelknowe	congregation seceded: Presbytery of Annandale and Eskdale
Clatt	Noth
Clayshant	Stoneykirk
Climpy	charge dissolved: Presbytery of Lanark
Clola	Deer
Clousta	Sandsting and Aithsting
Clova	The Glens and Kirriemuir: Old
Clydebank: Bank Street	Clydebank: St Cuthbert's
Clydebank: Boquhanran	Clydebank: Kilbowie St Andrew's
Clydebank: Hamilton Memorial	Clydebank: St Cuthbert's

Name no longer used	Present name of parish
Clydebank: Linnvale	Clydebank: St Cuthbert's
Clydebank: St James'	Clydebank: Abbotsford
Clydebank: Union	Clydebank: Kilbowie St Andrew's
Clydebank: West	Clydebank: Abbotsford
Coatbridge: Clifton	Coatbridge: New St Andrew's
Coatbridge: Cliftonhill	Coatbridge: New St Andrew's
Coatbridge: Coatdyke	Coatbridge: New St Andrew's
Coatbridge: Coats	Coatbridge: New St Andrew's
Coatbridge: Dunbeth	Coatbridge: New St Andrew's
Coatbridge: Gartsherrie	Coatbridge: New St Andrew's
Coatbridge: Garturk	Coatbridge: Calder
Coatbridge: Maxwell	Coatbridge: New St Andrew's
Coatbridge: Trinity	Coatbridge: New St Andrew's
Coatbridge: Whifflet	Coatbridge: Calder
Cobbinshaw	charge dissolved: Presbytery of West Lothian
Cockburnspath	Dunglass
Coigach	charge dissolved: Presbytery of Lochcarron – Skye
Coldstone	Cromar
Collessie	Howe of Fife
Corgarff	Upper Donside
Cortachy	The Glens and Kirriemuir: Old
Coull	Cromar
Covington	Cairngryffe
Cowdenbeath: Cairns	Cowdenbeath: Trinity
Cowdenbeath: Guthrie Memorial	Beath and Cowdenbeath: North
Cowdenbeath: West	Cowdenbeath: Trinity
Craggan	Tomintoul, Glenlivet and Inveraven
Craig	Inchbrayock
Craigdam	Tarves
Craigend	Perth: Craigie and Moncreiffe
Crailing	Ale and Teviot United
Cranshaws	Langton and Lammermuir Kirk
Cranstoun	Tyne Valley Parish
Crawford	Glencaple
Crawfordjohn	Glencaple
Cray	Kirkmichael, Straloch and Glenshee
Creetown	Kirkmabreck
Crichton	Tyne Valley Parish
Crofthead	Fauldhouse St Andrew's
Crombie	Culross and Torryburn
Crossgates	Cowdenbeath: Trinity
Cruggleton	Sorbie
Cuikston	Farnell
Culbin	Dyke
Cullicudden	Resolis and Urquhart
Cults	Howe of Fife
Cumbernauld: Baird	Cumbernauld: Old
Cumbernauld: Bridgend	Cumbernauld: Old
Cumbernauld: St Andrew's	Cumbernauld: Old
Dalgarno	Closeburn
Dalguise	Dunkeld
Daliburgh	South Uist
Dalkeith: Buccleuch Street	Dalkeith: St Nicholas Buccleuch
Dalkeith: West (C of S)	Dalkeith: St Nicholas Buccleuch
Dalkeith: West (UP)	Dalkeith: St John's and King's Park
Dalmeath	Huntly Cairnie Glass
Dalreoch	charge dissolved: Presbytery of Perth
Dalry: Courthill	Dalry: Trinity

Name no longer used	Present name of parish
Dalry: St Andrew's	Dalry: Trinity
Dalry: West	Dalry: Trinity
Deerness	East Mainland
Denholm	Ruberslaw
Denny: Broompark	Denny: Westpark
Denny: West	Denny: Westpark
Dennyloanhead	charge dissolved: Presbytery of Falkirk
Dolphinton	Black Mount
Douglas	The Douglas Valley Church
Douglas Water	The Douglas Valley Church
Dowally	Dunkeld
Drainie	Lossiemouth St Gerardine's High
Drumdelgie	Huntly Cairnie Glass
Dumbarrow	charge dissolved: Presbytery of Angus
Dumbarton: Bridgend	Dumbarton: West
Dumbarton: Dalreoch	Dumbarton: West
Dumbarton: High	Dumbarton: Riverside
Dumbarton: Knoxland	Dumbarton: Riverside
Dumbarton: North	Dumbarton: Riverside
Dumbarton: Old	Dumbarton: Riverside
Dumfries: Lincluden	Dumfries: Northwest
Dumfries: Lochside	Dumfries: Northwest
Dumfries: Maxwelltown Laurieknowe	Dumfries: Troqueer
Dumfries: Townhead	Dumfries: St Michael's and South
Dunbeath	The Parish of Latheron
Dunblane: East	Dunblane: St Blane's
Dunblane: Leighton	Dunblane: St Blane's
Dundee: Albert Square	Dundee: Meadowside St Paul's
Dundee: Baxter Park	Dundee: Trinity
Dundee: Broughty Ferry East	Dundee: Broughty Ferry New Kirk
Dundee: Broughty Ferry St Aidan's	Dundee: Broughty Ferry New Kirk
Dundee: Broughty Ferry Union	Dundee: Broughty Ferry St Stephen's and West
Dundee: Chapelshade (FC)	Dundee: Meadowside St Paul's
Dundee: Clepington	Dundee: Coldside
Dundee: Douglas and Angus	Dundee: Douglas and Mid Craigie
Dundee: Downfield North	Dundee: Strathmartine
Dundee: Fairmuir	Dundee: Coldside
Dundee: Hawkhill	Dundee: Meadowside St Paul's
Dundee: Martyrs'	Dundee: Balgay
Dundee: Maryfield	Dundee: Stobswell
Dundee: McCheyne Memorial	Dundee: West
Dundee: Ogilvie	Dundee: Stobswell
Dundee: Park	Dundee: Stobswell
Dundee: Roseangle	Dundee: West
Dundee: Ryehill	Dundee: West
Dundee: St Andrew's (FC)	Dundee: Meadowside St Paul's
Dundee: St Clement's Steeple	Dundee: Steeple
Dundee: St David's (C of S)	Dundee: Steeple
Dundee: St Enoch's	Dundee: Steeple
Dundee: St George's	Dundee: Meadowside St Paul's
Dundee: St John's	Dundee: West
Dundee: St Mark's	Dundee: West
Dundee: St Matthew's	Dundee: Trinity
Dundee: St Paul's	Dundee: Steeple
Dundee: St Peter's	Dundee: West
Dundee: Tay Square	Dundee: Meadowside St Paul's
Dundee: Victoria Street	Dundee: Stobswell
Dundee: Wallacetown	Dundee: Trinity

Name no longer used	Present name of parish
Dundee: Wishart Memorial	Dundee: Steeple
Dundurcas	charge suppressed: Presbytery of Moray
Duneaton	Glencaple
Dunfermline: Chalmers Street	Dunfermline: St Andrew's Erskine
Dunfermline: Maygate	Dunfermline: Gillespie Memorial
Dunfermline: Queen Anne Street	Dunfermline: St Andrew's Erskine
Dungree	Kirkpatrick Juxta
Duninald	Inchbrayock
Dunlappie	Brechin: Cathedral
Dunning	The Stewartry of Strathearn
Dunoon: Gaelic	Dunoon: St John's
Dunoon: Old	Dunoon: The High Kirk
Dunoon: St Cuthbert's	Dunoon: The High Kirk
Dunrod	Kirkcudbright
Dunsyre	Black Mount
Dupplin	The Stewartry of Strathearn
Ecclefechan	Hoddom, Kirtle-Eaglesfield and Middlebie
Ecclesjohn	Dun and Hillside
Ecclesmachan	Strathbrock
Ecclesmoghriodan	Abernethy and Dron and Arngask
Eckford	Ale and Teviot United
Edgerston	Jedburgh: Old and Trinity
Edinburgh: Abbey	Edinburgh: Greenside
Edinburgh: Abbeyhill	Edinburgh: Holyrood Abbey
Edinburgh: Arthur Street	Edinburgh: Kirk o' Field
Edinburgh: Barony	Edinburgh: Greenside
Edinburgh: Belford	Edinburgh: Palmerston Place
Edinburgh: Braid	Edinburgh: Morningside
Edinburgh: Bruntsfield	Edinburgh: Barclay Viewforth
Edinburgh: Buccleuch	Edinburgh: Kirk o' Field
Edinburgh: Cairns Memorial	Edinburgh: Gorgie Dalry
Edinburgh: Candlish	Edinburgh: Polwarth
Edinburgh: Canongate (FC, UP)	Edinburgh: Holy Trinity
Edinburgh: Chalmers	Edinburgh: Barclay Viewforth
Edinburgh: Charteris Memorial	Edinburgh: Kirk o' Field
Edinburgh: Cluny	Edinburgh: Morningside
Edinburgh: College	Edinburgh: Muirhouse St Andrew's
Edinburgh: College Street	Edinburgh: Muirhouse St Andrew's
Edinburgh: Cowgate (FC)	Edinburgh: Muirhouse St Andrew's
Edinburgh: Cowgate (R)	Edinburgh: Barclay Viewforth
Edinburgh: Cowgate (US)	Edinburgh: Mayfield Salisbury
Edinburgh: Davidson	Edinburgh: Stockbridge
Edinburgh: Dean (FC)	Edinburgh: Palmerston Place
Edinburgh: Dean Street	Edinburgh: Stockbridge
Edinburgh: Fountainhall Road	Edinburgh: Mayfield Salisbury
Edinburgh: Grange (C of S)	Edinburgh: Marchmont St Giles
Edinburgh: Grange (FC)	Edinburgh: St Catherine's Argyle
Edinburgh: Guthrie Memorial	Edinburgh: Greenside
Edinburgh: Haymarket	Edinburgh: Gorgie Dalry
Edinburgh: Henderson (C of S)	Edinburgh: Craigmillar Park
Edinburgh: Henderson (UP)	Edinburgh: Richmond Craigmillar
Edinburgh: Hillside	Edinburgh: Greenside
Edinburgh: Holyrood	Edinburgh: Holyrood Abbey
Edinburgh: Hope Park	Edinburgh: Mayfield Salisbury
Edinburgh: Hopetoun	Edinburgh: Greenside
Edinburgh: John Ker Memorial	Edinburgh: Polwarth
Edinburgh: Knox's	Edinburgh: Holy Trinity
Edinburgh: Lady Glenorchy's North	Edinburgh: Greenside

Name no longer used	Present name of parish
Edinburgh: Lady Glenorchy's South	Edinburgh: Holy Trinity
Edinburgh: Lady Yester's	Edinburgh: Greyfriars Tolbooth and Highland
Edinburgh: Lauriston	Edinburgh: Barclay Viewforth
Edinburgh: Lochend	Edinburgh: St Margaret's
Edinburgh: Lothian Road	Edinburgh: Palmerston Place
Edinburgh: Mayfield North	Edinburgh: Mayfield Salisbury
Edinburgh: Mayfield South	Edinburgh: Craigmillar Park
Edinburgh: McCrie	Edinburgh: Kirk o' Field
Edinburgh: McDonald Road	Edinburgh: Broughton St Mary's
Edinburgh: Moray	Edinburgh: Holy Trinity
Edinburgh: Morningside High	Edinburgh: Morningside
Edinburgh: New North (C of S)	Edinburgh: Marchmont St Giles
Edinburgh: New North (FC)	Edinburgh: Greyfriars Tolbooth and Highland
Edinburgh: Newington East	Edinburgh: Kirk o' Field
Edinburgh: Newington South	Edinburgh: Mayfield Salisbury
Edinburgh: Nicolson Street	Edinburgh: Kirk o' Field
Edinburgh: North Morningside	Edinburgh: Morningside United
Edinburgh: North Richmond Street	Edinburgh: Richmond Craigmillar
Edinburgh: Pleasance (FC)	Edinburgh: Muirhouse St Andrew's
Edinburgh: Pleasance (UF)	Edinburgh: Kirk o' Field
Edinburgh: Prestonfield	Edinburgh: Priestfield
Edinburgh: Queen Street (FC)	Edinburgh: St Andrew's and St George's West
Edinburgh: Queen Street (UP)	Edinburgh: Stockbridge
Edinburgh: Restalrig (C of S)	Edinburgh: St Margaret's
Edinburgh: Restalrig (FC)	Edinburgh: New Restalrig
Edinburgh: Rosehall	Edinburgh: Priestfield
Edinburgh: Roxburgh	Edinburgh: Kirk o' Field
Edinburgh: Roxburgh Terrace	Edinburgh: Kirk o' Field
Edinburgh: South Morningside	Edinburgh: Morningside
Edinburgh: St Bernard's	Edinburgh: Stockbridge
Edinburgh: St Bride's	Edinburgh: Gorgie Dalry
Edinburgh: St Colm's	Edinburgh: Gorgie Dalry
Edinburgh: St Columba's	Edinburgh: Greyfriars Tolbooth and Highland
Edinburgh: St David's (C of S)	Edinburgh: Barclay Viewforth
Edinburgh: St David's (FC)	Edinburgh: St David's Broomhouse
Edinburgh: St James' (C of S)	Edinburgh: Greenside
Edinburgh: St James' (FC)	Edinburgh: Inverleith
Edinburgh: St James' Place	Edinburgh: Greenside
Edinburgh: St John's	Edinburgh: Greyfriars Tolbooth and Highland
Edinburgh: St Luke's	Edinburgh: St Andrew's and St George's West
Edinburgh: St Matthew's	Edinburgh: Morningside
Edinburgh: St Oran's	Edinburgh: Greyfriars Tolbooth and Highland
Edinburgh: St Oswald's	Edinburgh: Barclay Viewforth
Edinburgh: St Paul's	Edinburgh: Kirk o' Field
Edinburgh: St Stephen's (C of S)	Edinburgh: Stockbridge
Edinburgh: St Stephen's (FC)	Edinburgh: St Stephen's Comely Bank
Edinburgh: Tolbooth (C of S)	Edinburgh: Greyfriars Tolbooth and Highland
Edinburgh: Tolbooth (FC)	Edinburgh: St Andrew's and St George's West
Edinburgh: Trinity College	Edinburgh: Holy Trinity
Edinburgh: Tynecastle	Edinburgh: Gorgie Dalry
Edinburgh: Warrender	Edinburgh: Marchmont St Giles
Edinburgh: West St Giles	Edinburgh: Marchmont St Giles
Eigg	North West Lochaber
Eilean Finain	Ardnamurchan
Elgin: Moss Street	Elgin: St Giles and St Columba's South
Elgin: South Street	Elgin: St Giles and St Columba's South
Ellem	Langton and Lammermuir Kirk
Elsrickle	Black Mount

Name no longer used	Present name of parish
Eshaness	Northmavine
Essie	Noth
Essil	Speymouth
Ethie	Inverkeilor and Lunan
Ettiltoun	Liddesdale
Ewes Durris	Langholm Eskdalemuir Ewes and Westerkirk
Fala	Tyne Valley Parish
Falkirk: Graham's Road	Falkirk: Grahamston United
Farnua	Kirkhill
Fergushill	Kilwinning: Mansefield Trinity
Ferryden	Inchbrayock
Fetterangus	Deer
Fettercairn	West Mearns
Fetternear	Blairdaff and Chapel of Garioch
Finzean	Birse and Feughside
Fochabers	Bellie
Forbes	Howe Trinity
Ford	Tyne Valley Parish
Fordoun	West Mearns
Forfar: South	Forfar: St Margaret's
Forfar: St James'	Forfar: St Margaret's
Forfar: West	Forfar: St Margaret's
Forgan	Newport-on-Tay
Forgue	Auchaber United
Forres: Castlehill	Forres: St Leonard's
Forres: High	Forres: St Leonard's
Forteviot	The Stewartry of Strathearn
Forvie	Ellon
Foula	Walls and Sandness
Galashiels: East	Galashiels: Trinity
Galashiels: Ladhope	Galashiels: Trinity
Galashiels: South	Galashiels: Trinity
Galashiels: St Aidan's	Galashiels: Trinity
Galashiels: St Andrew's	Galashiels: Trinity
Galashiels: St Columba's	Galashiels: Trinity
Galashiels: St Cuthbert's	Galashiels: Trinity
Galashiels: St Mark's	Galashiels: Trinity
Galashiels: St Ninian's	Galashiels: Trinity
Galtway	Kirkcudbright
Gamrie	charge dissolved: Presbytery of Buchan
Garmouth	Speymouth
Gartly	Noth
Garvell	Kirkmichael, Tinwald and Torthorwald
Garvock	Mearns Coastal
Gauldry	Balmerino
Gelston	Buittle and Kelton
Giffnock: Orchard Park	Giffnock: The Park
Girthon	Gatehouse of Fleet
Girvan: Chalmers	Girvan: North (Old and St Andrew's)
Girvan: Trinity	Girvan: North (Old and St Andrew's)
Glasgow: Abbotsford	Glasgow: Gorbals
Glasgow: Albert Drive	Glasgow: Pollokshields
Glasgow: Auldfield	Glasgow: Pollokshaws
Glasgow: Baillieston Old	Glasgow: Baillieston St Andrew's
Glasgow: Baillieston Rhinsdale	Glasgow: Baillieston St Andrew's
Glasgow: Balornock North	Glasgow: Wallacewell
Glasgow: Barmulloch	Glasgow: Wallacewell
Glasgow: Barrowfield (C of S)	Glasgow: Bridgeton St Francis in the East

Name no longer used	Present name of parish
Glasgow: Barrowfield (RP)	Glasgow: Gallowgate
Glasgow: Bath Street	Glasgow: Renfield St Stephen's
Glasgow: Battlefield East	Glasgow: Clincarthill
Glasgow: Battlefield West	Glasgow: Langside
Glasgow: Bellahouston	Glasgow: Ibrox
Glasgow: Bellgrove	Glasgow: Dennistoun New
Glasgow: Belmont	Glasgow: Kelvinside Hillhead
Glasgow: Berkeley Street	Glasgow: Renfield St Stephen's
Glasgow: Blackfriars	Glasgow: Dennistoun New
Glasgow: Bluevale	Glasgow: Dennistoun New
Glasgow: Blythswood	Glasgow: Renfield St Stephen's
Glasgow: Bridgeton East	Glasgow: Bridgeton St Francis in the East
Glasgow: Bridgeton West	Glasgow: Gallowgate
Glasgow: Buccleuch	Glasgow: Renfield St Stephen's
Glasgow: Burnbank	Glasgow: Lansdowne
Glasgow: Calton New	Glasgow: Gallowgate
Glasgow: Calton Old	Glasgow: Calton Parkhead
Glasgow: Calton Relief	Glasgow: Gallowgate
Glasgow: Cambridge Street	Bishopbriggs: Springfield Cambridge
Glasgow: Candlish Memorial	Glasgow: Govanhill Trinity
Glasgow: Carntyne Old	Glasgow: Shettleston New
Glasgow: Cathcart South	Glasgow: Cathcart Trinity
Glasgow: Central	Glasgow: Gallowgate
Glasgow: Cessnock	Glasgow: Kinning Park
Glasgow: Chalmers (C of S)	Glasgow: Gallowgate
Glasgow: Chalmers (FC)	Glasgow: Gorbals
Glasgow: Claremont	Glasgow: Anderston Kelvingrove
Glasgow: College	Glasgow: Anderston Kelvingrove
Glasgow: Copland Road	Glasgow: Govan and Linthouse
Glasgow: Cowcaddens	Glasgow: Renfield St Stephen's
Glasgow: Cowlairs	Glasgow: Springburn
Glasgow: Crosshill	Glasgow: Queen's Park
Glasgow: Dalmarnock (C of S)	Glasgow: Calton Parkhead
Glasgow: Dalmarnock (UF)	Rutherglen: Old
Glasgow: Dean Park	Glasgow: Govan and Linthouse
Glasgow: Dowanhill	Glasgow: Partick Trinity
Glasgow: Dowanvale	Glasgow: Partick South
Glasgow: Drumchapel Old	Glasgow: Drumchapel St Andrew's
Glasgow: East Campbell Street	Glasgow: Dennistoun New
Glasgow: East Park	Glasgow: Kelvin Stevenson Memorial
Glasgow: Eastbank	Glasgow: Shettleston New
Glasgow: Edgar Memorial	Glasgow: Gallowgate
Glasgow: Eglinton Street	Glasgow: Govanhill Trinity
Glasgow: Elder Park	Glasgow: Govan and Linthouse
Glasgow: Elgin Street	Glasgow: Govanhill Trinity
Glasgow: Erskine	Glasgow: Langside
Glasgow: Fairbairn	Rutherglen: Old
Glasgow: Fairfield	Glasgow: Govan and Linthouse
Glasgow: Finnieston	Glasgow: Anderston Kelvingrove
Glasgow: Garnethill	Glasgow: Renfield St Stephen's
Glasgow: Garscube Netherton	Glasgow: Knightswood St Margaret's
Glasgow: Gillespie	Glasgow: Gallowgate
Glasgow: Gordon Park	Glasgow: Whiteinch
Glasgow: Grant Street	Glasgow: Renfield St Stephen's
Glasgow: Greenhead	Glasgow: Gallowgate
Glasgow: Hall Memorial	Rutherglen: Old
Glasgow: Hamilton Crescent	Glasgow: Partick South
Glasgow: Highlanders' Memorial	Glasgow: Knightswood St Margaret's

Name no longer used	Present name of parish
Glasgow: Hyndland (UF)	Glasgow: St John's Renfield
Glasgow: John Knox's	Glasgow: Gorbals
Glasgow: Johnston	Glasgow: Springburn
Glasgow: Jordanvale	Glasgow: Whiteinch
Glasgow: Kelvinhaugh	Glasgow: Anderston Kelvingrove
Glasgow: Kelvinside Botanic Gardens	Glasgow: Kelvinside Hillhead
Glasgow: Kelvinside Old	Glasgow: Kelvin Stevenson Memorial
Glasgow: Kingston	Glasgow: Carnwadric
Glasgow: Lancefield	Glasgow: Anderston Kelvingrove
Glasgow: Langside Avenue	Glasgow: Shawlands
Glasgow: Langside Hill	Glasgow: Clincarthill
Glasgow: Langside Old	Glasgow: Langside
Glasgow: Laurieston (C of S)	Glasgow: Gorbals
Glasgow: Laurieston (FC)	Glasgow: Carnwadric
Glasgow: London Road	Glasgow: Bridgeton St Francis in the East
Glasgow: Lyon Street	Glasgow: Renfield St Stephen's
Glasgow: Macgregor Memorial	Glasgow: Govan and Linthouse
Glasgow: Macmillan	Glasgow: Gallowgate
Glasgow: Martyrs' East	Glasgow: Cathedral
Glasgow: Martyrs' West	Glasgow: Cathedral
Glasgow: Milton	Glasgow: Renfield St Stephen's
Glasgow: Mount Florida	Glasgow: Clincarthill
Glasgow: Netherton St Matthew's	Glasgow: Knightswood St Margaret's
Glasgow: New Cathcart	Glasgow: Cathcart Trinity
Glasgow: Newhall	Glasgow: Bridgeton St Francis in the East
Glasgow: Newton Place	Glasgow: Partick South
Glasgow: Nithsdale	Glasgow: Queen's Park
Glasgow: North Kelvinside	Glasgow: Ruchill Kelvinside
Glasgow: Old Partick	Glasgow: Partick Trinity
Glasgow: Paisley Road	Glasgow: Kinning Park
Glasgow: Partick Anderson	Glasgow: Partick South
Glasgow: Partick East	Glasgow: Partick Trinity
Glasgow: Partick High	Glasgow: Partick South
Glasgow: Phoenix Park	Glasgow: Springburn
Glasgow: Plantation	Glasgow: Kinning Park
Glasgow: Pollok St Aidan's	Glasgow: St James' Pollok
Glasgow: Pollok Street	Glasgow: Kinning Park
Glasgow: Polmadie	Glasgow: Govanhill Trinity
Glasgow: Queen's Cross	Glasgow: Ruchill Kelvinside
Glasgow: Renfield (C of S)	Glasgow: Renfield St Stephen's
Glasgow: Renfield (FC)	Glasgow: St John's Renfield
Glasgow: Renfield Street	Glasgow: Renfield St Stephen's
Glasgow: Renwick	Glasgow: Gorbals
Glasgow: Robertson Memorial	Glasgow: Cathedral
Glasgow: Rockcliffe	Rutherglen: Old
Glasgow: Rockvilla	Glasgow: Possilpark
Glasgow: Rose Street	Glasgow: Langside
Glasgow: Rutherford	Glasgow: Dennistoun New
Glasgow: Shamrock Street	Glasgow: Renfield St Stephen's
Glasgow: Shawholm	Glasgow: Pollokshaws
Glasgow: Shawlands Cross	Glasgow: Shawlands
Glasgow: Shawlands Old	Glasgow: Shawlands
Glasgow: Sighthill	Glasgow: Springburn
Glasgow: Somerville	Glasgow: Springburn
Glasgow: Springbank	Glasgow: Lansdowne
Glasgow: St Andrew's (C of S)	Glasgow: Gallowgate
Glasgow: St Andrew's (FC)	Glasgow: St Andrew's East
Glasgow: St Clement's	Glasgow: Bridgeton St Francis in the East

Name no longer used	Present name of parish
Glasgow: St Columba Gaelic	Glasgow: Govan and Linthouse
Glasgow: St Cuthbert's	Glasgow: Ruchill Kelvinside
Glasgow: St Enoch's (C of S)	Glasgow: St Enoch's Hogganfield
Glasgow: St Enoch's (FC)	Glasgow: Anderston Kelvingrove
Glasgow: St George's (C of S)	Glasgow: St George's Tron
Glasgow: St George's (FC)	Glasgow: Anderston Kelvingrove
Glasgow: St George's Road	Glasgow: Renfield St Stephen's
Glasgow: St James' (C of S)	Glasgow: St James' Pollok
Glasgow: St James' (FC)	Glasgow: Gallowgate
Glasgow: St John's (C of S)	Glasgow: Gallowgate
Glasgow: St John's (FC)	Glasgow: St John's Renfield
Glasgow: St Kenneth's	Glasgow: Govan and Linthouse
Glasgow: St Kiaran's	Glasgow: Govan and Linthouse
Glasgow: St Luke's	Glasgow: Gallowgate
Glasgow: St Mark's	Glasgow: Anderston Kelvingrove
Glasgow: St Mary's Partick	Glasgow: Partick South
Glasgow: St Matthew's (C of S)	Glasgow: Renfield St Stephen's
Glasgow: St Matthew's (FC)	Glasgow: Knightswood St Margaret's
Glasgow: St Ninian's	Glasgow: Gorbals
Glasgow: St Peter's	Glasgow: Anderston Kelvingrove
Glasgow: St Thomas'	Glasgow: Gallowgate
Glasgow: Steven Memorial	Glasgow: Ibrox
Glasgow: Strathbungo	Glasgow: Queen's Park
Glasgow: Summerfield	Rutherglen: Old
Glasgow: Summertown	Glasgow: Govan and Linthouse
Glasgow: Sydney Place	Glasgow: Dennistoun New
Glasgow: The Martyrs'	Glasgow: Cathedral
Glasgow: The Park	Giffnock: The Park
Glasgow: Titwood	Glasgow: Pollokshields
Glasgow: Tradeston	Glasgow: Gorbals
Glasgow: Trinity	Glasgow: Gallowgate
Glasgow: Trinity Duke Street	Glasgow: Dennistoun New
Glasgow: Tron St Anne's	Glasgow: St George's Tron
Glasgow: Union	Glasgow: Carnwadric
Glasgow: Victoria	Glasgow: Queen's Park
Glasgow: Wellfield	Glasgow: Springburn
Glasgow: Wellpark	Glasgow: Dennistoun New
Glasgow: West Scotland Street	Glasgow: Kinning Park
Glasgow: White Memorial	Glasgow: Kinning Park
Glasgow: Whitehill	Glasgow: Dennistoun New
Glasgow: Whitevale (FC)	Glasgow: Gallowgate
Glasgow: Whitevale (UP)	Glasgow: Dennistoun New
Glasgow: Wilton	Glasgow: Kelvin Stevenson Memorial
Glasgow: Woodlands	Glasgow: Wellington
Glasgow: Woodside	Glasgow: Lansdowne
Glasgow: Wynd (C of S)	Glasgow: Gallowgate
Glasgow: Wynd (FC)	Glasgow: Gorbals
Glasgow: Young Street	Glasgow: Dennistoun New
Glen Convinth	Kiltarlity
Glen Ussie	Fodderty and Strathpeffer
Glenapp	Ballantrae
Glenbervie	West Mearns
Glenbuchat	Upper Donside
Glenbuck	Muirkirk
Glencaple	Caerlaverock
Glendoick	St Madoes and Kinfauns
Glenfarg	Abernethy and Dron and Arngask
Glengairn	Glenmuick

Name no longer used	Present name of parish
Glengarnock	Kilbirnie: Auld Kirk
Glenisla	The Isla Parishes
Glenluce	Old Luce
Glenmoriston (FC)	Fort Augustus
Glenprosen	The Glens and Kirriemuir: Old
Glenrinnes	Mortlach and Cabrach
Glenshiel	Glenelg and Kintail
Glentanar	Aboyne and Dinnet
Gogar	Edinburgh: Corstorphine Old
Gordon	Monquhitter and New Byth
Graemsay	Stromness
Grangemouth: Dundas	Grangemouth: Abbotsgrange
Grangemouth: Grange	Grangemouth: Zetland
Grangemouth: Kerse	Grangemouth: Abbotsgrange
Grangemouth: Old	Grangemouth: Zetland
Greenloaning	Ardoch
Greenock: Ardgowan	Greenock: Lyle Kirk
Greenock: Augustine	Greenock: East End
Greenock: Cartsburn	Greenock: East End
Greenock: Cartsdyke	Greenock: East End
Greenock: Crawfordsburn	Greenock: East End
Greenock: Finnart	Greenock: Lyle Kirk
Greenock: Gaelic	Greenock: Westburn
Greenock: Greenbank	Greenock: Westburn
Greenock: Martyrs'	Greenock: Westburn
Greenock: Middle	Greenock: Westburn
Greenock: Mount Park	Greenock: Mount Kirk
Greenock: Mount Pleasant	Greenock: Mount Kirk
Greenock: North (C of S)	Greenock: Lyle Kirk
Greenock: North (FC)	Greenock: Westburn
Greenock: Old West	Greenock: Lyle Kirk
Greenock: Sir Michael Street	Greenock: Lyle Kirk
Greenock: South	Greenock: Mount Kirk
Greenock: South Park	Greenock: Mount Kirk
Greenock: St Andrew's	Greenock: Lyle Kirk
Greenock: St Columba's Gaelic	Greenock: Lyle Kirk
Greenock: St George's	Greenock: Westburn
Greenock: St Luke's	Greenock: Westburn
Greenock: St Mark's	Greenock: Westburn
Greenock: St Paul's	Greenock: Lyle Kirk
Greenock: St Thomas'	Greenock: Westburn
Greenock: The Old Kirk	Greenock: Westburn
Greenock: The Union Church	Greenock: Lyle Kirk
Greenock: Trinity	Greenock: Lyle Kirk
Greenock: Union Street	Greenock: Lyle Kirk
Greenock: West	Greenock: Westburn
Gress	Stornoway: St Columba
Guardbridge	Leuchars: St Athernase
Haddington: St John's	Haddington: West
Hamilton: Auchingramont North	Hamilton: North
Hamilton: Avon Street	Hamilton: St Andrew's
Hamilton: Brandon	Hamilton: St Andrew's
Hamilton: Saffronhall Assoc. Anti-Burgher	Hamilton: North
Hardgate	Urr
Hassendean	Ruberslaw
Hawick: East Bank	Hawick: Trinity
Hawick: Orrock	Hawick: St Mary's and Old
Hawick: St Andrew's	Hawick: Trinity

Name no longer used	Present name of parish
Hawick: St George's	Hawick: Teviot
Hawick: St George's West	Hawick: Teviot
Hawick: St John's	Hawick: Trinity
Hawick: St Margaret's	Hawick: Teviot
Hawick: West Port	Hawick: Teviot
Hawick: Wilton South	Hawick: Teviot
Haywood	Forth
Helensburgh: Old	Helensburgh: St Andrew's Kirk
Helensburgh: St Bride's	Helensburgh: St Andrew's Kirk
Helensburgh: St Columba's	Helensburgh: St Andrew's Kirk
Helensburgh: The West Kirk	Helensburgh: St Andrew's Kirk
Heylipol	Tiree
Hillside	Unst
Hillswick	Northmavine
Hilton	Whitsome
Holm	East Mainland
Holywell	The Border Kirk
Holywood	Dumfries: Northwest
Hope Kailzie	charge suppressed: Presbytery of Melrose and Peebles
Horndean	Ladykirk
Howford	charge dissolved: Presbytery of Inverness
Howmore	South Uist
Hume	Kelso Country Churches
Huntly: Princes Street	Strathbogie Drumblade
Inchkenneth	Kilfinichen and Kilvickeon and the Ross of Mull
Inchmartin	Errol
Innerleven: East	Methil: Wellesley
Innerwick	Dunglass
Inverallan	Grantown-on-Spey
Inverchaolain	Toward
Inverkeithny	Auchaber United
Inverness: Merkinch St Mark's	Inverness: Trinity
Inverness: Queen Street	Inverness: Trinity
Inverness: St Mary's	Inverness: Dalneigh and Bona
Inverness: West	Inverness: Inshes
Irving	Gretna, Half Morton and Kirkpatrick Fleming
Johnshaven	Mearns Coastal
Johnstone: East	Johnstone: St Paul's
Johnstone: West	Johnstone: St Paul's
Kames	Kyles
Kearn	Upper Donside
Keig	Howe Trinity
Keith Marischal	Humbie
Keith: South	Keith: North, Newmill, Boharm and Rothiemay
Kelso: East	Kelso: North and Ednam
Kelso: Edenside	Kelso: North and Ednam
Kelso: St John's	Kelso: North and Ednam
Kelso: Trinity	Kelso: North and Ednam
Kennethmont	Noth
Kettle	Howe of Fife
Kilbirnie: Barony	Kilbirnie: Auld Kirk
Kilbirnie: East	Kilbirnie: St Columba's
Kilbirnie: West	Kilbirnie: St Columba's
Kilblaan	Southend
Kilblane	Kirkmahoe
Kilbride (Cowal)	Kyles
Kilbride (Dumfries and Kirkcudbright)	Sanquhar
Kilbride (Lorn)	Kilmore and Oban

Name no longer used	Present name of parish
Kilbride (Stirling)	Dunblane: Cathedral
Kilchattan Bay	The United Church of Bute
Kilchousland	Campbeltown: Highland
Kilcolmkill (Kintyre)	Southend
Kilcolmkill (Lochaber)	Morvern
Kildrummy	Upper Donside
Kilkerran	Campbeltown: Highland
Kilkivan	Campbeltown: Highland
Killintag	Morvern
Kilmacolm: St James'	Kilmacolm: St Columba
Kilmahew	Cardross
Kilmahog	Callander
Kilmarnock: Grange	Kilmarnock: New Laigh Kirk
Kilmarnock: High (C of S)	Kilmarnock: Old High Kirk
Kilmarnock: High (FC)	Kilmarnock: New Laigh Kirk
Kilmarnock: Howard	Kilmarnock: St Andrew's and St Marnock's
Kilmarnock: King Street	Kilmarnock: St Andrew's and St Marnock's
Kilmarnock: Portland Road	Kilmarnock: St Andrew's and St Marnock's
Kilmarrow	Killean and Kilchenzie
Kilmichael (Inverness)	Urquhart and Glenmoriston
Kilmichael (Kintyre)	Campbeltown: Highland
Kilmoir	Brechin: Cathedral
Kilmore	Urquhart and Glenmoriston
Kilmoveonaig	Blair Atholl and Struan
Kilmun: St Andrew's	Strone and Ardentinny
Kilpheder	South Uist
Kilry	The Isla Parishes
Kilwinning: Abbey	Kilwinning: Old
Kilwinning: Erskine	Kilwinning: Old
Kinairney	Midmar
Kincardine O'Neil	Mid Deeside
Kincraig	Alvie and Insh
Kinedar	Lossiemouth: St Gerardine's High
Kingarth	The United Church of Bute
Kingoldrum	The Isla Parishes
Kininmonth	charge dissolved: Presbytery of Buchan
Kinkell	Fintray Kinellar Keithhall
Kinloch	Caputh and Clunie
Kinlochewe	Applecross, Lochcarron and Torridon
Kinlochluichart	Contin
Kinlochrannoch	Foss and Rannoch
Kinneil	Bo'ness: Old
Kinnettas	Fodderty and Strathpeffer
Kinnoir	Huntly Cairnie Glass
Kinrossie	Collace
Kirkandrews	Borgue
Kirkapol	Tiree
Kirkcaldy: Abbotsrood	Kirkcaldy: Bennochy
Kirkcaldy: Bethelfield	Kirkcaldy: Linktown
Kirkcaldy: Dunnikier	Kirkcaldy: Bennochy
Kirkcaldy: Gallatown	Dysart: St Clair
Kirkcaldy: Invertiel	Kirkcaldy: Linktown
Kirkcaldy: Old	Kirkcaldy: St Bryce Kirk
Kirkcaldy: Raith	Kirkcaldy: Abbotshall
Kirkcaldy: Sinclairtown	Dysart: St Clair
Kirkcaldy: St Andrew's	Kirkcaldy: Bennochy
Kirkcaldy: St Brycedale	Kirkcaldy: St Bryce Kirk
Kirkcaldy: St John's	Kirkcaldy: Bennochy

Name no longer used	Present name of parish
Kirkcaldy: Victoria Road	Kirkcaldy: Bennochy
Kirkcaldy: Viewforth	Dysart: St Clair
Kirkchrist	Tarff and Twynholm
Kirkconnel	Gretna, Half Morton and Kirkpatrick Fleming
Kirkcormick	Buittle and Kelton
Kirkdale	Kirkmabreck
Kirkforthar	Markinch
Kirkhope	Ettrick and Yarrow
Kirkintilloch: St Andrew's	Kirkintilloch: St Columba's
Kirkintilloch: St David's	Kirkintilloch: St Columba's
Kirkmadrine (Machars)	Sorbie
Kirkmadrine (Rhinns)	Stoneykirk
Kirkmaiden	Glasserton and Isle of Whithorn
Kirkmichael	Tomintoul, Glenlivet and Inveraven
Kirkpottie	Abernethy and Dron and Arngask
Kirkwall: King Street	Kirkwall: East
Kirkwall: Paterson	Kirkwall: East
Kirriemuir: Bank Street	The Glens and Kirriemuir: Old
Kirriemuir: Barony	The Glens and Kirriemuir: Old
Kirriemuir: Livingstone	Kirriemuir: St Andrew's
Kirriemuir: South	Kirriemuir: St Andrew's
Kirriemuir: St Ninian's	The Glens and Kirriemuir: Old
Kirriemuir: West	The Glens and Kirriemuir: Old
Knoydart	North West Lochaber
Ladybank	Howe of Fife
Lagganallochie	Dunkeld
Lamberton	Foulden and Mordington
Lamington	Glencaple
Lanark: Broomgate	Lanark: Greyfriars
Lanark: Cairns	Lanark: Greyfriars
Lanark: St Kentigern's	Lanark: Greyfriars
Lanark: St Leonard's	Lanark: St Nicholas'
Largieside	Killean and Kilchenzie
Lassodie	Dunfermline: Townhill and Kingseat
Lathones	Largoward
Laurieston	Balmaghie
Laxavoe	Delting
Leadhills	Lowther
Leith: Bonnington	Edinburgh: Leith North
Leith: Claremont	Edinburgh: Leith St Andrew's
Leith: Dalmeny Street	Edinburgh: Pilrig St Paul's
Leith: Elder Memorial	Edinburgh: St John's Oxgangs
Leith: Harper Memorial	Edinburgh: Leith North
Leith: Junction Road	Edinburgh: Leith St Andrew's
Leith: Kirkgate	Edinburgh: Leith South
Leith: South (FC)	Edinburgh: Leith St Andrew's
Leith: St Andrew's Place	Edinburgh: Leith St Andrew's
Leith: St John's	Edinburgh: St John's Oxgangs
Leith: St Nicholas	Edinburgh: Leith North
Leith: St Ninian's	Edinburgh: Leith North
Leith: St Thomas'	Edinburgh: Leith St Andrew's
Lemlair	Kiltearn
Lempitlaw	Kelso: Old and Sprouston
Leny	Callander
Leochel	Cushnie and Tough
Lesmahagow: Cordiner	Lesmahagow: Abbey Green
Lethendy	Caputh and Clunie
Lilliesleaf	Ale and Teviot United

Name no longer used	Present name of parish
Lindowan	Craigrownie
Linlithgow: East	Linlithgow: St Ninian's Craigmailen
Linlithgow: Trinity	Linlithgow: St Ninian's Craigmailen
Lintrathen	The Isla Parishes
Livingston: Tulloch	Livingston: Old
Livingston: West	Livingston: Old
Lochaline	Morvern
Lochcraig	Lochgelly and Benarty: St Serf's
Lochdonhead	Torosay and Kinlochspelvie
Lochearnhead	Balquhidder
Lochlee	Edzell Lethnot Glenesk
Lochryan	Inch
Logie (Dundee)	Fowlis and Liff
Logie (St Andrews)	charge dissolved: Presbytery of St Andrews
Logie Buchan	Ellon
Logie Mar	Cromar
Logie Pert	charge dissolved: Presbytery of Angus
Logie Wester	Ferintosh
Logiebride	Auchtergaven and Moneydie
Longcastle	Kirkinner
Longformacus	Langton and Lammermuir Kirk
Longnewton	Ale and Teviot United
Longridge	Breich Valley
Longtown	The Border Kirk
Luce	Hoddom, Kirtle-Eaglesfield and Middlebie
Lude	Blair Atholl and Struan
Lumphanan	Mid Deeside
Lumphinnans	Beath and Cowdenbeath: North
Lumsden	Upper Donside
Luncarty	Redgorton and Stanley
Lund	Unst
Lybster	The Parish of Latheron
Lynturk	Cushnie and Tough
Mailor	The Stewartry of Strathearn
Mainsriddle	Colvend, Southwick and Kirkbean
Makerstoun	Kelso Country Churches
Mallaig	North West Lochaber
Maryburgh	Ferintosh
Marykirk	Aberluthnott
Maryton	Inchbrayock
Meadowfield	Caldercruix and Longriggend
Meathie	Glamis, Inverarity and Kinnettles
Megget	Ettrick and Yarrow
Melville	charge suppressed: Presbytery of Lothian
Memus	The Glens and Kirriemuir: Old
Methil: East	Innerleven: East
Mid Calder: Bridgend	Kirk of Calder
Mid Calder: St John's	Kirk of Calder
Midholm	congregation seceded: Presbytery of Jedburgh
Migvie	Cromar
Millbrex	Fyvie
Millerston	charge dissolved: Presbytery of Glasgow
Millport	Cumbrae
Milnathort	Orwell and Portmoak
Minto	Ruberslaw
Monecht	charge dissolved: Presbytery of Gordon
Monifieth: North	Monikie and Newbigging and Murroes and Tealing
Montrose: Knox's	Montrose: Melville South

Name no longer used	Present name of parish
Montrose: St George's	Montrose: Old and St Andrew's
Montrose: St John's	Montrose: Old and St Andrew's
Montrose: St Luke's	Montrose: Old and St Andrew's
Montrose: St Paul's	Montrose: Melville South
Montrose: Trinity	Montrose: Old and St Andrew's
Monzievaird	Crieff
Moonzie	charge dissolved: Presbytery of St Andrews
Morton	Thornhill
Mossbank	Delting
Mossgreen	Cowdenbeath: Trinity
Motherwell: Brandon	Motherwell: Crosshill
Motherwell: Cairns	Motherwell: Crosshill
Motherwell: Manse Road	Motherwell: South
Motherwell: South Dalziel	Motherwell: South
Moulin	Pitlochry
Mount Kedar	Cummertrees, Mouswald and Ruthwell
Mow	Linton, Morebattle, Hownam and Yetholm
Moy	Dyke
Moyness	charge dissolved: Presbytery of Moray
Muckersie	The Stewartry of Strathearn
Muirton	Aberluthnott
Murthly	Caputh and Clunie
Musselburgh: Bridge Street	Musselburgh: St Andrew's High
Musselburgh: Millhill	Musselburgh: St Andrew's High
Nairn: High	Nairn: St Ninian's
Nairn: Rosebank	Nairn: St Ninian's
Navar	Edzell Lethnot Glenesk
Nenthorn	Kelso Country Churches
New Leeds	charge dissolved: Presbytery of Buchan
New Liston	Edinburgh: Kirkliston
Newcastleton	Liddesdale
Newdosk	Edzell Lethnot Glenesk
Newmills	Culross and Torryburn
Newseat	Rothienorman
Newton Stewart	Penninghame
Newtongrange	Newbattle
Nigg	charge dissolved: Presbytery of Aberdeen
Nisbet	Ale and Teviot United
North Bute	The United Church of Bute
Norwick	Unst
Ogston	Lossiemouth: St Gerardine's High
Old Cumnock: Crichton Memorial	Old Cumnock: Trinity
Old Cumnock: St Ninian's	Old Cumnock: Trinity
Old Cumnock: West	Old Cumnock: Trinity
Old Kilpatrick: Barclay	Dalmuir: Barclay
Oldhamstocks	Dunglass
Ollaberry	Northmavine
Olnafirth	Delting
Ord	Ordiquhill and Cornhill
Paisley: Canal Street	Paisley: Stow Brae Kirk
Paisley: Castlehead	Paisley: Stow Brae Kirk
Paisley: George Street	Paisley: Glenburn
Paisley: High	Paisley: Oakshaw Trinity
Paisley: Laigh Kirk	Paisley: Stow Brae Kirk
Paisley: Merksworth	Paisley: Wallneuk North
Paisley: Middle	Paisley: Stow Brae Kirk
Paisley: Mossvale	Paisley: Wallneuk North
Paisley: New Street	Paisley: Glenburn

Name no longer used	Present name of parish
Paisley: North	Paisley: Wallneuk North
Paisley: Oakshaw West	Paisley: St Luke's
Paisley: Orr Square	Paisley: Oakshaw Trinity
Paisley: South	Paisley: St Luke's
Paisley: St Andrew's	Paisley: Stow Brae Kirk
Paisley: St George's	Paisley: Stow Brae Kirk
Paisley: St John's	Paisley: Oakshaw Trinity
Paisley: Thread Street	Paisley: Martyrs' Sandyford
Papa Stour	Walls and Sandness
Park	Kinloch
Pathhead	Ormiston
Pathstruie	The Stewartry of Strathearn
Pearston	Dreghorn and Springside
Peebles: West	Peebles: St Andrew's Leckie
Pennersaughs	Hoddom, Kirtle-Eaglesfield and Middlebie
Pentland	Lasswade and Rosewell
Persie	Kirkmichael, Straloch and Glenshee
Perth: Bridgend	Perth: St Matthew's
Perth: East	Perth: St Leonard's-in-the-Fields
Perth: Knox's	Perth: St Leonard's-in-the-Fields
Perth: Middle	Perth: St Matthew's
Perth: St Andrew's	Perth: Riverside
Perth: St Columba's	Perth: North
Perth: St Leonard's	Perth: North
Perth: St Stephen's	Perth: Riverside
Perth: West	Perth: St Matthew's
Perth: Wilson	Perth: St Matthew's
Perth: York Place	Perth: St Leonard's-in-the-Fields
Peterhead: Charlotte Street	Peterhead: Trinity
Peterhead: East	Peterhead: St Andrew's
Peterhead: South	Peterhead: St Andrew's
Peterhead: St Peter's	Peterhead: Trinity
Peterhead: West Associate	Peterhead: Trinity
Pettinain	Cairngryffe
Pitcairn (C of S)	Redgorton and Stanley
Pitcairn (UF)	Almondbank Tibbermore
Pitlessie	Howe of Fife
Pitroddie	St Madoes and Kinfauns
Plockton	Lochalsh
Polmont South	Brightons
Polwarth	Langton and Lammermuir Kirk
Poolewe	Gairloch and Dundonnell
Port Bannatyne	The United Church of Bute
Port Ellen	Kildalton and Oa
Port Glasgow: Clune Park	Port Glasgow: St Andrew's
Port Glasgow: Newark	Port Glasgow: St Andrew's
Port Glasgow: Old	Port Glasgow: St Andrew's
Port Glasgow: Princes Street	Port Glasgow: St Andrew's
Port Glasgow: West	Port Glasgow: St Andrew's
Port Sonachan	Glenorchy and Inishail
Port William	Mochrum
Portobello: Regent Street	Edinburgh: Portobello Old
Portobello: Windsor Place	Edinburgh: Portobello Old
Portsoy	Fordyce
Prestonkirk	Traprain
Prinlaws	Leslie: Trinity
Quarrier's Mount Zion	Kilmacolm: St Columba
Raasay	Portree

Name no longer used	Present name of parish
Rathillet	Creich, Flisk and Kilmany
Rathmuriel	Noth
Reay	The North Coast Parish
Redcastle	Killearnan
Restenneth	Forfar: East and Old
Rhynd	Perth: Craigie and Moncreiffe
Rhynie	Noth
Rickarton	charge dissolved: Presbytery of Kincardine and Deeside
Rigg	Gretna, Half Morton and Kirkpatrick Fleming
Rigside	The Douglas Valley Church
Rinpatrick	Gretna, Half Morton and Kirkpatrick Fleming
Roberton	Glencaple
Rosehearty	Pitsligo
Rossie	Inchture and Kinnaird
Rothesay: Bridgend	The United Church of Bute
Rothesay: Craigmore High	Rothesay: Trinity
Rothesay: Craigmore St Brendan's	The United Church of Bute
Rothesay: High	The United Church of Bute
Rothesay: New	The United Church of Bute
Rothesay: St James'	Rothesay: Trinity
Rothesay: St John's	The United Church of Bute
Rothesay: West	Rothesay: Trinity
Roxburgh	Kelso Country Churches
Rutherglen: East	Rutherglen: Old
Rutherglen: Greenhill	Rutherglen: Old
Rutherglen: Munro	Rutherglen: West and Wardlawhill
Ruthven (Angus)	The Isla Parishes
Ruthven (Gordon)	Huntly Cairnie Glass
Saltcoats: Erskine	Saltcoats: New Trinity
Saltcoats: Landsborough	Saltcoats: New Trinity
Saltcoats: Middle	Saltcoats: New Trinity
Saltcoats: South Beach	Saltcoats: St Cuthbert's
Saltcoats: Trinity	Saltcoats: New Trinity
Saltcoats: West	Saltcoats: New Trinity
Sandhead	Stoneykirk
Saughtree	Liddesdale
Saulseat	Inch
Scalloway	Tingwall
Scatsta	Delting
Sclattie	Blairdaff and Chapel of Garioch
Scone: Abbey	Scone: New
Scone: West	Scone: New
Scoonie	Leven
Scourie	Eddrachillis
Seafield	Portknockie
Sennick	Borgue
Seton	Tranent
Shawbost	Carloway
Shebster	The North Coast Parish
Sheuchan	Stranraer: High
Shieldaig	Applecross, Lochcarron and Torridon
Shiels	Belhelvie
Shottsburn	Kirk o' Shotts
Shurrery	The North Coast Parish
Simprin	Fogo and Swinton
Skerrols	Kilarrow
Skinnet	Halkirk Westerdale
Slains	Ellon

Name no longer used	Present name of parish
Smailholm	Kelso Country Churches
Small Isles	North West Lochaber
South Ballachulish	charge dissolved: Presbytery of Lochaber
Soutra	Tyne Valley Parish
Spittal (Caithness)	Halkirk Westerdale
Spittal (Duns)	charge dissolved: Presbytery of Duns
Springfield	Gretna, Half Morton and Kirkpatrick Fleming
St Andrew's (Orkney)	East Mainland
St Cyrus	Mearns Coastal
St Ola	Kirkwall: St Magnus Cathedral
Stenton	Traprain
Stewartfield	Deer
Stewarton: Cairns	Stewarton: St Columba's
Stewarton: Laigh	Stewarton: St Columba's
Stichill	Kelso Country Churches
Stirling: Craigs	Stirling: St Columba's
Stirling: North (FC)	Stirling: St Columba's
Stobhill	Gorebridge
Stockbridge	Dunglass
Stonehaven: North	Stonehaven: South
Stoneyburn	Breich Valley
Stornoway: James Street	Stornoway: Martin's Memorial
Stracathro	Brechin: Cathedral
Strachan	Birse and Feughside
Stranraer: Bellevilla	Stranraer: St Ninian's
Stranraer: Bridge Street	Stranraer: St Ninian's
Stranraer: Ivy Place	Stranraer: Town Kirk
Stranraer: Old	Stranraer: Town Kirk
Stranraer: St Andrew's	Stranraer: Town Kirk
Stranraer: St Margaret's	Stranraer: High
Stranraer: St Mark's	Stranraer: Town Kirk
Strathaven: West	Strathaven: Avendale Old and Drumclog
Strathconon	Contin
Strathdeveron	Mortlach and Cabrach
Strathdon	Upper Donside
Stratherrick	Dores and Boleskine
Strathgarve	Contin
Strathglass	Kilmorack and Erchless
Strathmartine (C of S)	Dundee: Mains
Strathy	The North Coast Parish
Strowan	Comrie
Suddie	Knockbain
Tarfside	Edzell Lethnot Glenesk
Tarland	Cromar
Tarvit	Cupar: Old and St Michael of Tarvit
Temple	Gorebridge
Thankerton	Cairngryffe
The Bass	North Berwick: St Andrew Blackadder
Tighnabruaich	Kyles
Tongland	Tarff and Twynholm
Torphins	Mid Deeside
Torrance	East Kilbride: Old
Towie	Upper Donside
Trailflat	Kirkmichael, Tinwald and Torthorwald
Trailtrow	Cummertrees, Mouswald and Ruthwell
Trefontaine	Langton and Lammermuir Kirk
Trossachs	Callander
Trumisgarry	Berneray and Lochmaddy

Name no longer used	Present name of parish
Tullibole	Fossoway: St Serf's and Devonside
Tullich	Glenmuick
Tullichetil	Comrie
Tullynessle	Howe Trinity
Tummel	Foss and Rannoch
Tushielaw	Ettrick and Yarrow
Uddingston: Aitkenhead	Uddingston: Viewpark
Uddingston: Chalmers	Uddingston: Old
Uddingston: Trinity	Uddingston: Old
Uig	Snizort
Uphall: North	Strathbrock
Uyeasound	Unst
Walston	Black Mount
Wandel	Glencaple
Wanlockhead	Lowther
Waterbeck	charge dissolved: Presbytery of Annandale and Eskdale
Waternish	Bracadale and Duirinish
Wauchope	Langholm Eskdalemuir Ewes and Westerkirk
Waulkmill	Insch-Leslie-Premnay-Oyne
Weisdale	Tingwall
Wheelkirk	Liddesdale
Whitehill	New Pitsligo
Whiteness	Tingwall
Whittingehame	Traprain
Wick: Bridge Street	Wick: St Fergus
Wick: Central	Wick: Pulteneytown and Thrumster
Wick: Martyrs'	Wick: Pulteneytown and Thrumster
Wick: Old	Wick: St Fergus
Wick: St Andrew's	Wick: Pulteneytown and Thrumster
Wilkieston	Edinburgh: Ratho
Wilsontown	Forth
Wishaw: Chalmers	Wishaw: South Wishaw
Wishaw: Thornlie	Wishaw: South Wishaw
Wiston	Glencaple
Wolfhill	Cargill Burrelton
Wolflee	Hobkirk and Southdean
Woomet	Newton
Ythan Wells	Auchaber United

SECTION 10

Congregational
Statistics
2011

CHURCH OF SCOTLAND
Comparative Statistics: 1971–2011

	2011	*2001*	*1991*	*1981*	*1971*
Communicants	432,348	590,824	770,217	938,930	1,133,515
Elders	34,436	43,499	46,899	47,900	49,478

NOTES ON CONGREGATIONAL STATISTICS

Com Number of communicants at 31 December 2011.

Eld Number of elders at 31 December 2011.

G Membership of the Guild including Young Woman's Group and others as recorded on the 2011 annual return submitted to the Guild Office.

In 11 Ordinary General Income for 2011. Ordinary General Income consists of members' offerings, contributions from congregational organisations, regular fund-raising events, income from investments, deposits and so on. This figure does not include extraordinary or special income, or income from special collections and fund-raising for other charities.

M&M Final amount allocated to congregations after allowing for Presbytery-approved amendments up to 31 December 2011, but before deducting stipend endowments and normal allowances given for stipend purposes in a vacancy.

–18 This figure shows 'the number of children and young people aged 17 years and under who are involved in the life of the congregation'.

(NB: Figures may not be available for new charges created or for congregations which have entered into readjustment late in 2011 or during 2012. Figures might also not be available for congregations which failed to submit the appropriate schedule.)

Congregation	Com	Eld	G	In 11	M&M	–18
1. Edinburgh						
Albany Deaf Church of Edinburgh	115	6	–	–	–	–
Balerno	713	72	37	122,177	72,030	80
Barclay Viewforth	333	33	–	153,823	108,967	47
Blackhall St Columba's	940	82	32	185,351	100,301	53
Bristo Memorial Craigmillar	94	5	17	53,906	21,722	55
Broughton St Mary's	237	30	–	78,114	42,383	84
Canongate	385	42	–	106,028	65,030	20
Carrick Knowe	439	50	71	57,839	37,207	214
Colinton	925	77	–	–	118,503	102
Colinton Mains	177	15	–	53,302	31,840	50
Corstorphine Craigsbank	541	31	–	116,406	54,724	82
Corstorphine Old	473	53	53	88,541	65,357	58
Corstorphine St Anne's	393	46	66	109,230	58,342	64
Corstorphine St Ninian's	795	81	42	163,882	93,519	55
Craigentinny St Christopher's	99	12	–	26,185	19,978	15
Craiglockhart	484	55	30	159,122	91,153	55
Craigmillar Park	234	16	26	90,378	54,798	18
Cramond	1,093	95	–	208,522	151,578	88
Currie	625	44	87	169,281	82,441	65
Dalmeny	109	13	–	19,399	20,027	7
Queensferry	682	51	60	104,048	53,288	122
Davidson's Mains	676	16	40	203,422	110,657	100
Dean	207	22	–	–	37,522	20
Drylaw	123	14	–	20,754	12,354	5
Duddingston	847	54	44	117,890	66,289	140
Fairmilehead	679	62	37	90,143	60,225	70
Gorgie Dalry	308	36	21	88,908	79,092	48
Granton	244	17	–	–	30,171	11
Greenbank	836	83	39	289,742	133,671	82
Greenside	168	31	–	–	37,614	98
Greyfriars Tolbooth and Highland Kirk	356	45	14	–	74,655	25
High (St Giles')	522	39	–	268,375	145,607	8
Holyrood Abbey	218	23	–	217,861	83,590	80
Holy Trinity	227	22	–	149,848	63,709	50
Inverleith St Serf's	499	46	19	117,986	107,906	20
Juniper Green	308	26	–	93,929	59,598	40
Kaimes Lockhart Memorial	40	6	–	–	10,041	8
Liberton	765	80	47	182,676	102,885	90
Kirkliston	294	32	60	95,105	51,427	120
Kirk o' Field	150	21	–	30,743	31,407	1
Leith North	323	37	–	58,427	55,323	55
Leith St Andrew's	300	33	–	90,186	62,517	168
Leith South	438	66	–	118,605	69,659	99
Leith Wardie	556	69	32	149,111	75,755	153
Liberton Northfield	262	11	21	57,821	34,723	24
London Road	212	32	25	52,037	31,949	56
Marchmont St Giles'	240	37	29	112,283	53,272	41
Mayfield Salisbury	576	61	–	225,403	143,257	54

Congregation	Com	Eld	G	In 11	M&M	–18
Morningside	626	93	23	–	113,022	137
Morningside United	236	46	–	94,380	–	15
Muirhouse St Andrew's	49	10	–	18,270	516	80
Murrayfield	525	67	–	154,292	89,546	61
Newhaven	219	18	46	79,300	48,220	136
New Restalrig	163	14	18	–	66,750	34
Old Kirk	111	11	–	24,089	19,004	6
Palmerston Place	424	43	–	170,309	95,906	100
Pilrig St Paul's	259	19	30	41,450	35,458	4
Polwarth	220	25	15	63,738	56,423	25
Portobello Old	314	44	34	77,312	46,459	68
Portobello St James'	341	39	–	46,923	32,542	8
Portobello St Philip's Joppa	575	51	66	152,833	91,423	257
Priestfield	175	22	22	58,720	47,463	10
Ratho	205	18	–	43,471	27,707	21
Reid Memorial	323	21	–	105,096	60,447	20
Richmond Craigmillar	99	12	–	–	8,342	11
St Andrew's and St George's West	361	54	–	–	137,121	4
St Andrew's Clermiston	249	15	–	–	32,513	91
St Catherine's Argyle	294	26	–	161,945	77,564	200
St Cuthbert's	346	51	–	150,465	101,844	14
St David's Broomhouse	157	13	–	32,061	21,299	58
St John's Oxgangs	212	18	32	–	20,444	6
St Margaret's	373	35	18	48,109	34,019	62
St Martin's	97	11	–	18,622	4,687	40
St Michael's	364	29	–	71,379	34,390	15
St Nicholas' Sighthill	381	31	18	45,970	31,401	15
St Stephen's Comely Bank	339	19	–	148,068	67,259	115
Slateford Longstone	261	17	42	52,981	30,220	29
Stenhouse St Aidan's	87	10	–	25,334	19,183	4
Stockbridge	244	25	–	–	66,664	25
Tron Kirk (Gilmerton and Moredun)	106	13	–	25,255	5,721	90

2. West Lothian

Abercorn	75	9	–	14,713	11,932	–
Pardovan, Kingscavil and Winchburgh	276	27	15	52,692	30,585	69
Armadale	554	45	28	78,228	42,154	199
Avonbridge	81	9	–	12,591	6,301	4
Torphichen	247	18	–	63,186	23,116	84
Bathgate: Boghall	258	32	23	78,625	38,800	60
Bathgate: High	473	36	34	84,617	57,983	66
Bathgate: St John's	372	25	35	57,748	36,065	107
Blackburn and Seafield	437	29	–	60,210	37,285	95
Blackridge	85	5	–	33,314	11,132	–
Harthill: St Andrew's	214	12	33	56,044	39,968	75
Breich Valley	209	13	27	29,787	21,642	20
Broxburn	412	32	41	69,422	44,292	155
Fauldhouse: St Andrew's	218	11	–	50,903	30,468	11
Kirknewton and East Calder	346	37	28	110,861	60,001	77
Kirk of Calder	592	46	26	83,912	44,987	59

Congregation	Com	Eld	G	In 11	M&M	–18
Linlithgow: St Michael's	1,413	104	61	299,002	156,463	215
Linlithgow: St Ninian's Craigmailen	456	45	61	73,855	42,126	124
Livingston Ecumenical Parish	538	47	–	119,750	–	218
Livingston: Old	383	40	22	–	53,360	50
Polbeth Harwood	193	–	–	24,371	19,319	–
West Kirk of Calder	269	21	24	42,424	34,215	16
Strathbrock	337	34	20	98,567	66,715	90
Uphall: South	210	24	–	–	34,394	24
Whitburn: Brucefield	268	24	14	71,962	50,689	195
Whitburn: South	384	26	35	67,900	46,541	112

3. Lothian

Congregation	Com	Eld	G	In 11	M&M	–18
Aberlady	252	27	–	–	20,678	28
Gullane	385	34	30	60,863	37,072	68
Athelstaneford	205	13	–	25,238	11,954	9
Whitekirk and Tyninghame	147	14	–	–	20,979	2
Belhaven	684	36	52	75,141	41,505	40
Spott	109	8	–	13,099	6,655	6
Bilston	101	5	19	13,782	3,056	–
Glencorse	313	14	–	26,399	15,642	5
Roslin	252	9	–	24,830	19,933	15
Bolton and Saltoun	147	20	11	28,167	16,399	17
Humbie	82	9	–	17,774	11,104	8
Yester	196	18	11	–	15,612	3
Bonnyrigg	725	63	40	91,024	61,146	30
Cockenzie and Port Seton: Chalmers Memorial	216	36	32	–	46,118	30
Cockenzie and Port Seton: Old	402	15	16	–	21,036	24
Cockpen and Carrington	237	24	44	27,049	16,160	38
Lasswade and Rosewell	357	24	–	30,719	19,615	10
Dalkeith: St John's and King's Park	522	40	23	100,709	49,246	65
Dalkeith: St Nicholas' Buccleuch	403	27	–	77,175	29,722	12
Dirleton	231	15	–	30,424	32,385	10
North Berwick: Abbey	322	30	44	–	40,229	30
Dunbar	588	19	39	80,698	58,911	95
Dunglass	320	16	13	26,118	19,307	–
Garvald and Morham	47	10	–	11,256	4,776	17
Haddington: West	483	32	35	60,230	41,014	34
Gladsmuir	194	16	–	–	15,668	40
Longniddry	395	41	38	75,539	45,653	25
Gorebridge	432	16	–	90,492	51,686	50
Haddington: St Mary's	555	52	–	106,663	74,433	48
Howgate	42	6	–	19,252	7,701	15
Penicuik: South	138	14	–	72,722	51,658	40
Loanhead	333	24	33	58,183	35,664	35
Musselburgh: Northesk	351	35	42	75,388	38,068	108
Musselburgh: St Andrew's High	329	28	28	61,720	32,308	10
Musselburgh: St Clement's and St Ninian's	237	23	–	33,922	20,414	1
Musselburgh: St Michael's Inveresk	443	40	–	–	40,228	20
Newbattle	520	32	26	85,648	39,921	174
Newton	140	9	13	14,678	9,920	30

Congregation	Com	Eld	G	In 11	M&M	–18
North Berwick: St Andrew Blackadder	639	35	30	114,426	69,741	120
Ormiston	183	11	27	–	21,092	19
Pencaitland	260	7	–	–	30,010	38
Penicuik: North	571	36	–	83,268	51,972	85
Penicuik: St Mungo's	393	25	27	72,158	37,857	16
Prestonpans: Prestongrange	346	33	22	48,469	34,156	35
Tranent	244	15	29	47,133	30,453	25
Traprain	468	32	25	62,387	44,903	62
Tyne Valley Parish	363	33	–	60,961	50,643	42

4. Melrose and Peebles

Congregation	Com	Eld	G	In 11	M&M	–18
Ashkirk	60	5	7	11,934	3,470	1
Selkirk	513	18	–	64,036	39,813	16
Bowden and Melrose	921	49	34	113,894	80,084	37
Broughton, Glenholm and Kilbucho	156	11	25	19,290	10,012	–
Skirling	77	7	–	9,237	4,818	9
Stobo and Drumelzier	91	10	–	13,287	9,323	–
Tweedsmuir	36	6	–	–	3,526	7
Caddonfoot	217	17	–	19,884	7,318	12
Galashiels: Trinity	794	48	45	69,421	45,270	–
Carlops	63	15	–	20,452	6,343	–
Kirkurd and Newlands	107	11	19	27,907	11,582	–
West Linton: St Andrew's	228	23	–	39,324	19,014	–
Channelkirk and Lauder	442	29	28	68,698	31,088	25
Earlston	424	18	12	42,007	31,657	21
Eddleston	114	8	9	–	6,062	20
Peebles: Old	566	45	–	105,395	54,603	51
Ettrick and Yarrow	197	16	–	34,579	23,822	9
Galashiels: Old and St Paul's	291	21	29	61,605	39,624	35
Galashiels: St John's	226	14	–	–	28,764	86
Innerleithen, Traquair and Walkerburn	407	33	38	60,669	40,818	100
Lyne and Manor	109	10	–	26,632	16,906	9
Maxton and Mertoun	140	10	–	13,856	12,813	12
Newtown	148	11	–	14,234	6,758	1
St Boswells	226	27	26	36,500	24,820	45
Peebles: St Andrew's Leckie	626	37	–	96,253	53,892	71
Stow: St Mary of Wedale and Heriot	183	13	–	30,762	22,127	28

5. Duns

Congregation	Com	Eld	G	In 11	M&M	–18
Ayton and Burnmouth	173	11	–	17,124	10,109	14
Foulden and Mordington	80	9	–	5,563	5,961	–
Grantshouse and Houndwood and Reston	101	9	15	10,708	10,281	4
Berwick-upon-Tweed: St Andrew's Wallace Green and Lowick	405	24	29	52,699	42,593	12
Bonkyl and Preston	67	7	–	8,085	5,396	–
Chirnside	164	9	17	22,272	14,714	–
Edrom: Allanton	73	5	–	6,662	5,149	5
Coldingham and St Abb's	84	9	8	30,901	21,746	10
Eyemouth	188	19	35	33,990	24,178	2
Coldstream	390	26	–	43,808	25,915	30

Congregation	Com	Eld	G	In 11	M&M	–18
Eccles	76	11	17	9,480	6,231	6
Duns	504	25	36	50,529	29,062	31
Fogo and Swinton	118	4	–	8,293	8,822	2
Ladykirk	28	6	8	11,351	6,931	–
Leitholm	76	8	–	–	4,881	8
Whitsome	39	3	–	3,792	3,360	–
Gordon: St Michael's	70	7	–	–	7,267	8
Greenlaw	105	8	13	20,631	12,443	–
Legerwood	66	7	–	7,287	4,060	8
Westruther	43	8	14	7,119	3,669	30
Hutton and Fishwick and Paxton	74	8	15	14,792	7,397	4
Langton and Lammermuir Kirk	158	17	28	38,501	30,945	1

6. Jedburgh

Congregation	Com	Eld	G	In 11	M&M	–18
Ale and Teviot United	440	31	15	40,229	46,893	12
Cavers and Kirkton	135	10	–	10,829	8,820	–
Hawick: Trinity	783	29	52	53,777	26,874	74
Hawick: Burnfoot	115	12	12	33,496	16,149	98
Hawick: St Mary's and Old	481	26	26	44,189	27,186	96
Hawick: Teviot and Roberton	321	9	8	53,060	33,495	30
Hawick: Wilton	385	27	25	51,611	29,166	80
Teviothead	74	4	–	6,207	3,972	–
Hobkirk and Southdean	174	14	22	15,702	15,220	15
Ruberslaw	278	22	15	34,864	20,875	18
Jedburgh: Old and Trinity	733	19	40	67,449	46,314	3
Kelso Country Churches	218	21	17	31,453	30,356	–
Kelso: Old and Sprouston	568	33	–	51,764	31,649	7
Kelso: North and Ednam	1,213	75	38	145,873	68,301	97
Linton, Morebattle, Hownam and Yetholm	402	26	40	66,585	40,975	50
Oxnam	124	8	–	10,859	4,365	13

7. Annandale and Eskdale

Congregation	Com	Eld	G	In 11	M&M	–18
Annan: Old	393	43	42	75,857	45,447	32
Dornock	145	13	–	–	6,496	14
Annan: St Andrew's	685	45	63	61,760	36,546	104
Brydekirk	60	5	–	–	3,257	–
Applegarth, Sibbaldbie and Johnstone	177	9	6	10,559	11,038	–
Lochmaben	449	23	39	59,086	33,184	16
Canonbie United	121	13	–	33,964	–	18
Liddesdale	145	–	23	40,272	24,757	20
Dalton	109	9	–	11,639	6,748	–
Hightae	85	3	12	10,512	5,663	24
St Mungo	87	–	14	11,508	8,107	6
Gretna: Old, Gretna: St Andrew's Half Morton and Kirkpatrick Fleming	376	23	29	–	26,160	50
Hoddom, Kirtle-Eaglesfield and Middlebie	217	21	26	16,148	16,871	25
Kirkpatrick Juxta	153	8	–	16,121	9,727	–
Moffat: St Andrew's	430	43	27	70,760	45,697	60
Wamphray	54	7	–	9,017	2,738	9
Langholm Eskdalemuir Ewes and Westerkirk	482	39	16	50,573	35,407	–

Congregation	Com	Eld	G	In 11	M&M	–18
Lockerbie: Dryfesdale, Hutton and Corrie	831	48	35	63,160	39,926	28
The Border Kirk	346	45	41	68,533	32,255	25
Tundergarth	50	8	–	10,758	3,362	–
8. Dumfries and Kirkcudbright						
Auchencairn and Rerrick	69	7	–	10,143	6,797	–
Buittle and Kelton	165	16	–	18,220	18,997	–
Balmaclellan and Kells	76	7	17	16,934	15,436	–
Carsphairn	98	10	–	10,551	4,836	8
Dalry	154	13	16	15,895	7,608	2
Balmaghie	83	6	9	10,873	7,764	–
Tarff and Twynholm	168	14	27	27,874	17,383	4
Borgue	47	5	7	3,975	4,280	2
Gatehouse of Fleet	281	20	20	43,924	29,920	14
Caerlaverock	150	8	–	8,948	6,321	4
Dumfries: St Mary's-Greyfriars	606	37	36	70,960	46,417	8
Castle Douglas	403	27	13	56,866	35,139	16
Closeburn	234	13	–	–	17,179	18
Colvend, Southwick and Kirkbean	297	22	22	79,221	49,956	14
Corsock and Kirkpatrick Durham	96	15	21	20,682	14,744	6
Crossmichael and Parton	167	11	15	–	12,281	12
Cummertrees, Mouswald and Ruthwell	204	17	23	–	19,543	–
Dalbeattie	574	35	44	56,984	31,165	–
Urr	195	11	–	–	11,875	17
Dumfries: Maxwelltown West	639	49	49	93,382	52,169	125
Dumfries: Northwest	434	17	16	36,492	28,534	12
Dumfries: St George's	546	42	37	116,260	57,664	58
Dumfries: St Michael's and South	868	45	31	84,187	56,112	115
Dumfries: Troqueer	281	28	34	99,113	58,308	63
Dunscore	241	22	10	52,171	21,911	24
Glencairn and Moniaive	188	15	–	47,032	19,330	12
Durisdeer	153	6	18	19,782	12,757	8
Penpont, Keir and Tynron	174	9	–	22,364	20,798	30
Thornhill	203	12	15	27,041	19,538	–
Irongray, Lochrutton and Terregles	238	27	15	–	26,116	–
Kirkconnel	287	10	–	–	25,223	21
Kirkcudbright	581	28	–	–	53,720	42
Kirkgunzeon	55	6	–	6,829	3,069	–
Lochend and New Abbey	219	18	13	23,725	15,861	8
Kirkmahoe	328	18	32	–	17,481	6
Kirkmichael, Tinwald and Torthorwald	471	42	40	53,558	40,280	15
Sanquhar: St Bride's	441	24	15	39,261	23,893	27
9. Wigtown and Stranraer						
Ervie Kirkcolm	212	15	–	24,968	14,195	33
Leswalt	298	15	16	27,831	16,871	14
Glasserton and Isle of Whithorn	111	7	–	11,774	11,189	–
Whithorn: St Ninian's Priory	322	10	21	49,679	19,342	37
Inch	245	16	11	13,529	12,503	36
Stranraer: Town Kirk	565	47	–	61,274	56,291	52

Congregation	Com	Eld	G	In 11	M&M	–18
Kirkcowan	131	11	–	29,599	18,962	–
Wigtown	185	13	13	33,762	22,282	13
Kirkinner	153	8	14	14,278	9,131	–
Sorbie	141	9	–	18,399	10,120	12
Kirkmabreck	154	12	20	17,027	11,287	–
Monigaff	370	25	–	33,699	24,544	12
Kirkmaiden	220	19	10	25,169	16,417	6
Stoneykirk	335	19	14	45,543	23,138	12
Mochrum	282	21	26	32,831	16,447	29
New Luce	94	7	–	10,238	7,441	6
Old Luce	151	19	31	38,272	24,745	31
Penninghame	466	22	26	65,302	42,221	28
Portpatrick	228	9	25	19,895	13,612	–
Stranraer: St Ninian's	410	20	24	35,385	26,438	18
Stranraer: High Kirk	577	40	25	70,186	46,181	51

10. Ayr

Congregation	Com	Eld	G	In 11	M&M	–18
Alloway	1,182	102	18	202,529	118,945	170
Annbank	281	20	20	29,933	22,490	7
Tarbolton	472	30	25	46,022	31,159	12
Auchinleck	345	21	35	–	28,083	23
Catrine	133	13	23	25,852	14,269	1
Ayr: Auld Kirk of Ayr	544	45	41	76,235	54,019	34
Ayr: Castlehill	632	42	51	94,458	60,809	213
Ayr: Newton Wallacetown	437	55	61	119,851	75,502	229
Ayr: St Andrew's	354	30	9	65,441	47,648	80
Ayr: St Columba	1,353	130	58	227,096	117,464	125
Ayr: St James'	427	42	52	70,006	38,392	132
Ayr: St Leonard's	531	55	29	73,318	45,543	16
Dalrymple	251	17	–	24,195	14,536	–
Ayr: St Quivox	281	27	15	46,859	30,776	8
Ballantrae	250	20	31	34,479	26,520	21
St Colmon (Arnsheen Barrhill and Colmonell)	1,253	11	–	26,321	17,659	6
Barr	69	3	–	4,277	3,660	–
Dailly	157	10	12	14,111	11,847	5
Girvan: South	316	25	37	33,506	19,839	20
Coylton	317	19	–	45,368	18,086	15
Drongan: The Schaw Kirk	213	20	18	34,542	15,155	122
Craigie	119	9	–	11,737	8,059	12
Symington	346	21	23	53,795	32,975	11
Crosshill	183	–	16	16,443	11,054	–
Maybole	364	22	33	53,552	31,289	17
Dalmellington	247	26	52	46,319	28,436	50
Patna: Waterside	134	13	–	20,297	17,051	15
Dundonald	486	43	58	–	49,911	95
Fisherton	120	9	6	10,518	9,606	–
Kirkoswald	232	14	10	24,576	17,450	8
Girvan: North (Old and St Andrew's)	730	52	–	59,368	50,846	84
Kirkmichael	221	18	24	–	12,799	10
Straiton: St Cuthbert's	169	10	12	27,194	12,619	12

Congregation	Com	Eld	G	In 11	M&M	–18
Lugar	163	11	15	–	8,701	25
Old Cumnock: Old	381	20	35	62,011	40,570	43
Mauchline	472	24	46	81,163	50,357	35
Sorn	152	14	13	21,121	12,907	11
Monkton and Prestwick: North	396	30	44	–	60,885	36
Muirkirk	191	16	–	25,620	17,856	6
Old Cumnock: Trinity	377	21	35	60,277	35,338	22
New Cumnock	511	34	37	79,261	38,703	111
Ochiltree	258	20	20	34,569	21,122	16
Stair	217	16	15	30,799	18,120	43
Prestwick: Kingcase	702	82	72	118,998	84,003	232
Prestwick: St Nicholas'	710	77	68	110,786	65,590	189
Prestwick: South	303	37	38	91,176	49,420	85
Troon: Old	994	70	–	133,724	77,843	220
Troon: Portland	624	49	34	119,082	72,870	26
Troon: St Meddan's	951	102	49	178,357	99,744	27

11. Irvine and Kilmarnock

Caldwell	234	17	–	72,825	38,843	35
Dunlop	406	44	26	62,515	37,815	35
Crosshouse	309	34	21	52,848	27,986	79
Darvel	389	30	42	42,892	24,929	30
Dreghorn and Springside	515	48	32	68,708	45,858	40
Fenwick	342	26	28	62,477	44,235	25
Galston	683	61	72	101,892	69,523	75
Hurlford	404	22	33	60,469	36,508	16
Irvine: Fullarton	412	44	50	103,496	60,460	161
Irvine: Girdle Toll	171	14	28	–	20,249	110
Irvine: Mure	367	25	27	76,419	46,263	64
Irvine: Old	421	25	21	–	53,718	9
Irvine: Relief Bourtreehill	246	23	34	44,821	28,409	16
Irvine: St Andrew's	282	15	21	–	38,416	12
Kilmarnock: Henderson	504	63	47	128,509	65,339	–
Kilmarnock: New Laigh Kirk	1,145	82	76	163,253	120,902	181
Kilmarnock: Old High Kirk	147	13	15	32,129	27,296	13
Kilmarnock: Riccarton	283	30	23	69,050	41,675	59
Kilmarnock: St Andrew's and St Marnock's	994	88	45	157,668	97,902	491
Kilmarnock: St John's Onthank	263	22	24	45,724	28,279	125
Kilmarnock: St Kentigern's	285	23	–	58,313	32,690	117
Kilmarnock: St Ninian's Bellfield	206	14	23	30,147	19,542	45
Kilmarnock: Shortlees	96	8	–	20,044	15,700	–
Kilmaurs: St Maur's Glencairn	319	16	27	47,354	29,491	19
Newmilns: Loudoun	295	9	–	–	44,597	38
Stewarton: John Knox	283	33	21	84,082	42,748	40
Stewarton: St Columba's	474	42	37	–	46,308	124

12. Ardrossan

Ardrossan: Barony St John's	279	24	33	50,614	29,101	11
Ardrossan: Park	417	40	43	59,909	39,265	188
Beith	903	56	35	86,177	74,577	40

Congregation	Com	Eld	G	In 11	M&M	–18
Brodick	146	16	–	54,331	27,287	56
Corrie	48	5	–	18,688	9,146	3
Lochranza and Pirnmill	64	6	9	22,168	10,342	3
Shiskine	68	10	16	29,495	11,443	32
Cumbrae	261	25	63	51,937	33,876	68
Dalry: St Margaret's	700	53	31	133,444	68,673	120
Dalry: Trinity	222	18	–	82,696	47,139	44
Fairlie	254	35	42	–	42,983	25
Kilbirnie: Auld Kirk	371	–	14	64,243	27,309	9
Kilbirnie: St Columba's	576	34	20	65,230	35,358	73
Kilmory	42	6	–	13,241	5,038	5
Lamlash	118	15	26	30,653	20,961	17
Kilwinning: Mansefield Trinity	–	–	32	48,783	22,586	–
Kilwinning: Old	622	44	49	110,857	58,612	20
Largs: Clark Memorial	836	97	59	149,666	87,425	58
Largs: St Columba's	422	47	60	99,537	55,914	28
Largs: St John's	813	45	80	154,359	95,506	66
Saltcoats: New Trinity	262	40	22	53,396	37,011	5
Saltcoats: North	315	23	36	47,087	35,842	70
Saltcoats: St Cuthbert's	308	42	16	85,652	52,632	105
Stevenston: Ardeer	284	27	29	35,027	28,717	158
Stevenston: Livingstone	340	35	25	56,044	30,979	13
Stevenston: High	253	22	42	85,276	57,042	29
West Kilbride	699	55	38	121,999	81,437	51
Whiting Bay and Kildonan	102	8	–	42,964	27,025	18

13. Lanark

Congregation	Com	Eld	G	In 11	M&M	–18
Biggar	579	32	35	–	50,699	20
Black Mount	67	8	14	11,951	9,593	–
Culter	29	6	–	–	5,699	–
Libberton and Quothquan	84	12	–	17,262	5,228	10
Cairngryffe	172	14	18	24,153	20,784	10
Symington	198	20	18	32,716	22,070	9
Carluke: Kirkton	815	46	24	102,758	64,811	350
Carluke: St Andrew's	294	15	21	50,973	31,748	38
Carluke: St John's	750	41	40	90,181	51,440	42
Carnwath	276	17	22	34,856	27,585	38
Carstairs and Carstairs Junction	302	25	26	55,781	26,205	80
Coalburn	139	9	18	18,586	8,977	15
Lesmahagow: Old	449	23	23	75,470	42,445	13
Crossford	180	8	–	27,247	18,658	22
Kirkfieldbank	87	9	20	15,277	10,442	8
Forth: St Paul's	373	25	48	67,156	35,411	40
Glencaple	189	12	24	22,238	17,964	9
Lowther	36	4	–	4,744	2,761	3
Kirkmuirhill	297	20	43	99,269	72,210	100
Lanark: Greyfriars	594	40	38	99,916	52,647	196
Lanark: St Nicholas'	537	55	31	–	60,398	95
Law	200	16	32	–	21,340	114

Congregation	Com	Eld	G	In 11	M&M	–18
Lesmahagow: Abbeygreen	224	16	–	106,248	48,210	200
The Douglas Valley Church	361	38	45	57,321	29,395	10

14. Greenock and Paisley

Barrhead: Arthurlie	255	30	27	77,917	53,799	78
Barrhead: Bourock	456	42	47	96,064	53,563	263
Barrhead: South and Levern	402	28	19	81,211	46,720	126
Bishopton	670	55	–	94,509	58,566	106
Bridge of Weir: Freeland	416	52	–	129,440	65,570	78
Bridge of Weir: St Machar's Ranfurly	433	42	34	91,058	54,527	20
Elderslie Kirk	539	55	60	120,641	66,905	171
Erskine	328	32	72	113,747	59,717	226
Gourock: Old Gourock and Ashton	745	56	37	–	76,737	–
Gourock: St John's	596	68	17	126,455	60,075	–
Greenock: East End	57	6	–	11,608	2,200	13
Greenock: Lyle Kirk	919	93	34	–	137,645	346
Greenock: Mount Kirk	320	36	–	57,500	42,660	160
Greenock: St Margaret's	157	22	–	28,161	13,269	16
Greenock: St Ninian's	221	20	–	–	14,950	149
Greenock: Wellpark Mid Kirk	584	42	16	–	57,442	84
Greenock: Westburn	866	100	43	118,965	83,730	160
Houston and Killellan	677	62	72	155,152	88,889	240
Howwood	199	11	20	49,684	29,539	22
Inchinnan	357	36	29	70,156	42,576	140
Inverkip	392	27	28	56,905	34,390	20
Johnstone: High	245	31	40	95,107	52,363	122
Johnstone: St Andrew's Trinity	237	30	21	44,735	33,636	112
Johnstone: St Paul's	458	70	–	78,017	48,831	145
Kilbarchan: East	361	41	27	73,245	44,514	70
Kilbarchan: West	423	48	32	88,661	61,390	47
Kilmacolm: Old	504	50	–	118,505	69,354	30
Kilmacolm: St Columba	530	34	–	–	61,647	101
Langbank	142	13	–	–	19,981	10
Port Glasgow: St Andrew's	572	62	38	–	45,578	379
Linwood	359	24	15	–	39,238	12
Lochwinnoch	150	15	–	39,119	26,084	147
Neilston	611	40	22	–	56,798	–
Paisley: Abbey	737	47	–	–	88,864	95
Paisley: Glenburn	250	19	–	–	27,725	25
Paisley: Lylesland	373	50	36	94,761	50,415	33
Paisley: Martyrs' Sandyford	597	71	21	129,469	56,425	104
Paisley: Oakshaw Trinity	551	90	39	138,836	–	44
Paisley: St Columba Foxbar	187	25	21	30,465	21,965	141
Paisley: St James'	207	32	–	64,648	35,329	14
Paisley: St Luke's	243	25	–	–	35,486	9
Paisley: St Mark's Oldhall	538	60	69	107,805	66,546	45
Paisley: St Ninian's Ferguslie	61	–	–	13,752	1,500	15
Paisley: Sherwood Greenlaw	649	84	45	112,851	71,119	200
Paisley: Stow Brae Kirk	498	75	58	96,901	75,899	81
Paisley: Wallneuk North	415	39	–	–	46,076	16

Congregation	Com	Eld	G	In 11	M&M	–18
Port Glasgow: Hamilton Bardrainney	203	18	17	40,237	25,792	33
Port Glasgow: St Martin's	174	16	–	–	11,623	32
Renfrew: North	612	65	35	101,710	66,896	135
Renfrew: Old	473	26	37	78,813	44,481	178
Renfrew: Trinity	305	31	34	78,956	52,744	218
Skelmorlie and Wemyss Bay	343	35	–	90,547	45,352	14

16. Glasgow

Congregation	Com	Eld	G	In 11	M&M	–18
Banton	74	12	–	14,073	6,993	10
Twechar	70	12	–	16,937	7,726	10
Bishopbriggs: Kenmure	292	27	51	78,692	52,481	140
Bishopbriggs: Springfield Cambridge	689	47	91	119,313	62,405	178
Broom	611	54	34	138,976	87,857	290
Burnside Blairbeth	644	49	93	259,676	142,704	222
Busby	287	39	30	70,817	39,082	40
Cadder	805	83	57	148,908	86,503	208
Cambuslang: Flemington Hallside	313	16	20	48,669	23,581	80
Cambuslang Parish Church	786	66	45	137,400	101,939	141
Campsie	163	15	15	54,437	32,854	100
Chryston	638	34	17	190,442	100,870	110
Eaglesham	591	48	57	160,125	69,117	150
Fernhill and Cathkin	276	27	37	46,980	29,090	74
Gartcosh	140	9	–	21,121	8,996	71
Glenboig	119	11	13	–	7,243	10
Giffnock: Orchardhill	449	53	22	–	89,317	296
Giffnock: South	770	82	55	–	104,252	80
Giffnock: The Park	282	26	–	61,386	39,279	92
Greenbank	922	78	53	204,331	116,811	240
Kilsyth: Anderson	346	20	53	73,065	53,312	117
Kilsyth: Burns and Old	423	29	50	70,530	48,067	76
Kirkintilloch: Hillhead	112	8	14	17,322	7,804	28
Kirkintilloch: St Columba's	472	44	42	90,010	52,382	90
Kirkintilloch: St David's Memorial Park	648	51	34	–	77,961	165
Kirkintilloch: St Mary's	743	47	51	131,575	79,294	–
Lenzie: Old	464	45	–	107,164	64,857	26
Lenzie: Union	694	70	81	185,865	94,205	260
Maxwell Mearns Castle	283	37	–	152,431	89,514	62
Mearns	865	58	–	–	111,246	50
Milton of Campsie	347	38	56	65,829	41,174	108
Netherlee	734	68	36	200,598	110,231	315
Newton Mearns	554	52	20	119,208	70,677	119
Rutherglen: Old	334	30	–	62,457	35,219	39
Rutherglen: Stonelaw	373	38	32	147,167	73,179	48
Rutherglen: West and Wardlawhill	504	51	56	97,076	61,016	19
Stamperland	376	30	24	78,107	40,972	200
Stepps	344	26	–	–	32,408	120
Thornliebank	168	12	42	47,852	30,538	15
Torrance	311	14	–	100,987	47,326	140
Williamwood	439	69	37	113,524	73,851	463
Glasgow: Anderston Kelvingrove	64	10	12	–	17,197	17

Congregation	Com	Eld	G	In 11	M&M	–18
Glasgow: Baillieston Mure Memorial	468	29	94	91,763	50,226	188
Glasgow: Baillieston St Andrew's	331	17	38	59,948	38,863	136
Glasgow: Balshagray Victoria Park	211	35	19	94,308	60,520	59
Glasgow: Barlanark Greyfriars	113	20	15	42,961	24,813	253
Glasgow: Blawarthill	182	23	27	31,809	17,390	121
Glasgow: Bridgeton St Francis in the East	92	16	12	34,339	21,472	5
Glasgow: Broomhill	455	59	56	139,929	80,645	244
Glasgow: Calton Parkhead	87	12	–	33,684	10,253	51
Glasgow: Cardonald	419	41	68	115,672	72,059	243
Glasgow: Carmunnock	321	27	30	49,620	33,979	23
Glasgow: Carmyle	98	5	15	24,179	15,136	20
Glasgow: Kenmuir Mount Vernon	140	11	25	48,018	30,959	65
Glasgow: Carnwadric	147	16	–	35,017	17,881	45
Glasgow: Castlemilk East	126	11	7	16,781	17,008	10
Glasgow: Castlemilk West	92	19	–	21,669	11,160	26
Glasgow: Cathcart Old	269	48	45	98,454	59,042	364
Glasgow: Cathcart Trinity	485	56	55	–	108,821	138
Glasgow: Cathedral (High or St Mungo's)	421	58	–	92,508	77,069	13
Glasgow: Clincarthill	303	37	52	112,490	76,445	142
Glasgow: Colston Milton	80	11	–	25,825	16,054	20
Glasgow: Colston Wellpark	106	14	–	–	22,227	67
Glasgow: Cranhill	45	7	–	13,806	3,581	60
Glasgow: Croftfoot	285	44	42	–	43,742	61
Glasgow: Dennistoun New	301	36	25	106,342	55,276	90
Glasgow: Drumchapel St Andrew's	179	42	–	42,660	38,185	18
Glasgow: Drumchapel St Mark's	75	–	–	10,984	1,814	–
Glasgow: Easterhouse St George's and St Peter's	59	9	–	7,090	173	48
Glasgow: Eastwood	253	46	26	84,669	53,106	95
Glasgow: Gairbraid	177	14	14	34,206	20,098	15
Glasgow: Gallowgate	68	14	–	29,905	7,832	10
Glasgow: Gardner Street	37	–	–	–	–	–
Glasgow: Garthamlock and Craigend East	86	14	–	–	3,057	85
Glasgow: Gorbals	88	13	–	27,510	15,456	25
Glasgow: Govan and Linthouse	250	52	43	–	35,875	146
Glasgow: Govanhill Trinity	88	15	–	28,021	17,345	4
Glasgow: High Carntyne	299	25	58	74,984	44,361	10
Glasgow: Hillington Park	310	34	44	71,465	38,674	130
Glasgow: Househillwood St Christopher's	123	10	–	12,176	7,499	39
Glasgow: Hyndland	254	37	29	89,616	58,919	28
Glasgow: Ibrox	141	21	22	51,188	31,351	97
Glasgow: John Ross Memorial (for Deaf People)	59	6	–	–	–	–
Glasgow: Jordanhill	426	72	33	183,520	102,097	173
Glasgow: Kelvin Stevenson Memorial	139	24	15	36,120	27,923	86
Glasgow: Kelvinside Hillhead	167	27	–	95,816	49,415	99
Glasgow: King's Park	679	82	46	161,359	86,447	145
Glasgow: Kinning Park	138	12	–	37,852	19,203	7
Glasgow: Knightswood St Margaret's	242	29	32	53,133	35,895	53
Glasgow: Langside	195	40	18	79,179	46,346	178
Glasgow: Lansdowne	87	14	–	11,247	6,543	5
Glasgow: Lochwood	66	2	8	–	5,883	88

Congregation	Com	Eld	G	In 11	M&M	–18
Glasgow: Maryhill	166	18	12	42,555	22,723	117
Glasgow: Merrylea	348	66	35	77,176	51,196	125
Glasgow: Mosspark	145	29	39	52,191	34,054	62
Glasgow: Newlands South	532	65	24	170,818	95,790	24
Glasgow: Partick South	159	25	34	–	35,245	130
Glasgow: Partick Trinity	171	27	–	75,326	37,532	56
Glasgow: Penilee St Andrew's	124	23	–	36,847	23,162	125
Glasgow: Pollokshaws	134	22	22	40,709	27,174	49
Glasgow: Pollokshields	210	32	36	–	60,188	27
Glasgow: Possilpark	168	23	19	28,702	16,334	10
Glasgow: Priesthill and Nitshill	118	17	6	35,406	19,351	13
Glasgow: Queen's Park	205	29	33	80,912	47,520	25
Glasgow: Renfield St Stephen's	156	23	32	–	46,510	14
Glasgow: Robroyston	42	–	–	30,169	1,000	69
Glasgow: Ruchazie	31	9	–	5,492	4,959	87
Glasgow: Ruchill Kelvinside	111	19	–	69,119	60,091	21
Glasgow: St Andrew's East	71	16	21	38,245	19,490	37
Glasgow: St Columba	133	14	13	44,522	23,446	21
Glasgow: St David's Knightswood	332	31	32	86,784	57,652	21
Glasgow: St Enoch's Hogganfield	155	17	29	42,892	19,741	8
Glasgow: St George's Tron	380	24	–	61,861	112,681	70
Glasgow: St James' (Pollok)	154	25	21	47,884	32,013	89
Glasgow: St John's Renfield	364	49	–	159,863	90,884	184
Glasgow: St Margaret's Tollcross Park	135	6	–	–	14,758	15
Glasgow: St Nicholas' Cardonald	301	27	12	52,008	36,290	358
Glasgow: St Paul's	63	6	–	–	4,080	136
Glasgow: St Rollox	85	12	–	45,256	17,872	26
Glasgow: Sandyford Henderson Memorial	234	23	21	157,914	83,601	30
Glasgow: Sandyhills	312	29	52	–	41,539	39
Glasgow: Scotstoun	189	11	–	65,496	44,640	20
Glasgow: Shawlands	289	24	34	92,221	55,104	57
Glasgow: Sherbrooke St Gilbert's	375	46	–	126,914	75,841	140
Glasgow: Shettleston New	246	35	32	79,184	43,606	93
Glasgow: Shettleston Old	222	31	21	59,176	24,832	150
Glasgow: South Carntyne	66	7	–	24,654	17,787	32
Glasgow: South Shawlands	180	29	–	74,507	42,392	127
Glasgow: Springburn	232	34	27	58,130	43,149	128
Glasgow: Temple Anniesland	333	30	54	97,710	56,766	71
Glasgow: Toryglen	101	13	–	21,082	12,227	10
Glasgow: Trinity Possil and Henry Drummond	92	8	–	53,483	34,498	24
Glasgow: Tron St Mary's	134	18	–	38,944	25,909	120
Glasgow: Victoria Tollcross	124	14	22	–	15,232	91
Glasgow: Wallacewell	126	–	–	–	1,238	–
Glasgow: Wellington	237	24	–	95,329	58,214	32
Glasgow: Whiteinch	52	7	–	70,885	26,652	104
Glasgow: Yoker	95	11	–	23,122	17,899	7

17. Hamilton

Airdrie: Broomknoll	268	34	31	54,951	34,381	16
Calderbank	119	9	20	21,154	13,408	4

Congregation	Com	Eld	G	In 11	M&M	–18
Airdrie: Clarkston	368	35	25	67,940	32,381	101
Airdrie: Flowerhill	612	43	–	114,647	76,966	185
Airdrie: High	327	33	–	63,007	37,940	134
Airdrie: Jackson	343	51	23	80,993	39,223	207
Airdrie: New Monkland	302	30	18	51,539	27,239	135
Greengairs	132	9	–	22,689	13,832	–
Airdrie: St Columba's	234	–	–	–	11,317	–
Airdrie: The New Wellwynd	730	82	20	132,686	69,207	68
Bargeddie	125	9	–	59,600	36,217	11
Bellshill: Macdonald Memorial	258	17	17	45,748	27,000	12
Bellshill: Orbiston	202	18	13	14,303	8,408	6
Bellshill: West	551	54	30	76,956	41,435	30
Blantyre: Livingstone Memorial	254	24	22	59,055	33,169	165
Blantyre: Old	280	17	30	57,363	34,384	31
Blantyre: St Andrew's	249	24	26	62,259	35,966	55
Bothwell	493	50	34	103,752	63,050	147
Caldercruix and Longriggend	223	–	–	54,743	30,997	–
Carfin	43	–	–	4,446	4,331	–
Newarthill	383	27	23	–	34,399	166
Chapelhall	269	26	44	43,999	27,638	79
Chapelton	178	11	22	–	17,209	25
Strathaven: Rankin	556	60	41	85,277	47,832	65
Cleland	192	19	–	31,601	15,582	–
Coatbridge: Blairhill Dundyvan	296	25	29	62,873	37,059	144
Coatbridge: Calder	354	–	37	52,377	35,636	–
Coatbridge: Middle	367	34	32	64,322	28,699	178
Coatbridge: New St Andrew's	766	79	26	107,897	75,775	245
Coatbridge: Old Monkland	294	19	22	44,980	35,321	75
Coatbridge: Townhead	165	17	–	51,363	28,528	111
Dalserf	223	21	27	89,804	53,140	75
East Kilbride: Claremont	636	66	–	–	60,539	240
East Kilbride: Greenhills	174	15	33	30,628	19,162	30
East Kilbride: Moncreiff	702	65	56	118,176	66,432	250
East Kilbride: Mossneuk	260	15	–	34,094	25,649	155
East Kilbride: Old	704	62	41	113,212	59,071	120
East Kilbride: South	338	43	34	77,108	54,156	14
East Kilbride: Stewartfield	–	–	–	14,545	–	–
East Kilbride: West	427	37	55	63,977	42,031	150
East Kilbride: Westwood	575	43	–	81,435	47,767	247
Glasford	124	8	19	20,972	12,409	–
Strathaven: East	307	30	40	62,895	29,588	38
Hamilton: Burnbank	80	9	–	22,970	16,343	7
Hamilton: North	122	29	19	35,334	21,730	7
Hamilton: Cadzow	486	57	56	131,571	65,142	176
Hamilton: Gilmour and Whitehill	145	27	–	28,530	20,591	98
Hamilton: Hillhouse	385	52	31	75,494	35,694	35
Hamilton: Old	483	54	21	–	73,688	96
Hamilton: St Andrew's	200	34	24	58,797	35,358	134
Hamilton: St John's	527	57	56	111,325	67,119	270
Hamilton: South	252	29	28	56,914	31,242	31

Congregation	Com	Eld	G	In 11	M&M	−18
Quarter	103	16	22	24,018	13,781	18
Hamilton: Trinity	302	25	–	56,532	25,918	175
Hamilton: West	286	26	–	75,199	44,502	23
Holytown	188	20	30	44,880	25,746	89
New Stevenston: Wrangholm Kirk	106	10	19	35,105	23,055	65
Kirk o' Shotts	167	11	9	27,958	19,534	20
Larkhall: Chalmers	122	11	30	29,877	18,529	8
Larkhall: St Machan's	459	50	42	99,633	60,137	95
Larkhall: Trinity	199	19	27	62,376	26,868	162
Motherwell: Crosshill	454	54	57	85,156	47,117	65
Motherwell: Dalziel St Andrew's	539	67	55	136,089	78,514	200
Motherwell: North	205	–	–	47,067	31,784	–
Motherwell: St Margaret's	357	–	20	–	24,662	–
Motherwell: St Mary's	845	91	71	124,915	67,124	247
Motherwell: South	444	–	104	109,632	61,235	–
Newmains: Bonkle	146	21	–	37,726	22,262	17
Newmains: Coltness Memorial	218	27	19	–	39,326	72
Overtown	279	32	50	46,856	27,624	207
Shotts: Calderhead Erskine	486	31	33	73,674	49,421	14
Stonehouse: St Ninian's	364	36	36	80,245	46,116	50
Strathaven: Avendale Old and Drumclog	847	–	55	–	103,029	–
Uddingston: Burnhead	267	21	11	47,880	17,787	88
Uddingston: Old	633	70	53	106,303	71,926	20
Uddingston: Viewpark	450	57	35	92,937	51,611	200
Wishaw: Cambusnethan North	486	32	–	72,599	48,839	130
Wishaw: Cambusnethan Old and Morningside	495	39	23	70,789	41,028	212
Wishaw: Craigneuk and Belhaven	165	28	23	48,338	31,342	24
Wishaw: Old	252	29	–	45,938	29,851	75
Wishaw: St Mark's	376	35	41	69,542	45,511	101
Wishaw: South Wishaw	494	38	38	87,559	55,135	78

18. Dumbarton

Alexandria	312	37	22	78,469	43,496	37
Arrochar	66	11	17	26,546	15,753	54
Luss	109	15	20	48,762	32,724	61
Baldernock	194	–	–	39,133	24,554	–
Bearsden: Baljaffray	354	30	60	73,382	37,262	80
Bearsden: Cross	934	–	38	188,095	109,101	–
Bearsden: Killermont	653	61	66	151,200	85,045	210
Bearsden: New Kilpatrick	1,550	134	125	290,037	155,911	111
Bearsden: Westerton Fairlie Memorial	391	46	41	87,626	45,782	82
Bonhill	863	–	–	77,783	44,537	–
Cardross	410	36	29	94,674	53,723	25
Clydebank: Abbotsford	290	18	–	53,281	34,096	37
Clydebank: Faifley	196	14	35	43,111	21,406	31
Clydebank: Kilbowie St Andrew's	281	25	19	47,436	28,809	85
Clydebank: Radnor Park	183	23	33	47,257	31,274	–
Clydebank: St Cuthbert's	122	14	23	13,520	14,988	14
Duntocher	266	–	29	46,436	33,450	–
Craigrownie	196	20	24	35,935	27,611	15

Congregation	Com	Eld	G	In 11	M&M	–18
Rosneath: St Modan's	137	11	29	26,660	16,403	2
Dalmuir: Barclay	230	16	24	44,191	26,169	26
Dumbarton: Riverside	537	66	65	113,634	60,333	239
Dumbarton: St Andrew's	134	33	–	–	18,842	2
Dumbarton: West Kirk	299	–	–	–	28,007	–
Garelochhead	177	–	–	61,356	33,850	–
Helensburgh: Park	413	38	17	74,400	45,384	18
Helensburgh: St Andrew's Kirk	1,082	–	59	220,522	130,486	–
Jamestown	356	–	21	–	32,826	–
Kilmaronock Gartocharn	263	–	–	25,724	17,561	–
Renton: Trinity	258	20	–	32,984	18,540	2
Milngavie: Cairns	504	41	–	124,906	74,778	16
Milngavie: St Luke's	394	37	27	78,346	39,903	59
Milngavie: St Paul's	1,014	–	89	221,074	115,961	–
Old Kilpatrick Bowling	253	28	25	39,829	38,269	113
Rhu and Shandon	281	–	34	66,532	49,280	–

19. Argyll

Appin	97	14	18	19,753	9,910	20
Lismore	53	6	12	12,927	6,408	9
Ardchattan	121	–	8	21,456	11,720	–
Ardrishaig	147	22	31	34,262	21,845	18
South Knapdale	35	6	–	–	3,163	–
Campbeltown: Highland	430	–	–	68,852	35,102	–
Campbeltown: Lorne and Lowland	859	61	50	82,781	52,039	36
Coll	15	3	–	4,358	1,142	–
Connel	128	22	10	44,126	26,374	4
Colonsay and Oronsay	14	2	–	–	5,090	–
Craignish	50	–	–	–	5,441	–
Kilbrandon and Kilchattan	95	–	–	30,056	13,395	–
Kilninver and Kilmelford	63	7	–	12,300	5,910	12
Cumlodden, Lochfyneside and Lochgair	94	–	12	29,705	12,193	–
Dunoon: St John's	195	24	40	40,109	30,531	15
Kirn	312	33	–	66,591	44,664	22
Sandbank	119	13	–	14,511	11,783	3
Dunoon: The High Kirk	347	–	40	–	34,725	–
Innellan	99	12	–	21,595	14,191	6
Toward	96	12	–	19,073	11,426	26
Gigha and Cara	36	–	–	8,249	4,553	–
Glassary, Kilmartin and Ford	103	13	–	19,912	16,479	25
North Knapdale	55	6	–	23,604	23,507	1
Glenaray and Inveraray	117	–	–	26,963	15,039	–
Glenorchy and Innishael	67	9	–	16,850	4,208	5
Strathfillan	43	6	–	13,547	4,474	1
Iona	19	–	–	5,320	3,177	–
Kilfinichen and Kilvickeon and the Ross of Mull	32	–	–	12,262	5,150	–
Jura	40	7	–	11,499	6,441	2
Kilarrow	81	–	–	24,912	21,075	–
Kildalton and Oa	110	–	–	41,063	20,038	–
Kilberry	8	2	–	1,560	566	–

Congregation	Com	Eld	G	In 11	M&M	–18
Tarbert (Loch Fyne)	153	16	20	–	20,328	10
Kilcalmonell	49	15	12	11,332	3,219	5
Killean and Kilchenzie	161	14	20	20,628	20,344	18
Kilchoman	88	–	–	13,889	16,266	–
Kilmeny	33	5	–	10,829	4,469	–
Portnahaven	24	5	12	6,656	2,065	–
Kilchrenan and Dalavich	25	5	7	9,380	8,104	–
Muckairn	144	19	11	32,775	13,328	13
Kilfinan	29	4	–	10,191	2,196	–
Kilmodan and Colintraive	91	11	–	18,892	11,066	11
Kyles	143	17	24	26,995	16,359	10
Kilmore and Oban	558	–	41	–	57,435	–
Kilmun (St Munn's)	93	8	17	15,786	9,627	–
Strone and Ardentinny	121	12	16	27,256	18,302	15
Lochgilphead	217	–	21	–	17,944	–
Lochgoilhead and Kilmorich	69	14	14	24,511	20,120	1
Mull, Isle of, Kilninian and Kilmore	26	4	–	9,649	6,512	–
Salen and Ulva	37	5	–	14,978	5,345	26
Tobermory	67	12	–	21,184	11,182	9
Torosay and Kinlochspelvie	25	–	–	5,507	2,662	–
Rothesay: Trinity	404	39	24	–	37,956	50
Saddell and Carradale	200	14	23	–	18,853	6
Skipness	24	3	–	6,038	3,117	9
Southend	239	11	15	–	20,501	12
Strachur and Strachlachlan	97	16	18	32,098	25,688	8
The United Church of Bute	570	47	47	73,210	51,730	42
Tiree	91	13	20	25,887	13,540	4

22. Falkirk

Airth	149	6	18	–	24,383	30
Blackbraes and Shieldhill	172	17	17	33,585	15,528	15
Muiravonside	201	21	–	–	23,383	6
Bo'ness: Old	404	33	16	66,240	39,854	53
Bo'ness: St Andrew's	515	26	–	106,432	49,658	114
Bonnybridge: St Helen's	355	21	23	57,578	32,787	34
Bothkennar and Carronshore	246	27	–	32,643	20,037	13
Brightons	682	39	58	–	79,003	232
Carriden	461	41	22	48,582	31,286	19
Cumbernauld: Abronhill	276	25	32	66,393	44,559	129
Cumbernauld: Condorrat	419	31	33	65,557	43,483	105
Cumbernauld: Kildrum	327	41	–	53,918	33,650	221
Cumbernauld: Old	378	43	–	–	49,786	120
Cumbernauld: St Mungo's	286	25	–	37,095	29,401	25
Denny: Old	398	41	30	–	42,463	90
Denny: Westpark	544	34	39	78,111	53,721	120
Dunipace	370	34	15	59,967	36,265	97
Falkirk: Bainsford	217	15	–	42,475	23,533	70
Falkirk: Camelon	336	21	–	77,424	52,817	22
Falkirk: Erskine	430	46	29	79,407	45,399	35
Falkirk: Grahamston United	366	39	38	67,892	–	24

Congregation	Com	Eld	G	In 11	M&M	–18
Falkirk: Laurieston	230	21	29	31,918	22,187	19
Redding and Westquarter	165	13	29	30,231	17,090	15
Falkirk: Old and St Modan's	512	58	7	128,259	65,975	90
Falkirk: St Andrew's West	506	36	–	100,442	63,370	65
Falkirk: St James'	249	25	8	31,330	19,987	55
Grangemouth: Abbotsgrange	543	55	27	61,807	43,411	121
Grangemouth: Kirk of the Holy Rood	471	47	–	60,717	42,137	61
Grangemouth: Zetland	804	74	67	112,775	70,801	160
Haggs	269	28	18	39,805	24,483	86
Larbert: East	664	51	49	110,165	61,484	220
Larbert: Old	467	33	19	–	55,909	260
Larbert: West	434	42	38	76,950	49,414	147
Polmont: Old	402	30	60	85,978	52,147	275
Slamannan	220	7	–	–	20,204	14
Stenhouse and Carron	406	36	24	–	46,932	17

23. Stirling

Congregation	Com	Eld	G	In 11	M&M	–18
Aberfoyle	114	10	23	25,641	15,058	14
Port of Menteith	61	9	–	14,868	5,705	3
Alloa: Ludgate	334	22	30	75,909	55,412	15
Alloa: St Mungo's	398	41	50	61,143	41,252	16
Alva	533	54	30	77,485	44,543	60
Balfron	145	19	22	–	37,292	15
Fintry	122	10	16	15,244	12,873	9
Balquhidder	80	3	–	17,354	14,303	5
Killin and Ardeonaig	112	8	9	23,451	15,987	12
Bannockburn: Allan	420	34	–	58,742	39,096	32
Bannockburn: Ladywell	415	20	–	–	17,798	9
Bridge of Allan	763	52	48	124,238	77,557	223
Buchanan	96	9	–	42,803	14,597	7
Drymen	266	22	–	69,677	33,629	50
Buchlyvie	216	14	18	26,797	18,505	7
Gartmore	67	10	–	15,247	13,805	6
Callander	607	36	38	102,358	73,842	50
Cambusbarron: The Bruce Memorial	335	17	–	–	26,595	63
Clackmannan	441	32	38	76,261	46,432	46
Cowie and Plean	209	10	6	–	15,067	–
Fallin	248	8	–	–	19,859	60
Dollar	421	36	60	83,043	57,869	19
Glendevon	44	3	–	6,126	2,622	–
Muckhart	123	8	–	23,266	9,751	10
Dunblane: Cathedral	905	82	58	224,279	121,714	325
Dunblane: St Blane's	368	39	33	104,937	58,181	25
Gargunnock	152	14	–	23,066	16,772	14
Kilmadock	100	14	–	12,218	8,315	3
Kincardine-in-Menteith	79	8	–	14,316	7,903	16
Killearn	426	30	41	85,929	57,621	39
Kippen	255	18	20	30,545	24,241	–
Norrieston	122	13	13	16,665	13,006	3
Lecropt	216	17	–	46,962	26,352	21

Congregation	Com	Eld	G	In 11	M&M	–18
Logie	552	62	34	93,945	55,811	35
Menstrie	387	25	22	68,803	39,972	15
Sauchie and Coalsnaughton	665	32	10	53,505	40,379	8
Stirling: Allan Park South	202	34	–	47,490	28,695	21
Stirling: Church of the Holy Rude	194	26	–	–	30,596	6
Stirling: Viewfield Erskine	337	22	31	43,532	32,103	20
Stirling: North	384	36	23	80,578	43,798	76
Stirling: St Columba's	521	58	–	92,127	57,453	14
Stirling: St Mark's	231	11	–	27,801	19,926	46
Stirling: St Ninian's Old	739	61	–	94,313	47,211	63
Strathblane	192	23	43	73,577	46,825	27
Tillicoultry	740	65	35	90,693	56,607	101
Tullibody: St Serf's	422	14	25	47,552	37,065	60

24. Dunfermline

Aberdour: St Fillan's	412	28	–	70,398	47,654	61
Beath and Cowdenbeath: North	220	22	16	56,091	30,284	32
Cairneyhill	114	17	–	25,282	13,574	12
Limekilns	286	50	–	–	43,312	12
Carnock and Oakley	211	20	20	58,432	32,048	42
Cowdenbeath: Trinity	362	27	14	60,948	36,565	77
Culross and Torryburn	251	18	–	52,648	29,264	24
Dalgety	546	36	27	102,195	68,769	81
Dunfermline: Abbey	683	75	–	139,699	81,895	160
Dunfermline: East	–	–	–	15,998	–	50
Dunfermline: Gillespie Memorial	299	68	19	94,822	65,134	40
Dunfermline: North	195	13	–	33,889	22,444	7
Dunfermline: St Andrew's Erskine	200	27	23	43,605	28,244	20
Dunfermline: St Leonard's	375	31	33	72,643	40,529	40
Dunfermline: St Margaret's	243	50	20	69,416	34,628	34
Dunfermline: St Ninian's	201	22	33	51,538	24,258	44
Dunfermline: Townhill and Kingseat	347	27	27	67,002	37,726	30
Inverkeithing	339	36	–	56,941	37,428	102
North Queensferry	65	8	–	16,631	9,989	18
Kelty	300	28	40	60,801	45,330	15
Lochgelly and Benarty: St Serf's	442	41	–	66,384	45,015	24
Rosyth	258	27	–	40,862	21,295	48
Saline and Blairingone	158	13	16	39,588	29,473	20
Tulliallan and Kincardine	477	26	40	51,645	33,330	7

25. Kirkcaldy

Auchterderran: St Fothad's	262	20	13	37,801	28,995	19
Kinglassie	154	11	–	–	13,493	7
Auchtertool	71	7	–	10,648	4,014	8
Kirkcaldy: Linktown	283	36	31	54,855	36,822	26
Buckhaven and Wemyss	279	28	25	48,419	32,358	7
Burntisland	460	36	16	53,524	41,160	23
Dysart	319	29	16	49,261	30,925	24
Glenrothes: Christ's Kirk	240	21	35	53,166	28,355	12
Glenrothes: St Columba's	512	33	8	55,033	33,196	33

Congregation	Com	Eld	G	In 11	M&M	–18
Glenrothes: St Margaret's	322	26	40	61,525	37,329	64
Glenrothes: St Ninian's	272	39	12	67,132	38,101	17
Innerleven: East	109	7	14	–	16,463	62
Kennoway, Windygates and Balgonie: St Kenneth's	662	45	71	93,813	51,647	35
Kinghorn	386	–	–	72,411	44,974	–
Kirkcaldy: Abbotshall	544	46	–	79,539	49,538	14
Kirkcaldy: Bennochy	520	64	58	98,935	65,754	5
Kirkcaldy: Pathhead	386	36	43	71,078	50,265	109
Kirkcaldy: St Bryce Kirk	438	29	40	96,467	63,343	66
Kirkcaldy: Templehall	207	18	19	41,121	28,616	12
Kirkcaldy: Torbain	245	31	17	43,385	24,359	108
Kirkcaldy: Viewforth	245	8	–	23,887	19,067	10
Thornton	169	7	–	17,167	12,946	6
Leslie: Trinity	222	21	19	35,056	21,826	5
Leven	534	36	34	114,803	64,411	10
Markinch	547	34	–	68,611	51,298	50
Methil	272	25	20	–	18,351	86
Methilhill and Denbeath	213	21	38	27,132	21,259	10

26. St Andrews

Congregation	Com	Eld	G	In 11	M&M	–18
Abdie and Dunbog	165	19	–	18,244	14,059	21
Newburgh	242	14	–	18,633	14,429	30
Anstruther	230	20	–	47,564	26,451	16
Cellardyke	274	22	48	50,090	26,613	11
Kilrenny	125	14	18	26,992	18,412	14
Auchtermuchty	294	17	22	45,465	20,228	5
Edenshead and Strathmiglo	177	12	–	–	16,908	5
Balmerino	135	14	15	24,474	16,460	10
Wormit	272	20	36	44,508	19,185	14
Boarhills and Dunino	160	9	–	18,368	14,443	–
Cameron	95	12	13	19,411	11,963	14
St Andrews: St Leonard's	585	45	32	131,854	74,125	33
Carnbee	109	15	20	16,152	11,852	6
Pittenweem	279	16	18	27,129	22,187	15
Ceres, Kemback and Springfield	429	39	26	49,985	71,951	14
Crail	408	30	35	–	39,490	52
Kingsbarns	89	10	–	–	11,301	–
Creich, Flisk and Kilmany	115	13	16	21,554	13,887	11
Monimail	95	12	–	26,960	14,890	10
Cupar: Old and St Michael of Tarvit	625	44	29	–	68,277	180
Cupar: St John's and Dairsie United	782	52	47	90,825	60,110	27
Elie Kilconquhar and Colinsburgh	536	44	61	93,260	63,968	32
Falkland	260	17	–	32,890	23,260	4
Freuchie	209	14	18	20,902	14,851	14
Howe of Fife	521	30	–	56,214	36,951	38
Largo and Newburn	273	23	–	50,180	26,342	21
Largo: St David's	169	18	44	32,175	19,196	20
Largoward	85	–	–	12,410	4,551	–
St Monans	283	14	47	–	37,163	45
Leuchars: St Athernase	473	29	37	44,750	40,272	10

Congregation	Com	Eld	G	In 11	M&M	–18
Newport-on-Tay	389	–	–	63,929	45,771	–
St Andrews: Holy Trinity	491	36	53	129,309	63,883	47
St Andrews: Hope Park and Martyrs'	711	69	37	137,653	76,339	–
Strathkinness	103	12	–	18,436	11,753	–
Tayport	427	31	24	41,681	32,438	15

27. Dunkeld and Meigle

Congregation	Com	Eld	G	In 11	M&M	–18
Aberfeldy	214	15	13	–	27,322	160
Amulree and Strathbraan	21	3	–	–	3,055	–
Dull and Weem	103	10	20	16,968	13,487	12
Alyth	721	33	35	–	47,320	17
Ardler, Kettins and Meigle	433	26	32	43,594	35,453	26
Bendochy	93	14	–	23,751	12,585	3
Coupar Angus: Abbey	302	20	–	43,788	25,069	76
Blair Atholl and Struan	149	16	13	15,724	20,345	3
Tenandry	54	11	–	20,621	13,080	5
Blairgowrie	929	57	42	113,714	61,560	28
Braes of Rannoch	30	6	–	15,613	8,379	–
Foss and Rannoch	98	12	11	19,048	14,118	–
Caputh and Clunie	167	18	18	16,636	18,872	–
Kinclaven	154	14	14	29,723	12,387	–
Dunkeld	393	31	16	79,144	59,339	45
Fortingall and Glenlyon	47	9	–	14,569	13,217	5
Kenmore and Lawers	87	9	21	28,582	22,072	25
Grantully, Logierait and Strathtay	148	13	13	37,825	26,293	12
Kirkmichael, Straloch and Glenshee	109	5	–	13,256	10,538	7
Rattray	379	17	28	34,099	20,540	2
Pitlochry	418	32	24	87,767	47,903	16

28. Perth

Congregation	Com	Eld	G	In 11	M&M	–18
Abernethy and Dron and Arngask	328	26	14	38,730	37,234	14
Almondbank Tibbermore	299	23	35	–	24,818	9
Methven and Logiealmond	300	20	18	–	20,778	–
Ardoch	173	19	27	23,825	23,795	24
Blackford	112	16	–	27,637	10,683	48
Auchterarder	585	30	47	99,864	53,162	30
Auchtergaven and Moneydie	506	28	35	47,469	28,406	112
Redgorton and Stanley	369	23	33	41,661	27,142	30
Cargill Burrelton	295	12	26	29,761	26,129	1
Collace	118	8	18	16,262	10,938	–
Cleish	246	–	19	60,347	34,629	–
Fossoway: St Serf's and Devonside	254	20	–	40,601	25,777	30
Comrie	434	27	24	79,947	43,766	23
Dundurn	61	11	–	13,272	10,220	–
Crieff	819	51	38	103,340	63,146	120
Dunbarney and Forgandenny	595	34	13	79,011	44,949	17
Errol	302	17	19	41,483	24,183	20
Kilspindie and Rait	65	6	–	–	7,931	–
Fowlis Wester, Madderty and Monzie	313	30	12	48,834	27,071	19
Gask	126	12	15	18,289	17,460	6

Congregation	Com	Eld	G	In 11	M&M	–18
Kinross	691	43	45	106,057	49,830	166
Muthill	279	24	17	38,156	24,658	14
Trinity Gask and Kinkell	55	4	–	8,085	3,581	–
Orwell and Portmoak	476	37	26	63,062	44,250	9
Perth: Craigie and Moncreiffe	762	37	40	76,910	49,637	30
Perth: Kinnoull	447	38	26	–	43,967	25
Perth: Letham St Mark's	561	11	24	100,052	53,197	80
Perth: North	1,135	96	23	215,228	107,097	55
Perth: Riverside	69	–	–	59,202	–	–
Perth: St John's Kirk of Perth	521	29	–	97,145	61,518	–
Perth: St Leonard's-in-the-Fields	500	49	–	93,838	60,324	10
Perth: St Matthew's	810	58	27	–	64,524	202
St Madoes and Kinfauns	335	29	25	49,262	23,830	58
St Martins	178	6	10	11,071	5,729	2
Scone: New	468	38	–	66,157	36,177	9
Scone: Old	566	36	34	72,283	40,060	86
The Stewartry of Strathearn	444	31	–	55,858	50,062	15

29. Dundee

Congregation	Com	Eld	G	In 11	M&M	–18
Abernyte	93	9	–	17,316	8,710	14
Inchture and Kinnaird	210	29	–	33,934	17,680	12
Longforgan	194	18	24	–	20,068	23
Auchterhouse	150	15	17	25,103	16,539	12
Monikie and Newbigging and Murroes and Tealing	571	33	26	56,160	42,866	8
Dundee: Balgay	421	36	23	78,559	52,051	45
Dundee: Barnhill St Margaret's	795	55	62	–	74,468	31
Dundee: Broughty Ferry New Kirk	855	62	47	112,380	67,742	35
Dundee: Broughty Ferry St James'	264	13	25	–	33,292	46
Dundee: Broughty Ferry St Luke's and Queen Street	461	53	34	79,204	49,714	40
Dundee: Broughty Ferry St Stephen's and West	338	27	–	52,269	22,326	32
Dundee: Camperdown	156	13	12	–	20,453	10
Dundee: Chalmers Ardler	233	19	37	83,609	44,690	88
Dundee: Clepington and Fairmuir	364	27	–	48,071	36,545	62
Dundee: Craigiebank	216	12	–	38,473	28,276	115
Dundee: Douglas and Mid Craigie	165	15	16	43,298	19,046	110
Dundee: Downfield South	309	33	22	76,313	46,038	30
Dundee: Dundee (St Mary's)	585	55	26	93,900	59,330	13
Dundee: Fintry Parish Church	106	9	–	57,801	29,740	29
Dundee: Lochee	616	34	31	70,863	45,644	222
Dundee: Logie and St John's Cross	312	17	23	–	69,683	64
Dundee: Mains	119	8	–	19,440	9,696	40
Dundee: Meadowside St Paul's	521	27	25	69,302	48,137	42
Dundee: Menzieshill	281	18	–	47,170	23,167	19
Dundee: St Andrew's	525	63	29	122,024	55,578	24
Dundee: St David's High Kirk	326	51	34	55,256	34,426	56
Dundee: Steeple	324	34	–	119,717	76,862	15
Dundee: Stobswell	480	41	–	65,782	46,372	7
Dundee: Strathmartine	310	21	32	46,869	34,181	5
Dundee: Trinity	533	37	34	–	34,416	76
Dundee: West	339	24	21	84,741	46,992	4

Congregation	Com	Eld	G	In 11	M&M	–18
Dundee: Whitfield	41	8	–	18,078	4,277	130
Fowlis and Liff	152	14	13	–	27,776	18
Lundie and Muirhead	321	31	–	43,651	25,870	34
Invergowrie	428	53	51	69,119	37,660	102
Monifieth	1,205	71	55	150,369	86,726	102

30. Angus

Aberlemno	194	–	–	18,683	11,887	18
Guthrie and Rescobie	224	10	11	19,479	14,291	15
Arbirlot	187	12	–	21,230	14,440	10
Carmyllie	118	12	5	–	16,976	5
Arbroath: Knox's	329	25	36	38,319	28,077	10
Arbroath: St Vigeans	582	45	29	69,637	43,099	13
Arbroath: Old and Abbey	559	40	34	107,023	65,895	50
Arbroath: St Andrew's	636	65	35	137,942	70,811	100
Arbroath: West Kirk	875	81	54	80,504	53,601	70
Barry	217	13	12	28,264	15,685	–
Carnoustie	404	30	22	73,568	43,667	26
Brechin: Cathedral	795	39	18	–	50,293	–
Brechin: Gardner Memorial	500	24	–	46,460	34,513	12
Farnell	116	11	–	6,415	9,743	1
Carnoustie: Panbride	719	33	–	78,787	39,685	58
Colliston	184	9	10	19,163	11,122	5
Friockheim Kinnell	204	17	17	18,912	11,171	8
Inverkeilor and Lunan	147	8	22	20,598	15,394	11
Dun and Hillside	441	52	36	63,916	36,512	30
Dunnichen, Letham and Kirkden	311	18	35	37,718	28,219	8
Eassie, Nevay and Newtyle	322	20	22	27,857	24,220	27
Edzell Lethnot Glenesk	364	24	26	38,886	36,071	20
Fern Careston Menmuir	–	–	–	17,421	14,990	–
Forfar: East and Old	877	47	41	84,256	54,367	57
Forfar: Lowson Memorial	937	40	18	85,051	43,959	140
Forfar: St Margaret's	581	30	23	–	48,300	120
Glamis, Inverarity and Kinnettles	393	22	–	45,670	38,333	50
Inchbrayock	200	11	–	33,725	29,343	16
Montrose: Melville South	300	18	–	–	21,527	8
Kirriemuir: St Andrew's	343	27	39	60,691	38,677	12
Oathlaw Tannadice	171	9	–	17,812	18,017	12
Montrose: Old and St Andrew's	781	49	34	101,648	67,822	42
The Glens and Kirriemuir: Old	1,081	70	40	–	96,138	40
The Isla Parishes	254	20	19	39,565	27,542	15

31. Aberdeen

Aberdeen: Bridge of Don Oldmachar	236	11	–	69,923	44,385	14
Aberdeen: Cove	86	6	–	26,349	3,885	30
Aberdeen: Craigiebuckler	809	75	56	–	66,741	150
Aberdeen: Ferryhill	414	57	27	88,787	52,129	36
Aberdeen: Garthdee	235	15	12	–	15,736	13
Aberdeen: Ruthrieston West	369	32	24	62,027	39,702	11
Aberdeen: Gilcomston South	321	27	–	176,221	105,402	47

Congregation	Com	Eld	G	In 11	M&M	–18
Aberdeen: High Hilton	410	16	32	–	87,456	180
Aberdeen: Holburn West	469	–	27	108,909	59,232	–
Aberdeen: Mannofield	1,267	124	58	168,599	103,600	187
Aberdeen: Mastrick	305	17	15	40,084	28,311	–
Aberdeen: Middlefield	117	8	–	14,327	1,615	5
Aberdeen: Midstocket	632	56	46	112,446	69,542	25
Aberdeen: New Stockethill	92	–	–	27,515	2,500	14
Aberdeen: Northfield	262	12	15	25,033	16,095	60
Aberdeen: Queen Street	659	54	43	–	62,160	67
Aberdeen: Queen's Cross	458	50	30	153,756	86,379	132
Aberdeen: Rubislaw	598	78	46	148,134	82,664	107
Aberdeen: St Columba's Bridge of Don	339	–	–	–	57,218	–
Aberdeen: St George's Tillydrone	115	–	16	15,204	8,002	–
Aberdeen: St John's Church for Deaf People	96	–	–	–	–	–
Aberdeen: St Machar's Cathedral	647	49	–	125,123	70,402	20
Aberdeen: St Mark's	441	39	25	96,787	57,973	35
Aberdeen: St Mary's	447	35	14	59,249	35,813	70
Aberdeen: St Nicholas Kincorth, South of	371	26	27	67,098	32,424	45
Aberdeen: St Nicholas Uniting, Kirk of	411	48	15	–	–	8
Aberdeen: St Stephen's	191	21	12	–	40,941	50
Aberdeen: South Holburn	650	54	82	87,814	71,607	59
Aberdeen: Summerhill	146	21	–	29,551	18,806	3
Aberdeen: Torry St Fittick's	423	26	22	51,151	28,919	–
Aberdeen: Woodside	300	31	24	–	29,023	30
Bucksburn Stoneywood	499	–	18	44,365	30,486	–
Cults	813	66	49	155,133	82,091	40
Dyce	1,139	71	36	–	52,122	243
Kingswells	420	–	25	54,845	30,055	–
Newhills	483	51	63	114,305	68,588	25
Peterculter	614	47	–	114,098	57,104	200

32. Kincardine and Deeside

Aberluthnott	208	7	14	15,061	12,202	3
Laurencekirk	475	–	33	33,787	21,914	–
Aboyne and Dinnet	341	6	27	–	37,822	15
Cromar	242	13	–	–	17,103	–
Arbuthnott, Bervie and Kinneff	702	41	35	84,197	48,697	24
Banchory-Devenick and Maryculter/Cookney	196	16	9	37,140	34,901	5
Banchory-Ternan: East	586	41	26	117,869	61,024	40
Banchory-Ternan: West	583	31	29	107,118	63,326	68
Birse and Feughside	235	21	13	35,882	30,341	17
Braemar and Crathie	243	40	15	68,647	46,739	19
Drumoak-Durris	425	24	38	72,976	47,374	44
Glenmuick (Ballater)	307	23	30	40,416	26,787	–
Mearns Coastal	292	17	21	25,607	22,146	5
Mid Deeside	713	37	27	51,443	50,062	25
Newtonhill	365	12	14	24,549	20,677	94
Portlethen	458	14	–	58,137	47,484	165
Stonehaven: Dunnottar	743	32	26	98,780	47,835	16
Stonehaven: Fetteresso	864	34	38	–	97,742	130

Congregation	Com	Eld	G	In 11	M&M	–18
Stonehaven: South	281	21	–	38,841	25,577	20
West Mearns	522	–	30	52,351	37,170	–

33. Gordon

Barthol Chapel	99	10	10	14,462	3,239	16
Tarves	412	23	34	35,754	23,782	11
Belhelvie	393	36	20	–	47,982	50
Blairdaff and Chapel of Garioch	403	36	14	–	27,780	44
Cluny	211	11	7	28,664	14,120	15
Monymusk	122	6	–	19,973	10,070	14
Culsalmond and Rayne	183	8	–	13,801	8,413	26
Daviot	142	9	–	15,017	12,409	15
Cushnie and Tough	286	19	7	28,853	21,463	13
Echt	251	9	–	20,207	17,146	8
Midmar	154	7	–	12,855	10,340	7
Ellon	1,606	94	–	142,340	88,076	195
Fintray Kinellar Keithhall	216	20	14	–	24,815	–
Foveran	333	17	–	56,218	21,161	42
Howe Trinity	613	26	33	47,589	33,098	32
Huntly Cairnie Glass	692	14	21	39,362	30,940	10
Insch-Leslie-Premnay-Oyne	352	30	24	–	27,389	20
Inverurie: St Andrew's	1,066	37	35	248,941	62,490	230
Inverurie: West	725	42	32	92,414	54,079	52
Kemnay	571	45	–	59,981	41,159	135
Kintore	739	50	21	–	68,494	102
Meldrum and Bourtie	470	34	41	63,681	46,647	26
Methlick	359	22	20	56,464	33,585	20
New Machar	475	18	18	55,544	43,361	42
Noth	301	14	–	26,952	19,062	11
Skene	1,402	97	51	130,860	81,258	145
Strathbogie Drumblade	556	41	31	69,184	41,710	55
Udny and Pitmedden	280	26	12	75,602	35,829	18
Upper Donside	412	25	–	39,703	31,610	61

34. Buchan

Aberdour	127	9	12	10,659	6,487	12
Pitsligo	98	10	–	–	8,431	–
Auchaber United	166	14	11	16,069	13,333	7
Auchterless	186	18	13	19,382	15,402	4
Banff	659	30	24	61,389	51,841	150
King Edward	156	17	10	–	14,854	13
Crimond	214	11	–	19,183	11,516	–
Lonmay	112	12	13	11,730	9,967	55
Cruden	435	27	27	56,884	33,697	26
Deer	776	31	19	54,420	44,343	10
Fordyce	434	18	36	50,856	45,034	2
Fraserburgh: Old	625	62	72	111,331	72,112	221
Fraserburgh: South	296	20	–	–	23,777	8
Inverallochy and Rathen: East	93	11	–	–	5,573	6
Fraserburgh: West	558	48	–	61,995	40,105	155

Congregation	Com	Eld	G	In 11	M&M	–18
Rathen: West	102	10	–	12,357	4,156	27
Fyvie	352	22	29	36,690	26,081	2
Rothienorman	138	10	13	13,908	7,393	15
Gardenstown	68	10	29	53,612	33,031	59
Longside	520	29	–	57,245	38,490	100
Macduff	690	36	45	91,200	53,587	169
Marnoch	411	14	16	33,900	23,996	2
Maud and Savoch	216	14	19	23,782	16,987	6
New Deer: St Kane's	393	26	17	59,184	33,198	57
Monquhitter and New Byth	332	20	14	25,627	20,300	12
Turriff: St Andrew's	553	31	12	–	27,902	66
New Pitsligo	298	6	–	23,764	16,936	31
Strichen and Tyrie	542	20	23	37,290	28,370	60
Ordiquhill and Cornhill	142	10	11	13,120	8,569	18
Whitehills	298	19	23	39,567	24,089	2
Peterhead: Old	410	26	26	62,220	40,595	40
Peterhead: St Andrew's	500	37	36	63,056	34,810	33
Peterhead: Trinity	322	26	27	148,152	69,238	8
St Fergus	183	13	13	14,104	5,746	12
Sandhaven	73	7	–	9,317	3,799	54
Turriff: St Ninian's and Forglen	821	30	40	71,836	49,393	30

35. Moray

Congregation	Com	Eld	G	In 11	M&M	–18
Aberlour	317	–	23	42,095	27,718	–
Alves and Burghead	155	–	37	26,049	15,740	–
Kinloss and Findhorn	94	–	11	27,209	13,006	–
Bellie	315	–	34	50,323	34,509	–
Speymouth	205	–	12	22,424	11,867	–
Birnie and Pluscarden	288	–	48	–	22,657	–
Elgin: High	595	–	–	76,154	40,981	–
Buckie: North	439	–	59	58,068	35,856	–
Buckie: South and West	305	–	36	42,444	23,607	–
Enzie	91	–	15	10,612	10,129	–
Cullen and Deskford	364	–	24	–	31,781	–
Dallas	60	–	13	10,201	7,747	–
Forres: St Leonard's	242	–	42	–	32,815	–
Rafford	78	–	–	13,372	6,023	–
Duffus, Spynie and Hopeman	319	–	16	45,864	30,274	–
Dyke	139	–	9	30,797	12,078	–
Edinkillie	91	–	–	13,792	12,460	–
Elgin: St Giles' and St Columba's South	1,109	–	43	134,083	86,847	–
Findochty	49	–	9	17,236	12,647	–
Portknockie	77	–	22	21,541	15,018	–
Rathven	97	–	22	18,140	12,712	–
Forres: St Laurence	437	–	41	86,097	48,646	–
Keith: North, Newmill, Boharm and Rothiemay	632	–	27	59,794	70,451	–
Keith: St Rufus, Botriphnie and Grange	1,034	–	30	86,516	51,016	–
Knockando, Elchies and Archiestown	252	–	13	29,894	21,093	–
Rothes	318	–	13	40,908	21,894	–
Lossiemouth: St Gerardine's High	381	–	28	40,208	34,791	–

Congregation	Com	Eld	G	In 11	M&M	–18
Lossiemouth: St James'	339	–	35	51,730	29,172	–
Mortlach and Cabrach	383	–	11	26,066	21,264	–
St Andrew's-Lhanbryd and Urquhart	479	–	32	66,629	41,937	–
36. Abernethy						
Abernethy	150	14	–	43,126	24,897	85
Cromdale and Advie	84	2	–	22,550	14,024	–
Alvie and Insh	66	7	–	–	17,429	35
Rothiemurchus and Aviemore	80	7	–	21,442	10,250	–
Boat of Garten, Duthil and Kincardine	154	16	30	31,717	20,203	6
Dulnain Bridge	35	5	–	11,473	9,459	–
Grantown-on-Spey	219	16	14	39,729	24,474	20
Kingussie	102	14	–	30,330	19,439	5
Laggan	40	7	–	14,591	9,910	–
Newtonmore	84	12	–	28,689	16,696	6
Tomintoul, Glenlivet and Inveraven	155	11	–	–	19,848	8
37. Inverness						
Ardersier	60	–	–	18,891	10,988	–
Petty	69	–	10	18,496	10,903	–
Auldearn and Dalmore	69	5	12	12,455	8,405	8
Nairn: St Ninian's	234	16	25	50,336	28,943	20
Cawdor	160	17	–	32,671	22,070	12
Croy and Dalcross	56	–	11	14,947	8,064	–
Culloden: The Barn	258	19	24	81,904	48,023	140
Daviot and Dunlichity	62	7	11	17,361	10,741	9
Moy, Dalarossie and Tomatin	32	5	12	11,790	9,158	–
Dores and Boleskine	73	–	–	18,049	12,136	–
Inverness: Crown	593	74	48	145,187	80,057	180
Inverness: Dalneigh and Bona	268	26	24	81,289	58,013	93
Inverness: East	281	31	–	119,248	73,431	93
Inverness: Hilton	270	10	–	86,563	44,319	84
Inverness: Inshes	220	19	–	133,682	68,533	74
Inverness: Kinmylies	104	10	–	52,913	21,308	30
Inverness: Ness Bank	616	65	33	133,739	66,294	158
Inverness: Old High St Stephen's	433	42	–	119,094	72,525	57
Inverness: St Columba	93	–	–	35,834	–	–
Inverness: Trinity	252	27	19	75,159	47,537	74
Kilmorack and Erchless	105	11	18	–	26,173	50
Kiltarlity	52	7	8	20,904	12,730	17
Kirkhill	81	12	10	22,026	7,520	5
Nairn: Old	795	52	25	111,251	65,593	51
Urquhart and Glenmoriston	132	7	–	57,270	33,923	60
38. Lochaber						
Acharacle	41	–	–	16,529	11,177	–
Ardnamurchan	19	–	–	6,056	3,674	–
Ardgour	53	–	14	11,942	8,389	–
Morvern	44	–	11	9,885	6,657	–
Strontian	32	–	–	9,133	3,576	–

Congregation	Com	Eld	G	In 11	M&M	–18
Duror	39	–	13	16,530	5,985	–
Glencoe: St Munda's	53	–	–	13,524	9,021	–
Fort Augustus	76	–	9	21,033	13,393	–
Glengarry	29	–	10	–	8,336	–
Fort William: Duncansburgh MacIntosh	426	–	22	89,380	58,975	–
Kilmonivaig	77	–	12	20,465	17,917	–
Kilmallie	137	–	23	32,327	31,483	–
Kinlochleven	59	–	19	22,629	10,535	–
Nether Lochaber	47	–	–	18,241	10,515	–
North West Lochaber	101	–	21	30,990	23,587	–
39. Ross						
Alness	88	8	–	32,828	21,393	25
Avoch	18	4	11	17,408	9,294	12
Fortrose and Rosemarkie	117	15	–	44,934	24,895	9
Contin	56	12	–	15,718	17,589	3
Fodderty and Strathpeffer	122	14	–	26,913	18,393	28
Cromarty	47	6	–	11,565	2,800	14
Resolis and Urquhart	69	7	–	–	17,800	6
Dingwall: Castle Street	138	22	28	55,118	28,695	22
Dingwall: St Clement's	228	30	27	56,175	33,650	16
Fearn Abbey and Nigg	92	11	–	–	21,157	2
Tarbat	59	9	–	15,724	10,014	–
Ferintosh	174	22	21	45,593	28,656	41
Invergordon	159	11	–	53,564	29,246	16
Killearnan	132	18	–	26,943	27,352	10
Knockbain	56	10	–	–	14,017	–
Kilmuir and Logie Easter	73	9	24	25,056	19,307	6
Kiltearn	58	6	–	33,361	16,509	28
Lochbroom and Ullapool	41	6	8	–	16,613	10
Rosskeen	130	10	18	57,592	30,939	61
Tain	123	8	19	55,653	37,848	4
Urray and Kilchrist	78	13	16	49,193	24,521	110
40. Sutherland						
Altnaharra and Farr	22	2	–	–	7,379	1
Assynt and Stoer	11	1	–	–	7,925	7
Clyne	69	11	–	27,660	13,523	5
Kildonan and Loth Helmsdale	33	5	–	14,412	5,035	9
Dornoch Cathedral	333	34	48	120,415	71,594	67
Durness and Kinlochbervie	19	2	–	22,319	12,117	4
Eddrachillis	12	2	–	15,641	7,857	2
Golspie	80	20	10	–	20,983	3
Kincardine Croick and Edderton	65	13	15	23,441	16,567	26
Creich	25	6	–	9,858	13,569	–
Rosehall	20	3	–	8,258	4,399	8
Lairg	49	7	17	–	14,685	–
Rogart	19	3	–	13,751	9,978	2
Melness and Tongue	46	8	–	19,529	11,912	15

Congregation	Com	Eld	G	In 11	M&M	–18
41. Caithness						
Bower	36	10	11	13,504	5,828	–
Halkirk Westerdale	59	7	13	15,436	10,195	9
Watten	40	5	–	10,102	8,756	11
Canisbay	45	7	14	–	6,059	12
Dunnet	18	3	8	–	3,598	20
Keiss	27	1	10	10,718	3,877	3
Olrig	51	3	7	7,949	4,836	12
Thurso: St Peter's and St Andrew's	191	15	31	–	35,959	17
The North Coast Parish	54	13	29	23,502	13,286	10
The Parish of Latheron	71	14	17	20,407	18,277	24
Thurso: West	219	27	28	48,078	46,886	17
Wick: Pulteneytown and Thrumster	240	19	28	52,093	30,128	80
Wick: St Fergus	269	38	35	62,013	40,502	12
42. Lochcarron – Skye						
Applecross, Lochcarron and Torridon	87	5	21	36,655	25,251	38
Bracadale and Duirinish	69	9	12	32,565	17,652	9
Gairloch and Dundonnell	84	–	–	65,150	44,392	–
Glenelg and Kintail	53	7	–	28,629	21,541	30
Kilmuir and Stenscholl	67	6	–	–	27,368	12
Lochalsh	67	6	17	38,718	26,208	15
Portree	82	9	–	55,844	35,780	19
Snizort	48	4	–	38,517	23,195	11
Strath and Sleat	180	9	13	94,027	59,060	64
43. Uist						
Barra	39	4	–	21,383	6,476	64
Benbecula	69	11	8	35,848	23,339	50
Berneray and Lochmaddy	53	4	11	24,827	20,294	5
Carinish	73	7	14	51,447	29,747	6
Kilmuir and Paible	26	4	–	31,329	20,741	15
Manish-Scarista	37	5	–	40,958	22,277	20
South Uist	55	11	–	17,787	18,759	27
Tarbert	137	12	–	66,275	47,894	61
44. Lewis						
Barvas	83	8	–	60,776	46,057	21
Carloway	50	5	–	35,273	15,869	40
Cross Ness	69	7	–	57,595	28,609	46
Kinloch	46	10	–	36,938	19,539	27
Knock	52	2	–	43,314	25,307	5
Lochs-Crossbost	26	–	–	27,976	12,552	–
Lochs-in-Bernera	24	2	–	16,807	11,675	11
Uig	30	4	–	27,339	16,575	4
Stornoway: High	250	15	–	127,445	74,527	85
Stornoway: Martin's Memorial	270	12	–	166,511	41,131	80
Stornoway: St Columba	124	17	43	81,040	44,816	89

Congregation	Com	Eld	G	In 11	M&M	–18
45. Orkney						
Birsay, Harray and Sandwick	326	28	33	33,448	27,941	12
East Mainland	247	20	21	29,386	23,667	15
Eday	10	3	–	6,492	1,160	4
Stronsay: Moncur Memorial	83	8	–	15,430	8,184	15
Evie	34	4	–	5,351	7,651	7
Firth	94	10	–	28,235	14,124	43
Rendall	45	4	–	7,308	6,727	20
Rousay	18	2	–	1,918	3,781	–
Flotta	25	7	–	5,229	1,737	–
Hoy and Walls	58	11	14	5,865	2,170	2
Orphir and Stenness	156	12	15	11,355	16,414	10
Kirkwall: East	404	43	31	66,694	46,518	32
Shapinsay	54	8	–	6,269	4,052	11
Kirkwall: St Magnus Cathedral	587	46	19	–	42,949	–
North Ronaldsay	12	–	–	–	1,294	–
Sanday	76	9	9	7,730	7,051	–
Papa Westray	8	4	–	4,275	2,689	5
Westray	78	18	27	23,392	13,614	35
South Ronaldsay and Burray	143	11	12	16,120	11,952	14
Stromness	331	27	26	41,768	31,645	15
46. Shetland						
Burra Isle	37	6	17	12,176	3,562	15
Tingwall	141	17	11	29,309	20,754	–
Delting	84	8	13	15,527	9,125	14
Northmavine	67	9	–	–	6,484	10
Dunrossness and St Ninian's	53	13	–	–	11,910	52
Sandwick, Cunningsburgh and Quarff	82	10	6	22,577	15,833	27
Fetlar	17	5	–	637	866	–
Unst	116	7	20	21,263	11,904	–
Yell	112	–	14	12,630	9,370	–
Lerwick and Bressay	395	30	10	78,321	47,259	57
Nesting and Lunnasting	35	5	16	5,604	7,061	–
Whalsay and Skerries	200	16	15	26,772	14,236	20
Sandsting and Aithsting	44	9	–	8,290	3,044	12
Walls and Sandness	35	10	–	8,957	3,475	–
47. England						
Corby: St Andrew's	279	13	33	53,112	24,643	9
Corby: St Ninian's	210	19	–	37,619	27,923	4
Guernsey: St Andrew's in the Grange	205	21	–	63,533	37,485	20
Jersey: St Columba's	128	16	–	70,678	39,611	21
Liverpool: St Andrew's	35	4	–	22,976	10,463	8
London: Crown Court	252	30	8	–	53,523	12
London: St Columba's	1,007	51	–	291,429	149,595	86
Newcastle: St Andrew's	100	20	–	–	5,504	26

INDEX OF ADVERTISERS

INDEX OF MINISTERS

NOTE: Ministers who are members of a Presbytery are designated 'A' if holding a parochial appointment in that Presbytery, or 'B' if otherwise qualifying for membership. 'A-1, A-2' etc. indicate the numerical order of congregations in the Presbyteries of Edinburgh, Glasgow and Hamilton.

Also included are:

(1) Ministers who have resigned their seat in Presbytery (List 6-H)
(2) Ministers who hold a Practising Certificate (List 6-I)
(3) Ministers serving overseas (List 6-K)
(4) Auxiliary Ministers (List 6-A)
(5) Ministers ordained for sixty years and upwards (List 6-Q)
(6) Ministers who have died since the publication of the last *Year Book* (List 6-R)

NB *For a list of the Diaconate, see List 6-G.*

INDEX OF PARISHES AND PLACES

NOTE: Numbers on the right of the column refer to the Presbytery in which the district lies. Names in brackets are given for ease of identification. They may refer to the name of the parish, which may be different from that of the district, or they distinguish places with the same name, or they indicate the first named charge in a union.

INDEX OF SUBJECTS